Modern Studies in Property Law

This book is a collection of papers given at the seventh biennial conference held at the University of Cambridge in March 2008, and is the fifth in the series Modern Studies in Property Law. The Property Law conference has become well known as a unique opportunity for property lawyers to meet and confer both formally and informally. This volume is a refereed and revised selection of the papers given there. It covers a broad range of topics of immediate importance, not only in domestic law but also on a worldwide scale.

Previous volumes in this series:

Modern Studies in Property Law: Volume 1
Edited by Elizabeth Cooke

Modern Studies in Property Law: Volume 2
Edited by Elizabeth Cooke

Modern Studies in Property Law: Volume 3
Edited by Elizabeth Cooke

Modern Studies in Property Law: Volume 4
Edited by Elizabeth Cooke

Modern Studies in Property Law

Volume 5

Edited by

Martin Dixon

·H A R T·
PUBLISHING

OXFORD AND PORTLAND, OREGON
2009

Published in North America (US and Canada) by
Hart Publishing
c/o International Specialized Book Services
920 NE 58th Avenue, Suite 300
Portland, OR 97213-3786
USA
Tel: +1 (503) 287-3093 or toll-free: +1 (800) 944-6190
Fax: +1 (503) 280-8832
E-mail: orders@isbs.com
Website: www.isbs.com

Hart Publishing, 16C Worcester Place, Oxford, OX1 2JW, United Kingdom
Telephone: +44 (0)1865-517530 Fax: +44 (0)1865-510710
E-mail: mail@hartpub.co.uk
Website: http://www.hartpub.co.uk

British Library Cataloguing in Publication Data
Data Available

ISBN: 978-1-84113-960-9

Typeset by Compuscript Ltd, Shannon
Printed and bound in Great Britain by
CPI Antony Rowe Ltd, Chippenham, Wiltshire

Preface

The 7th Biennial Conference on Property Law was held at Queens' College, Cambridge in April 2008 and this collection of essays contains the revised and updated versions of a number of the papers presented there. It is the fifth volume in the series *Modern Studies in Property Law*, published by Hart Publishing who continue to give generous support to the *Modern Studies* programme. The Conferences on Property Law have their origin in the work of the Centre for Property Law at the University of Reading and without their work, particularly that of Sandi Murdoch, Letitia Crabb and Elizabeth Cooke, the Conferences would not have the international reputation that they currently enjoy. The 7th Conference was the first to be held away from Reading and now operates under an inter-University Editorial and Management Board and its work will continue at the 8th Conference to be held in Oxford in 2010.

The papers in this collection cover a wide spectrum of topics within the canon of property law and all have been subject to peer review. The authors come from the four corners of the legal world—both common law and civilian—and a good portion of the analysis is comparative in outlook. In Part I, four essays deal with questions at the heart of the matter for hard-bitten chancery lawyers—questions concerning the operation of a system of land registration in the twenty-first century. The sanctity of title registration is examined in Matthew Harding and Michael Bryan's *Responding to Fraud in Title Registration Systems: A Comparative Study* and Simon Cooper provides a comparative analysis of what can be done in the event of errors in the register in *The Versatility of State Indemnity Provisions*. Part I continues with a thorough examination of a problem common to all registration systems (*Easements and Servitudes Created by Implied Grant, Implied Reservation or Prescription and Title-by-Registration Systems*: Fiona Burns) and then ends with something challenging for those among us who relish the history of land law: *Feudal Law: The Case for Reform* by Judith Bray.

Part II contains essays on the great invention of the common law: trusts and equitable remedies. In *Restrictions on Dispositions of Charity Property—Protection or Undue Burden?* (Jean Warburton), *'You Just Gotta Keep the Customer Satisfied': Where Stands the Beneficiary's Right to Information?* (Gerwyn Griffiths) and *Territorial Extremism in Awards of Specific Performance* (Peter Sparkes), the authors examine three modern controversies in the enforcement of trusts while Roger Kerridge (*Draftsmen and Suspicious Wills*) provides a fascinating insight into a modern problem through the prism of historical analysis.

The ever present conflict between occupiers of land and those seeking to enforce third party rights over that land is examined in Part III: *Family Homes*. Rules and principles designed to ensure the free flow of capital and the realisation of the economic value of land are often in conflict with the needs and rights of those for whom the land is a home and a family asset. *Constructive Trusts and Constructing Intention* by Nick Piska focuses on the doctrinal aspects of co-ownership problems while Justice Berna Collier in *Bankrupt Husbands and the Application of the Doctrine of Exoneration in Australian Law: Moving into the 21st Century* provides a comparative analysis of how the family asset can be apportioned when something goes badly wrong. These are accompanied by a paper which examines a very modern phenomenon. *The Elderly, Their Homes and the Unconscionable Bargain Doctrine* by Lorna Fox and James Devenney analyses the social, policy and legal questions surrounding equity release schemes and similar financial transactions which can be both a boon and a curse for the elderly land owner.

Parts IV and V of the collection consider the nature of property rights and different conceptions of property. The fluid nature of property concepts is considered in Jill Morgan's piece on *Leases: Property, Contract or More?* and John Mee's *The Role of Expectation in the Determination of Proprietary Estoppel Remedies*. They take us into the nuts and bolts of these critical property tools while at the same time reminding us that real problems cannot be compartmentalised neatly in the way that academics seem to favour. Indeed, understanding what we mean by 'property' is a final theme of the essays. Paul McHugh's *The Property Rights of Tribes* and Sue Farran's *Selling the Land: Should It Stop? A Case Study from the South Pacific* examine the meaning of 'property' in different societies and contexts, while Charlotte Woodhead (*Ownership, Possession, Title and Transfer: Human Remains in Museum Collections*), Pamela O'Connor (*The Extension of Land Registration Principles to New Property Rights in Environmental Goods*) and Sarah William & Jamie Glister (*Protection of Cultural Property in Times of Armed Conflict*) challenge our conception of what we mean by 'property' and ask whether our existing concepts are as transferable and durable as we would like to think they are.

The Biennial Conferences provide an opportunity for property lawyers from around the world to gather and learn. As much is done outside the formal sessions as within them. Of course, they present challenges of organisation and I am grateful to the many people who made the 7th Conference a success and the team at Hart Publishing who have managed the publication of this collection. The collection stands alone as a work of scholarship and it will be judged by others on that basis. That said, I also hope that the volume encourages those who read it to engage in their own research into the fascinating, perplexing and challenging world of property law.

Martin Dixon
Queens' College
Cambridge
Michaelmas 2009

Table of Contents

Preface v

I. A System of Land Law for the 21st Century

1. Responding to Fraud in Title Registration Systems:
   A Comparative Study 3
   Matthew Harding and Michael Bryan

2. The Versatility of State Indemnity Provisions 35
   Simon Cooper

3. Easements and Servitudes Created by Implied Grant, Implied
   Reservation or Prescription and Title-by-Registration
   Systems 61
   Fiona R Burns

4. Feudal Law: The Case for Reform 99
   Judith Bray

II. Trusts and Equitable Remedies

5. Restrictions on Dispositions of Charity Property—Protection
   or Undue Burden? 125
   Jean Warburton

6. 'You Just Gotta Keep the Customer Satisfied': Where Stands the
   Beneficiary's Right to Information? 145
   Gerwyn Ll H Griffiths

7. Draftsmen and Suspicious Wills 159
   Roger Kerridge

8. Territorial Extremism in Awards of Specific Performance 183
   Peter Sparkes

III. Family Homes

9. Constructive Trusts and Constructing Intention 203
   Nick Piška

10. Bankrupt Husbands and the Application of the Doctrine
    of Exoneration in Australian Law: Moving into the
    21st Century 235
    Justice Berna Collier

11. The Elderly, Their Homes and the Unconscionable
    Bargain Doctrine 265
    Lorna Fox O'Mahony and James Devenney

IV. Different Conceptions of Property

12. Selling the Land: Should It Stop? A Case Study
    from the South Pacific 289
    Sue Farran

13. Ownership, Possession, Title and Transfer: Human Remains
    in Museum Collections 313
    Charlotte Woodhead

14. Protection of Cultural Property in Times of Armed Conflict:
    UK Ratification of the Hague Convention 1954 337
    Sarah Williams and Jamie Glister

15. The Extension of Land Registration Principles to New
    Property Rights in Environmental Goods 363
    Pamela O'Connor

V. The Nature of Property Rights

16. The Role of Expectation in the Determination of Proprietary
    Estoppel Remedies 389
    John Mee

17. Leases: Property, Contract or More? 419
    Jill Morgan

18. The Property Rights of Tribes 433
    Dr PG McHugh

Index.. 473

I

A System of Land Law
for the 21st Century

1

Responding to Fraud in Title Registration Systems: A Comparative Study

MATTHEW HARDING AND MICHAEL BRYAN*

I. INTRODUCTION

L AST YEAR WAS the 150th anniversary of the South Australian Real
Property Act of 1858, the statute that introduced the world's first
Torrens title registration system. As the Torrens model turns 150,
it is appropriate to pause and reflect, not only on the revolution that
Torrens thinking has already achieved in land law, but also on the work
that remains to be done in Torrens jurisdictions if the Torrens model is to
operate as well as it can. This, in a broad sense, is the aim of our chapter.
The chapter has a narrower aim as well: to compare how title registration
systems, including Torrens systems, respond to fraud in the various jurisdictions of England and Wales, New Zealand, Australia and Canada.[1] In
comparing and evaluating these responses to fraud, the chapter identifies
some matters on which legislators, judges and other participants in Torrens

* Melbourne Law School. We thank Mr Robert Walker for his excellent research assistance.
[1] The Torrens systems are: New Zealand (Land Transfer Act 1952 (NZ)); the Australian
Capital Territory (Land Titles Act 1925 (ACT)); New South Wales (Real Property Act 1900
(NSW)); the Northern Territory (Land Title Act 2000 (NT)); Queensland (Land Title Act
1994 (Qld)); South Australia (Real Property Act 1886 (SA)); Tasmania (Land Titles Act 1980
(Tas)); Victoria (Transfer of Land Act 1958 (Vic)); Western Australia (Transfer of Land Act
1893 (WA)); Alberta (Land Titles Act RSA 2000 c L-4 (Alb)); British Columbia (Land Title
Act RSBC 1996 c C-250 (BC)); Manitoba (The Real Property Act CCSM 1988 c R-30 (Man));
New Brunswick (Land Titles Act RSNB 1981 c L-11 (NB)); the Northwest Territories (Land
Titles Act RSNWT 1988 c 8 (Supp) (NWT)); Nova Scotia (Land Registration Act SNS 2001
c C-6 (NS)); Nunavut (Land Titles Act RSNWT 1988 c 8 (Supp) (Nun)); Saskatchewan (The
Land Titles Act 2000 SS 2000 c L-51 (Sask)); and the Yukon (Land Titles Act RSY 2002 c
130 (Yuk)). The non-Torrens systems are England and Wales (Land Registration Act 2002
c 9 (EW)); and Ontario (Land Titles Act 1990 c L-5 (Ont)). NS shares characteristics with
English and Welsh land law and to that extent it may be more accurate to describe it as a
hybrid rather than a Torrens statute. For present purposes, we are content to classify it as a
Torrens statute.

systems might reflect with the future development of those systems in mind. As a result, rather than pointing out what the Torrens model has to offer other title registration systems, the chapter suggests that Torrens systems may themselves learn from the responses to fraud developed within non-Torrens frameworks.

A. Fraud

First, it is important to be clear about what we mean by fraud. Torrens statutes typically make reference to fraud as a basis on which a registered title may be impugned.[2] It has been clear for over a century that fraud in this statutory sense depends on the dishonesty of the defendant.[3] However, we do not confine our study to fraud as understood in Torrens statutes. Fraud in that sense means something different from common law fraud, which depends on the deliberate or reckless making of a false representation,[4] and from equitable fraud, which depends on the requirements of conscience as understood by the Courts of Chancery before the judicature reforms.[5] Our concern in this chapter is with responses to cases that may be thought of as answering descriptions of fraud either at common law, in equity, or with reference to Torrens statutes. In other words, we take a broad view of fraud.

B. Responses to Fraud

Two types of response to fraud, so understood, may be identified in title registration systems. First, a court may award a remedy that has proprietary consequences either because it requires a rectification of the register or because it requires the defendant to perform actions that will bring about the loss of their registered title. Rectification of the register may be ordered in Torrens systems on the basis of, inter alia, a finding of statutory fraud,[6] in England and Wales based on the fact that the register contains a mistake, including one caused by fraud,[7] and in Ontario on the basis of fraud, mistake or the court's opinion that rectification is just in light of an unregistered

---

[2] NZ s 62; ACT s 58(1); NSW s 42(1); NT s 188(3)(b); Qld s 184(3)(b); SA ss 69(a) and 187; Tas s 40(3)(a); Vic ss 42(1) and 43; WA s 68; Alb s 60(1); BC s 23(2)(i); Man s 59(1); NB s 16; NWT s 66(1); NS ss 4, 20(3)(b) and 49(1)(b); Nun s 66(1); Sask s 15(1); Yuk s 66(1).

[3] *Assets Company v Mere Roihi* [1905] AC 176 (PC).

[4] *Derry v Peek* (1889) 14 App Cas 337 (HL).

[5] *Nocton v Lord Ashburton* [1914] AC 932 (HL).

[6] NZ s 85; ACT s 161; NSW s 138; NT s 191; Qld s 187; SA s 64; Tas s 141; Vic (by implication) ss 44 and 106; WA s 200; Alb s 190; Man s 176(1); NB s 70(1); NWT s 175; NS s 33; Nun s 175; Sask s 109(1); Yuk s 151. Note that BC makes no explicit provision for court ordered rectification.

[7] EW Sch 4.

interest.[8] Orders requiring the defendant to bring about the loss of their registered title are, in Torrens jurisdictions and (in theory) in England and Wales and Ontario, made in response to what in Torrens parlance are called *in personam* claims. *In personam* claims, so understood, are claims based on the conduct of a registered title-holder that do not take the form of claims of statutory fraud and that seek remedies with proprietary consequences.[9]

Secondly, a court may award a remedy that does not have proprietary consequences. Such remedies usually take the form of an order that the defendant pay to the claimant a sum of money. As a matter of classification, remedies without proprietary consequences may result from personal claims, but they may not result from *in personam* claims. In our view, for the avoidance of confusion the phrase '*in personam* claims' is best reserved only for those claims that seek remedies with proprietary consequences. In what follows, we consider responses to fraud in the form both of remedies with proprietary consequences and of remedies without proprietary consequences.

We examine the two types of response to fraud—in shorthand, proprietary remedies and personal remedies—with respect to three types of case that arise in title registration systems and that, from one or more perspectives, may be said to entail fraud. First, there is the case where a defendant gets registered pursuant to a forged instrument of transfer or mortgage. Secondly, there is the case where a defendant accepts that an unregistered interest exists in land, then becomes the registered owner of that land, and then repudiates the unregistered interest. And thirdly, there is the case where a defendant becomes the registered holder of a title that was, prior to registration, held on trust or subject to fiduciary obligation and that has been transferred to the defendant as a consequence of a breach of that trust or fiduciary obligation. We consider these three types of case through the study of three actual cases: one a recent decision of the Ontario Court of Appeal; one a leading authority of the High Court of Australia; and one the latest Australian contribution to the unsettled law relating to knowing receipt.

II. FORGERY

Our first case study is *Lawrence v Wright*.[10] A woman pretending to be Susan Lawrence purported to sell land owned by the real Susan Lawrence to a man using the alias 'Thomas Wright'. A forged transfer in favour of Wright was registered and almost immediately afterwards so was a mortgage over the land in favour of Maple Trust. Maple Trust had lent money to Wright on the security of that mortgage; presumably there was a conspiracy

---

[8] Ont Pt X.

[9] *Breskvar v Wall* (1971) 126 CLR 376 (HCA) 385 (Barwick CJ).

[10] *Lawrence v Wright* (2007) 278 DLR (4th) 698 (Ont CA).

on the part of the woman pretending to be Ms Lawrence, and Wright, to defraud Maple Trust. The real Ms Lawrence subsequently discovered what had happened, and sought to have the transfer to Wright and the mortgage in favour of Maple Trust set aside. It is not clear from the judgment of the Ontario Court of Appeal whether rectification of the register was sought, or whether orders against Wright and Maple Trust were sought, although it is likely that rectification was sought given that in Ontario rectification may be ordered in a wide range of circumstances.

A. Proprietary Remedies

Forgery cases tend to fall into three categories. First, there is the case where X's land is transferred or mortgaged to Z pursuant to a forged instrument, and Z gets registered as transferee or mortgagee. Call this case X-Z. Secondly, there is the case where X's land is transferred to Y pursuant to a forged instrument, and Y gets registered as transferee, and Y then transfers or mortgages the land to Z who gets registered. Call this case X-Y-Z. Finally, there is the case where X's land is transferred to a fictitious Y pursuant to a forged instrument, and the registration of the fictitious Y is procured, and then so is the transfer or mortgage of the land from the fictitious Y to Z who gets registered. Call this case X-'Y'-Z.

In X-Z, if Z has acted dishonestly, say by forging the instrument pursuant to which they were registered, X is entitled to rectification of the register or to orders against Z requiring the execution and lodgment of a form of transfer or discharge. The same is true in X-Y-Z and X-'Y'-Z, if Z has acted dishonestly. That is because in all jurisdictions a person will be divested of a registered title owing to their own dishonesty in getting registered. However, in *Lawrence v Wright*, a proprietary remedy was not sought against a dishonest defendant. The mortgagee, Maple Trust, was itself an unwitting victim of fraud, and this meant that *Lawrence v Wright* entailed a dispute between two innocent persons—the real Susan Lawrence, and Maple Trust—over the consequences of the dishonesty of third parties.

(i) Immediate Indefeasibility

In New Zealand and Australia, cases of the type X-Z and X-Y-Z—assuming now that Z is honest—are resolved by the application of the principle of immediate indefeasibility.[11] The same appears to be true in Saskatchewan[12] and may be taken to be true in the other Torrens jurisdictions of Canada

---

[11] *Frazer v Walker* [1967] 1 AC 569 (PC); *Breskvar v Wall* (1971) 126 CLR 376 (HCA).
[12] *Hermanson v Martin* (1987) 33 DLR (4th) 12 (Sask CA) although see now *CIBC Mortgages Inc v Saskatchewan (Registrar of Titles)* [2006] 9 WWR 556 (Sask C of QB).

except for British Columbia, New Brunswick and Nova Scotia, although there is no authority on point in those jurisdictions except for Alberta, where some older authority actually points the other way.[13] (British Columbia and New Brunswick adopt a principle of deferred indefeasibility, and Nova Scotia adopts a principle of discretionary indefeasibility, as discussed below.) According to the principle of immediate indefeasibility, from the moment of registration the honest transferee or mortgagee gains an immunity. This immunity protects the transferee or mortgagee from proprietary remedies that would otherwise have been enforceable against them owing to the fact that the instrument effecting the transfer or mortgage was void. This principle of immediate indefeasibility protects the transferee or mortgagee irrespective of the reason why the instrument was void—forgery, the doctrine of non est factum, because a party to the instrument acted ultra vires by executing it,[14] or perhaps something else—so long as the transferee or mortgagee has been honest. Immediate indefeasibility means that in X-Z and X-Y-Z cases, proprietary remedies may not be awarded against Z if Z acted honestly.[15]

Jurisdictions that apply the principle of immediate indefeasibility appear to treat differently the case of X-'Y'-Z, permitting proprietary remedies to be awarded against Z even if they were honest.[16] However, there appears to be no reason why X-'Y'-Z should be treated differently once the need for immediate indefeasibility is accepted. It is said that immediate indefeasibility is justified because it protects a registered title-holder against defects in an instrument that they did not know about. It is also said that this protection helps to ensure the security of title that is desirable in any community characterised by the private ownership of land. Assuming that this is an adequate justification of immediate indefeasibility, it is not clear why a registered title-holder should not be protected against a defective instrument simply because the defect took one form rather than another. Indeed, given that it is the defect that counts, and not its form, the case of X-'Y'-Z is really just the case of X-Z where X-Z consists of two void instruments rather than one.

All of this is irrelevant to the case of *Lawrence v Wright*, because *Lawrence v Wright* was neither a case of X-Z nor a case of X-'Y'-Z. Instead, it was a

---

[13] *Adams v McFarland* (1914) 20 DLR 293 (Alb SC); *Essery v Essery* [1947] 2 WWR 1044 (Alb SC, App Div).

[14] See *Boyd v Mayor of Wellington* [1924] NZLR 1174 (NZCA).

[15] Strictly, this is not true as an in personam claim may be brought successfully against Z and a remedy with proprietary consequences may follow. However, if Z has acted honestly, such a claim is very unlikely to succeed. The well-known Australian case of *Mercantile Mutual Life Insurance Co Ltd v Gosper* (1991) 25 NSWLR 32 (NSWCA), in which such a claim did succeed in a variant of X-Z, has not been followed. See, eg, *Spina v Conran Associates Pty Ltd* [2008] NSWSC 326 (Austin J).

[16] *Gibbs v Messer* [1891] AC 248 (PC).

case of *X-Y-Z*:[17] *X* was the real Susan Lawrence; *Y* was Wright; and *Z* was Maple Trust. If the principle of immediate indefeasibility had been applied by the Ontario Court of Appeal in *Lawrence v Wright*—and, for reasons we shall come to shortly, it was not—the outcome of the case would have been clear: Maple Trust would have had an indefeasible title. To begin with, the mortgage was not void because Wright was the registered owner of the land for the purposes of the mortgage. Moreover, even if the mortgage had been void, Maple Trust was honest and that, in light of the principle of immediate indefeasibility, was sufficient to entitle it to immunity from proprietary remedies in favour of the real Susan Lawrence.

(ii) Deferred Indefeasibility

Lawrence v Wright was decided in Ontario, where the principle of immediate indefeasibility is not applied. Courts in Ontario, like those in British Columbia[18] and New Brunswick,[19] apply a principle of deferred indefeasibility instead; indeed, *Lawrence v Wright* itself has now confirmed the applicability of deferred indefeasibility in Ontario, after a period of doubt about whether it still applied there.[20] Deferred indefeasibility yields a different outcome than immediate indefeasibility in cases of the type *X-Z* and *X-'Y'-Z*. That is because, according to the principle of deferred indefeasibility, a transferee or mortgagee whose transfer or mortgage has been effected by a void instrument gains no immunity on registration, even if they have been honest. Such a person is susceptible to whatever proprietary remedies may be enforced against them owing to the fact that the instrument in question was void. So, in *X-Z* the register may be rectified to *Z*'s detriment, and *Z* may be ordered to perform actions which will bring about the loss of their registered title. And in *X-'Y'-Z*—which, as we have already seen is just *X-Z* in disguise—the outcome is the same.

What about *X-Y-Z*? In the typical case of *X-Y-Z*, deferred indefeasibility yields the same outcome as immediate indefeasibility, assuming again that

---

[17] For the purpose of working out precisely when *Z*'s interest came into existence, it might be correct to say that a case like *Lawrence v Wright* is an X-Z (or an X-Y/Z) case: see *Abbey National Building Society v Cann* [1991] 1 AC 56 (HL). However, that does not affect the status of *Z*'s interest as against X.

[18] In British Columbia, deferred indefeasibility is applied except where *Z* is a good faith purchaser of an ownership interest: BC s 25.1.

[19] NB s 71.

[20] In *CIBC Mortgages Inc v Chan* (2005) 261 DLR (4th) 679 (Ont CA), the Ontario Court of Appeal seemed to establish immediate indefeasibility for the province. However, in *Rabi v Rosu* (2006) 277 DLR (4th) 54 (Ont SCJ) and *Home Trust Co v Zivic* (2006) CarswellOnt 7125 (Ont SCJ), the Ontario Superior Court of Justice refused to follow *CIBC Mortgages Inc v Chan* on analogous facts. In 2007, *Lawrence v Wright* re-established deferred indefeasibility, as did the *Ministry of Government Services* Consumer Protection and Service Modernization Act 2006, which amended s 155 of the Ontario Land Titles Act 1990 specifically to undo the effect of *CIBC Mortgages Inc v Chan*.

Z has been honest. That is because, although the transfer X-Y is void in the typical X-Y-Z case, the transfer or mortgage Y-Z is not, because Y-Z does not typically entail a forgery and because Y has a registered interest to transfer or mortgage at the time of Y-Z. Z, unless they have been dishonest, gains an immunity protecting them against any proprietary remedies that might otherwise be enforceable by X. As we have seen already, *Lawrence v Wright* was a case of X-Y-Z in which Y-Z was not void owing to forgery or for any other reason. It follows that an application of the principle of deferred indefeasibility in *Lawrence v Wright* ought to have yielded an immunity for Maple Trust in respect of its mortgage vis-à-vis the real Susan Lawrence. However, that is not how the Ontario Court of Appeal decided the case. Instead, the Court permitted the real Ms Lawrence to enforce a proprietary remedy against Maple Trust. In doing so, the Court appears to have mistakenly viewed the case as an X-Z case.[21] This was a mistake because even though Wright was using an alias, he was a real person, not a fictitious one, and he was the registered owner of the land at the time when the mortgage was registered. Had Wright been a fictitious person, *Lawrence v Wright* would have been an X-'Y'-Z case—an X-Z case in disguise—and the principle of deferred indefeasibility, properly applied, would have rendered Maple Trust susceptible to proprietary remedies. But Wright being a real person, the Ontario Court of Appeal's reasoning in *Lawrence v Wright* was defective, even if—as we suggest below—the outcome of the case was desirable.[22]

(iii) Discretionary Indefeasibility

There can be little doubt that the outcome in *Lawrence v Wright*, even though the product of defective reasoning, was more desirable than the outcome that would have been delivered by an application of the principle of immediate indefeasibility or a proper application of the principle of deferred indefeasibility. That is because the real Ms Lawrence lived on the land in dispute. Had Maple Trust been permitted to exercise its power of sale as mortgagee, she would have lost her home. By denying Maple Trust the right to exercise that power, the Ontario Court of Appeal ensured that Ms Lawrence kept her home. Maple Trust was left to seek compensation from the state for its financial loss. Such an outcome is desirable both because of the value that is placed on the settled occupation of land, and because of efficiency considerations: ordinarily, compensation is, if easily accessed and sufficient, as satisfactory an outcome as possession, and one that costs less to obtain, for a typical mortgagee in a case like *Lawrence*

---

[21] *Lawrence v Wright* (2007) 278 DLR (4th) 698 (Ont CA) [22] (Gillese JA for the Court).
[22] See generally Bruce Ziff, 'Looking for Mr Wright: A Comment on *Lawrence v Wright* (2007) 51 *Real Property Reports (4th series)* 22.

v Wright. Nonetheless, it is also easy to imagine X-Z, X-'Y'-Z and X-Y-Z
cases in which the most desirable outcome is that delivered by immediate or
(in the case of X-Y-Z) deferred indefeasibility of title. For example, think of
an X-Z case in which X has never lived on the land in dispute and has only
discovered the forged transfer to Z—a forgery of which Z was unaware and
could not reasonably have been aware—five years after Z got registered and
made the land in question their family home.

Law reform commissions and scholars have proposed that, irrespective
of which of immediate and deferred indefeasibility is adopted, it should be
supplemented by a discretion to displace it on grounds like the fact that one
of the parties to the dispute is in occupation of the land in question.[23] A
default principle of immediate or deferred indefeasibility, plus such a supplemental discretion, has been described as discretionary indefeasibility. It
is the prevailing approach in Nova Scotia. Nova Scotia's Land Registration
Act 2001 adopts a default principle of deferred indefeasibility but then
states that a court may determine that it is 'just and equitable' to uphold
the title of a person who was registered pursuant to a void instrument. In
making this determination, a court in Nova Scotia is required to consider
the following: the nature of the parties' interests; the circumstances of the
impugned registration; the characteristics and significance of the land to the
parties; the willingness of the parties to receive compensation rather than a
title; the ease with which compensation for a loss may be determined; and
any other circumstances that strike the court as relevant.[24]

Discretionary indefeasibility is also the prevailing approach in the Torrens
jurisdiction of Queensland when it comes to the registered titles of mortgagees. According to the Queensland Land Title Act 1994, the default principle
is immediate indefeasibility.[25] However, where a mortgagee has failed to
take reasonable steps to ensure that the person executing a mortgage instrument is the registered owner of land,[26] and the mortgage turns out to have
been forged, a court is granted a supplemental discretion to 'make the order
it considers just' with respect to the registered mortgage.[27] This enables the

---

[23] New Zealand Property Law and Equity Reform Committee, *The Decision in Frazer v
Walker* (June 1977); Victorian Law Reform Commission, *Report on the Torrens Register
Book* (Report No 12, 1987); Canadian Joint Titles Committee, *Renovating the Foundation:
Proposals for a Model Recording and Registration Act for the Provinces and Territories of
Canada* (July 1990); Elizabeth Toomey, 'Fraud and Forgery in the 1990s: Can *Frazer v Walker*
Survive the Strain?' (1994) 5 *Canterbury Law Review* 424; Anthony Mason, 'Indefeasibility:
Logic or Legend?' in David Grinlinton (ed), *Torrens in the Twenty-First Century* (Wellington,
LexisNexis, 2003) 3.

[24] NS s 35.

[25] Qld s 184.

[26] A mortgagee has obligations to take such steps under ss 11A and 11B of the Land Title
Act 1994.

[27] Qld s 187. For a discussion of these provisions, see Michael Weir, 'Indefeasibility:
Queensland Style' (2007) 15 *Australian Property Law Journal* 79.

desirable outcome to be reached in a case where, for instance, an innocent person stands to lose their home because a mortgagee has been careless with respect to a forged mortgage.

Discretionary indefeasibility has the advantage of enabling courts to deliver the most desirable outcome in *X-Z* and *X-'Y'-Z* cases, particularly where *X* stands to lose their home to a mortgagee who was registered pursuant to a forged mortgage and immediate indefeasibility would ordinarily apply. However, in an *X-Y-Z* case like *Lawrence v Wright*, discretionary indefeasibility, whether in the form applied in Nova Scotia or in Queensland, does not yield the most desirable outcome. In Nova Scotia, the default principle is deferred indefeasibility. This, applied to the facts of *Lawrence v Wright*, already protects Maple Trust's title as mortgagee; there is no need to resort to the discretionary considerations by which an otherwise defeasible title might be upheld in Nova Scotia. And in Queensland, Maple Trust is protected because discretionary indefeasibility is triggered in that jurisdiction only where a mortgage has been registered pursuant to a void instrument and in *Lawrence v Wright* the mortgage was not void.

(iv) Qualified Indefeasibility

The fact that Susan Lawrence stood to lose her home would have been relevant had *Lawrence v Wright* been decided under the law of England and Wales. There was no mistake in the registration of Maple Trust as mortgagee, because Wright was the registered owner of the land in dispute at the time when the mortgage was registered, and the mortgage was not void for any other reason. Therefore, Ms Lawrence was not entitled to rectification of the register on the basis of a mistake in the registration of the mortgage. However, Ms Lawrence was entitled to rectification of the register on the basis of a mistake in the registration of Wright as owner, because that registration had occurred pursuant to a void instrument. Under the law of England and Wales, this right to rectification of the register would have ensured that Ms Lawrence was once again registered as the owner of the land. However, a question remains. Did Ms Lawrence's right to rectification of the register mean that, under the law of England and Wales, she would have regained her title free from Maple Trust's mortgage?

Because Ms Lawrence was in actual and apparent occupation of the land in dispute—it was her home—any interest that she had in the land at the time of registration of the mortgage would override the mortgage according to section 29 and Schedule 3 of the Land Registration Act 2002.[28] The fact that the interest of a person in occupation of land may override a registered

---

[28] See Simon Gardner, *An Introduction to Land Law* (Oxford, Hart Publishing, 2007) 36–9.

title in this way has led to the title registration system of England and Wales being described as a system of qualified indefeasibility.[29] According to this principle of qualified indefeasibility, if Ms Lawrence's right to rectification of the register based on the mistake caused by the void transfer to Wright was an interest in the land, then, according to the Land Registration Act, the right to rectification would override Maple Trust's mortgage. Put another way, Ms Lawrence's right to be restored through rectification of the register as the unencumbered owner of the land in dispute would be enforceable against Maple Trust, which would be unable as a consequence to resist the cancellation of its registered mortgage pursuant to the rectification.

However, none of this could happen unless Ms Lawrence's right to rectification of the register was an interest in the land. According to section 116 of the Land Registration Act, a mere equity is an interest in land. Therefore, it would appear that whether or not a right to rectification of the register is an interest capable of overriding if held by a person in occupation of land depends on whether or not such a right is a mere equity. It would seem that this is a matter on which opinions differ.[30] However, we suggest that there is no good reason why a right to rectification of the register may not be described as a mere equity for the purposes of the Land Registration Act. A right to seek rescission of a voidable transaction, where rescission will have proprietary consequences, is a mere equity.[31] So is a right to seek rectification of an instrument to correct a mistake.[32] If a right to rectification of the register were not also regarded as a mere equity, then the rights of a defrauded person in the position of Ms Lawrence would depend on the form that the fraud happened to take. To illustrate, imagine that in *Lawrence v Wright*, the transfer to Wright had been induced by a fraudulent misrepresentation. That transfer would have been voidable, not void. Ms Lawrence's right to rescind it would have been a mere equity, enforceable against Maple Trust because Ms Lawrence was in occupation of the land. Why should the outcome of the case be any different just because the fraud took the form of forgery, rendering the transaction by which Wright got registered void, not voidable? We cannot think of any reason of policy or principle for such a distinction. It might be objected that Ms Lawrence should not be permitted to enforce proprietary remedies in either the case of fraudulent misrepresentation or the case of forgery. For reasons of policy

---

[29] Elizabeth Cooke, *Land Law* (Oxford, Oxford University Press, 2006) 57.

[30] See *Malory Enterprises Ltd v Cheshire Homes Ltd* [2002] Ch 216 (CA); Duncan Sheehan, 'Rights to Rectify the Land Register as Interests in Land' (2003) 119 *Law Quarterly Review* 31; Elizabeth Cooke, 'Land Registration: Void and Voidable Titles—A Discussion of the Scottish Law Commission's Paper' [2004] *Conveyancer and Property Lawyer* 482; David Fox, 'Forgery and Alteration of the Register under the Land Registration Act 2002' in Elizabeth Cooke (ed), *Modern Studies in Property Law: Volume III* (Oxford, Hart Publishing, 2005) 25.

[31] *Latec Investments Ltd v Hotel Terrigal Pty Ltd* (1965) 113 CLR 265 (HCA).

[32] *Smith v Jones* [1954] 1 WLR 1089 (Ch).

to do with security of title, this objection has force. But it is not an objection to regarding a right to rectification of the register as a mere equity. It is an objection to regarding mere equities as interests in land, and there is no doubt that they are currently so regarded under the Land Registration Act.

Even if mere equities were not interests in land under the Land Registration Act, Ms Lawrence might still have been able to enforce a proprietary remedy against Maple Trust if *Lawrence v Wright* had been decided under the law of England and Wales. Robert Chambers argues that the right to rescind a transaction or rectify an instrument under which title to property has passed gives rise to a resulting trust in favour of the claimant seeking to regain that title. The resulting trust arises because, whatever reason entitled the claimant to rescission or rectification, the claimant did not intend the benefit of the property in question to pass to the defendant.[33]

Professor Chambers' reasoning may be applied, a fortiori, in the case of a void, rather than a voidable, instrument under which title to registered land has passed, where that instrument is void owing to forgery. Applying Professor Chambers's analysis to the facts of *Lawrence v Wright* in light of the Land Registration Act, it is clear that the real Susan Lawrence did not intend the benefit of her land to pass to Wright because she was completely ignorant of the transfer pursuant to which Wright became the registered owner of that land. As a result, Wright held his title on resulting trust for the real Susan Lawrence from the moment when he became the registered owner. Almost immediately afterwards, when Maple Trust got registered as mortgagee, it acquired its mortgage subject to any interest that Ms Lawrence retained in the land notwithstanding that she was no longer the registered owner, because Ms Lawrence was in occupation of the land. Her resulting trust interest was such an interest and therefore was enforceable against Maple Trust. On this analysis, the question whether a right to rectification of the register is a mere equity for the purposes of section 116 of the Land Transfer Act, although interesting, is irrelevant.

B. Personal Remedies

Suppose that Susan Lawrence cannot recover her land, either because the jurisdiction in question applies the principle of immediate or deferred indefeasibility or because her claim does not meet the specific statutory

---

[33] Robert Chambers, *Resulting Trusts* (Oxford, Clarendon Press, 1997) ch 7. In their recent book on rescission, Dominic O'Sullivan, Steven Elliot and Rafal Zakrzewski appear to disagree with Professor Chambers' view, pointing out that there is no authority for regarding a right to seek rescission of a voidable agreement or instrument as giving rise to a resulting trust: *The Law of Rescission* (Oxford, Oxford University Press, 2008) [16.12]–[16.17]. However, the authors of *The Law of Rescission* do not discuss whether a resulting trust may arise where title has passed pursuant to an instrument that is void because of forgery.

requirements of a system of discretionary or qualified indefeasibility. Will she be entitled to a personal restitutionary remedy against Maple Trust on the ground that Maple Trust has been unjustly enriched at her expense?

Texts on the law of unjust enrichment seldom discuss restitutionary claims brought against registered title-holders. If indefeasibility is discussed at all it is in terms of its application as a defence to a proprietary restitutionary claim. For example, James Edelman and Elise Bant treat registration of interests in land under the Torrens system in a chapter on defences to claims in unjust enrichment.[34] The authors conclude that registration constitutes a defence to a proprietary claim[35] but that Torrens statutes 'plainly do not exclude any personal claim for restitution in unjust enrichment'.[36]

Although title registration statutes, including Torrens statutes, do not themselves exclude the possibility of bringing a personal claim against the holder of a registered title, some authorities have held that a personal claim will only be permitted where relief would be consistent with the indefeasibility principle. In *Registrar of Titles (WA) v Franzon*,[37] the High Court of Australia considered section 201 of the Western Australian Transfer of Land Act 1893, entitling any person deprived of an interest in land by reason of registration to bring 'an action at law for the recovery of damages' against the registered title-holder where the latter had acquired title through 'fraud, error or misdescription'.[38] The claimants' solicitor obtained a loan by forging the claimants' signatures on a mortgage of their land to the defendant finance company. The claimants brought an action under section 201 against the defendant finance company. The latter had obtained a valid mortgage over the land under the doctrine of immediate indefeasibility. The High Court of Australia held that a registered title-holder was not liable to pay compensation under the statute unless the claimant could also have recovered the land by the application of an exception, such as the fraud exception, to the indefeasibility principle. Justice Mason stated that compensation under the statute must be 'complementary' to the principles of proprietary relief.

Although section 201 is not a provision which relates directly to indefeasibility of title, it is complementary to those provisions which regulate indefeasibility of title and it provides for compensation for loss of indefeasible title.[39]

---

[34] James Edelman and Elise Bant, *Unjust Enrichment in Australia* (Melbourne, Oxford University Press, 2006) 352–5.

[35] A conclusion now reinforced by the decision of the High Court of Australia in *Farah Constructions Pty Ltd v Say-Dee Pty Ltd* (2007) 232 ALR 209 (HCA), which we discuss below in Part IV.

[36] Edelman and Bant, above n 34, at 354.

[37] *Registrar of Titles (WA) v Franzon* (1975) 132 CLR 611 (HCA).

[38] WA s 201.

[39] *Registrar of Titles (WA) v Franzon* (1975) 132 CLR 611 (HCA) 618.

The High Court in *Registrar of Titles (WA) v Franzon* was construing a statute which authorised the payment of compensation to a claimant deprived of an interest in land; the decision is not authority on the availability of restitutionary claims for unjust enrichment. Nonetheless, the decision articulates a policy that awards of personal relief should be congruent with the principles governing the recovery of land held under a title registration system. This policy is the mirror opposite of the policy identified by Professors Edelman and Bant, namely that a personal restitutionary claim should be available against the registered title-holder where it is independent of the proprietary claim. The law of unjust enrichment is indeed independent of contractual and proprietary claims, but it is suggested that this independence can result in the law pursuing inconsistent policy objectives. 'Independence' here means that a registered title-holder is not bound to return an interest in land to a claimant who has been deprived of it by fraud but must nonetheless make restitution of the value of the interest on the ground that they have been unjustly enriched at the expense of the claimant. What is unjust about obtaining an indefeasible title if none of the exceptions to indefeasibility applies?

Graham Virgo has argued that a personal restitutionary claim against the registered title-holder is based not on the law of unjust enrichment but on the claimant's vindication of a property right by the award of a personal restitutionary remedy.[40] But this analysis does not eliminate the lack of congruity between the principles governing proprietary and personal relief; indeed, it highlights the inconsistency. If Professor Virgo is right, the claimant can vindicate a property right by the award of a personal remedy even though they have been lawfully deprived of that right by the operation of the principle of indefeasibility. If, as Mason J stated, the principles of personal relief should complement the principles of proprietary recovery, indefeasibility ought to bar a personal, as well as a proprietary, restitutionary claim.

The principle that the personal liability of registered title-holders should be consistent with the principles of proprietary recovery is recognised by some Torrens statutes, although admittedly the provisions, like the provision discussed in *Registrar of Titles (WA) v Franzon*, apply to claims to compensation, not to restitution. An example is section 44(2) of the Victorian Transfer of Land Act 1958, which states that

> nothing in this Act shall be so interpreted as to leave subject to an action of ejectment *or for recovery of damages* or for deprivation of the estate or interest in respect of which he is registered any bona fide purchaser for valuable consideration of land.[41] (emphasis added)

---

[40] Graham Virgo, *The Principles of the Law of Restitution*, 2nd edn (Oxford, Oxford University Press, 2005) 11–18; 645–6. The analysis was applied in *Foskett v McKeown* [2001] 1 AC 102 (HL).

[41] Vic s 44(2).

These 'ejectment' provisions are found only in the older Torrens statutes.[42] They have been omitted from the 'new generation' title registration legislation. But they reflect a policy, recognised early in the history of Torrens legislation, that the indefeasible title obtained by a good faith purchaser should be protected from adverse personal, as well as proprietary, claims. We shall return to the question of congruity of personal and proprietary remedies in Part IV.

III. ACKNOWLEDGEMENT AND REPUDIATION

Our second case study is *Bahr v Nicolay (No 2)*.[43] Walter and Joanna Bahr sold land to Marcus Nicolay. In the contract of sale, Nicolay promised to re-sell the land to the Bahrs for a specified price after three years had expired. Nicolay subsequently sold the land to David and Thelma Thompson and this time the contract of sale contained an acknowledgement of the Bahrs' right to re-purchase. Three years from the date of their original contract with Nicolay, the Bahrs sought to exercise their right to re-purchase, but the Thompsons repudiated that right. The Bahrs sought an order of specific performance with proprietary consequences, requiring the Thompsons to take the steps necessary to effect the Bahrs' re-purchase of the land on the terms set out in their contract with Nicolay.

A. Proprietary Remedies

(i) The Torrens Response

(a) Statutory Fraud

The first and principal component of the Torrens response to a case like *Bahr v Nicolay (No 2)* in which a proprietary remedy is sought is to determine whether or not the conduct of the defendant amounts to statutory fraud. As we have seen, in Torrens statutes, fraud means dishonesty. Actual knowledge or constructive notice of an unregistered interest at the time of registration, coupled with a repudiation of that interest after registration, does not amount to fraud and does not for any other reason render the registered title-holder susceptible to the interest in question.[44] Only dishonesty will do. Dishonesty is an inference that must be drawn from

---

[42] NZ s 183(1); NSW s 45(2); BC s 294.2; NWT s 164; Nun 164; Yuk s 138.

[43] *Bahr v Nicolay (No 2)* (1988) 164 CLR 604 (HCA).

[44] NZ s 182; ACT s 59; NSW s 43; NT s 188(2)(a); Qld s 184(2)(a); SA ss 186 and 187; Tas s 41; Vic s 43; WA s 134; Alb s 203; BC s 29; Man s 80; NB s 61; NWT s 75; Nun s 75; Sask ss 23 and 24; Yuk s 162.

established facts. In a case like *Bahr v Nicolay (No 2)*, it has been assumed that in Torrens jurisdictions an inference of dishonesty will be drawn only from an exceptional set of facts.[45] Those who would make this assumption may point to a long line of authority revealing a judicial reluctance to make a finding of statutory fraud.[46] However, it is also possible to point to authority where an inference of dishonesty, grounding a finding of statutory fraud, was drawn or contemplated from what were arguably slender facts.[47] Moreover, it is possible to identify, in leading cases like *Bahr v Nicolay (No 2)*, differing views from members of the same appellate bench on whether or not an inference of dishonesty should be drawn.[48] In *Bahr v Nicolay (No 2)* itself, the High Court of Australia was divided both on whether the Thompsons' acknowledgement and subsequent repudiation of the Bahrs' unregistered interest amounted to facts from which an inference of dishonesty might properly be drawn,[49] and also on whether the inference had to be of dishonesty leading up to registration of the Thompsons' interest or whether it was sufficient that dishonesty could be inferred after the time of registration.[50]

These difficulties are to be expected. A finding of statutory fraud is a finding of fact. Moreover, it is a finding of fact that depends on an inference as to the state of mind of the defendant, whether assessed with reference to what the court takes to be the defendant's beliefs, or with reference to the standard of conduct that may reasonably be demanded of the honest person, or both.[51] Making findings of fact and drawing inferences from established facts are exercises that inevitably generate uncertainty, because reasonable minds may disagree about whether a finding of fact or an inference is justified. And uncertainty in the resolution of disputes over land is to be minimised in any title registration system, because it undermines the fundamental aim of all

---

[45] Douglas J Whalan, 'The Meaning of Fraud under the Torrens System' (1975) 6 *New Zealand Universities Law Review* 207.

[46] *Assets Company v Mere Roihi* [1905] AC 176 (PC); *Waimiha Sawmilling Co Ltd v Waione Timber Co Ltd* [1926] AC 101 (PC); *Wicks v Bennett* (1921) 30 CLR 80 (HCA); *Mills v Stokman* (1967) 116 CLR 61 (HCA); *RM Hosking Properties Pty Ltd v Barnes* [1971] SASR 100 (SASC); *Szabo v Janeil Enterprises Ltd* (2006) 55 BCLR (4th) 188 (BCSC).

[47] *Waimiha Sawmilling Co Ltd (in liq) v Waione Timber Co Ltd* [1923] NZLR 1137 (NZCA); *McCrae v Wheeler* [1969] NZLR 333 (NZSC); *Efstratiou, H Glantschnig and Petrovic v Christine Glantschnig* [1972] NZLR 594 (NZCA).

[48] *Hackworth v Baker* [1936] 1 WWR 321 (Sask CA); *Sutton v O'Kane* [1973] 2 NZLR 304 (NZCA); *Holt Renfrew and Co Ltd v Henry Singer Ltd* (1982) 135 DLR (3d) 391 (Alb CA); *Bunt v Hallinan* [1985] 1 NZLR 450 (NZCA); and of course *Bahr v Nicolay (No 2)* itself.

[49] *Bahr v Nicolay (No 2)* (1988) 164 CLR 604 (HCA) 615–16 (Mason CJ and Dawson J); *contra* 636–7 (Wilson and Toohey JJ).

[50] *Bahr v Nicolay (No 2)* (1988) 164 CLR 604 (HCA) 615–16 (Mason CJ and Dawson J); *contra* 633 (Wilson and Toohey JJ).

[51] *Royal Brunei Airlines Sdn Bhd v Tan* [1995] 2 AC 378 (PC); *Twinsectra Ltd v Yardley* [2002] 2 AC 164 (HL); *Barlowe Clowes International Ltd (in liq) v Eurotrust International Ltd* [2006] 1 All ER 333 (PC).

title registration systems: to ensure certainty in land transactions and security of title to the greatest degree possible. If there is some way of dealing with a case like *Bahr v Nicolay (No 2)* that does not entail drawing an inference of dishonesty but nonetheless leaves open the door to proprietary remedies, it might be more easily reconciled with the demands of certainty and security while giving claimants a chance, where appropriate, to enforce their unregistered interests. One such way is via an *in personam* claim.

(b) An *In Personam* Claim

Remember that an *in personam* claim is one based on the conduct of a registered title-holder that, if successful, results in a remedy with proprietary consequences. In a case like *Bahr v Nicolay (No 2)* only two *in personam* claims seem possible. The first is a claim in proprietary—or, in Australia, equitable—estoppel. However, such a claim is only feasible where the holder of the unregistered interest has been induced by the defendant into some act of detrimental reliance.[52] In a case where the defendant has, by acknowledging an unregistered interest in some way, persuaded the holder of that unregistered interest not to protect the interest in some other way, say by lodging a caveat in a Torrens jurisdiction, it may be possible to prove detrimental reliance. However, that will not always be the case and it certainty was not the case in *Bahr v Nicolay (No 2)*. There, the Bahrs failed to lodge a caveat prior to the transfer to the Thompsons, but the Thompsons did not induce them to stay their hand in this fashion.

The second possible *in personam* claim in a case like *Bahr v Nicolay (No 2)* is an action for breach of trust. Indeed, in the High Court of Australia, all five judges who decided the case thought that the Bahrs could enforce a trust against the Thompsons. Chief Justice Mason and Dawson J thought that an inference of intention to create an express trust could be drawn out of the acknowledgement of the Bahrs' interest that was in the contract between Nicolay and the Thompsons.[53] In light of this express trust, it would seem that, rather than an order of specific performance, what the Bahrs sought against the Thompsons was really an order compelling the Thompsons to carry out the trust according to its terms, an order to which the Bahrs were entitled according to the rule in *Saunders v Vautier*,[54] and which would have proprietary consequences by causing a transfer of title from the Thompsons to the Bahrs. However, the express trust analysis of *Bahr v Nicolay (No 2)* is troubling. First, it appears unclear from the evidence whether the Thompsons intended to create a trust of the land itself,

---

[52] *Inwards v Baker* [1965] 2 QB 29 (CA); *Crabb v Arun District Council* [1976] Ch 197 (CA); *Yeoman's Row Management Limited v Cobbe* [2008] UKHL 55; and, in Australia, *Waltons Stores (Interstate) Ltd v Maher* (1988) 164 CLR 387 (HCA).
[53] *Bahr v Nicolay (No 2)* (1988) 164 CLR 604 (HCA) 618–19.
[54] *Saunders v Vautier* (1841) 4 Beav 115 (Ch).

or a trust of a contractual promise given to Nicolay for the benefit of the Bahrs.[55] And secondly, it is doubtful that there was sufficient evidence from which an inference of intention to create a trust could be drawn at all;[56] the fact that three of the five High Court judges who heard the case thought that an express trust had not arisen illustrates this.

These three judges, Wilson and Toohey JJ, and Brennan J, thought that in *Bahr v Nicolay (No 2)*, the Thompsons' conduct was such that equity ought to impose a constructive trust on them, again entitling the Bahrs to seek orders compelling the discharge of the trust.[57] In doing so, their Honours relied on the line of English authority beginning with *Rochefoucauld v Boustead* and ending with *Ashburn Anstalt v WJ Arnold & Co.*[58] That line of authority is easy to apply in two types of case. In the first type of case, A, the registered owner of land, holds it on trust for C and sells it to B. B orally promises A that B will, after registration, hold the land on trust for C. B repudiates that trust after registration. Here, B shelters improperly behind the writing requirements of the Statute of Frauds, and equity will not tolerate that. B's conduct offends conscience sufficiently to justify the imposition of a constructive trust.[59] In the second type of case, B makes no promise to A and performs no other acts, but B knows that A holds the land subject to C's unregistered interest, and B repudiates the unregistered interest after registration. Here, the line of English authority is clear that B's conduct is not sufficiently unconscionable to justify the imposition of a constructive trust. However, although these two types of case are capable of clear resolution, difficulties arise in other types of case where a court must work out what, in addition to B's knowledge of C's unregistered interest, might suffice to justify the imposition of a constructive trust on B in a case where B has not orally promised to hold land on trust after registration. Will it be sufficient that the sale from A to B is expressed to be 'subject to' C's unregistered interest? Will the fact that B 'acknowledges' C's unregistered interest—as in *Bahr v Nicolay (No 2)*—suffice?[60] Will the price that B pays to A be evidence of probative value in cases of this type?[61]

---

[55] See *Trident General Insurance Co Ltd v McNiece Bros Pty Ltd* (1988) 165 CLR 107 (HCA).

[56] See the oft-cited passage from the judgment of du Parcq J in *Re Schebsman; Official Receiver v Cargo Superintendents (London) Ltd* [1944] Ch 83 (CA) 104.

[57] *Bahr v Nicolay (No 2)* (1988) 164 CLR 604 (HCA) 638–9 (Wilson and Toohey JJ); 654–6 (Brennan J).

[58] *Rochefoucauld v Boustead* [1897] 1 Ch 196 (CA); *Bannister v Bannister* [1948] 2 All ER 133 (CA); *Binions v Evans* [1972] Ch 359 (CA); *Lyus v Prowsa Developments Ltd* [1982] 1 WLR 1044 (Ch); *Ashburn Anstalt v WJ Arnold & Co* [1989] Ch 1 (CA).

[59] *Rochefoucauld v Boustead* [1897] 1 Ch 196 (CA).

[60] *Bahr v Nicolay (No 2)* (1988) 164 CLR 604 (HCA) 626.

[61] Difficulties like these are discussed in Ben McFarlane, 'Constructive Trusts Arising on a Receipt of Property *Sub Conditione* (2004) 120 *Law Quarterly Review* 667; Gardner, above n 28, at 128–34; Nicholas Hopkins, 'How Should We Respond to Unconscionability? Unpacking the Relationship between Conscience and the Constructive Trust' in Martin Dixon

These, of course, are questions of fact that will fall to be determined by trial judges. They are not questions that are incapable of satisfactory resolution in individual cases. However, cases that turn on the answers to these questions are inevitably characterised by the same uncertainty as emerges from an inquiry into whether or not a person has engaged in statutory fraud, the uncertainty that arises once a court is required to draw an inference from established facts. This time, the inference is one of unconscionable conduct, not dishonesty, but it is surrounded by uncertainty nonetheless.

(ii) Ontario and Nova Scotia

(a) Ontario

If *Bahr v Nicolay (No 2)* were to arise in Ontario today, the resolution of the case would be straightforward. Unlike Torrens statutes, the Ontario Land Titles Act 1990 is silent on the question whether getting registered with actual knowledge or constructive notice of a prior unregistered interest amounts to fraud. However, in *United Trust Co v Dominion Stores Ltd*, a case that was analogous to *Bahr v Nicolay (No 2)*, a majority of the Supreme Court of Canada took that silence to mean that the Ontario legislature intended to leave undisturbed the general law principle that a transferee is bound by actual knowledge of a prior unregistered interest.[62] The Thompsons had actual knowledge of the Bahrs' unregistered right to re-purchase. Under Ontario law, they would therefore have been bound by that right and could have been ordered to take the steps necessary to effect the re-sale of the land to the Bahrs.

(b) Nova Scotia

In Nova Scotia, the Land Registration Act 2001 defines fraud expansively. That definition includes getting registered with: (i) actual knowledge of a prior unregistered interest; (ii) actual knowledge of the fact that the transaction by which one is getting registered was not authorised by the prior unregistered interest holder; and (iii) constructive notice that the transaction will prejudice the prior unregistered interest holder.[63] This opens the door to proprietary remedies in fewer cases than in Ontario. For example, it does not extend to cases where a transferee thought that a transaction was authorised but it turns out not to have been. However, it opens the door to proprietary

---

and Gerwyn LlH Griffiths (eds), *Contemporary Perspectives on Property, Equity and Trusts Law* (Oxford, Oxford University Press, 2007) 3.

[62] *United Trust Co v Dominion Stores Ltd* (1977) 71 DLR (3d) 72 (SCC) (Spence J; Judson, Ritchie and Beetz JJ concurring, Laskin CJC dissenting). See also Marcia Neave, 'The Concept of Notice under the Ontario Land Titles Act' (1976) 54 *Canadian Bar Review* 132.

[63] NS s 4(4). The definition does not extend to getting registered with constructive notice of a prior unregistered interest: NS s 4(2).

remedies in a much wider range of cases than does the Torrens response. In a case like *Bahr v Nicolay (No 2)*, where no question of authorisation of the transaction arises, the Nova Scotia definition of fraud appears to be satisfied whenever there is evidence that the transferee had actual knowledge of the prior unregistered interest at the time of registration. This is because it is difficult to imagine circumstances where such knowledge would be insufficient to support a finding of constructive notice that the transaction would prejudice the prior unregistered interest holder. In *Bahr v Nicolay (No 2)* itself, it is clear that the Thompsons' conduct in getting registered would have amounted to fraud under the Nova Scotia Land Registration Act. They knew of the Bahr's unregistered right to re-purchase, and the evidence shows that the reasonable person in their position would have known that the transaction would prejudice that unregistered right. Indeed, the Thompsons appeared to have actual knowledge, prior to registration, of the potential for prejudice to the Bahrs' interest: why else would they have bothered to acknowledge that interest in their contract with Nicolay?

The title registration systems of Ontario and Nova Scotia are able to handle cases like *Bahr v Nicolay (No 2)* with a greater degree of certainty than typical Torrens systems. That is because their responses to such cases depend on straightforward findings of fact relating to what defendants in the position of the Thompsons knew at the time of registration. Inferences of dishonesty need not be drawn from established facts (including facts relating to knowledge). Nor is it necessary to demonstrate that detrimental reliance has been induced, or that an intention to create a trust may be inferred, or that the conduct of the defendant justifies the imposition of a constructive trust.

To the Torrens mind, such certainty is gained at too high a price. As we have seen, it is a fundamental principle of the Torrens system that a registered title-holder is not bound by a prior unregistered interest of which they had actual knowledge or constructive notice at the time of registration, except where they have engaged in statutory fraud or an *in personam* claim may be brought against them. Justifications of this principle usually point to the desirability of protecting a transferee against unregistered interests of which they did not know and which they could not reasonably have discovered. It is therefore unclear why the principle extends to unregistered interests of which a transferee actually knew.[64] Nonetheless, for present purposes, we are content to concede that the responses of the title registration systems of Ontario and Nova Scotia to a case like *Bahr v Nicolay (No 2)* are at odds with the fundamentals that ought to underpin

---

[64] DW McMorland, 'Notice, Knowledge and Fraud' in David Grinlinton (ed), *Torrens in the Twenty-First Century* (Wellington, LexisNexis, 2003) 67, 96 points out that it was, after all, only the doctrine of constructive notice that created problems with general law conveyancing.

title registrations systems. We turn instead to a possible response to *Bahr v Nicolay (No 2)* that may lead to the award of a proprietary remedy, but that does not depend on dishonesty, detrimental reliance, intention, unconscionable conduct, or knowledge.

(iii) England and Wales

One fact about *Bahr v Nicolay (No 2)* is critical to understanding how the case might be dealt with if it arose today in England and Wales, but that fact was not considered relevant by the High Court of Australia in its determination of the case. The Bahrs were in actual and apparent occupation of the land in question prior to and at the time of the Thompsons' registration. They had been lessees of the land since the time when they sold it to Nicolay and they had conducted the business of a general store, post office and newsagency there.[65] The fact of occupation in a case like *Bahr v Nicolay (No 2)* means that the case can be determined under the law of England and Wales, such that a proprietary remedy is awarded, without resort to the notion of statutory fraud or *in personam* claims, thus avoiding the uncertainty generated by those approaches.

As we have seen, the combined effect of section 29 and Schedule 3 of the Land Registration Act 2002 is that an unregistered interest in land held by a person in occupation of that land is overriding and therefore enforceable against a person who gets registered as the owner of the land. A contractual right to compel the transfer of an ownership interest in land, such as the right that the Bahrs ultimately had pursuant to their contract with Nicolay, gives rise to an interest in that land under a constructive trust.[66] Because they were in occupation of the land, the Bahrs could enforce that interest against the Thompsons by way of an order requiring the Thompsons to transfer the land to the Bahrs on the terms set out in the Bahrs' contract with Nicolay. Thus, the resolution of *Bahr v Nicolay (No 2)* would have been straightforward under the law of England and Wales.

But what would have happened had the Bahrs not been in occupation of the land? Let us imagine a new case that falls to be determined according to the law of England and Wales, identical to *Bahr v Nicolay (No 2)* except that now the Bahrs are not in occupation. Their interest is not overriding according to the provisions of the Land Registration Act. They will most likely pursue an *in personam* claim, arguing that a constructive trust ought to be imposed on the Thompsons owing to the Thompsons' unconscionable conduct. But as we have seen, such a claim will generate uncertainty and, indeed, did generate uncertainty in *Bahr v Nicolay (No 2)* itself. Putting that

---

[65] *Bahr v Nicolay (No 2)* (1988) 164 CLR 604 (HCA) 606.
[66] *Lysaght v Edwards* (1876) 2 Ch D 499 (CA).

in personam claim to one side, in this variation on *Bahr v Nicolay (No 2)* there appears to be no reason in the law of England and Wales to allow the Bahrs access to the proprietary remedy that they seek. Is this desirable?

In his recent account of land law in England and Wales, Simon Gardner draws a distinction between what he calls 'organised' and 'disorganised' ways of creating interests in land. Organised interests are the product of intention and planning. Disorganised interests are not the product of intention and planning, but they arise anyway because—for one of any number of reasons—justice requires them. Mr Gardner points out that the Land Registration Act adopts one strategy for ensuring the protection of organised interests, and another strategy for ensuring the protection of disorganised interests. Organised interests, because they are the product of intention and planning, may be protected by registering, recording, or otherwise protecting them on the register and if they are not so protected, the statute assumes that they are postponed to interests that are registered or recorded. But in the case of disorganised interests, because they are not the product of intention and planning, it would be unreasonable to expect their holders to take actions to protect them on the register. Instead, to the extent that they are regarded as worthy of protection, they override under Schedule 3 of the Land Registration Act.[67] Underlying the adoption of these two strategies that Mr Gardner identifies in the Land Registration Act is an assumption. The assumption is that, where a person acquires an organised interest, they *ought* to protect it on the register and if they fail to do so they bear the risk of it being unenforceable. Another way of putting this is to say that individuals in a community that has adopted a title registration system have a social responsibility to use the register to protect organised interests in land and contribute thereby to maximising the accuracy of the register.[68]

If a social responsibility to protect organised interests on the register is accepted—and it appears to be accepted in the Land Registration Act—then there appears to be no reason why, in the variation on *Bahr v Nicolay (No 2)*, the Bahrs' inability to enforce their interest against the Thompsons under the law of England and Wales should generate unease. They have failed to use the register to protect the interest that they acquired pursuant to their contract with Nicolay.[69] Yet that interest has arisen because of the

---

[67] Gardner, above n 28, at 39–47.

[68] Murray Raff, *Private Property and Environmental Responsibility: A Comparative Study of German Real Property Law* (The Hague, Kluwer Law International, 2003) ch 1.

[69] In the real *Bahr v Nicolay (No 2)*, arising as it did in the Torrens jurisdiction of Western Australia, it was the Bahrs' failure to lodge a caveat that left their interest unprotected. Strictly, in Australia at least, lodging a caveat does not entail using the register to protect an interest, because a caveat is considered to be a private direction to the registrar: see *J & H Just Holdings Pty Ltd v Bank of New South Wales* (1971) 125 CLR 546 (HCA). However, in England and Wales, an unregistrable interest is protected either by entering a notice of it and thereby recording it on the register or by applying for a restriction preventing inconsistent dealing, which restriction will also be entered on the register: see EW, Pt 4.

intentional and planned execution of a contract. In Mr Gardner's language, it is an organised interest. The Bahrs ought to have protected it on the register and their failure to discharge their social responsibility to do so has quite properly rendered the interest unenforceable against the Thompsons now that the Thompsons are the registered owners of the land. It is true that if, in the variation on *Bahr v Nicolay (No 2)*, the Bahrs' interest arises under a constructive trust,[70] that interest may not be recorded by entering a notice of it on the register.[71] However, the interest may be protected by applying for a restriction preventing the registration of any inconsistent interest until the Bahrs are at least allowed an opportunity to protect their interest further.[72] The demand of the Land Registration Act that such a mechanism for protection be utilised if an unregistered interest is to be enforceable, is reasonable in light of the social responsibility to contribute to the accuracy of the register in cases—like the variation on *Bahr v Nicolay (No 2)*—where the unregistered interest-holder is not in occupation of the land.

B. Personal Remedies

Suppose that the Bahrs are not entitled to recover their land on any of the approaches discussed above. Will they be entitled to personal relief against either Nicolay or the Thompsons? Cases of acknowledgement and repudiation of the claimant's interest do not give rise to any question of restitution for unjust enrichment. In *Bahr v Nicolay (No 2)* itself, the basis of the Bahrs' claim to personal relief will be loss of the opportunity to re-purchase the land after three years, and damages will be compensatory.

Nicolay will be liable for breach of contract if, being under an absolute obligation to permit the Bahrs to re-purchase the land, he transfers the land to the Thompsons who repudiate the obligation. It is immaterial that Nicolay, as was in fact the case in *Bahr v Nicolay (No 2)* itself, honestly believed that the Thompsons would respect the obligation. However, no breach will have been committed if Nicolay was under an obligation to use his best efforts to ensure that the Bahrs were able to re-purchase the land, since he had clearly taken all reasonable steps to do so.[73]

An alternative for the Bahrs is to sue the Thompsons in tort for inducing Nicolay to commit a breach of contract, but this claim is also likely to fail. The requirements of this tort, established in *Lumley v Gye*,[74] have recently

---

[70] *Lysaght v Edwards* (1876) 2 Ch D 499 (CA).
[71] EW s 33(a)(i).
[72] EW ss 40-3.
[73] *British Motor Trade Association v Salvadori* [1949] Ch 556 (CA); *Tophams Ltd v Earl of Sefton* [1967] 1 AC 50 (HL); Robert Megarry and HWR Wade, *The Law of Real Property*, 5th edn (London, Stevens, 1984) 777.
[74] *Lumley v Gye* (1853) 2 E & B 216 (QB).

been considered by the House of Lords in *OBG v Allan*; *Mainstream Properties v Young*.[75] Their Lordships reaffirmed the principle that the liability of the procuring party is accessory to liability for breach of contract.[76] Without a breach of contract, there can be no liability for this tort. Previous decisions and dicta to the effect that liability can be imposed for interference with contractual relations where there has been no breach of contract were overruled.[77] If Nicolay has not committed a breach of contract by transferring the land to the Thompsons, the latter cannot be held liable under *Lumley v Gye*, even if they have procured the transfer with every intention of defeating the Bahrs' rights in the land.

The Bahrs are little better placed if the transfer to the Thompsons is a breach of contract. Liability will then depend on whether the Thompsons 'actually realize' that procuring the transfer will cause Nicolay to be in breach of contract.[78] There was no evidence in *Bahr v Nicolay (No 2)* itself that the Thompsons intended to defeat the Bahrs' right to re-purchase when they bought the land from Nicolay; the idea of repudiating that right only occurred to them later.

Personal liability under *Lumley v Gye* will therefore only be imposed if: first, the land was transferred to the Thompsons in breach of contract; and secondly, the Thompsons realised that they had procured the breach. In Part II.B, we argued that the principles of personal liability should complement, or be congruent with, the principles applicable to proprietary recovery. Liability under *Lumley v Gye* has of course developed independently from the principles of title registration, and there is no special reason to expect to find congruity of legal principle in cases of acknowledgement and repudiation like *Bahr v Nicolay (No 2)*. Proprietary recovery is restitutionary whereas liability under *Lumley v Gye* is compensatory. Nonetheless, the application of this tort to property transactions is consistent with the application of the principle of indefeasibility and its exceptions. A transferee of land who gives an undertaking to respect the transferor's contractual obligations to a third party, and who repudiates those obligations in circumstances in which the repudiation will be a breach of contract, will have acted dishonestly for the purposes of the fraud exception to indefeasibility, and will have incurred liability for inducing breach of contract. Personal liability therefore reinforces, and does not undercut, the principles of title registration in acknowledgement and repudiation cases.

---

[75] *OBG v Allan*; *Mainstream Properties v Young* [2007] UKHL 21. See also Janet O'Sullivan, 'Intentional Economic Torts in the House of Lords' [2007] *Cambridge Law Journal* 503.

[76] *OBG v Allan*; *Mainstream Properties v Young* [2007] UKHL 21, [5] (Lord Hoffmann).

[77] *OBG v Allan*; *Mainstream Properties v Young* [2007] UKHL 21, [44] (Lord Hoffmann, overruling *Torquay Hotel Co Ltd v Cousins* [1969] 2 Ch 106 (CA); disapproving *Merkur v Island Shipping Corp* [1983] 2 AC 570 (HL) 607–8 (Lord Diplock)).

[78] *OBG v Allan*; *Mainstream Properties v Young* [2007] UKHL 21, [39] (Lord Hoffmann).

IV. BREACH OF TRUST OR FIDUCIARY OBLIGATION

Our final case study is *Farah Constructions Pty Ltd v Say-Dee Pty Ltd.*[79] Farah and Say-Dee owned land in Sydney, which they held for the purposes of a property development joint venture that they had entered into. Farah had undertaken to manage the development project, including applying for necessary planning permissions from the local council. Its applications were refused for the reason that the proposed development was too large for the site. According to Say-Dee, Farah acted in breach of fiduciary obligation by failing to disclose to Say-Dee the reason for the council's refusal and by then procuring the acquisition of adjacent land with a view to developing for its own benefit a larger site. Some of the adjacent land was acquired by the wife and daughters of the controlling mind of Farah, and the wife and daughters were subsequently registered as the owners of that land. Say-Dee sought a declaration that the wife and daughters held their registered titles on constructive trust and consequential orders requiring the wife and daughters to divest themselves of those titles. For the purposes of the following analysis, we assume that Farah did act in breach of fiduciary obligation when it procured the acquisition of the adjacent land by the wife and daughters of its controlling mind, notwithstanding that the High Court of Australia found that the facts disclosed no such breach.[80]

A. Proprietary Remedies

(i) The Torrens Response

(a) Statutory Fraud

As we have seen, in a Torrens system a finding of statutory fraud entails an inference of dishonesty being drawn from facts relating to the knowledge and the conduct of the defendant. In the rare case where a defendant has dishonestly assisted in a breach of trust or fiduciary obligation pursuant to which they have become the registered holder of a title previously held subject to the trust or fiduciary obligation, such an inference may be drawn and a finding of statutory fraud may be made, opening the door to proprietary remedies.[81] However, that rare case was not *Farah Constructions* itself.

---

[79] *Farah Constructions Pty Ltd v Say-Dee Pty Ltd* (2007) 236 ALR 209 (HCA) ('*Farah Constructions*').

[80] On the fiduciary aspects of the case, see Matthew Harding, 'Two Fiduciary Fallacies' (2007) 2 *Journal of Equity* 1.

[81] Whether or not a defendant has *dishonestly* assisted in a breach of trust or fiduciary obligation is not a question of interest to Australian courts, particularly in light of *Farah Constructions*. Rather, Australian courts are interested in the question whether a defendant has assisted in a dishonest breach of trust or fiduciary obligation with actual knowledge or

There was no evidence that the defendants in that case dishonestly assisted in a breach of fiduciary obligation and, indeed, the claimant did not even plead dishonesty. In the equally rare case where, on agency principles, the dishonesty of a defaulting trustee or fiduciary may be brought home to the defendant who received a title as a consequence of the breach of trust or fiduciary obligation, a finding of statutory fraud may be made. However, there was no evidence of dishonesty on Farah's part in *Farah Constructions* and, although the New South Wales Court of Appeal was prepared to find an agency relationship between Farah and the wife and daughters of its controlling mind, the High Court of Australia rejected that finding.[82] As a result, nothing could be imputed to the defendants on agency principles.

Even in Nova Scotia, where the statutory definition of fraud is more expansive than in other Torrens jurisdictions, it seems clear that *Farah Constructions* would not be treated as a case of statutory fraud. Remember that statutory fraud in Nova Scotia includes getting registered with, inter alia, actual knowledge of the existence of an unregistered interest in the land in question.[83] There was no evidence in *Farah Constructions* that the defendants had actual knowledge of a prior unregistered interest in the disputed land, except on the agency principles whose application to the case was rejected by the High Court of Australia. No finding of statutory fraud based on the law of Nova Scotia could follow.

(b) Volunteer Status

In Torrens jurisdictions, the second possible path to proprietary remedies in a case like *Farah Constructions* is through a finding that the defendant received as a volunteer (ie without providing valuable consideration) a title that was encumbered by a prior unregistered interest and that therefore might be subject to proprietary remedies in favour of the holder of the prior unregistered interest.[84] This is a path to proprietary remedies only in some Torrens jurisdictions. In New South Wales, the Northern Territory, Queensland and Western Australia, a volunteer, on registration, gains the benefit of the immunity from proprietary remedies otherwise enforceable against them that is known in Torrens language as indefeasibility of title.[85] In Victoria, Alberta, New Brunswick, and Nova Scotia, that immunity is

---

constructive notice of the facts constituting the breach: *Farah Constructions* (2007) 236 ALR 209, [174]–[179].

[82] Compare *Say-Dee Pty Ltd v Farah Constructions Pty Ltd* [2005] NSWCA 309, [214]–[215] and *Farah Constructions* (2007) 236 ALR 209, [100], [122]–[129].

[83] NS s 4(4).

[84] Michael Bryan, 'Recipient Liability under the Torrens System: Some Category Errors' in Charles Rickett and Ross Grantham (eds), *Structure and Justification in Private Law: Essays for Peter Birks* (Oxford, Hart Publishing, 2008) 339.

[85] *Bogdanovic v Koteff* (1988) 12 NSWLR 472 (NSWCA); NT s 183; Qld s 180; *Conlan v Registrar of Titles* (2001) 24 WAR 299 (WASC).

not extended to a volunteer.[86] In other Torrens jurisdictions, the status of volunteers is unclear at present.[87] New South Wales, the jurisdiction in which *Farah Constructions* arose, extends indefeasibility of title to volunteers, all else being equal.[88] Therefore, had the defendants in *Farah Constructions* received their titles as volunteers, they would have been protected. However, the question of volunteer status was, ultimately, irrelevant in *Farah Constructions*, because the High Court of Australia found that the defendants gave valuable consideration for their titles.[89] On the basis of that finding, the defendants in *Farah Constructions* would have been immune from proprietary remedies in any Torrens jurisdiction, even one that makes available proprietary remedies against volunteers qua volunteers.

(c) An *In Personam* Claim

In a case like *Farah Constructions*, the third possible path to proprietary remedies in Torrens jurisdictions is also the most controversial. It is the pursuit of an *in personam* claim. Given the facts of *Farah Constructions*, *in personam* claims based on duress, undue influence and misrepresentation may be ruled out. Nor was there evidence on the basis of which the equitable doctrine of *Barclay's Bank plc v O'Brien* might be applied.[90] There was no breach of any contract between the claimant and the defendants; nor did a relationship of express trust or a fiduciary relationship of any other type exist between those parties. And there was no evidence on the basis of which a constructive trust might be imposed because of the defendants' unconscionable conduct, as happened in *Bahr v Nicolay (No 2)*. If an *in personam* claim is to succeed in a case like *Farah Constructions*, it must take the form of a claim of knowing receipt. Whether such claims may bring about the loss of a registered Torrens title in a case like *Farah Constructions* has been the subject of considerable debate in Australia in recent years.[91]

The debate has concentrated on whether allowing an *in personam* claim based on the receipt of a title, previously held subject to a trust or fiduciary obligation, with actual knowledge or constructive notice of the breach of

---

[86] *King v Smail* [1958] VR 273 (Vic SC); *Rasmussen v Rasmussen* [1995] 1 VR 613 (Vic SC); *Kaup v Imperial Oil Co* (1962) 32 DLR (2d) 38 (SCC, on appeal from Alb); NB s 15(4); NS s 20(3). The same is true of Ontario, which is not a Torrens jurisdiction: Ont s 90.

[87] For example, New Zealand: GW Hinde and DW McMorland (eds), *Hinde, McMorland and Sim: Land Law in New Zealand* (looseleaf, Wellington, LexisNexis, 2004) [9.079]; and Saskatchewan: Roger Carter, 'Does Indefeasibility Protect the Title of a Volunteer?' (1984–85) 49 *Saskatechewan Law Review* 329.

[88] *Bogdanovic v Koteff* (1988) 12 NSWLR 472 (NSWCA).

[89] *Farah Constructions* (2007) 236 ALR 209, [188].

[90] *Barclay's Bank plc v O'Brien* [1994] 1 AC 180 (HL).

[91] See Bryan, above n 84; Matthew Harding, '*Barnes v Addy* Claims and the Indefeasibility of Torrens Title' (2007) 31 *Melbourne University Law Review* 343, where we discuss the case law and the issues.

trust or fiduciary obligation, undermines the fundamental principle of the Torrens system that the security of title of a registered title-holder is not affected by knowledge or notice of an unregistered interest. In our view, the High Court of Australia was right in thinking that *Farah Constructions* was not a case of knowing receipt, irrespective of whether the elements of knowing receipt are consistent with the immunity given to registered title-holders in Torrens systems. The defendants in *Farah Constructions* were found by the High Court to have had no knowledge or notice of any kind either of the unregistered interest claimed by the claimant or of the breach of fiduciary obligation that we are here assuming was entailed in the circumstances in which the defendants acquired their titles.[92] Moreover, their Honours found that the acquisition of the titles by the defendants did not amount to receipt for the purposes of knowing receipt, because the claimant never had an interest in relevant property that was exchanged for those titles and was subject to a trust or fiduciary obligation.[93] Thus, the defendants could not have been liable for knowing receipt in either a Torrens system where there may be a conflict between the elements of knowing receipt and the immunity known as indefeasibility of title, or even in a non-Torrens system like Ontario's in which a registered title-holder is bound by unregistered interests of which they had actual knowledge at the time of registration.

The many hurdles facing a claimant who makes a claim of knowing receipt in a case like *Farah Constructions* suggest that such a claim is not a desirable path to proprietary remedies, even if it is correct to say that in a Torrens jurisdiction such remedies may be awarded against a registered title-holder in a knowing receipt case. The possibility remains, perhaps only in theory at present at least in Australian law, that an *in personam* claim might be brought in a case like *Farah Constructions* based on the unjust enrichment of the defendant. There is insufficient space here to consider such a claim in detail; suffice it to say that if the principle of indefeasibility of title rules out an *in personam* claim based on knowing receipt, it is difficult to see how that principle could be consistent with proprietary restitution of unjust enrichment. Whether it might be consistent with restitution in the form of personal relief we take up below.

(ii) England and Wales

That leaves England and Wales. Once, the availability in England and Wales of proprietary remedies in a case like *Farah Constructions* would have depended on whether the defendants had actual knowledge of the

---

[92] *Farah Constructions* (2007) 236 ALR 209, [122]–[129].
[93] *Farah Constructions* (2007) 236 ALR 209, [117]–[118].

claimant's interest.[94] However, under the Land Registration Act 2002, that is no longer the case. Proprietary remedies in a case like *Farah Constructions* are now available only if: the claimant's interest is overriding; the defendants acquired their titles as volunteers; or an *in personam* claim may be brought. We have discussed already all but the first of these possibilities, and either ruled them out or concluded that they are subject to much uncertainty. In *Farah Constructions*, the defendants were not volunteers, nor did they have any knowledge of the claimant's interest. Was the claimant's interest in *Farah Constructions* overriding? Say-Dee was not in actual and apparent occupation of the land in dispute; it is not known who occupied that land. Nor did its interest—as claimed—fall within any of the other categories of overriding interest in Schedule 3 of the Land Registration Act. As a result, that interest was not enforceable against the defendants under section 29 of the Land Registration Act.

It seems, therefore, that if the claimant had sought proprietary remedies under the law of England and Wales in *Farah Constructions*, the outcome of the case would have been the same as it was in the High Court of Australia. One aspect of the case suggests that this outcome ought to generate a little disquiet. The claimant's interest in *Farah Constructions*—assuming now that the claimant had an interest in the land in dispute—arose in a disorganised way. It was not the product of intention and planning. Therefore, it cannot be said that the claimant in *Farah Constructions* had only itself to blame because it did not protect its interest by lodging a caveat or, as might have occurred in England and Wales, applying for a restriction to be entered on the register. At the same time, the claimant's interest was not of a type that could have been overriding under Schedule 3 of the Land Registration Act, because the claimant was not in occupation of the land. The title registration system of England and Wales is silent when it comes to the enforceability of interests that are not overriding but that cannot reasonably be protected on the register because they are disorganised. This silence suggests one of two conclusions: either such interests are appropriately postponed in cases like *Farah Constructions*, or they are appropriately protected in (at least some) such cases through awarding proprietary remedies in response to *in personam* claims.[95] If the latter conclusion is correct, the smooth functioning of the system envisaged by the Land Registration Act depends, in cases like *Farah Constructions*, on the present uncertainty surrounding knowing receipt being cleared up.

---

[94]   *Pfeffer v Rigg* [1977] 1 WLR 285 (Ch).
[95]   Elizabeth Cooke and Pamela O'Connor take the latter view: 'Purchaser Liability to Third Parties in the English Land Registration System: A Comparative Perspective' (2004) 120 *Law Quarterly Review* 640, 664.

B. Personal Remedies

In *Farah Constructions*, a personal claim based on knowing receipt against the wife and daughters for the value of the properties they acquired would have failed for the same reasons that the *in personam* claim based on knowing receipt failed. First, the wife and daughters had received, in consequence of the assumed breach of fiduciary duty, not titles to land, but only non-confidential information (which is not, in law, property) in light of which they acquired those titles. Secondly, they had no knowledge of any breach of fiduciary obligation. Even though what constitutes knowledge for this purpose is a notoriously difficult question to which common law jurisdictions have given a variety of answers,[96] there is no suggestion that the defendants knew of a breach of fiduciary obligation on any of the tests currently applied.

Debate rages about whether a claimant in a case like *Farah Constuctions* should be entitled to a strict liability claim against the recipient which would either replace the existing knowledge-based equitable claim or supplement it.[97] Moreover, there are cases (although *Farah Constructions* is not one of them) in which the claimant will have a common law claim for money had and received.[98] Arguments about whether the claim is founded in unjust enrichment or enforces property rights can be put to one side for the moment.[99] On either view, a strict liability claim is being put forward as an alternative to an 'equitable tort' which requires proof of some kind of knowledge.

For present purposes, the critical question is whether a defendant should be strictly liable to pay the value of property received to a victim of a breach of fiduciary obligation when the defendant enjoys an indefeasible title to the property. In a casenote on *Farah Constructions*, Matthew Conaglen and Richard Nolan suggest that the finding that the wife and daughters were not personally liable for having knowingly received their titles as a consequence of Farah's breach of fiduciary obligation prevented the indefeasibility

---

[96] *Equiticorp Industries Group Ltd v Hawkins* [1991] 3 NZLR 700 (NZCA); *Citadel General Assurance Co v Lloyds Bank Canada* (1997) 152 DLR (4th) 411 (SCC); *Bank of Credit and Commerce International (Overseas) Ltd v Akindele* [2001] Ch 437 (CA); *Farah Constructions*.

[97] *Criterion Properties plc v Stratford UK Properties LLC* [2004] 1 WLR 1846 (HL) 1848 (noted by Robert Stevens in [2004] *Lloyd's Commercial and Maritime Law Quarterly* 421); Lord Nicholls, 'Knowing Receipt: the Need for a New Landmark' in W Cornish et al (eds), *Restitution, Past, Present and Future: Essays in Honour of Gareth Jones* (Oxford, Hart Publishing, 1998) ch 15; Jill Martin, 'Recipient Liability after *Westdeutsche*' [1998] *Conveyancer* 13; Robert Chambers, 'Knowing Receipt: Frozen in Australia' (2007) 2 *Journal of Equity* 40.

[98] *Lipkin Gorman (a firm) v Karpnale Ltd* [1991] 2 AC 548 (HL); *Spangaro v Corporate Investment Funds Management Ltd* (2003) 47 ACSR 285 (FCA, Finkelstein J).

[99] Virgo, above n 40.

principle from being undermined surreptitiously.[100] The claimant recovered neither the properties nor the value of the properties in a personal restitutionary claim.

The suggestion is important, and returns us to the policy question discussed in connection with *Lawrence v Wright* in Part II.B above. In what circumstances should a claimant be entitled to a restitutionary remedy, based on the value of an interest in land, when a proprietary claim to that interest itself would fail? We have already argued that the grounds of personal liability should be consistent with the principles of proprietary recovery and not independent of them. In the rich academic literature on the equitable response to cases of receipt there are many persuasive arguments for and against the imposition of strict liability on recipients. But from a title registration perspective the arguments for the imposition of liability based on fault—and preferably requiring the recipient to have a high degree of cognition of the breach of trust or fiduciary obligation in question[101]—are more consistent with the principles of title registration than the arguments for strict liability. The fraud or *in personam* exceptions to indefeasibility will apply only if the recipient deliberately facilitated the breach of trust or fiduciary obligation in taking title to the property, or engaged in some other unconscionable conduct which contributed to the property being transferred to them. Alternatively, if the arguments for strict liability in equity are accepted the recipient's indefeasible title should defeat a personal, as well as a proprietary, claim based on the value of the property received. If the law compels the innocent registered title-holder to pay the value of the property received to the claimant who has been deprived of it by a breach of trust or fiduciary obligation, the title-holder will enjoy the form of indefeasibility of title but not its economic substance.

V. CONCLUSION

Pamela O'Connor has argued that the 'key parameter' for a comparative study of title registration systems is the balance that each system strikes between protecting holders of interests in land and protecting purchasers of interests in land: what she calls the balance between 'static security'

---

[100] Matthew Conaglen and Richard Nolan, 'Recipient Liability in Equity' [2007] *Cambridge Law Journal* 515, 517.

[101] Arguably down to the third point on the scale of knowledge expounded by Peter Gibson J in *Baden, Delvaux and Lecuit v Société Générale pour Favoriser le Développement du Commerce et de l'Industrie en France SA* [1983] BCLC 325; [1993] 1 WLR 509 (Ch). However, a case can be made that knowledge of circumstances that would indicate a breach of trust or fiduciary obligation to an honest and reasonable person—the fourth point on the scale—should also suffice. See Fox, above n 30, at 41.

and 'dynamic security'.[102] In addition to that parameter for analysis, we would add two others. First, there is the extent to which the operation of a title registration system is consistent with the aims of static *and* dynamic security, whatever their correct balance might be. And secondly, there is the extent to which the availability of personal remedies against the holders of registered titles is consistent with the availability of proprietary remedies against such persons.

In light of these three parameters, three conclusions emerge from our comparative analysis of responses to fraud in title registration systems. First, the typical Torrens response to forgery cases is insufficiently sensitive to the static security of title of those in occupation of land, especially in cases where there is a dispute between the person in occupation and a mortgagee seeking to exercise their power of sale. Secondly, in acceptance and repudiation cases, the Torrens emphasis on fraud and the *in personam* exception generates uncertainty that is at odds with the aim of security of titles whether that aim be static or dynamic security. And finally, consistency of personal and proprietary relief is not achieved to the extent that a personal restitutionary remedy may be awarded against the holder of an indefeasible title, requiring that title-holder to pay the value of the property in respect of which the title is held. As land lawyers in Torrens jurisdictions reflect on where the Torrens model is situated after 150 years, they would do well to note that, in the case of the first and second of these conclusions, lessons might be learned from non-Torrens models. And in the case of the third conclusion, lessons may need to be learned in all title registration systems about the proper relationship of statutory and general law.

---

[102] Pamela O'Connor, 'Registration of Title in England and Australia: A Theoretical and Comparative Analysis' in Elizabeth Cooke (ed), *Modern Studies in Property Law: Volume II* (Oxford, Hart Publishing, 2003) 81, 99.

2

The Versatility of State Indemnity Provisions

SIMON COOPER[*]

I. INTRODUCTION

S YSTEMS FOR REGISTRATION of title commonly include a
provision making available an indemnity by the state for losses which
occur in the course of dealings with registered land. Often the rationale for these indemnity provisions is explained summarily as a supplement
to indefeasibility of title, taking the stance that any property rights taken
away by the state's registration system ought to be replaced with a monetary substitute from the state. But regardless of its value in supporting a
concept of security of wealth through the protection of property rights via
their substituted value in monetary terms, this paper argues that indemnity is also to be justified on account of its function as a policy tool to
manipulate the attitudes and behaviour of those involved in land dealings.
Challenging the view that indemnity merely reflects the doctrine of indefeasible title in monetary terms, this paper argues that indemnity's merit lies
in its versatile character, which enables it to implement a range of specific
policy objectives.

II. DANGERS TO THE PROPRIETOR

Indemnity is usually expressed in the statutes as a state liability to pay in the
event of some particular type of loss, so it is helpful first to identify what
dangers present themselves to the holder of rights in land under a system
of registered title. In order to do this, the registered proprietor must look
not only at the current state of the land title register but, Janus-like, must
look into the future to seek potential sources of prospective deprivation
occurring due to future events, and into the past to discern events before

---

[*] Dr Simon Cooper is Senior Lecturer at the Cayman Islands Law School and Visiting
Professor at Stetson University, Florida.

acquisition which might have generated claims derogating from the state of title as currently appearing in the register. These two sets of dangers[1] to the integrity of the registered title will be considered in turn.

First, the danger of future deprivation of registered title is a necessary part of every system of title by registration: the system which gives to the current registered proprietor an indefeasible title is the very same system which can take it away in order to allocate it to a new registered proprietor. It is consequently possible for a registered proprietor to lose land through the future registration of another person who secures indefeasible title.[2] A particular variety of this type of deprivation can be seen when a parcel undergoes the transition from unregistered to registered title. If, at first compilation of the register, the existing common law rights are not entered on the register, the usual rule in registration systems is that they lose their priority vis-à-vis the first registered proprietor. In this way, first registration can constitute a future event with the potential to deprive the owner of title.

Secondly, deprivations of registered title caused by future events occurring only after the moment of acquisition must be clearly differentiated from any defects in title which are rooted in past events. A system for registration of title need not stipulate that the title as currently shown in the register is absolutely definitive and exhaustive, and the reality is that all registration systems have at least some circumstances in which property rights not entered on the register at the time of acquisition are nevertheless permitted to be enforced against a registered proprietor. It is the enforcement of these property rights, pre-dating the moment of the proprietor's registration, or arising at the moment of and because of the proprietor's registration, which constitutes a second source of danger to the integrity of the land title register as a description of the rights of the registered proprietor.

III. INDEMNITY FOR FUTURE-EVENT DEPRIVATIONS: POLICY OBJECTIVES

If a registered proprietor suffers a deprivation due to the acquisition of indefeasible title by another, and the deprivation occurred without consent or the proper operation of some overriding general law, then in English and Torrens registration systems the former registered proprietor will generally be entitled to a statutory indemnity. The remaining part of this segment will seek to identify the objectives which justify the availability of indemnity in this case.

---

[1] Other sources of losses, such as loss of registry documents and issue of erroneous certificates, do not alter the vesting of property rights and are not dealt with in this paper.

[2] Classic examples are *Frazer v Walker* [1967] 1 AC 569, decided under the Land Transfer Act 1952 (New Zealand), and *Norwich & Peterborough Building Society v Steed* [1993] Ch 116, decided under the Land Registration Act 1925 (England).

A. Promoting Acceptance of Registration

The first purpose ascribed to indemnity is to promote acceptance of a registration system. Ceding compensation in such cases has been perceived as critical in securing enactment of a registration bill. The possibility of loss of land under the indefeasibility provisions without redress was one of the chief grounds on which the South Australian legal profession opposed the original Torrens Bill; indemnity was vital to 'inspire confidence' and to 'draw the fangs of the opposition'.[3] This had earlier been recognised by the English commission reporting on the first proposed registration of title regime in England,[4] and again when the Torrens system spread to the African colonies.[5]

Once the relevant land registration bill has been enacted and has secured general acceptance, it may be the case that the other advantages of title registration are recognised as sufficient to entice the public to accept registration without indemnity. If so, consideration needs to be given to the continuing justifications for indemnity, whether it has served its purpose and may be abrogated. While it can be argued that the initial idea of palliating the objectors may have passed, there remains of course the possibility that if the indemnity provision were repealed the registration system would cease to command the confidence of the population. In England, for example, when it was realised that the statutory bars to indemnity would prohibit indemnity payment on the basis of an innocent contribution to an erroneous registration, the resulting expression of concern[6] led quickly to amendment of the terms of the statutory indemnity bar.[7] Several other imperfections in the indemnity provision, primarily in the method of quantifying indemnity awards, have been improved[8] in response to critical comment.[9] Other jurisdictions, including Scotland,[10]

---

[3] DJ Whalan, *The Torrens System in Australia* (Sydney, Law Book Co, 1982) 345. See also D Pike, 'Introduction of the Real Property Act in South Australia' (1961) *Adelaide Law Review* 169; *pace* R Stein, 'The Torrens System Assurance Fund in New South Wales' (1981) 55 *ALJ* 150, 151.

[4] See 'Report of the Commissioners to Consider the Subject of the Registration of Title with Reference to the Sale and Transfer of Land' (1857, c 2215), paras 26, 30, 57, 86.

[5] Eg JF Spry, 'Notes on the Tanganyika Land Registration Bill', para 9, contained in Appendix II of SR Simpson, IE Morgan and JE Jardin, *A Report on the Registration of Title to Land in Kenya* (Nairobi, Unpublished, 1961).

[6] S Cretney and G Dworkin, 'Rectification and Indemnity: Illusion and Reality' (1968) 84 *Law Quarterly Review* 528, 555.

[7] Land Registration and Land Charges Act 1971 (England) s 3(1).

[8] By the Land Registration Act 1997 (England).

[9] Including DJ Hayton, *Registered Land* (London, Sweet & Maxwell, 1973) ch 9. See also Law Commission, *Land Registration* (Law Comm Working Paper No 45, 1972) and Law Commission, *Third Report on Land Registration* (Law Comm Report No 158, 1987).

[10] Scottish Law Commission, *Discussion Paper on Land Registration: Registration, Rectification and Indemnity* (Discussion Paper No 128, Edinburgh, 2005).

Australian[11] and Canadian[12] states, have also shown an on-going interest in keeping under review the adequacy of their indemnity provisions.

In order to promote acceptance of the registration system, a registration bill must, at the very least, confer indemnity in those cases where the registration system is capable of making a person worse off. The principal danger not encountered at common law is that the statutory scheme of indefeasibility can cause an owner to relinquish priority in circumstances where the common law principle of *nemo dat quod non habet* would have allowed that owner to prevail. An indemnity provision which seeks merely to compensate for the losses that follow from the revised priority rules contained in a land registration statute could be drafted so as to indemnify simply for those deprivations which have been caused by the statute. This causation-based approach is taken in one of the constituent limbs of the traditional indemnity provision in Torrens statutes, as seen in the Land Transfer Act 1952 of New Zealand, which confers an indemnity claim on

> [a]ny person ...
>
> (b) who is deprived of any land, or of any estate or interest in land, through ... the registration of any other person as proprietor of that land ... and who by this Act is barred from bringing an action for possession or other action for the recovery of that land, estate, or interest.[13]

An illustration of the restrictive scope of this style of indemnity provision is presented by those Canadian states where the doctrine of deferred indefeasibility prevails. If a fraudster were to impersonate the registered proprietor of land in a sale, the purchaser becoming registered under a forged transfer, then the purchaser's registered title would be subject to revision. No indemnity would be paid since the loss of title would not be a deprivation caused by the operation of the statute: as the loss would have occurred at common law under the principle of *nemo dat*, the registration statute cannot be said to have caused the loss. Where immediate indefeasibility prevails, in contrast, the common law result is reversed in favour of the purchaser and indemnity would be payable to the ousted proprietor. Regardless of whether the regime in question is one of immediate or deferred indefeasibility, indemnity can be linked in this way to the reversal of priority caused by

---

[11] Examples include: New South Wales Law Reform Commission, *Torrens Title: Compensation for Loss* (Report No 76, Sydney, 1996); Queensland Law Reform Commission, *Consolidation of the Real Property Acts* (Report No 40, Victoria, 1991); Land Law Review Committee of the Northern Territory, *Guarantee of Torrens Title in the Northern Territory* (Report No 5, Darwin, 1991).

[12] Joint Land Titles Committee of Canada, *Renovating the Foundation: Proposals for a Model Land Recording and Registration Act for the Provinces and Territories of Canada* (Edmonton, JLTC, 1990); Alberta Law Reform Institute, *Proposals for a Land Recording and Registration Act for Alberta* Report No 69 (Edmonton, 1993).

[13] Land Transfer Act 1952 (New Zealand) s 172.

the new registered land regime. Some dissatisfaction has been expressed over the comparison with common law priority rules to determine the availability of indemnity and a movement has developed which prefers to substitute new rules referring to the validity of the transaction which led to the disputed registration.[14] While this approach possesses certain practical and technical advantages, it inevitably involves a slight departure from the technique of measuring loss by reference to the common law. To that extent, it falls short of the ideal of compensating deprivations caused by the registration system, and correspondingly diminishes its ability to promote acceptance of the registration statute.

B. Easing Registry Examinations of Instruments

As well as promoting the acceptance of a new registration regime, indemnity may also be used as an instrument to control the behaviour of those involved in the land transfer process. In particular, the presence of an indemnity clause may influence the operations of the registry. By introducing a power to accept less than perfect titles, coupled with an indemnity provision to cover any losses that may arise from that approach, a registry is prompted to accept instruments for registration which are imperfect. The registry may then take a less stringent approach to the examination and registration of instruments, avoiding inquiries into possible imperfections which might require an impracticably costly and time-consuming effort.

The scope for doubts to arise upon registry examination is substantially reduced where submissions consist only of instruments dealing with a title which has already been registered. Registration systems tend to go hand in hand with reforms to simplify titles, instruments and conveyancing, so it is rare that a registry would need to rely on indemnity to justify taking a calculated risk in registering a doubtful instrument. Only seldom might there be any query over a disposition which justifies the registry placing a conscious reliance on indemnity, although the aim of easing registry examinations may have a minor role in relation to questions over the validity of execution of instruments.[15]

---

[14] See the 'government undertakings' approach to indemnity proposed in Land Law Review Committee of the Northern Territories, *Guarantee of Torrens Title in the Northern Territories* (Report No 5, Darwin, 1991) 5; the 'system malfunction' approach in Part 7 of the Model Land Recording and Registration Bill recommended in Joint Land Titles Committee of Canada (above n 12); the 'mistake' based approach to rectification, upon which indemnity largely depends, under the Land Registration Act 2002 (England) Sch 4 para 2 and Sch 8 para 1(1).

[15] Author's interview with RC Buchanan, Cayman Islands Registrar of Lands, 10 July 2001; TW Mapp, *Torrens' Elusive Title* (Edmonton, Alberta Institute for Law Research and Reform, 1978) 70; Alberta Law Reform Institute (above n 12) at 154.

IV. INDEMNITY FOR FUTURE-EVENT DEPRIVATIONS: COUNTERPOLICIES

Having identified some policy objectives attributable to the availability of indemnity for future-event deprivations, it remains to consider how those objectives may conflict with other objectives of the registration system. The following subheadings describe potential countervailing objectives which militate against indemnity in certain areas, and which are therefore occasionally found as express restraints on the ambit of an indemnity clause.

A. Sanctity of Property

One of the policy objectives of indemnity mentioned above was the easing of the registry's examination of instruments submitted for registration. This policy must be balanced against the associated risk of destroying a subsisting property right when it is not detected by an abridged examination at registration.[16] Although monetary compensation could be offered through indemnity, this is not always a satisfactory substitute for the property right, and the security of wealth afforded by indemnity may be only one element in determining whether the system fulfills constitutional guarantees of protection against interference with property.

B. Suppressing Land Transaction Costs

One of the primary goals of land registration is to promote an efficient land market and to reduce the disincentives to trafficking in land, particularly those disincentives lying in the process of transaction itself, such as expense and delay. The need to set up and maintain an indemnity fund will inevitably lead to extra transactional costs in the guise of premiums taken by the registry for maintenance of the fund. If the premiums are allowed to escalate, this has a detrimental effect on overall transaction costs, and could frustrate indemnity's goal of cheapening conveyancing. The basic precautions taken by conveyancers and the registry should limit the number of indemnifiable future deprivations caused by imposters and simple forgeries (particularly the requirement in Torrens systems for notarised execution of transfers[17]), but various statutory constraints on indemnity have been imposed which are designed to keep premiums low. They include the techniques of correlating payments into the indemnity fund with payments out, and imposing limits on indemnity awards.

---

[16] CT Emery, 'The Chief Land Registrar's Power to Approve of a Good Holding Title' (1976) 40 *Conveyancer* 122, 129.

[17] For example, the original Real Property Act 1858 (South Australia) ss 88–90.

(i) Correlating Premiums and Awards

For so long as the indemnity system is administered in accordance with an insurance model, the costs attributable to indemnity should be low in comparison with private title insurance covering the same risks. Once the indemnity system deviates from an insurance model, there is the likelihood that the cost of the indemnity programme will cease to be correlated to the achievement of its objectives. A common situation (seen in England[18] and Torrens states[19]) is for a separate indemnity fund to be abolished and indemnity premium revenues paid directly to general government funds without any attempt to make an appraisal on an actuarial basis of the likely payments out upon successful claims. Where a substantial surplus is simply appropriated to general funds it may be characterised as no longer reflecting an insurance system but a form of disguised taxation of land transactions. The result is that the cost of land transactions may increase without delivering improvements in return.

(ii) Limits on Indemnity

Certain limits on the availability of indemnity in exceptional cases may be tolerated so long as the general effectiveness of indemnity as a policy tool is achieved in the broad run of cases by influencing the behaviour of conveyancers and registry title examiners. Limits on indemnity could assist in the preservation of the indemnity fund against exceptionally large claims and in keeping down the costs of indemnity premiums. Capping individual indemnity claims[20], for example, would still permit the fulfillment of the indemnity policy objectives in common dealings, leaving parties involved in especially large transactions to consider the desirability of private title insurance.[21] Other methods may be employed to relate payments out to payments in, such as providing for pro rata indemnity payments proportional to the standing of the indemnity fund, or simple non-payment upon the fund becoming exhausted.[22] Restrictions on quantum or outright bars

---

[18] The Land Registration Act 1936 ss 4 and 6 uncoupled the size of the indemnity fund from the level of payments in, and the Land Registration and Land Charges Act 1971 s 1 amalgamated the indemnity fund with the Consolidated Fund.

[19] For example, the Land Transfer Act 1870 (New Zealand) and its successors established the Assurance Fund which, after various mutations, was transferred to the Consolidated Fund by the Finance Act 1930 (New Zealand) s 53.

[20] For example, the Land Titles Act 2000 (Alberta) s 179(1).

[21] See Alberta Law Reform Institute (above n 12) at para 8(f).

[22] See the Land Registration Act 1925 (England), proviso to s 75(4), repealed by the Land Registration Act 1936 s 3(2). The indemnity under the Land Registration Act 1925 (England) s 75(4) was repealed by the Land Registration and Land Charges Act 1971 s 14.

to indemnity could also be imposed for particular types of loss, such as mineral titles.[23]

C. Encouraging Basic Self-Protection by the Proprietor

A danger in conferring indemnity is that it may tend to encourage a proprietor to neglect to take obvious and simple steps to safeguard his or her position against the possibility of future deprivation. A suitable response to this could be to deny indemnity where such steps have not been taken. One technique, seen in England[24], New Zealand[25] and New South Wales[26] amongst many others, has been to create a bar to indemnity, or to reduce its amount, in the event that the negligence of the indemnity claimant or his agent has contributed to the deprivation in respect of which indemnity would otherwise have been payable.

A clear illustration of negligent conduct would be the failure to protect a newly-acquired right on the register. If the land registration system were to permit indemnity upon an unprotected right being overridden by a later registered disposition, then the loss could be attributed exclusively to the failure to take the elementary precaution of registering; registration is the type of simple, cheap and speedy step that should not be discouraged by rewarding the irresponsible purchaser with indemnity. Omission to register was expressly declared to be a form of negligence barring entitlement to indemnity under the English Land Transfer Act 1897[27], and it has been suggested that the same conclusion ought to have been reached under the 1925 English statute.[28] The leading work on New Zealand land titles suggests a similar response on the interpretation of the New Zealand Torrens provisions[29], and an equivalent provision has been incorporated into the proposed Alberta reforms.[30]

---

[23]   For example, the Land Registration Act 2002 (England) Sch 8 para 2; Land Titles Act, 2000 (SS 2000. c L-51) (Saskatchewan) s 86; Land Titles Act (RSA 2000, c L-4) (Alberta) s 185.

[24]   Land Registration Act 2002 Sch 8 para 5 (formerly the Land Registration Act 1925 s 83(5)(a)).

[25]   Recognised as a total defence in *Miller v Davy* (1889) 7 NZLR 515; following the Contributory Negligence Act 1947 (New Zealand), a proportionate defence only: *Registrar-General v Marshall* [1995] 2 NZLR 189.

[26]   S 129(2)(a) of the Real Property Act 1900 (NSW), as amended by the Real Property Amendment (Compensation) Act 2000 (NSW).

[27]   Land Transfer Act 1897 (England) s 7(3).

[28]   RJ Smith, 'Land Registration Reform' [1987] *Conveyancer* 334, 343. Indemnity was expressly barred in respect of loss of company charges that had not been registered at the Land Registry: Land Registration Act 1925 (England) s 60(2).

[29]   GW Hinde, DW McMorland and PBA Sim, *Land Law in New Zealand* (Wellington, Lexis Nexis, 2003) paras 9.092, 9.096, relying on the Land Transfer Act 1952 (New Zealand) s 60.

[30]   Clause 7.4 of the Model Land Recording and Registration Bill proposed by Alberta Law Reform Institute (above n 12).

In those registration systems issuing land certificates to registered proprietors which must be submitted upon a transfer, another example of
negligent conduct encouraged by the ready availability of indemnity might
be a proprietor's failure to guard the land certificate against the risk of theft
or unauthorised usage.[31] In England, placing it in the hands of an untrust-
worthy agent has been regarded as the sort of invitation to fraud or unauthorised dealing that should be discouraged by the denial of indemnity[32],
and precisely the same conclusion has been suggested in those Torrens
systems issuing duplicate certificates of title.[33] The position would be even
clearer where the proprietor puts both the certificate and a transfer form
signed in blank into the hands of an unreliable agent. To the extent that
indemnity is barred by such negligent conduct, the policy of encouraging
the proprietor to guard against fraud could, however, impinge on the objective of promoting the acceptance of registration by indemnifying losses that
could not occur at common law, where the failure by the victim to safeguard the muniments of title does not, without more, prevent the recovery
of the property. For this reason, Torrens authors have recommended that,
in a regime where indemnity's goal is to compensate losses that would not
have occurred at common law, full indemnity should be awarded without
any negligence-based bar for this type of careless conduct.[34]

V. INDEMNITY FOR LOSSES CAUSED BY FIRST REGISTRATION

Where the registered proprietor in question is the first registered proprietor following initial compilation of the register for a parcel, he or she may
be subject to the risk of a past defect in title if some outstanding interest
which pre-dated the first registration can still be asserted (whether through
rectification or otherwise). The availability of indemnity in that situation will be considered below. If, on the other hand, the first registered
proprietor is protected by indefeasibility and the earlier right is incapable
of enforcement, then the interest of the unregistered common law rightholder suffers a future-event deprivation caused by the first registration.
Indemnity for this type of loss possesses its own particular objectives and
constraints.

---

[31] See L Griggs 'The Assurance Fund: Government Funded or Private?' (2002) 76 *ALJ* 250,
254–5.
[32] CF Brickdale and JS Stewart-Wallace, *Land Registration Act 1925*, 4th edn (London,
Stevens, 1939) 220.
[33] L McCrimmon, 'Compensation Provisions in Torrens Statutes: The Existing Structure
and Proposals for Change' (1993) 67 *ALJ* 904, 910.
[34] AE Wallace and CAC MacDonald, 'A New Era in Torrens Title in Queensland' (1994)
68 *ALJ* 675, 680.

A. Promoting Acceptance of Registration

The availability of indemnity tends to promote acceptance of registration by ensuring that unregistered common law owners at the time of introducing the registration system, who might be deprived of title upon registration of another, will not go uncompensated.

B. Easing Registry Examinations of Root of Title at First Registration

The presence of this type of indemnity may strongly influence the operations of the registry. Where there is a power to accept less than perfect titles, coupled with an indemnity provision to cover any losses that may arise from that approach, a registry may then take a business-like approach to the examination of titles, avoiding uneconomic examinations of title which seek to inquire into all possible imperfections, where an 'impracticably costly and stringent'[35] investigation of title might have revealed the flaw. By extensive reliance on indemnity, 'the once formidable difficulty of first registration with absolute title can be almost entirely eliminated.'[36]

The effect of omitting an indemnity clause is dramatically revealed by the tale of the English Land Registry Act 1862. The indemnity clause in the original bill[37] was eventually jettisoned in the light of Treasury objections[38], forcing the registry to adopt a painstaking procedure for proof of title. The applicant was required to show the standard of good marketable title, which reformers had already warned was 'unattainably high'[39], leading to a negligible number of titles being registered under the Act. An inquest carried out by subsequent Royal Commission reported that its failure could be attributed, amongst others matters, to the registrar lacking the discretion to ignore blemishes on title that prospective purchasers would be willing to risk.[40] Accordingly, the registration system later propounded in the Land

---

[35] John Stewart-Wallace, *Introduction to the Principles of Land Registration* (London, Stevens, 1937) 50. See also Law Commission, *Third Report on Land Registration* (Law Comm Report No 158, 1987), para 3.23, and NSW Law Reform Commission (above n 11) at para 1.12.

[36] CF Brickdale and JS Stewart-Wallace, *The Land Registration Act 1925*, 3rd edn (London, Stevens, 1927) 274. See also AH Withers, 'Twenty Years' Experience of the Property Legislation of 1925' (1946) 62 *Law Quarterly Review* 167, 169.

[37] 'Report of the Commissioners Appointed to Consider the Subject of the Registration of Title with Reference to the Sale and Transfer of Land' (1857, c 2215), para XXX. See the proposed Transfer of Land Bill in Appendix A to the Report.

[38] JS Anderson, *Lawyers and the Making of English Land Law 1832–1940* (Oxford, Oxford University Press, 1992) 110.

[39] Anderson (above n 38) at 111. See also HW Elphinstone, 'Transfer of Land' (1886) 2 *Law Quarterly Review* 12, 17.

[40] Report of the Royal Commissioners appointed to inquire into the operation of the Land Transfer Act (1870, c 20) paras 44, 77. See HW Elphinstone, 'Reviews and Notices' (1886) 2 *Law Quarterly Review* 237, 238; W Strachan, 'Land Transfer Registries' (1899) 15 *Law*

Transfer Act 1875 included the express provision that the registrar was empowered to approve for registration a 'safe holding title'.[41] Pursuing the same policy to which these provisions were directed, indemnity was introduced in the Land Transfer Act 1897[42] when registration was first made compulsory on sale. This ensured that if some pre-registration entitlement had been overlooked or discounted by the registry upon examination, then either the registered title could subsequently be amended through rectification, or, if rectification was unavailable, compensation would be forthcoming for the dispossessed former rightholder. Although stigmatised as the replacement of absolute title by a merely guaranteed title[43], the reforms operated to encourage a policy of abridged registry examination of title since the motivation to carry out the fullest scrutiny of titles before registering was significantly weakened by the availability of compensation for any rights overlooked.[44] The regime's structure of either rectifying or indemnifying was subsequently carried through into the Land Registration Act 1925[45] and formed the basis for the successful expansion of title registration in England throughout the twentieth century[46], the early Chief Land Registrars noting that 'the once formidable difficulty of first registration with absolute title can be almost entirely eliminated.'[47]

The value of indemnity in easing the task of the registry was not confined to the English experience. Even for the supposedly simple land titles of the Australasian colonies, with their short roots of title derived from a perfect Crown grant, the land registration statutes generally contained a provision for indemnity if an interest was omitted when the parcel was brought under the registration system.[48] Once again, indemnity was perceived as a significant tool in easing examination of titles in the registry. Baalman explained one of the two principal reasons for the institution of the Torrens Assurance Fund as being 'to afford to the administration such a measure of latitude in its approach to conveyancing problems as was considered essential

---

Quarterly Review 15, 17; DJ Whalan, 'Immediate Success of Registration of Title to Land in Australia and Early Failures in England' (1967) 2 *New Zealand Universities Law Review* 416.

[41] Land Transfer Act 1875 (England) s 17(3). See now the Land Registration Act 2002 s 9(3).

[42] Land Transfer Act 1897 ss 7(1), 21. Various indemnity clauses had been proposed in the bills presented in the interim.

[43] BL Cherry and HW Marigold, *The Land Transfer Acts 1875 & 1897* (London, Sweet & Maxwell, 1899) 10, 168.

[44] 'Royal Commission on the Land Transfer Acts: Second and Final Report of the Commissioners' (St Aldwyn Commission) (Cd 5483, 1911) para 82.

[45] Land Registration Act 1925 (England) ss 82, 83.

[46] W Strachan, 'Land Transfer Registries' (1899) 15 *Law Quarterly Review* 15 and 'Registration of Title along Business Lines' (1915) 31 *Law Quarterly Review* 404, 407.

[47] *Brickdale and Stewart-Wallace on the Land Registration Act 1925*, 3rd edn (London, Stevens, 1927) 274. See also AH Withers, 'Twenty Years' Experience of the Property Legislation of 1925' (1946) 62 *Law Quarterly Review* 167, 169.

[48] For example, the Land Transfer Act 1952 (New Zealand) s 172(b).

to the smooth and economic flow of business'[49] although the full advantages seem not to have been realised in all Torrens states[50] because of registries' insistence on strict proof of good title.[51] The provisions recently introduced in Victoria[52] to encourage rapid conversion to Torrens title assume a less thorough analysis of title by the registry, predicated on 'compensation being freely available for persons who suffer loss as a result.'[53]

C. Removal of Blemishes in the Root of Title

There is a further beneficial effect to the strategy of liberally granting unqualified grade of title under a regime of abbreviated registry examination of title at first registration: it tends to clear off blemishes from titles. If a title submitted for registration appears to be afflicted by some blemish which may reflect an outstanding adverse interest, then the existence of indemnity, coupled with the discretion to accept imperfect titles for registration, enables the registry to create a registered title with absolute grade of title notwithstanding the blemish. When this opportunity is taken, the blemish is removed from the title forever, subject only to the possibility of rectification (a route which is usually strictly limited for claims arising from circumstances existing prior to adjudication), so that a title which before registration may have been regarded as nothing more than a safe holding title may be elevated to a good marketable title. The importance of this objective of registration was emphasised by former registrars in England, who had described it as their 'prime and justifiable aim to endeavour to cure for all time the greatest possible number of defective titles,'[54] and who regarded it as 'one of the most useful functions of HM Land Registry.'[55]

---

[49] RA Woodman and PJ Grimes, *Baalman's Torrens System in New South Wales*, 2nd edn (Sydney, Law Book Co, 1974) 389. See also Whalan (above n 3) at 59.

[50] Whalan (above n 3) at 59; PW Young 'Compensation under the Torrens System' (1996) 70 *ALJ* 786, 788. This cautious approach dismayed the former registrar in England: TBF Ruoff, *An Englishman Looks at the Torrens System* (Sydney, Law Book Co, 1957) ch 5.

[51] Good marketable title is generally required: *Smith v Auckland District Land Registrar* (1905) 24 NZLR 862; *Beck v Auerbach* (1985–86) 6 New South Wales LR 454. Exceptionally, Tasmania and Manitoba demand proof of a mere safe holding title: Land Titles Act 1980 (Tasmania) ss 12(3), 17; and Real Property Act 1988 (Manitoba) ss 37, 43. Under a popular New Zealand innovation, titles falling short of the marketable title standard could receive a limited Certificate of Title without prejudice to paramount rights: Land Transfer Act 1952 (New Zealand) ss 190(3), 191, 199.

[52] Transfer of Land (Conversion) Act 1986 (Victoria).

[53] AJ Bradbrook, SV McCallum and AP Moore, *Australian Real Property Law* (Sydney, Law Book Co, 1991) 194.

[54] TBF Ruoff and RB Roper (eds), *Ruoff & Roper on The Law and Practice of Registered Conveyancing* (London, Sweet & Maxwell, 1998 Looseleaf) para 12–47 (omitted from latest edition).

[55] TBF Ruoff, *An Englishman Looks at the Torrens System* (Sydney, Law Book Co, 1957) 83.

D. Sanctity of Property

To the extent that the registry staff abridge their examination of title at first registration, there is a heightened risk that some overlooked common law right will be destroyed. The aim of reducing the risk of destruction can be seen as a counterpolicy to indemnity. From the time of Lord Westbury's 1862 registration bill[56], concerns had been raised in England at the prospect of a bureaucratic registry exercising judicial powers at first registration[57] and the point was emphasised by the early English registrars, who recognised the constitutional importance in 'safeguarding landowners from the risk of the Executive unjustly, illegally, mistakenly or tyrannically depriving them of their land by declaring itself or some other persons to have absolute title to their land.'[58] In South Australia, similar concerns were raised at the third reading of Torrens' Real Property Bill when it was argued that the bill would place a 'dangerous and unconstitutional power in the hands of an irresponsible person.'[59] In the United States, moreover, the constitutional provision[60] for due process in relation to the deprivation of property compelled the inclusion in its Torrens systems of an expensive and time-consuming judicial hearing before first registration with absolute title, leading to doubts over the cost-effectiveness of the entire land registration system.[61]

VI. INDEMNITY FOR PAST-EVENT DEFECTS IN TITLE: POLICY OBJECTIVES

Some registration systems provide indemnity to a registered proprietor where a past event or state of affairs led to the register misrepresenting the totality of proprietary interests in the land at the time of acquisition. This is an altogether different function from indemnifying losses caused by future events removing the registered proprietor from the register without consent or proper operation of the general law.

---

[56] 'Report of the Commissioners Appointed to Consider the Subject of the Registration of Title with Reference to the Sale and Transfer of Land' (1857, c 2215) para 86. Later critical comment is expressed in T Key, 'Registration of Title to Land' (1886) 2 *Law Quarterly Review* 324, 335, W Strachan, 'Land Transfer Registries' (1899) 15 *Law Quarterly Review* 15 and C Sweet, 'The Land Transfer Act' (1908) 24 *Law Quarterly Review* 25, 31.

[57] 'Report of the Commissioners Appointed to Consider the Subject of the Registration of Title with Reference to the Sale and Transfer of Land' (1857, c 2215), dissent of Mr Wilson in Appendix A.

[58] John Stewart Stewart-Wallace, *Introduction to the Principles of Land Registration* (London, Stevens, 1937) 44.

[59] RR Torrens, *Speeches of Robert R. Torrens Esq* (Adelaide, 1858) 19, reporting Torrens's rebuttal of the criticism.

[60] The Due Process Clause of the Fourteenth Amendment of the United States Constitution.

[61] BC Shick and IH Plotkin, *Torrens in the United States: A Legal and Economic History and Analysis of American Land-Registration Systems* (Lexington, Lexington Books, 1978) 10, 22.

Torrens systems generally, but not universally, protect a registered proprietor against title defects originating prior to his or her registration. For example, a registered proprietor is protected against an unregistered mortgage subsisting at the time of acquisition, but not an unregistered legal easement.[62] Indemnity is allowed here to the registered proprietor who fails to secure the clear title initially promised by the register[63] under the typical Torrens indemnity provision compensating a 'loss' caused by an 'error, omission or misdescription' in the register.[64] As with the English statutes, the Torrens statutes have tended to intertwine the different indemnity heads, and few Torrens authors have stressed the two, fundamentally unrelated, functions of indemnity in compensating future deprivations of title and past defects in title.[65]

In England, indemnity for certain defects in title has been available since 1897[66], but the later indemnity clauses have taken a circuitous route in determining the availability of indemnity by linking it to the principle of statutory vesting and the rectification power. The English system awards indemnity for 'loss'[67] and then contrives to manufacture the necessary 'loss' in cases of a failure to acquire the desired title on account of unregistered interests existing before registration. This is achieved by declaring that a registered proprietor takes free from registrable but unregistered interests[68] and then introducing the possibility of rectification to re-establish those interests.[69] By reviving the binding status of an unregistered interest through the event of rectification, the English system[70] takes a defect in the registered title arising from a past event and, by a statutory sleight of hand, converts it into a future-event deprivation. The technique of taking what is, in substance, a defect in title based on past events and treating it as a future deprivation conceals the nature of the two component limbs of the English

---

[62] For example, the Land Transfer Act 1952 (New Zealand) s 172(b); applied in *Millns v Borck* [1986] 1 NZLR 302.

[63] Views conflict on whether compensation is dependent or not upon the unregistered right being one that is registrable and submitted for registration: *Trieste Investments Pty Ltd v Watson* (1963) 64 SR (NSW) 98 and *Voudouris v Registrar General* (1993) 30 NSWLR 195.

[64] For example, the Land Transfer Act 1952 (New Zealand) s 172(b).

[65] The division is most clearly set out in B Ziff, *Principles of Property Law*, 4th edn (Toronto, Thomson, 2006) 447.

[66] Land Transfer Act 1897 (England) s 7(2).

[67] Land Registration Act 2002 (England) Sch 8 para 1(1).

[68] Land Registration Act 2002 (England) ss 29, 30.

[69] Land Registration Act 2002 (England) Sch 4 para 2.

[70] This approach will be seen in Torrens systems if they move towards discretionary indefeasibility: see A Mason, 'Indefeasibility—Logic or Legend' in D Grinlinton (ed), *Torrens in the Twenty-First Century* (Wellington, Lexis Nexis, 2003); E Toomey, 'Fraud and Forgery in the 1990s' (1994) 5 *Canterbury Law Review* 424. See Métis Settlements Land Registry Regulation 361/91 (Alberta) r 34(3), and the Land Titles Act, SNB, 1981 (New Brunswick) ss 68–74, embodying discretionary indefeasibility in registration statutes which otherwise draw on a Torrens system heritage.

indemnity provision, which must be carefully separated when examining their respective justifications and objectives.[71]

The following subheadings will attempt to deduce various policy objectives from the availability of indemnity to a registered proprietor upon the assertion of an unregistered interest arising from events before or at the moment of acquisition.

A. Promoting Acceptance of Registration and Abridging Registry Examinations of Instruments

Some of the policy objectives mentioned earlier in relation to indemnity for future-event deprivations are equally applicable to indemnity for past-event defects in title. In the latter case, the availability of indemnity promotes acceptance of the registration system by ensuring that certain losses arising from historic defects in title can be the subject of compensation which may have no equivalent in a system of unregistered land. Indemnity for past-event defects may also tend to ease the registry examination of instruments submitted as staff may be more willing to abbreviate examination and run the risk of improperly omitting to register certain new rights (or of improperly failing to preserve the registration of certain existing rights) if the rightholder could subsequently assert those rights against a registered proprietor who could, in turn, secure indemnity.

B. Easing Conveyancers' Investigations into Title and Validity of Transaction

The reassurance afforded to purchasers by the availability of indemnity may be accepted by conveyancers as a substitute for their investigations into certain categories of possible title defect, yielding the advantage of reducing time and expense associated with the acquisition of interests in land.[72] To take maximum advantage of this effect of indemnity, the indemnity clause should be directed at deterring conveyancers from indulging in investigations of title beyond the face of the register for the relevant parcel, relying on the knowledge that compensation will be awarded if a defect does materialise.

Early Torrens cases promoted this objective by linking the availability of indemnity to title searches: one judgment awarded indemnity despite

---

[71] Recent reform proposals conceive indemnity for past defects as a warranty, in favour of the registered proprietor, that the title at acquisition was as expressed in the register: Scottish Law Commission (above n 10) at para 7.26.

[72] See P O'Connor 'Double Indemnity' (2003) 3 *Queensland University of Technology Law and Justice Journal* 1, 17–18.

the fact that the purchaser could have discovered the title defect by careful examination of the conflicting registered plans for the lot and the lease of part, with the words, 'If purchasers under the Land Transfer system have to search and ascertain the title of the transferring party or of his transferor, the beneficial effect of the Land Transfer Act will be much impaired.'[73] The use of indemnity in order to encourage reliance on the register was seen[74] as one of the principal functions of the land registration scheme in England where the guarantee was provided 'in order to limit the extent of investigation of title without undue risk to the purchaser...'[75] The same policy of encouraging reliance is seen elsewhere in provisions allowing a conveyancer to rely on a certified copy of the register[76] and the former English rule prohibiting a purchaser from demanding proof of matters lying behind registered entries.[77]

While the need to discourage conveyancers from inquiring into the validity of register entries is conceptually fundamental to title registration, the impracticality of making any such inquiries would probably tend to discourage that activity regardless of any indemnity clause. Perhaps the most feasible source of inquiry would be examining the bundle submitted at first registration to ensure that the register was correctly compiled, and for later dealings with the land, a conveyancer may, depending on the particular system, be permitted to investigate the earlier registered instruments stored at the registry in order to verify that their content had been accurately transcribed onto the register. Apart from these matters, there is little more a conveyancer could realistically do; if prior registered instruments are available, it might be possible to check their execution for signs of forgery but this would no doubt be expensive, time consuming and ultimately inconclusive. There is virtually nothing that could be done to uncover any past frauds which induced the execution of an instrument.[78] In Torrens systems, however, it might be possible to discover the issue of a prior conflicting

---

[73] *Russell v Registrar-General of Land* (1906) 26 NZLR 1223, 1228 (Stout CJ). *Racoon Ltd v Turnbull* [1996] 3 WLR 353 (PC, British Virgin Islands) was criticised for requiring similar inquiries: SAA Cooper, 'Indefeasibility of Title in the British Dependent Territories' (1995) 20 *West Indies Law Journal* 22. *Dempster v Richardson* (1930) 44 CLR 576 (Tasmania) was criticised as potentially inducing purchasers to investigate the history of register entries to determine their validity: SR Robinson, *Transfer of Land in Victoria* (Melbourne, Law Book Co, 1979) 419.

[74] H Potter, 'Registered Conveyancing and the Land Law' (1949) 12 *Modern Law Review* 205, 207.

[75] H Potter, *Key & Elphinstone's Precedents in Conveyancing: Registered Land*, 15th edn, vol 3 (London, Sweet & Maxwell, 1954) 93–4.

[76] For example, the Land Registration Act 2002 (England) s 67(2); and the Registered Land Law (2004 Revision) (Cayman Islands) s 36(2).

[77] Land Registration Act 1925 (England) s 110.

[78] TW Mapp, *Torrens' Elusive Title* (Edmonton, Alberta Institute for Law Research and Reform, 1978) 14; EJ Cooke, *The New Law of Land Registration* (Oxford, Hart Publishing, 2003) 105.

certificate (a common exception to indefeasibility[79]) by tracing the chain of registered title back to the original Crown grant.[80]

If an objective of indemnity is to encourage conduct which will quicken or cheapen conveyancing, then the indemnity provision need not be limited to matters which are mentioned on the register. The policy of discouraging conveyancers from engaging in investigations of title could be pursued regardless of the cause of the title defect and whether or not the registry was involved in the defect's creation or detection. For example, indemnity could in principle be awarded to compensate for overriding interests[81] (or exceptions to indefeasibility) simply to save the time and cost associated with investigating them. This point highlights the difficult relationship between indemnity and conveyancing professional standards. To the extent that indemnity is used as a tool to ease title investigations by a purchaser's conveyancer, it necessarily discourages the fuller investigation of title traditionally undertaken in accordance with established professional practice. It is possible to envisage the use of indemnity to encourage conveyancers to dispense with almost all title investigations, a solution which would be of greatest appeal to those whose interests lie primarily in the economic value of their rights, such as mortgagees.[82] If indemnity were designed for this breadth of policy objective, the corresponding professional standards should be recast in order to prevent the conveyancers continuing to employ the fullest investigations of title because of the perceived risk of professional negligence liability.

For similar reasons, any bar to indemnity based on fault or contribution to the loss should be addressed only in conjunction with an appraisal of the professional standards. Where such a bar to indemnity is enacted, the effect of indemnity in discouraging title investigations could be diminished by a perception that the very steps being discouraged by indemnity were the same steps whose omission would lead to the indemnity being barred on the ground of fault or contribution to the loss. A similar dilution of the effect of indemnity would follow if conveyancers were ultimately liable to reimburse the state under some form of subrogation following an indemnity award. It has also been recognised that a similar counter-productive

---

[79] For example, the Land Transfer Act 1952 (New Zealand) s 62(c).

[80] Considered in IL Head, 'The Torrens System in Alberta: A Dream in Operation' (1957) 35 *Canadian Bar Review* 1, 13. Alberta Law Reform Institute (above n 12) at 37 proposed that historical searches to detect prior certificates be discouraged through the provision of indemnity, a rare case of a Torrens bill indemnifying against the risk of an exception to indefeasibility materialising.

[81] A limited version was proposed in Law Commission, *Third Report on Land Registration* (Law Comm Report No 158, 1987), para 3.39.

[82] See, for example, P O'Connor, 'Double Indemnity' (2003) 3 *Queensland University of Technology Law and Justice Journal* 1, 7–8; J Flaws, 'Compensation for Loss under the Torrens System' 18–21, and B Ziff, 'Title Insurance: The Big Print Giveth but the Small Print Taketh Away?' in D Grinlinton (ed), *Torrens in the Twenty-First Century* (Wellington, Lexis Nexis, 2003).

effect would follow if a vendor or any other former registered proprietor were liable to the registry for recoupment.[83] For indemnity to function effectively in discouraging investigation of title behind the land register, it is therefore necessary to integrate the indemnity provision, the indemnity bar, rights of subrogation and relevant professional standards. Without a unified approach achieved by the integration of these matters, it must be doubted whether indemnity could have any causative influence in altering conveyancing practices concerning the investigation of title.

The attempt of indemnity to change conveyancing behaviour could extend beyond investigating defects in the root of title and include the conveyancer's activity in assessing the validity of the registrable instrument. Some indemnity reforms have been explicitly justified by indemnity's capacity to ease investigations into the circumstances of the transfer: 'If the system requires every purchaser to conduct elaborate investigations to determine that the conveyances they receive are binding upon his or her vendor, it will tend to obstruct rather than facilitate the transfer of interests.'[84]

VII. INDEMNITY FOR PAST-EVENT DEFECTS: COUNTERPOLICIES

The following subheadings describe possible objectives of land registration which are capable of conflicting with the objectives of indemnity, and which consequently might be used to circumscribe an indemnity clause.

A. Suppressing Transaction Costs

The ready availability of indemnity for past-event defects would raise the indemnity premium payable on land transactions and, if allowed to escalate, could lead to a potentially counterproductive impact on the land market. Various techniques for suppressing the cost of indemnity premiums have been noted above: correlating premiums to indemnity awards; imposing arbitrary caps; excluding certain interests or high-value transactions. When considered in the context of indemnity for past-event defects in title, further possible strategies exist for suppressing premiums, particularly in avoiding superfluous awards by tailoring the availability of indemnity to

---

[83] A Underhill, 'Land Transfer Commissioners' Report' (1911) 27 *Law Quarterly Review* 173, 177–8.

[84] Joint Land Titles Committee of Canada, above n 12, at 25. See also 'Report of a Working Party on Registration of Ownership of Land in Lagos' (Lagos, Federation of Nigeria, 1960) 37: 'the Registry should be as prepared to guarantee that the persons shown on the Register are the persons who sign the instrument as they are to guarantee the title itself'. The Lagos recommendations underlie the Foreign and Commonwealth Office model statute in the British overseas territories.

its policy objectives in changing behaviour, and in discouraging purchasers from taking excessive risks in conveyancing. These two categories will be dealt with under the following subheadings.

B. Tailoring Indemnity to its Policy Objectives

One obvious solution to suppress indemnity premiums is to ensure that the statutory indemnity clause is narrowly tailored to the pursuit of indemnity's policy objectives, targeting the behaviour only of those whom it is specifically sought to influence. This is particularly relevant to indemnity for past-event defects in title which could potentially be inquired into by conveyancers at the time of purchase: indemnity would be inefficient if it were available in circumstances where conveyancers and registry examiners had not placed any reliance on it in determining their practices for investigating title. Two broad classes may be identified in which conveyancers are likely not to place reliance on the availability of indemnity and which therefore demonstrate circumstances in which indemnity is superfluous.

The first class is where a conveyancer could not practically take suitable precautionary steps as part of relevant conveyancing practice. In this type of case, there is no precautionary behaviour that could be deterred by making indemnity available. It follows that any indemnity provision here would lack any effect as a policy instrument.[85] This can be demonstrated by a source of risk to a purchaser that could, at least in theory, be detected by investigation but which is not sought out by the purchaser in practice. In such circumstances there is no conveyancing behaviour that indemnity needs to remodel in accordance with the overall goal of improving land transfer. One of those risks is the risk of negligence or fraud by the professional conveyancer. In practice, clients are rarely likely to seek to verify professional competence or *bona fides* when instructing a new conveyancer or dealing with the other side's conveyancer, and even if they were, there would be some difficulty in determining what sources would yield material on which this could be adjudged.[86] The lack of any impact on existing practices suggests that indemnity would be fruitless here.[87]

---

[85] For similar reason indemnity should also be denied for administrative mistakes by the registry after submission of instruments: Scottish Law Commission, *Discussion Paper on Land Registration: Void and Voidable Titles* (Discussion Paper No 125, Edinburgh, 2004) paras 3.35–3.41.

[86] NSW Law Reform Commission (above n 11) at para 4.34.

[87] Similarly, where a purchase triggers first registration of title and the register is subsequently rectified on account of a pre-registration title defect, the purchaser could not have relied on the register; indemnity therefore could not promote reliance on the register and should not be awarded: see 'Royal Commission on the Land Transfer Acts: Second and Final Report of the Commissioners' (St Aldwyn Commission) (1911, Cd 5483) para 57; EJ Harvey,

The second class where participants are likely not to place reliance on the availability of indemnity is where there are external influences on the relevant conveyancing practices which are so compelling that the availability of indemnity is unlikely to have a causative effect in changing practices. The effectiveness of indemnity is diminished in this manner when compensation is forthcoming from other sources, such as certain forms of insurance for conveyancers.[88] State indemnity may be superfluous here as the desired influence on behaviour is already achieved through private sources of compensation. To reflect this, a statutory indemnity clause might be cut down by barring any indemnity claims by insurers who have paid out and are seeking to transfer their loss to the state indemnity fund.[89]

Professional standards for conveyancers are another external influence prompting conveyancers to resist the more liberal practices encouraged by an indemnity regime. To the extent that indemnity is employed as a tool to ease the title investigations of a purchaser's conveyancer, it necessarily discourages the fuller investigation of title and other precautionary steps which might be traditionally undertaken in accordance with established professional practice. While the risks associated with abandoning these steps could fall within the ambit of an indemnity provision, conveyancers may be reluctant to transgress established professional standards by incurring the risk of land rights being lost with only monetary compensation as a substitute.

C. Discouraging Excessive Risk-Taking in Conveyancing

One of the primary objectives attributed to indemnity is to ease the land transfer process by discouraging certain investigations into title and other precautionary measures of conveyancers. Taken to an extreme, this could encourage a reckless approach to the risks encountered in a land transaction[90], so a balance ought to be struck between deterring conveyancers' excessive, inefficient inquiries into risks, and shifting easily avoidable losses onto the indemnity fund. Conveyancers should not be discouraged from

---

'The Land Transfer Report II' (1912) 28 *Law Quarterly Review* 26, 33–4; SR Simpson, *Land Law and Registration* (Cambridge, Cambridge University Press 1976) 596.

[88] See P O'Connor, 'Double Indemnity' (2003) 3 *Queensland University of Technology Law and Justice Journal* 1, 7–8; P O'Connor, 'Title Insurance—Is there a Catch?' (2003) 10 *Australian Property Law Journal* 8, 22–3. The papers supply examples of insurance taken out for the purpose of enabling purchasers to dispense with certain title investigations.

[89] Applied in relation to future-event deprivations: s 129(2)(b)(ii) of the Real Property Act 1900 as amended by Real Property Amendment (Compensation) Act 2000 (New South Wales). See NSW Law Reform Commission (above n 11) at para 3.20.

[90] HL Robinson, 'The Assurance Fund in British Columbia' (1952) 30 *Canadian Bar Review* 445, 456.

making elementary checks to increase the likelihood of ensuring that the client obtains the land rather than mere monetary compensation. In reality, it is thought that reckless risk-taking is unlikely, having regard to the external influences canvassed above, particularly negligence liability, that tend to resist the most extreme effects of indemnity.

One technique to counteract reckless risk-taking is to bar indemnity, or reduce quantum, where the negligence of the indemnity claimant or his agent has contributed to the error or omission in respect of which indemnity would otherwise have been payable.[91] In the most obvious case, it would block any indemnity claim where the defect was already visible from either the face of the register[92] or the daily record of pending instruments.[93] In less clear-cut cases, the use of contributory negligence may suffer from difficulty in predicting what constitutes negligence within the registration scheme. This must be determined whilst bearing in mind that it is the very function of indemnity to influence the practices to be carried out by conveyancers. Any lack of predictability in indemnity would stimulate conveyancers to behave defensively, increasing the degree of caution in their conveyancing and detracting from the effectiveness of indemnity in easing their title investigations.

A contributory negligence bar could be aimed either at penalising the negligence of purchasers personally, or at the negligence of both purchasers and their agents. If negligence of a conveyancing agent were to affect a purchaser's indemnity, the prospect of an uncompensated loss might have little impact on the client's behaviour because of the difficulty[94] in taking steps to forestall fraud or negligence by the agent.[95] Because a purchaser is practically unable to make an informed assessment of the risks in employing a particular conveyancer, or because he lacks any choice in selecting conveyancers, withholding indemnity here would penalise the purchaser without achieving any policy objective in controlling behaviour.[96]

---

[91] Land Registration Act 2002 (England) sch 8 para 5.

[92] *Miller v Davy* (1889) 7 NZLR 515. The better route to the same result might have been to hold that the content of the register was the standard by which the existence of a title defect was to be measured, otherwise there is difficulty in identifying what constitutes the necessary statutory 'loss.'

[93] *Re Jackson's Claim* (1890) 10 NZLR 148.

[94] PBA Sim, 'The Compensation Provsions of the Act' in GW Hinde (ed), *The New Zealand Torrens System Centennial Essays* (Wellington, Butterworths, 1971) 159. See P O'Connor, 'Double Indemnity' (2003) 3 *Queensland University of Technology Law and Justice Journal* 1, 20–21.

[95] In England, a registration pursuant to fraud in e-conveyancing will pass title as if authorised, and it has been queried whether the deemed authorisation attributes the solicitor's fraud to the client as principal: EJ Cooke, 'E-Conveyancing in England: Enthusiasms and Reluctance' in D Grinlinton (ed), *Torrens in the Twenty-First Century* (Wellington, Lexis Nexis, 2003) 287.

[96] NSW Law Reform Commission (above n 11) at paras 4.28–4.34 In the event, the legislature did not find these policies sufficiently compelling to displace the indemnity bar for the contributory negligence of agents: s 129 of the Real Property Act 1900 as amended by Real Property Amendment (Compensation) Act 2000 (NSW). The same principle applies under the

Even if a contributory negligence bar were to operate only upon the negligence of the claimant personally, and not that of his or her conveyancer, a similar counter-productive effect on the behaviour of conveyancers would result if such a bar were to be supplemented by a provision allowing the state to exercise subrogated rights as insurer against a negligent agent. Such a scheme for indemnity would exert the same influences on conveyancing practice as a contributory negligence bar based on the negligence of agents: that is, from fear of liability, a conveyancer would feel impelled to maintain higher, traditional standards in investigating title and other precautionary steps. The Alberta solution was to prevent the exercise of any subrogated rights by the state in cases of mere negligence by conveyancers[97], on the ground that it would otherwise encourage conveyancers to undertake defensive practices to save themselves from recoupment after a successful indemnity claim. The English scheme does not go that far but at least limits the recoupment to cases of fault.[98]

A contributory negligence bar is a blunt instrument to implement the policy objectives as it lacks focus in its effort to change behaviour and causes problems of uncertainty. But it is not the only device available for the strategic denial of indemnity in order to limit the excessive effects of indemnity on conveyancing practices. Other discriminatory approaches to indemnity are found which are targetted more specifically, constructively stimulating care in particular aspects of the conveyancing process by removing the safety-net afforded by indemnity. For example, indemnity could be removed in relation to loss attributable to fraud in which the purchaser's conveyancer failed to verify that the identity of the vendor matched the registered proprietor; to encourage the highest standards in investigating this matter, an indemnity bar could impose an absolute standard and need not be limited to circumstances of negligence by the purchaser's conveyancer.[99]

In England, there was formerly an indemnity bar which precluded indemnity where the claimant had caused or substantially contributed to the loss by his act, neglect or default.[100] While the concepts of neglect and default established a contributory negligence-based indemnity bar, the

---

Land Title Act 1994 (Queensland) s 174; see AE Wallace and CAC MacDonald, 'A New Era in Torrens Title in Queensland' (1994) 68 *ALJ* 75, 680.

[97] Clause 7.8(1) of the Model Land Recording and Registration Bill proposed by Alberta Law Reform Institute (above n 12).

[98] Under the English Land Registration Act 2002, 'subrogation will only be sought against somebody who is at fault through fraud or negligence. A particular assurance to this effect was given in the passage of the Bill through the House of Lords by Baroness Scotland': PN Kenny, *Current Law Statutes 2002* vol 1 (London, Thomson, 2002) 9–97.

[99] T Key, 'Registration of Title to Land' (1886) 2 *Law Quarterly Review* 324, 346.

[100] Land Transfer Act 1897 (England) s 7(3), repealed by the Land Registration Act 1925 s 83(5)(a). The act/neglect/default bar was reinstated by the Land Registration Act 1966 s 1(4) before being repealed again by the Land Registration and Land Charges Act 1971.

concept of the 'act' was interpreted in *Attorney-General v Odell*[101] to preclude indemnity for an innocent involvement in causing the loss, even by the mere act of lodging for registration an instrument which had been signed by an imposter. In determining the allocation of loss between the two possible victims—the original rightholder or the purchaser from the fraudster—it may be contended that the purchaser was better placed to discover the risk of fraud and so, as a matter of promoting care in verifying identity, the risk of loss ought to be borne by the purchaser.[102] The effect[103] of the innocent indemnity bar was that it tended to encourage conveyancers to take precautions against the possibility of forgery and impersonation by a vendor.

A similar effect to the indemnity bar based on an innocent contribution could be achieved by cutting down the indefeasibility provisions and allowing the assertion of unregistered rights without indemnity. The withdrawal of title protection could be implemented either through a regime of deferred indefeasibility or by the specific withholding of indefeasibility for a particular type of interest, such as a charge.[104] This would again operate to encourage absolute care by the person taking under the relevant disposition. Examples of the application of these provisions were seen under English and Torrens systems in *Attorney-General v Odell*[105] and *Gibbs v Messer*[106] respectively. In both cases, a forged disposition entered on the register was denied the protection of indefeasibility, the register was revised, and the stricken purchaser denied indemnity. While the denial of indemnity in these cases would discourage conveyancers from taking risks over the vendor's identity[107], they were later regarded as unsatisfactory for

---

[101] *Attorney-General v Odell* [1906] 2 Ch 47 (CA).

[102] Such was counsel's argument for the indemnity fund in *Attorney-General v Odell* [1906] 2 Ch 47, 59. See also 'Royal Commission on the Land Transfer Acts: Second and Final Report of the Commissioners' (St Aldwyn Commission) (1911, Cd 5483) para 54; Scottish Law Commission, *Discussion Paper on Land Registration: Void and Voidable Titles* (Discussion Paper No 125, Edinburgh, 2004) paras 3.31, 4.45. That approach was criticised in TBF Ruoff, *An Englishman Looks at the Torrens System* (Sydney, Law Book Co, 1957) 47 on the basis of the difficulty to the purchaser in verifying the vendor's identity.

[103] Although apparently not intentional: JS Stewart-Wallace, *Introduction to the Principles of Land Registration* (London, Stevens & Sons, 1937) 47.

[104] Charges were not included in the statutory vesting provisions of the Land Transfer Act 1875 (England) and remain excluded from the statutory vesting provisions in the Foreign and Commonwealth Office model statute in the British overseas territories: see, for example, the Registered Land Law (2004 Revision) (Cayman Islands) s 23.

[105] *Attorney-General v Odell* [1906] 2 Ch 47 (CA) interpreting the English Land Transfer Act 1897.

[106] *Gibbs v Messer* [1891] AC 248 (PC) interpreting the Transfer of Land Act 1866 (Victoria).

[107] W Taylor, 'Scotching *Frazer v Walker*' (1970) 44 *Australian LJ* 248, 254. See also GW Hinde, 'Indefeasibility of Title since *Frazer v Walker*' in GW Hinde (ed), *The New Zealand Torrens System Centennial Essays* (Wellington, Butterworths, 1971) 71; P O'Connor, 'Registration of Invalid Dispositions: Who Gets the Property?' ch 3 in E Cooke, *Modern Studies in Property Law*, vol 3 (Oxford, Hart Publishing, 2005) 60–61.

jeopardising the reliability of the land register and imposing too onerous duties on conveyancers[108] and efforts were made to reverse both.[109] The chequered history of these provisions reflects the concern in striking the right balance between confidence in the land title register and the establishment of minimum levels of care in conveyancing. In Torrens systems outside Victoria (where *Gibbs v Messer* was decided), a further encouragement to care in verifying identity and the circumstances of the dealing is found in the requirement of the conveyancer's certificate of correctness[110] on instruments submitted for registration.

Another illustration of promoting care in a particular sphere of conveyancing behaviour is seen in those systems which subjugate a purchaser's registered title to some particular paramount or overriding interest without indemnity. While overriding interests may serve many purposes, the significance of their exclusion from the indemnity regime is that the burden on the indemnity fund is diminished and premiums suppressed[111], while at the same time forcing conveyancers to inquire into them as a possible source of title defect. If the overriding interest is justified by the desire to deter conveyancers from throwing the most easily avoidable losses onto the indemnity fund, then the overriding interest need only comprise those rights which are likely to be discovered by basic conveyancing inquiries which are rapid, inexpensive and yield reliable results. In England, for example, the class of overriding interest based on actual occupation[112] is constrained by a telling concept of 'discoverability'[113], revealing the link between the overriding interest and conveyancing standards requiring a reasonable inspection of the land.

---

[108] R Sackville, 'The Torrens System—Some Thoughts on Indefeasibility and Priorities' (1973) *Australian LJ* 526, 531 and see also M Neave, 'Indefeasibility of Title in the Canadian Context' (1976) 23 *University of Toronto LJ* 173, 192.

[109] Land Registration Act 1925 (England) s 83(4), as explained in *Brickdale and Stewart-Wallace on the Land Registration Act 1925*, 3rd edn (London, Stevens, 1927) 280–81; the Transfer of Land (Forgeries) Act 1939 (Victoria), following the split decision in *Clements v Ellis* (1934) 51 CLR 217.

[110] Eg, Land Transfer Act 1952 (New Zealand) s 164.

[111] Overriding interests were advocated explicitly for the purpose of protecting the indemnity fund: 'Royal Commission on the Land Transfer Acts: First Report of the Commissioners' (1909, Cd 4510), Minutes of Evidence of CF Brickdale. See JS Anderson, 'The 1925 Property Legislation: Setting Contexts' in S Bright and J Dewar (ed), *Land Law Themes and Perspectives* (Oxford, Oxford University Press, 1998) 124; Anderson (above n 38) at 277–80. Indemnity for certain overriding interests was later rejected on cost grounds: Law Commission & HM Land Registry, *Land Registration for the Twenty-First Century: A Consultative Document* (Law Comm Report No 254, 1998), para 4.19.

[112] Land Registration Act 2002 Sch 3 para 2.

[113] Land Registration Act 2002 Sch 3 para 2(c), referring to a person whose occupation 'would not have been obvious on a reasonably careful inspection of the land'.

D. Sanctity of Property

Notions of sanctity of property, described above, may exert a restraining force on the willingness of the registry to abridge examination of submitted documents in reliance on the availability of rectification and indemnity for past-event defects in title.

E. Enhancing Comprehensiveness in First Compilation of the Register

While indemnity may protect proprietors generally against past-event defects in title, special considerations are at play when the registered proprietor was entered as such at the first compilation of the register for the parcel. In land registration systems which are based upon systematic adjudication of a territory, great importance may be attached to the unique and exhaustive adjudication of all titles under a finite project for its staffing, funding and the practical and legal administration.[114] Participation of local communities, extensive notification procedures and public advertising may be employed to ensure that all rightholders present their claims. As part of the package of inducements and penalties to encourage potential claimants both to submit claims and ensure proper entry on the register, indemnity could be withheld from claims arising from alleged interests existing prior to first registration which were not made in timely fashion during the adjudication process.[115] By denying indemnity where an unregistered right is subsequently asserted against the first registered proprietor, an indemnity bar tends to provide an added incentive to ensure proper participation in the adjudication process and thereby enhance the comprehensiveness of the register. This type of indemnity bar is, conversely, quite unsuited to the traditional regimes of sporadic adjudication of title, where there may be no broad public inquisition into land rights, no public education of the need to raise claims on pain of loss and no widespread programme of advertising for claimants, but instead a primary reliance by the registry on the deeds and declarations supplied by the applicant whose transaction triggers first registration.[116]

VIII. CONCLUSION

Indemnity functions as a versatile policy instrument. This versatility is in stark contrast to the rigidity of the rules of priority found in common law and in title registration systems, which tend to allocate the land to one of

---

[114] Exemplified by the comprehensive programme of systematic adjudication and registration of titles in the British overseas territories of the Caribbean during the 1970s.

[115] Illustrated by Registered Land Law (2004 Revision) (Cayman Islands) s 141(1)(b).

[116] For example, the Land Registration Rules 2003 (England) rr 23–38.

the competing claimants leaving the loser with nothing. There is rarely any scope in property priority rules to exercise a judgment of Solomon and divide the proprietary rights between competing claimants, and there may be various reasons why the successful claimant is quite undeserving. Indemnity has the advantage in these cases: it may be available to multiple claimants; it can be removed entirely to punish or encourage certain types of behaviour; it can be reduced in quantum on grounds of negligence, fault, contribution, and so on; it can be increased beyond the value of the lost land rights so as to cover consequential losses. It follows that indefeasible title and indemnity are not opposite sides of the same coin[117]: the one need not necessarily substitute for the other. In those cases where indemnity is awarded as a substitute, it need not reflect the value of the property rights lost but can be a lesser or greater sum. It is these flexible characteristics which allow it to pursue the diverse policy objectives identified in this work: namely, promoting acceptance of registration, easing land registry examination of titles at first registration and examination of dealings thereafter, removal of blemishes in title, and easing conveyancers' investigation of title and validity of dealings.

Despite its versatility, however, indemnity may be only a weak force in moulding behaviour. Those involved in land dealings may operate under much more potent forces that influence their conduct in an opposing direction. For example, despite the availability of indemnity for past-event defects, a purchaser's conveyancer might nevertheless continue to carry out investigations beyond the register in order to provide good client service, avoid the possibility of professional censure, give a certificate of correctness, or reduce the risk of liability upon the registry exercising its rights of subrogation. On the other hand, indemnity can be seen as ineffectual and superfluous where a person's conduct is already influenced in the same direction by external factors. For example, a purchaser's conveyancer might refrain from certain aspects of title investigations solely in reliance on a private insurance policy or on account of the factual impracticalities attending such investigations. In both sets of cases, factors are at work amongst which indemnity is only one force and one which may not be sufficiently compelling to change behaviour.

---

[117] Reform proposals in Scotland have recently emphasised the desirability of severing the dependency of indemnity on rectification altogether and linking indemnity instead to inaccuracy in the register: Scottish Law Commission (above n 10) at para.7.17.

3

Easements and Servitudes Created by Implied Grant, Implied Reservation or Prescription and Title-by-Registration Systems

FIONA R BURNS*

I. INTRODUCTION

THIS PAPER WILL consider the present role and continued effectiveness of implied and prescriptive easements[1] and servitudes[2] in three jurisdictions which have embraced title-by-registration—England, Australia and Scotland. Implied and prescriptive easements and servitudes do not fit well into title-by-registration systems because they legitimately arise and exist outside the norms of acquisition of title-by-registration. A comparison and contrast of these jurisdictions will demonstrate that there has not been one common response to whether these kinds of easements and servitudes ought to continue to exist. Instead, any solution has been determined by a series of important variables, such as the nature and extent of the interest, the inherent logic of and legal bases for the interest, the extent to which a particular title-by-registration system is expected to constitute a complete title system and any external obligations.

---

* Senior Lecturer, Faculty of Law, University of Sydney: F.Burns@usyd.edu.au.
[1] In England and Australia the legal term 'easement' is used.
[2] In Scotland, the legal term 'servitude' is used. According to Scottish authors, the word 'easement' has been used in Scottish law and it featured in Scottish law even before the word 'servitude': Douglas J Cusine and Roderick RM Paisley, *Servitudes and Rights of Way* (Edinburgh, W Green & Son Ltd, 1998) para [1.03]. In modern times, Scottish law has referred to servitudes, although statutes which apply to both England and Scotland will make it clear that easements also denote Scottish servitudes. Sara has suggested that it would be better to see easements as the English version of servitudes rather than servitudes as the Scottish version of easements: Colin Sara, *Boundaries and Easements*, 2nd edn (London, Sweet & Maxwell, 1996) 169–70.

The paper will be divided into three parts. In Part II, the paper will briefly consider the nature of easements and servitudes, and the historical origins and legal bases for them. In Part III, the paper will consider how title-by-registration has affected the way law reform bodies and legislatures have interpreted and dealt with implied and prescriptive easements and servitudes in each jurisdiction. It will be argued that the position taken in these jurisdictions has differed markedly, depending to some extent on whether the goal is a streamlined and hard-edged title-by-registration scheme. In Part IV, the paper will consider possible future trends. It will be argued that there are two separate issues here. First, it will be contended that it will still be necessary to take into account human rights obligations, particularly in England and Scotland, which are subject to the European Convention on Human Rights. Secondly, there is also a practical dimension. Both the reform and abolition of prescriptive and implied easements could leave a significant practical and legal vacuum, which will necessitate a re-appraisal of what avenues ought to be available to a party seeking easement access. A test of 'reasonableness' is beginning to surface not only in jurisdictions where implied and prescriptive easements and servitudes have been effectively abolished, but also in the recent recommendations of the Law Commission with regard to implied easements. It will be contended that easements based on what is reasonable and necessary may become increasingly important in the future.

II. PRESCRIPTIVE AND IMPLIED EASEMENTS AND SERVITUDES

A. England

(i) Definition

Halsbury's Laws of England defines the modern easement as:

> a right annexed to land to utilise other land of different ownership in a particular manner (not involving the taking of any part of the natural produce of that land or any part of its soil) or to prevent the owner of the other land from utilising his land in a particular manner.[3]

Such rights have been either positive in character, such as rights of way,[4] or negative, such as rights to air[5] or light.[6] An easement is an estate or

---

[3] 14 *Halsbury's Laws of England*, 4th edn (London, Butterworths, 1975) 4. For other definitions generally consistent with this one, see Kevin Gray and Susan Francis Gray, *Elements of Land Law*, 4th edn (Oxford, Oxford University Press, 2005) para [8.7]; and Jonathan Gaunt and Paul Morgan, *Gale on Easements*, 17th edn (London, Sweet & Maxwell, 2002) para [1-01].

[4] Gaunt and Morgan, above n 3, ch 9. For a helpful list see: Gaunt and Morgan, above n 3, at para [1-65]; Gray and Gray, above n 3, at para [8.89].

[5] *Bass v Gregory* (1890) 25 QBD 481; Gaunt and Morgan, above n 3, at para [1-66]; ch 8.

[6] Gaunt and Morgan, above n 3, at paras [1-66], [7-01]; Gray and Gray, above n 3, at para [8.103].

interest in the servient land which is proprietary in character.[7] Generally, easements are legal interests in land,[8] although equitable easements may arise in some circumstances.[9] Any alleged easement must comply with strict requirements.[10]

(ii) Prescriptive Easements

Prescriptive easements[11] may be acquired at common law or under statute on three grounds. If a claimant can demonstrate that the user commenced before 1189, it will be assumed that the user was based in lawful origins. However, this has become almost impossible to satisfy[12] and it is more likely that a claimant will rely on the doctrine of lost modern grant[13] and/or the Prescription Act 1832.[14] Under the doctrine of lost modern grant, it is assumed that sometime after 1189 the servient owner granted the alleged easement to the dominant owner, but that the deed was since misplaced or lost.[15] The doctrine is a fiction because it applies where there is no evidence whatsoever that a deed creating an easement was signed.[16] A person may also rely on the Prescription Act 1832, which does not replace the other two grounds, but supplements them.[17] It protects easements generally[18] and prescriptive easements for light in particular.[19]

Prescriptive easements have been criticised because of their reliance on fictions and the lack of doctrinal coherence. Some eminent judges[20] and commentators[21] contend that the central rationale for prescription was

---

[7] Gaunt and Morgan, above n 3, at para [1-01]; Gray and Gray, above n 3, at para [8.8].

[8] Gaunt and Morgan, above n 3, at para [2-01].

[9] The kind of circumstances are: when a grantor has only an equitable interest in land; Gray and Gray, above n 3, at paras [9.88]; where there has been an agreement to create an easement which did not comply with statutory formalities; Gaunt and Morgan, above n 3, at paras [2-16]–[2-221]; where the claimant relies on proprietary estoppel: *Crabb v Arun District Council* [1976] Ch 179; Gaunt and Morgan, above n 3, at paras [2-03]–[2-05]; where the easement is created for a period which is neither fixed nor perpetual: Gray and Gray, above n 3, at para [9.90].

[10] *Re Ellenborough Park* [1956] Ch 131. For a helpful overview of the case see: Gaunt and Morgan, above n 3, at paras [1-05]–[1-63].

[11] See generally Gaunt and Morgan, above n 3, ch 4.

[12] WS Holdsworth, *A History of English Law*, 13 vols (London, Methuen & Co Ltd, 1922–52) vol 7, 346–8; Gray and Gray, above n 3, at para [8.189].

[13] Gaunt and Morgan, above n 3, at paras [4-06]–[4-16].

[14] *ibid*, paras [4-17]–[4-49].

[15] Eg *Tehidy Minerals Ltd v Norman* [1971] 2 QB 528, 552.

[16] Eg *Dalton v Angus & Co* [1881] 6 App Cas 740.

[17] Gaunt and Morgan, above n 3, at paras [4–18].

[18] Prescription Act 1832 s 2. Helpful cases are *Dalton v Angus & Co* (1881) 6 App Cas 740, 798; *Bass v Gregory* (1890) 25 QBD 481.

[19] Prescription Act 1832 s 3.

[20] *Dalton v Angus & Co* (1881) 6 App Cas 740, 773 (Fry J); *Mills v Silver* [1991] Ch 271 (CA) 281 (Dillon LJ); *Oxford County Council: Ex parte Sunningwell Parish Council* [2000] AC 335 (HL) 351 (Lord Hoffman).

[21] EH Burn, *Cheshire and Burn's Modern Law of Real Property*, 16th edn (London, Butterworths, 2000) 25.

the acquiescence of the servient owner, who ought to have taken steps to prevent the exercise of the alleged prescriptive right before it crystallised. However, in *Dalton v Angus*[22] Lord Blackburn held that prescription was a pragmatic doctrine which addressed competing claims and quietened title.[23] Recently Sara[24] has argued that reliance on acquiescence simply confused prescription with proprietary estoppel; while expedience did not address why prescription was necessary in the first place. He has contended that traversing the land belonging to another is the exercise of freedom of movement, which constitutes an important human right[25] (although it does not appear that such a human right, so broadly expressed, was adopted in the European Convention of Human Rights).[26]

(iii) Implied Easements

The precise scope of implied easements differs depending on the commentary.[27] For the purposes of this paper, English law has three categories of implied easements which aid and assist the smooth operation of the grant where one has not been formally created: easements which have been inferred from the language of description in the grant;[28] easements arising from the particular use that was intended by the parties but not stated or reserved in the grant;[29] and easements implied under the doctrine of non-derogation of the grant (the single most important being the rule in *Wheeldon v Burrows*[30] for continuous and apparent easements). The court is required to determine whether the easement may be implied from the underlying contract (including the surrounding conditions) and is necessary to give effect to it. In *Wheeldon v Burrows* easements, the question whether the easement was necessary for the reasonable enjoyment of the property has also pre-figured.[31]

There are also easements of necessity, which are implied where otherwise the owner of the land would be unable to obtain access to the land after severence. The criteria for such easements have been strictly

---

[22] *Dalton v Angus* [1881] 6 App Cas 740 (HL).
[23] *ibid*, 820–22. Interestingly, Lord Blackburn relied on Scottish law.
[24] Colin Sara, 'Prescription—What is it for?' (2004) 68 *Conveyancer and Property Lawyer* 13.
[25] *ibid*, 16–17.
[26] It is highly debatable whether inchoate prescriptive acts would fall for protection under Art 2 of Protocol 4 of the *European Convention on Human Rights*: consider Clare Ovey and Robin White (eds), *Jacobs and White, The European Convention on Human Rights*, 4th edn (Oxford, Oxford University Press, 2006) 401–6.
[27] Consider Gaunt and Morgan, above n 3, at paras [3-17]–[3-118].
[28] Eg *Roberts v Karr* (1809) 1 Taunt 495; 127 ER 926; Gaunt and Morgan, above n 3, at paras [3-20]–[3-25].
[29] Eg, *Pwllbach Colliery Co v Woodman* [1915] AC 634 (HL) 646 (Lord Parker); Gaunt and Morgan, above n 3, at paras [3-26]–[3-30].
[30] *Wheeldon v Burrows* (1879) 12 Ch D 31.
[31] *ibid*, 49 (Thesiger LJ).

construed and applied because the dominant owner is seeking a proprietary interest which may have been denied by the putative servient owner.[32] Easements of necessity ensure essential attributes of ownership—access and possession.[33]

B. Australia

(i) Definition

Australian land law was derived from English law because it was assumed that there was no established law and that the settlers took with them such English law as necessary.[34] Australian judges and commentators[35] have adopted definitions and criteria in regard to easements which are in accordance with the modern description in *Halsbury's Laws of England*.[36] However, this is subject to state legislative amendments[37] and diverging developments in the case law.[38]

(ii) Prescriptive Easements

Australia adopted a significant proportion of the English law of prescription, so that the general principles which apply in England also pertain to Australia.[39] However, there is no uniform approach to prescription because each state and territory regulates its own land law. Moreover, the grounds for acquiring an easement by prescription are more limited. Prescription based at common law is not part of Australian law because the grant could not have occurred before 1189.[40] The Prescription Act 1832 never applied

---

[32] Gaunt and Morgan, above n 3, at paras [3-109]–[3-118].

[33] In some cases, the claims may be against land belonging to third parties: Gray and Gray, above n 3, at para [8.132], fn 6.

[34] Peter Butt, *Land Law*, 5th edn (Sydney, Law Book Co, 2006) para [102].

[35] Eg, *Concord Municipal Council v Coles* (1906) 3 CLR 96, 110 (Barton J) quoted with approval in *Mitcham City Council v Clothier* (1994) 62 SASR 394, 397 (Olsson J); Adrian J Bradbrook and Marcia A Neave, *Easements and Restrictive Covenants in Australia*, 2nd edn (Sydney, Butterworths, 2000) para [1.2].

[36] Eg Butt, above n 24, at para [1607].

[37] Some states have permitted easements in gross: Bradbrook and Neave, above n 35, at para [1.13] while other states allow easements to continue although one party owns both the dominant and servient tenement: Conveyancing Act 1919 (NSW) s 88B; Real Property Act 1900 (NSW) s 46A.

[38] Australia Act 1986 (UK) s 11, which abolished all rights of appeal to the Privy Council.

[39] Eg Butt, above n 34, at paras [1667]–[1682]. Note also *Delohery v Permanent Trustee Co of New South Wales* (1904) 1 CLR 283.

[40] *Stevens v McClung* (1859) 2 Legge 1226; *Richardson v Browning* (1936) 31 Tas LR 78, 140–41.

in New South Wales (NSW), Queensland or Victoria,[41] although applying in Western Australia (WA)[42] and possibly in South Australia (SA).[43] In all states and territories, except Tasmania, it is theoretically possible (at least in some circumstances) to make a claim under the doctrine of lost modern grant, which was endorsed in an early High Court decision.[44] In contrast, Tasmania has abolished the doctrine of lost modern grant and has set up a statutory scheme of prescription.[45] There has also been some dramatic legislative abolition of certain easements by prescription, particularly prescriptive rights to light[46] and air.[47] Individual states and territories have also abolished or modified prescriptive rights of way[48] and rights of support.[49]

(iii) Implied Easements

Australia adopted and broadly followed the English approach to implied easements outlined above.[50]

C. Scotland

(i) Definition

Bell's definition of a servitude, which has been generally regarded as authoritative,[51] states that

> '[s]ervitude' is a burden on land or houses, imposed by agreement—express or implied—in favour of the owners of other tenements; whereby the owner of the burdened or 'servient' tenement, and his heirs and singular successors in the

---

[41] *Cooper v Corporation of Sydney* (1853) 1 Legge 765, 771 (Stephen CJ); *Delohery v Permanent Trustee Co of New South Wales* (1904) 1 CLR 283.

[42] It was implemented under Imperial legislation: Prescription Act 1832 (Imp) 2 & 3 Wm 4, c 71; and applied in Western Australia: *Austin v Wright* (1926) 29 WALR 55; *Hough v Taylor* (1927) 29 WALR 97; *Piromalli v Di Masi* [1980] WAR 173. It is still in force: *Wayella Nominees* [2003] WASC 210 (Unreported, Roberts-Smith J, 4 November 2003).

[43] According to the Supreme Court of South Australia: *White v McLean* (1890) 24 SASR 97, 101 (Boucat J); *Golding v Tanner* (1991) 56 SASR 482, 483 (King CJ).

[44] *Delohery v Permanent Trustee Co of New South Wales* (1904) 1 CLR 283.

[45] Land Titles Act 1980 (Tas) ss 138L and 138J.

[46] Eg Conveyancing Act 1919 (NSW) s 179; Property Law Act 1974 (Qld) s 178.

[47] Eg Conveyancing Act 1919 (NSW) s 179; Property Law Act 1974 (Qld) s 178; Property Law Act 1958 (Vic) s 196; Property Law Act 1969 (WA) s 121.

[48] Eg Law of Property Act 1974 (Qld) s 198A(1); Adrian J Bradbrook, Susan V MacCallum and Anthony P Moore, *Australian Real Property Law*, 4th edn (Sydney, Law Book Co, 2007) para [18.115].

[49] Eg Conveyancing Act 1919 (NSW) s 177; Law of Property Act 2000 (NT) s 162.

[50] Butt, above n 34, at paras [1643]–[1661].

[51] AGM Duncan, 'Servitudes and Public Rights of Way' in Kenneth GC Reid (ed), *The Law of Property in Scotland* (Edinburgh, Law Society of Scotland, 1996) para [440]; Cusine and Paisley, above n 2, at para [1.33].

subject, must submit to certain uses to be exercised by the owner of the other or 'dominant' tenement; or must suffer restraint in his own use or occupation of property. Presupposing those extensions or restraints of the exclusive or absolute right of use which naturally proceed from the situation of coterminous properties, a servitude is a further limitation of that right in favour of the owner of another subject.[52]

Servitudes bind the servient land irrespective of changes of ownership[53] and must comply with strict criteria.[54] However, modern Scottish law no longer recognises the negative servitudes alluded to in Bell's definition.

Although there are some similarities between servitudes and English and Australian easements,[55] there are significant differences. As Sara has noted, Scottish servitudes are obligations which burden the land whereas easements are rights annexed to and incidental to land.[56] Although in practical terms the effect may be similar, the English definition suggests the tangential nature of some easements, whereas the Scottish definition has stressed the inherent connection between the land and the servitude[57] and the links between servitudes and real burdens.[58] Such connections have been strengthened under the Title Conditions (Scotland) Act 2003 because negative servitudes are in the process of being converted into real burdens.[59]

English law and Australian law are arguably broader than Scottish law because both permit negative easements (although such categories may be closing because of serious concerns about the impact of negative prescriptive easements).[60] Until recently, Scottish law also recognised negative servitudes. It was possible to establish negative servitudes by grant or implication,[61] but

---

[52] George Joseph Bell, *Principles of the Law of Scotland*, 10th edn reprinted (Edinburgh, Law Society of Scotland/Butterworths, 1989) para [979].

[53] William M Gordon, *Scottish Land Law*, 2nd edn (Edinburgh, W Green & Son Ltd, 1999) para [24-07] and ch 21.

[54] *ibid*, paras [24-09]–[24-24].

[55] All jurisdictions require that the burden or right is not merely personal. For England see Gaunt and Morgan, above n 3, at para [1-01]; for Australia see Bradbrook and Neave, above n 35, at paras [1.2]–[1.3]; for Scotland see Gordon, above n 53, at para [24-16].

[56] Sara, above n 2, at 169–70.

[57] *Yaxley v Morrison* 2007 SLT 756, para [48].

[58] Real burdens are encumbrances on land which are created as an obligation to do something (including an obligation to defray or contribute towards some cost) or an obligation to refrain from doing something: Title Conditions (Scotland) Act 2003 ss 1(1), 2(1). They can perform some of the same functions as servitudes, however the real burdens had to appear on the title of the burdened land and the real burden had to be clearly stated on the title without reference to other documentation: WM Gordon and MJ De Waal, 'Servitudes and Real Burdens' in Reinhard Zimmerman, DP Visser and Kenneth Reid (eds), *Mixed Legal Systems in Comparative Perspective* (Oxford, Oxford University Press, 2004) 735, 750–51; Cusine and Paisley, above n 2, at para [1-06].

[59] Title Conditions (Scotland) Act 2003 s 80.

[60] *Hunter v Canary Wharf Ltd* [1997] AC 655. Bradbrook and Neave, above n 35, at para [1.48].

[61] Duncan, above n 51, at para [441].

not by prescription.[62] However, statute precludes the creation of negative servitudes after 28 November 2004.[63]

However, the Scottish law of servitudes is also broader than English or Australian law. Scottish rural servitudes[64] may include rights separately classified and treated as profits à prendre in England and Australia.[65] Moreover, an agreement not to build on land or not to grow trees to a certain height is treated as a servitude in Scotland, whereas in England and Australia the agreement would constitute a restrictive covenant.[66]

(ii) Prescriptive Servitudes

The basis for prescription in Scottish law appears to be an uninterrupted consent for a period recognised by law, rather than, for example, a presumed grant.[67]

The Scottish law of servitudes was and is statutory prescription[68] because there was no recognition of prescription in customary or common law and the doctrine of lost modern grant was not adopted.[69] Prescription was not limited to the acquisition of servitudes because it was and remains in some circumstances an important factor in fortifying claims for title to land. In the mid-twentieth century there was an overhaul of the statutory system and its replacement, inter alia, with a regime for positive prescriptive servitudes.[70] It is strongly arguable that because of the fundamental role of prescription in land ownership and the modern reforms, the modern Scottish

---

[62]   *ibid*, para [458].

[63]   *Title Conditions (Scotland) Act 2003* s 79. Note also Keepers Office, 'The Registers and the Appointed Day' *The Journal Magazine: The Journal of the Law Society of Scotland*, November 2004 available at http://www.journalonline.co.uk/Magazine/1001245.aspx; John McNeil, 'The New Law of Real Burdens' The Journal Magazine: The Journal of the Law Society of Scotland, June 2004 available at http://www.journalonline.co.uk/Magazine/10000235.aspx.

[64]   Such as the right to enter the servient land and remove building materials such as stone, slate, sand or gravel, the right to fuel, feal and divot: Gordon, above n 53, at para [24-22].

[65]   Although legislatures and commentators in these jurisdictions will often make twin consideration of easements and profits à prendre: Gray and Gray, above n 3, at paras [8.110]–[8.129]; Butt, above n 34, at paras [16135]–[16149].

[66]   Sara, above n 2, at 170; Gordon, above n 53, at para [24-23]. Restrictive covenants will not be discussed in this paper.

[67]   Cusine and Paisley, above n 2, at para [10.03]; cf *Grierson v Sandsting & Aithsting School Board* (1882) 9R 437 (HL) 442–3 (Lord Young) quoted with approval in *Nationwide Building Society v Walter D Allan Ltd* [2004] ScotCS 198, paras [32]–[35].

[68]   However, some authors have suggested that prescription in Scottish law was older than the statutes: Cusine and Paisley, above n 2, at para [10.01]. Scotland developed a complex system of prescription which began by a series of statutes beginning in the 16th century: David M Walker, *The Law of Prescription and Limitations of Actions in Scotland*, 4th edn (Edinburgh, W Green & Son Ltd, 1990) 2–3.

[69]   In respect to customary law note Walker, above n 68, at 1; Cusine and Paisley, above n 2, at para [10.03].

[70]   *ibid*, 7–8. Prescription and Limitation (Scotland) Act 1973 s 3(b).

law of prescription has not been subject to the same degree of derision as its English and Australian counterparts.

The Scottish law of prescription has always been limited to positive servitudes.[71] Positive prescription, in the form of continuous possession for 20 or more years, may be relied on to establish a servitude.[72] Prescription may also 'fortify' a written grant of a servitude,[73] so that if a valid deed expressly or implicitly grants a servitude, then after the prescriptive period has passed, the servitude is recognised.[74] This may, in part, explain why the Scottish law of implied servitudes is narrower than its English and Australian counterparts.

(iii) Implied Servitudes

It has been commented that Scottish law looks upon implied servitudes 'with disfavour'.[75] As indicated above, servitudes may be implied from the terms of a deed.[76] However, the main form of implied servitude recognised in Scottish law is akin to the continuous and apparent easement recognised in English law[77] (although the servitude has been described as a servitude based on necessity).[78] A servitude will be implied when it is in existence at the time the dominant and servient tenements are severed and the servitude is reasonably necessary for the comfortable enjoyment of land obtained by the grantee.[79] It remains uncertain whether other servitudes based on the circumstances and conduct of the parties would succeed in Scottish law.[80]

---

[71] *Anderson v Robertson* 1958 SC 367.

[72] Prescription and Limitation (Scotland) Act 1973 s 3(2). Gordon, above n 53, at para [24-44]; Cusine and Paisley, above n 2, at paras [10.11]–[10.22]; *Carstairs v Spence* 1924 SLT 300.

[73] Prescription and Limitation (Scotland) Act 1973 s 3(1). Gordon, above n 53, at para [24-43]; Cusine and Paisley, above n 2, at paras [10.06]–[10.10].

[74] Cusine and Paisley, above n 2, at paras [10.06]–[10.10]; and Walker, above n 68, at 38–41.

[75] Gordon, above n 53, at para [24-34]. The reason is that there is a presumption in favour of the freedom of the servient tenement: Cusine and Paisley, above n 2, at para [8.02].

[76] Part II A(iii).

[77] Some Scottish cases also referred to the English law on this subject: *Cochrane v Ewart* (1860) 23 D (HL) 3; 4 Macq 117; *Shearer v Peddie* (1899) 1 F 1201; Gordon, above n 53, at para [24-34]; Cusine and Paisley, above n 2, at para [8.09]. Modern examples based substantially on necessity are *Middletweed v Murray* 1989 SLT 11; *Bowers v Kennedy* 2000 SC 555 and *Inverness Seafield Development Co Ltd v Mackintosh* 2001 SC 406; Roderick R M Paisley, 'Bower of Bliss?' (2002) 6 *Edinburgh Law Review* 101.

[78] *Inverness Seafield Development Co Ltd v Mackintosh* 2001 SC 406; *Yaxley v Morrison* 2007 SLT 756, para [33]. According to Rennie, this has caused confusion because it may be a natural civil right which relates to ownership rather than constituting a servitude: Robert Rennie, 'A Matter of Opinion' *The Journal Magazine: The Journal of the Law Society of Scotland*, May 2003, available at http://www.journalonline.co.uk/Magazine/48-5/1000015. aspx. Other cases where an easement of necessity has been considered: *Bell v Campbell* [2004] ScotCS 14.

[79] *Inglis v Clark* (1901) 4 F 288; Gordon, above n 53, at paras [24-35]–[24-40].

[80] Gordon, above n 53, at para [24-41].

III. TITLE-BY-REGISTRATION SYSTEMS AND PRESCRIPTIVE AND IMPLIED EASEMENTS AND SERVITUDES

A. Land Title Registration and Title-by-Registration

Despite the significant dissimilarities between prescriptive and implied easements and servitudes in the jurisdictions surveyed, one common element is that they developed in eras well before the introduction of title-by-registration. The concept of prescription arose in an era where possession or some kind of physical nexus to the land determined the nature and extent of the right claimed. Implied easements developed to give effect to the deed of grant or permit a landowner to gain access to the land where otherwise no access would be possible.

Each jurisdiction under consideration adopted a registration-of-title system by the nineteenth century.[81] Although the registration-of-title systems may have appeared innovative at the time, landowners still depended on the validity and efficacy of the underlying title documentation and the register did not purport to disclose all interests which could affect the land. In England and Australia, the registration of title system did not challenge the existence of prescriptive or implied easements. However, it has been suggested that a system of public registration of real burdens in Scotland inhibited the development of servitudes which could be created without registration.[82]

Although it is impossible to discuss fully the features of title-by-registration in this paper,[83] two characteristics need to be highlighted. One feature is the 'mirror' principle. A register will contain a separate title (for each parcel of land), which will state who is registered as the proprietor of the land and what other interests affecting the land are registered or noted.[84] Bona fide purchasers for value without notice ought to be able to rely on the register without investigating behind the immediate details on the register. Upon registration, new proprietors acquire their interests free from interests which are not registered even though these interests

---

[81] For England: see AWB Simpson, *A History of the Land Law*, 2nd edn (Oxford, Clarendon Press, 1986) 280–83; and Australia: Butt, above n 34, at paras [1988]–[1989]. Scotland was well ahead of England in this regard: Gordon, above n 53, at paras [2-32]–[2-34]; Registers of Scotland, *Registration of Title Practice Book* available at http://www.ros.gov.uk/rotbook/index.html, ch 1.

[82] MJ De Waal, 'Servitudes' in Reinhard Zimmerman and Kenneth Reid (eds), *A History of Private Law in Scotland*, vol 1 (Oxford, Oxford University Press, 2000) 305, 331.

[83] Gray and Gray, above n 3, at paras [2.103]–[2.110]; AM Honoré, 'Ownership' in A G Guest (ed), *Oxford Essays in Jurisprudence* (Oxford, Oxford University Press, 1961) 107; Elizabeth Cooke, 'The Land Registration Act 2002 and the Nature of Ownership' in Alistair Hudson (ed), *New Perspectives on Property Law, Obligations and Restitution* (London, Cavendish Publishing, 2004) 117.

[84] Gray and Gray, above n 3, at para [6.11].

may have been enforceable against the previous owner. Neither physical possession nor the terms of the original grant are determinative of owner-ship or ancillary rights.

The other feature is the potential for a 'crack in the mirror', which is the extent to which interests which arise outside the registration process are given institutionalised protection. In Australia, such 'cracks' may take the form of statutory exceptions to indefeasibility.[85] In England and Scotland, they are 'overriding interests'. As prescriptive and implied easements and servitudes arise outside or off-the-register, they represent potential 'cracks in the mirror'. The extent to which 'cracks in the mirror' are tolerated will demonstrate the extent to which governments demand and the public desires a comprehensive or hard-edged title-by-registration system.

As Australia implemented title-by-registration first, the Australian approach to prescriptive and implied easements will be considered before the reactions of England and Scotland, both of which adopted title-by-registration systems in the twentieth century.

B. Prescriptive and Implied Easements and the Torrens System in Australia

(i) No Uniform Approach

In Australia, there has been neither a uniform approach to exceptions to indefeasibility generally nor a common approach to prescriptive and implied easements as exceptions to indefeasibility.[86] There are probably two reasons for this. One is that both implied easements and the law of pre-scription were acquired and later modified differently by colonial and state legislatures. The other is that for nearly 150 years, Australian legislatures, the judiciary and law reform bodies have taken the original Torrens inheri-tance and gradually transformed it to suit modern conditions. The rate of reform in each state and territory has been dependent upon the extent to which prescriptive and implied easements have been considered tolerable 'cracks in the mirror'. It is fairly certain that Torrens's main desire was to set up an efficient and cheap method of land dealing rather than to elimi-nate all interests which arose outside the registration process. Indeed, the early drafters of the Torrens system envisaged that land under the system would be subject to unregistered interests.[87] Early in the twentieth century

---

[85] There are also overriding statutes: *South Eastern Drainage Board v Savings Bank of South Australia* (1939) 62 CLR 603; *Hillpalm Pty Ltd v Heaven's Door Pty Ltd* (2004) 79 ALJR 282; Butt, above n 34, at paras [20116]–[20118]; and possible *in personam* actions in equity: *ibid*, paras [20102]–[20106]. These will not be discussed.

[86] Bradbrook and Neave, above n 35, at paras [11.12]–[11.46].

[87] *Dobbie v Davidson* (1991) 23 NSWLR 625, 648–56.

the High Court observed that prescriptive easements and ancient lights were compatible with the Torrens system, pointing out that the Torrens legislation in all the states

> expressly mention easements, and provide that as to them the register is not con-clusive evidence of title. This is a plain recognition of the existence of a law under which interests can be created otherwise than by written instruments, since there could have been no difficulty in providing for the registration of grants on agree-ment for the creation of easements if it had been desired to do so.[88]

Later, a majority of the High Court also endorsed an easement by implica-tion even though it arose in the context of the Torrens system.[89] Since then, there have been some significant legislative changes.

(ii) Law Reform

The law reform bodies in Victoria,[90] South Australia[91] and Tasmania[92] advocated the direct abolition of prescriptive easements for a number of reasons, including the following: the law of prescriptive easements was complex; prescriptive easements were no longer necessary, particularly in a conveyancing system which is simple and accessible; an owner may not be aware that prescriptive use has taken place; parties ought to be able to negotiate easements and obtain a grant for a price; and prescription is incompatible with the workings of title-by-registration.[93] The underlying assumptions of the reports were that parties ought to be able to negotiate and deal with their land as they see fit; and any agreement ought to take the form of a registered easement. Nevertheless, neither Victoria nor South Australia has taken steps to either abolish prescriptive easements or remove them as exceptions to indefeasibility. Tasmania has abolished the doctrine of lost modern grant, but immediately replaced it with a statutory scheme of prescription, which will be discussed below.[94]

In NSW the Law Reform Commission advocated amendments to the law which would give neighbours greater access to land—falling short of a

---

[88] *Delohery v Permanent Trustee Co of NSW* (1904) 1 CLR 283, 312.

[89] *Dabbs v Seaman* (1925) 36 CLR 538.

[90] Law Reform Commission of Victoria, *Easements and Covenants*, Discussion Paper No 15 (1989) para [10].

[91] Law Reform Committee of South Australia, *Prescription and Limitation of Actions*, Report No 76 (1987) 54.

[92] Law Reform Commission of Tasmania, *Report and Recommendations for Reform of Fifteen Conveyancing Matters*, Report No 36 (1984) para [2.6]. The Tasmanian Law Reform Institute was preparing an Issues Paper titled *Easements and Analogous Rights* which was due for publica-tion in 2008. At the date of writing in 2008–early 2009 it was not available for comment.

[93] Law Reform Commission of Victoria, above n 90, at para [9]. This was also implied by the finding that easements should be required to be noted on the Certificate of Title: Law Reform Committee of South Australia, above n 91, at 52.

[94] Part III B (iii)(d).

statutory right of user[95]—and greater security of support for land without the need to rely on prescription.[96] The consequent legislation for access[97] and support[98] had some limited impact on prescriptive and implied easements because it is no longer necessary to rely on easements for temporary access or prescription for support. However, as will be shown below, the amendments to the indefeasibility provisions in 1995 have significantly affected the status of prescriptive and implied easements in that state.[99]

There has been a dearth of law reform proposals in respect of implied easements, possibly because it is assumed that implied easements are unacceptable 'cracks in the mirror'. However, the Law Reform Commission of Victoria made recommendations for the abolition of implied easements by grant and reservation. The Commission argued that implied easements were developed in an earlier period when conveyancing was complex and a clear picture of the land and any interests exercised over it was unavailable. In comparison, title-by-registration and land management practices obviated reliance on implied easements, as there would be maps, a certificate of title and the opportunity for inspection. Implied easements undermined the protection afforded by title-by-registration.[100] The Commission recommended instead that the Registrar have the power to grant easements which were necessary for the reasonable enjoyment of land so long as there was adequate compensation payable to the servient owner. There would be room for an administrative appeal against the decision of the Registrar.[101] However, the analysis was arguably flawed because it was exclusively focused on land-locked land rather than all the categories of implied easements outlined above; and it was assumed that it was appropriate for an administrative official to have the power to impose a proprietary interest.

(iii) Legislative and Judicial Approaches

At present, there are four major approaches to prescriptive and implied easements in Australia. The discussion will commence with what was probably the original approach to such easements within the original Torrens legislation and continue through to modern attitudes to them.

---

[95] Law Reform Commission of New South Wales, *Right of Access to Neighbouring Land*, Report No 71 (1994).

[96] Law Reform Commission of New South Wales, *The Right to Support from Adjoining Land*, Report No 84 (1997). It was clear that the Commission considered the law which relied on *Dalton v Angus & Co* (1881) 6 App Cas 740 as unsatisfactory for modern conditions: paras [3.23]–[3.31].

[97] Access to Neighbouring Land Act 2000 (NSW).

[98] Conveyancing Amendment (Law of Support) Act 2000 (NSW).

[99] Property Legislation Amendment (Easements) Act 1995 (NSW) s 2, sch 13.

[100] Law Reform Commission of Victoria, above n 90, at paras [12]–[13].

[101] *ibid*, para [13].

(a) Exceptions to Indefeasibility

In Victoria[102] and WA,[103] the legislation is broadly framed to permit both prescriptive[104] and implied[105] easements, which existed not only in respect of land which will be converted from old system (or common law) title to land under the Torrens register,[106] but also in respect of land which has always been regulated by the Torrens system.[107] The wide drafting of the legislation together with no evidence of a legislative curb on implied or prescriptive easements[108] has led the courts to determine that they may operate as exceptions to indefeasibility[109] or tolerable 'cracks in the mirror'.

(b) *In Personam* or Equitable Obligations

When the legislation governing setting up the Torrens system is ambiguous about the status of prescriptive or implied easements or courts do not wish to erase them completely, courts have construed them as equitable easements. The rationale is that these easements cannot be legal interests because legal interests are only acquired by registration. However, consistent with the kind of conduct on the part of registered proprietors creating *in personam* rights in others,[110] the conduct of the registered proprietor in respect of the prescriptive or implied easement has had a sufficient binding quality. Therefore, the owner of dominant land who used a right of way over servient land for a prescriptive period recognised by law would be entitled to rely on the law of prescription against the servient owner. However, the right would be only equitable in character and would not be exercisable against the servient owner's successors in title.[111] Equally, where a continuous and apparent easement arose on standard principles, the court would treat it as an equitable easement which would be extinguished when the servient land was transferred to a new registered proprietor.[112] The problem is that this interpretation is focused on non-registration, whereas under orthodox principles neither prescriptive nor implied easements are ever created by registration. It is an artificial compromise, which takes into

---

[102] Transfer of Land Act 1958 (Vic) s 42 (2)(d). This provision refers to 'any easements however acquired subsisting over or upon or affecting the land even though they are not specifically notified on the register.' Note also Transfer of Land Act 1958 (Vic) s 3.

[103] Transfer of Land Act 1893 (WA) s 68.

[104] In regard to Victoria note *Nelson v Hughes* [1947] VLR 227; *National Trustees Executors and Agency Co of Australasia Ltd v Long* [1939] VLR 33.

[105] *Taylor v Browning* (1885) 11 VLR 158; *Stevens v Allan* (1955) 58 WALR 1 in respect of a *Wheeldon v Burrows* easement.

[106] *Stevens v Allan* (1955) 58 WALR 1.

[107] *Di Masi v Piromalli* [1980] WAR 57.

[108] Other than in respect of light: Property Law Act 1958 (Vic) s 195, Property Law Act 1969 (WA) s 121; and air: Property Law Act 1958 (Vic) s 196, Property Law Act 1969 (WA) s 121.

[109] WA has the widest scope for prescriptive easements as exceptions to indefeasibility as a claimant may rely on either the doctrine of lost modern grant or the Prescription Act 1832.

[110] *Frazer v Walker* [1967] 1 AC 569 (PC) 585.

[111] *Golding v Tanner* (1991) SASR 482.

[112] *Australian Hi-Fi Publications Pty Ltd* [1979] 2 NSWLR 618.

account the centrality of registration and ensures that the easement does not burden subsequent acquirers of the servient land.

The extent to which this *in personam* concession applies in Australia is unclear. It may operate in SA in respect of both prescriptive and implied easements.[113] However, in NSW it does not apply to prescriptive easements,[114] but the matter is still open in respect of implied easements.[115]

(c) Virtual Abolition?

Prescriptive and implied easements always have been subjects of controversy in NSW. In early cases, the courts questioned the legality and practicality of prescriptive easements and their operation within the Torrens system.[116] Implied easements were accepted, but still with some misgivings about whether they were consistent with the Torrens system.[117]

While the original Torrens legislation in NSW envisaged that prescriptive and implied easements would constitute exceptions to indefeasibility of title,[118] subsequent amendments[119] persistently narrowed down the range of easements which could constitute exceptions to indefeasibility.[120] As the legislation became stricter, commentators in NSW also argued that prescriptive easements were incongruous and ought not to be permitted in the Torrens system.[121] They also contended that implied easements ought to be restricted to the kind specifically endorsed by High Court authority,[122] although they conceded that in respect of *Wheeldon v Burrows* easements, the purchaser may acquire a personal equity requiring the vendor to execute a transfer granting an easement.[123]

---

[113] *Golding v Tanner* (1991) SASR 482; Bradbrook, MacCallum and Moore, above n 48, at para [18.215].

[114] *Williams v State Transit Authority of New South Wales* (2004) 60 NSWLR 286, 301–2 (Mason P).

[115] *McGrath v Campbell* (2006) 68 NSWLR 229, 252–3 (Tobias JA).

[116] *Sheehy v Edwards, Dunlop & Co* (1897) 13 WN (NSW) 165; *Delohery v Permanent Trustee Co of NSW* (1903) 4 SR (NSW) 1.

[117] *Seaman v Dabbs* (1924) 24 SR (NSW) 481.

[118] Real Property Act 1862 (26 Vic No 9) s 40. Also note the commentary of JG Beckingham and Lewis A Harris, *The Real Property Act NSW (as amended to the end of 1928)* (Sydney, The Law Book of Australasia Ltd, 1929) 96–7.

[119] Section 42 of the Real Property Act 1900 (NSW) set down specific statutory exceptions to indefeasibility including para (b) which stated: 'in the case of the omission or misdescription of any right-of-way or other easement created in or existing upon any land.' Thereafter, a new section 42 (1) (a1) was inserted in the Real Property Act 1900 (NSW).

[120] Some cases had left the way open for easements which were not created by registration to constitute exceptions to indefeasibility: *Australian Hi-Fi Publications v Gehl* [1979] NSWLR 618; *Dobbie v Davidson* (1991) 23 NSWLR 625.

[121] John Baalman, *The Torrens System in New South Wales* (Sydney, The Law Book of Australasia Ltd, 1951) 202; RA Woodman and PJ Grimes, *Baalman: The Torrens System in New South Wales*, 2nd edn (Sydney, The Law Book Company Ltd, 1974) 186.

[122] When an easement arises by the description of conveyed property: *Dabbs v Seaman* (1925) 36 CLR 538; Butt, above n 34, at para [2093].

[123] Baalman, above n 121, at 202.

The present legislation is two tiered.[124] Prescriptive and implied easements which were acquired *before* the servient land was converted from old system to Torrens title remain valid and effective exceptions to indefeasibility as 'omitted' easements. However, the only other easement exception to indefeasibility will be those easements which were validly created by registration or statute and later omitted or mis-described. The centrality of registration and the protection of newly-registered owners of land, rather than any inherent benefits of off-the-register easements to claimants, has been the focus of legislative action.

The immediate issue has been whether prescriptive and implied easements could constitute validly omitted easements. In respect of prescriptive easements there was a significant line of authority which considered that they could not be acquired under the Torrens system.[125] A recent Court of Appeal decision has unequivocally held that prescriptive easements can no longer be acquired in the Torrens system because it was impossible to contort the doctrine of lost modern grant to meet the process of registration.[126] Therefore, subject to the narrow first exemption in the legislation, an owner of land under the Torrens systems can no longer rely on a prescriptive easement.

The position in respect of implied easements remains complex. The problem has been that the legislation has not sufficiently differentiated prescriptive and implied easements because both arise outside the title-by-registration system and are assumed to be unnecessary 'cracks in the mirror'. Accordingly, some decisions have aligned implied easements with prescriptive easements because they arise outside the registration process. The result has been that the courts have relied on decisions in respect of prescriptive easements and found that the implied easement did not constitute an exception to indefeasibility.[127] However, there are different kinds of easements which fall under the classification and there have been other judicial responses which have been more accommodating.[128] At present, the situation is open-ended because of a recent decision[129] in which the Court of Appeal did not have to make a firm determination because no implied easement was initially found to exist. The Court considered that such unregistered implied easements constituted equitable

---

[124] Real Property Act 1900 (NSW) s 42(1)(a1).

[125] *Jobson v Nankervis* (1943) 44 SR (NSW) 277; *Kostis v Devitt* (1979) 1 BPR 9231; *Dewhirst v Edwards* [1983] 1 NSWLR 34.

[126] *Williams v State Transit Authority of New South Wales* (2004) 60 NSWLR 286, 300 (Mason P).

[127] Eg the decisions of Powell J in *Dewhirst v Edwards* [1983] 1 NSWLR 34 and *Torrisi v Magame Pty Ltd* [1984] 1 NSWLR 14.

[128] Eg *Australian Hi-Fi Publications Pty Ltd v Gehl* [1979] 2 NSWLR 618; *Lamos Pty Ltd v Hutchison* (1984) NSW Conv R 55–183; *Kebewar Pty Ltd v Harkin* (1987) 9 NSWLR 738; *Wilcox v Richardson* (1997) 43 NSWLR 4.

[129] *McGrath v Campbell* (2006) 68 NSWLR 229.

easements when they were raised against the original servient owner.[130] However, the Court also acknowledged that there was a question of consistency, particularly as prescriptive easements had been found incompatible with the Torrens system.[131] It is submitted that the centrality of registration in NSW law and the alternative avenue of a statutory right of user (which will be discussed below) are likely to lead to a future determination that implied easements cannot be acquired over land under the Torrens system.

The legislation in Queensland[132] and the Northern Territory (NT)[133] is broadly similar to the provisions in NSW. However, there are potential differences in treatment. First, it is strongly arguable that the definition of omitted easements in NSW is marginally narrower than that either in Queensland or the Northern Territory.[134] Secondly, in respect of Queensland, commentators have suggested either that both prescriptive and implied easements are unlikely to prevail in the Torrens system in that state[135] or that those easements will be *in personam* rights which are unenforceable against subsequent proprietors of the servient land.[136]

(d) A Statutory Scheme of Prescription; Implied Easements as Exceptions to Indefeasibility

The Tasmanian attitude to prescriptive and implied easements is an unusual one. The first three Australian approaches either have a consistent attitude towards prescriptive and implied easements or, as in the case of NSW and Queensland, promise a uniform stance if current legal reasoning is consistently applied.

---

[130] *ibid*, 245.

[131] *ibid*, 251.

[132] Land Title Act 1994 (Qld) ss 184 and 185. Like NSW, significant amendments to earlier Torrens legislation have precluded the prescriptive and implied easements arising land administered under the Torrens system: cf *Pryce and Irving v McGuinness* [1966] Qd R 591.

[133] Land Title Act 2000 (NT) s 189(1)(c); *cf* Bradbrook, MacCallum and Moore, above n 48, at para [18.200] in respect to implied reservations.

[134] Unlike in NSW, in Queensland omitted and misdescribed easements include easements which were the subject of instruments lodged for registration, but because of the error of the registrar were never registered: Land Title Act 1994 (Qld) s 185(3)(c). In the NT omissions are statutorily limited to easements in existence at the time land was brought on the register or easements which were registered but later omitted by an error of the Registrar-General: Land Title Act 2000 (NT) s 189 (3). It has been suggested that s 58(1)(b) of the Land Titles Act 1925 (ACT) is similar to earlier legislation in NSW which was sufficiently broad to allow prescriptive and implied easements to affect land under the Torrens title system: Bradbrook and Neave, above n 35, at para [11.46]. However, a narrow interpretation would be that the exception is limited to easements which were originally created but then not described or misdescribed on the certificate of title.

[135] Bradbrook and Neave, above n 35, at paras [11.24]–[11.29].

[136] Carmel MacDonald, Les McCrimmon, Anne Wallace, Michael Weir and Sally Sheldon, *Real Property Law in Queensland*, 2nd edn (Sydney, Law Book Co, 2005) paras [15.149] and [15.210].

However, Tasmania has adopted two different positions in respect of prescriptive and implied easements. The state has abolished the doctrine of lost modern grant and instituted a statutory scheme, which is based on the principles of prescription and is bureaucratically administered.[137] The law of prescription is abolished, re-invented and appropriated to the Torrens system. It is still necessary for a claimant to provide the kind of evidence required under the doctrine of lost modern grant,[138] but in addition the claimant must satisfy other requirements such as verification of the user by at least one other person.[139] Moreover, the successful application is still dependent upon the decision of the Recorder, and the servient owner may object to the application, which in many cases will probably bring the application to an end.[140] It is likely that it will be difficult to make a claim for statutory prescription.

However, Tasmania has not abolished or modified the law of implied easements. Instead, the Torrens legislation expressly allows easements arising by implication to constitute exceptions to indefeasibility, so long as the easement would have constituted a legal easement if the servient land had not been under the Torrens system.[141] As all implied easements are legal easements under orthodox principles, they all ought to constitute exceptions to indefeasibility.[142]

C. Prescriptive and Implied Easements and Title-by-Registration in England

(i) A Uniform Approach

In comparison to Australia, the introduction of title-by-registration into England was slow and incomplete.[143] However, modern law reform has been more uniform than in Australia because the legislative reforms of the title-by-registration system apply to prescriptive and implied easements throughout the country.

---

[137] Land Titles Act 1980 (Tas) ss 138I–138L.

[138] Land Titles Act 1980 (Tas) s 138L(1). However, it is important to note that the period of user is 15 years or 30 years for a person under a disability: Land Titles Act 1980 (Tas) s 138J.

[139] Land Titles Act 1980 (Tas) s 138L(1).

[140] Land Titles Act 1980 (Tas) s 138K(2).

[141] Land Titles Act 1980 (Tas) s 40(3)(e)(i). This provision does not exempt from indefeasibility an easement which was created by grant before the servient land was registered in the Torrens system: *Parramore v Duggan* (1995) 183 CLR 633. The legislation was subsequently amended to cover this situation: Land Titles Act 1980 (Tas) s 40(3)(e)(ia); Bradbrook and Neave, above n 35, at para [11.44].

[142] However, if the implied easement in question was regarded as equitable it could still constitute an exception to indefeasibility as long as it was not raised against a bona fide purchaser for value who had lodged a transfer for registration: Land Titles Act 1980 (Tas) s 40(3)(e)(ii): Bradbrook, MacCallum and Moore, above n 48, at para [18.180].

[143] Simpson, above n 81, at 281–3.

The Land Registration Act 1925 began the implementation of a comprehensive title-by-registration system. Prescriptive and (probably) implied easements[144] were overriding interests because legal easements bound the registered land although they were not stated on the register.[145]

(ii) Land Registration Act 2002[146]

The present Land Registration Act 2002 does not limit the grounds upon which prescriptive or implied easements can arise. It confirms that legal easements may constitute overriding interests, although it has added qualifying criteria;[147] and it is anticipated that such interests will proceed to registration.[148] Equitable easements no longer constitute overriding interests.[149]

Legal easements which were created after 13 October 2003 constitute overriding interests until 12 October 2006.[150] After that date these easements will continue to be overriding interests in certain circumstances, but only when the easement was:

(a)   'within the actual knowledge' of the disponee;[151]
(b)   'obvious on a reasonably careful inspection of the land over which the easement or profit is exercisable';[152]
(c)   exercised within a year preceding the date of disposition;[153] or
(d)   registered under the Commons Registration Act 1965.[154]

These criteria represented an interesting compromise. The centrality of the register was not jettisoned by these additional conditions. The function of the register is to operate as a mirror which, as far as possible, reflects the true

---

[144] Law Commission and HM Land Registry, *Land Registration for the Twenty-First Century: A Consultative Document*, Law Com No 254 (1998), para [5.11]. Note also Gaunt and Morgan, above n 3, at paras [5-07]–[5-08] and *Sommer v Sweet* [2004] EWHC 1504 (Ch); [2005] EWCA Civ 227.

[145] Land Registration Act 1925 s 70(1)(a); Land Registration Rules, r 258; Gaunt and Morgan, above n 3, at para [5-10]; *Celsteel Ltd v Alton House Holdings Ltd* [1985] 1 WLR 204.

[146] Law Commission and HM Land Registry, *Land Registration for the Twenty-First Century: A Conveyancing Revolution*, Law Com No 271 (2001). See generally Martin Dixon, 'The Reform of Property Law and the Land Registration Act 2002: A Risk Assessment' [2003] 63 *The Conveyancer and Property Lawyer* 136; Phillip Kenny, 'Vanishing Easements in Registered Land' [2003] 67 *The Conveyancer and Property Lawyer* 304; Graham Battersby, 'More Thoughts on Easements under the Land Registration Act 2002 [2005] 69 *The Conveyancer and Property Lawyer* 195.

[147] Law Commission and HM Land Registry, above n 146, at paras [8.68]–[8.72].

[148] *ibid*, para [8.73].

[149] *ibid*, para [8.67].

[150] *ibid*.

[151] Land Registration Act 2002 sch 3 para 3(1)(a).

[152] Land Registration Act 2002 sch 3 para 3(1)(b).

[153] Land Registration Act 2002 sch 3 para 3(2).

[154] Land Registration Act 2002 sch 3 para 3(1).

state of the title and any interests burdening it. These criteria supplement the information on the register and, like the register, refer to data which is objectively observable and obtainable. It is arguable that the imposition of such criteria began the slow process of eliminating most forms of prescriptive and implied easements from the title-by-registration system. However, this observation must be read in conjunction with the Commission's latest paper on the issue.

(iii) The Law Commission Consultation Paper No 186[155]

(a) Introduction

The recently published Consultation Paper has demonstrated the development of several important trends when dealing with prescriptive and implied easements as overriding interests. The Commission has decided that easements in the basic form outlined in the beginning of this paper[156] ought to remain part of the legal system.[157] However, the Law Commission has shown a willingness to reform directly the underlying legal bases for prescriptive and implied easements. This has meant that the Commission has reviewed the policy reasons for and against such easements in significantly greater depth than in earlier reports. Moreover, the Commission has not automatically assumed that prescriptive and implied easements as 'overriding interests' are necessarily antithetical to the operation of a title-by-registration system. Instead, the Commission has investigated prescriptive and implied easements as separate entities requiring different treatment and reform. This approach greatly enhances the prospect that a workable integration of prescriptive and implied easements may be possible in a title-by-registration system.

(b) Prescriptive Easements

Recognising that the present grounds for prescriptive easements were defective, the Commission determined that it was not desirable to retain the present law.[158] However, the Commission also did not consider that outright abolition was desirable because it considered that prescription continued to play a useful role, as land was a social resource requiring co-operation between neighbours.[159] The Commission acknowledged

---

[155] Law Commission, *Easements, Covenants and Profits à Prendre: A Consultation Paper*, Consultation Paper No 186 (March 2008).
[156] *ibid*, ch 3. However, the Law Commission suggested that where an easement is registered, there ought to be no requirement that the owners be different person, provided that the dominant and servient estates are registered with different title numbers. The Commission adopted the position applying in Scotland: *ibid*, paras [3.62]–[3.65]. This is already the basic position in Australia: Butt, above n 34, at para [1619].
[157] *ibid*, paras [15.2], [15.16]–[15.17] and [15.21]–[15.25].
[158] *ibid*, paras [4.172]–[4.174].
[159] *ibid*, paras [4.182]–[4.183].

that negative easements caused great difficulty because claims were easy to make but difficult to refute. It suggested two alternative avenues for reform: abolishing all rights capable of existing as negative easements, or reducing the rights capable of existing as negative easements. The intent would be to subsume negative easements under a new concept of 'Land Obligations', which would require express creation and registration.[160] Such a recommendation is broadly similar to the approach that the Scots have recently taken towards negative servitudes, which, subject to transitional provisions, must be expressly created and registered.[161]

Briefly stated, the Commission also recommended that the old grounds for prescription would be prospectively abolished and a statutory scheme for prescriptive acquisition would be implemented. The claimant would be required only to demonstrate long use (but not acquiescence) for a period of 20 years' continuous qualifying use.[162] Such use would be required to continue to within 12 months of application being made to the Registrar for registration. This would ensure that there was a period of limitation under which the claimant would be required to make an application.[163] The Commission left open the possibility that the owner of the servient land could enter a notice on the dominant land objecting to the qualifying use.[164] However, until registration, the easement would not constitute a legal interest.[165] Accordingly, unlike the presumption of lost modern grant the use would not give rise to the easement; rather registration would create a legal easement which would be a proprietary interest attached to the land. Once evidence of the qualifying use had been presented, the putative dominant owner would be entitled to have the easement registered. The servient owner would not be permitted to veto the prescriptive acquisition of the easement because it could mean that the servient owner would 'hold dominant landowners hostage to their demands'.[166]

It appears that the new statutory scheme would operate in conjunction with Schedule 3 of the 2002 Act. A purchaser of the servient land would take subject to the putative dominant owner's inchoate right to have the easement entered on the register, particularly as an easement can override a registered disposition when the easement has been exercised in the period of one year before the date of the disposition.[167] However, the Commission did not explicitly state how the alternative knowledge and inspection requirements would apply.

[160] *ibid*, paras [4.184]–[4.186].
[161] *ibid*, paras [15.36]–[15.39].
[162] *ibid*, paras [4.202]–[4.205], [15.32]–[15.42].
[163] *ibid*, para [4.212]–[4.217].
[164] *ibid*, para [4.220].
[165] *ibid*, para [4.222].
[166] *ibid*, para [4.229].
[167] *ibid*, paras [4.235]–[4.236].

The Commission's proposal is an attempt to retain prescription, but directly control, streamline and integrate it within the title-by-registration system. In this respect, it has some general similarities with the approaches taken in Scotland[168] and Tasmania[169] in the sense that the right to a prescriptive easement would be declared and determined by reference to legislative criteria. Further, like Tasmania, traditional grounds for prescription would be abolished and prescription would be re-packaged to take into account the existence of the title-by-registration system. An administrator, rather than a judge, would determine whether the statutory requirements have been satisfied and take action to register the putative easement. However, it is likely that the Commission's proposals are more weighted in favour of the putative dominant owner than the Tasmanian scheme because under the latter the servient owner is formally notified of the objection and may object to the application, which in many cases will halt the process. Moreover, the Tasmanian scheme requires third-party proof of the requisite user for the prescribed period. If putative servient owners under the English scheme were able to place a notice on the title of the dominant land stating an objection to the use, then this might address potential dual concerns that the emphasis on mere use rather than the servient owner's acquiescence and the lack of a veto mechanism unjustifiably favour the dominant owner.

However, a clear advantage of the proposal from the perspective of title-by-registration is that the legal easement would not come into being until registration. Therefore, all easement rights would be registered and prospective servient owners would only be required to investigate possible inchoate claims and if possible, lodge an objection to the qualifying use.

(c) Implied Easements

The Commission considered that the current law which governed when easements could be implied was unsatisfactory because it had developed in a piecemeal and uncoordinated fashion.[170] It emphasised that parties are expected to consider and negotiate for rights that are intended to be granted and reserved. Courts ought not to be expected to re-write the terms of transactions, although the law ought to give effect to the intentions of the parties.[171]

The Commission proffered several possible options for reform without expressing a final preference for any. One possibility would be to allow for implied easements based on intention.[172] Considering that actual intention may be difficult to demonstrate, the Commission preferred a set of

---

[168] Part II B (iii).
[169] Part III B (iii)(d).
[170] Law Commission, above n 155, at paras [4.98]–[4.99].
[171] *ibid*, para [4.100].
[172] *ibid*, paras [4.108]–[4.109].

statutory default presumptions of intention.[173] Another suggestion was a contract-like implication of terms based on the individual contract, on standardised terms,[174] necessity[175] or on a reasonable use rule.[176] Alternatively, the current law could be modified and codified, setting out an exhaustive basis for implication which would exclude intention or non-derogation from the grant.[177] In effect, there would be a statutory scheme for implied easements based on one underlying theme such as intention or reasonableness; or one set of legislative criteria broadly encompassing the various kinds of implied easements.

The Commission's acknowledgement that the law could be streamlined is a further step towards the integration of implied easements within the title-by-registration system. The strength of the proposals is that the Commission considered a wide variety of possible criteria, which would be 'objectified' in the statutory context. None of the other jurisdictions which have been considered have taken this approach. They have been content instead to rely on the existing statement of the law in cases. However, unlike the position in respect of prescription, the Commission's recommendations do not propose any amendment of the present registration rules for implied easements.[178] Accordingly, the means by which an implied easement arose would change, but it would become an overriding interest and legal easement so long as it conformed to one of the criterion in Schedule 3.

D. Prescriptive and Implied Servitudes and Title-by-Registration in Scotland

(i) The Scottish Context

Scotland has been slower than either Australia or England to adopt a title-by-registration system. Moreover, it appears that the practical conversion to title-by-registration has been measured.[179]

In order to understand how the Scots have dealt with prescriptive and implied servitudes, it is necessary to appreciate the different context in which title-by-registration operates. First, it is clear that the Scots have not been so ready to accept the alleged merits of title-by-registration.[180] Moreover, the

---

[173] *ibid*, paras [4.110]–[4.121].
[174] *ibid*, paras [4.122]–[4.131].
[175] *ibid*, paras [4.132]–[4.136].
[176] *ibid*, paras [4.140]–[4.141].
[177] *ibid*, paras [4.142]–[4.144].
[178] *ibid*, para [4.146].
[179] Todds Murray LPP, 'Land Registration in Scotland' available at http://www.todsmurray.com/aNews.aspx?News ID =268.
[180] Indeed, the view as been expressed that the adoption of an English scheme of title-by-registration was not necessarily the best solution for Scotland: Gordon, above n 53, at para

Scottish Law Commission has considered that easy facility of transfer and security of title are irreconcilable under title-by-registration. Briefly stated, it has argued that title-by-registration systems tend to favour the acquirer of land, rather than the owner of land and provide a result in conflict with traditional property norms. It has advocated a title-by-registration system based on conventional property rules.[181] The focus of Scottish reform generally has been a balance between the rights of the owner and the acquirer of the land. It has not been assumed that registration can or ought to provide automatically the correct answer in property disputes. In comparison, England and Australia have endorsed a title-by-registration system in which in most cases, the state of the register ought to determine proprietary rights in order to impart certainty and speed in land transactions. In broad principle, if the acquirer of the land is a bona fide purchaser without notice of the alleged interest, then upon registration it is assumed that her title ought to prevail unencumbered by the alleged interest, whatever its merits.

Secondly, in England and Australia there has been a determined effort to limit the number and range of off-the-register interests, so that the register may more accurately reflect the state of the title.[182] In Scotland, there are also 'overriding interests' which may affect the registered title, even though such interests may not appear in the register.[183] Over time the list of overriding interests has been amended and expanded, rather than deliberately reduced.[184]

Thirdly, in Australian and English law the importance of possession as an indicator of title and ownership has been diminished and the advent of title-by-registration has accelerated this trend.[185] In Scotland, where title-by-registration operates it can be generally said that reliance on possession is neither necessary nor possible,[186] although there are some specific circumstances where possession may assist to determine rights under the title-by-registration legislation.[187] However, prescriptive possession is not only the foundation for prescriptive servitudes. Title to unregistered

---

[12-10]. Moreover, it is clear that Scottish courts are also aware of problems associated with or generated by title by registration in the context of rectification or applications for reduction: *Laing (Trust on the sequestrated estates of Alexander Short) v Keeper of the Registers of Scotland*, [1995] UKHL 21; 1996 SCLR 571; *Kaur v Singh* 1999 SC 180; *Safeway Stores Plc v Tesco Stores Ltd* 2004 SC 29; *Yaxley v Morrison* 2007 SLT 756.

[181] Scottish Law Commission, *Discussion Paper on Land Registration: Miscellaneous Issues*, Discussion Paper No 130, paras [1.3]–[1.10].

[182] Law Commission and HM Land Registry, above n 146, at paras [1.4]–[1.14]. In Australia the legislation is not a perfect list of exceptions: Butt, above n 34, at paras [20102]–[20106], [20116]–[20117].

[183] Land Registration (Scotland) Act 1979 ss 28, 6(4).

[184] See Scottish Law Commission, above n 181, at para [5.18].

[185] *Cf* native title in Australia: *Mabo v Queensland (No 2)* (1992) 175 CLR 1; Butt, above n 34, ch 25.

[186] Gordon, above n 53, at para [12-16].

[187] *ibid*, para [12-17].

land is dependent on two factors: the existence of title and prescriptive possession.[188]

(ii) Recommendations for Reform

Scottish plans for reform are not focused on specifically changing the scope of prescriptive or implied servitudes in the context of the title-by-registration system. There are several possible reasons: the Scottish law of servitudes is already more streamlined than its English and Australian counterparts and therefore arguably less contentious; negative servitudes cannot be acquired prescriptively and negative servitudes generally are being phased out; there is a single legislative ground for acquiring easements prescriptively; and the range of implied easements is narrow.[189]

The Scots also do not automatically consider that servitudes by prescription or implication necessarily constitute intolerable problems for a title-by-registration system, particularly as they emphasise the need to balance the rights of owners and acquirers by reference to property law rather than the act of registration. The Scottish Law Commission observed:

> [T]he issues are not straightforward. It is true, of course, that a reduction in off-register rights would benefit the acquirer of land. But ... the interests of acquirers must be balanced against those of the holders of rights which pre-date the acquisition. In fact there are usually good reasons for allowing real rights in question, the need to allow informal acquisition of rights which in practice are unlikely to be the subject of express grant, the fact that the right is sufficiently publicized in some other way (typically possession) and so on.[190]

While the Scots have been less intense about ridding the title-by-registration system of off-the-register interests, they have still been very concerned about improving the integrity of the register and imparting more accurate knowledge to persons seeking to acquire land. In particular, the Scottish Law Commission has recommended: encouraging the registration of overriding interests; abandoning the concept of overriding interests in favour of unregistered real rights; and implementing a new system for the noting of unregistered real rights on the title sheet of land.[191]

At present, prescriptive and implied servitudes are off-the-register real rights which have been accorded the status of overriding interests in the

---

[188] *ibid*, para [12-19].

[189] Parts II B(iii) and II C(iii).

[190] Scottish Law Commission, above n 181, at para [5.25]. While the Commission noted that these issues were beyond the scope of its study, this viewpoint has been generally influential.

[191] For example, the Scottish Law Commission has recommended that the term overriding interest be replaced by the term 'unregistered real right' and that there should no longer be a supplemental list of examples of overriding interests or unregistered real right because they do not reflect the changing nature of Scottish land law: Scottish Law Commission, above n 181, at paras [5.23] and [5.28].

title-by-registration system.[192] One overriding interest in relation to land includes

the right or interest over it of—

(d) the proprietor of the dominant tenement in any servitude which was not created by registration in accordance with section 75(1) of the Title Conditions (Scotland) Act 2003 (asp 9).[193]

Servitudes may appear on the register in three ways: by registration, by entering and by noting. The entering and noting of servitudes can be important for prescriptive or implied servitudes.

Simply stated, a servitude is only entered against the benefited or dominant land.[194] The effect of entering is that it potentially engages provisions which create and protect real rights like servitudes.[195] The Keeper of the register initially entered servitudes in favour of the benefited property. However this led to unfortunate results, including the entering of servitudes which were subsequently found not to exist or to be exaggerated. Therefore, the administrative process was tightened so that it is unlikely that off-the-register servitudes will be entered on the title sheet of the benefited property.[196] On the other hand, off-the-register servitudes may be noted on the title sheet for the burdened or servient land.[197] According to the Scottish Law Commission, noting does not change or enhance the validity of the right claimed. It has no legal effect and is for information only.[198] Nevertheless, it must have some bearing on the question of notice. In respect of knowledge, noting must fortify notice of prescriptive servitudes (which must be *nec vi*)[199] and the existence of implied grants which are based on continuous use.[200]

The Scottish Law Commission has criticised the noting of servitudes in respect of burdened land only. It has argued that this limitation is enshrined in the definition of overriding interests, which are confined to servitudes which are rights or interests *over* land.[201] It has recommended that servitudes

---

[192] Generally speaking, overriding interests are rights which have been made real other than by registration: Land Registration Act (Scotland) 1979 s 28(1)(h).

[193] Land Registration Act (Scotland) 1979 s 28(1)(d) as amended.

[194] Land Registration Act (Scotland) 1979 s 6(1).

[195] Land Registration Act (Scotland) 1979 s 3(1)(a); *Yaxley v Morrison* 2007 SLT 756.

[196] Scottish Law Commission, above n 181, at paras [4.33]–[4.35]; *M R S Hamilton Ltd v Keeper of the Registers of Scotland* 2000 SC 271; *Griffiths v Keeper of the Registers of Scotland* (Unreported, Lands Tribunal Scotland, 20 December 2002); Registers of Scotland, *Registration of Title Practice Book* available at http://www.ros.gov.uk/rotbook/index.html, paras [6.51]–[6.61].

[197] Land Registration Act (Scotland) 1979 s 6(4).

[198] No indemnity is payable in respect of the noting of servitudes as overriding interests: Scottish Law Commission, above n 181, at para [5.31].

[199] Gordon, above n 53, at para [24-46].

[200] *ibid*, para [24-35].

[201] Scottish Law Commission, above n 181, at para [5.40] and fn 79.

as unregistered real rights could be noted for both the burdened and the benefited land.[202] Moreover, as an application to note the servitude is more likely to be made by the dominant owner, the Commission recommended that on the receipt of such an application, the Keeper would notify the servient owner and give that person eight weeks to reply. If the servient owner supported the application or did not reply, the Keeper would note the right. If the servient owner objected to the application, then the Keeper would not note the servitude unless the Keeper was satisfied that the right did exist. Otherwise the applicant could appeal against the rejection or seek a declaration that the right exists.[203] Where a servitude was noted on the title sheet of one property, the Commission recommended that the Keeper ought to make a corresponding entry in the title of the other.[204] The Commission argued:

> Our proposals attempt to balance the interests of the different parties. For the servitude holder, they make it more likely that an entry on the Register will be made; for the owner of the burdened property, they offer notice and a chance to object; and for the Keeper, they provide a system which is virtually mechanical and which does not put his indemnity at risk.[205]

The Scottish Law Commission sought neither to change the intrinsic nature of prescriptive or implied easements nor to eliminate them from the legal landscape. Instead, Scottish law accommodates the title-by-registration system to the pre-existing law of prescriptive and implied servitudes, and the Commission preferred to further this accommodation by encouraging registration and modifying the administrative process by which such interests may be noted on the register.

Until recently, the Scottish approach stood in sharp contrast to the English stance (and the attitude of several Australian states). The recent Law Commission Consultation Paper represents a moderation of the English attitude, but still contrasts with the Scottish approach to the extent that it recommends refashioning of the legal grounds for both prescriptive and implied easements. However, the differences between the English and Scottish standpoints ought not to be overstated for four reasons. First, the Law Commission recommends a form of statutory 20-year prescription which is akin to that in the Scottish legislation, except that in Scotland it is unnecessary to register the easement in order for it to achieve a legal status. Secondly, the Scots do not have a broad concept of implied servitudes, so a contrast would be unhelpful in this regard anyway. Thirdly, influenced by the Scottish approach to negative servitudes and real burdens, the Law Commission has broached

---

[202] *ibid*, para [5.40].
[203] *ibid*, paras [5.38] and [5.41].
[204] *ibid*, para [5.42].
[205] *ibid*, para [5.41].

the possibility of abolishing negative easements with prospective effect and replacing them with Land Obligations which would be expressly created and registered.[206] Fourthly, unlike in NSW or Queensland, the prescriptive and implied easements as fundamental entities are retained in Scotland and would be preserved (albeit modified) under the Law Commission's recommendations.

IV. FUTURE ISSUES

A. Diverse Reactions

The vastly different approaches to the role and function of prescriptive and implied easements in title-by-registration systems were considered in Part III. At one end of the continuum are those jurisdictions where the orthodox principles for prescriptive and implied easements and servitudes remain largely unaffected by title-by-registration. Easements and servitudes are apparently considered compatible with title-by-registration and the system has been accommodated to them.[207] In the middle of the continuum are those jurisdictions which have attempted to modify the impact of prescriptive and implied easements on the title-by-registration system by: the introduction of or recommendation for a separate scheme to scrutinise claims; the reduction of the grounds upon which a claim can be made; the rationalisation of the legal principles which govern them; or the implementation of additional criteria for validity.[208] At the other end of the spectrum, there are jurisdictions which have either ignored or indirectly abolished prescriptive and implied easements so that when title-by-registration becomes the predominant or only form of title, such easements will virtually become historical relics.[209] These last two categories are the result of a commitment to the protection of bona fide purchasers of land, a growing unease about off-the-register interests and a belief in the register as a mirror of title best able to resolve title disputes.

The proprietary nature of easements and servitudes was outlined briefly in Part I. For dominant and servient owners, there are significant property rights involved. Any retention or reform of prescriptive and implied easements and servitudes must take into account the impact upon both present and future dominant and servient tenement owners within the broader context of human rights, particularly in Europe. Australia provides little assistance in respect of human rights and land law. There the concept of human

---

[206] Law Commission, above n 155, at paras [15.35]–[15.39].
[207] Such as Scotland, Victoria and Western Australia.
[208] Such jurisdictions as England and Tasmania.
[209] Such jurisdictions as NSW, Queensland and the NT.

rights, particularly in relation to property is at a very early stage.[210] There are only two jurisdictions which have implemented legislation dealing with human rights and these rights are essentially civil and political only.[211]

B. European Human Rights

(i) England

(a) Article 1 of the First Protocol

Article 1 of the First Protocol of the European Convention for the Protection of Human Rights ('Article 1') applies in the United Kingdom[212] and provides:

> Every natural or legal person is entitled to the peaceful enjoyment of his posses-sions. No one shall be deprived of his possessions except in the public interest and subject to the conditions provided for by law and by the general principles of international law.
>
> The preceding provisions shall not, however, in any way impair the right of a State to enforce such laws as it deems necessary to control the use of property in accordance with the general interest or to secure the payment of taxes or other contributions or penalties.

The Protocol has three rules.[213] First, the Protocol protects the effec-tive use of property where there is no deprivation or control of property involved.[214] Secondly it protects against the deprivation or extinguishment of some legal right in respect of property,[215] unless it is in the public interest. It has been contended that such deprivation of property rights must amount to a shift in proprietary entitlement from one party to another, rather than simply the recognition of a pre-existing limitation on the use of the prop-erty.[216] If this is the case (and for the purpose of the discussion below it will be assumed) then pre-existing prescriptive or implied easements will

---

[210] Lynden Griggs, 'Real Property and Human Rights' *8th Real Property Teachers' Conference 2007*, Faculty of Law, University of Tasmania.

[211] Human Rights Act 2004 (ACT) Pt 3; Charter of Human Rights and Responsibilities Act 2006 (Vic); Tasmania Law Reform Institute, *A Charter of Rights for Tasmania?* (Issues Paper No 11, 2006).

[212] Human Rights Act 1998 (c 42).

[213] Ovey and White, above n 26, at 346; Jean Howell, 'Land and Human Rights' [1999] 63 *The Conveyancer and Property Lawyer* 287, 296–8; Law Commission and HM Land Registry, above n 144, at paras [4.27]–[4.30].

[214] *Sporrong v Lönnroth v Sweden* (1983) 5 EHRR 35.

[215] *James v United Kingdom* (1986) 8 EHRR 123.

[216] Amy Goymour, 'Proprietary Claims and Human Rights—A "Reservoir of Entitlement"' (2006) 65 *Cambridge Law Journal* 696, 711–16, who argues that the courts have drawn a distinction between inherent limitations in the property ownership which will not trigger the operation of Art 1 and proprietary shifts which could breach Art 1.

not constitute potential breaches of Article 1. However, it is arguable that a reliance on a proprietary shift is not sufficiently extensive because the retention of off-the-register interests could be considered a fundamental challenge to the right to own property, particularly when the register is supposed to operate on a mirror principle and the registered owner on acquisition of the land was unaware that a valid unregistered easement or servitude already existed. Thirdly, the state may enforce laws necessary for the control of property which do not constitute a deprivation of property, but are in accord with the general interest.[217] These three rules protect possessions, a concept which has been broadly interpreted to include restrictive covenants[218] and licences.[219] It has been suggested that an easement would constitute a possession.[220]

The state will enjoy a 'margin of appreciation' to make an assessment about what action ought to be taken.[221] However, the deprivation of possessions must be proportionate to the aim and must be in the public interest.[222] Generally, the taking of property without compensation will not be countenanced other than in exceptional circumstances.[223] However, where the issue is one of control of property, then the right to compensation may not be automatic, though it may be necessary for the requirement of proportionality.[224]

(b) The Influence of Article 1

In England, Article 1 has had an impact on land law, although this impact appears to have been curtailed by a recent decision on adverse possession.[225] Prescriptive or implied easements do not appear to have been challenged by putative servient owners under Article 1. However, in 1998 the Law Commission considered the scope of overriding interests, including prescriptive and implied easements, from the perspective of Article 1. It contended that the reduction of the range and status of pre-existing overriding interests

---

[217] Consider *Pine Valley Developments v Ireland* (1992) 14 EHHR 319.
[218] *S v UK* [1986] 51 DR 195.
[219] *Fredin v Sweden* (1991) 13 EHRR 784. See also Ovey and White, above n 26, at 352–3.
[220] Howell, above n 213, at 295.
[221] *James v United Kingdom* (1986) 8 EHRR 123, 142.
[222] *ibid*, 145.
[223] *ibid*, 147; *Holy Monasteries v Greece* (1995) 20 EHRR 1.
[224] Ovey and White, above n 26, at 371–3. However, note *JA Pye (Oxford) v United Kingdom* (2007) 41 EG 200, [2007] ECHR 700, para [79].
[225] Initially, a majority of the European Court of Human Rights held that legislation which regulated claims for adverse possession constituted a breach of Art 1 because it permitted the deprivation of property (or a proprietary shift) without adequate notice or proportionate compensation: *JA Pye (Oxford) Ltd v United Kingdom* (2006) 43 EHRR 3. On appeal, the matter was referred to the Grand Chamber which reversed the earlier decision and determined that the legislative provisions dealing with adverse possession were an exercise of control under rule 3 and were a fair balance required by Art 1: *JA Pye (Oxford) Ltd v United Kingdom* [2007] 41 EG 200, [2007] ECHR 700, paras [64]–[85].

would probably fall within the public interest exception of the second rule because it would simplify and cheapen the transfer of land. However, even if this were the case, there was still the question of compensation payable by the servient owner to the dominant owner under the second or third rules.[226] The Commission implicitly considered that stripping pre-existing prescriptive and implied easements of their overriding status could constitute a breach of Article 1.

In 2001 the Law Commission took a more robust approach to the removal and reduction of overriding interests, and the Land Registration Act 2002 reflects this. The legislation encourages the disclosure, notification and registration of overriding interests. The Commission argued that the reduction in the nature and extent of overriding interests constituted a control of, rather than a deprivation of, property because the removal of the overriding status has no effect on the right per se.[227] Presently, prescriptive and implied easements are not phased out but merely modified under the current law.

In 2008, the Law Commission considered that Article 1 would have little impact on its recommendations for the reform of prescriptive and implied easements due to the wide margin of appreciation which has been given to legislatures to modify the law.[228] Certainly, as the Commission does not recommend the abolition of either prescriptive or implied easements, but rather a coherent statutory regulation of them, it is arguable that the Commission is correct. In the light of the recent decision of the European Court of Human Rights in which adverse possession (as regulated by statute)[229] was found not to breach Article 1, it can be contended that putative servient owners may find it difficult to rely on Article 1.

Nevertheless, servient owners may be able to argue breach of Article 1, depending on what legislative rights they may acquire to prevent the registration of a prescriptive easement. Moreover, the recommendations of the Commission make no provision for the compensation of servient owners in respect of prescriptive or implied easements. The servient owner could maintain that that the principles of prescriptive or implied easements (albeit modified by statute) triggered a proprietary deprivation for which he was not recompensed.[230] A claim that there ought to be some form of compensation could be particularly compelling if the statutory prescriptive easement was not based on the acquiescence of the servient owner, or the implied easement was not based on the actual or likely intention of the parties to the original disposition of land.

---

[226] Law Commission and HM Land Registry, above n 144, at para [4.30].
[227] Law Commission and HM Land Registry, above n 146, at para [8.89].
[228] Law Commission, above n 155, at paras [1.27]–[1.28].
[229] *JA Pye (Oxford) Ltd v United Kingdom* [2007] 41 EG 200, [2007] ECHR 700.
[230] Note Goymour, above n 216, at 716.

It is also arguable that if ongoing negative easements were abolished and subsumed under a different scheme requiring express creation and registration,[231] a dominant owner could argue that this constituted a proprietary deprivation. Equally, a dominant owner could argue that the limited 12-month period effectively permitted for registration of the prescriptive easement constituted an abuse of the margin of appreciation accorded to states.

(ii) Scotland

Scotland is also subject to Article 1. As Scotland has not seriously considered the complete abolition or modification of prescriptive and implied servitudes, the major problem is whether the legislation regulating prescriptive servitudes constitutes a deprivation of, or a control over, property because it lacks a scheme of compensation. One issue may be whether the extinguishment of unconverted and unregistered negative servitudes[232] will constitute a breach of Article 1 because it amounts to a deprivation without compensation. As implied servitudes are limited, it is less likely that such easements would constitute a breach of Article 1 if they were ascertainable before acquisition and registration. However, it is arguable that there would be a breach if the easement were imposed on the basis of necessity and it was not continuous and apparent.

C. Statutory Rights or Rights of Statutory User

While some Australian states have retained common law principles for both prescriptive and implied easements, it is important to comment upon two developments which are the direct outcome of the interface between the law of easements and title-by-registration: statutory rights of prescriptive and implied easements; and rights of statutory user. Although different in nature and scope, in both the legislature assumes greater responsibility for prescribing the criteria and process needed to be satisfied before an easement is acquired.

(i) Statutory Rights

Leaving aside the particular situation in Scotland, it is clear that jurisdictions which wish to retain prescription or implied easements, but are dissatisfied with the current law, may decide to make statutory amendments

---

[231] See the Law Commission, above n 155, at paras [15.32]–[15.39].
[232] *Title Conditions (Scotland) Act 2003* s 80(2).

to the intrinsic nature of prescriptive or implied easements and the bases upon which they may be registered or achieve an overriding status. The recent recommendations of the Law Commission are an important example of this trend. Moreover, if these recommendations were implemented, then a significant collateral effect would be the shift from a system of criteria which had evolved from judicial decisions to a statutory system of entitlement which would be bureaucratically managed.

In respect of prescriptive easements, the new statutory form of prescription would be relatively unambiguous and easier to apply than the present system. Once the qualifying user had been established, it would simply be a matter of administrative evaluation and then registration.

The recommendations in respect of implied easements may also lead to a strict system of statutory implication. Implied easements, which are currently created in a number of ways, would either be determined by one broad criterion or at the very least set down in one statutory instrument. However, several matters would have to be determined: what the criterion or criteria would be; and the extent to which the relevant statute would minutely define the criteria and prescribe how it will apply. In particular, a significant issue will be whether to legislate for a subjective (or intention-based) approach or an objective (or some kind of necessity or reasonable use) approach. The scope of implied easements based only on intention or imputed intention may be too narrow, particularly from the perspective of the putative dominant tenement. As the Commission has acknowledged the need for neighbourliness elsewhere in the Consultation Paper,[233] an objective approach to need and reasonable use may be preferable. Certainly, it would be in keeping with the criteria of reasonable enjoyment evidenced in some implied easement cases[234] and the tendency for modern land law to moderate an ideology of absolute ownership.[235]

If an objective test of necessity and reasonable use were adopted, it could be argued that through the concept of statutory implied easements, the Commission had laid the seeds of a statutory system of easement creation justified by necessity and reasonable use. So far, the Commission's suggestions appear rudimentary compared to the rights of statutory user, considered below. Nevertheless, this would be broadly consistent with what has occurred in several Australian jurisdictions where, in the absence of express agreement, objective entitlement is determined by reference to reasonable necessity, the public interest and compensation.

---

[233] Law Commission, above 155, at para [4.182].
[234] *Wheeldon v Burrows* (1879) 12 Ch D 31(CA) 49 (Thesiger LJ).
[235] Kevin Gray and Susan Francis Gray, 'The Rhetoric of Realty' in Joshua Getzler (ed), *Rationalizing Property, Equity and Trusts: Essays in Honour of Edward Burn* (London, LexisNexis UK, 2003) 204, 253.

(ii) Rights of Statutory User

Where prescriptive and implied easements have been virtually abolished or circumscribed as exceptions to indefeasibility, law reform bodies and legislatures in Australia have increasingly resorted to the implementation of statutory rights of user (or court-imposed easements).[236]

The Law Commission in England in 1971 recommended that a person ought to be able to make an application for the imposition of certain 'Land Obligations'[237] including easements, provided that the applicant demonstrated that: the land obligation was in the public interest; the land obligation was necessary for the development of the land; the servient owner could be compensated for the loss and disadvantage caused; and the servient owner had unreasonably refused to agree with the proposal. These recommendations were not implemented in England, arguably because the legal conditions were not apposite: the reduction or elimination of overriding interests was not an urgent priority.

However, the conditions were different in several Australian states which had begun the process of virtually abolishing prescriptive and implied easements as exceptions to indefeasibility. The dilemma was that in earlier times, such easements had a practical and communitarian role to play even if the grounds upon which they were claimed were no longer defensible. In 1973, the Queensland Law Reform Commission commented:

> In Queensland such problems have arisen not so much in the sphere of estate development where owners can generally be induced by the offer of a substantial consideration to grant the rights required, but in relation to individual residential or commercial properties requiring access to or for utilities and services on to public highways—these problems are accentuated by the titles registration system, which precludes recognition of easements which would ordinarily be implied or imposed at law or in equity.
>
> There seems to be no reason why the court should not have power to create such rights in favour of the dominant land and to impose them on the servient land where this is necessary in the interest of effective user of the dominant land.[238]

Section 180 of the Property Law Act 1974 (Qld) was implemented and several states and territories followed,[239] including NSW which enacted section

---

[236] A right of statutory user is different from orders for temporary access to a neighbour's land which is regulated by separate legislation, eg Access to Neighbouring Land Act 2000 (NSW): Butt, above n 34, at para [214].

[237] Law Commission, *Appurtenant Rights* (Working Paper No 36, 1971) 118, proposal 15. The concept of 'Land Obligations' contemplated by the Law Commission in 1971 was very different from that presented in the recent Consultation Paper: Law Commission, above n 155, at paras [15.26]–[15.30].

[238] Queensland Law Reform Commission, *A Bill to Consolidate, Amend and Reform the Law relating to Conveyancing Property and Contract and to Terminate the Application of Certain Imperial Statutes* (Report 16, Brisbane, 1973) para 180.

[239] Conveyancing and Law of Property Act 1886 (Tas) s 84J; Law of Property Act 2000 (NT) s 164.

88K of the Conveyancing Act 1919 (NSW). The developments in New South Wales are interesting in the light of the ongoing debate about prescriptive and implied easements as exceptions to indefeasibility. The statutory right of user was implemented in the same legislation that set the present limits on easements as exceptions to indefeasibility and indirectly abolished prescriptive easements in the Torrens system.[240] Therefore, it can be said that in respect of both Queensland and NSW (and probably the NT) the limitation of prescriptive and implied easements as exception to indefeasibility has a direct correlation with the implementation of a right of statutory user.[241]

Upon a putative dominant owner's application, the state Supreme Court has power to impose an easement where it is reasonably necessary for the development of the benefited land.[242] It is not necessary for the easement to be absolutely necessary,[243] but it must be substantially preferable for the proposed use.[244] The easement must be consistent with the public interest,[245] although it is not necessary that the public interest will be advanced.[246] As a precondition to the exercise of power, the court must be satisfied that the servient owner can be satisfactorily compensated for the loss or disadvantage incurred.[247] The calculation of the compensation is flexible so that the court may compensate for the devaluation of the servient land, impediments to future development,[248] disturbances and further access for maintenance.[249] The applicant must have made reasonable, but unsuccessful, efforts to acquire the easement.[250]

It is difficult to acquire a statutory right of user, as the order amounts to a compulsory acquisition of a proprietary right.[251] However, if the requirements of the legislation are fulfilled on an objective basis, then a right of statutory user must be imposed, subject to the court's discretion.[252] Under the Torrens system, the easement takes effect when it is registered.[253]

---

[240] Property Legislation Amendment (Easements) Act 1995 (NSW) s 2, sch 13.

[241] Tasmania does not follow this pattern: Land Titles Act 1980 (Tas) ss 138J–138L; Land Titles Act 1980 (Tas) s 40(3)(e)(i).

[242] Eg, Conveyancing Act 1919 (NSW) s 88K; Property Law Act 1974 (Qld) s 180(1).

[243] *117 York Street Pty Ltd v Proprietors Strata Plan 16123* (1998) 43 NSWLR 504, 508.

[244] Something more than merely desirable: *117 York Street Pty Ltd v Proprietors Strata Plan 16123* (1998) 43 NSWLR 504, 509.

[245] Eg, Property Law Act 1974 (Qld) s 180(3)(a). In NSW the easement is not to be inconsistent with the public interest: Conveyancing Act 1919 (NSW) s 88K(2)(a).

[246] *Ex parte Edward Street Properties Pty Ltd* [1977] Qd R 86, 90; *Re Worthston Pty Ltd* (1987) 1 Qd R 400, 403.

[247] Eg, Conveyancing Act 1919 (NSW) s 88K(2)(b); Property Law Act 1974(Qld) s 180(4)(a) and (b).

[248] *King v Carr-Gregg* [2002] NSWSC 379 (Unreported, Foster JA, 2 May 2002), para [66].

[249] *Tregoyd Gardens Pty Ltd v Jervis* (1997) 8 BPR 15,845, 15,851.

[250] Eg, Conveyancing Act 1919 (NSW) s 88K(2)(c); Property Law Act 1974 (Qld) s 180(3)(c).

[251] *Durack v DeWinton* (1998) 9 BPR 16403, 16449.

[252] *Busways Management Pty Ltd v Milner* (2002) 11 BPR 20,385, para [22].

[253] Eg Conveyancing Act 1919 (NSW) s 88K(7); Property Law Act 1974 (Qld) s 180(4)(c)(e).

A system of court-imposed easements has drawbacks. It is still novel and lacks a predictive quality. The determining criteria are different from long user or the need to fill or rectify gaps in contractual negotiations. It is triggered by a reasonable necessity, which is not as restrictively interpreted as in the case of easements of necessity. Unlike prescriptive and implied easements, conformity with the criteria does not create immediate rights. An application to and evaluation by the court, taking into account the public interest, is indispensable.

However, it is strongly arguable that the merits of court-imposed easements outweigh any disadvantages; and may in the long term be preferable to statutorily regulated prescriptive or implied easements. First, the process is an open one. The parties have an opportunity to present their views about the proposed easement. It cannot be contended by the servient owner that the existence of the easement was a complete surprise. Secondly, the court determines the matter with reference to the facts of the case rather than historical records, previous use or descriptions of land on title deeds (although these matters may be relevant). Thirdly, instead of the disparate strands of various kinds of easements, statutory rights of user are centrally and judicially evaluated by reference to broad and modern criteria, particularly the public interest and compensation. Neither prescriptive nor implied easements (either under common law or statute) are sourced in an acknowledgment of the general public interest or the fairness of compensation. Fourthly, a statutory right of user fits neatly into a streamlined title-by-registration system where the 'cracks in the mirror' are minimised. Either parties successfully negotiate and register an easement, or an impartial gatekeeper determines that an easement ought to be imposed and registered. Events which do not result in registration do not create a legal proprietary interest in the land. Fifthly, court-imposed easements restrict unreasonable reliance on absolute ownership and restore a balance between ownership of land and broader social needs and goals.[254]

V. CONCLUSION

It is erroneously assumed that land law is a necessary, but settled and uninspiring area of the law. This is far from the case. As Gray and Gray observed from an English perspective in 2005,

> [m]any of the familiar features of 20th century land law have now been removed, sidelined or transformed beyond recognition ... The Land Registration Act 2002 ... promises to alter the legal landscape in hugely significant ways. Modern land law is also being reshaped by the impact of the Human Rights

---

[254] Gray and Gray, above n 235.

Act ... Far-reaching reformulations of the law of easements and the codes regulating domestic lettings and mortgages are now well within view. Suddenly the land law of the immediately foreseeable future appears markedly different from the law we have known in the past.[255]

In all three jurisdictions considered, the future treatment of prescriptive and implied easements will be an important indicator of the extent of change in the legal landscape. In varying degrees in all three jurisdictions, prescriptive and implied easements and servitudes have been stable mainstays of land law so that it is difficult to imagine land law without them.

Any perceived inadequacies or flaws in implied and prescriptive easements and servitudes were not the stimuli for title-by-registration. Yet neither has been immune from the significant shifts wrought by title-by-registration or to a lesser extent, human rights legislation.

In some jurisdictions like New South Wales one of the collateral impacts of title-by-registration has been the virtual abolition of prescriptive easements and the creation of a statutory right of user based on reasonable necessity, the public interest and compensation. In England, the advent of title-by-registration has placed serious pressure on the current law of prescriptive and implied easements. The implementation of the broad recommendations made by the Law Commission in the Consultation Paper would preserve prescriptive easements and some statutory form of implied easements. However, these adjustments would constitute significant breaks from the past. Even in jurisdictions where title-by-registration has been moderately implemented, such as Scotland or Victoria, it has still been necessary to determine to what extent such servitudes and easements are compatible with the title-by-registration system and to make or recommend changes accordingly.

Prior to the implementation of human rights legislation in England and Scotland, it was automatically assumed that prescriptive and implied easements and servitudes were valid even though servient owners were subject to a legally enforceable proprietary shifts without compensation. Although concerns about the impact of human rights law on land law have recently abated, the fact that prescriptive and implied easements constitute proprietary shifts in favour of the putative dominant owners will require a careful balancing of rights between parties in any statutory scheme.

---

[255] Gray and Gray, above n 3, at para [1.8].

4

Feudal Law: The Case for Reform

JUDITH BRAY[*]

I. INTRODUCTION

FEUDAL LAW PLAYS a very limited role in the application of land law today. Nevertheless there is sufficient residual effect for the Law Commission to have contemplated its abolition. Indeed this was recognised in an earlier report, which in very strong terms called for wholesale reform as the present law was, in the words of the report, 'indefensible'[1]. In June 2008 the Law Commission published its 10th programme of reform but yet again the reform of feudal law was not included. It was said to be a deferral, suggesting that it may be included in a future programme. This paper intends to consider the historical principles of feudal law, its gradual erosion and what, if any, part it plays in the structure of land law today. Finally, it will consider whether the part feudal law plays is of sufficient importance for the Law Commission to devote time in the future to consideration of its reform?[2]

II. BASIC PRINCIPLES OF FEUDAL LAW

Feudal Law has always been difficult to define. Historically it meant something rather different from what Feudal Law has come to mean today. This has given rise to some divergence amongst academics as to how the feudal system can be defined. Professor JH Baker comments in his *Introduction to Legal History*[3] that the term feudal system is really an anachronism, a useful modern label for certain common features of medieval life which had no contemporary name given to them. He suggests

[*] J Bray, Senior Lecturer in Law, University of Buckingham (April 2008).
[1] Land Registration for the Twenty-First Century—A Conveyancing Revolution (Law Com No 271).
[2] With thanks to Dr Mary Welstead, Visiting Professor of Law at the University of Buckingham, for her comments on an earlier draft of this paper and thanks to Paul Hogarth-Blood for his assistance with the initial research, in particular on the law of escheat.
[3] JH Baker, *An Introduction to Legal History*, 3rd edn (London, Butterworths, 1990) 256.

that it was the lawyers who took feudalism to mean the law of tenures and that is the modern assumption today. JGA Pocock comments that the phrases feudal system and feudalism were not regularly used until the eighteenth century and nineteenth century[4] and, more significantly, EH Burn suggests that feudalism is a word of some vagueness and ambiguity and one that was certainly unknown to the peoples or people to whom it is applied.[5] For Maitland feudalism is 'a state of society in which the main social bond is between lord and man, a relation implying on the lord's part protection and defence; on the man's part protection, service and reverence'.[6]

For centuries it was accepted that feudal land-holding was based on the principle that the king had ultimate rights over all land. However, as Simpson suggests, rights were not necessarily equated with ownership of land:

> The lawyers never adopted the premise that the king owned all the land; such a dogma is of very modern appearance. It was sufficient for them to note that the king was lord, ultimately, of all the tenants in the realm, and that as lord he had many rights common to other lords ... and some peculiar to his position as supreme lord.[7]

The view that the king owned all land is of much more modern origin. However, in recent years ownership derived from the exertion of force has lost credibility as any basis for legal title in land.[8] It has been suggested that force alone cannot eradicate title.[9] The king asserted ownership over the land and used it as a way of rewarding those who had shown him support in troubled times. The king distributed rights in land to loyal supporters, known as tenants in chief, and in return they provided services to him. The system of feudal law, which had worked successfully in Norman France and had been imported into England, was a system of law where ownership of land was linked to duties owed to someone who had superior title. Initially these duties were owed to the king and then to a Tenant in Chief who took his land from the king. This aspect of reciprocal rights and duties has grown to have some resonance today where land use by the Government and large organisations could be said to carry some social responsibility,[10]

---

[4] JGA Pocock, *The Ancient Constitution and the Feudal Law*, (Cambridge, Publisher, 1957).

[5] *Cheshire and Burn's Modern Law of Real Property*, 15th edn (London, Butterworths, 1994) 9.

[6] Maitland, *Constitutional History of England* (1908) 143.

[7] AWB Simpson, *A History of The Land Law*, 2nd edn (Oxford, Oxford University Press, 1986) 47.

[8] *Mabo v Queensland (No 2)* (1993) 175 CLR 1.

[9] Gray and Gray, *Elements of Land Law*, 4th edn (Oxford, Oxford University Press, 2005) 69 and generally.

[10] *ibid*, 82 and 147.

such obligations ranging from controlling emissions from power stations to the maintenance of a footpath by a local authority or the maintenance of land within the National Parks. However the duties owed in medieval times were often much more individualised. These were duties owed from and to a particular Lord or Tenant in Chief.

Services varied from the provision of men (knights) who would serve the king for a minimum number of days a year, called 'knight service', to the provision of some highly personal service such as the personal delivery of letters. It is generally agreed that military service was at the core of the relationship between the feudal Lord and his tenant.[11] This incident of feudal tenure rested on the constant need of the king and also the tenants in chief to retain a force to protect them. Once the land was granted to the tenant in chief he, in his turn, might make a further grant of land to someone to work on his land. Other tenures included spiritual tenures called frankalmoign,[12] where land was granted to Ecclesiastical bodies and in exchange prayers and masses were said for the souls of the grantor of land and his heirs and successors.

The relationship between the king and others can be likened to a pyramid. The king was placed at the top with ultimate ownership of all land. Everyone below the king only held land subject to 'tenure' or agreement concerning services with the king or with someone lower in the pyramid. Everyone had his place in the hierarchy: tenure, rank and economic position were interdependent.[13] The complexity of feudal law in England contrasted with that in other countries in Europe where the feudal system was less complex.[14]

Tenures could be subdivided further into free and unfree tenures. The free tenures were part of the feudal structure, albeit at the lower end of the ladder, but the holders of unfree tenures were held by common labourers or villein tenants and had no place on this giant feudal ladder. Villein tenants could acquire land but their claim to the land was precarious and subject to the superior claim of the Lord.[15] This type of tenure gradually came to

---

[11] JMW Bean, *The Decline of English Feudalism*, (Manchester, Manchester University Press, 1968) 2.

[12] 'No definite or specified services could be reserved to the lord on a gift in frankalmoigne, but a general obligation was implied to say prayers and masses for the souls of him and his heirs. If any definite or specified ecclesiastical service was annexed to the gift, the tenure was not properly frankalmoigne, but by Divine Service': HW Challis, *Law of Real Property*, 3rd edn (London, Charles Sweet, 1911) 11–12.

[13] JH Baker, *An Introduction to English Legal History*, 3rd edn (London, Butterworths, 1990) 260.

[14] See generally S Reynolds, *Fiefs and Vassals: The Medieval Evidence Reinterpreted* (Oxford, Oxford University Press, 1994).

[15] 'It was a popular saying that villeins owned only what they had in their bellies; but this was an exaggeration, because until seizure by the lord any real or personal acquisitions belonged to the villein and he could pass good title to a third party': JH Baker, *An Introduction to English Legal History*, above n 13, at 533.

be recognised as villeinage and then later copyhold tenure. Unlike villeinage copyhold tenure gave some security to the holder and was the last form of tenure to be abolished.[16]

One particular problem of feudalism was the right to alienate the land. The tenant of the land could not freely deal in his land but he could convey that land to another by the use of subinfeudation. Subinfeudation allowed the transfer of land by the tenant but only on the basis that after the transfer the new tenant held the land as his tenant and a new tenurial relationship was added. This made the pyramid very complex and was soon disallowed. The Statute *Quia Emptores* was passed in 1290. This expressly prohibited the alienation of land through subinfeudation. After 1290 only the Crown held the right to grant new tenures. Alienation of land remained a problem and as a result a second method of transfer was introduced called substitution. This allowed rights to pass from one to another by substituting the new tenant rather than adding new rights in further tenurial layers. On acceding to the land the new tenant accepted the feudal duties which had been exercised by the previous tenant. This method had the advantage of restricting the growth of the pyramid.

The abolition of subinfeudation through the Statute *Quia Emptores* marks the start of the decline in feudalism. By 1600 most tenures ceased to have practical effect and the Tenures Abolition Act 1660 reduced the number of tenures. Land was no longer held in the pyramid of duties but simply held directly in relation to the Crown. The one significant form of tenure that did continue after 1600 was villeinage or copyhold tenure and that was not finally abolished until 1922. This was held by farm labourers and the services which they performed in return for land rights were later exchanged for money.

So in practical terms the feudal system ceased in the seventeenth century but the feudal pyramid which we consider to be at the heart of the feudal system was never formally abolished. Today the Crown still technically holds title to all land and all freehold owners are tenants of the Crown.

> It is the Statute *Quia Emptores* which—quite unnoticed—still regulates fee simple transfers of land today. Each transfer is merely a process of substitution of the transferee in the shoes of the transferor. The operation of the Statute during the last seven centuries has tended towards a gradual levelling of the feudal pyramid so that all tenants in fee simple are today presumed (in the absence of contrary evidence) to hold directly of the crown as 'tenants in chief'.[17]

This remnant of feudal law is largely irrelevant to most landowners in the United Kingdom and formal abolition of this aspect of the feudal system

---

[16] The Law of Property Act 1922 s 128.
[17] Gray and Gray, above n 9, at 81.

would have little or no effect on land ownership of the vast majority of people. This seems a sensible and simple step that the Law Commission could adopt by varying the terminology of registration of title. Ownership of land is still based on an estate. The terminology of section 1(1) Law of Property Act 1925 speaks of an estate in land.

> The doctrine of estates is regarded as the cornerstone of land holding since it manages to overcome the difficulty of the crown as ultimate owner of all land. The notional entity of the estate was interposed between the tenant and the land, with the consequence that each tenant owned (and still owns) not land itself but an *estate* in land, each estate being graded with reference to its temporal duration ... All proprietary relationships with land thus fall to be analysed at one remove—through the intermediacy of an *estate*—the tenant always having ownership of an intangible right (ie an *estate*) rather than ownership of a tangible thing (ie the land).[18]

An estate is thus based on a relationship with another rather than the absolute ownership which freehold owners believe they hold. Section 1(1) would therefore need to repealed and replaced by a new definition of freehold and leasehold ownership which incorporates the principle of an estate in time or 'slice of time' as laid down in *Walsingham's Case*[19] but does not rely on the ownership of the intangible estate granted from the Crown but ownership of a tangible right in the land itself. This issue is not without precedent since the problem has been confronted fairly recently in Scotland. Although the feudal system in Scotland was somewhat different in many respects to that of England there are certain lessons to be drawn from their recent experience in following through a programme of reform of feudal law.

Feudal ownership of land in Scotland has its roots in the eleventh and twelfth centuries. The Crown granted rights over land called *feu* charters to members of the Scottish nobility (superiors) in return for either obligations to the supply of men for the army or financial obligations. They in turn granted land to others (vassals). Under the feudal system in Scotland all land was held of the Crown as the paramount superior, and ownership was conditional upon the rights and interests of the paramount superior. However a key difference in the Scottish feudal system is that the rights and interests held by the Crown as paramount superior were rights and interests held in the public interest. An aspect of reform was the move from ownership where the public had a direct stake to absolute ownership and this could be considered as a retrograde step. This aspect is relevant to the issue of reform of Crown land and land owned by the Duchies in England. The relationship long outlived that in England and *feu* duties continued to

---

[18] *ibid*, 68.
[19] *Walsingham's Case* (1573) 2 Plowd 547, 75 ER 805.

be exacted by superiors up until abolition. There had been earlier piecemeal reform[20] with the limiting of *feu* duties but feudalism itself continued. The important reform under the 2000 Act is the removal of the relationship of feudal tenure under section 2.

2. Consequences of abolition

(1) An estate of *dominium utile* of land shall, on the appointed day, cease to exist as a feudal estate but shall forthwith become the ownership of the land and, in so far as is consistent with the provisions of this Act, the land shall be subject to the same subordinate real rights and other encumbrances as was the estate of *dominium utile*.

(2) Every other feudal estate in land shall, on that day, cease to exist.

(3) It shall, on that day, cease to be possible to create a feudal estate in land.[21]

These provisions ensure that existing vassals will immediately cease to be vassals and will become absolute owners of property. This important provision took effect in November 2004 and marked a dramatic change in land ownership in Scotland.[22] As Professor Hector MacQueen stated,

from now on, in law as well as in social and economic reality, there will be out-right ownership of land, in line with the civilian principles generally applying in Scots property law rather than the divided or double dominium in which the dominium utile is held of the dominium directum, both estates being regarded as ones of ownership of the land in question, without the ownership being either joint or common.[23]

However, the Scottish reforms may only have limited applications to the reform of English Feudal Law.

Scotland started, so far as the available sources are concerned, from a basis which was admittedly that of a very different system of land law. Sometimes the employ-ment of Roman law terms has been successful and helpful more particularly in showing that the term 'landowner' has a legal basis in Scotland which it lacks in England.[24]

The doctrine of estates in England has given ownership of land a flexibility lacking in Scots law but it also acts as a strait jacket in some ways when the most fundamental reform of English land law is contemplated. The

---

[20] The Land Tenure Reform (Scotland) Act 1974. Vassals were given the chance to pay off feu duties in a one-off payment and it introduced a prohibition on the creation of new feu duties.

[21] Abolition of Feudal Tenure etc (Scotland) Act 2000, Pt 1 Abolition of Feudal Tenure, s 2.

[22] Deputy Justice Minister Hugh Henry commented, 'These Acts represent both a symbolic change and practical reform. For the first time since the 12th century Scots can own their property, rather than being at the bottom of a pyramid of feudal superiors'.

[23] H McQueen, 'Tears of a Legal Historian: Scottish Feudalism and the *IUS COMMUNE*' (2003) *Juridical Review* 2.

[24] CF Kolbert and NAM MacKay, *History of Scots and English Land Law* (Geographical Publications Ltd, 1977) 161.

issue to be grasped is whether under English law the landowner can own 'the land itself' rather than 'an estate in the land'. However following the Scottish experience there seems little reason to retain the most significant relic of the feudal system in England, namely the Crown's ultimate claim on all titles.

Apart from this reform there remains a strange collection of issues which have the potential to affect landownership in ways which are thoroughly unsatisfactory where recent attempts have been made to systematise land-ownership and to open it to public scrutiny.[25] The legacy of feudal law is largely one of uncertainty and obscurity.

III. RESIDUAL FEUDAL LAW AND ITS CONSEQUENCES

The main areas where feudalism still has a residual effect fall into three main categories:

The Law of Escheat;
Manorial Rights; and
Ownership of land by the Crown, including land held by the Royal Duchies.

IV. ESCHEAT

The Law of Escheat is expressly mentioned in the Law Commission's ninth programme for reform. It referred to the Law of Escheat and that of *bona vacantia* as processes which 'create undue complexity and place responsibility for ownerless land in too many agencies', clearly highlight-ing the need for reform. Escheat itself is fairly unusual as it affects less than 400–500 properties annually.[26] However property passing *bona vacantia* to the Crown is more common. The main difficulties in this area lie in the overlap of the present rules and the arbitrary nature of their application.

Escheat can be described as the reversion of an estate in land to the grantor on the occurrence of certain events. Under feudal law all land had to have a tenant, it could not be ownerless, so if someone died without leaving an heir or if someone lost the right to own land, the land would

---

[25] The Land Registration Act 1988 s 1(1).
[26] Law Com No. 271 (2001) para 11.22.

revert back to the Lord who had granted the land. Where the land was held directly of the Crown then the land would revert back to the Crown:

> The Lord's rights have been there all along; the tenant's rights disappear; the lord has all along been entitled to the land; he is entitled to it now, and, since he has no tenant, he can enjoy it in demesne.[27]

When land was transferred to a tenant a ceremony of homage took place, which transferred rights to the tenant. In exchange the tenant took an oath of fealty under which the tenant swore to be faithful to his Lord. The relationship of Lord and tenant was therefore reciprocal with duties owed by each to the other. The Lord promised to protect the tenant and to defend him from attacks either by force or more subtly by legal proceedings. Holdsworth writes:

> the ceremony of homage cements those associations of lords and men which in the days of the weakness or the infancy of the state of necessity assume many public duties and causing landowning to be a matter of public law.[28]

The tenant could lose the protection from his Lord if he committed a felony, which originally constituted any breach of obligations but then assumed the more modern concept of a serious criminal offence. This was *escheat propter delictum tenentis* and if it were committed then the estate of the felon would revert to his immediate Lord and later to the Crown.[29] This aspect of feudalism was finally abolished by the Forfeiture Act 1870. The other form of escheat *escheat propter defectum sanguinis* would occur on the death of a tenant without heirs. In these circumstances it was held that the lord had a better claim than anyone else. The modern equivalent of this can be found in the Administration of Estates Act 1925,[30] which allows property, including freehold land, to pass to the Crown as *bona vacantia* where an individual dies intestate and without an heir.

True escheat still applies in one or two limited circumstances, namely insolvency both personal and corporate. Where a company is dissolved and land belonging to the company has been overlooked then that land passes to the Crown. In cases of personal bankruptcy a trustee in bankruptcy may disclaim property which makes it a liability rather than an asset. It may, for example, carry repairing covenants which would make it a burden rather than a benefit.

There are isolated examples in more modern case law of escheat applying, *Re Wells*[31] being one example. In this case a company on its dissolution

---

[27] Pollock and Maitland, *The History of English Law*, 2nd edn, SFC Milsom (ed) (Cambridge, Cambridge University Press, 1968) vol 2, 82.

[28] WS Holdsworth, A History of English Land Law, 2nd edn (1932) vol III, 54.

[29] *ibid*, 69.

[30] Administration of Estates Act 1925 s 46(1)(vi).

[31] *Re Sir Thomas Spencer Wells* [1933] Ch 29.

continued to own leasehold land under a mortgage. The rent received was so low that it would not cover the interest payable on the mortgage so the liquidator did not claim the equity of redemption, as it appeared to be worthless. The rents later increased and so exceeded the interest due on the mortgage, which meant the equity of redemption had some value. Since the liquidator had already disclaimed the equity of redemption, the mortgagees decided to claim it. There was some logic in this argument, since there was now no one to whom it could be returned. The Court of Appeal held that the equity of redemption was a proprietary interest which had never passed to the mortgagees and the interest therefore passed to the Crown.

Originally, where escheat applied, the title reverted back free of third party rights. So for instance, if the grantee had taken out a mortgage, the grantor would receive the land back without the burden of the mortgage and the mortgagee would lose the important security that he held in the land. The Land Registration Act 2002 failed to include the wholesale reform of feudal law which was originally intended by the Law Commission,[32] but it did have one important effect on the law of escheat. Entries on the Register were to be allowed to remain against escheated land and so a mortgage or any other third-party right could still take effect against the escheated land.[33] It was recognised that the rights of a third party had been seriously undermined where the title to escheated registered land had been wiped clean. However, in spite of this reform, escheat still remains. As pointed out above, it rarely occurs today mainly because freehold ownership of land gives the owner rights not only in his/her lifetime but also after death, and even where the owner dies intestate the property will pass to a person's heir and successors under statute. If there are no heirs and successors then the property will pass to the Crown.

Escheated land will pass to the Crown and today it is held by the Treasury Solicitor, who has authority to sell it, and until it is sold the title to the land can remain on the register. However, where the land passing under escheat is situated in the Duchy of Lancaster or the Duchy of Cornwall, it will pass to the relevant Duchy. The Crown holds this but the rules are different and inconsistent. Although the number of cases involved is small, it would make sense to introduce some simple reforms. Reform of the law on escheat cannot be undertaken in isolation from the law concerning *bona vacantia*.

First, if ownership of land ceases to rest on tenure where the Crown has the ultimate claim it would challenge the justification for automatic reversion to the Crown where land has been deemed ownerless. There is a logic in the state taking control and dealing in the land but it could pass to another body such as the Charity Commission. Reform of the Crown's

---

[32] *Land Registration for the Twenty-First Century—A Conveyancing Revolution* (Law Com No 271).
[33] Land Registration Act 2002 s 82.

claim on land would open up debate on these alternatives. Secondly, the various agencies which deal in such land need to be rationalised so that all land passing under these rules are dealt within one agency: either the Treasury Solicitor, which currently deals with most of the property passing under escheat or *bona vacantia*, or a new agency dedicated to administering such property. An important reform would be to remove the right of the Duchies to such land. Finally it would be appropriate to confer a special interim registrable status on the land.

V. MANORIAL RIGHTS

The Law Commission has stated that land law has, in most respects, moved on from ancient concepts and practices, and so it is inconsistent that remnants of feudal law remain in operation.[34] It has also stated that it makes little sense to have partial retention of feudal land law for twenty-first-century land holdings. It says that the remnants that remain cause uncertainty to the general public, legal practitioners and the courts. One such area of uncertainty is the nature and extent of manorial rights. However the Law Commission did not include manorial rights in its remit for reform in 2007, which seems an unfortunate omission and it is hoped they will be included when feudal law eventually returns to the Law Commission's working agenda.

The manor played a role in the feudal system but it was not part of the pyramid of rights described earlier. Rather it existed independently as a complete administrative unit. It was already in existence at the time of the Norman Conquest. 'The Manor had been an economic and social unit before the conquest, comprising a vill or hamlet of perhaps a hundred or so inhabitants, centred upon the mansion house or hall of a lord'.[35] A manor could denote a geographical area similar to a village today or it could denote a jurisdictional or economic entity.[36] It is probably better to regard the manor in relation to the rights held by the Lord as a geographical area of land. There were huge variations in the size of manors: some parishes had more than one manor but others, such as Taunton Dean in Somerset, were very large indeed. The manor could consist of several houses as well as one large manor inhabited by the Lord of the Manor, large areas of farmland and also some wasteland. Some of these areas of wasteland became common land, still in existence today, and continue to cause problems to lawyers today particularly in relation to rights of access.[37] Important grantees of the Crown such as Tenants in Chief or the

---

[34] See www.lawcom.gov.uk Feudal Law.
[35] Baker, *An Introduction to English Legal History*, above n 13, at 258.
[36] Simpson, *A History of the Land Law*, above n 7, at 157 and generally.
[37] See *Bakewell Management Ltd v Brandwood* [2004] 2 WLR 955.

Church held manors. The more wealthy and influential Tenants in Chief held more than one manor.

The Lord of the Manor had an important role in society, which gave him certain rights over those living in the manor and to whom he also owed reciprocal duties. Within the manor some held the land as free men owing duties similar to feudal duties such as knight service or agricultural work, whereas others had the status of unfree men called villeins. This class had no independent rights over their land. The distinction between the two groups lay in whether they had villein tenure or not. If someone held with villein tenure then they were recognised as unfree. Bracton comments that the distinguishing feature of an unfree tenant was that 'he did not know when he went to bed, what work he would have to do in the morning'.[38] By the fourteenth century the tenants of the Lord of the Manor rarely provided services but instead provided money payments.[39] The term villein tenure was replaced by the term copyhold tenure, which arose because copies of the entry recording the rights of these tenants were recorded on the court rolls. The court roll recorded the title of each tenant and was proof of rights of each tenant. Copyhold tenure was finally abolished in 1922.[40] There had been a gradual erosion of copyhold tenure throughout the nineteenth century, so the passage of the Act was merely a culmination of this. As a result of the 1922 Act all copyhold tenure was automatically converted into freehold tenure.[41] However, abolition of the tenure did not abolish rights that were still in existence. These have lived on.

The Lord of the Manor retained rights over any land within the manor and control over his tenant's use of the land whether they were free or unfree. His role also carried certain duties within the manor; many were associated with the enforcement of law and order, such as holding a manorial court from time to time, which his tenants had to attend. He also offered protection to his tenants. Today these duties have all but disappeared save for some liability to repair dykes, ditches and canals but the rights over the tenants have remained. Although these rights arose through ownership of 'the manor' the rights were capable of being separated from the ownership of land. An owner of land who was short of money might agree to sell the land but retain the rights of the Lord of the Manor, often providing an income for the Lord. These rights might include fishing or mineral rights. The 1922 Act was both far-reaching and also very conservative in the manner that it approached manorial rights. Some rights were abolished either immediately or within a specific time-frame but others

---

[38] Bracton, *On the Law and Customs of England*, GE Woodbine and SE Thorne (eds) (1968–77) vol II, 89.

[39] Simpson, *A History of the Land Law*, above n 7, at 261.

[40] The Law of Property Act 1922.

[41] The Law of Property Act 1922 s 128.

were retained and some have proved to be more controversial than others. Examples include the right to manorial waste, giving the Lord of the Manor rights over strips of land, many of which may allow access for others who live within the manorial boundaries. By contrast the right to hold fairs and markets and fishing and sporting rights are less controversial. After the abolition of copyhold tenure most land became owned under freehold tenure but parcels of wasteland or common land may still carry rights for the 'Lord' whoever he/she may be.

Since the separation of the title from the land there has grown up a ready market for purchase of these titles. In a number of notorious cases the rights of the Lord of the Manor have been purchased at auction thus allowing the owner to resurrect the rights. The new Lord of the Manor can reclaim rights over land which was originally part of the manor and which has existed for centuries as common land or wasteland. In 1999, manorial rights were purchased over land in a small village called Peterstone Wentloog and the new Lord of the Manor sought to exercise ancient rights against villagers, using land which he claimed to be land of the original Manor. He refused to allow the villagers use of an access route, enjoyed for years, unless they made substantial payments. The villagers believed the route to be over common land. The new Lord supported his claim by registering a caution against their titles at the Land Registry.[42] The villagers were spared the payments but only after intervention of Parliament.[43] Manorial rights were described by one person involved in the case 'as a minefield of uncertainty involving lawyers, civil servants, [and] Land Registry officials leaving people wide open to exploitation by unscrupulous individuals'. This is by no means an isolated case. There are several ongoing cases where disputes such as this continue.[44] Recent cases such as *Crown Estates Commissioners v Mark Andrew Tudor Roberts, Trelleck Estate Ltd*[45] and *Roberts v Swangrove Estates Ltd*[46] continue to show that complex issues of law are involved.

The Land Registration Act 2002 has to some extent addressed the issue of manorial rights in the long term, by holding that their status as rights that override the register shall only last until 12 October 2013, when they must all be brought on to the Register in order to be binding.[47] However, this is only

---

[42] Such a caution would have been registered under the Land Registration Act 1925 s 54, now repealed and replaced by s 15 (cautions against first registration) and s 35 (the entry of a unilateral notice).

[43] House of Commons Debates Hansard 3 February 2004.

[44] Alstonefield in Staffordshire is one example. Here the title of Lord Alstonefield was purchased at auction in 1999 by a Cardiff-based businessman. The title carried mineral rights, hunting and fishing rights and rights over areas giving access to land.

[45] *Crown Estates Commissioners v Mark Andrew Tudor Roberts, Trelleck Estate Ltd* [2008] EWHC 1302 (Ch).

[46] *Roberts v Swangrove Estates Ltd* [2007] 2 P & CR 17.

[47] Land Registration Act 2002 s 117(1), sch 3 para 11.

a partial solution. Abolition of such rights would afford far greater protection for innocent members of the public affected. The main obstacle for total abolition rests with potential violation of human rights.[48] Article 1 Protocol 1 of the European Convention on Human Rights protects rights in property. This issue was considered during the passage of the Land Registration Act. Examples were cited of those who may lose their rights in 2013 because they were unaware of the need to register. It was suggested that people would be deprived of their property simply because they are unaware of the relevant provision.[49] The Land Registration Act 2002 affected many such rights in land and manors are just one right[50] given a timescale of 10 years in order to bring such rights on to the register. Such a lengthy timescale was introduced in order to address the issue of potential violation of human rights. However the abolition of such rights presents a more drastic reform altogether. There are some analogies to be drawn with the abolition of the feudal system in Scotland. A key feature of the Scottish system was the payment of *feu* duties. These were feudal conditions which had been converted into monetary payments. The payment of such sums had been addressed in earlier legislation[51] and largely abolished but the 2000 Act removed any that remained. The Act allowed for a period of transition when payments could still be required and feudal superiors could claim compensation. Under section 7 any *feu* duty still in existence when the Act came into force was extinguished with immediate effect. However under section 7 provision was made for compensation to be paid by the vassal to the superior Lord. After a period of two years all rights to such duties would cease. A further point of comparison is the approach to feudal burdens, which bear a similarity to the rights of the Lord of the Manor. Feudal burdens consisted of conditions which would be set out in the title deeds, limiting the use that could be made of property by the owner. There is a striking similarity to restrictive covenants. The key feature, however, of feudal burdens was the fact that they would remain enforceable by the superior even where they ceased to have any meaningful connection with the land. The feudal burden can allow considerable control over the use of the land made by a purchaser where such a burden exists.

A feudal superior owning no neighbouring land, and whose sole interest in the burdened land is a right of *dominium directum*, could claim payment of a waiver consenting to the carrying out of work contrary to the burden. The superior

---

[48] European Convention for the Protection of Human Rights and Fundamental Freedoms, Protocol 1 Art 1.

[49] Hansard debate 11 February 2002 pt 11.

[50] Land Registration Act 2002 schs 1 and 3 include such rights as franchises, rights in respect of an embankment or sea or river wall or a right in respect of the repair of a church chancel.

[51] Land Tenure Reform (Scotland) Act 1974.

would have no interest to enforce the burden other than to charge for payment for the waiver.[52]

By contrast the enforcement of the benefit of a covenant within English law has always relied on the ownership of a legal estate in the land by the covenantee and his/her successor in title.[53] The feudal burdens were largely extinguished by the 2000 Act. In limited cases a superior could take action to preserve them.[54] There are provisions within the Act which must be met in order for such feudal burdens to be preserved. For instance, under section 19 the superior and vassal must have come to a mutual agreement, or under section 20 the superior must have convinced the Land Tribunal that he or she will suffer substantial loss or disadvantage if the burden is lost. In this way the abolition of feudal burdens in Scotland has foreseen the possibility of challenges under the European Convention of Human Rights.

A contrast between the recent cases concerning the purchase of manorial rights and the feudal burdens within the Scottish system can be made. The uncompromising approach of the Scottish legislation could be applied in any reform of manorial rights. The removal of such rights could be justified if compensation were offered. However unlike the Scottish system where compensation can be demanded from the vassal, in England compensation for the loss of manorial rights would require some Government funding. If compensation were to be based on loss then such loss would require proof. For those rights which have lain dormant for years or even centuries then the purchaser of such rights would have difficulty in proving loss.

VI. CROWN LAND

Finally, there is the complex question of Crown land. Ownership of land by the Crown has its roots firmly in feudal law and is a highly complex issue, principally because the Crown owns land in many different capacities.

There has long been a distinction drawn between the hereditary land and personal land of the monarch. Any land that can be described as personal can be disposed of freely as he or she wishes. It was expected that hereditary land would be passed on to the monarch's successor. Halsbury mentions an example of this, possibly the first, in the will of Alfred King of the West Saxons, who died in 899 AD. That will drew a distinction between the hereditary lands of the monarch, which he was expected to pass on to his successor, and his own lands acquired by gift or inheritance, which he

---

[52] Scott Wortley and Andrew Steven, *The Modernisation of Real Burdens and Servitudes: Some Observations on the Title Conditions (Scotland) Bill Consultation Paper* (2001) 6 *Scottish Law and Practice Quarterly* 261.

[53] *Webb v Russell* (1789) 3 TR 393; *Smith and Snipes Hall Farm Ltd v River Douglas Catchment Board* [1949] 2 KB 500.

[54] The Abolition of Feudal Tenure etc (Scotland) Act 2000 ss 19, 20.

was free to dispose of as he wished.[55] However this distinction was not always clear and Halsbury states that following the Norman Conquest in 1066 it became established that all royal lands were of the same nature—at the disposal of the monarch. Royal lands formed part of the revenues of the Crown out of which the monarch was expected to carry on the normal administration of the country.[56] So revenue from the royal estates which might be termed personal estates went towards the huge cost of defence and administration of the country. Also royal lands were by no means static and were constantly increased by such means as escheats, forfeitures and inheritances[57] and also decreased through grants where necessary to a royal servant or a royal son. A clear distinction between hereditary land and personal land has only evolved over a relatively recent period of time. Vernon Bogdanor observes that 'Until the seventeenth century, it was difficult to draw any distinction at all between the finances of the sovereign and those of government'.[58]

Today Crown land can be conveniently split into three separate categories:

1. Land held by the monarchy in its political capacity;
2. Land held by the monarchy in its private capacity; and
3. The Royal Duchies.

A. Land Held by the Monarchy in its Political Capacity

First, land held in the Crown's political capacity such as Buckingham Palace, St James's Palace and Windsor Castle. Such land passes from monarch to monarch and could usefully be referred to as land vested in the monarch in his/her body politic. This land is largely managed as part of the national revenues either in the hands of the Crown Estates, the Department for Culture, Media and Sport or in some cases the Forestry Commission. There can be real problems for anyone wishing to buy or deal in this land. Historically, when the Crown separated from the executive, fear grew that the monarch would sell Crown land and gain a private profit. Peter Sparkes suggests that this was to prevent William of Orange joining in the frenzy of property speculation prevalent at the time.[59] Certainly, Parliament regarded the ownership of land by the Crown with increasing suspicion after the restoration

---

[55] 12(1) *Halsburys Laws of England* (Crown Property), para 203.
[56] *ibid.*
[57] *ibid.*
[58] Vernon Bogdanor, *The Monarchy and the Constitution*, (Oxford, Clarendon Press, 1995) 183.
[59] Peter Sparkes, *A New Land Law*, 2nd edn (Oxford, Hart Publishing, 2003) 49.

of the monarchy in 1660. Crown land, especially that within the Duchies, had been sold during the Commonwealth and so the monarchy was short of revenue. Parliament may have been justified in their suspicions but their reaction was to pass a statute that effectively prevented any sale of Crown land at all. The Crown Lands Act 1702 forbade any sale of land or any grant of a lease of land for a term of over 31 years subject to the Act. In spite of subsequent reforming legislation, this Act still applies today and has a serious effect on anyone attempting to deal in land subject to the Act. It has meant that special rules must be applied in order to pass ownership of land within the definition to a third party. In 2002 an Act of Parliament had to be passed in order for a very small parcel of land adjoining Kensington Palace to be sold to the Royal Garden Hotel in Kensington. More general repeal of this Act would prevent such an absurd situation arising in the future.[60] This surely goes against the principles laid down in 1925 that conveyancing should enable the purchaser to purchase land freely. Repeal of the Act would address the issues arising in this special case but it would, however, open the possibility of more comprehensive sale of Crown land once the fetters had been removed.

B. Land Held by the Monarchy in its Private Capacity

Land can also be held by the monarch in his/her private capacity, eg Balmoral and Sandringham. Although the distinction was apparent very early, as illustrated above by Alfred's Will in 899, the formalisation of this distinction is relatively recent and is governed by the Crown Private Estates Act 1800. A sovereign can own land and can deal freely in land and now, since the Land Registration Act 2002, can even register title to land.[61] So it has been accepted that—subject to limitations within the 1800 Act, the Crown Lands Act 1823 and section 1 of the Crown Private Estates Act 1862—the monarch enjoys certain estates in his/her natural capacity as distinct from his/her political capacity and such land would not be subject to any hereditary rights associated with the monarch.

Only land purchased out of money issued and applied for the use of the Privy Purse or coming to the monarch other than in their capacity as king or queen of the realm can be enjoyed privately. This property may be disposed of freely by sale, gift or by will. There is no particular distinction here with purchase or dealings with any other person.

There is often a problem in distinguishing the Crown's private land where the overall use inevitably involves some political use and enjoyment of that

---

[60] Land at Palace Avenue, Kensington (Acquisition of Freehold) Act 2000.
[61] Land Registration Act 2002 s 79.

land.[62] For instance, some of those employed at Sandringham are treated as employees of the State. If the land were to be sold then would it be subject to capital gains tax exemption? The distinction is often blurred today. Windsor Castle is held for the monarch in his/her official capacity and yet the Queen funded repairs after the fire in 1992.

C. Land Held in the Royal Duchies of Lancaster and Cornwall

The most complex issues of Crown land and its ownership lie with the land held in the two Royal Duchies, the Duchy of Cornwall and the Duchy of Lancaster. To uncover the rules of these two royal holdings is to tap into a very rich but highly complex mix of history, feudal law and constitutional law.[63] The position of the two Duchies is somewhat different and so the relevant rules concerning land within each Duchy have taken differing paths. Although dealings in Duchy land were effectively frozen in 1702 after the passage of the Crown Lands Act there has been a gradual loosening of those ties that prevent the free dealing in property held in the Duchies. It would be appropriate to look at each separately and then to draw some analogies between the two.

(i) The Duchy of Lancaster

The Duchy of Lancaster originated with a simple grant of land from Henry III to his son in 1265. Simon de Montfort, Earl of Leicester had been defeated in battle at Evesham and died leaving no issue so his land was given to Edmund, the youngest son of Henry III. It would have been the first grant in the feudal ladder similar to many other grants to persons of merit or strength. Formal transfer was made four years later on 22 April 1269.[64] The estates diminished as a result of the rules of escheat[65] and expanded as a result of the king's bounty or through marriage.[66] The Duchy of Lancaster came into existence some years later, probably when Edmund's son Henry was created Duke of Lancaster in 1351 and was given sovereign rights over the county Palatine in such areas as administration and justice.

---

[62] 'It is, however, not easy to distinguish in the case of the sovereign between income used for public expenditure and income used for private expenditure. Balmoral and Sandringham for example are privately owned by the sovereign, but he or she continues to carry out official constitutional duties when staying there'. Vernon Bogdanor, *The Monarchy and the Constitution* (Oxford, Clarendon Press, 1995) 193.

[63] I am much indebted to: Elisabeth Stuart, archivist at the Duchy of Cornwall and Roy Smith, archivist at the Duchy of Lancaster, for their assistance in my research.

[64] *Quo Warranto* Rolls, Parl Writs II ii 252.

[65] Edmund's first wife, Aveline, died at the age of 15 and her land had escheated to the Crown.

[66] Edmund married Blanche of Artois in 1276.

However, some argue that the Duchy truly assumed its separate identity in 1361 when Henry died and the lands passed to John of Gaunt.[67]

Crucially in 1399 the Duchy of Lancaster ceased to be held independently. Henry IV, having assumed the throne, wanted to keep the lands under the Duchy of Lancaster separate from the rest of the estates of the Crown.[68] It was an insurance policy in order to ensure that these interests would remain his, if he ever lost the throne. This clever fourteenth-century plan laid the foundations of the Duchy as it stands today. The Duchy could be enjoyed by the Crown in its personal capacity for the monarch but managed quite independently. From then on the lands and associated rights would always be kept quite separate from other land of the Crown. This raised a problem as to the capacity in which the Crown held the land.

> Did the King have two capacities in respect of the Duchy of Lancaster? Did he hold the Duchy as king or Duke of Lancaster? If he held as it as Duke had he in his Duchy none of the rights he possessed as King?[69]

This could be more than a mere theoretical problem. If land was granted within the Duchy did the Crown grant it or was it granted by the Duke of Lancaster? The evidence from contemporary case law conflicts, but it leaves us with a difficult issue today. Does the Queen own the land in the Duchy of Lancaster as the monarch or as Duke of Lancaster? And is that land owned in her personal or political capacity? One observation that can be made is that the Crown in 1399 had enjoyment and control and the right to deal in the land, which continued for some 300 years.

Parliament had gradually placed limits on the way the Crown could raise revenue. This presented problems for high-spending kings such as James I, as Robert Somerville put it:

> The Stuart Kings were by no means economical; James I indeed was extravagant to a degree. He and Charles I were not merely relatively short of resources, but actually on the verge of bankruptcy ... the ordinary income failed to meet the ordinary expenses; thus large debts were incurred, some of which were repaid by the sale of Crown lands.[70]

The Crown Lands Act 1702 is significant as an attempt to control 'for the first time in history the sovereign's power of freely disposing of his lands'.[71] It affected land within both Duchies as well as land held by the monarchy in its political capacity as discussed earlier. The Act made it hard for land

---

[67] See R Somerville, *History of the Duchy of Lancaster* (London, The Chancellor and Council of the Duchy of Lancaster, 1953) vol I.

[68] The Hereford Charter; the Lancaster Charter presented before Parliament 14 October 1399 later referred to as the Charter of Duchy Liberties.

[69] Somerville, above n 67, vol I p 144.

[70] Somerville, above n 67, vol II p 1.

[71] RB Pugh, *The Crown Estate: An Historical Essay* (London, HMSO, 1960).

to be sold which was at best inconvenient and at worst tied the hands of those trying to manage the estates.

When George III ascended the throne an attempt was made to clarify the financing of the monarchy and in particular the ownership of land by the Crown. This was the formal introduction of the civil list, although there had already been a Civil List Act passed in 1697 introducing the idea of the monarch foregoing certain property in exchange for a regular annual payment of money from the Government. Crown land would now be managed by the Government and eventually, in order to avoid the inevitable confusion in status of that land and Government land, the Crown Estate was introduced and regularised by legislation.[72] The civil list introduced for George III was rather different from the civil list of the twenty-first century. Bognador further observes that 'the sovereign retained sufficient independent revenues to be able to exert influence—which was sometimes corrupt influence—on ministers and on parliament'.[73] Somerville records that the Chancellor of the Exchequer informed Parliament of an arrangement that in exchange for Government support of the royal household it could dispose of His Majesty's interest in the hereditary revenues of the Crown.[74] These included rents of Crown lands. The Duchy of Cornwall was expressly excluded but the Duchy of Lancaster was simply not mentioned. This omission is subject to speculation but the main reason could be that the Duchy revenues were not hereditary revenues of the Crown.

The land still had the millstone of being inalienable as a result of the Crown Lands Act 1702. Since then legislation has slowly chipped away at the strict regime tying the hands of the monarchy in its ability to deal in the Duchy land. The Duchy of Lancaster Lands Act 1855 lifted the bar on sale of freehold land but subject to strict limits, so only land which in the judgement of the Chancellor and Council is inconvenient to be held with other Duchy possessions could therefore be sold. The money received had to be invested or used for improvements to other Duchy land. There has been further significant reform such as the Duchy of Lancaster Act 1988. Overall the power of disposal still remains limited so that core estates are not affected.

Where land within the Duchy of Lancaster falls into the hands of the Crown under the law of escheat then it is treated as land belonging to the Duchy and is treated quite separately. Such treatment is unique to the Duchy of Lancaster and the Duchy of Cornwall.

The income from Duchy land is taxable in the hands of the monarch although the Duchy itself does not pay tax. Its financial affairs have had

---

[72] The Crown Estates Acts 1951 and 1961.

[73] Vernon Bogdanor, *The Monarchy and the Constitution* (Oxford, Clarendon Press, 1995) 184.

[74] Somerville, *History of the Duchy of Lancaster*, above n 67, vol II p 121.

transparency since legislation[75] required the officers of the Duchy of Lancaster to prepare accounts and submit them to the Treasury. The Duchy of Lancaster remains a capital asset of the Crown. However, although the Crown is not entitled to the Duchy's capital or to capital profits, its revenue is paid directly to the Keeper of the Privy Purse, which in turn is used to finance the monarch's private expenditure as sovereign. This reflects the 1399 position even today. The first issue for the Law Commission is to identify the exact status of this land, since it neither lies with the Crown nor with the Crown Estates. Until this question has been addressed it is difficult to see how reform of the ownership of Duchy land holdings can be made.

(ii) The Duchy of Cornwall

The main difference between the two Duchies lies in the fact that for most of its history The Duchy of Cornwall has been managed for, and often by, the monarch's eldest son.

The Duchy of Cornwall was formally created by Edward III by Royal Charter in 1337,[76] when he granted land to his son and heir, Prince Edward (the Black Prince), to provide him with an income. Land in Cornwall belonging to the Earl of Cornwall, one John of Eltham, had escheated to the Crown in 1336, when he died without an heir. Edward also created the title of Duke of Cornwall. The charter laid down strict terms of the grant. The land and the title were to pass to the eldest surviving son of the monarch and the heir to the throne and the terms remain today. No daughter can inherit the land and the title in spite of the fact that the monarch can be a woman. Where the monarch has no son it will revert to the Crown. For instance, the Duchy reverted to the Crown when Edward VIII became king in 1936 and the Duchy of Cornwall was held by the Crown until the Queen ascended to the throne in 1952 and Charles became Duke of Cornwall aged four. However, whenever the Duchy reverts, it continues to be kept separate from the assets of the Crown in the same way as the Duchy of Lancaster.

The core land within the Duchy in 1337 was 17 manors, known as assessionable manors, within Cornwall itself but there were also holdings of land around the country, such as Yorkshire and Norfolk.[77] The lands within the Duchy have constantly changed in the same way as the land within the Duchy of Lancaster. Much of the land was sold during the Commonwealth but some was recovered later when the monarchy was restored.

The Duchy has even less freedom to deal in the capital assets than the Duchy of Lancaster. The Charter of 1337 itself limited the right of the

---

[75] The Duchy of Cornwall and Duchy of Lancaster Act 1838.

[76] The Great Charter, 17 March 1337.

[77] E Stuart, *Dukes of Cornwall and Princes of Wales* (Duchy of Cornwall, 2001).

Duke of Cornwall to deal in the capital assets, which was compounded by the Crown Lands Act 1702. These controls caused particular problems for the Duchy when land tax was introduced.[78] Revenue from the estates could not meet the tax and it was necessary to raise capital. Legislation was introduced specifically to allow the Duchy to sell land in order to repay the tax.[79] Several further Acts gave the Duchy power to deal in the Duchy lands, such as the Duchy of Cornwall Management Act 1863, giving power to sell land within certain limitations which still exist today. For example, land can be sold but the Treasury must approve transactions with a value in excess of £200,000.

What makes the Duchy of Cornwall different from the Duchy of Lancaster is its primary purpose, which is to ensure that the heir apparent to the throne receives an income rather than solely for the benefit of the monarch. Along with the income it is apparently there to act as a training ground for the eldest son to exercise some management skills as a landowner. It constituted part of the training for kingship. Historically it was recognised that the heavy onus of monarchy required gradual succession to power.[80] Today the Duke of Cornwall does not receive Civil List funding; he relies exclusively on the income from the Duchy for himself and other members of his family. There must be an incentive for any landowner to maximise the assets held and the present Duke of Cornwall has shown himself to address issues of management proactively. The development at Poundbury on land owned by the Crown since 1342 and now within the Duchy reflects a very modern approach to land use.[81]

It must also been seen in the context of the length of time that the present Duke of Cornwall has enjoyed the Duchy lands.[82] However, if the real justification for separate ownership lies in its training ground for monarchy then it breaks down where the heir apparent is a woman, such

---

[78] Land Tax was introduced in 1692 as a way to increase revenue. The amount to be raised by an individual county was fixed by the Government. Local assessors within each county would then decide how much should be raised by each parish. The more rural parishes carried a heavier burden which was a particularly heavy burden for the Duchy of Cornwall whose land lay at that time in predominantly rural areas.

[79] The Redemption of Land Tax Act 1798 was introduced by Pitt and it specifically allowed the sale of Duchy land in order to raise revenue.

[80] See James I's *Basilikon Doron or His Majesties Instructions To His Dearest Sonne, Henry the Prince* (Edinburgh 1599).

[81] See Poundbury fact sheet (January 2008). 'In 1987 the local planning authority, West Dorset District Council, selected Duchy land to the west of Dorchester for future expansion of the town. As Duke of Cornwall, The Prince of Wales—who re-examined many of the precepts of urban and rural planning in his book "A Vision of Britain", took the opportunity to work with the council to contribute to exemplary urban addition to this market town. In 1988, The Prince of Wales appointed the architect and urban planner, Leon Krier ... his challenge was to create an autonomous new extension to the town within the context of traditional Dorset architecture'.

[82] There are only two Dukes of Cornwall that have enjoyed the title for longer than the current Duke of Cornwall, ie George IV (1762–1820) and Edward VII (1841–1901).

as Queen Elizabeth II or Queen Victoria. Neither Queen succeeded to the throne with the opportunity to exercise these management skills. A far more persuasive argument lies in the fact that the revenue from the Duchy allows the Duke of Cornwall a measure of financial independence and it is this question that needs to be addressed at the same time as addressing the reform of the Duchy ownership of land.

VII. CONCLUSIONS

Should the Law Commission commit itself to reform of feudal law?

The role of feudalism in ownership of land in England has largely disappeared. There remain, however, small pockets of uncertainty such as escheat and manorial rights, which cause confusion and muddy the much-sought-after clarity of land ownership. It is possible to address reform of these more easily than the reform of Crown ownership of land.

Crown ownership of land has its roots firmly in feudal law. The details are extremely complex because, as stated earlier, the Crown owns land in so many different capacities. However, it is an extremely important issue in the context of land ownership in England and Wales today. The extent of Crown lands is very considerable. The value of the land in the Duchies alone runs to over £834 million. The estates held by the Crown are managed estates with transactions running into millions of pounds each year. It is hardly surprising that the Law Commission should hesitate before intervening in this area. Because the role of feudalism in England has largely disappeared it might seem tempting to remove the last areas of uncertainty by abolishing the right of the Crown to own land within the Royal Duchies. The land held as Crown land has been partially addressed in the Land Registration Act 2002 but there are still a host of ancient rules which cause confusion. Most important of all is the fact that the ownership tends to undermine the principle behind land registration, which is that the Land Register should be a complete picture of all land and all owners of land held in England and Wales.

Other countries have already been successful in sweeping away the remnants of the feudal system. The revolution in France and its aftermath led to a complete abolition of the feudal system in the nineteenth century by Napoleon. More recently Scotland abolished feudal law in its entirety in 2000.[83] In the case of Scotland, however, it was a slow process, the Law Commission started work on the abolition of the feudal system, which culminated with the final report in 1999 and the subsequent Act passed in 2000.

---

[83] The Abolition of Feudal Tenure etc (Scotland) Act 2000, The Title Conditions (Scotland) Act 2003 and the Tenements (Scotland) Act 2004.

However, the issues raised concerning Crown land are not simply matters of land law and registration. They are important historical, constitutional and fiscal issues, which are intertwined. Reform in this area cannot be seen in a legal vacuum separate from the role and duties of the monarch and in particular the constitutionally significant fact that the monarch's eldest son has always held the position of the Duke of Cornwall until he succeeds to the throne. His powers and duties in managing these huge estates have been regarded as an invaluable training for his future position as monarch. So whereas there are useful reforms which could be carried out in the area of escheat and manorial rights, the Law Commission would be well advised to tread softly in the area of the Duchies and Crown lands. Undoubtedly reform is needed but apart from the property law issues there appears to be a constitutional and fiscal minefield ahead.

II

Trusts and Equitable Remedies

5

Restrictions on Dispositions of Charity Property—Protection or Undue Burden?

JEAN WARBURTON*

I. INTRODUCTION

THE CHARITIES ACT 2006 makes some amendments to the restrictions on the disposition of charity land in sections 36 to 39 of the Charities Act 1993. The amendments are clarifications of the extent of the controls, not deregulation. At the same time, the 2006 Act eases considerably the rules which restrict the powers of charities to spend capital, including permanent endowment. This juxtaposition raises an apparent conflict between control and liberalisation of the powers of charity trustees.

It is the purpose of this paper to examine the rules in sections 36 to 39 of the 1993 Act in order to determine if it is still necessary or appropriate to retain a separate, strict regime controlling the disposition of charity land. The rules will be analysed in three ways. First, the rules will be placed in their historical context to determine to what extent the present statutory regime deviates from the original judicial controls. Secondly, the rules will be compared with the rules which govern the disposition of other investments by charity trustees. Thirdly, the rules will be examined against the changing wider legal, economic and social context in which charities operate, including changing investment patterns, registration of title to land, deregulation, transparency and empowerment of trustees.

The paper will then consider whether and to what extent there should still be a system of scrutiny and control over the disposal of charity land. Finally, the paper will seek to suggest a more appropriate set of restrictions which are consistent with the way in which charities operate and are controlled in the twenty-first century.

---

* J Warburton LLD, Solicitor, Emeritus Professor of Law, Liverpool Law School.

II. RESTRICTIONS ON THE DISPOSITION OF CHARITY LAND

Statutory restrictions apply whenever charity trustees sell, mortgage, lease or otherwise dispose[1] of any land.[2] The restrictions differentiate between sales and leases for terms of more than seven years, leases for seven years or less, sales and leases of specie land and mortgages. The restrictions do not apply if the charity is an exempt charity.[3]

The starting point for sales and leases of land held in trust for a charity is that an order of the court or the Charity Commission is necessary unless the two relevant conditions are complied with.[4] The first condition is complied with if the disposition is not to a connected person.[5] Compliance with the second condition depends on the nature of the disposition and the type of land.

In the case of a sale or lease for more than seven years the condition is complied with if three requirements are met[6] before contracts are exchanged.[7] First, the trustees must have obtained and considered a written report[8] on the proposed disposition from a qualified surveyor[9] who has been instructed by them and who is acting exclusively for the charity. Secondly, the trustees must have advertised the sale or lease in accordance with the surveyor's advice. Thirdly, the trustees must have decided that they are satisfied that the terms of the sale or lease are the best that can reasonably be obtained for the charity.

In the case of a lease for seven years or less, there are two requirements.[10] First, the trustees must have obtained and considered the advice of a person they reasonably believe to have the requisite ability and experience to provide them with competent advice on the lease. Secondly, the trustees must have decided that the terms are the best that can reasonably be obtained for the charity.[11]

---

[1] 'Dispose' requires an interest in land to be created, so the grant of a licence is not caught—see *Gray v Taylor* [1998] 1 WLR 1093 (almshouse resident).

[2] Charities Act 1993 ss 36(1), 38(1).

[3] Charities Act 1993 ss 36(10)(a), 38(7).

[4] Charities Act 1993 s 36(1).

[5] Charities Act 1993 s 36(2)(a). A very wide definition of 'connected person' is given in sch 5.

[6] Charities Act 1993 36(3).

[7] See *Bayoumi v Women's Total Abstinence Educational Union Ltd* [2003] EWCA Civ 1548, [2004] All ER 110, [25].

[8] The Charities (Qualified Surveyor's Reports) Regulations 1992, SI 1992/2980, sets out the required contents of the report.

[9] 'Qualified surveyor' is defined in s 36(4) of the 1993 Act and, as well as those professionally qualified, includes someone reasonably believed by the trustees to have ability in and experience of valuation of the land in question.

[10] Charities Act 1993 s 36(5).

[11] The rent can be less than best rent if the lease is to a beneficiary with the intention that the property should be occupied for the purposes of the charity—Charities Act 1993 s 36(9)(c).

Where the land is held on trusts which stipulate that it must be used for the purposes of the charity, ie, it is designated or specie land, in addition to the usual three requirements for a sale or lease of land, the trustees must also give public notice of the proposed disposition and consider any representations made as a result of such notice.[12] The additional requirement need not be complied with if the disposition is with a view to acquiring replacement property or if it is a lease for two years or less.[13]

A similar regime applies to mortgages of charity land. The trustees must obtain an order of the court or the Charity Commission unless they have obtained and considered proper advice on the relevant matters[14] from a person they reasonably believe to be qualified by ability and experience in financial matters and who has no financial interest in the making of the loan or grant in question.[15] In the case of a mortgage to secure the repayment of a loan or grant, there are three relevant matters: first, whether the proposed loan or grant is necessary in order for the charity to pursue the course of action for which it is seeking the loan or grant; secondly, whether the terms of the loan or grant are reasonable having regard to the fact the borrower or grantee is a charity; and, thirdly, the ability of the charity to repay the loan or grant on the terms proposed.[16] In the case of a mortgage to secure the discharge of any other obligations—for example, guaranteeing the obligations of a charity's trading company—there is only one relevant matter; whether it is reasonable for the charity trustees to undertake to discharge the obligation having regard to the charity's purposes.[17]

There are provisions in sections 37 and 39 of the 1993 Act to ensure that charity trustees comply with the statutory restrictions on the disposal of land. Any contract for the sale, lease or other disposition of charity land and any conveyance, transfer or lease of charity land must state[18] that the land is held by or in trust for a charity and either that restrictions on its disposition apply or that it is exempt.[19] In addition, the charity trustees must certify[20] in the instrument of disposition,[21] as appropriate, either that the consent of the court or the Charity Commission has been obtained or that they have power to effect the relevant disposition and the relevant conditions have

---

[12] Charities Act 1993 s 36(6).
[13] Charities Act 1993 s 36(7).
[14] Charities Act 1993 s 38(1), (2).
[15] Charities Act 1993 s 38(4). Such a person may be an officer or employee of the charity.
[16] Charities Act 1993 s 38(3).
[17] Charities Act 1993 s 38(3A).
[18] For the relevant wording see the Land Registration Rules 2003, SI 2003/1417, r 180.
[19] Charities Act 1993 s 37(1). For the requirement for exempt charities, see Trusts of Land and Appointment of Trustees Act 1996 sch 1 para 4(2).
[20] For the relevant wording see Land Registry Practice Guide 14, *Charities* (2007) para 6.2.3.
[21] But not in the contract for sale or lease: See *Bayoumi v Women's Total Abstinence Education Union Ltd* [2003] EWCA Civ 1548, [2004] 3 All ER 110, [29].

been complied with, ie the conditions in section 36(3) or 36(5) of the 1993 Act.[22] If the land is registered, or is a disposition which triggers registration, the Registrar must enter a restriction on the Land Register.[23] Section 39 applies very similar provisions as to statements and certificates on mortgage of charity land.[24]

The elaborate system of conditions and requirements to be complied with and the necessity for statements and certificates designed to protect charities is undermined to a certain extent by provisions designed to protect purchasers. By sections 37(3) and 39(3) of the 1993 Act, the facts stated in a certificate are conclusively presumed to be correct in favour of a person who acquires an interest in land for money or money's worth.[25] Further, in favour of a purchaser in good faith acquiring an interest in charity land for money or money's worth, a disposition is valid whether or not the court or Charity Commission by order have sanctioned the transaction or whether or not the conditions have been complied with.[26] These latter provisions can only assist someone who is not aware that they are acquiring an interest in charity land.

III. HISTORICAL CONTEXT OF RESTRICTIONS ON THE DISPOSITION OF CHARITY LAND

The courts did not impose any restrictions on the powers of charity trustees to sell, lease or mortgage charity land.[27] A transaction, however, was liable to be set aside in equity unless it was shown by the purchaser to be beneficial to the charity.[28] This caused considerable uncertainty despite the court allowing purchasers, where appropriate, to rely on the defence of purchaser for value without notice or the Statute of Limitations.[29] The first statutory

---

[22] Charities Act 1993 s 37(2).

[23] Charities Act 1993 s 37(8). For the form of the restriction see the Land Registry Rules 2003, SI 2003/1417, sch 4 Form E.

[24] Charities Act 1993 s 39(1)(2). See also Charity Commission OG 22 C1 *Borrowings and Mortgages: Statements and Certificates in Mortgages Required by s 39*.

[25] These provisions only provide protection once a transaction has been completed: *Bayoumi v Women's Total Abstinence Educational Union Ltd* [2003] EWCA Civ 1548, [2004] 3 All ER 110, [43].

[26] Charities Act 1993 ss 37(4), 39(4).

[27] *Re Manchester New College* (1853) Beav 610, 628, 629; *Re Mason's Orphanage and London and North Western Railway Co* [1896] 1 Ch 596, 604; *Re Howard Street Congregational Chapel, Sheffield* [1913] 2 Ch 690, 695.

[28] *Att-Gen v Warren* (1818) 2 Swan 291, 303; *Att-Gen v Hungerford* (1834) 2 Cl & Fin 357, 374–5; *Att-Gen v Brettingham* (1840) Beav 91, 95; *Att-Gen v South Sea Co* (1841) 4 Beav 453, 458; *Att-Gen v Pilgrim* (1849) 12 Beav 57, 60; *Re Manchester New College* (1853) 16 Beav 610, 628, 629; *Att-Gen v Davey* (1854) 19 Beav 521, 525; *Re Clergy Orphan Corporation* [1894] 3 Ch 145 and see D Dennis, 'Dispositions of Charitable Land' [2006] Conv 219, 220.

[29] *St Mary Magdalen College Oxford v Att-Gen* [1857] 6 HL Cas 189.

intervention was in sections 21 and 24 of the Charitable Trusts Act 1853, which authorised the newly-established Charity Commissioners to sanction sales, leases, mortgages and exchanges of charity lands.

Restriction on the disposition of charity land soon followed in section 29 of the Charitable Trusts Amendment Act 1855. That section prohibited any sale or other disposition of charity land without the authority of Parliament, the courts or the Charity Commissioners. Any disposition of charity land without the required authority was void.[30] The restriction did not apply if the charity was wholly or partially exempted from the operation of the 1853 Act.[31] Although the application of the exemption could be difficult,[32] the effect was to limit the restriction to the disposition of land that formed part of the endowment of a charity.[33]

The rationale for the introduction of the restriction in 1855 was said by Stirling J in *Re Mason's Orphanage and London and North Western Railway Co*[34] to be the prevention of abuse.[35] More particularly, the Court of Appeal in the same case identified the problem of small charities dealing with their property in an arbitrary manner.[36]

Section 29 of the 1855 Act was replaced by section 29 of the Charities Act 1960, which provided that no property which was permanent endowment or functional land could be disposed of without an order of the court or the Charity Commissioners. The restriction in the 1960 Act was narrower in that the definition of 'permanent endowment' in sections 45(3) and 46 was more restrictive than that given to endowment in *Re Clergy Orphan Corporation*[37] for the purposes of the 1855 Act.[38] Land occupied for the purposes of the charity,[39] ie functional land, almost invariably came within the old definition of endowment.[40] The 1960 Act imposed no restriction on the disposal of land purchased as an investment by charity trustees out of funds expendable as income which was not occupied by the charity. The restriction was also diluted by the provision in section 29(2) that a purchaser of functional land, where there had been no order, was protected

---

[30] *Bishop of Bangor v Parry* [1891] 2 QB 277.

[31] Charitable Trusts Amendment Act 1855 s 48 and Charitable Trusts Act 1853 s 62.

[32] See SG Maurice and DB Parker (eds), *Tudor on Charities*, 7th edn (London, Sweet & Maxwell,1984) 558.

[33] See *Re Clergy Orphan Corporation* [1894] 3 Ch 145, 154–5.

[34] *Re Mason's Orphanage and London and North Western Railway* Co [1896] 1 Ch 54, 61.

[35] Examples can be found in the report of the Brougham Commissioners which preceded the Charitable Trusts Acts 1853–60, see D Owen, *English Philanthropy 1660–1960* (London, OUP, 1964) 194–5.

[36] *Re Mason's Orphanage and London and North Western Railway* Co [1896] 1 Ch 596 (CA) 605.

[37] *Re Clergy Orphan Corporation* [1894] 3 Ch 145.

[38] See *Bayoumi v Women's Total Abstinence Educational Union Ltd* [2003] EWCA Civ 1548, [2004] 3 All ER 110 at [22].

[39] Charities Act 1960 s 29(2).

[40] See Maurice and Parker, *Tudor on Charities*, above n 32, at 558.

if he, in good faith, acquired an interest in the land for money or money's worth.[41]

The rationale for the imposition of restrictions on the sale of land forming part of permanent endowment was said to be to retain the capital value of the endowment. The reason why consent was needed for the sale of land more generally was said to be that, unlike investments which were quoted on the Stock Exchange, it provided a check that a reasonable price was being obtained. Further, the fact that land was being sold was often a sign of a radical change in the policy and state of a charity and consent ensured that the proceeds of sale were applied cy-pres.[42]

The statutory requirement for consent on the disposal of charity land came under scrutiny in the 1980s as to whether it amounted to an undue restriction on trustees' powers and was an effective and valid use of the resources of the Charity Commissioners. The reasoning behind the original 1855 restrictions and later 1960 restrictions was still regarded as valid. It was accepted that the provisions safeguarded beneficiaries and helped to prevent abuse by trustees and exploitation by prospective purchasers, local authorities and developers.[43] In 1984, it was estimated that intervention by the Charity Commissioners on applications for consent had resulted in an additional £800,000 being obtained by charities on disposals of land.[44] The requirement for consent also alerted the Charity Commissioners to charities whose purposes needed a cy-pres scheme to allow for more effective application of their income.[45]

The Charity Commissioners, in their 1986 Annual Report, suggested that charity trustees should have a general power to sell subject to compliance with statutory requirements such as acting on the advice of a surveyor. They considered that consent should still be needed for the disposition of functional land. The Woodfield Report, *Efficiency Scrutiny of the Supervision of Charities*, highlighted the long delays in obtaining consent which could damage the interests of charities,[46] and recommended that the consent of the Charity Commissioners should no longer be necessary for the disposal of land, provided statutory conditions were complied with, even if the land was functional land.[47] The recommendation was accepted in the White Paper,

---

[41] The protection was included because a purchaser was inevitably reliant on the charity in determining if the land was functional land or not: *Hansard* Commons Standing Committee A, 28 June 1960, col 324, Solicitor-General (Sir Joscelyn Simon).

[42] *Hansard* Commons Standing Committee A, 28 June 1960, col 325, Solicitor-General (Sir Joscelyn Simon).

[43] Charity Commission Annual Report 1986, para 30.

[44] Woodfield Report, *Efficiency Scrutiny of the Supervision of Charities* (1987), para 97.

[45] Charity Commission Annual Report 1986, para 30; *Charities: A Framework for the Future* (Cm 694, 1989) para 7.2.

[46] Woodfield Report, above n 44, at para 97.

[47] *ibid*, para 98.

Charities: A Framework for the Future,[48] subject to a flagging procedure to alert third parties that the trustees they were dealing with were subject to a special regime. The White Paper stressed that the recommendation was consistent with the aim of fostering among trustees a greater sense of their own responsibilities.

The detail of the resultant restrictions imposed by sections 32 to 35 of the Charities Act 1992 has already been noted.[49] The same regime applies to the disposal of all land,[50] the only differentiation being that there must be public notice of a sale of specie land unless replacement land is being purchased.[51] In essence, it is unlawful for charity trustees to enter into an agreement for the disposal of charity land unless they have complied with the requirements in section 36(3) of the 1993 Act as to a surveyor's report etc. If the disposal is to a connected person, the agreement cannot be performed without an order of the court or the Charity Commission; if it is to anyone else the disposal can be completed without reference to the court or the Commission.[52]

The provisions have not been free from difficulty as to both interpretation and application. It was not clear if the reference to land being 'sold' in section 36(1) included entry into a contract of sale and hence the status of a contract not complying with section 36(3) was unclear. The clarification in *Bayoumi v Women's Total Abstinence Educational Union Ltd*,[53] that an uncompleted contract for the sale of charity land was not a 'disposition' of the land within section 36(1), necessitated amendment of the section by the Charities Act 2006.[54] There is also lack of clarity as to who are the 'charity trustees' for the purposes of section 36 when there are both holding trustees and trustees of the benefiting charity, and as to how precisely the provisions apply when land is held for more than one charity.[55]

Section 38 permitted charity trustees to mortgage land without an order of the court or the Charity Commissioners if statutory conditions were complied with, but only to secure repayment of a loan. It is not unusual for grant givers to require security, which necessitated charities having to seek

---

[48] *Charities: A Framework for the Future*, above n 45, at 38–40.

[49] See the text at nn 1–16 above. The sections became ss 36–39 of the 1993 Act on the consolidation of the 1992 and 1960 Acts.

[50] Charities Act 1993 ss 36(1), 38(1).

[51] Charities Act 1993 s 36(6) and (7).

[52] See *Bayoumi v Women's Total Abstinence Educational Union Ltd* [2003] EWCA Civ 1548, [2004] 3 All ER 110, [25], not following *Milner v Staffordshire Congregational Union (Inc)* [1956] 1 All ER 494.

[53] *Bayoumi* [2003] EWCA Civ 1548, [2004] 3 All ER 110 and see S Roberts and E Millington, 'Disposals of Land by Charities' (2006) 9(2) CL & PR 1.

[54] Charities Act 2006 s 75(1), sch 8 paras 96, 128.

[55] See the evidence of the Charity Law Association to the Joint Committee on the Draft Charities Bill, *Report of the Joint Committee on the Draft Charities Bill* vol 11 (2004) HL Paper 167-11 HC Paper 660-11, Ev 86 para 134 *et seq*.

an order from the Charity Commissioners in order to enter into the relevant mortgage.[56] The section was amended by the Charities Act 2006[57] to widen the circumstances in which an order of the court or the Commission need not be sought if statutory conditions are complied with.

The historical context of the restrictions on the disposal of charity land also includes the parallel developments in relation to the power of charity trustees to dispose of land. The attempt to deal with the uncertainty of powers by authorising the Charity Commissioners to sanction disposal has already been noted.[58] Charity trustees received statutory power to dispose of land by section 29 of the Settled Land Act 1925, although the powers were restricted and the Charity Commission still had to authorise some dispositions.[59] Land held on charitable trusts is now held on a trust of land.[60] Thus charity trustees have all the powers of an absolute owner in relation to charity land,[61] including wide powers of disposal which cannot be restricted by provisions in the trust instrument.[62]

An historical analysis of the statutory restrictions on the disposal of charity land shows a surprising lack of consistency both as to categories of land affected and the reasons for the imposition of the restrictions. This is in contrast to steadily increasing powers of sale. The present regime, whilst simpler in that it applies to all land, shows a worrying complexity in the detail of the rules; rules which have required amendment to clarify meaning, to meet the needs of charities and to reflect changing social conditions.[63]

IV. RESTRICTIONS ON SALES OF INVESTMENTS OTHER THAN LAND

There is no separate statutory regime, akin to sections 36 to 39 of the 1993 Act, covering the sale of investments other than land. Similarly, there are no statutory controls on mortgaging property other than land. Charity trustees are subject to the same controls and restrictions as any other trustees. The statutory restrictions imposed on trustees by the Trustee Act 2000 apply when trustees are investing[64] or when they are appointing agents, nominees

---

[56] *ibid*, para 142.
[57] Section 27.
[58] See the text following n 29 above.
[59] See D Dennis, 'Dispositions of Charitable Land' [2006] *Conveyancer* 219, 223.
[60] Trusts of Land and Appointment of Trustees Act 1997 ss 1(1), 2(5).
[61] *ibid*, s 6(1).
[62] *ibid*, s 8(3) and see D Dennis, 'Dispositions of Charitable Land' [2006] *Conveyancer* 219, 224–5.
[63] See amendments to Charities Act 1993 sch 5 (defining 'connected person' for the purposes of s 36(1))—Civil Partnership Act 2004 s 26(1), sch 27 para 147; Charities Act 2006 s 75(1), sch 8 paras 96, 178.
[64] Trustee Act 2000 ss 3, 4 and 5.

or custodians.[65] Thus in the case of a simple sale of an existing investment, the only restrictions are those imposed by case law.

Case law imposes on trustees a duty to obtain the best price for the particular investment.[66] They are also under the usual duty not to sell to themselves[67] or to a connected person such as a relative[68] or to a nominee.[69] The trustees' actual decision to sell must be guided by purely financial criteria and not, for example, by the effect on the work-force of a sale of a major shareholding in a company.[70] It is not unusual for charities to be set up with an initial endowment of shares in the founder's company.[71] There are also generous tax reliefs on gifts of shares to charities.[72] Accordingly, sales of investments by charities subject only to restrictions imposed by case law are not unusual.

If the sale of the investment arises out of a review of investments by the trustees, the Trustee Act 2000 requires that the review must be taken with proper advice[73] and the trustees must exercise the statutory duty of care.[74] In practice, the decision to sell and the sale are far more likely to be made by an agent to whom the investment function has been delegated. Whilst charity trustees' powers of delegation are limited, they may delegate the investment function.[75] The statutory duty of care applies to trustees when appointing and reviewing an agent.[76] The trustees are obliged to enter into an agreement with any such agent, which sets out guidance in the form of a policy statement as to how the investment function is to be carried out.[77] The policy statement must be directed to ensuring that the investment function is exercised in the best interests of the trust.[78] It is perhaps interesting to note that, prior to the passing of the Trustee Act 2000, the Charity Commissioners were prepared to grant by order, as a matter of course, power to charity trustees to delegate their investment function to investment managers, subject to constraints similar to those now found

---

[65] Trustee Act 2000 ss 11, 16 and 17.
[66] *Buttle v Saunders* [1950] 2 All ER 193 (Ch).
[67] *Tito v Waddell (No 2)* [1977] Ch 106. For details of the self-dealing rule see DJ Hayton (ed), *Underhill and Hayton Law of Trusts and Trustees*, 16th edn (London, Butterworths, 2003) 661 *et seq*; A Hudson, *Equity and Trusts*, 5th edn (London, Routledge-Cavendish, 2007) 332 *et seq*.
[68] *Coles v Trecothick* (1804) 9 Ves 234.
[69] *Silkstone & Haigh Moor Coal Co v Edey* [1900] 1 Ch 167.
[70] See *Public Trustee v Cooper* (2000) 2 WTLR 901.
[71] For an extreme example, see *Wellcome Trust Ltd v Customs and Excise Commissioners* [1996] STC 945.
[72] Taxation of Chargeable Gains Act 1992 s 257; Income Tax Act 2007 ss 431–433.
[73] Trustee Act 2000 s 5(2).
[74] Trustee Act 2000 s 1, sch 1 para 1(b).
[75] Trustee Act 2000 s 11(3)(b).
[76] Trustee Act 2000 ss 1, 11, 22, sch 1 paras 3(1)(a) and (e).
[77] Trustee Act 2000 s 15(1)(2).
[78] Trustee Act 2000 s 15(3).

in section 15 of the 2000 Act.[79] Thus, many charity trustees had a more liberal regime in relation to investment management ahead of trustees of non-charitable trusts.

V. CHANGING WIDER LEGAL, SOCIAL
AND ECONOMIC CONTEXT

Charities do not exist isolated from the rest of the legal, social and economic world. The major change in the social context for charities at the present time is their increasing involvement in the delivery of public services[80] with all the resultant pressure of tendering, employing staff and acquiring premises. Specific legal changes which potentially impact on the restrictions on the disposal of charity land are those relating to registration of title, increased requirements for reporting and transparency by charities and enhancement of trustees' powers. The legal changes need to be seen in the context of moves towards deregulation. The main economic context to be considered is the changing pattern of investment by charities.

A. Land Registration

The Land Registration Act 2002[81] increases the number of events which trigger registration, with a resultant steady increase in the amount of land the title to which is registered.[82] In particular, the appointment of a new trustee and the vesting of trust property in that trustee is now a trigger event.[83] This is the practical manifestation of the objective behind the 2002 Act that all remaining unregistered land should be phased out as quickly as possible.[84]

The register is open to public inspection and has been since 1988.[85] The public have the right to inspect and make copies of any part of any register of title.[86] This means that the purchase price of any title is in the public domain and available via the Land Registry website.[87]

---

[79] See (1994) 2 CC Decisions p 28 *et seq*. The order was made under the Charities Act 1993 s 26.

[80] See A Blackmore, *The reform of public services: the role of the voluntary sector* (2005); HM Treasury, Cabinet Office, Office of the Third Sector, *The future role of the third sector in social and economic regeneration* (2007).

[81] Land Registration Act 2002 s 4.

[82] For example in 2003 there were 18.87 million registered titles and 20.5 million in 2006: Land Registry Annual Reports 2002–03, 2005–06.

[83] Land Registration Act 2002 (Amendment) Order 2008, SI 2008/2872.

[84] Law Commission Report No 271, *Land Registration for the Twenty-First Century—A Conveyancing Revolution* (2001) para 2.9.

[85] Land Registration Act 1988.

[86] Land Registration Act 2002 s 66.

[87] www.landreg.gov.uk.

B. Reporting and Transparency

Prior to the passing of the Charities Act 1992, only about 11 per cent[88] of charities submitted their accounts to the Charity Commissioners.[89] The 1992 Act introduced not only a universal obligation to submit accounts but also requirements for those accounts to be in a specific form and to be audited or independently examined.[90] Transparency in relation to charities' property and activities was increased by a concurrent obligation to prepare and submit an annual report to the Charity Commissioners.[91] The detail required in the annual report was increased in 2005.[92] The requirements do not go so far, however, as to require sales of major assets to be set out specifically in the report.[93]

The Charity Commission has made considerable efforts to ensure that charities file both accounts and reports. In 2007, the Charity Commission held the most recent due accounts for 88 per cent of charities obliged to file accounts.[94] All filed accounts and reports are available on the Charity Commission website against each registered charity's entry.[95] Thus it is now possible for any major movement of capital in a charity with an income of more than £10,000 to be seen within 10 months of the end of its financial year.[96]

C. Trustee Autonomy

One of the objectives of the Charities Act 1992, which introduced the present restrictions on the disposal of charity land, was 'to encourage trustees to shoulder their responsibilities'.[97] The transfer of responsibility for the disposal of charity land from the Charity Commissioners to

---

[88] See National Audit Office report, *Monitoring and control of charities in England and Wales* (1999) para 19.

[89] Charities Act 1960 s 8(1) required only permanently endowed charities to submit accounts to the Charity Commissioners although the Charitable Trusts Act 1853 s 10 and the Charitable Trusts Act 1855 ss 44–45 had required all charities, unless exempt from the Acts, to submit accounts—a wider category.

[90] Charities Act 1992 ss 20–23.The relevant provisions are now in Part VI Charities Act 1993 as amended by Charities Act 2006.

[91] Charities Act 1993 s 45.

[92] Charities (Accounts and Reports) Regulations 2005, SI 2005/572 reg 11 and Statement of Recommended Practice 2005, paras 41–59.

[93] Statement of Recommended Practice 2005, paras 53 and 55 require reporting only of investment performance, policy and objectives.

[94] Charity Commission Annual Report 2007–08, p 19.

[95] The Charity Commission has a very strong policy of ensuring accounts and reports are filed on time. This includes naming defaulting charities on the website—Charity Commissioners' Annual Report 2004–05, pp 6–7.

[96] Charities Act 1993 s 45(3).

[97] *Charities: A Framework For The Future* (Cm 694, 1989) para 1.18.

charity trustees was one manifestation of that objective;[98] another was the divestment of charity property, other than land, held by the Official Custodian for Charities.[99]

After the passing of the 1992 Act, the Charity Commissioners in a number of cases exercised their powers in a way which increased the autonomy of charity trustees. The granting of power to trustees to appoint managing agents for investments has already been noted.[100] Another instance is in relation to the Charity Commissioners' power under section 26 of the Charities Act 1993 to sanction by order an action not otherwise within the power of a charity. The Charity Commissioners developed a policy of not simply granting the order requested but of also including a general power of amendment for the trustees to amend their own governing instrument in the future.[101]

The Charities Act 2006 has followed the pattern of devolving greater power to trustees. The original powers in the 1993 Act, which allowed trustees of small charities to resolve to transfer property and modify objects,[102] have been expanded both in terms of financial limits and the need for the Charity Commission to positively consent to the resolution.[103] More fundamental is the granting to trustees of unincorporated charities of a wide general power to spend the capital of an endowed fund.[104] However, this may not be as great a change as it first appears. The Charity Commissioners had for some time ceased to presume that assets were permanent endowment where the terms on which those assets were held were not clear; thus to a certain extent pre-empting the new transfer to trustees of power to spend capital.[105]

Hand in hand with this transfer of responsibilities to trustees have been concerted efforts to educate trustees as to their overall responsibilities and to provide them with sources of assistance. The Charity Commission provides a wide range of detailed guidance for trustees, which is readily available on its website.[106] The government has made available funds, in the context of capacity building of the voluntary sector,[107] which have been used to provide better sources of information on governance for charities.[108]

---

[98] See Woodfield Report, *Efficiency Report on the Supervision of Charities* (1987) 36.
[99] Charities Act 1992 s 29.
[100] See the text at n 79 above.
[101] See J Warburton (ed), *Tudor on Charities*, 9th edn (London, Thomson 2003) para 9–007.
[102] Charities Act 1993 s 74.
[103] Charities Act 2006 ss 40–42, inserting ss 74–74D in the Charities Act 1993.
[104] Charities Act 2006 s 43, inserting ss 75–75B in the Charities Act 1993.
[105] See S Robert, 'The Charity Commission's Powers and Policy on Expenditure of Permanent Endowment' (2007) 10(2) Charity Law & Practice Review 17, 20.
[106] See www.charity-commission.gov.uk/publications.
[107] See Home Office, *Change Up: Capacity Building and Infrastructure Framework for the Voluntary and Community Sector* (2004).
[108] See the Governance Hub, www.governancehub.org.uk.

D. Deregulation

There has been concern for a number of years about the level of regulation imposed on the charity sector. This concern is directed partly at complying with charity law and the requirements of the Charity Commission and partly at complying with the law and regulations which govern the particular area in which a charity works, for example, provision for children or the elderly.[109] These concerns were recognised in the Strategy Unit Report, *Private Action Public Benefit. A Review of Charities and the Wider Not-For-Profit Sector*, which stated that one of the principles which ought to underpin any reform of charity law was that regulation should be carefully targeted and proportionate to risk.[110] Reacting to the concerns of the wider voluntary and community sector, the Better Regulation Task Force undertook a review of regulation of the sector in 2005.[111] In their response to the report the Government said:[112]

> The Government has a responsibility to ensure that the legal and regulatory framework within which the third sector operates, does not stifle the sector with unnecessary or disproportionate regulation, and does not inhibit the sector's ability to benefit society.

The need to avoid burdening charities with undue regulation was recognised in the Charities Act 2006, which imposes a general duty on the Charity Commission to have regard to the principles of best regulatory practice. Those principles include that regulatory activities should be proportionate, accountable, consistent, transparent and targeted only at cases in which action is needed.[113]

E. Changing Investment Patterns

The legal regime governing the type of investment available to charitable trusts changed dramatically with the passing of the Trustee Act 2000. Trustees were given power to make any type of investment[114] and a specific power to acquire freehold and leasehold land in the United Kingdom.[115]

---

[109] See *Report of the Joint Committee on the Draft Charities Bill* vol 1, (2004) HL Paper 167-1, HC Paper 660-1 pp 36–8.

[110] Cabinet Office, Strategy Unit, *Private Action, Public Benefit. A Review of Charities and the Wider Not-For-Profit Sector* (2002) para 3.10.

[111] Better Regulation Task Force, *Better Regulation for Civil Society* (2005).

[112] Cabinet Office, Office of the Third Sector, '*Better Regulation for Civil Society*' The *Government's Response* (2006) p 2.

[113] Charities Act 2006 s 6, inserting s 1D(2)4 in the Charities Act 1993.

[114] Trustee Act 2000 s 3; compare the restricted powers under the Trustee Investment Act 1961.

[115] Trustee Act 2000 s 8.

Many charities, of course, prior to 2000 had either acquired,[116] or were set up with wider powers of investment. Those without specific wider powers of investment used Common Investment Funds[117] to gain some diversity in investments, particularly equities other than in larger United Kingdom companies.[118]

In the context of this paper, what is important is the type of investment chosen by charities and, in particular, the recent rise of property as a favoured category of investment.[119] JP Morgan Asset Management conducts an annual survey of investment by charities. The 2004 survey shows 44 per cent of charities investing in property, with that figure remaining relatively constant to 2006 at 42 per cent and then a rise to 49 per cent in 2007. The surveys also show a large number of charities increasing their holdings in property.[120] The rise in property as an important investment for charities in recent years can also be seen from the establishment of four property common investment funds since 1999 with none before that date[121] and the holding, in 2008, of the first conference specifically focusing on charities' investments in property.[122] The present market volatility has emphasised the need for charities to have diversification of investments, including holdings in property.[123]

VI. THE RULES IN A CHANGING CONTEXT

A number of different reasons were propounded over the years for the imposition of restrictions on charity trustees' powers to dispose of charity land. It has to be asked whether those restrictions are still valid today in the changing environment in which charities now operate. Even if there are still sound reasons to impose restrictions, the question remains as to whether the present regime is the correct one. Are there sufficient countervailing reasons to say that charity trustees' powers of disposition should be unfettered by a separate statutory regime?

This paper seeks to question the value and effectiveness of retaining restrictions on charity trustees' powers of disposition beyond those imposed by case law. Any consideration of the value of a separate statutory regime

---

[116] See *Trustees of the British Museum v Att-Gen* [1984] 1 WLR 1471 and J Warburton (ed), *Tudor on Charities*, 8th edn (London, Sweet & Maxwell, 1995) 248.
[117] Charities Act 1993 s 24.
[118] See Trustee Investment Act 1961 s 1, sch1.
[119] See C Mesquita, 'On the Property Ladder' [2007] *Charity Finance* (July) 30.
[120] JP Morgan Fleming Asset Management, *Charity Investment Industry Survey* (2004) p 7; JP Morgan Fleming Asset Management, *Charity Survey* (2006) p 7; JP Morgan Asset Management, *Charity Investment Industry Survey* (2007) p 8.
[121] Charity Finance, *Pooled Funds: A Guide for Charity Investors 2007*, (2007).
[122] Plaza Publishing, Charities Property Conference 2008.
[123] *Rathbones Charity Review*, Autumn 2008, p 3.

should be firmly in the context of charity trustees' overriding duty to carry out the trust according to the terms set out in the trust instrument[124] and the particular duties to obtain the best consideration on any disposal of charity land[125] and to avoid any conflict of interest[126] by not selling to a connected person.[127] These duties can be enforced by the Attorney General[128] or the Charity Commission[129] bringing an action for breach of trust. In practice, enforcement is far more likely to be by the Charity Commission using their temporary and protective powers under section 18 of the 1993 Act after carrying out a section 8 inquiry.[130]

One reason given for the imposition of restrictions on the disposal of land in the 1960 Act was that it ensured a reasonable price was obtained.[131] This was on the basis that the price of land was not publicly available and that the price of investments was as investments were quoted on the Stock Exchange. This reasoning is no longer valid. The fact that the public can inspect the Land Register[132] means that it is relatively easy to ascertain the value of any particular plot of land. The widening of powers of investment by the Trustee Act 2000[133] means that charities can legitimately hold a variety of investments which are not quoted on a recognised stock exchange. Some of these, for example, large holdings in a private company, can be difficult to value.[134] The need to check that a reasonable price has been obtained no longer provides a reason to differentiate between disposals of land and other investments.

Another reason given for the provisions in 1960 Act was that the sale of land was an indication of change in a charity and the possible need for a cy-pres scheme.[135] Charities are now required to submit annually a report and accounts to the Charity Commission.[136] The accounts will show any large receipt of capital during the last financial year and the report must set out the main activities of the charity.[137] This increased transparency in

---

[124] G Duke, *The Law of Charitable Uses* (1676) 116.

[125] *Buttle v Saunders* [1950] 2 All ER 193 (Ch).

[126] *Bray v Ford* [1896] AC 44 (HL) 51; *Boardman v Phipps* [1967] 2 AC 46 (HL).

[127] *Tito v Waddell (No 2)* [1977] Ch 106; for details of the self-dealing rule see DJ Hayton (ed), *Underhill and Hayton Law of Trusts and Trustees*, 16th edn (London, Butterworths, 2003) 661 *et seq* and A Hudson, *Equity and Trusts*, 5th edn (London, Routledge-Cavendish, 2007) 332 *et seq*.

[128] See *Att-Gen v Wright* [1988] 1 WLR 164 (injunction to restrain the disposition of charity property in breach of trust).

[129] Charities Act 1993 s 32(1)(a).

[130] For details of the Charity Commission's enforcement powers see J Warburton (ed), *Tudor on Charities*, 9th edn (London, Thomson, 2003) paras 9-043–9-045.

[131] See the text at n 42 above.

[132] See the text at n 85 above.

[133] See the text at n 114 above.

[134] See *Public Trustee v Cooper* (2000) 2 WTLR 901.

[135] See the text at n 42 above.

[136] See the text at n 91 above.

[137] Charities (Accounts and Reports) Regulations 2005, SI 2005/572 reg 11.

relation to charities means that the potential need for a cy-pres scheme no longer provides a reason for imposing a separate statutory regime on the disposal of charity land.

The importance of maintaining the capital value of permanent endowment was a further reason put forward for the imposition of restrictions in the 1960 Act.[138] This argument reflected the model of charities funded from the income of endowed funds and the importance attached to the retention of permanent endowment.[139] What has changed since 1960 is the attitude taken to permanent endowment by both Parliament and the Charity Commission. The Charity Commission has for some time ceased to regard permanent endowment as sacred. In 2001, the Commissioners began to authorise charity trustees, by order under section 26 of the 1993 Act, to adopt a total return investment policy with the inevitable consequence of some expenditure of capital.[140] The Commission has also taken a more liberal approach to requiring replacement of permanent endowment out of income where there has been capital expenditure.[141] The greatest change has been brought about by the Charities Act 2006, which now empowers charity trustees to spend the capital of a permanently endowed fund if that is a more effective way of carrying out the purposes of the charity.[142] In the light of this change to regarding permanent endowment as something to be used, rather than preserved, it is considered that there is no longer a valid reason for imposing a separate regime restricting the disposal of land forming part of the permanent endowment of a charity.

The rationale behind the imposition of restrictions on the disposal of charity land in 1855 was the prevention of abuse.[143] The validity of that reason was recognised in the 1980s with the addition of the avoidance of exploitation by purchasers, local authorities and developers.[144] The temptation for trustees to make a personal profit from the sale of charity land has not gone, nor has the temptation for a developer to make an apparently generous offer for overgrown allotments owned by a charity, secure in the knowledge that the land is a prime site for a supermarket.[145]

---

[138] See the text at n 42 above.

[139] See *Re Faraker* [1912] 2 Ch 488 and the Charities Act 1960 s 23(4) (now the Charities Act 1993 s 26(4)), power for the Charity Commissioners to required expenditure charged to capital to be recouped out of income.

[140] See Warburton (ed), *Tudor on Charities*, 9th edn, para 6-027.

[141] See S Roberts, 'The Charity Commission's Power and Policy on Expenditure of Permanent Endowment' (2007) 10(2) Charity Law & Practice Review 17, 23.

[142] Charities Act 1993 s 75, inserted by the Charities Act 2006 s 43. There are limitations if the fund was given by a particular individual or institution and the fund exceeds £10,000: s 75A.

[143] See the text at n 35 above.

[144] See the text at n 43 above.

[145] See *Richmond upon Thames LBC v Rogers* [1989] Ch 484 (*Hampton Fuel Allotment Society*).

The question is whether, in the circumstances in which charities now operate, the prevention of abuse remains a sufficient reason to impose a separate statutory regime of restrictions on the disposal of charity land.

In considering that question, relevant factors are: the greater autonomy and knowledge of trustees;[146] the increasing use of land as part of a spread of investments;[147] easier public access to land values;[148] greater transparency and reporting of the activities of charities;[149] and the recent moves to reduce the burden of regulation on charities.[150] Two additional factors need to be considered. First, charities now have much better access to both general advice provided by the regulator[151] and sector umbrella bodies,[152] and professional advice for specific cases.[153] Secondly, charities vary enormously in size and type of activity and a detailed statutory set of requirements fails to recognise this diversity.[154]

The form of the present statutory regime also needs to be considered. The provisions set out a list of conditions to be complied with, which are focused on the terms on which the disposition is to be made. It can be argued that this distracts trustees from the importance of the decision as to whether the transaction should be entered into in the first place. In the one instance where focus is placed on the transaction itself—a sale of designated or specie land[155]—the statutory regime removes any requirement for public notice where replacement land is being bought even though the sale of any such land has implications well beyond the terms on which it is sold.[156] The regime also underplays the importance of the decision as to the specific form of the disposal. It may, for example, be better for trustees to raise funds by means of leasing rather than a sale or entering into a mortgage. The setting of a list of conditions to be complied with can also be said to engender a 'tick box' approach which discourages trustees from considering further or wider issues such as the environmental implications of a particular disposal.[157]

---

[146] See the text at nn 97–108 above.

[147] See the text at nn 119–123 above.

[148] See the text at nn 85–87 above.

[149] See the text at nn 90–96 above.

[150] See the text at nn 109–113 above.

[151] See the text at n 106 above.

[152] See, eg, www.ncvo-vol.org.uk (National Council of Voluntary Organisations); www.navca.org.uk (National Association for Voluntary and Community Action); www.trusteenet.org.uk (Charity Trustee Network).

[153] The Charity Law Association was founded in 1992 and now has over 850 members who advice on charity law.

[154] See O Reichardt, D Kane, B Pratten and K Wilding, *The UK Civil Society Almanac 2008*.

[155] See the text at nn 12–13 above.

[156] See *Oldham Metropolitan BC v Att-Gen* [1993] Ch 210.

[157] See Charity Commission, *Environmental responsibility: what role should charities play?* (2007); S Leather, 'Waking up to warming' [2007] *Charity Finance* (October) 37.

It could be argued that all these factors point towards the retention of a separate statutory regime for disposals of permanent endowment and specie or designated land, but the removal of the regime from disposals of investment land. Such an approach recognises changing investment patterns.[158] It also recognises that abuse, in the form of sales at an undervalue, and strong views about the retention of land regarded as important in the locality are more likely to occur where land has been held by a charity for a long time. The problem with this approach is the need for the categorisation of land holdings which can be difficult in itself[159] and can change over time.[160] For those reasons, limited retention of the statutory regime is not advocated.

It is submitted that the better view, after consideration of all the factors, is that there is no longer sufficient justification for the imposition of additional statutory restrictions on the disposal of any charity land. Abolition of the statutory regime does not mean that there would be no controls on the disposal of land. The obligations imposed by case law would still apply.[161] The question is how and to what extent those obligations should be enforced.

VII. A NEW REGIME?

The regime imposed by sections 36 to 39 of the 1993 Act can be seen as merely one, somewhat mechanistic, method of ensuring charity trustees carry out some of the obligations imposed on them by case law. What is important is that charity trustees consider carefully whether a particular disposal is in the interest of their charity, that the consideration is the best that can be obtained and that the disposal is not to a connected person.[162]

The deregulatory approach would be to leave the obligations in relation to the disposal of land to be enforced in the same way as those in relation to investments, ie by the Attorney General or the Charity Commission.[163] An examination of the various rationales for the imposition of a separate statutory regime has shown,[164] however, that the prevention of abuse, whether by trustees or prospective purchasers, is still regarded as a real concern. Bearing in mind that charitable trusts are public and not private trusts,[165] it is considered, therefore, that some steps should be taken to ensure compliance by charity trustees with their obligations in relation to land.

---

[158] See the text at nn 119–123 above.
[159] See the text at n 41 above.
[160] See the text at n 105 above.
[161] See the text at nn 124–127 above.
[162] See Charity Commission, 28 *Disposals of Charity Land* para 11 *et seq.*
[163] See the text at nn 128–30 above.
[164] See the text at n 143 *et seq* above.
[165] *Gaudiya v Brahmachary* [1997] 4 All ER 957, 963.

There is clearly a danger that, in the absence of a detailed statutory regime, some trustees will be confused as to what is necessary in order to comply with the general obligations and do either too little or too much; the latter resulting in unnecessary expenditure of charitable funds. It is proposed, therefore, that the obligations should be supplemented by guidance from the Charity Commission, setting out the general principles and providing examples of steps to be taken in common situations. This allows for far more flexibility than the present two sets of requirements on a disposal: one for sales and leases for terms of more than seven years and one for leases of seven years or less.[166] It also allows for as much emphasis to be placed on the decision to dispose of land as on the terms on which the disposal takes place. Another advantage of using Charity Commission guidance, rather than a statutory regime, is that guidance, unlike statute, can be altered easily as new situations arise. As charities move to mixed funding regimes and seek to use their property more actively to support income generation in different ways,[167] flexibility becomes more important.

The proposed method for ensuring compliance with the obligations is based on the retention of the requirement in section 37(1) of the 1993 Act for both a contract for, and a document effecting, the disposal of land to state that the land is held by a charity. It is also assumed that all land which has been registered in the names of charity trustees is the subject of a restriction in the register.[168] To ensure that charity trustees direct their minds to the relevant matters, it is proposed that the restriction should be in the form that no disposition be registered unless the charity trustees[169] certify that they have had regard to the guidance of the Charity Commission.[170] Any purchaser is protected under the usual land registration principles that a registered proprietor is deemed to have unfettered powers unless there is a limitation on the register.[171] The charity is protected by the entry of the restriction preventing disposal until the conditions set out in the restriction are complied with.[172] It is clearly less easy to ensure compliance with the obligations in the case of unregistered land. Whilst a requirement of a certificate of compliance in the conveyance, lease or mortgage can be retained,[173] there is no automatic bar on completion as in the case of

---

[166] See the text at nn 6–11 above.

[167] See, eg, G Collins and C Glossop, *An introduction to sustainable funding – understanding your options* (NCVO, 2006).

[168] For the obligation to impose a restriction see Charities Act 1993 s 37(8).

[169] To be specified as the trustees of the charity and not the holding trustees, if any—see the text at n 55 above.

[170] For a precedent for requiring charity trustees to have regard to Charity Commission guidance when exercising their powers, see Charities Act 2006 s 4(6) (Guidance on the public benefit requirement).

[171] Land Registration Act 2002 s 26(1).

[172] Land Registration Act 2002 s 40.

[173] Charities Act 1993 ss 37(2), 39(2).

registered land but rather a transaction which is open to challenge on the grounds of validity.

This proposal keeps the existing regime to the extent that a disposal in breach of the obligations, for example to a connected person or for less than full consideration, would still require the consent of the Charity Commission. If the statutory regime in sections 36 to 39 were repealed, consent would have to be given, as for any other potentially unauthorised action, under section 26 of the 1993 Act.

As an additional safeguard against abuse, it is proposed that charity trustees should be required to set out in their annual report if they have sold land in the preceding financial year. To ensure proportionate regulation, this could be limited to disposals of land above a certain value.

VIII. CONCLUSION

The statutory controls on the disposal of charity land are unduly complex and rigid. The changed legal, economic and social environment in which charities now operate calls for a much lighter regulatory regime which takes a more proportionate response to the risk of abuse in relation to charity property.

6

'You Just Gotta Keep the Customer Satisfied': Where Stands the Beneficiary's Right to Information?

GERWYN LL H GRIFFITHS[*]

I. INTRODUCTION: BALANCING FIDUCIARY OBLIGATIONS WITH A PRODUCT-ORIENTATED EXPECTATION

A T FIRST SIGHT, the words of the American singer/songwriter Paul Simon would appear to have little or no relevance to the position of a trustee towards the beneficiaries of the trust and the rights and obligations arising from that relationship. In classical terms, the trust is essentially an obligation based upon a fiduciary duty; an obligation to act properly and impartially, regulated by a very clear set of duties and obligations on either side.[1] Moreover, although the settler may seek to exert influence and make his views known indirectly by devices such as letters or memoranda of wishes[2] or the appointment of a protector,[3] the independence of the trustee is paramount—indeed, this parting with ownership and control is the 'price' that the settlor pays in order that the funds, assets or property transferred to the trustee have the 'ring fencing' which make the trust so attractive.

In reality—and certainly in the field of the international or offshore trust—the picture may sometimes be markedly different. The flexibility of the trust is a major part of its attraction and a reason for its growth. Yet that very flexibility means that in many cases settlors (and to a lesser extent beneficiaries), having as their principle concern the preservation of family wealth and paying considerable fees to professional trustee

---

[*] Professor of Equity and The Law of Property, University of Glamorgan; Visiting Senior Fellow University of Cambridge; Consultant, Butterfield Trust (Malta).

[1] *Armitage v Nourse* [1998] Ch 241 (CA) 253 (Millett LJ).

[2] See generally P Matthews, 'Letters of Wishes' (1995) 5 *Offshore Tax Planning Review* 181.

[3] DWM Waters, 'The Protector: New Wine in Old Bottles' in AJ Oakley (ed), *Trends in Contemporary Trust Law* (Oxford, Clarendon Press, 1996).

companies to achieve this, will inevitably view the trust in terms of a 'product' and themselves as 'customers' or 'clients'. Thus, a cursory glance at recent issues of professional journals such as *The Society of Trust and Estate Practitioners' Journal* and *Trusts and Trustees* reveals a total of no less than 67 firms advertising a range of trustee and trustee-related services.[4] Indeed, many trust jurisdictions regard such services as a valuable and entirely legitimate component of a successful and vibrant financial services industry. It is not surprising, therefore, that the Government regulator of one of the most recent jurisdictions to embrace the concept of the trust could observe; 'Creating a new legal platform for trusts is perhaps the final piece in the jigsaw of the rapid development of an international industry'.[5]

In general terms, as long as a trust is being properly administered and is continuing a beneficiary has no right to interfere in its administration but has to wait passively to receive the benefits to which he is entitled under the trust. If, however, it is not being properly administered he will want to take steps to compel its proper administration and to preserve his position. Even more so, he will not be able to do anything unless he knows he is a beneficiary in the first place. Against this background, the trustee's duty to account and provide information and the beneficiary's ability to demand it become of extreme importance, but, on occasion, the two competing philosophies above may mean that the trustee can be faced with a delicate balancing act as to how far and in what way he may carry out his office.

II. THREE CENTRAL QUESTIONS

The obligation to provide financial accounts is, of course, central to the relationship of trustee and beneficiary. Whether the beneficiary's interest is fixed, or discretionary, in possession or not, the trustee must, as Plumer MR observed in *Pearse v Green*, 'be constantly ready with his accounts'.[6] Indeed, the opportunity for such an inspection will often be the beneficiary's first warning of some irregularity or breach. Beyond this, however, there will be situations where other types and categories of information are required.

---

[4] A very good discussion of the practical marketing strategies involved can be found in Larder, 'Marketing Trust Services: A Hard Sell', a paper presented to the Caribbean STEP Conference, 19–20 April 1999.

[5] Joe Bannister, Chairman, Malta Financial Services Authority (2005) 11(6) *Trusts and Trustees* 12.

[6] (1819) 1 Jac & W 135, 140. For a detailed discussion, see A Hudson, *Equity and Trusts*, 5th edn (London, Routledge Cavendish, 2007) ch 18.

Essentially, legal debate and practice in this wider area can be summarised in the following, often overlapping, questions.[7] Is the right or obligation essentially proactive, requiring trustees actually to seek out those entitled and volunteer information, or reactive in that trustees only have to respond to requests for information received? What information is covered by the right? To whom does this right of information extend?

Each of these questions now falls for consideration.

III. PROACTIVE OR REACTIVE?

The obligation upon the trustees is, essentially reactive; an obligation to respond to requests. Any requirement to be proactive in the sense of initiating the process of information-giving is limited to a duty to give general information as to the existence of the trust, the identity of the trustees and the overall nature of the trust. Unlike the situation in a will, where until the will is probated, the executors are under no duty to inform the beneficiaries under the will of their rights, trustees of a fixed trust, whether it is inter-vivos or testamentary, are under a duty to inform the beneficiaries of both the existence of the trust and the nature of the beneficiaries' entitlement under it.[8] The courts—perhaps motivated by concerns not only that to do so would be to give advantage to one beneficiary over others and recognising the potentially fraught relationship in the event of some breaches of trust such as occur in pension fund trusts[9]—do not require them to go further and explain the meaning of those interests. It is reasonable to assume that the same approach applies in the case of a discretionary trust if it is one with a relatively small group or class of beneficiaries, such as 'all my family and dependants'.

If, however, as may well be the situation in many modern discretionary trusts, there is a very large class of potential beneficiaries, then it will clearly be impracticable to notify every single member of his potential right under it. The most that trustees could conceivably be expected to do would be to advertise for potential beneficiaries to present themselves.[10]

---

[7] For a similar approach, see DA Steele, 'The Beneficiary's Right to Know', A paper presented to the Law Society of Upper Canada Fourth Annual Estates and Trusts Forum (November 2001).

[8] *Hawkesley v May* [1956] 1 QB 304. For other, earlier, English authorities to the same effect, see *Brittlebank v Goodwin* (1868) LR 5 Eq 545, 550 (Sir GM Giffard VC)—loan by trustees on insufficient security; *Burrows v Walls* (1855) 5 De GM & G 231, 253 (Lord Cranworth LC)—improper delegation of investment funds among co-trustees.

[9] *Hamar v Pensions Ombudsman* [1996] PLR 1; *NHS Pensions v Beechinor* [1997] OPLR 99. For a discussion of the pensions trust as *sui generis*, see DJ Hayton, 'Pension Trusts and Traditional Trusts: Drastically Different Species of Trusts' [2005] 69 *Conveyancer* 229.

[10] *Re Hay's Settlement Trusts* [1982] 1 WLR 202 (Ch D).

What if the trustee (or indeed the settlor) is presented with the slightly different situation of a potential beneficiary who actually makes an enquiry to him? There can be no real doubt that the trustee or settlor is obliged to give a truthful answer to any such person. Similarly, where a person knows that he is a beneficiary or a potential beneficiary of a discretionary trust but does not know the identity of the current trustees he is able to oblige the settlor to disclose this information to him.

So much is clear from the case of *Murphy v Murphy*,[11] which concerned a family trust dispute. The trust was a discretionary trust and one of the beneficiaries wanted information as to the nature and value of the trust property, the income earned, its distribution and the investment of the trust fund. The beneficiary did not know the identity of the trustees. The court confirmed that the beneficiary was entitled to the information requested and ordered the settlor to disclose the identity of the trustee to enable the beneficiary to contact the trustee for information.

IV. WHAT INFORMATION IS COVERED?

A number of jurisdictions have enacted specific statutory provisions dealing with this issue and seeking to define its scope,[12] but it is equally clear that in some of these same jurisdictions these statutory enactments do not replace or oust what might be termed the beneficiary's 'underlying' or 'common law' rights to information.[13] It is these principles which must, therefore, be the focus of our investigation.

A. Defining 'Trust Documents'

At first glance, an answer to this question is to be found in the words of Lord Wrenbury in *O'Rourke v Darbishire*.[14] He observed that '[a beneficiary] is entitled to see all the trust documents because they are trust documents and because he is a beneficiary'. This is, however, more apparent than real because, while stressing that generally beneficiaries have a right to view documentation dealing with the management and administration of the trust, the cases provide no single, definitive list of 'trust documents'

---

[11] *Murphy v Murphy* [1999] 1 WLR 282 (Court).
[12] For example, Art 29 of the Trusts (Jersey) Law 1984, as amended and s 22 of the Trusts (Guernsey) Law 1989, as amended. For a comprehensive list, see E Campbell and J Hilliard, 'Disclosure of Information by Trustees' in J Glasson and G Thomas (eds), *The International Trust*, 2nd edn (Place, Jordans, 2006).
[13] *Stuart-Hutcheson v Spread Trustee Co Ltd* (2002) 5 ITELR 140 (Guernsey Court of Appeal).
[14] *O'Rourke v Darbishire* [1920] AC 581 (HL) 626.

which must be disclosed, and it is respectfully suggested that Salmon LJ's categorisation of them in *Re Londonderry's Settlement*,[15] as documents in possession of the trustees containing information about the trust which the beneficiaries are entitled to know, adds little in the search for clarity.

Because of this difficulty, the illustrations given cannot be a comprehensive, definitive list but it is nevertheless established that trustees will be obliged to provide the following information: the trust deed, deeds of appointment, retirement and removal together with deeds exercising their dispositive powers of appointment and any related application of trust capital. In terms of any trust investments, they must provide details such as who is in occupation of trust property[16] and any mortgage deeds or other formal documentation[17] and, a little more generally, any changes to such investments. In *Re Londonderry's Settlement*[18] it was also made clear that legal opinions and instructions to solicitors and counsel concerning the terms of the trust and the duties of the trustees should be similarly disclosed but, as Salmon LJ averred in the same case, this is not an obligation which extends to all legal advice provided and so, arguably, would not extend to opinions provided in connection with hostile litigation between those same trustees and beneficiaries.[19]

In contrast, no such obligation to disclose exists in respect of the agenda and minutes of trustee meetings nor, in the absence any specific statutory requirement (such as may sometimes be found in pension trusts[20]) can the trustees be compelled to give reasons for dispositive and administrative decisions they may make. Similarly, correspondence, be it between the trustees or donees of a power or between either of these parties and the beneficiaries, will not be within the meaning of trust documents.

B. 'Defences' and Overriding Considerations

In the case of certain kinds or items of information there will be circumstances when, even if by virtue of their classification there is an initial presumption of disclosure, certain 'defences'[21] will be available which will prevent it.

---

[15] *Re Londonderry's Settlement* [1965] Ch 918 (CA) 938.
[16] *Chaine Nicholson v Bank of Ireland* [1976] IR 393.
[17] *Re Tillott* [1892] 1 Ch 86.
[18] *Re Londonderry's Settlement* [1965] Ch 918.
[19] *ibid*.
[20] Eg The UK's Pensions Act 1995 requires trustees of an occupational pension scheme to provide a statement of investment principles. See *Wilson v Law Debenture Trust Corporation* [1995] 2 All ER 337.
[21] This characterisation is utilised by Campbell and Hilliard, above n 12.

(i) The Sanctity of 'Reasoning'

The first of these limitations is well established, since it has been clear as early as the decision in *Re Beloved Wilkes' Charity*[22] in 1851 that, unless it is in the course of civil proceedings founded upon an allegation of exercising their discretion in an improper manner,[23] a trustee is not required to disclose his or her reasons for exercising a discretionary power.

Perhaps the classic exposition of this limitation is illustrated by the Court of Appeal decision in *Re Londonderry's Settlement*.[24] Here, the trustees had determined that it would not be in the interests of family harmony to disclose documents which included minutes and agendas of trust meetings and correspondence between the trustees and their agents. Reversing Plowman J in the Chancery Division and in a judgment which arguably can really only be understood in policy terms,[25] all three judges of the appellate court refused the beneficiary access to documentation that would show why the trustees chose to distribute the fund in the way that they did. In the view of the Court, the trustees of a discretionary family settlement such as the one before them could not effectively discharge their sensitive role if, 'at any moment there is likely to be an investigation for the purpose of seeing whether they have exercised their discretion in the best possible manner'.[26] That the courts have continued to show a higher regard for this principle than any requirement of disclosure can be seen very clearly from the judgment of Rattee J in *Wilson v Law Debenture Trust Corporation*,[27] where he felt compelled to give effect to settled principles of trust law and so would not order the trustees of a pension scheme to disclose their reasons for exercising their discretion.

(ii) Confidentiality, Exclusion and Commercial Sensitivity

What is the status or efficacy of a clause inserted by the settler into his settlement which requires the trustees to treat certain documents as confidential or indeed which seeks to remove the information rights of the beneficiaries completely? The balance of opinion is that, in such a case, the court would recognise and give effect to the clause but only within certain limits.[28] Thus, in *Tierney v King*[29] the Supreme Court of Queensland was prepared

---

[22] *Re Beloved Wilkes' Charity* (1851) 3 Mac & G 440 (Ch D).

[23] *Talbot v Marshfield* (1865) 2 Dr & Sm 549.

[24] *Re Londonderry's Settlement* [1965] Ch 918 (CA).

[25] My conclusion stems from the problems their Lordships had in shedding any meaningful light on what actually constituted a 'trust document' and even more so in explaining how a document which had been generated in the administration of the trust could not be so classified!

[26] *Re Londonderry's Settlement* [1965] Ch 918 (CA) 935.

[27] *Wilson v Law Debenture Trust Corporation* [1995] 2 All ER 337 (Ch).

[28] *Bathurst v Kleinwort Benson (Channel Islands) Trustees Ltd*, 4 August 2004, Unreported (Royal Court of Guernsey).

[29] *Tierney v King* [1893] 2 Qd R 580.

to recognise and give weight to a clause which instructed the trustees of an occupational pension trust to 'observe strict secrecy with regard to the affairs, accounts and transactions' of the scheme and, in an admittedly analogous case, the Privy Council has accepted the validity of a clause in a will which sought to remove the trustees' obligations in respect of a specified piece of property for a limited and fixed time.

On the other hand, a clause which seeks to restrict per se the court's right to make appropriate orders for disclosure must be void because to hold otherwise is nothing short of an attempt to oust the jurisdiction of the court to oversee the trust and a contravention of the beneficiary principle.[30]

In addition to documents which are expressly or indeed impliedly confidential, the trustee will be able to refuse to disclose any documents or information which relates to a corporation or other business owned or controlled by the trust if the information at issue is commercially sensitive or the effect of disclosure would be to disrupt the carrying on of its business. To do otherwise, as Romer LJ made clear in *Butt v Kelson*,[31] '[m]ight be very prejudicial to the company and the interests of ... [the other] beneficiaries who might not wish [the requesting beneficiary] to have access to the documents'.

(iii) A Particular Issue: Letters of Wishes

Although not beloved of all trust lawyers,[32] letters (or memoranda) of wishes are a common feature in the trust world. As their name suggests these are documents which exist outside the formal trust documents and, although they set out the wishes of the settlor, they are not generally binding on the trustees[33] and the trustees are free to follow, be guided by or indeed completely ignore them. The question for present purposes is, do letters of wishes have to be disclosed? There is established law, emanating from the decision of the New South Wales Court of Appeal in *Hartigan Nominees Pty Ltd v Rydge*[34] that they do not. *Hartigan* involved a letter of wishes in a discretionary family trust, the letter having been prepared by Sir Norman Rydge, the instigator of the trust. The trustees of the family trust had refused to permit the plaintiff beneficiary to inspect the letter of wishes, which apparently disclosed Sir Norman's preferences regarding

---

[30] *Jones et al v Shipping Federation of British Columbia et al* (1963) 37 DLR (2d) 373 (British Columbia Supreme Court).

[31] *Butt v Kelson* [1952] Ch 197, 205. Later considered and approved by the Cayman Islands Grand Court in *In The Matter of the Ojjeh Trust* (1992–93) CILR 348.

[32] See J Wadham, *Willoughby's Misplaced Trust*, 2nd edn (Saffron Walden, Gostick Hall, 2002) 41.

[33] For a detailed examination of the concepts of 'legally binding', 'legally significant' and 'morally binding', see Hayton, Matthews and Mitchell (eds), *Underhill and Hayton Law of Trusts and Trustees*, 17th edn (London, Butterworth LexisNexis, 2007) 835–40.

[34] *Hartigan Nominees Pty Ltd v Rydge* (1992) NSWLR 405 (NSWCA).

discretionary distributions from the trust. On appeal, the majority of a three-judge panel[35] held that the trustees were not obliged to disclose the letter of wishes. Very recently, this same approach—that letters of wishes should not, subject only to the court's discretion, be disclosable—was taken by Briggs J in *Breakspear v Acland*.[36]

Such a conclusion is logical when using 'trust document' as a measure but nevertheless, there is significant support for the contrary or perhaps modified, principle that while there is a strong presumption that such letters should not be disclosed it may be ordered in circumstances where there are clear and valid grounds to do so. This has certainly been the prevailing view, with both the Royal Courts of Jersey and Guernsey having held that there can be disclosure where there are strong reasons for so doing,[37] and such an argument seems even stronger when viewed in the light of the current basis for disclosure, which is considered later in this paper.[38] Accordingly, it is suggested that trustees cannot assume they will never be ordered to disclose a letter of wishes.

V. TO WHOM DOES THE DUTY EXTEND?

A. The Traditional 'Proprietary' Approach

As with our second question, in traditional terms at least, a starting point for our final enquiry is provided by Lord Wrenbury's judgment in *O' Rourke v Darbishire*.[39] As will be recalled, he framed eligibility in terms of who was a beneficiary. Thus, emphasis was placed on the status of the claimant. The rationale underlying this was essentially proprietary in nature. As Lord Wrenbury himself said: '[t]hey are in a sense his own. Action or no action he is entitled to see them. The proprietary right is a right to access documents which are your own'.[40] It is the view of the author of this paper (and indeed many others) that, while it might have been appropriate in the case itself—because the beneficiary in question would have been entitled to the entire trust fund—predicating the right to disclosure on this basis was and is flawed. For example, if, as may often be the case, the trust contains different classes of beneficiaries, entitled to different parts of the trust fund, then those beneficiaries may only have 'ownership' of the documents

---

[35] Sheller and Mahoney JJ A with Kirby P dissenting.

[36] *Breakspear v Acland* [2008] EWHC 220; [2008] All ER 260. Considered below.

[37] *Re Rabaiotti 1989 Settlement* [2000] 2 ITELR 763; *Bathurst v Kleinwort Benson (Channel Islands) Trustees Ltd*, above n 28 (Disclosure was limited only to claimant's lawyer).

[38] See also, Lightman J, 'The Trustees' Duty to Provide Information to Beneficiaries' *The Withers Lecture 2003*.

[39] *O' Rourke v Darbishire* [1920] AC 581.

[40] *ibid*, 626–7.

relevant to that part. To put it into context, although he might have need of information regarding the trustees' dealings with income in order to assess whether they were properly managing the trust, the capital beneficiary should, logically, only be entitled to information regarding the capital of the fund.

Moreover, what was also certainly the case was that while beneficiaries under fixed trusts and probably small-scale family discretionary trusts[41] could seek disclosure, objects of discretionary powers of appointment could not.

B. A New Basis: The Court's Inherent Jurisdiction to Supervise

As the foregoing account has shown, the proprietary analogy attracted great (and, it is submitted, justifiable) criticism. The Southern hemisphere courts in particular have always adopted a robustly sceptical approach to it[42] and this is echoed by commentators such as Ford and Lee, who comment: '[T]he beneficiaries' rights to inspect trust documents are founded not upon any equitable proprietary interest in relation to a particular trust document, but upon the trustee's duty to keep the beneficiary informed'.[43] Among the most telling of arguments was that of David Hayton, who advocated an approach which effectively shifted emphasis from the status of the beneficiary seeking disclosure to the role of the court in carrying out its supervisory function. Only in this way could the beneficiaries' right to enforce the trust—'irreducible core content of trusteeship'[44]—be adequately safeguarded. In 2003, seven years after Professor (as then was) Hayton's argument was aired, the Judicial Committee of the Privy Council, in *Schmidt v Rosewood Trust Ltd*[45] rejected the proprietary argument and established what must now be the current rationale for disclosure.

The case, which has been described as a tale 'of oil-rich Russians able and willing to give orders when it suited them concerning many millions they had safely tucked away in a respectable part of the world',[46] has been the subject of extensive commentary but, for present purposes the facts may be stated as follows. Two discretionary trusts ('Angora' and 'Everest') had been set up in the Isle of Man. The effective objects of these were

---

[41] *Re Londonderry's Settlement* [1965] Ch 918.

[42] *Inter alia, Spellson v George* (1992) 26 NSWLR 666.

[43] *Principles of the Law of Trusts*, 3rd edn (Sydney, The Law Book Company, 1995).

[44] See Oakley (ed), *Trends in Contemporary Trust Law* (Oxford, Clarendon Press, 1996) 46–62.

[45] *Schmidt v Rosewood Trust Ltd* [2003] 2 AC 709 (PC) (Nicholls, Hope, Hutton, Hobhouse and Walker LJJ). The case concerned an appeal from the Staff of Government Division in the Isle of Man.

[46] JD Davies, 'Integrity of Trusteeship' (2004) 120 *Law Quarterly Review* 1.

Russian businessmen associated with Lukoil, one of the largest privatised oil companies in Russia. One of them, Vitali Schmidt, was also protector of the first trust. They and the Royal National Lifeboat Institution were beneficiaries of both trusts and under each trust the trustees had a power to accumulate income and an overriding power of appointment in favour of the beneficiaries, which was exercisable with the written consent of the protector. In the Angora trust, there was a provision for each beneficiary's portion of the trust fund to be held on his death for the persons notified by him to the trustees and in default for his closest relatives. The Everest trust, on the other hand, contained a power to add beneficiaries and a discretionary trust of income in favour of the beneficiaries in default of accumulation or appointment.

The appellant, Vadim Schmidt, was the son of the now-deceased Vitali. He sought to obtain trust accounts and other information from the trustees of two settlements[47] and made this claim for disclosure in two capacities: personally and as administrator of his father's estate. It was argued that since the appellant had no proprietary interest in the trust property, he was not entitled to any disclosure of information. So far as the proprietary issue was concerned, the Judicial Committee reached the same conclusion. As administrator, Vadim's status was simply that of representing a person who had benefited from the exercise of a power during his lifetime, while in his personal capacity, he had no actual interest of any kind in the trusts. Yet this was not fatal to his claim because, in their Lordships' view, such a proprietary right was neither necessary nor sufficient. The court was clear: it would act wherever it felt that, on the facts, intervention was needed and for this purpose, a beneficiary under a discretionary trust and a person entitled to benefit under a power were in the same position.

C. *Rosewood Trust*: An Assessment

There can be little doubt that the approach in *Rosewood* now provides the juridical basis upon which disclosure or otherwise will be ordered. Of even more importance, it is suggested, is how this will operate in practice. Thus, questions such as the binding nature or other wise of the decision, its interpretation and how far, if at all, it will provide different results from the test which preceded it must be considered.

It is, of course, a decision of the Judicial Committee of the Privy Council and so not strictly binding but it is clear that this does not prevent it being adopted as the relevant paradigm. Evidence for this exists both at general

---

[47] The Judicial Committee's task was not made easier by the muddled drafting in these settlements.

and specific levels. As a general principle, one can point to the judgment of Lawrence Collins J in *Daraydan Holdings Ltd v Solland International Ltd*,[48] holding that the High Court and the Court of Appeal can follow Privy Council decisions even though they depart from previous Court of Appeal decisions.

More specifically, a number of later decisions confirm its applicability. The first of these is the decision of the New Zealand High Court in *Foreman v Kingstone and Cave* which, coming as it did so soon after *Schmidt v Rosewood Trust*,[49] provides a particularly valuable illustration. Bill Foreman, a successful businessman, married three times and had children of each marriage. Over time, three family trusts were established: by Bill himself in 1959, by his second wife in 1986 and by Bill and his third wife in 1999. The majority of the trust assets derived from the value of shares in a company, Trigon Ltd, which Bill developed and subsequently sold. The discretionary beneficiaries included children of each marriage. The four from the first union became increasingly concerned about a number of aspects of the trust administration, including the validity of distributions made to Bill himself, the winding up of the 1986 trust and a resettlement carried out in respect of the 1959 trust.

In order to allay their worries, they requested from the trustees some 13 categories of documentation and information including financial statements, investment details and details relating to the trustees themselves. While, as they made clear, they accepted that there would be particular circumstances where disclosure might be refused or limited, they argued that when, as here, the beneficiaries had a significant interest certain documents should always be made available by the trustees because to allow otherwise was completely contrary to the irreducible core[50] of obligations owed by those same trustees.

The trustees, however, while they were happy to provide copies of the trust deeds, refused to furnish any other information, essentially basing their refusal on twin arguments that to do so in a personal family trust could lead only to conflict and disharmony and that in any event such disclosure was only being sought here in order to find a basis upon which to challenge the exercise of their (the trustees') discretions.

These latter arguments found little support from the New Zealand High Court, which concluded that a right to information had been established, and ordered that all financial statements relating to the trust, including matters such as details of distributions (of both capital and income, on

---

[48] *Daraydan Holdings Ltd v Solland International Ltd* [2004] EWHC 622.
[49] *Foreman v Kingstone and Cave* [2005] WTLR 823; [2004] 1 NZLR 841; see also, *Crowe v Stevedoring Employees Retirement Fund Pty Ltd* [2003] PLR 343 (Supreme Court of Victoria).
[50] See above n 1.

winding up or otherwise), assets and liabilities and deeds of appointment be disclosed.

The question of how far the application of the principles in *Rosewood* will produce a different result to that under the former regime was considered in *Breakspear v Ackland*.[51] In the case itself, in early 1995, Basil Dunning created[52] a discretionary family settlement, the trust property consisting of an area of farmland and buildings, shares and cash. The trustees were Basil himself and his accountant and friend Robert Ackland. At the time the settlement was made, Basil was in poor health and also in the process of separating from his second wife. The beneficiaries were Basil, his children and remoter issue, with Basil's future third wife, Patricia, subsequently being added under a clause in the settlement. Shortly after the trust was settled, Basil told Robert Ackland of his wish that Patricia be adequately provided for if she survived him and subsequently signed a letter of wishes to this effect in the first week of March. Basil Dunning died late in November 2002 but the claimants (who were three of his children by his first marriage)[53] were not made aware that the settlement existed until January 2005 and did not receive copies of the settlement or notification that a letter of wishes existed until a further 10 months had passed. They then sought disclosure of the letter of wishes but the trustees declined their request, arguing that not only did the letter contain confidential information but that the disclosure would lead to discord within the family and, in any event, at least one of the claimants did not, as the object of a mere power, have any entitlement. In the Chancery Division, Briggs J upheld the trustees' refusal, holding that the letter was, prima facie, confidential and so non-disclosable.

The judgment of Briggs J is dominated by a detailed and closely argued investigation into the relationship of what might be termed the 'old' and 'new' principles governing disclosure as it affects letters of wishes, not only considering how such letters should be treated and how far that treatment might or should differ under the discretionary approach of *Rosewood* but also examining the extent to which the former rules survive that Privy Council decision.

Having established the case for the non-disclosure of letters of wishes under the previous regime, Briggs J then turned his attention to the question of how far, if at all, principles derived under that regime are of relevance after the *Rosewood* decision. A powerful argument that they are not is to be found in The Withers Lecture for 2003, delivered by Mr Justice Lightman. Referring to letters or memoranda of wishes, he commented extra-judicially, 'I would suggest that the principles stated in earlier cases (and particular

---

[51] Above n 36.
[52] De facto if not de jure. See *Breakspear v Ackland* [2008] EWHC 220, [25].
[53] They were also default beneficiaries of the settlement.

Londonderry) may no longer apply at least with the same stringency'.[54] Rather, it was now necessary to undertake a 'balancing exercise', which might, in appropriate cases, require disclosure.

Acknowledging these views, Briggs J responded to them on two grounds. The first of these was that in his judgment in *Rosewood*, Lord Walker had characterised the need to protect confidentiality as 'one of the most important limitations on the right to disclosure of trust documents'.[55] Furthermore, as the judge observed, there could be no question of *Rosewood* overruling the established principle as to confidentiality because, given the actual facts in the case, confidentiality was simply not an issue. For these reasons, he said, he was 'bound to continue to treat the *Londonderry* principle as still being good law'[56] and letters of wishes should, subject only to the court's overriding discretion, be regarded as confidential and not disclosable.[57]

VI. SOME CONCLUSIONS

In any attempted evaluation as to the way the *Rosewood* principle will operate, perhaps the most important feature is the fact that the former 'right' to disclosure is now replaced by a 'discretion'. Lord Walker expressed this approach as follows: 'no beneficiary has any entitlement as of right to disclosure of anything which can plausibly be described as a trust document'.[58] And so the key question becomes, how will this discretion be applied and with what results? One cannot look to the decision itself for comprehensive guidance. (Indeed, given that the Privy Council were not required to decide whether the object of the power of appointment in question should be entitled to the disclosure he sought, it would have been strange if they had.)

In his judgment, however, Lord Walker did suggest that limits and safeguards may have to be put in place and among the factors governing these would be issues of personal confidentiality, the need to balance competing interests and the strength of the particular claimant's case.[59] The abandonment of the old proprietary paradigm is to be welcomed on jurisprudential grounds, but it is vital both for those seeking advice and those giving it that this discretion is exercised in a consistent manner. In the light of all the

[54] Lightman J, *The Withers Lecture* (2003) p 5.
[55] *Schmidt v Rosewood Trust Ltd* [2003] 2 AC 709 (PC) 728. Cited *Breakspear v Ackland* [2008] EWHC 220, [40].
[56] *Breakspear v Ackland* [2008] EWHC 220 [53].
[57] In taking this view, he preferred the view of the authors of *Lewin*, above n 9, at 818–24 to that of the authors of Underhill. See Hayton, Matthews and Mitchell (eds), *Underhill and Hayton—Law of Trusts and Trustees*, 17th edn (London, LexisNexis Butterworths, 2006) 837–9.
[58] *Schmidt v Rosewood Trust Ltd* [2003] 2 AC 709 (PC) 734.
[59] *ibid*, 734–5.

evidence available, the following observations as to how this discretion will operate would appear appropriate.

In terms of *who* may be entitled, because the court is freed from the necessity to limit information to those who have a definite or vested interest in the trust, it will be neither surprising nor objectionable that beneficiaries under a discretionary trust—in particular a small family trust—will have the locus standi to seek information. Indeed the judgment in *Foreman* makes it absolutely clear that

> [i]n the case of persons named or included by definition as discretionary beneficiaries under a trust instrument, circumstances that might exclude them from relief would be limited, because to decline disclosure of accounts and information would be a direct conflict with the trustees fundamental obligation to be accountable to the beneficiaries.[60]

This will extend to objects of a fiduciary power but only if there is, in practical terms a real possibility they will benefit. Such might not always be the case in very large discretionary trusts and objects of dispositive powers.

So far as the issue of *what* a claimant may obtain is concerned, it is when considering this question that the discretion which the court uses when exercising its inherent power to supervise a trust may be most relevant. The traditionally very powerful ground that any documents giving reasons for the trustees' decisions need not be disclosed will still have a major part to play. Parallel to that is a recognition that certain types of documents go to the very essence or core of the trust and its operation. Into this category will fall trust deeds, deeds of appointment, resettlement and removal, and financial statements containing information about matters such as assets liabilities and financial transactions. In such cases, arguments based on confidentiality or avoiding potential conflict will need to be extremely strong if a claim for disclosure made by a beneficiary with a realistic expectation is to be refused. If the information is sought by a beneficiary whose claim is weaker by reason of being more remote, then he or she may have to make a case before disclosure is ordered.

There will be some documents—such as letters of wishes and legal opinions which have been funded out of trust moneys and were obtained for purposes connected with the trust—which are less clear cut and the court will have to decide whether such disclosure should be whole or partial and what if any safeguards are required.

---

[60] *Foreman v Kingstone and Cave* [2004] 1 NZLR 841, 859 (Potter J).

7

Draftsmen and Suspicious Wills*

ROGER KERRIDGE**

I. THE PROBLEM

ENGLISH LAW DOES not deal well with the situation which arises when a beneficiary becomes involved in the preparation of a will. Or, to put it another way, it is too easy, in England, to obtain probate of a will which is tainted by a beneficiary's influence and which, in many other systems, would stand no chance of being recognised as a valid testamentary disposition.[1] There is no rule in English law to the effect that a will prepared by a beneficiary, or in the preparation of which a beneficiary has played a part, shall be void or of no effect. Section 15 of the Wills Act 1837 does say that a gift to an attesting witness or to his or her spouse shall be 'utterly null and void' but that only covers the situation where the beneficiary is a witness—it covers nothing else.[2] Section 15 may sometimes operate too harshly, and there is much to be said for providing for some kind of relief in cases where the witness-beneficiary can demonstrate that there is nothing amiss.[3] But the problem is the opposite one. There is no clear prohibition against a beneficiary's preparing a draft of a will, having it typed out on his computer,[4] writing out the entire will in his (the beneficiary's) handwriting,[5] and/or being present when the will is prepared and executed.[6] There is something wrong somewhere.

---

* The writer would like to thank his colleagues Gwen Seabourne and Stephen Watterson for commenting on earlier drafts of this paper. The usual disclaimers apply.
** Professor of Law, University of Bristol.

[1] In Roman Law, a gift to a person who had assisted in the preparation of the will was normally void; Dig XXXIIII.8.1, and the would-be beneficiary would normally be liable to the penalty for forgery under the *Lex Cornelia*; Dig XXXXVIII 10.6 pr, 15 pr.

[2] *O'Brien v Seagrave* [2007] 1 WLR 2002 (will witnessed by partner and friend of sole beneficiary).

[3] See DECYale, 'Witnessing Wills and Losing Legacies' (1984) 100 *Law Quarterly Review* 453.

[4] *Re Dabbs, Hart v Dabbs* [2001] WTLR 527.

[5] *Fuller v Strum* [2002] 1 WLR 1097.

[6] *Wood v Smith* [1993] Ch 90—this will failed to obtain probate, *but not* because of the beneficiary's conduct—on the basis of lack of capacity—see also *Sherrington v Sherrington* [2005] WTLR 587.

In a recent article in the *Law Quarterly Review*, Pauline Ridge suggests[7] that the origins of the problem can be traced back to 'the values and attitudes of a particular culture and place, namely, mid-nineteenth century England'. She is an Australian, so she is distancing herself from the people involved, but she seems to be saying that the rules are not brutal enough. By contrast, Chadwick LJ, in the Court of Appeal in *Fuller v Strum*,[8] criticised the trial judge[9] for adopting an expression used by Lord Hatherley in *Fulton v Andrew*,[10] where Lord Hatherley spoke of the 'righteousness of the transaction'. Chadwick LJ referred to this as 'redolent of morality' as if it were a criticism. Pauline Ridge and Chadwick LJ appear to have taken opposed approaches. She seems to suggest that Victorian attitudes were too easy-going, whereas he seemed to think that at least one Victorian judge was too austere. There may be ways of reconciling the two views, but it is suggested that they are both wrong—his more significantly than hers. In so far as Lord Hatherley referred, in *Fulton v Andrew*, to the 'righteousness of the transaction', and, by so doing, implied that some transactions might be *un*righteous, he was, it is submitted, correct. The preparation of a will by a beneficiary *is* an unrighteous transaction and the fact that a judge in the Court of Appeal can criticise the use of that expression in this context is an illustration of what has gone wrong. A major problem here is the way in which many judges appear unwilling to criticise conduct which deserves to be criticised. As to Pauline Ridge, in so far that she implies there is a lack of rigour, she is completely correct *but* she is wrong to blame *England* in the mid-nineteenth century. The fault lies not with *England*, but with a particular group of people who happen to have lived, and still live here—these people were and are *lawyers*. The one real cause of confusion in all this is that the problem has been created not by one set of lawyers, but by two separate groups who have operated apart, but in what appears to be a form of subconscious co-operation. In so far as there is a problem understanding what has happened, it is due in part to the difficulties created by attempting to disentangle the input of these two groups.

II. THE LAWYERS

A. The Two Groups of Lawyers

And so who are these two groups of lawyers? On the one hand there are those who are concerned with challenging wills—the contentious probate

---

[7] P Ridge, 'Equitable Undue Influence and Wills' (2004) 120 *Law Quarterly Review* 617, 618.
[8] *Fuller v Strum* [2002] 1 WLR 1097; casenote in (2003) 119 *Law Quarterly Review* 39.
[9] Jules Sher QC.
[10] *Fulton v Andrew* (1875) LR 7 HL 448.

practitioners—who conduct the litigation, fight the cases. And, on the other hand, there are those who draft the wills. They, it is suggested, are the two groups who have created the confusion and difficulty in which we now find ourselves—and neither group comes out of this story in a light which can be described as heroic. This paper is principally concerned with the second group—the will draftsmen—but it is not possible to refer to them without fitting them into context, and so it is necessary to say something also about the contentious probate practitioners—though it is only a brief account of the part they have played.

(i) The Contentious Probate Practitioners

Contentious probate practitioners, the barristers involved in challenging wills, are nowadays, members of the Chancery Bar. But Chancery barristers have handled contentious probate only since 1971. The earliest reported cases of challenges to wills date back to the first half of the nineteenth century.[11] In the early years of the nineteenth century wills of personalty had to be challenged in the ecclesiastical courts, wills of realty were challenged in the Common Law courts, and Chancery could intervene in either case. Having said this, there are very few reported cases in the Common Law courts[12] and Chancery[13] was reluctant to become involved in will cases. As a result, virtually all the will cases were in the ecclesiastical courts, and the reported cases are those heard in the Prerogative Court, the court of the Archdiocese of Canterbury.[14] In the Prerogative Court, there was confusion over the rules governing the grounds upon which a will could be challenged, confusion over the presumptions which applied when a will had been prepared by a beneficiary, and confusion over the rules covering costs. As a result of these various confusions, the cases dragged on and generated significant amounts of work for the lawyers involved.[15] In 1858, probate, including contentious probate, was transferred from the Prerogative Court to the newly-founded Court of Probate. Those who practised in the newly-founded court were, by and large,

---

[11] There were two eighteenth century cases, but *Middleton v Forbes* (1787) is not properly reported while *Lamkin v Babb* (1752) 1 Lee 1, 161 ER 1 was a standard case of a wife exercising undue influence over her husband—eighteenth and nineteenth century wives were not always politically correct.

[12] *Probably* because land would usually be held in settlement.

[13] In spite of what Dickens wrote in *Bleak House.*

[14] *Matrimonial* cases would normally be heard in the Consistory Court—the Court of the Diocese of London. Both courts sat in London, in the court-room at Doctors' Commons.

[15] *Bleak House* could, perfectly well, have been played out in the Prerogative Court, rather than Chancery. The lawyers who practised in the Prerogative Court were, of course, trained in Roman Law. Yet they chose *not* to adopt the Roman Law rule applicable to a will in the preparation of which a beneficiary had taken part. The rule was referred to by Sir John Nicholl, the Judge of the Prerogative Court, both in *Paske v Ollatt* (below n 22) and in *Ingram v Wyatt* (below n 23). For the Roman Law rule itself, see above n 1.

those who had previously practised in the ecclesiastical courts. Once things got under way in the new court, it was clear that there was still confusion as to the grounds upon which a will could be challenged[16] and, in 1865, in *Hastilow v Stobie*[17] Sir JP Wilde introduced the plea of 'lack of knowledge and approval'. He claimed that he was able to trace this plea back to *Barry v Butlin*.[18] That was historically incorrect, but there is insufficient time to deal with this in detail here.[19] In 1875, the Court of Probate was abolished and probate work moved to the newly-established Probate, Divorce and Admiralty Division of the Supreme Court, where it remained until 1971. In 1971, non-contentious probate went to the Family Division, while contentious probate was transferred to Chancery. But the significant point is that the origins of almost all the problems in this area lie in the ecclesiastical courts and with the doctors of Doctors' Commons.[20] The blame for what has gone wrong lies not with mid-nineteenth century England, but with the ecclesiastical lawyers, and what is to be regretted is that later generations of lawyers have not put right what they managed, for their own benefit, to get wrong.

(ii) The Will Draftsmen

The other group of lawyers who have been involved in the problem, and who are the principal interest of this paper, are the will draftsmen—the solicitors. It was, in England, until the 1950s, standard practice for them to draft wills in their own favour. A solicitor who, in the nineteenth century, or early twentieth century, had a client who did not know to whom to leave his property on death, had no problem. He drafted a will in his own favour.[21]

---

[16] The problem had existed before 1858, but came into sharper focus when the new Court of Probate took over.

[17] *Hastilow v Stobie* (1865) LR 1 P & D 64.

[18] *Barry v Butlin* (1837–38) 1 Curt 614, 163 ER 215; 2 Moo PC 480, 12 ER 1089.

[19] There were references in *Barry v Butlin* to 'knowledge and approval' but they were not to a *plea* of *lack* of knowledge and approval. This is back-to-front. In *Barry v Butlin* it was not the son, who was challenging the will, who raised *lack* of knowledge and approval, but the propounders, those seeking to uphold the will, who claimed that there *was* knowledge and approval: this was not a plea, it was, in effect, their *defence* to the son's *pleas* of *lack of capacity* and *undue influence*. What makes this absolutely clear is that, before Sir JP Wilde, the second Judge Ordinary of the Court of Probate, admitted the plea of lack of knowledge and approval in 1865, Sir Cresswell Cresswell, the first Judge Ordinary, had held in *Middlehurst v Johnson* (1861) 30 LJ (PMA) 14, and again in *Cunliffe v Cross* (1863) 3 Sw & Tr 37, that no such plea existed. Nobody would have better understood what had happened in *Barry v Butlin* than Sir Cresswell Cresswell. He had acted in the case; he was leading counsel for the son. Had there been a plea of lack of knowledge and approval in *Barry v Butlin*, it would have been his team who would have pleaded it. In July 1863, six months after *Cunliffe v Cross*, Sir Cresswell Cresswell was thrown by his horse and killed. This was an unlucky chance, which had a significant and unfortunate effect on the way in which this branch of the law then developed.

[20] The doctors were doctors of law or of civil law and were the advocates who practised before the ecclesiastical courts.

[21] See below for details. It is *assumed*, in favour of the solicitors, that their clients did not know what to do with their property—in some cases it may have been worse than this.

B. Interaction of the Two Groups

Now look at the cases where wills were challenged in the Prerogative Court between 1800 and 1858, and an interesting statistic emerges. There are nine cases of challenges to wills which had been prepared by beneficiaries and in four of the nine cases the wills obtained probate, whereas in five they did not—that is a 50 per cent success/failure rate and such a rate would suit the doctors who practised in the Prerogative Court. Then look again at the nine cases. Three out of the four cases where the propounders succeeded were concerned with wills in favour of solicitors—*Paske v Ollat*,[22] *Ingram v Wyatt*,[23] and *Barry v Butlin*.[24] The most outrageous of these was *Ingram v Wyatt*, where the will was refused probate at first instance and an appeal to the High Court of Delegates[25] succeeded—no reasons given. But what about those who were refused probate? Four out of these five cases were in favour of people who were not solicitors, *Billinghurst v Vickers*,[26] *Baker v Batt*,[27] *Harwood v Baker*[28] and *Greville v Tylee*.[29] The *Greville* case concerned a will in favour of a doctor, but he failed, so there was no class bias in favour of the professions. It was much more straightforward than that; there was a bias in favour of solicitors. There was an almost perfect fit between being a lawyer and succeeding, and the two cases which appear to be out of line *are*, when examined properly, special. The one case where a lawyer failed to obtain probate of a will (it was actually a codicil) in his own favour was *Croft v Day*,[30] but the solicitor was *not* the testator's family solicitor. The family solicitor opposed granting probate to this codicil, so it is not surprising that the interloping solicitor did not succeed. And the one case where someone other than a solicitor did obtain probate, *Constable v Tufnell*,[31] is also unusual. This was a dispute between two groups of people, each of whom had been involved in preparing a will which had been tainted by a degree of undue influence. The earlier will was in favour of the parson and the servants; the later will was in favour of the testator's family. In that kind of situation, the family was almost bound to succeed, and it did. So, if these two unusual cases are discounted, there is

---

[22] *Paske v Ollat* (1815) 2 Phill Ecc 187, 161 ER 956.
[23] *Ingram v Wyatt* (1828–29) 1 Hagg Ecc 382, 162 ER 621; 3 Hagg Ecc 466, 162 ER 1228.
[24] *Barry v Butlin* (1837–38) 1 Curt 614, 163 ER 215; 2 Moo PC 480, 12 ER 1089.
[25] The High Court of Delegates was the court which, until a third of the way through the nineteenth century, dealt with appeals from the ecclesiastical courts. It conducted itself in a way which was little short of scandalous and its functions were transferred to the Privy Council in 1833.
[26] *Billinghurst v Vickers* (1810) 1 Phill Ecc 187, 161 ER 956.
[27] *Baker v Batt* (1836–38) 1 Curt 125, 163 ER 42; 2 Moo PC 317, 12 ER 1026.
[28] *Harwood v Baker* (1840) 3 Moo PC 282, 13 ER 117.
[29] *Greville v Tylee* (1851) 7 Moo PC 320, 13 ER 904.
[30] *Croft v Day* (1838) 1 Curt 782, 163 ER 271.
[31] *Constable v Tufnell* (1833) 4 Hagg Ecc 465, 162 ER 1516.

a perfect match between solicitor-drawn wills, which all obtained probate, and wills not prepared by solicitors, which all failed.

III. PRE-1960 CASES

A. Cases Between the 1850s and the 1950s

There are not many reported cases of challenges to beneficiary-made wills in the period between 1858, when the Court of Probate took over from the Prerogative Court, and the 1950s, when we come to *Wintle v Nye*.[32] The pattern remained the same, except that this was the period during which there were further complications over the pleadings, the grounds on which wills could be challenged: these problems do not form part of the present discussion. During this period, there were two reasonably straightforward[33] cases in which wills which were not in favour of solicitors were set aside—*Hall v Hall*[34] and *Fulton v Andrew*.[35] And there were two straightforward[36] cases in which wills prepared by solicitors in their own favour were granted probate—*Mitchell and Mitchell v Gard and Kingwell*[37] and *In the Estate of Osment*.[38] *Osment* was particularly unpleasant and in some ways the shape of things to come. Most of the victims in these cases had tended to be single and childless, so did not have dependants. Osment was a married man with infant children, and his vice was drink. His drinking companion was Child, and Child introduced Osment to Jarvis, a solicitor, who prepared a will for Osment in which Osment left £1,000 to Jarvis, the solicitor, £200 to Jarvis's clerk (to keep the people in the office happy),[39] and then an unspecified, and presumably much larger, sum to Child. Osment died, presumably of drink, two months after the will was executed. The family challenged the will—the trial was before a special jury—and the will was upheld. This outcome seems to have been too much for the trial judge, Sir Samuel Evans P, and so he granted costs to the losers (the dead man's children) and *from* the legacies to Jarvis and Child. That step might seem hard to justify in logic, but there is little in this case which can be described as logical.

Another case during this period where a judge and jury failed to see eye to eye was *Atter v Atkinson*,[40] a case of a solicitor-beneficiary. The judge,

---

[32] *Wintle v Nye* [1959] 1 WLR 284.
[33] Reasonably straightforward in the present context.
[34] *Hall v Hall* (1868) LR 1 P & D 481.
[35] *Fulton v Andrew* (1875) LR 7 HL 448.
[36] Straightforward in the present context.
[37] *Mitchell and Mitchell v Gard and Kingwell* (1863) 3 Sw & Tr 275, 164 ER 1280.
[38] *In the Estate of Osment* [1914] P 129.
[39] There is no indication that Osment knew the clerk.
[40] *Atter v Atkinson* (1869) LR 1 P & D 665.

Sir JP Wilde, followed the standard approach and did what he could to uphold the will, but the jury were not willing to go along with this and ended up by failing to agree a verdict. Then there was *Goodacre and Taylor v Smith*,[41] which was the sole reported example during this 100-year period of a case where probate was obtained of a beneficiary-prepared will by someone who was not a solicitor.[42] A case which may *appear* to be out of line on the other side is the Australian case of *Farrelly v Corrigan*,[43] where a will drafted by a lawyer in his own favour was refused probate. In fact, *Farrelly* is more confusing than out of line. The draftsman was not, strictly speaking, a solicitor—he was an articled clerk, learning the tricks of the trade at the start of his career. He prepared a will, in his own favour, for an illiterate testator to whom he did not bother to read it over, and he then lied about this on oath. That was too much for an Australian jury, though one can only speculate on what verdict an English jury would have reached.

B. *Wintle v Nye*

Speaking of juries leads to the great case of *Wintle v Nye*.[44] This is a case of which anyone who has ever had the slightest interest in succession must have heard, but it may well be that some of the circumstances surrounding it are not fully appreciated by those who have read it quickly.

Kathleen Helen (Kitty) Wells, who lived in East Grinstead,[45] was unmarried, childless, reclusive, and rich. She died in 1947,[46] leaving a will which had been prepared for her by her solicitor, Nye;[47] and this will devised and bequeathed almost her entire estate to (not hard to guess) Nye. Kitty's next of kin was her sister, Mildred (Millie), to whom Kitty left only a small annuity. But Millie had displeased their mother, so she had not expected to be treated generously and was not particularly surprised: she did not challenge the will. Millie then died, intestate, about a year after Kitty, and Millie's estate passed to her first cousins, the Wellses. They had had hardly any dealings with Kitty or with Millie; they had expected nothing, so they made no fuss either. *But* Kitty had some first half-cousins[48] who

---

[41] *Goodacre and Taylor v Smith* (1867) LR 1 P & D 359.

[42] This is only the second case on record of a will prepared by a non-solicitor beneficiary obtaining probate—the first was *Constable v Tufnell*—see above n 31.

[43] *Farrelly v Corrigan* [1899] AC 563 (PC).

[44] *Wintle v Nye* [1959] 1 WLR 284 (HL).

[45] And Hove.

[46] Not in East Grinstead, or Hove, but in Penge; she did not die in either of her own houses. The detail, as in many succession cases, matters, but there is no space in this paper to go further into this.

[47] Her attestation was witnessed by his clerks.

[48] Described, incorrectly, in the judgments, as second cousins—this is not important in the context.

were very upset. One of these first half-cousins, Marjorie Wintle, had (so she claimed) been Kitty's companion and, according to the Wintles, Kitty had promised Marjorie that she would make provision for her in her will. Marjorie was, herself, not the kind of person to challenge a will—that takes courage bordering on foolhardiness—but Marjorie's brother, Freddie,[49] who was a retired half-colonel in the Dragoons, did it for her. Colonel Wintle persuaded one of the Wells cousins to assign to him a share in Millie's, and therefore Kitty's, estate and he then issued proceedings. There was a jury trial, and the jury decided in Nye's favour. So far, this case was following the standard pattern. Colonel Wintle then appealed to the Court of Appeal, alleging misdirection by the trial judge, he lost again.[50] Undeterred, he appealed to the House of Lords and won there—5-0.

That is a quick resumé of the case and someone who reads this account fast gets the impression that all's well that ends well—it is a happy ending. But there are a number of misconceptions. Colonel Wintle was a litigant in person—in the House of Lords. It is easy for the reader to come away with the impression that he was a litigant in person at all stages. But he was not, he was *not* a litigant in person at first instance; at that stage he had the assistance, if it can be called that, of two silks, two junior counsel, solicitors etc. The legal team and their part in what happened are important for a number of reasons—though they emerge from the story with little credit. It was they, not the colonel, who decided on the grounds on which this will should be challenged, and they chose to allege 'lack of knowledge and approval'. Since *Wintle v Nye*, this has become the preferred ground on which to challenge a beneficiary-made will, and this appears to be because it was the ground on which Wintle won his case. In a later case, *In the Estate of Fuld dec'd*,[51] Scarman J seemed to say, obiter, that when wills are challenged, they should be challenged as Kitty Wells's will was challenged—on the basis of lack of knowledge and approval. But he forgot to mention (i) the fact that Wintle *lost* the case at first instance; (ii) that when the case was lost at first instance the colonel and his legal team parted company, on bad terms; and (iii) that he, Scarman, had been a member of the team. As Wintle himself put it, they, the lawyers, having requested an 'outlaying of thousands of pounds ... spilled at the first ditch'. So, if Colonel Wintle were to tell the story he would say that Scarman drafted the pleadings and lost. Winners are supposed to write history. In fact, strictly speaking, nobody 'won'. When the case reached the Lords, they held that there had been a misdirection, and that should have led to a re-trial. There was no such re-trial because Nye surrendered, but he did so because of the publicity

---

[49] Alfred Daniel Wintle.

[50] Statistically, wills were (and still are) more likely to be upheld on appeal than at first instance, so the odds were not on the colonel's side.

[51] *In the Estate of Fuld dec'd* [1968] P 675, 722.

surrounding the case, certainly no thanks to Wintle's former legal team. Having said this, the whole question of the pleadings is of only incidental relevance to the point being investigated here. What is important is what happened to Nye.

C. What Happened to Nye?

In an article in the *Cambridge Law Journal* in 2000[52] it is stated that *after* the case of *Wintle v Nye* the Law Society changed the way in which they were interpreting the rules they applied to solicitors[53] who drafted wills in their own favour; and references are made in that article to a case in the 1970s, *Re A Solicitor*,[54] where two solicitors were struck off for drafting a will in their own favour. It is implied in the article that the solicitors in the 1975 case were struck off, but that no disciplinary action was taken against Nye. This is the impression obtained from a straightforward reading of the two cases. But, if the cases are re-read carefully, it is apparent that there is something wrong somewhere. The hearing in *Re A Solicitor* is about 20 years after the litigation in *Wintle v Nye* and so it is easy to assume that there was a change in rules, or in the way in which they were interpreted or applied, *after Wintle v Nye* had gone through the courts and *before* anything happened in *Re A Solicitor*. But that is wrong: the time-scale is longer than at first sight it appears. The solicitors in *Re A Solicitor* were judged to have misbehaved, in that they prepared a will in their own favour, but they did this in 1949, shortly after Kitty Wells died and some years *before* the litigation in *Wintle v Nye* began. There could have been no change in the rules, or in the way they were interpreted, as a result of what had happened in *Wintle v Nye*, at the stage when they prepared their will. Having carried out further investigations, the writer[55] has discovered that the rules were not re-interpreted *after Wintle v Nye*—they were re-interpreted at the end of *Wintle v Nye* itself; and Frederick Harry Nye was struck off the roll on 7 April 1960.[56]

So what is wrong? Did Nye not deserve to be struck off?

The point which is being made here is that Frederick Harry Nye *did* deserve to be struck off, but that the timing of the striking off was little

---

[52] R Kerridge, 'Wills Made in Suspicious Circumstances: The Problem of the Vulnerable Testator' (2000) 59 *Cambridge Law Journal* 310.

[53] See Pt IV, below.

[54] *Re A Solicitor* [1975] 1 QB 475.

[55] Who was also the author of the 2000 article in the *Cambridge Law Journal*.

[56] The Solicitors Regulation Authority who have, reluctantly, confirmed that Nye was struck off, say that they do not have a record which sets out the ground, nor do they have a transcript of the proceedings. It is easy to guess the ground—Frederick Harry Nye was struck off for serious professional misconduct in drafting a client's will in his own favour.

better than a farce. Striking him off in April 1960 was a waste of time. Striking Nye off *after Wintle v Nye* had finished was an empty gesture: he could not possibly have practised anyway. Nye was admitted as a solicitor in July 1906[57] and so he must have been at least 75 years old in 1960. He had just lost a very well-publicised court case, which had brought him (and the entire legal profession) into serious disrepute. He could not possibly have gone on practising.

The question is not why Nye *was* struck off in April 1960; it is why he was *not* struck off 10 years earlier.

Go back in history: Kitty Wells died in 1947 and after she died Colonel Wintle started making a fuss. If the various accounts of what happened are put together, it is clear that virtually the entire legal profession began by treating Colonel Wintle as crazy. What was he doing complaining about this solicitor (Nye) whose only alleged offence was to have drafted a will in his own favour, when his client clearly did not know what to do with her money? Nye had 150 years of precedents saying that this kind of thing was perfectly alright. Who was this colonel fellow who dared to suggest otherwise?

Note the following passage from Wintle's autobiography:

> I consulted one lawyer after another, visited the Law Society, the Solicitor-General and Scotland Yard ... I chased my own tail for ages. Everyone agreed that something should be done but not by him. It was pointed out to me that—although no honourable solicitor would do what Nye had done in the way he had done it—nothing downright illegal seemed to have occurred.

That was the position in or about 1950. *Nobody* was prepared to do anything for Wintle. And because nobody would do anything, Wintle took the law into his own hands, assaulted Nye and spent six months in jail. The lawyers thought that that would shut him up—it did nothing of the sort *and*, in a way that the lawyers completely failed to grasp, it generated publicity in his favour.

Look (again) at the stages of what happened in *Wintle v Nye*:

(i)   Kitty Wells died, leaving a will drafted by Nye in his own favour.
(ii) Colonel Wintle went round trying to get someone to do something— and nobody, including in particular the Law Society, took any action.
(iii) Wintle assaulted Nye and was jailed for six months.
(iv) When he was released from prison, Wintle was contacted by Millie's (and therefore Kitty's) next of kin and it was agreed that one of them would assign to him a share in Millie's/Kitty's estate so that he could challenge the will.

---

[57] The Solicitors Regulation Authority *does* have a record of that.

(v)   Colonel Wintle assembled a team of lawyers who challenged the will on the ground of lack of knowledge and approval. This was *not* the appropriate approach if Nye had misbehaved. Had he misbehaved, the appropriate and logical attack would have been on the basis of undue influence and/or fraud.

(vi)   At the end of his summing up to the jury, the trial judge, Barnard J,[58] having referred to the Scottish case of *Lowe v Guthrie*,[59] said as follows:

> Colonel Wintle's admitted motive in starting this action was to bring Mr Nye into court and expose him. No doubt the jury will have little sympathy with that, but they should not let it affect their minds and should forget any question of motive in reaching their verdict.

Translate that back into plain English and it means that Colonel Wintle's motive was to bring Mr Nye into court and to expose him; that this was something with which the jury should have no sympathy whatsoever; and that Barnard J confidently hoped that it *would* affect their minds. The jury took the hint and found in Nye's favour.

(vii) At that point, Barnard J had to deal with costs and he *again* referred to Colonel Wintle's attempts to expose Nye:

> As to costs, His Lordship said that the general rule was that costs should follow the event, but there were certain well-known exceptions. The one relevant to the present case was that an unsuccessful party was usually given costs when one of the principal beneficiaries had been engaged in the preparation of the will and had not shown, by disinterested evidence, that the will had been read over and explained to the testator … So far as Colonel Wintle was concerned, nobody could say that this was the usual case. He was not a next of kin and not entitled to contest the will until, at quite a late stage, he had persuaded one of the next of kin to assign his interest to him. He (His Lordship) thought he was entitled to take Colonel Wintle's motives into account in this respect. He had said frankly that his motive was to drag Mr Nye into court and expose him. His Lordship thought he ought to pay for that pleasure. There would, therefore, be no order as to Colonel Wintle's costs.[60]

(viii) This meant that Colonel Wintle had to pay his legal team for losing the case.[61]

---

[58] Barnard J was the son of Barnard KC, who happened to be counsel in *Osment* (see above n 38) in 1914. Barnard senior acted in that case for the solicitor who had drawn up the will in favour of himself and Child.

[59] *Lowe v Guthrie* [1909] AC 278 (HL Sc), why did he refer to a *Scottish* case?

[60] This report is taken from *The Times*.

[61] Which, it has just been suggested, they pleaded incorrectly – but this point ties in with the question of exposing Nye. The costs almost bankrupted Wintle.

(ix)   Wintle went on, as a litigant in person, to lose in the Court of Appeal, but to win in the House of Lords. The House of Lords held that there had been a series of misdirections by Barnard J, but they did *not* refer to any of the points he made about exposing Nye.

What is noteworthy, from the present point of view, is not what the House of Lords *did* criticise, but what they did not. There was no criticism of Barnard J for *twice* attacking Wintle on the ground that he had attempted to expose Nye. And yet, in 1960, Nye was struck off. Wintle had been right all the time, Nye ought to have been 'dragged into court and exposed'.

IV. THE 1960 RULES

A. The Rules Covering Solicitors and Wills

So, now look at the rules under which Nye, having been exposed, not by his fellow lawyers but by the colonel, was struck off. The problem with the rules under which Nye was struck off is that they were put together at the end of *Wintle v Nye* and were then applied retrospectively. Because they were to be applied retrospectively, and because solicitors had got away with so much for so long, it was impossible to draft them so that they were both clear and brutal. They were, from the outset, at least in relation to wills, a 'fudge'. They were first set out in the first edition of the Law Society's 'Guide to the Professional Conduct of Solicitors', dated 1960[62] and they appear never to have been significantly amended. In their present (2007) form they are as follows:

Solicitors Code of Conduct 2007

Rule 2—Client Relations

2.01 Taking on Clients

(1)   ...

(c) where instructions are given by someone other than the client ... you must not proceed without checking that all clients agree with the instructions given; or

(d) where you know or have reasonable grounds for believing that the instructions are affected by duress or undue influence, you must not act on those instructions until you have satisfied yourself that they represent the client's wishes.

---

[62] Before 1960, the only published Practice Rules for solicitors dealt with handling clients' money and touting for business. There were no published rules on wills.

Guidance to Rule 2—Client Relations

(c) Duress or undue influence

It is important to be satisfied that clients give their instructions freely. Some clients, such as the elderly, those with language or learning difficulties and those with disabilities are particularly vulnerable to pressure from others. If you suspect that a client's instructions are the result of undue influence you need to exercise your judgment as to whether you can proceed on the client's behalf. For example, if you suspect that a friend or relative who accompanies the client is exerting undue influence, you should arrange to see the client alone or if appropriate with an independent third party or interpreter ...

Rule 3—Conflict of Interests

3.04 Accepting gifts from clients

Where a client proposes to make a lifetime gift or a gift on death to, or for the benefit of:

(a) you;

... and the gift is of a significant amount, either in itself or having regard to the size of the client's estate and the reasonable expectations of the prospective beneficiaries, you must advise the client to take independent advice about the gift, unless the client is a member of the beneficiary's family. If the client refuses, you must stop acting for the client in relation to the gift.

Guidance on Rule 3

Accepting gifts from clients—3.04

57. Subrule 3.04 allows you to prepare a will for a family member under which you receive a significant gift without requiring the client to seek independent advice on that gift. However, extreme caution should always be exercised in these circumstances as your ability to give independent, dispassionate advice could easily be undermined by your relationship with others within, and outside, the family. The risk of conflict, therefore, is very high.

B. The Aftermath of *Wintle v Nye*

The theme of this paper is that lawyers have never really understood the significance of permitting beneficiaries to take part in the preparation of wills. When *Wintle v Nye* was over, Nye was sacrificed, but it was a meaningless sacrifice because he would not have been able to practise anyway. But what was missing at the conclusion of the case was genuine contrition—there was little more than a cover-up, an attempt to put the Press off the scent. There was no general understanding that beneficiary-made wills are wrong—and that lawyers should not get involved with them.

V. THE POST-1960 CASES

A. Should Professional Will Draftsmen be Considered at Fault When Wills They Have Drafted are Set Aside?

There are five principal grounds on which a will may be refused probate:

(i)   lack of due execution;
(ii) lack of capacity;
(iii) undue influence;
(iv) fraud;
(v)   lack of knowledge and approval.

If a professional draftsman is involved in the will-making process, he or she may or may not be at fault where a will is refused probate for lack of due execution.[63] As to fraud, it is seldom pleaded and *never* successfully. That is a condemnation of the system, but for present purposes fraud may be disregarded. In the case of the three other pleas, lack of capacity, undue influence, and lack of knowledge and approval (which is, itself, usually a disguised plea of fraud or undue influence), *if* a professionally-drawn will fails on one of these grounds, the draftsman is prima facie at fault. In a system which operates properly, a draftsman should not allow a situation to arise where a client who lacks capacity, or who does not understand what is happening, or who does not really intend to do what he is somehow being persuaded into doing, executes a purported will.

What should be happening, but is not, is that solicitors and other professional will draftsmen should be strongly discouraged by their professional associations (in the case of solicitors, the Law Society, or now, the Solicitors Regulation Authority)[64] from taking part in the preparation of wills where they suspect, or ought to suspect, that their clients, the persons making wills, lack either capacity or complete freedom to make the dispositions which they, the testators, want to make.

B. Where Do We Begin?

There have recently been a significant number of reported cases[65] where professionally drawn wills have not obtained probate as a result of circumstances

---

[63] A draftsman may send a will to a testator for execution, with clear instructions, and the testator may not follow them. This may not be the draftsman's fault.

[64] The change in the regulation procedures for solicitors from regulation by the Law Society to regulation by the Solicitors Regulation Authority appears to have no significance in the present context.

[65] The sudden jump in the number of *reported* cases is probably due to the appearance of the Wills and Trusts Law Reports which first appeared in 2000.

which reflect no credit on those who should have been looking after the testators' interests. And these reported cases may well be only the tip of an iceberg. Many cases of suspicious wills will not reach the courts; some will be compromised; in other cases the challengers will not dare to risk the costs.[66] And most cases which do reach the courts will not be reported. But, against that background, look at some cases which have been reported—and note that in none of these cases, referred to from now on, does any disciplinary action appear to have been taken against the draftsmen.

C. Draftsmen Who Do Not Bother to See Their Clients, the Testators

In *Re Stott*,[67] Lady Stott, who was 91 years old and suffering from senile dementia, entered a nursing home. Less than a month later, someone called Davey, who was linked with the nursing home proprietress, contacted a firm of solicitors with whom Lady Stott had had no previous contact and asked the solicitors to prepare a will for her. Under this will, the proprietress of the nursing home was the residuary beneficiary. The solicitors at no time saw their client, and they must have allowed the 'will' to be executed in the nursing home under the control of the principal beneficiary.[68] It is hard to see how any professional draftsmen could permit a situation like this to arise.[69]

Stott was an example of solicitors preparing a will without seeing the client. If that appears grim, move on to the more recent case of *Reynolds*.[70] Here, the solicitor took instructions from the beneficiary, never saw the testatrix at all, and then lied about it on oath. His misfortune was that the trial judge was Rimer J—someone who does not waste time with fictions. Note the following passage from his judgment:

> If I were to accept [the beneficiary's] and [the solicitor's] evidence about the occasion when [the solicitor] drew the will, then I would be disposed to accept that it would go a long way, probably all the way, to discharging the burden of proof of knowledge and approval. However, I do not accept that evidence. I was wholly unconvinced by [the solicitor's] evidence that he took his instructions from [the

[66] Challengers are more likely to be deterred, where a will is professionally drawn.

[67] *Re Stott* [1980] 1 WLR 246.

[68] After Lady Stott's death, the will was challenged by members of her family and the report of the case is concerned chiefly with pleadings. Some facts are inferred.

[69] The more closely many succession cases are examined, the worse they look. *Stott* is linked with another case, *Re Davey* [1981] 1 WLR 164, involving the same people from the same nursing home, except that they played different roles. Davey married one of the patients. His bride, Miss St Barbe, was 93 years old, and in such a poor state at the time of the 'marriage' ceremony that she could not sign her name; all she could do was to make a mark. These two cases, *Stott* and *Davey*, do not refer to one another—that seems all to be part of a polite fiction. It seems to be considered bad taste to suggest that anyone misbehaved, but when the two cases are read side by side, the evidence is overwhelming.

[70] *Reynolds* [2005] EWHC 6; [2005] All ER (D) 70 Jan.

testatrix] directly. I regret to say that I did not believe a word of it ... I do not accept [the solicitor's] evidence that he ever saw [the testatrix], let alone that he took his instructions from her.

So what happens to a solicitor who behaves like this, who takes instructions from a beneficiary, has no contact at all with the testatrix, and who then lies about it on oath? Nothing! This solicitor was not in private practice, but worked for the Citizens Advice Bureau and, for the work he did, or was supposed to do, did not need a Practising Certificate. After the case was over, he, having lied on oath about his part in the preparation of the will, permitted himself to be removed from the roll. But that is retirement. This solicitor should not have been allowed to retire. He should have been made an example of; he should have been punished.

D. Taking Instructions from Beneficiaries

Stott and *Reynolds* are cases of solicitors who did not see their clients, but who simply took instructions from beneficiaries. There are a larger number of cases where draftsmen have seen the clients, but have still taken instructions from others. In *Buckenham v Dickinson*,[71] a 93-year-old, who was very deaf, almost blind, and close to death, had a will prepared for him by a solicitor who asked him leading questions fed to the solicitor by the man's second wife—she and her grandchildren were, of course, the beneficiaries. Note the following passage from the judgment in this case:

I have hesitated as to whether one can say that this is really something where [the solicitor's] own behaviour was unreasonable. I find it difficult quite to go so far as that. But I think there were things [the solicitor] could have done and should have done but didn't, but I think he acted in all good faith, and I don't disbelieve a word of what he says.

What the judge[72] appears to be saying is that solicitors who take instructions from beneficiaries, but who do not go as far as to lie about it afterwards,[73] will only get a gentle rap over the knuckles.

Another case where the trial judge seems to have been indulgent towards the solicitor draftsman was *Richards v Allan*.[74] The will here was prepared for an 84-year-old diabetic, under the influence of medication, while her sister was out of the house. It was (unsurprisingly) set aside for lack of capacity and for lack of knowledge and approval. The solicitor involved

---

[71] *Buckenham v Dickinson*, a 1997 High Court case reported in [2000] WTLR 1083.
[72] Judge Roger Cooke.
[73] For solicitors who *do* lie about it afterwards, see below.
[74] *Richards v Allan* [2001] WTLR 1031.

was the beneficiary's brother-in-law and he *did not charge for preparing the will*. The trial judge noted as follows:

> No file was opened for the matter and no fee was charged. He [the solicitor] said he was not dealing with it through his firm; he regarded it as more of a family matter, which would tend to suggest that he subconsciously viewed [the beneficiary] as more in the nature of the client than [the testatrix] … His [the solicitor's] demeanour in the witness box was such as to suggest to me that he felt rather uncomfortable about what had happened in this case.

It is hardly surprising that a solicitor who prepared a will which disinherited the testatrix's sister and benefited his sister-in-law, and who, subconsciously or otherwise, viewed the beneficiary as more in the nature of a client than the testatrix, should feel *uncomfortable*.

All the cases mentioned so far have been concerned with solicitors. In true free market tradition, it is now time to refer to one where the professional draftsmen were not solicitors, but bank employees. In *d'Eye v Avery*,[75] the victim (he can only be described that way) had had a massive stroke and a receiver had been appointed for him. Unbeknown to the receiver, the victim's dancing partner took him to the Midland Bank in Horsham where a will was prepared for him and then not read to him before he executed it—reading it out would have been pointless. The will was set aside for lack of knowledge and approval.[76] What on earth did the bank employees think that they were doing?

Another case involving a draftsman who was not a solicitor, but a retired solicitor who ran a will-drafting business, was *Re Loxston*.[77] Here, the testatrix was the donor of an enduring power of attorney, and it had been registered. Her carer summoned the draftsman, but said nothing to him about the EPA. The draftsman duly prepared a will which devised the testatrix's house to the carer, and for this he was paid his fixed standard fee of £55 in cash. The will was, at enormous cost, set aside for lack of capacity. The trial judge[78] was indulgent towards both the carer and the draftsman. There is no reference in the judgment to suspicions raised, or which should have been raised, by a £55 payment in cash, presumably by the carer herself, to the draftsman.[79] Who did the draftsman think was paying him? He was not to know that he had not been the first person to be approached about preparing a will for this testatrix;[80] but, even without this knowledge, there

---

[75] *D'Eye v Avery*. A 1997 High Court case reported in [2001] WTLR 227.
[76] Nothing is said in the report about costs.
[77] *Re Loxston* [2006] WTLR 1567.
[78] Nicholas Strauss QC sitting as a High Court judge.
[79] Given that the testatrix was subject to a registered EPA, it is almost inconceivable that she had access to anything other than insignificant amounts of money.
[80] Another solicitor had been involved earlier, but, for reasons which are not entirely clear, it was decided not to ask him to proceed.

should have been enough to make him hesitate, and at least to insist that a doctor be summoned to confirm whether the testatrix did or did not have capacity. The combination of cut-price will drafting services together with a market which provides no formal, or necessary, record of 'shopping around' makes it relatively easy for someone who is anxious to have a particular will prepared to find an obliging practitioner.

Other cases of beneficiaries who appear to have shopped around for draftsmen willing to act in the preparation of wills are *Vaughan v Vaughan*,[81] *Re Simpson*,[82] and *Tchilingirian v Ouzounian*.[83]

VI. THE SIGNIFICANCE OF WHAT HAS (NOT) HAPPENED

A. Why Does This Matter?

What has been said in this article may appear to some readers as an attack on professional will draftsmen. In fact, it is the opposite. The writer believes that home-made wills are a bad thing and that all testators should be encouraged to have their wills prepared by professionals. Home-made wills should be discouraged, cut-price wills should be discouraged; the making of a will is hugely important and the will-making process should be regarded as something requiring a high degree of expertise. But one of the things which the client, the would-be testator, is entitled to expect from a draftsman, is that his or her interests will be paramount. It is a betrayal for any will draftsman, particularly one dealing with a vulnerable testator, to put himself in a position where there is the merest suspicion that he has paid attention to anyone else's interests or wishes. And it is in the long-term interest of the legal profession, and of all professional will draftsmen, that draftsmen are perceived to serve only the interests of those who are their clients. They are not so perceived and, to make matters worse, their professional governing bodies do not appear to understand the damage which has been, and is being, done.

English law does not do what Roman Law did, and automatically void beneficiary-made wills.[84] That is unfortunate, but it is too late to put it right. It would be impossible now suddenly to adopt a rule to the effect that all wills in the making of which beneficiaries have played a part are to be void.

---

[81] *Vaughan v Vaughan*. A 2002 High Court case reported in [2005] WTLR 401 where a solicitor prepared a will for someone who mended his car, but without knowing that another solicitor had refused to make any more wills for the car-mender's mother on the basis that he realised that she had been put under improper pressure.

[82] *Re Simpson (dec'd): Schaniel v Simpson* (1977) 121 *Solicitors Journal* 224.

[83] *Tchilingirian v Ouzounian* [2003] WTLR 709 (Court answer = High Court, Chancery Division) where three wills prepared by two different firms were all set aside.

[84] For the position in Roman Law, see above nn 1 and 15.

There are some existing wills, in the making of which beneficiaries have played a part, which are above board.[85] It is too late now to introduce into England a rule which voids all beneficiary-prepared wills. We have a system which is in a mess, and we need to sort out the pleadings, the presumptions, the costs rules—all the things which the doctors of Doctors' Commons managed to confuse, and which have never been properly sorted out. But, whether or not we succeed in this, we need also to encourage testators (particularly those who are vulnerable) to feel confident that when they have their wills drawn up by solicitors, or other professional will draftsmen, they will be protected.

Will draftsmen can, if they conduct themselves properly, do much to stop things from happening which should not happen, and there have been cases where lawyers have acted correctly.[86] But set these cases against the others referred to above and the balance sheet is horribly negative.

Returning for a moment to home-made wills, and to their being discouraged, it ought to be possible, in a system which is operating sensibly, to draw an adverse inference from the fact that a vulnerable testator has had a non-professionally drawn will prepared for him: it ought to be possible to suggest that there is something odd about expecting an old or feeble person to make a will without a draftsman's protection. But that can only be the case if professional draftsmen can be trusted to look after testators. Look again at *Fuller v Strum*, the case where Chadwick LJ appeared to ridicule the reference to the 'righteousness of the transaction'. That was a case of a home-made will, written out entirely in the handwriting of a beneficiary, and the two attesting witnesses were that beneficiary's aunt and one of his friends. As to the testator's signature, it was said by a court-appointed handwriting expert that there was 'very strong positive evidence' that it had been forged. But, in spite of all this, that will obtained probate.[87] One of the things missing from that case was any suggestion that it was odd for someone in the testator's position to become involved in the making of a home-made will, let alone one prepared by a beneficiary.

B. Costs

It might be suggested that nothing needs to be done because will draftsmen will be deterred from acting improperly by the risk of having to pay the

---

[85] There will, for example, be wills openly prepared by children for their parents, where everyone in the family knows what has happened.

[86] Examples are *Simpson v Simpson* [1992] 1 FLR 601 and *Wood v Smith* [1993] Ch 90.

[87] Counsel for the challenger failed to notice that the testator was domiciled in Israel at the time of his death. The substantive law applicable should have been Israeli Law, and Israeli Law (quite sensibly) voids all gifts to those 'concerned in [the] preparation' of a will. Section 35 of the Israeli Succession Order 1965.

costs of successful challenges to wills which are set aside. That is not sufficient. In most of the recent reported cases where wills have successfully been challenged, there is no reference to costs as between the parties; and, in any case, professional will draftsmen are not parties to the original litigation when a will is challenged, so their costs involvement would not be spelled out in that litigation. One can only guess as to how many will draftsmen have been obliged to contribute towards the costs of setting aside the wills they have helped to prepare. But, even assuming that the threat of having to pay towards the costs of setting their wills aside is something which occurs to will draftsmen, it may occur too late, and at that stage the fear of the costs order may operate in such a way as to make things worse.

If a draftsman has acted, in the preparation of a will, in a way which, after the event, he realises was unwise, the knowledge that if the will is successfully challenged he may be asked to contribute towards the costs of such challenge may influence his evidence. It is likely to encourage him to assist in the upholding of will. His evidence will not be that of a neutral bystander.

There is only one recent case recording an award of costs against a draftsman; it is *Sifri v Clough & Willis*.[88] In *Sifri*, the draftsman took instructions directly from the beneficiary, the testator's second wife, and excluded the testator's daughter by his first marriage. He did this in the case of two successive wills, which were both set aside. The daughter then sued the solicitor and recovered part of her costs. Only part, because she had alleged lack of capacity, undue influence, lack of due execution, and lack of knowledge and approval, and had succeeded *only* on the last of the four pleas. This seems to be hard on the daughter, because the pleas overlap[89] and, anyway, there would have been no need to sue at all had the solicitor not taken instructions from the beneficiary.[90]

Draftsmen should pay the costs of most successful challenges to wills they have drawn, but this, by itself, is not a sufficient disincentive to bad behaviour. What is needed are unambiguous rules, laid down by the professional bodies, which make it absolutely clear that any involvement in the making of a suspicious will by a professional draftsman will make him

---

[88] *Sifri v Clough & Willis* [2007] WTLR 1453 (Ch D).

[89] To a considerable extent.

[90] There is insufficient space in this paper to discuss whether an action for costs against the draftsman should be brought by the beneficiaries who successfully challenged the will, as happened in *Sifri*, or by the personal representatives, as the Court of Appeal in *Worby v Rosser*, [1999] Lloyd's Rep PN 972, held should have happened. Another possibility is to join the personal representatives and the beneficiaries, see *Chappell v Somers & Blake* [2004] Ch 19. But none of this matters in the present context. The draftsman's conduct will be in no way influenced by considerations as to who is going to ask him to pay for the litigation which has taken place.

subject to severe penalties. This would be of advantage to draftsmen who were anxious to maintain reasonable standards. A draftsman who, for example, suspected that a testator was under pressure from a family member who appeared reluctant to permit such testator to communicate with the draftsman outside his hearing, could tell the family member that the rules of his profession forbade him to proceed with the drafting of a will. In many cases, this would simplify things for the draftsman—there would be no need for false delicacy.

C. A Recent Case

In case the reader may think that what has been said so far has been in any way exaggerated, and that solicitor draftsmen are subject to a reasonable code at the present time, it might be a good idea to end with a recent case, *Franks v Sinclair*.[91] In spite of the changes to the way in the rules have been interpreted since *Wintle v Nye*, it is possible for a solicitor to prepare a will for himself where the testator or testatrix is a member of his family. In this case, the solicitor, knowing that his mother did not intend to benefit him by her will, prepared a will for her, under which he took half her estate. The will was challenged, successfully. The trial judge's finding was that the mother did not understand the effect of the will and that she did not know and approve of its contents. There are several passages in the judgment to the effect that the solicitor had lied on oath.[92] So what happened to him? It is true that he lost the case and that had to pay the costs on an indemnity basis,[93] but it is submitted that this, given what he had attempted, was an inadequate penalty. The trial judge appeared to think[94] that being found to have prepared a will which was not based on his client's instructions and wishes, and then making false statements about this on oath, would have caused problems in his practice and for his standing in the profession, but there is no sign, at the time of writing, that the Solicitors Regulation Authority are thinking of taking any action in this matter. Sixty years after Colonel Wintle tried to get the Law Society to take action against Frederick Harry Nye, things have changed less than some would have us believe.

---

[91] *Franks v Sinclair* [2007] WTLR 339, [2006] All ER (D) 340 (Ch D).

[92] See, in particular, para 97, where David Richards J says 'I am satisfied that Mr F was not telling the truth in this evidence', and para 105, where he says 'These matters going to Mr F's credibility vary in their weight and significance, but overall they have brought me to the reluctant conclusion that he is not a witness on whose evidence I can rely'.

[93] *Franks v Sinclair* [2007] WTLR 1453 (Ch D). This is one of the rare cases where the costs position is reported.

[94] See, eg, para 69 of the judgment.

POSTSCRIPT

This paper was delivered at the Cambridge Conference in April in 2008 and was, to the writer's knowledge, up-to-date at the time of delivery. But there have been two developments since (this Postscript is written in September 2008).

I.   It is said in footnote 56 of the paper (above) that 'the Solicitors Regulation Authority who have, reluctantly, confirmed that Nye was struck off, say that they do not have a record which sets out the ground, nor do they have a transcript of the proceedings'. In fact, the writer wrote a series of letters to the Solicitors Regulation Authority about Nye's striking off and they claimed (i) that they did not have a record of the grounds on which Nye was struck off and (ii) that they could 'think of no other organisations or individuals that might hold the information' (letter of 15 March 2007 from the Solicitors Regulation Authority to the writer). The writer always believed that someone must have a record, and went on to discuss this with other solicitors who were in practice, and who were more helpful than the Solicitors Regulation Authority. At long last, the writer's former colleague (and co-editor), Alastair Brierley, discovered that the Solicitors Disciplinary Tribunal *were*, after all, able to supply a transcript of the proceedings in which Nye was struck off. He was struck off as the result of an application made by the Law Society on the ground that he 'had been guilty of conduct unbefitting a solicitor in that he took advantage of the inexperience, lack of understanding and un-businesslike habits of his client, Miss Kathleen Helen Wells, for his own benefit'. There is, unsurprisingly, no indication as to why the proceedings were brought by the Law Society 10 years after they should have been brought, and it may also seem odd that the Solicitors Regulation Society told the writer, in March 2007, that they could 'think of no other organisations or individuals that might have the information' when they should have been aware that the Solicitors' Disciplinary Tribunal had the record.

II. The paper ends with a discussion of the *Franks* case. The writer made various attempts to find out whether any action was being taken here. He had no help from the Solicitors Regulation Authority. He contacted prominent people at the Law Society, who said that they would try to find out whether anything was happening, and from whom he then heard nothing further. He was aware that other solicitors were also making enquiries and getting nowhere. This led both him and others to believe that nothing was happening. And then, by chance, the writer had a conversation with Joshua Rozenberg, the legal journalist. Joshua Rozenberg said that he would enquire. He did so, and *he* was informed (very quickly) that some form of action is now being taken in the *Franks* case. Further details appear almost impossible to come by but, if proceedings are in progress, it would be improper to say more at this time, except to note that, if something is happening, it will be the first case of its kind since *Re A Solicitor* (see above, footnote 54) a generation ago.

8

Territorial Extremism in Awards of Specific Performance

PETER SPARKES*

I. INTRODUCTION

S HOULD ENGLISH COURTS order the performance of a contract to sell land in Europe? Equity assumes this power as part of its '*in personam*' jurisdiction, reliance being placed on *Penn v Lord Baltimore*[1] in almost all modern equity texts.[2] Assertion of a wide non-territorial jurisdiction is exorbitant and started from a misplaced 'arrogance' towards foreign legal systems. An order for performance of a contract to sell land overseas is real, but only a neutered '*in personam*' form of the remedy is available when the land is overseas.[3]

II. SPECIFIC PERFORMANCE IN EUROPE

Forum rules for European contract cases are laid down in the Regulation commonly known as Brussels I,[4] which applies to European Union Member States, including the United Kingdom[5] and more recently Denmark, with

---

* University of Southampton. The author wishes to thank his colleagues Nicholas Hopkins and Dr Remi Nwabueze for very helpful comments on an earlier draft.

[1] *Penn v Baltimore* (1750) 1 Ves Sen 444, 27 ER 1132; also *Penn* (interlocutory) Ridg temp Hardwicke 333, 27 ER 847; *Penn* (decree) (1750) Ves Sen Supp 194, 28 ER 498.

[2] GW Keeton and LA Sheridan (eds), *Equity*, 3rd edn (London, Rose, 1987) 10–14; G Jones and W Goodhart, *Specific Performance*, 2nd edn (London, Butterworths, 2001) 136–41; ICF Spry, *Principles of Equitable Remedies* 6th edn (London, Sweet & Maxwell, 2001) 36–50; PH Pettit, *Equity & the Law of Trusts*, 10th edn (Oxford, Oxford University Press, 2006) 665–6; J McGhee (ed), *Snell's Equity*, 31st edn (London, Sweet & Maxwell, 2005) para [5.28].

[3] FT White and OD Tudor (eds), *Leading Cases in Equity* (London, Sweet & Maxwell, 1910) I 814ff; *Hanbury & Martin's Modern Equity*, 17th edn (London, Sweet & Maxwell, 2005) para [24-004], though see at paras [1-018] and [1-036].

[4] Regulation on Jurisdiction and the Enforcement of Judgments in Civil and Commercial Matters (EC) 44/2001, [2001] OJ L12/1.

[5] Civil Jurisdiction and Judgments Act 1982 (c 27) as amended; internal allocations occur under sch 4, which is broadly similar.

the amended version set to extend to the European Economic Area in 2009.[6] Land disputes are subject to the exclusive forum of the courts of the Member State in which the land is sited 'in proceedings which have as their objects rights in rem in immovable property or tenancies of immovable property'.[7]

Contractual actions between owners (freeholders) are non-exclusive.[8] This leaves a nice question about whether or not specific performance is exclusive, a question rarely discussed in equity texts[9] and for which one needs to turn to conflicts texts for an accurate picture.[10] Specific performance in its 'real' form is exclusive but a contracting party can opt out of the exclusive forum by restricting his claim to personal aspects of the overall remedy, with disastrous results.

Ashburner stated the general principle that 'Equity acts on the person'.[11] A landowner with an overburdened conscience is offered the chance during Chancery litigation for moral regeneration but if he spurns his chance he can be forced to convey his land and, if he refuses could be imprisoned 'with the windows of his cells barred up' and, if that did not work, he could be 'put into irons'.[12] Maitland is a superhero to academics,[13] but his deduction that equity was constrained to operate *only in personam* cannot sit with Lord Cottenham's observation that: 'in this country contracts for sale ... are in certain cases made by the Courts of equity to act in rem'.[14] Specific performance demonstrates these real effects. Cambridge undergraduates could not help thinking in terms of equitable interests,[15] and they are joined by a lot of distinguished equity lawyers who might have failed the Cambridge tripos of the time.[16]

---

[6] P Sparkes, *European Land Law* (Oxford, Hart Publishing, 2007) para [4.04ff].

[7] Civil Jurisdiction Regulation, above n 4, §22[1]; this is not subject to submission or choice of forum; exclusive forum over public registers is conferred by §22[3].

[8] Case C-518/99 *Gaillard v Checkili* [2001] I ECR 2771 (ECJ); P Schlosser, *Report on UK etc Accession to the Brussels Convention* [1979] OJ C59/71 [169ff].

[9] Except Jones and Goodhart, above n 2, at 136.

[10] JJ Fawcett (ed), *Cheshire & North's Private International Law*, 13th edn (London, Butterworths, 1999) 375–86; L Collins (ed), *Dicey & Morris's Conflicts of Law*, 16th edn (London, Sweet & Maxwell, 2006) [23R-021ff]. The author wishes to acknowledge his special debt to JD Falconbridge *Essays on the Conflict of Laws*, 2nd edn (Toronto, Canada Law Books, 1954) 594ff.

[11] M Ashburner, *Principles of Equity*, 2nd edn, D Browne (ed) (London, Butterworths, 1933) 44. Hardwicke LC gives this as '*agit in personam*' where *agit* derives from *agito* (to set in continuous motion); ie the originating process was personal.

[12] Ashburner, above n 11, at 44 (was he writing historically?); Hanbury & Martin, above n 3, at para [1-036]; Falconbridge, above n 10, at 602.

[13] CHS Fifoot, *Life of FW Maitland* (Cambridge MA, Harvard University Press, 1971) 183.

[14] *Ex parte Pollard* (1838) 4 Deacon 27, 40 (Cottenham LC).

[15] Brunyate (ed), *Maitland's Equity*, 2nd edn (Cambridge, Cambridge University Press, 1947) 106, 314–15.

[16] HG Hanbury, 'Ius in Personam and Ad Rem' (1928) 44 *Law Quarterly Review* 68; Falconbridge, above n 10, at 601; RP Meagher, JD Heydon and MJ Leeming, *Equity,*

Without question equity had power to determine personal issues with foreign facts. A foreign landlord can sue an English tenant for rent but cannot do so to effect an English distress on West Indian land.[17] The personal 'substratum'[18] of the action must be a personal privity falling within one of four recognised heads—fraud, privity, contract and trust[19]—to which may be added family redistributions.[20] Thus a fraud carried out in England can be detected by the English Chancery Division, which must then leave it to the courts of the site of the land to decide whether the grant is rendered void or voidable.[21] This procedure is wholly unobjectionable provided that fraud means fraud.[22] In trusts there is the same distinction between supervising the trustees of foreign trusts and vesting foreign land in English trustees.[23]

Some aspects of specific performance are personal as is shown by the decree in *Penn v Baltimore*.[24] The parties were ordered, after the surveying was complete, to execute releases settled by the Master to confirm legal title to the newly-defined boundaries, a personal order to execute a conveyance.[25] This was to go back to the form of specific performance awarded at the start of the reign of James I, when the order to execute a conveyance was backed up by indefinite imprisonment in Ashburner's 'irons' and perhaps the (near real) sequestration but excluding any orders about possession.

Jurisdiction rules for contractual actions in Europe are complex. An express choice of forum may be made, and possibly appropriately where, say, one English family sells a Spanish holiday home to another English family, and any choice that is made will be presumed to be exclusive.[26] An English forum may follow from a choice of English law for contractual aspects of a transaction, though a choice of law cannot extend to the land

---

Doctrines and Remedies, 4th edn (NSW, Butterworths Australia, 2002) para [3.224]; PBH Birks, 'In Rem or In Personam?' (1994) 8 *Trust Law International* 99–101.

[17] *Vincent v Godson* (1854) 4 De GM & G 546, 43 ER 620 (Cranworth LC). European site-based courts have exclusive forum over actions derived from leases: Civil Jurisdiction Regulation, above n 4, §22[1].

[18] RC Horne (ed), *Lewin on Trusts*, 15th edn (London, Sweet & Maxwell, 1950) 36.

[19] *Deschamps v Miller* [1908] 1 Ch 856, 863 (Parker J); Spry, above n 2, at 45.

[20] *Hamlin v Hamlin* [1986] Fam 11 (CA).

[21] *Arglass v Muschamp* (1682) 1 Vern 76, 23 ER 322 (Nottingham LC); (1682?) 1 Vern 135, 23 ER 369; (1684) 1 Vern 237, 23 ER 438 (North LK); *Innes v Mitchell* (1857) 4 Drew 56, 62 ER 22.

[22] 'There is ... some danger of doing injustice if the strict rules which the English Court of Chancery has applied to dealings with trust property are applied to a case between foreigners under foreign law': *Concha v Concha* [1892] AC 670 (HL) 675 (Lord Macnaghten); this statement would be improved by omission of the word 'some'.

[23] *Chellaram v Chellaram* [1985] Ch 409 (Ch) 427, 428 (Scott J); also many other cases.

[24] *Penn* (decree), above n 1.

[25] *Penn v Baltimore*, above n 1; *Richardson v Hamilton* (1735) cited in 2 Hare 643n, 67 ER 265; *Annesley v Anglesey* (1743) Dick 90, 21 ER 202 (Hardwicke LC); *Portarlington v Soulby* (1834) 3 My & K 103, 108; 40 ER 40 (Brougham LC); White and Tudor, above n 3, at 814.

[26] Civil Jurisdiction Regulation, above n 4, §23.

law aspects.[27] In the absence of an explicit choice, a forum may be deduced from the place of performance of the principal obligation of the contract, though here there is an ambiguity about whether that means the site as the place where possession of the land is to be handed over, or whether it can be the place of execution of a transfer, which is not necessarily site-based. A defaulting party can also be sued where he is domiciled[28] or where he has submitted to the court's jurisdiction[29] and amongst the multiplicity of possible actions a first seised rule applies.[30] An English contract to sell Spanish land is determined in England if action is taken there first but sent to the Spanish courts if the Spanish action has priority, with substantive results that may vary wildly.

Traditional equity was based on personal presence in England. Even a casual day trip could found jurisdiction, so debtors had to go to Boulogne and stay there, and once served with proceedings a writ *ne exeat regno* would prevent a defendant from leaving the kingdom.[31] Casual presence no longer suffices without domicile. In *Penn v Baltimore* itself the parties were resident in America where the negotiation took place, but the agreement was sealed in London and the parties submitted to the jurisdiction of the King's Council.[32] Power has existed since the nineteenth century to serve overseas when a case is connected to England, for example, by a choice of English law.[33] Equitable *in personam* jurisdiction must now flex again to fit with the European conceits.

Brussels I has distorted the whole question of equitable jurisdiction, since too many equitable actions are treated as personal, and the consequence has been to reopen the possibility of equity ruling, or overruling, the whole of Europe. An eccentric view was taken in the European Court of Justice in *Webb v Webb*.[34] In 1971, a father had purchased a flat at

---

[27] Rome Convention on the Law Applicable to Contractual Obligations [2005] OJ C334/1 §4; Sparkes, *English Land Law*, above n 6, ch 10. Dicey & Morris, above n 10, at para [33-237] state that the law of the contract determines (1) whether an equitable mortgage or equitable charge exists and (2) whether specific performance should be awarded and how the discretion should be exercised; but the situation is complicated by the fact that the mandatory rules and public policy exception ensure that a core of any land contract is site based. Dicey & Morris overstate the position because all civilian systems have a numerus clausus of proprietary rights which precludes recognition of equities.

[28] Civil Jurisdiction Regulation, above n 4, §2[1] (unless an exclusive choice of forum has been made). This paper assumes that the buyer is not a consumer.

[29] Civil Jurisdiction Regulation, above n 4, §24.

[30] Civil Jurisdiction Regulation, above n 4, §27[1] ('involving the same cause of action and between the same parties').

[31] This overcame the problem in *Archer v Preston* (Nottingham LC), cited in *Arglass v Muschamp* (1682) 1 Vern 76, 23 ER 322.

[32] *Penn v Baltimore*, above n 1, at 446–7.

[33] *Duder v Amsterdamsch Trustees Kantnor* [1902] 2 Ch 132 (Byrne J).

[34] Case C–294/92 *Webb v Webb* [1994] I ECR 1717 (ECJ). Searching criticism by A Briggs, 'Trusts of Land and the Brussels Convention' (1994) 110 *Law Quarterly Review* 526–31 represents the sense of the vast majority of the English comment.

Antibes on the French Riviera, the transfer being taken in the name of his son who became registered as owner. Twenty years later, in 1991, the father sought a declaration from the English Chancery Division that the son held the apartment on a resulting trust and an order requiring the son to transfer the legal title to the father, though not a (real) vesting order.[35] The issue of whether or not there had been an advancement had to wait until forum was decided. The European Court of Justice held that the action did not aim to establish rights *in rem* in French immovable property and so was not the exclusive property of the courts of the Alpes Maritimes. Thus a declaration of ownership, an order to effect a transfer and a claim to be registered are personal in Europe, as, strangely, is an order for sale.[36] If these claims had related to the legal estate they must all have been within the exclusive French jurisdiction. It is one thing to enforce a true trust against French land, but a long stride further to a case like *Webb* which concerns a claim to a bare trust of the *Saunders v Vautier* type,[37] and if there was no gift the result would be an order to pass the legal estate. This decision distorted the original intention of the framers of the Brussels rulebook.

In *Webb*[38] English and French proceedings might have involved the same cause of action but the English action was not 'principally concerned with' the ownership of land[39] because of the limited remedies claimed. Cut-down real actions are personal. An '*in personam*' order for specific performance of a contract to sell the legal estate has to be classified as personal in the erroneous European sense of the word personal and, in that wide sense, even real specific performance might be personal.

III. ORDERING POSSESSION

Full specific performance is real because it passes possession and precisely for this reason it cannot be awarded for land sited overseas, since equity does nothing in vain. Hardwicke LC's decree in *Penn v Baltimore*[40] ordered the appointment of surveyors in England and also execution of releases settled by the Master to confirm legal title to the newly-surveyed

---

[35] *Re Hayward* [1997] Ch 45, 56–7 Rattee J (villa in Minorca). Query whether it was open to the son in *Webb*, above n 34, to enter a torpedo defence ie an application for a negative declaration that the father was not entitled to be registered.

[36] *Ashurst v Pollard* [2001] Ch 595 (CA); JM Carruthers, *Transfer of Property in the Conflict of Law* (Oxford, Oxford University Press, 2005) para [2.39ff] (should be real).

[37] *Saunders v Vautier* (1841) Cr & Ph 240, 41 ER 482; Birks, above n 16.

[38] *Webb v Webb*, above n 34.

[39] Civil Jurisdiction Regulation, above n 4, §§25, 27[1].

[40] *Penn* (decree), above n 1.

boundaries, an *in personam* power that was no novelty as early as 1750.[41] White and Tudor[42] deserve a belated gold star for preserving a distinction lost in most modern discussions derived primarily from the modes of enforcement.[43]

Three aspects of the execution of a decree of specific performance might be seen as real. If imprisonment failed to secure compliance a sequestration would be laid on the contemnor's land, commissioners being appointed to take possession of the defendant's goods and also of the rents and profits from his land.[44] Since this was done by writ of possession, it was almost real. It seems to demonstrate that: 'A decree of the Court of Chancery, *unless it was for land*, originally operated only in personam' (emphasis added).[45] Power to sequestrate was contested vigorously by the common lawyers—who treated equitable sequestrators as mere trespassers with the implication that it was justifiable homicide to kill one[46]—and was not available overseas.[47]

Possession[48] and the appointment of a full receiver[49] are real remedies of the kind that are refused against foreign land, as is partition.[50] Orders to quiet possession were a part of specific performance after the time of James I. A writ to execute a decree was accompanied by an injunction ordering the losing party not to interfere with the winner's possession and a writ of assistance was directed to the sheriff instructing him to provide the muscle

---

[41] *Penn v Baltimorei*, above n 1; *Richardson v Hamilton*, above n 25; *Annesley v Angleseyi*, above n 25.

[42] White and Tudor, above n 3, at 814; Cheshire & North, above n 10, at 375–86.

[43] The form of the action must be irrelevant (to all except the ultra wing of the Hohfeldians) since the common law used a (personal) action in trespass for the (real) object of the recovery of land (ejectment).

[44] *Company of Horners in London* (1625) 2 Rolle 471, 81 ER 923; Jones & Goodhart, above n 2, at 256.

[45] ER Daniell, *Pleading & Practice in the High Court of Chancery*, 2nd edn, T Headlam (ed) (Boston MA, Little & Brown, 1846) vol I 789ff. Priority existed on bankruptcy and sequestration was supported by sale but was less than fully proprietary in that it was not to be had against an heir.

[46] '20 Jac Elwes. Indictment for a murder for laying on a sequestration, one being killed: Question if justifiable or not, Pardon sued out': *Colston v Gardner* (1680) 2 Ch Cas 43, 22 ER 838 (Nottingham LC); WW Cook, 'Powers of Courts of Equity' (1915) 15 *Columbia Law Review* 106, 167.

[47] *Fryer v Bernard* (1724) 2 P Wms 261, 24 ER 722, was doubted in *Portarlington v Soulby*, above n 25. Power lay in the King in Council.

[48] *Angus v Angus* (1737) West temp Hardwicke 23, 25 ER 800; *Roberdeau v Rous* (1738) 1 Atk 545, 26 ER 342; *Black Point Syndicate v Eastern Concession* (1898) 79 LT 658 (Ch) 661 (Stirling J); Cook, above n 46, at 128.

[49] *Reiner v Salisbury* (1875) 2 Ch D 378, 385 (Malins V-C).

[50] *Cartwright v Pettus* (1676) 2 Ch Cas 214, 22 ER 916; also as *Carterett v Pettie* Rep temp Finch 242, 23 ER 133; (1818) 2 Swans 313, 323–4; 36 ER 635. But why could there not be a personal order to partition?

needed to enforce the transfer of possession.[51] Possession is not granted as a matter of course today but rather it is obtained under a supplementary order executed by writ of possession.[52]

Such an order *in rem* could not be made in relation to the Maryland-Pennsylvania border, and it would have been vain to attempt enforcement.[53] Hence the refusal in *Penn v Baltimore* to order the quiet enjoyment of land in America, which could only result in repeated applications for contempt. 'If the parties want more to be done they must resort to another jurisdiction'.[54] For the same reason it would be wrong to order the inspection of land overseas.[55]

American courts view decrees quieting possession as real[56] and so limited to the American State where the land is sited, although this doctrine remains controversial.[57]

A further step towards reality was the power, originally proposed by Sir Edward Sugden,[58] to vest property itself. This power is now available after a High Court[59] judgment directing a person to execute a conveyance, contract or other document in cases of neglect, refusal[60] or absence. The Court appoints a 'master extraordinary' out of London to execute the document and if there is no explicit territorial limitation there is also no sign of cases where the power has been used overseas. In American law the power is *in rem*.[61]

An English court considering performance in specie of a contract relating to foreign land inevitably treads on the toes of a foreign court holding full powers.[62]

---

[51] *Stribley v Hawkie* (1744) 3 Atk 275, 26 ER 961; *Huguenin v Baseley* (1808) 15 Ves 180, 33 ER 722 (Eldon LC).

[52] Rules of the Supreme Court Order 46; *Mir v Mir* [1992] Fam 79 Scott (Baker J) (execution of document ordered in support of sequestration).

[53] *Norris v Chambres* (1861) 3 De GF & J 581, 45 ER 1004 (Lord Campbell).

[54] *Penn v Baltimorei*, above n 1, at 454 (Hardwicke LC).

[55] As Templeman J did in *Cook Industries v Galliher* [1979] Ch 439 (flat in Paris); Jones and Goodhart, above n 2, at 138.

[56] *Fall v Eastin* 215 US 1 (1909) (Washington divorce court ordered husband to convey to wife 160 acres of Nebraska).

[57] W Barbour, 'Extra Territorial Effect of Equitable Decrees' (1918) 17 *Michigan Law Review* 527; EG Lorenzen, 'Equitable Decrees Conveying Foreign Land' (1924) 34 *Yale Law Journal* 591; B Currie, 'Full Faith and Credit to Foreign Land Decrees' (1953) 21 *University of Chicago Law Review* 620; M Hancock, 'The Supreme Court and the Land Taboo' (1965) 18 *Stanford Law Review* 1299.

[58] Sir Edward Sugden's Act 1830 (11 Geo IV &1 Wm IV c 36) s 15 rule 15; Daniell, above n 45, vol II 1334–5.

[59] Supreme Court Act 1981 c 54 s 39; Rules of the Supreme Court Order 45 r 7; each is to be renamed 'Senior Courts'.

[60] *Beale v Bragg* [1902] 1 IR 99 V-C (solicitor conveys in name of party refusing); *Savage v Norton* [1908] 1 Ch 290 (Parker J).

[61] *Fall v Eastin*, above n 56, US Supreme Court; Cook (above n 46) at 126ff.

[62] Falconbridge, above n 10, at 603–5.

IV. WANT OF A (SUITABLE) COURT AT THE SITE

The case commonly cited for an '*in personam*' approach to specific performance is *Penn v Lord Baltimore*[63] in which Lord Hardwicke LC, 'the most consummate judge who ever sat in the Court of Chancery',[64] settled the boundaries of Maryland and Pennsylvania while sitting in London.[65] The case does not, in itself, support a general power to award specific performance of contracts affecting foreign land.

Delaware, known at the time as the 'Three Lower Counties', was acquired from Dutch settlers by the Duke of York and then sold on to Penn. Hence the more or less northerly State line splitting the Delaware Peninsular, which was settled by the Board of Plantations on reference by the King's Council. At its northern limit this straight line hit a unique circular boundary drawn to a radius of 12 miles round New Castle, a distance insisted upon by the Catholic Duke of York to keep Penn's Quakers[66] at arm's length. This 12-mile radius was afterwards transferred to Penn by a feoffment with full livery of seisin,[67] creating a ticklish problem of estoppel.[68] Disputes remained about the join between the straight Delaware-Maryland line and the curved line round New Castle until 1922.

Pennsylvania to the north was separated from Maryland to the south by a line fixed by Lord Hardwicke LC and settled on the ground as the Mason-Dixon line[69] more or less along a line of parallel at North 39 degrees, 43 minutes and 20 seconds. Maryland had been granted in 1632 to the second Lord Baltimore up to the 40th degree of latitude, so a literal interpretation would move the State line 20 miles to the north and would cause Gettysburg to switch State along with half of Philadelphia. Uncertainty was compounded when Charles II made a conflicting grant to William Penn, son of an admiral to whom Charles owed money, seeming to fix a line 20 miles further to the south. A compromise was eventually agreed in 1732 between Penn's sons and the fifth Lord Baltimore.[70] This effectively

---

[63] *Penn v Baltimore*, above n 1.

[64] J Campbell, *Lives of the Lord Chancellors* (London, John Murray, 1846) V 1.

[65] Chancery generally sat in Westminster Hall, but it is often said that this case was heard in the Old Hall of Lincoln's Inn perhaps based on the statement in Campbell, *ibid*, 39–40, that Hardwicke once sat as Lord Chancellor in Lincoln's Inn and as Chief Justice in Westminster Hall on the same day.

[66] Penn is not, as is popularly believed, pictured on the Quaker's Oats porridge packet.

[67] By symbolic delivery of turf, a twig, a porringer of river water and some soil.

[68] York's de facto title was only perfected later by a grant from his brother, Charles II, and when York acceded as the ill-fated James II, an estoppel was held to arise against the monarch, affirmed in *New Jersey v Delaware* 291 US 361 (1933) US Supreme Court; the papers cover 25 volumes.

[69] Charles Mason was surveyor and assistant at Greenwich and Jeremiah Dixon was an astronomer from Durham; their work was undertaken between 1763 and 1767.

[70] Agreement was reached between principals resident in the Americas, but the agreement was sealed in England and personal jurisdiction was also based on submission to the Council;

split the difference and is what was decreed by Hardwicke LC and carried into effect on the ground by Mason and Dixon. Baltimore reneged and the Hanoverian Council instructed the parties to litigate. A bill for specific performance of the boundary settlement was filed in Chancery in 1735 and came to court after a leisurely 15 years devoted to pleadings but Lord Hardwicke dispatched it in five days[71] with a comprehensive victory for the Penns.[72]

In course of time *Penn v Baltimore* has become authority for the proposition that the jurisdiction to award specific performance of a contract for land overseas is the same as if the land were situated in England.[73] There are a few dissenters.[74] Taken to an extreme it seemed to suggest that '*in personam*' equity could rule, even overrule, the world, making London the specific performance capital of the world in preference to the courts of America or Scotland or France.[75] These absurd results find no support in the case itself, which did not infringe any other territorial jurisdiction.[76] Had the case been fought out after independence in 1776 the whole case would have been left to the American Federal courts.[77] Before a constitution was adopted there was no court in America that could resolve rival claims to Maryland and Pennsylvania, which were separate 'provinces' owned by proprietors with power to wage war, on each other, as they did (in Cresap's War). Absence of a court would have been a ground for the Court of Chancery to step in within the Crown's dominions,[78] though this

---

Pen (interlocutory), above n 1, at 335 (Hardwicke LC); TM Yeo, *Choice of Law for Equitable Doctrines* (Oxford, Oxford University Press, 2004) para [4.23].

[71] Hardwicke LC 'abstaining his bottle at lunchtime', unlike his contemporaries, often sat in the afternoon or evening: Campbell, above n 64, at 49.

[72] Factors were poor work by Baltimore's solicitors and strong work for the Penns by William Murray, the future Lord Mansfield: J Carroll Hayes, 'A Brief for the Penns' (1940) 7–8 *Pennsylvania History* 278.

[73] E Fry, *Specific Performance*, 6th edn, GR Northcote (ed) (London, Sweet & Maxwell, 1920) para [126]; Keeton, above n 2, at para [5.28]; Spry, above n 2, at 36; Yeo, above n 70, at para [4.23].

[74] Falconbridge, above n 10, at 616 ('embarrassing questions'); Jones and Goodhart, above n 2, at 138ff; Hanbury & Martin, above n 3, at para [24-004].

[75] Civilian systems vary about whether to order performance in specie, but the English courts ignore such matters.

[76] Territoriality may have been infringed in *Toller v Carteret* (1705) 2 Vern 494, 23 ER 916; *Derby v Athol* (1748) 1 Ves Sen 202, 204; 27 ER 982; *Paget v Ede* (1874) LR 18 Eq 118 (Bacon V-C). A mortgage of Sark was foreclosed in Chancery when Guernsey was the proper forum; however, Sark was a fief of the Duke of Normandy (the Crown) so again the Crown's feudal court was arguably proper; this is why the case emphasises that the mortgage was of the whole island.

[77] *New Jersey v Delaware*, above n 68, at 363 (Justice Cardozo) (original jurisdiction of the Supreme Court).

[78] *Admiral Palliser's case* Lord Mansfield, discussed in *Mostyn v Fabrigas* (1774) 1 Comp 161, 181; 98 ER 1021; *Skinner v East India Co* (1666) 6 State Trials 710, 719 (dispossession of an Indian house and the island of 'Barella' not justiciable at law).

may not survive the *Moçambique* case.[79] Modern courts cannot impinge on sovereign immunity by determining international boundaries, nor any transactions by foreign states.[80] At the time of *Penn* a dispute about boundaries had to be settled in the feudal court of the English King, either the Board of Plantations or the King in Council,[81] and it was indeed the Hanoverian Council which transferred the main dispute to Chancery in 1735.[82] Hardwicke LC was thus acting in support of a properly seised and best placed court.[83]

Wider early cases were explicable on the basis that 'the foreign court was a colonial court and the English judges viewed them as inferior'.[84] Was this arrogance or a desire to be over-inclusive rather than to deny justice altogether? English judges once thought of themselves as the proper exponents of the law of Ireland,[85] before appeals and reviews were prohibited,[86] but the same arrogance continued towards America,[87] the West Indies,[88] India and Scotland.[89] Today former colonies are as one with foreign countries.[90]

Shadwell V-C stretched all this out to form a world view in a memorable dictum, all too easy to misquote, that in the contemplation of the Court of Chancery, 'every foreign court is an Inferior Court'.[91] Capitalisation of the final two words makes clear that he was using an unfortunate way of stating a truth—that discovery could not be called in aid of foreign courts technically called 'Inferior'. This becomes an unfortunate untruth when the case of the final words is switched,[92] but even when read in its

---

[79] *British South African Co v Compania de Moçambique* [1892] 2 QB 358 (Div Ct & CA); [1893] AC 602 (HL); contrast (1) Div Ct at 366–7 (Wright J) and HL at 619–20 (Herschell LC) with (2) HL at 625 (Herschell LC).

[80] *Buttes Gas & Oil Co v Hammer* [1982] AC 888 (HL) 926, 931 (Lord Wilberforce).

[81] *Penn v Baltimore*, above n 1, at 446; note to *Innes v Mitchell*, above n 21; *Bishop of Sodor & Man v Derby* (1751) 2 Ves Sen 337, 28 ER 217 (Hardwicke LC); Hanbury & Martin, above n 3, at para [24-004].

[82] *Penn* (interlocutory), above n 1, at 337; *Penn v Baltimore*, above n 1, at 447. Hardwicke LC at 446 likened his position as decision maker to that of the Roman Senate.

[83] *Penn v Baltimore*, (above n 1, at 447–8; *Morgan's case* (1737) 1 Atk 408, 26 ER 259; *Re Kooperman* [1928] WN 101.

[84] Jones and Goodhart, above n 2, at 141 fn 4; Spry, above n 2, at 40.

[85] *Kildare v Eustace* (1686) 1 Vern 419, 23 ER 559; *Foster v Vassal* (1747) 3 Atk 587, 26 ER 1138; *Roberdeau*, above n 48; White and Tudor, above n 3, at 821.

[86] Irish Appeals Act 1783 (George III c 28) s 2; *Portarlington* (above n 25) at 109 (Brougham LC).

[87] *Richardson v Hamilton*, above n 25, (personal process ordered in Pennsylvania).

[88] *Cranstown v Johnston* (1796) 3 Ves 170, 182; 30 ER 952 (Arden MR); *Tulloch v Hartley* (1841) 1 Y & CCC 114, 62 ER 84 (Knight Bruce LJ).

[89] 'One equity' suggested the argument (albeit unsuccessful) in *Holmes v The Queen* (1861) 31 LJ Ch 58 (Wood V-C) that the Queen could be sued in England in relation to Canadian land because of deemed residence throughout her Dominions.

[90] White and Tudor, above n 3, at 816.

[91] *Bent v Young* (1839) 9 Sim 180, 191, 59 ER 327.

[92] Dicey & Morris, above n 10, at para [23-050].

technical sense still supports the charge of 'arrogance'. *Penn v Baltimore*[93] is very narrow, but provides the excuse for territorial expansionism when subverted by wily Chancery practitioners eager for fees. The modern tendency is to limit *in personam* equity for fear of doing indirectly what the court dare not do directly.[94]

V. FOREIGN TITLE

English courts should not adjudicate on the title or right to possession of immovable property out of the jurisdiction, so performance abroad can generally be blocked by challenging title, and *in personam* specific performance lacks mutuality.

The title bar at common law precludes an action for recovery of (that is 'ejectment' from) foreign land.[95] This, *Doulson v Matthews*[96] decided, was an action local to the shire within which the land was sited, but still prohibited after the abolition of the localness of actions.[97] Damages cannot be claimed where the title is in issue; thus in the *Moçambique* case the claim was to damages of £250,000 (at 1893 values) arising from rival Portuguese and English grants of mining rights in Manica, Portuguese territory near the Mozambique border. Modern legislation has taken a backward step to allow damages where title and possession are *not* in issue.[98]

Equity followed the law's[99] self-denying ordinance since it determined uncertain titles by enquiry,[100] in that way mimicking the common law.[101] In *Moçambique* itself a declaration of title and injunction were refused at first instance and the claim for these remedies was abandoned before the appellate courts.[102] *Deschamps v Miller*[103] is often cited for a dictum of Parker J justifying an '*in personam*' jurisdiction rather than its ratio.

---

[93] *Penn v Baltimore*, above n 1.

[94] *Moçambique* (CA), above n 79, at 404–5 (Lord Esher MR), subsequently affirmed by HL; *Black Point*, above n 48, at 661 (Stirling J); Jones and Goodhart, above n 2, at 45, 138 fn 2, 139; GW Keeton, 'Trusts in the Conflict of Laws' [1951] *Current Legal Problems* 107, 109.

[95] *Moçambique* (HL), above n 79; *Hesperides Hotels v Muftizade* [1979] AC 508 (HL). Contrast trespass to the person: *Mostyn v Fabrigas* (above n 78).

[96] *Doulson v Matthews* (1792) 4 Term R 503, 100 ER 1143 (Lord Kenyon CJ and Buller J) (house in Canada); *Moçambique* (HL), above n 79, at 633 (Herschell LC).

[97] *Moçambique* (HL), above n 79, at 628–9 (Herschell LC).

[98] Civil Jurisdiction and Judgments Act 1982, above n 5 s 30; *Re Polly Peck International (No 2)* [1998] 3 All ER 812 (CA) 828g–829h (Mummery LJ); Cheshire & North, above n 10, at 384.

[99] *Moçambique* (CA), above n 79, at 404–5 (Esher MR); Spry, above n 2, at 39.

[100] Daniell, above n 45, vol II 1203–4.

[101] Charles Yorke's opinion on Lord Clive's jaghire I in F Hargrave, *Collectanea Juridica* (London, 1792) 246, 248 (available on Google Books).

[102] *Moçambique* (CA), above n 79, at 415 (Lopes LJ).

[103] *Deschamps v Miller*, above n 19, at 863 (Parker J).

An English administrator failed to secure possession of land in India already vested in an Indian administrator and this was all to the good because the argument to be run was that the settlement in favour of a second wife infringed the French matrimonial regime of the first wife. What could English courts know about that? Sale should not be ordered[104] nor an account of the proceeds of sale of a house.[105] Peripheral issues of title were decided, for example the ownership of land on a Pacific island as the necessary qualification for a plaintiff to succeed in his claim to benefit under a trust.[106] Courts of equity could act on the conscience of residents and doing so could affect mediately (but not immediately) rights to land abroad.[107]

Growth of equitable powers over foreign land was effectively curbed since few states allowed foreigners unrestrained access to the domestic market in land. Specific performance could not be awarded in London of a contract whose vitality depended upon the licence of a foreign land-control board. Any restraint on alienation (meaning acquisition) scuppered equity unless a preliminary enquiry removed the uncertainty.[108] Equity was kept at bay by limiting free purchase to nationals. Reforms of the internal market implemented at Maastricht have made it more likely that access to European markets will be unrestricted, though controls may still exist and may be internal market compliant.[109] Issues of capacity raise the same substantive bar.[110]

Any issue of third-party title or priority must be left to the courts of the site.[111] Privity is lacking when a purchaser sues a third party to whom the vendor has sold,[112] when rent is claimed from an assignee,[113] and when registration of a mortgage has been overlooked.[114] Had Maitland been right a personal equity could be imposed on a buyer with notice but this

---

[104] *Grey v Manitoba Railway* [1897] AC 254 (PC) (Manitoba courts cannot order sale of stretch of railway which crosses into the North West Territory).

[105] *Re Hawthorne* (1883) 23 Ch D 743 (Kay J); Falconbridge, above n 10, at 618.

[106] *Tito v Waddell* [1977] Ch 106, 262–3 (Megarry V-C).

[107] *Houlditch v Donegal* (1834) 8 Bli NS 955, 5 ER 955 (HL Ireland); *Moçambique* (HL), above n 79, at 626 (Herschell LC).

[108] *Waterhouse v Stansfield* (1851) 9 Hare 234, 68 ER 489, (1852) 10 Hare 254, 68 ER 921; *Ex parte Pollard*, above n 14, at 40 (Cottenham LC); *Hicks v Powell* (1868) LR 4 Ch App 741 (CA in Chancery).

[109] Sparkes, *European Land Law*, above n 6, ch 2.

[110] *Bank of Africa v Cohen* [1909] 2 Ch 129 (CA) (guarantee by South African woman of husband's debts required prior warnings); the case is criticised by Dicey & Morris, above n 10, at para [23-067].

[111] *Innes v Mitchell*, above n 21, fn at 99; Fry, above n 73, at para [128].

[112] *Norris v Chambres*, above n 53.

[113] *Vincent v Godson*, above n 17.

[114] White and Tudor, above n 3, at 820ff; *Norton v Florence Land & Public Works Co* (1877) 7 Ch D 332, Jessel MR (registration of mortgage in Florence not proved).

step has been taken in only a single, egregious, decision.[115] It is wrong to impose notice on an immoral world. Third-party title to chattels may be a question of choice of law but the core of a land contract must be site-based even where a choice of law is made.[116]

Want of title can be manipulated by a buyer, but not by the seller, so the doctrine that results from specific performance on vacation is a misshapen beast lacking mutuality. When the seller's title is not accepted there must be a reference as to title,[117] a wily buyer challenges the seller's title,[118] and only a buyer sued at a late stage after the concession of title can be compelled *in personam.*[119]

Walsh v Lonsdale[120] is a 'somewhat difficult and dangerous case'.[121] A contract for a lease of a mill for seven years failed at law for want of formality, but was held to create a lease in equity under which the landlord could distrain for rent in advance. Availability of specific performance justifies a substantivisation[122] or reification of the equity, which overcomes problems such as 'unclean hands' on the part of the tenant.[123] If 'equity treats as done that which ought to be done' the equity may be applied with prospectivity, overcoming the then prevalent delays. And so, to misquote Maitland, 'an agreement for a lease is as good as a lease'.[124] That was the doctrine applied to a contract for a lease of a mill in Darwen just south of Blackburn, but would the equity have been the same if the land had been just south of Madrid or of Aix en Provence? The answer is a very limited yes. First it applies in practice only to an agreement to create a charge,[125] since the lender is not going to dispute title but will grab whatever title is on offer.[126] Secondly it applies only when the existence of the equitable

---

[115] *Mercantile Investment & General Trust Co v River Plate Trust Loan & Agency Co* [1892] 2 Ch 303 North J (charge on 17.5 million acres of Lower California); Cheshire & North, above n 10, at 382–3. The point was overlooked by Brougham LC in *Portarlington,* above n 25; and *Griggs Group v Evans* [2004] EWHC 1088, [2005] Ch 153, [110–111] Peter Prescott QC must be doubted.

[116] *Macmillan v Bishopsgate Investment Trust (No 3)* [1995] 1 WLR 978 (Ch) 980–90 (Millett J), affirmed on other grounds [1996] 1 WLR 387 (CA).

[117] Fry, above n 73, at paras [878ff], [1145], [1316].

[118] *Enolin v Wylie* (1862) 10 HLC 1, 11 ER 924.

[119] *Richard West & Partners (Inverness) v Dick* [1969] 2 Ch 424, 429 Megarry V-C, approved in CA (title had been approved and the conveyance executed in escrow when expensive fire requirements were discovered).

[120] *Walsh v Lonsdale* (1882) 21 Ch D 9 (CA).

[121] *Maitland's Equity,* above n 15, at 156.

[122] Yeo, above n 70, at para [4.24ff].

[123] *Coatsworth v Johnston* (1886) 55 LJQB 220 (CA); this has been reversed by statute: P Sparkes 'Forfeiture of Equitable Leases' (1987) 16 *Anglo-American Law Review* 160.

[124] *Maitland's Equity,* above n 15, at 158; this was stated by Maitland as a fallacy, but the succeeding passage makes clear that it is broadly true inter partes.

[125] *United Bank of Kuwait v Sahib* [1997] Ch 107 (CA) decides that the basis of the equitable mortgage is an agreement to charge; contrast Fry, above n 73, at para [38].

[126] Falconbridge, above n 10, at 605.

charge is in issue on an English insolvency;[127] an equitable charge cannot be imposed in a state blissfully ignorant of equity. No property right is created in the land.

Failure of a foreign court to recognise an equitable charge ought to be a complete bar of title—as would be the case if the claimed right was legal—but the '*in personam*' theory allows equities unknown locally.[128]

> The courts ... in administering equities between parties residing here act upon their own rules and are not influenced by any consideration of what the effects of such contracts might be in the country where the lands are situate, or of the manner in which the courts of such countries might deal with such equities.[129]

Courts of the site of the land should be able 'to grant or to deny acquisitive effect to the contract itself'.[130]

Hence the strange concept of a security not secured on the security. Thus we have the mortgage by deposit of the title deeds to land in Scotland[131] carrying no right to possession,[132] the mortgage by deposit of a house in Shanghai[133] or Brazil[134] contrary to the respective site-based laws, an '*in personam*' floating charge,[135] receivers without possession,[136] and mortgages of West Indian land redeemed in England but still subsisting in the West Indies.[137] Not to mention '*in personam*' foreclosure,[138] a strange beast lacking the usual order for possession,[139] or common-law ejectment[140] and

---

[127] *Re Scheibler* (1873) LR 9 Ch App 722, 728 (Mellish LJ). The Insolvency Proceedings Regulation (EC) 1346/2000, [2000] OJ L160/1, §5, requires that security rights (described as 'rights in rem' but including equitable security) recognised at the site of the land be respected elsewhere in Europe: Sparkes, *European Land Law*, above n 6, at para [9.49ff]. This suggests also the converse that English proceedings should not recognise '*in personam*' security against French land.

[128] *Ex parte Pollard*, above n 14, at 40–41 Lord Cottenham LC; Yeo, above n 73, at para [1.34ff]; *Re The Anchor Line* [1937] Ch 483, 488 Luxmoore J; Spry, above n 2, at 40–41. What is the difference between non registration of a mortgage, above n 114, and its non existence?

[129] White and Tudor, above n 3, at 820ff.

[130] GC Venturini, 'Property' ch 21 in *International Encyclopaedia of Comparative Law* (Tubingen, Germany, Mohr; The Hague, Netherlands, Mouton, 1976) vol III 23; Carruthers, above n 36, at para [4.03]; Falconbridge, above n 10, at 608.

[131] *Coote v Jecks* (1872) LR 13 Eq 597 (Bacon V-C).

[132] *Angus*, above n 48. The personal character was shown by refusing possession; *Innes v Mitchell* (above n 21) note suggests that the decision rests on the interlocutory stage at which it was decided.

[133] *Re Scheibler*, above n 127, CA in Chancery.

[134] *Duder v Amsterdamsch Trustees Kantnor*, above n 33.

[135] *The Anchor Line*, above n 128.

[136] *Re Maudslay Sons & Field* [1900] 1 Ch 602 (Cozens-Hardy J).

[137] *Cranstown v Johnston*, above n 88.

[138] See above n 76; these cases were subjected to searching criticism by Falconbridge, above n 10, at 618–20.

[139] Daniell, above n 45, vol II 1212, 1227–8.

[140] *Heath v Pugh* (1880) LR 6 QB 345 (CA) 360, 362 (Selborne LC), approved (1881) 7 App Cas 235 (HL).

in any event substituted by a (real?) order for sale when the land affected by the foreclosure was overseas.[141] Nowadays a true foreclosure moves the legal estate and must be real in every sense. Lack of coherence is a problem with common-law mortgages[142] and an insurmountable hurdle with civilian hypothecs.[143]

Almost all of the sting is removed from the theoretical possibility of territorial expansionism by the removal from *Walsh v Lonsdale*[144] of proprietary effect overseas. A formal bar would better avoid the odd results just demonstrated.

VI. LIMITING THE INCONVENIENCE OF EXTRA-TERRITORIALITY

Scotland remains an independent, foreign, and often hostile kingdom.[145] Lord Hardwicke's *in personam* jurisdiction must have been received with considerable suspicion north of the border. George II was summering in Hanover when the Young Pretender landed in 1745, so Hardwicke, his Lord Chancellor, was head of the regency. He presided at the trials of the principal Scottish 'traitors' after Culloden and afterwards imposed the 'Coercion Act', banning Highland dress and forcing the inhabitants 'to wear breeches', though sadly he stopped short of banning the bagpipe![146]

At the time of the Union Scotland forgot to tell equity to stay away. Thus in *Richard West & Partners (Inverness) v Dick*[147] Megarry V-C granted English specific performance of a contract for the sale of land in Scotland to a Scottish firm because the purchaser was resident in England. The decision was affirmed by the Court of Appeal after the buyer, arguing in person, failed to dent the Vice Chancellor's judgment. Snell[148] showed that there was an undoubted jurisdiction, but Sir Robert was puzzled that counsel had not been able to produce a single case in which foreign specific performance had been awarded of a straightforward contract of sale. His puzzlement resulted from a limited citation of *Ewing v Orr Ewing*. A Scottish testator died leaving land in Scotland and personalty of both persuasions

---

[141] *Beckford v Kemble* (1822) 1 Sim & Stu 15, 57 ER 3 as explained in *Cranstown v Johnston* (1796) 1 Ves Jun Supp 355 n [5], 34 ER 824.

[142] *Harrison v Gurney* (1821) 2 Jac & Walk 563, 37 ER 743 (Lord Eldon LC); *Clarke v Ormonde* (1821) Jac 108, 546; 37 ER 791, 956; *Jenny v Mackintosh* (1886) 33 Ch D 595; *Duder* (above n 33).

[143] Falconbridge, above n 10, at 619.

[144] *Walsh v Lonsdale*, above n 121; Insolvency Proceedings Regulation, above n 127, §8.

[145] Though there is a UK conflicts regime and common service area.

[146] Campbell, above n 64, at 114ff.

[147] *Richard West & Partners (Inverness) v Dick*, above n 119; Carruthers, above n 36, at para [2.33]; Yeo, above n 70, at para [4.23] (question of proper law not addressed).

[148] Snell, above n 2, has a very '*in personam*' approach.

on trust for a beneficiary who was an English minor. The trust was Scots and the trustees divided equally between the two jurisdictions. An action in England reached the House of Lords, which confirmed that the English court had jurisdiction to administer the trusts of the Scottish land.[149] That was in November 1883. Were we to stop there we would have the decision relied upon by Megarry V-C to order English performance of a contract for Scottish land, but we must go on.

Earlier that same year, in July 1883, an action had begun in Scotland for a declaration that the trustees were bound to administer the same trust according to Scottish law and that they were not entitled to place the case under a foreign tribunal 'furth of Scotland'. After all, Scots law applied to the trust. The Lord Ordinary gave judgment in trenchant terms in December 1884 and his declaration for the Scots courts was watered down only slightly by the Inner House. The English Chancery Division ordered the trustees to appeal and so the case came back to the House of Lords;[150] Scottish this time and differently constituted. Exclusive competency of the Scottish courts was repudiated,[151] but the power of the Scottish court to sequestrate Scots land was affirmed, as was the prima facie case of convenience established in favour of the courts of Scotland. The trustees may have been comforted by knowing that the unsatisfactory English law could only be corrected by legislation. They must have wondered about Lord Fitzgerald's suggestion that there was no conflict between the two cases,[152] and surely the Lord Ordinary came closer to the mark with his suggestion that the English Lords left room for violations of international law. In essence, then, Scots law determined the natural forum whereas the backward English law at that time did not.

The really vicious aspect of Chancery was the issue of anti-suit injunctions. English Chancery could not assume direct jurisdiction over foreign trustees of foreign land[153] but from the early nineteenth century it could and did restrain English trustees from litigating overseas, or, what amounts to the same, in the Court of Session.[154] 'Convenience', in a loose sense, was in play because English anti-suit injunctions would only issue where

---

[149] *Ewing v Orr Ewing* (1883) 9 App Cas 34 (HL England); the panel consisted of the Earl of Selborne LC and Lords Blackburn and Watson.

[150] *Ewing v Orr Ewing* (1884) 10 App Cas 453 (HL Scotland); the panel consisted of the Earl of Selborne LC and Lords Blackburn, Watson and Fitzgerald. English terminology is adopted in this paper since the language of the two reports makes it sound as if two completely different cases are under discussion.

[151] Scotland had long asserted an in personam jurisdiction over foreign land: *Johnston v Johnston* (1579) *Morison's Dictionary of Decisions* 4788.

[152] *Ewing* (HL Scotland), above n 150, at 546 (Lord Fitzgerald).

[153] *Kennedy v Cassillis* (1818) 2 Swan 319, 36 ER 635.

[154] *Beckford v Kemble* (1822) 1 Sim & Stu 15, 57 ER 3; *Bushby v Munday* (1821) 5 Mad 297, 56 ER 908; *Harrison v Gurney* (1821) 2 Jac & Walk 565, 37 ER 743, Eldon LC (Ireland).

England was the natural forum and foreign proceedings would be vexatious and oppressive, and they have subsequently been banned altogether in European cases.[155]

The immediate issue in *Ewing* was resolved by a rule change,[156] unsurprisingly lost to modern writers who cite the English House of Lords as final confirmation that the Lord Chancellor's writ runs across the world. More generally convenience was grafted from Scottish into English law.[157] A Chilean landlord should no longer claim against companies trading exclusively in South America for rent due on shops in Santiago de Chile under a lease in Spanish, executed in Paris, under which all parties elected Chilean domicile.[158] The English decision in *Ewing v Orr Ewing*[159] was clearly wrong and the jurisdiction exercised in *Richard West*[160] would today be excluded. Comity must displace chauvinism.[161]

European first seised rules produce counter-intuitive results, since the naturalness of the forum is irrelevant.[162] Removal of convenience in European cases brings us back to a lop-sided equity conducive to gross inequity. Convenience and discretion have become mixed up and need to be disentangled so as to impose a substantive block to European proceedings away from the natural forum, when *in personam* cases affecting land overseas would cease to work injustice.

Ask not what actions can be brought but rather when our courts will (be forced to) recognise foreign judgments.[163] With that question the jingoism of the English courts becomes clear, for English courts decide cases affecting foreign land but do not reciprocally recognise foreign decisions affecting English land.[164] Recognition of foreign non-money judgments, such as specific performance, applies within the European conflicts club[165] and between parts of the United Kingdom.[166] Recognition of a non-site

---

[155] Case C-159/02 *Turner v Grovit* [2004] I ECR 3565 (ECJ).

[156] Rules of the Supreme Court 1883 Order 55 r 10; White and Tudor, above n 3, at 820; convenience became a factor in orders to administer trusts.

[157] *Spiliades Maritime Corp v Consulex* [1987] AC 460 (HL); Dicey & Morris, above n 10, ch 12; of course 'convenience' does not mean 'convenience'.

[158] *St Pierre v South American Stores (Gath & Chaves)* [1936] 1 KB 382 (CA); Dicey & Morris, above n 10, at para [12-008].

[159] *Ewing* (English HL), above n 149.

[160] *Richard West*, above n 119.

[161] *Abidin Daver* [1984] AC 398 (HL) 411 (Lord Diplock).

[162] Case C-281/02 *Owusu v Jackson* [2005] I ECR 1383 (ECJ).

[163] Falconbridge, above n 10, at 612.

[164] *Houlditch v Donegal*, above n 107; *Boyse v Colclough* (1854) 1 K & J 124, 502; 69 ER 396, 557; DM Gordon, 'The Converse of *Penn v Lord Baltimore*' (1933) 49 *LQR* 547; RW White, 'Enforcement of Foreign Judgments in Equity' (1982) 9 *Sydney Law Review* 630.

[165] Civil Jurisdiction Regulation, above n 4, §33; Dicey & Morris, above n 10, at para [14-188]. Otherwise it is necessary to sue on the judgment which may or may not be res judicata; recognition precludes review of the merits.

[166] Civil Jurisdiction and Judgments Act 1982, above n 5, s 18, sch 7.

judgment[167] is subject to the inherent limitation of the lack of jurisdiction to determine the *in rem* issue and so the *in personam* aspects have to be recognised. Non-site courts can decide that there is a contract and that the seller has broken his contract by failing to convey, but cannot determine that the buyer should become owner. It is not clear whether the real issue can be re-litigated in the courts appropriate to the site. *Houlditch v Donegal* certainly allowed an English decision to be challenged in the Irish courts where it is to be enforced. An English receiver was appointed of land in Ireland to recover a peer's debts,[168] but it proved impracticable to execute the decree and a separate action had to be started in the Court of Chancery in Ireland. In that suit the merits of the English decree could be re-examined, since it purported to decide a non-site title.[169] Renewed argument of the *in personam* issue would be blocked by issue estoppel[170] but no estoppel should arise in relation to the *in rem* issue.[171] So it was in *Duke v Andler*[172] that the Canadian courts would not recognise a decree of the Californian courts that ordered the defendants to re-convey land in British Columbia. The Canadian Registrar was entitled to refuse to register a conveyance effected under American court order, since the Californian judgment was personal and had no effect at the site of the land. Site-based rules encourage the courts of the site to disregard earlier court hearings.[173]

VII. CONCLUSION

Equity acts *in rem*. Specific performance between the parties creates lop-sided doctrine and in the modern world the entire matter would be better left to the courts and the law of the site of the land. It is wasteful to allow litigation of part issues in incomplete forums and '*in personam*' specific performance should be abolished.

---

[167] Dicey & Morris, above n 10, at para [14R-099].
[168] *Houlditch v Donegal* (HL Ireland), above n 107, at 343–4.
[169] *Houlditch v Donegal*, above n 107, at 338 (Brougham LC).
[170] *Godard v Gray* (1870) LR 6 QB 139; Dicey & Morris, above n 10, at para [14-110]; *Newland v Horsman* (1681) 2 Ch Cas 75, 22 ER 853; *Burrows v Jemino* (1727) 2 Str 733, 93 ER 815.
[171] Civil Jurisdiction Regulation, above n 4, §35[1] (non recognition of judgment impinging on an exclusive jurisdiction); the position was less clear at common law: *Castrique v Imrie* (1870) LR 4 HL 414, 429 Blackburn J, approved (at 448) Hartherley LC.
[172] *Duke v Andler* [1932] 4 DLR 529 (Supreme Court of Canada); Falconbridge, n 10 above, at 612, 614; *Raeburn v Raeburn*, 20 March 2007, Benjamin J (English decision is not accepted in West Indies); W Anderson, 'Foreign Orders and Local Land' (1999) 48 *International Comparative Law Quarterly* 167.
[173] Carruthers, above n 36, at para [2.44].

III

Family Homes

9

Constructive Trusts and Constructing Intention

NICK PIŠKA*

I. INTRODUCTION

IN *STACK V DOWDEN*[1] intention was reasserted as central to the distribution of interests in the family home following the breakdown of intimate relationships, which was simultaneously to reassert the significance of property in liberal ideology. In this paper I critically examine the role and construction of intention in the context of the 'common intention' constructive trust, and the influence of liberal ideology in the role and construction of intention, linking this critical re-examination to contemporary debates in the taxonomy of private law.

II. THE PROPERTY PARADIGM AND THE IDEOLOGY OF LIBERALISM

> Behind the concept of the trust ... stands an even more fundamental [concept] of great significance and universally recognised ideological significance—the concept of property.[2]

In the introduction to an article on the law of tracing Craig Rotherham stated that the law 'cannot be explained without first comprehending the meaning ascribed to and the function performed by 'property' in our legal discourse'.[3] The law relating to the ownership of the family home likewise

---

* Kent Law School, University of Kent. I would like to thank Sir Terence Etherton for the long and fruitful discussions we had during 2007 on the nature of the constructive trust. I would also like to thank Stuart Bridge, Lizzie Cooke, Matt Jolley and Brian Sloan for their comments on various drafts of this paper.

[1] *Stack v Dowden* [2007] UKHL 17.

[2] R Cotterrell, 'Power, Property and the Law of Trusts' (1987) 14 *Journal of Law and Society* 77, 82.

[3] C Rotherham, 'The Metaphysics of Tracing: Substituted Title and Property Rhetoric' (1996) 34 *Osgoode Hall Law Journal* 321, 324.

cannot be explained without first considering the meaning and function of 'property'. Moreover, the modern idea of property in law cannot be comprehended without an understanding of the ideology from which it developed.

A. The Ideology of Liberalism

At its most general an ideology 'is a set of ideas and values'.[4] These ideas and values may form part of an explicit political creed, but are more likely to be implicit and acted out as part of a way of life, unnoticed by the vast majority.[5] The political ideology of liberalism usually falls into the implicit category. As Anthony Arblaster states,

> Liberalism in its contemporary form is not so much a set of ideals or doctrines to which people subscribe by conscious choice; it is a way of seeing the social world, and a set of assumptions about it, which are absorbed by the individual in so natural and gradual manner that he or she is not conscious of their being assumptions at all.[6]

Charles Fried has recently written that liberalism is individuality made normative, 'a refusal to be subject to anyone—even everyone—or anything, except as we choose to be'.[7] This captures the essence of liberalism: a greater concern with the individual than communities or groups.[8] From this, further interrelated ideas or values emerge. First it provides the metaphysical and ontological foundation for a concern with individual freedom and autonomy. Freedom has both a positive and negative sense.[9] In the positive sense it means freedom of the individual to determine his own ends, to do as he wishes so long as he does not harm others.[10] However, it is the negative sense that is far more prominent in the liberal tradition, where freedom is couched in terms of 'freedom from', an area of non-interference by others, 'a condition in which one is *not* compelled, *not* restricted, *not* interfered with, and *not* pressurized'.[11]

---

[4] J Adams and R Brownsword, 'The Ideologies of Contract' (1987) 7 *Legal Studies* 205. *cf* D McLellan, *Ideology*, 2nd edn (Buckingham, Open University Press, 1995) and R Cotterrell, *Law's Community* (Oxford, Clarendon Press, 1995) 7–14 and ch 12.

[5] A Arblaster, *The Rise and Decline of Western Liberalism* (Oxford, Basil Blackwell Publishing, 1984) 9.

[6] *ibid*, 6.

[7] C Fried, *Modern Liberty and the Limits of Government* (New York, WW Norton and Co, 2007) 180.

[8] *cf* Arblaster, above n 5, ch 2.

[9] *cf* I Berlin, 'Two Concepts of Liberty' in *Four Essays on Liberty* (London, Oxford University Press, 1969).

[10] *cf* JS Mill, *On Liberty* (London, JW Parker & Son, 1859).

[11] Arblaster, above n 5, at 55–6.

The answer to the question 'freedom from whom?' provides the basis for the second value of liberalism, a sharp distinction between the private and public domains: 'freedom from control, compulsion, restriction, and interference by the state'.[12] Martin Loughlin describes the traditional image of the state within liberal ideology:

> The State thus devises rules ... which define property rights and regulate its transfer, and otherwise promote voluntary transactions amongst citizens; and the courts are established as those special institutions of the State which exist to ensure the proper enforcement of those rules of just conduct.[13]

This draws attention to a number of points. First, it highlights the centrality of private rights, in particular private property rights. Secondly, the role of the state is purely facilitative of the protection and transfer of those rights.[14] Thirdly, the state includes the judiciary and as such the judiciary's role is limited to corrective and not distributive justice. According to Atiyah this view was shared by nineteenth-century judges:

> [T]he function of the civil law came to be seen as largely a negative one. Its main object was to enable people to 'realise their wills', or, in more prosaic language, to leave them to get on with their business, to conduct their commercial affairs as they thought best, to lead their own lives unhampered by government interference, and so forth.[15]

Distributive justice was something that was to be left to the markets to determine or perhaps Government, but definitely not the courts.[16] Insofar as the courts were concerned, the public/private distinction separated law and politics, 'creating a neutral and apolitical system of legal doctrine and legal reasoning free from what was thought to be the dangerous and unstable redistributive tendencies of democratic politics'.[17]

B. The Property Paradigm and Trust Law

The overlapping values of individualism and the public/private divide in liberal ideology were most prevalent in the nineteenth century and greatly influenced the development of contract and property law, and continue

---

[12] Arblaster, above n 5, at 57–8, and ch 13 generally. *cf* PS Atiyah, *An Introduction to the Law of Contract* (Oxford, Clarendon Press, 1995) 7–15.

[13] M Loughlin, *Sword and Scales: an Examination of the Relationship between Law and Politics* (Oxford, Hart Publishing, 2000) 95.

[14] *cf* J Locke, *Second Treatise of Government* (New York, Prometheus Books, 1986).

[15] Atiyah, above n 12, at 8.

[16] *cf* JAG Griffith, *The Politics of the Judiciary*, 3rd revised edn (London, Fontana Press, 1985) 202–3.

[17] MJ Horwitz, 'The History of the Public/Private Distinction' (1982) 130 *University of Pennsylvania Law Review* 1423.

to encapsulate our paradigmatic ideas about 'property'.[18] The property paradigm conjures the image of an individual owner who has the right to deny the rest of the world access to a specific thing. In his analysis of the idea of property in law, James Penner argues that while 'property' does not necessarily entail the right to enter binding agreements for the transfer of property, the right does entail the liberty to dispose of things as one wishes.[19] The central example for Penner was the right to transfer rights by gift through a manifestation of the owner's intention.[20] In the introduction to his series on *Liberty, Property and the Law*, Epstein states that '[v]irtually all legal systems in the English (or common law) tradition … start from the central proposition that each person is entitled to exclusive control of his or her property, free from invasions by other individuals'.[21] The ideas of liberty and property are inseparable, and it is no surprise to find the central values of classic liberalism reflected in the property paradigm, which emphasises ownership and voluntary exchange.[22]

Voluntary exchange falls within that sphere of law that concerns itself with self-imposed obligations (voluntary obligations), as distinct from those obligations imposed by law (involuntary obligations). This distinction may be mapped onto a taxonomy of private law, with voluntary obligations generally arising in the causative category of consent and involuntary obligations arising in response to wrongs and unjust enrichment.[23] The 'core case' of consent, and therefore voluntary obligations, is contract.[24] As with property, contract was also imbued with the liberal ideology of the nineteenth century judiciary:

> Contractual obligations came to be treated as being almost exclusively about promises, agreements, intentions, acts of will. The function of the law came to be seen as that of merely giving effect to the private autonomy of contracting parties to make their own legal arrangements.[25]

---

[18] It also influenced the development of contract. See PS Atiyah, 'Contracts, Promises and the Law of Obligations' in *Essays on Contract* (Oxford, Clarendon Press, 1986). For a recent discussion of the key themes in the liberal conception of property see M Davies, *Property: Meanings, histories, theories* (Oxford, Routledge-Cavendish, 2007) 10–12.

[19] JE Penner, *The Idea of Property in Law* (Oxford, Oxford University Press, 1997) ch 4. *cf* AM Honore, 'Ownership' in AG Guest (ed), *Oxford Essays in Jurisprudence* (Oxford, Oxford University Press, 1961).

[20] Penner, above n 19, at 88–90.

[21] RA Epstein, *Liberty, Property and the Law* (London, Garland Publishing, 2000) vii.

[22] *ibid*, viii–x; *cf* C Rotherham, *Proprietary Remedies in Context: a Study of the Judicial Redistribution of Property Rights* (Oxford, Hart Publishing, 2002) ch 10.

[23] P Birks, *Unjust Enrichment*, 2nd edn (Oxford, Oxford University Press, 2005); Atiyah, *An Introduction to the Law of Contract*, above n 12, at 1–2.

[24] P Birks, 'The Concept of a Civil Wrong' in DG Owen (ed), *Philosophical Foundations of Tort Law* (Oxford, Oxford University Press, 1995).

[25] Atiyah, 'Contracts, Promises and the Law of Obligations', above n 18, at 10–11.

Voluntary exchange, as exemplified by contract, came to be dominated by a concern with 'acts of will'.[26] The twin pillars of freedom of contract and sanctity of contract developed to give effect to the autonomy of the individual and manifestations of his intention. The public/private divide was reinforced by the view that the individual voluntarily imposed obligations on him or herself through an exercise of free will that the courts were bound to respect.[27] The function of the court was merely 'to discover what the parties [had] agreed, or what their joint intention was, and give effect to it'.[28]

The heavy reliance on intention had four consequences. First, courts were not concerned with broad notions of fairness or justice; it was for the individual contractor to look after his or her own interests.[29] Secondly, 'there was a reluctance to impose obligations on those who had not voluntarily assumed them'.[30] Thirdly, where obligations were imposed there was a tendency to express them in terms of intentions, a prime example being implied terms.[31] This allowed the courts formally to respect liberal ideology while at the same time subverting it. Fourthly, the obligations were said to arise from the moment of the exercise of the will (or, rather, the moment of intention), and not from the later judgment of the court. Voluntary legal obligations therefore existed outside of the courtroom, the consequence for property rights being that property rights were transferred at the moment of intention and the role of the court was merely declaratory of pre-existing property entitlements.[32]

The property paradigm is normative in both cause and effect, by which I mean that the idea of property influences both how the legal rules are constructed and also how they function. The property paradigm tends towards the construction of property rules in terms of intentions, which is to downplay the role of the judiciary.[33] Once facts fit the property paradigm the normative basis is provided for third parties to be bound by pre-existing

---

[26] See PS Atiyah, *The Rise and Fall of Freedom of Contract* (Oxford, Clarendon Press, 1979) 405–19.

[27] PS Atiyah, 'The Liberal Theory of Contract' in *Essays on Contract* (Oxford, Clarendon Press, 1986) 121, referring to the liberal theory of justice embodied by Charles Fried's *Contract as Promise: a Theory of Contractual Obligation* (London, Harvard University Press, 1981).

[28] AWB Simpson, 'Innovation in Nineteenth Century Contract Law' (1975) 91 *Law Quarterly Review* 247, 265.

[29] Atiyah, *An Introduction to the Law of Contract*, above n 12, at 8–9.

[30] *ibid*, 10.

[31] *ibid*, 10.

[32] That certain formalities may or may not have been required does not detract from the ideology.

[33] *cf* M Halliwell, 'Equity as Injustice: the Cohabitant's Case' (1991) 20 *Anglo-American Law Review* 500: 'The rationale of the institutions of express trust is nowadays usually identified by intention and equity is working well on a principled basis to prevent intention being defeated'.

rights and obligations.[34] This can be seen in trust law. For example, settlor intention is central to the express trust, as embodied in the requirement of certainty of intention. The settlor, as owner of private property, may voluntarily transfer his property as he wishes. The court will look to the terms of the trust to decipher the settlor's intention, which in turn determines beneficiaries' respective property interests, which in turn bind the world. Equally the resulting trust, at least formally,[35] functions within the bounds of the property paradigm, unwinding non-consensual transfers of wealth, and consequently binding third parties.[36] The constructive trust is also a property institution, in the same way as the express trust,[37] with the ability to bind third parties, arising as facts happen rather than as the consequence of a court order.[38] Operating within the property paradigm, the court's function is merely declaratory of prior interests and not discretionary.[39] Andrew Hicks has noted the normative effect of the institutional nature of the constructive trust, the 'apparent inevitability of the outcome' which is 'bolstered by the power of property':

> [A]t the time the court adjudicates on the dispute the claimant already owns the asset. The court cannot therefore order an alternative form of relief and refuse to recognise the claimant's right, for to do so would be tantamount to an illegitimate judicial expropriation of property. The idea that something is already the property of the claimant thus exerts greater leverage than competing normative considerations that may suggest an alternative outcome.[40]

Working within the model of private ordering, the court's role is to declare the order of things but apparently takes no role in the ordering.[41] In

---

[34] On the normative force of property see C Rotherham, 'The Metaphysics of Tracing: Substituted Title and Property Rhetoric' (1996) 34 *Osgoode Hall Law Journal* 321, 325; AD Hicks, 'Conceptualising the Constructive Trust' (2005) 56 *Northern Ireland Legal Quarterly* 521; RB Grantham and CEF Rickett, 'Property Rights as a Legally Significant Event' (2003) 62 *Cambridge Law Journal* 717; and generally JE Penner, *The Idea of Property in Law* (Oxford, Oxford University Press, 1997).

[35] See R Chambers, *Resulting Trusts* (Oxford, Clarendon Press, 1997) on the relationship between the resulting trust and unjust enrichment. It can be seen as within the tradition in the sense of protecting property, but outside the tradition by imposing involuntary obligations. *cf* W Swadling, 'Explaining Resulting Trusts' (2008) 124 *Law Quarterly Review* 72.

[36] It rests on the intentions of the private owner based on a rebuttable presumption that shields the judiciary from censure for intermeddling in property interests.

[37] DWM Waters, 'The Nature of the Remedial Constructive Trust' in P Birks (ed), *The Frontiers of Liability Volume 2* (Oxford, Oxford University Press, 1994).

[38] P Birks, 'The End of the Remedial Constructive Trust' (1998) 12 *Trust Law International* 202.

[39] S Gardner, 'The Element of Discretion' in P Birks (ed), *The Frontiers of Liability Volume 2* (Oxford, Oxford University Press, 1994).

[40] AD Hicks, 'Conceptualising the Constructive Trust' (2005) 56 *Northern Ireland Legal Quarterly* 521, 524–5.

[41] See C Rotherham, 'The Metaphysics of Tracing: Substituted Title and Property Rhetoric' (1996) 34 *Osgoode Hall Law Journal* 321, 324; C Rotherham, 'Proprietary Relief for Enrichment by Wrongs: Some Realism about Property Talk' (1996) 19 *University of New South Wales Law Journal* 378, 381; AD Hicks, 'Conceptualising the Constructive Trust'

the remainder of this paper I will demonstrate how the court is always implicated in the ordering of entitlements, how various incursions have been made into the property paradigm in the context of the family home, and the consequences this has for the taxonomy of private law.

III. *STACK* AND THE CENTRALITY OF INTENTION

A. Fairness or Intention?

The distribution of the family home has long been based on the common intentions of the parties, situating it firmly within the property paradigm. The question has not so much been the correct principles but rather how to construct those intentions. In *Lloyd's Bank v Rosset*[42] Lord Bridge held that there are two ways of proving the necessary intention to share. The common intention could either be demonstrated by evidence of an express 'agreement, arrangement or understanding' reached by the parties 'at any time prior to acquisition' or could be inferred from 'direct contributions to the purchase price by the partner who is not the legal owner, whether initially or by payment of mortgage instalments'. The question that dominated the Court of Appeal after *Rosset* was how to quantify the beneficial interest. This raised two related questions. First, is the search for what the parties intended or should the beneficial interest be quantified according to what the court considers fair? Answers to this question differed according to whether or not the property was held by the parties as legal joint tenants or in the name of only one party. Secondly, where there is no evidence of an express intention regarding the beneficial interest, are parties' intentions to be inferred from their financial contributions alone or is a broader approach available? In *Oxley v Hiscock*, a sole legal owner case, Chadwick LJ held that 'each is entitled to that share which the court considers fair having regard to the whole course of dealing between them in relation to the property'.[43] He applied the same approach to joint legal owners in *Stack*.[44]

This reliance on the common intention of parties has been subject to much comment, most of which criticises the search for intention as 'unrealistic and highly artificial'.[45] As Simon Gardner has pointed out, such '[a]greements are in reality found or denied in a manner quite unconnected

---

(2005) 56 *Northern Ireland Legal Quarterly* 521; RB Grantham and CEF Rickett, 'Property Rights as a Legally Significant Event' (2003) 62 *Cambridge Law Journal* 717, 719.

[42] *Lloyd's Bank v Rosset* [1991] 1 AC 107 (HL).

[43] *Oxley v Hiscock* [2004] EWCA Civ 546, para [69].

[44] *Stack v Dowden* [2005] EWCA Civ 857.

[45] K Gray and SF Gray, *Elements of Land Law*, 4th edn (Oxford, Oxford University Press, 2005) para 10.92.

with their actual presence or absence'.[46] He considered the inference of an agreement, arrangement or understanding from financial contributions to highlight the point: 'There may very well be no agreement truly to be found here either, yet one routinely is discovered—that is to say, invented, in disregard of the prohibition'.[47] Marcia Neave has stated such 'assertions of intention or expectation are often *ex post facto* rationalizations of a course of conduct in which the issue of ownership was never seriously considered'.[48] With the continued reliance on common intentions and real bargains in the post-*Rosset* quantification cases, the strain was beginning to be noticed at both a judicial level and in the commentaries. In *Oxley* Chadwick LJ referred to the reliance on intention as 'artificial and an unnecessary fiction',[49] whilst in his case note on *Oxley* Gardner stated that 'an invented common intention that the claimant shall have an interest at all will sometimes strain credulity, but one that her interest shall be of a particular size will do so even more readily'.[50] Gray and Gray note that 'it has become painfully obvious in recent years that the inference of intended beneficial ownership almost invariably collapses back into something approaching an assessment of fair outcome'.[51]

Sooner or later the House of Lords were going to be presented with a choice: either it could follow the lead of the Court of Appeal in rejecting the fiction of intention and apply a broad-brush 'fairness' approach to the quantification of beneficial interests, or it could reject that in favour of a narrower approach rooted in the parties' intentions. When *Stack* reached the House of Lords the majority seemingly took the latter approach. Baroness Hale held that the starting point is that equity follows the law and that there is a heavy burden on the person seeking to show that the beneficial ownership is different from the legal ownership. But how is this done? Baroness Hale states that '[t]he search is to ascertain the parties' shared intentions, actual, inferred or imputed, with respect to the property in the light of their whole course of conduct in relation to it'.[52] In rejecting Chadwick LJ's formulation of the question in terms of fairness she explains that the court cannot 'abandon that search in favour of the result which the court itself considers fair'.[53]

---

[46] S Gardner, 'Rethinking Family Property' (1993) 109 *Law Quarterly Review* 263, 264.

[47] *ibid*, 264.

[48] M Neave, 'Three Approaches to Family Property Disputes—Intention/Belief, Unjust Enrichment and Unconscionability' in TG Youdan (ed), *Equity, Fiduciaries and Trusts* (Toronto, Carswell, 1989) 249.

[49] *Oxley v Hiscock* [2004] EWCA Civ 546, para [71].

[50] S Gardner, 'Quantum in *Gissing v Gissing* Constructive Trusts' (2004) 120 *Law Quarterly Review* 541, 543.

[51] K Gray and SF Gray, *Elements of Land Law*, 4th edn (Oxford, Oxford University Press, 2005) para 10.142.

[52] *Stack v Dowden* [2007] UKHL 17, para [60].

[53] *ibid*, para [61].

B. Unleashing Intention

Despite the explicit rejection of an approach based on fairness, three fragments are suggestive of a broader approach to intention: the widening of the evidence from which an intention can be inferred; the development of a factors-based approach to intention; and the apparent acceptance of imputed intentions.

In *Rosset* Lord Bridge had limited the existence question to express intentions and financial contributions, and had doubted whether anything less would do. In his concurring opinion in *Stack* Lord Walker stated that whether or not Lord Bridge's observation had been justified in 1990, the law had moved on, and, moreover, that their Lordships should move it a little more in the same direction.[54] Baroness Hale, while noting that *Stack* was not concerned with the establishment of a beneficial interest, noted that *Rosset* may have set the first hurdle rather too high.[55] Importantly, she stated that the presumption of resulting trust, and with it an approach to intention rooted in inference from financial contributions, is of less importance and '[m]any more factors than financial contributions may be relevant to divining the parties' true intentions'.[56] This was confirmed by the Privy Council shortly after *Stack* in *Abbott v Abbott*.[57] That case concerned the beneficial ownership of the former matrimonial home, which was held in the sole name of Mr Abbott. In considering the existence question, Baroness Hale re-emphasised that 'the law has undoubtedly moved on' from the days when financial contributions were the only evidence from which a common intention could be inferred. Rather, 'the parties' whole course of conduct in relation to the property must be taken into account in determining their shared intentions as to its ownership'.[58]

The second strand suggesting a broader enquiry is Baroness Hale's factor-based approach to the divination of the parties' true intentions. She provided a long list of factors apparently relevant to the determination of intention, including the purpose for which the home was acquired, the nature of the parties' relationship, whether they had children, and the parties' individual characters and personalities.[59] Such an approach is reminiscent of the wide factor-based discretion available under the Matrimonial Causes Act 1973, only couched in terms of the search for intentions.

Finally, despite reference to the parties' 'true intentions' Baroness Hale expressly allows the imputation of intentions, which is supported by her

---

[54] *ibid*, para [26].
[55] *ibid*, para [63].
[56] *ibid*, para [69].
[57] *Abbott v Abbott* [2007] UKPC 53.
[58] *ibid*, para [19].
[59] *Stack v Dowden* [2007] UKHL 17, paras [69]–[70].

statement that 'the search is still for the result which reflects what the parties must, in the light of their conduct, be taken to have intended'.[60] The suggestion is that if the court cannot find an actual or inferred intention, they may nevertheless impute to the parties the intention that the court considers that they would have had, had they directed their minds to the question. If this is what the majority intended, then it would allow relief to be provided in a wider range of circumstances than if evidence of a real bargain was required.

C. Imputed Intentions: Inferring or Inventing?

In *Stack* Lord Walker explained that most of the controversy since *Pettitt*[61] and *Gissing*[62] really boils down to 'whether the court must find a real bargain between the parties, or whether it can (in the absence of any sufficient evidence as to their real intentions) infer or impute a bargain'.[63] However, instead of resolving the controversy *Stack* embodies the controversy. In this very quote Lord Walker contrasted inferred and imputed intentions with real bargains, which he seems to equate with actual intentions. Noting that in *Pettitt* 'there was a clear majority as to the need for an actual bargain',[64] he stated that in *Gissing* Lord Diplock's replacement of 'impute' with the 'rather ambiguous (and perhaps deliberately ambiguous) language of "inference"'[65] constituted a departure from the requirement of an actual bargain. The acceptance of invented intentions was perpetuated in the second limb of *Rosset*, where it was agreed that 'a "common intention" trust could be inferred even when there was no evidence of an actual agreement' from financial contributions.[66] Consequently Lord Walker concluded that, despite *Pettitt*, the court might infer or impute a bargain. Indeed, he considered that the law had moved on since *Rosset* and the court may infer or impute a bargain from wider circumstances than just financial contributions.

Unlike Lord Walker, Lord Neuberger distinguished inferred and imputed intentions:

> An inferred intention is one which is objectively deduced to be the subjective actual intention of the parties, in the light of their actions and statements. An imputed intention is one which is attributed to the parties, even though no such actual intention can be deduced from their actions and statements, and even

---

[60] *ibid*, para [61].
[61] *Pettitt v Pettitt* [1970] AC 777 (HL).
[62] *Gissing v Gissing* [1971] AC 886 (HL).
[63] *Stack v Dowden* [2007] UKHL 17, para [17].
[64] *ibid*, para [22].
[65] *ibid*, para [21].
[66] *ibid*, para [25].

though they had no such intention. Imputation involves concluding what the parties would have intended, whereas inference involves concluding what they did intend.[67]

This is similar to Lord Reid's distinction between inferred and imputed intentions in *Gissing*.[68] The difference between Lord Neuberger and Lord Walker is that they draw the line between real and invented intentions in different places. Whereas Lord Walker draws the line between actual intentions on the one hand, and inferred and imputed intentions on the other, Lord Neuberger draws the line between actual and inferred intentions, and imputed intentions. For Lord Neuberger, both actual and inferred intentions are concerned with 'actual subjective intention' whereas imputed intention is an intention attributed to the parties but does not really exist.

Importantly, for both Lord Walker and Lord Neuberger, an imputed intention seems to equate to an invented intention. Lord Reid in *Pettitt* stated that such an intention consists of what reasonable people in the parties' shoes would have agreed.[69] Lord Neuberger was uncertain as to whether such a deemed intention would be constructed from 'a hypothetical negotiation between the actual parties, or what reasonable parties would have agreed'.[70] The former would require the judge to consider how the actual parties would have decided the matter, which would involve the judge taking into account various factors, such as the nature of the relationship, but also the particular characteristics of the parties. For this reason Lord Neuberger considered that whilst it would be more logical, 'it would redound to the advantage of an unreasonable party'.[71] The latter approach does not have this problem, as it considers what 'reasonable parties would have agreed'. However, Lord Neuberger considered that this approach was 'inconsistent with the principle ... that the court's view of fairness is not the correct yardstick for determining the parties' shares'.[72] Given that neither Lord Walker nor Baroness Hale defined what they meant by imputed intention, Lord Neuberger's definition must be accepted as authoritative.

IV. IMPUTED INTENTIONS AND LEGAL FICTIONS

Much of the post-*Stack* commentary has focused on imputed intentions. For example Rebecca Lee complained that '[t]o impute an intention is ... to disregard the normative value of agreement protected by the constructive

---

[67] *ibid*, para [126].
[68] *Gissing v Gissing* [1971] AC 886 (HL) 897.
[69] See *Pettitt v Pettitt* [1970] AC 777 (HL) 795.
[70] *Stack v Dowden* [2007] UKHL 17, para [127].
[71] *ibid*.
[72] *ibid*.

trust doctrine'.[73] Edmund Cullen stated that the rejection of fairness in favour of imputed intention has revived the fiction of intention.[74] In his dissenting opinion, Lord Neuberger criticised the imputation of intentions not only as contrary to principle, but as involving judges in an exercise that is 'difficult, subjective and uncertain'. Sir Terence Etherton has stated that '[i]t is impossible to disagree with Lord Neuberger that an imputed intention is not the same as, but rather is to be contrasted with, express or inferred intention', and that the majority's reliance on the fiction of an common intention 'to legitimate legal analysis is unsatisfactory'.[75] He goes on to state, in a similar vein to modern legal taxonomists, 'fiction in the law prevents the coherent development of the law in accordance with principle, and indicates an immaturity of legal development'.[76]

Central to each of these objections to imputed intention is the accusation that it rests on a legal fiction. The Oxford English Dictionary's entries on 'fiction' suggest that a fiction is an invention as opposed to a fact. In the legal context, it defines a fiction as 'a supposition known to be at variance with fact, but conventionally accepted for some reason of practical convenience'. The most comprehensive work on legal fictions is Lon Fuller's *Legal Fictions*.[77] Fuller distinguishes fictions from lies; whereas a lie is intended to deceive people into believing that it is true, a fiction is not. Indeed, central to the fiction for Fuller is consciousness or recognition of the falsity of the statement. Relying on the earlier work of Hans Vaihinger on the instrumentality of fictions, Fuller explains that 'a fiction is an "expedient, but *consciously false*, assumption"'.[78] He goes on to give a two-fold definition of a legal fiction: 'A fiction is either (1) a statement propounded with a complete or partial consciousness of its falsity, or (2) a false statement recognised as having utility'.[79] Both definitions rest on two premises. First, 'a statement must be false before it can be a fiction'. Secondly, consciousness of the falsehood is necessary to its utility and renders it safe. In assessing the criticism that common intention rests on a fiction it is necessary to first consider what we mean by 'common intention'.

---

[73] R Lee, '*Stack v Dowden*: a Sequel' (2008) 124 *Law Quarterly Review* 209, 212.

[74] E Cullen, '*Stack v Dowden*: an End to Uncertainty?' (2008) 21 *Insolvency Intelligence* 43, 44.

[75] T Etherton, 'Constructive Trusts: a New Model for Equity and Unjust Enrichment' (2008) 67 *Cambridge Law Journal* 265, 279.

[76] *ibid*.

[77] L Fuller, *Legal Fictions* (Stanford, Stanford University Press, 1967). *cf* L Harmon, 'Falling Off the Vine: Legal Fictions and the Doctrine of Substituted Judgment' (1990) 100 *Yale Law Journal* 1.

[78] Fuller, above n 77, at 7, quoting Hans Vaihinger. See further H Vaihinger, *The Philosophy of 'As-If': a System of the Theoretical, Practical, and Religious Fictions of Mankind*, (tr) CK Ogden, 1924 (London, Routledge, 2001).

[79] Fuller, above n 77, at 9.

A. Real Bargains, Actual Intentions and The Concept of Intention

Whilst Lord Walker and Lord Neuberger disagreed as to where to draw the line between inference and imputation regarding 'real bargains', they implicitly agreed that a real bargain is constructed from actual intentions. The common view is that 'actual intention' is a state of mind, a thing, that judges 'discover' directly from the evidence. This picture of 'actual intention' is illustrated by Lord Morris' rejection of imputed intention in *Pettitt* and *Gissing*. In *Pettitt* he stated that 'the court does not find and, indeed, cannot find that there was some thought in the mind of a person which never was there at all'.[80] In *Gissing* he was even more clear not only in his rejection of imputation but also acceptance that the court's role is to find actual intentions:

> The court does not decide how the parties might have ordered their affairs; it only finds how they did. The court cannot devise arrangements which the parties never made. The court cannot ascribe intentions the parties in fact never had.[81]

In *Stack*, Lord Neuberger held a similar view; the court's role is to find actual subjective intentions, which are discoverable directly from written or oral agreements, arrangements or understandings. This is what Lord Walker would describe as a 'real bargain', and is taken to be something existing in the minds of the parties.

But what is meant by 'intention'? In her monograph *Intention* Anscombe distinguishes three meanings of intention: the expression of an intention to do something in the future, intention as a reason for action (ie intentional action or actions that are voluntary), and action with an intention.[82] For example, if Mike states 'I am going to go to the shop' this is an expression of intention to do something in the future, ie go to the shop. When Mike actually gets up and starts walking to the shop we can infer that he intends to go to shop in the sense that his walking is voluntary. Slightly less obviously, if Mike returns with a bottle of wine we can infer not only that Mike intended to purchase the wine (in the voluntary sense) but that he went to the shops with the intention of purchasing the wine. This is action with an intention, and is concerned with the purpose or meaning of an action. Private law is mainly concerned with the second and third senses of intention, in that it requires that acts are both voluntary and that in deciphering voluntary obligations the search is for what the parties intended, ie the meaning or purpose of words and conduct. This is what is referred to as 'speaker meaning' or 'subjective intended meaning'. It is with this that we are immediately concerned.

---

[80] *Pettitt v Pettitt* [1970] AC 777 (HL) 804–5.
[81] *Gissing v Gissing* [1971] AC 886 (HL) 898.
[82] GEM Anscombe, *Intention*, 2nd edn (New York, Cornell University Press, 1963) § 1.

Lord Neuberger's reference to 'actual subjective intention' is a reference to 'subjective intended meaning'. The problem is that we do not have direct access to the mind and therefore cannot discover subjective intended meaning directly. As Lord Hoffmann has said, 'for the purposes of interpreting what other people say, we have no direct access to their subjective mental states, no window into their minds'.[83] Consequently we are forced to discover intention indirectly through external manifestations in words and conduct. The search for subjective intended meaning is therefore an inferential one, and bound to objectivity. Again quoting Lord Hoffmann:

> In the end ... our interpretation is bound to be objective in the sense that it will be our best effort to construe what such a person, using those words against that background, would have meant. We may hope that our interpretation corresponds with his or her subjective intentions, but we cannot be sure.[84]

To return to the example of Mike going to the shops, we infer from his statement that he intends to go to the shop, from his action of going to the shop, and from his returning from the shop with a bottle of wine, that he intended to go to the shop to buy a bottle of wine. On this approach to intention, each of these facts render it more probable that Mike subjectively intended to go to the shops to buy a bottle of wine, and this 'intention' existed in Mike's mind. However, we cannot be sure; there is no way of verifying the conclusion. Whilst we may consider it very likely that Mike intended to go to the shops to buy a bottle of wine, he may have subjectively intended to go to the shops to buy something else, or he may have only intended to go to the shops to meet some friends or take a stroll.

The question arises as to how we choose between these various conclusions. We do this through a process of interpretation, deducing the existence of certain facts from the existence of other facts that we know to exist.[85] Whilst formally an inductive process, it involves a series of background generalisations and prejudices that convert the inferential process from an inductive to a deductive process. William Twining states that '[g]eneralisations are warrants that serve as the "glue" that links an item of evidence to a particular interim or ultimate probandum by showing that it is relevant'.[86] These generalisations usually go unstated and unnoticed. The legitimacy of any given generalisation, and consequently any fact that

---

[83] L Hoffmann, 'The Intolerable Wrestle with Words and Meanings' (1997) 113 *South African Law Journal* 656, 661.

[84] *ibid.*

[85] See generally T Anderson, D Schum and W Twining, *Analysis of Evidence*, 2nd edn (Cambridge, Cambridge University Press, 2005) and AAS Zuckerman, *The Principles of Criminal Evidence* (Oxford, Clarendon Press, 1989) ch 2. See further HG Gadamer, *Truth and Method*, 2nd revised edn, (tr) J Weinsheimer and DG Marshall (London, Continuum, 2004).

[86] T Anderson, D Schum and W Twining, *Analysis of Evidence*, 2nd edn (Cambridge, Cambridge University Press, 2005) 262. See further GEM Anscombe, 'On Brute Facts' (1958) 18(3) *Analysis* 69.

the generalisation helps to construct, depends on the extent of consensus underpinning the generalisation. Twining explains that most generalisations are not in fact dangerous, as for the most part they are 'too essential a part of our culture for there to be any serious disagreement about them'.[87] This stems from the fact that generalisations are rooted in shared cultural experiences which create a common 'stock of knowledge' consisting of

> ill-defined agglomerations of beliefs that typically consist of a complex soup of more or less well-grounded information, sophisticated models, anecdotal memories, impressions, stories, myths, proverbs, wishes, stereotypes, speculations, and prejudices.[88]

To return to our example of Mike going to the shops, we can infer that he intended to go to the shops from his statement 'I intend to go to the shops'. Whilst on the face of it this does not employ any background assumptions, that is not the case. First, it relies on the assumption that people mean what they say, which is to assume that every action has a meaning (purposive action assumption) and that every action has only one meaning (determined actor assumption). However, this does not get us very far, as part of what we are trying to do is discover the meaning of what was said. As such, and secondly, it employs the assumption that people say what they mean; that people convey the meaning of their actions in a form recognised by a given community. This rests on a further assumption, that people do not lie or trick us as to their intended meaning. In our example, it may be that Mike was in fact going to meet a secret girlfriend somewhere other than the shops, but chose to tell us that he was going to the shops. The assumptions usually employed are 'assumptions of normality',[89] but this itself raises questions as to the meaning of normality. As Twining has stated,

> [a] high degree of consensus about the contents of the social 'stock of knowledge' or beliefs cannot be taken for granted, especially in a plural or a stratified society. Moreover, so much of 'common sense' that is indeed common in a given society is relative to time, place, and subject matter.[90]

This draws our attention to a further point. If, in creating rights and obligations, the law is concerned with subjective speaker meaning, it is necessary to reconcile these initial prejudices with the speaker's prejudices and background assumptions. In other words, the extent to which our conclusions

---

[87] LJ Cohen, *The Probable and the Provable* (Oxford, Oxford University Press 1977) quoted in T Anderson, D Schum and W Twining, *Analysis of Evidence*, 2nd edn (Cambridge, Cambridge University Press, 2005) 274.

[88] W Twining, 'Narrative and Generalizations in Argumentation about Questions of Fact' (1999) 40 *South Texas Law Review* 351, 362.

[89] A Kramer, 'Common Sense Principles of Contract Interpretation (And How We've Been Using Them All Along)' (2003) 23 *Oxford Journal of Legal Studies* 173, 181.

[90] W Twining, 'Narrative and Generalizations in Argumentation about Questions of Fact' (1999) 40 *South Texas Law Review* 351, 362.

correspond with speaker meaning is dependent on the extent to which the interpreter places himself in the context of the speaker. The relevance of context in interpretation has received judicial recognition. Extra-judicially Lord Hoffmann has stated that '[n]o utterance is ever complete in itself to convey the intended meaning',[91] and consequently a certain amount of background evidence is necessary. In another article Lord Steyn has said that '[i]n everyday life words receive their colour from their context ... Time, place and circumstances are relevant to the process of selecting the appropriate meaning'.[92] The importance of context was emphasised in *Investor Compensation Scheme v West Bromwich Building Society*,[93] where Lord Hoffmann gave his ideas on interpretation legal force in relation to the interpretation of written contracts. In that case he emphasised that interpretation is the ascertainment of meaning in context, which includes the background knowledge reasonably available to the parties. In *Stack* itself Baroness Hale emphasised that 'context is everything'.[94] But how much context should be available in determining speaker intention? As Kramer has stated in relation to contractual interpretation, 'by harnessing, and then processing, more information than merely the text, more meaning can be extracted at the other end of the interpretive process'.[95] Paradoxically, by admitting more context to discover more accurately speaker intention we may create the possibility for a wider range of possible subjective intended meanings.

At this point an additional element should be introduced: that of the 'other' party, the 'hearer'. So far we have been considering intention as a fact residing in the mind of a single party, with the interpretative process described aimed at 'discovering' that fact. However, this may be to misunderstand the nature of the problem. In any given dispute there will exist two relevant parties: the speaker and the hearer, or in contractual terms the promisor and the promisee. So far the analysis has been concerned with the speaker's subjective intended meaning in the abstract, or from the perspective of the court; the interpretation has not concerned itself with the context of who the speaker is addressing. Recognising the hearer is important for a number of reasons. First it demonstrates that, prior to any court interpretation, it is the hearer who must interpret the words and

---

[91] L Hoffmann, 'The Intolerable Wrestle with Words and Meanings' (1997) 113 *South African Law Journal* 656, 658.

[92] J Steyn, 'Written Contracts: To What Extent May Evidence Control Language?' [1988] *Current Legal Problems* 23, 25.

[93] *Investor Compensation Scheme v West Bromwich Building Society* [1998] 1 WLR 896 (HL).

[94] *Stack v Dowden* [2007] UKHL 17, para [69]. See also *Staden v Jones* [2008] EWCA Civ 936.

[95] A Kramer, 'Common Sense Principles of Contract Interpretation (And How We've Been Using Them All Along)' (2003) 23 *Oxford Journal of Legal Studies* 173, 177.

conduct of the speaker to discover what they mean. It is the hearer who experiences the manifestations and the context in real time, and must also interpret subjective intended meanings in real time. Secondly, it draws our attention to the fact that the speaker's subjective intended meaning and the hearer's interpretation may be in conflict. A gap in intention may emerge between speaker and hearer. Thirdly, if the issue comes before the court a choice emerges as to whether the search is for the speaker's subjective intended meaning or the understanding created in the hearer. If the latter, this introduces a further stage in the process of interpretation, as it becomes necessary to then interpret the range of possible understandings available to the particular hearer, based on the hearer's particular prejudices and background assumptions.

Of course, all this assumes that one party is the speaker and the other the hearer. In many if not all cases both parties are simultaneously speaker and hearer.[96] Intention is thus a multifaceted complex, consisting of numerous projected meanings and interpretations. How is intention to be constructed given all these possibilities? In contract law—the area in which issues of interpretation are most often played out—these problems are resolved by placing certain restraints on the interpretive exercise. As Lord Hoffmann has said, objective interpretation really means the artificial restriction of the amount of background which can be used in aid of construction.[97] In *Investor Compensation Scheme* Lord Hoffmann explained that 'context' includes 'absolutely anything which would have affected the way in which the language of the document would have been understood by a reasonable man'.[98] This illustrates the first of the arbitrary constraints used in the contract law: the parties are converted from real persons into fictional 'reasonable persons', which means that background evidence as to the particular characteristics of the parties is suppressed: 'They are imaginary in the sense that the law removes their personal quirks and assumes them both, probably quite contrary to the facts, to be reasonable men'.[99]

The second technique is to suppress certain other kinds of background evidence for practical policy reasons. In contract law, evidence of prior negotiations and subsequent conduct have generally been looked upon sceptically, leading to the criticism of 'judicial tunnel vision' in the adoption

---

[96] *cf* W Howarth, 'The Meaning of Objectivity in Contract' (1984) 100 *Law Quarterly Review* 265 and JP Vorster, 'A Comment on the Meaning of Objectivity in Contract' (1987) 104 *Law Quarterly Review* 274.

[97] L Hoffmann, 'The Intolerable Wrestle with Words and Meanings' (1997) 113 *South African Law Journal* 656, 661.

[98] *Investor Compensation Scheme v West Bromwich Building Society* [1998] 1 WLR 896 (HL) 912–13.

[99] L Hoffmann, 'The Intolerable Wrestle with Words and Meanings' (1997) 113 *South African Law Journal* 656, 662.

of a 'single moment' theory of contract.[100] The reason for the exclusion is that English law is concerned with providing an objective interpretation of the words used in the contract. Lord Steyn suggests one way of looking at the issue: 'In relation to that enquiry evidence of the actual intentions of the parties, or of their pre-contractual communications is unhelpful'.[101]

Contrary to Lord Steyn's view, it is not that evidence of the parties' actual intentions is unhelpful—as we have seen such evidence is not actually direct evidence of the parties' intentions—but rather that the inferences that may be drawn from such evidence makes the enquiry unnecessarily complex and the conclusions to be drawn less certain.

In *Gissing* Lord Diplock explained what is meant by an objective approach to intention which navigates the speaker's meaning and hearer's interpretation:

> As in so many branches of English law in which legal rights and obligations depend upon the intention of the parties to a transaction, the relevant intention of each party is the intention which was reasonably understood by the other party to be manifested by that party's words or conduct notwithstanding that he did not consciously formulate that intention in his own mind or even acted with some different intention which he did not communicate to the other party. On the other hand, he is not bound by any inference which the other party draws as to his intention unless that inference is one which can reasonably be drawn from his words or conduct.[102]

This passage makes it clear that the boundaries of intention are set by the range of possible subjectively intended meanings and the possible objective interpretations, 'and not ... [by] any subjective intention or absence of intention which was not made manifest at the time of the transaction itself'.[103]

B. Intention: The Real Issue

It is impossible to disagree with the assertion that an imputed intention is a legal fiction. However, the analysis of the concept of intention and the

---

[100] See G McMeel, 'Prior Negotiations and Subsequent Conduct—the Next Step Forward for Contractual Interpretation' (2003) 119 *Law Quarterly Review* 272.

[101] J Steyn, 'Written Contracts: To What Extent May Evidence Control Language?' [1988] *Current Legal Problems* 23, 28–9.

[102] *Gissing v Gissing* [1971] AC 886 (HL) 906.

[103] *ibid*, 906. In the context of oral assurances and agreements it has been suggested that the parties' subjective intentions and understandings of the assurance or agreement may be relevant to determining the terms of the agreement: see *Carmichael v National Power Plc* [1999] 1 WLR 2042 (HL) 2048-2051 (oral agreement for employment) and *Thorner v Majors* [2009] UKHL 18, paras [80]–[83] (oral assurance of inheritance). It is unclear whether the same reasoning applies to the common intention constructive trust: see *Gissing v Gissing* [1971] AC 886 (HL) 906 and *Fowler v Barron* [2008] EWCA Civ 377, paras [36]–[37].

process of interpretation highlights a number of points. First, if 'intention' is taken to refer to 'subjective intended meaning' but only an objective approach to interpretation can be taken then it follows that actual intentions are inferred intentions, and that all 'findings' of intention may or may not correspond to subjective intended meaning. To the extent that the constructed intention departs from identity with the subjective intended meaning it can be regarded as false, and consequently a legal fiction. As such, the criticism that an imputed intention is fictional potentially applies equally to all findings of intention. This conclusion is bolstered by the fact that intention need only be established on the balance of probabilities.[104]

Secondly, the difference between an inferred and an imputed intention will usually be a fine one. If, on the one hand, an imputed intention is constructed from a hypothetical negotiation between the actual parties, then it will take into account the actual parties' particular prejudices and beliefs; the imputation will be grounded by the parties' belief structures. As we have seen, this additional evidence may allow the interpreter to close the gap between subjective intended meaning and objective interpretation, by placing the interpreter in the position of the actual parties.[105] Whilst Lord Neuberger criticised this approach as redounding to the advantage of the unreasonable party, arguably this approach is closer in structure to realising the wills of the parties than an inferential approach where the underpinning generalisations may go unstated. On the other hand, if the imputed intention is constructed from what reasonable parties would have done, we have seen that the notion of the 'reasonable man' is ever-present in the process of interpretation in any case. Imputation therefore crosses the boundaries and enters the forbidden territories of fairness only to the extent that notions of fairness are implicated in interpretation generally.

This links with a third point, that the finding of intention in any given case will implicate the court through the process of interpretation: 'Values inevitably pervade fact-finding, just as fact-finding is sometimes a kind of law-making. Herein lies the truth of the assertion that facts are *made*, as much as found, in legal process'.[106] The process is not one of finding facts, nor is it wholly the invention or construction of facts, but involves the court in moulding facts from the raw materials presented in court. Here we can see that intention has always confronted the property paradigm, as the court has always been implicated in the construction of intention. The real distinction between an inferred and imputed intention is actually the judicial consciousness of the construction of intention and therefore its

---

[104] cf *Fowler v Barron* [2008] EWCA Civ 377.

[105] HG Gadamer, *Truth and Method*, 2nd revised edn, (tr) J Weinsheimer and DG Marshall (London, Continuum, 2004)).

[106] P Roberts and A Zuckerman, *Criminal Evidence* (Oxford, Oxford University Press, 2004) 138.

potential falsity. But why, then, is imputation regarded with more hostility than actual and inferred intentions? The answer lies in its direct confrontation with the property paradigm. Whereas reference to actual and inferred intentions hide the role of the court, and with it its constructed nature, imputed intention directly and explicitly recognised its constructed nature, and with it its falsity. And here is the central point: it is its explicit recognition of its falsity that renders the fiction of imputed intention less dangerous than actual and inferred intention. As Fuller states,

> [a] fiction taken seriously, ie 'believed', becomes dangerous and loses its utility. It ceases to be a fiction under either alternative of the definition given above ... A fiction becomes wholly safe only when it is used with a complete consciousness of its falsity.[107]

The real problem does not lie in the recognition of imputed intentions, but rather in the related question: how is intention constructed, or interpretation constrained (which amounts to the same thing), after *Stack*?

V. CONSTRAINING INTERPRETATION AND CONSTRUCTING INTENTION

The analysis of the concept of intention suggests that the key question that must be asked in the construction of common intention is what is the range of legitimate or permissible meanings that can be placed on the parties' words and conduct? It is this question which I am concerned with and this section addresses. There is a second question that is equally important which the analysis suggests: did the claimant hold a legitimate interpretation of the words and conduct? Space precludes an analysis of this question.

A. Constraints, Objectivity and Discretion

We have already seen that intention is bound to objectivity, and that part of that process is the artificial restriction of evidence admitted in the construction of intention. This artificial restriction is important as it not only provides the framework for interpretation, and therefore for the range of legitimate meanings, but also the conditions that render the decision reviewable, predictable and certain. As MacCallum has said, 'talk about the "correctness" of judicial decisions makes clear sense only where there is a fairly well-established accumulation of policies, principles, rules, etc, which judges are expected to apply and which guide judges in making

---

[107] Fuller, above n 77, at 9–10.

decisions'.[108] Moreover, the extent to which intention is constrained or unconstrained determines the extent to which the constructive trust imposed is rule-based or discretionary.[109] We must focus on the constraints involved in order to assess any given rule or discretion:

> Constraining adjudication promotes judicial efficiency, and also consistency of decision-making, so that like cases are treated alike, and unlike cases differently ... When the constraints are publicly known, they typically allow those affected by the branch of law in question to plan their activities with assurance so as to prevent disputes arising, and also so as to resolve them efficiently if they do arise. When the constraint lies in private regularising factors, however, this will not be case.[110]

There are certain inbuilt constraints on judicial decision-making, including upbringing, training and socialisation,[111] but explicit constraints are also usually present.

This has wider implications as 'so long as a judicial remedy is described as discretionary, it cannot logically be said that the particular form of practical help which the remedy implies is part of the plaintiff's entitlement'.[112] Thus the extent of the constraints operating on the construction of intention implicates the property paradigm, as the more constrained the jurisdiction the less discretionary, whilst the less constrained the more discretionary, which means the remedy is not concerned with confirming pre-existing entitlement but re-arranging pre-existing entitlements contrary to the property paradigm.[113]

B. From Intention to Discretion?

Before *Stack* the range of evidence from which a permissible interpretation as to beneficial ownership could be made was very limited. *Rosset* limited the intentions which could be legitimately be inferred from express agreements, arrangements or understandings and financial contributions to the

---

[108] GC MacCallum, 'Dworkin on Judicial Discretion: Comments' (1963) 60 *The Journal of Philosophy* 638, 640 commenting on R Dworkin, 'Judicial Discretion' (1963) 60 *The Journal of Philosophy* 624.

[109] It is important to note that 'in reality, the distinction between rules and discretions is by no means an absolute one. It is rather a matter of degree: a matter of being more or less constrained, but never totally constrained or unconstrained': S Gardner, 'The Element of Discretion' in P Birks (ed), *The Frontiers of Liability Volume 2* (Oxford, Oxford University Press, 1994) 193.

[110] *ibid*, 195.

[111] *ibid*, 197. *cf* Griffith, above n 16.

[112] P Birks 'Proprietary Rights as Remedies' in P Birks (ed), *The Frontiers of Liability Volume 2* (Oxford, Oxford University Press, 1994), p 217.

[113] *cf ibid*, 223.

purchase of the property. Unlike contract law, the evidence from which an agreement, arrangement or understanding could be inferred was not limited to a singular point in time, but included both discussions prior to the acquisition of property and subsequent discussions.[114] The generalisation underpinning the inference of intention from financial contributions was premised on the importance of individual property investment for gain, rather than gift-giving, and the protection of the autonomy of the individual, both central aspects of the property paradigm. Despite the limitations placed on the interpretative process by *Rosset*, subsequent cases still found room to manoeuvre. For example, in *Hammond v Mitchell*[115] relatively slight evidence of an agreement was sufficient to establish a common intention. In other cases, such as *Midland Bank v Cooke*,[116] relatively small financial contributions to the purchase of property were increasingly found to be sufficient evidence from which to infer a common intention to share. And in *Le Foe v Le Foe*[117] it was found to be legitimate to infer the existence of a common intention from non-financial contributions to the family home.

These explicit restrictions were swept away in *Stack*, and now any evidence may be relevant to the determination of the parties' intentions and the determination of intention is constrained only by the implicit constraints of judicial assumptions and prejudices. For example, Baroness Hale's background in family law and her ideas of family property clearly influenced how she constructed intention in *Stack*. In her list of factors that may be relevant to divining the parties' true intention, the following cluster of factors suggest that an intention to share will depend on whether the parties' relationship indicates a shared life:

> [T]he purpose for which the home was acquired; the nature of the parties' relationship; whether they had children for whom they both had responsibility to provide a home; how the purchase was financed, both initially and subsequently; how the parties arranged their finances, whether separately or together or a bit of both; how they discharged the outgoings on the property and their other household expenses.[118]

In other words, evidence of a shared life is evidence of shared property, even if the parties contributed in different proportions and in different ways:

> It will be easier to draw the inference that they intended that each should contribute as much to the household as they reasonably could and that they would share the eventual benefit and burden equally ... Mercenary considerations ...

---

114 See *Gissing v Gissing* [1971] AC 886 (HL) 908.
115 *Hammond v Mitchell* [1991] 1 WLR 1127.
116 *Midland Bank v Cooke* [1995] 4 All ER 562.
117 *Le Foe v Le Foe* [2001] All ER 325.
118 *Stack v Dowden* [2007] UKHL 17, para [69].

should not be assumed [to] always take pride and place over natural love and affection.[119]

In applying the facts to the case, the sub-text to Baroness Hale's decision is clear: this was not a case of a 'real domestic partnership'.[120] Despite criticising the trial judge for looking at the relationship between the parties rather than matters relevant to intention,[121] Baroness Hale's opinion is underpinned by a discussion of the nature of the relationship. Mr Stack appears as a lazy free-loader, uninterested in his children, unconcerned with family responsibilities, and undertaking no financial responsibilities. Near the beginning of Baroness Hale's statement of the facts we learn that 'Mr Stack was "self-employed" as a builder/decorator, claiming no benefits but making no tax returns and keeping no records. Ms Dowden's evidence was that he did not want to take responsibility for the mortgage'.[122] The quotation marks around 'self-employed' indicate an element of disapproval, and the reference to Mr Stack not claiming benefits seemingly unnecessary and irrelevant to the question of intention which Baroness Hale had set. Ms Dowden, on the other hand, is portrayed as a hard-working, successful and independent woman. She took on a mortgage over property on her own,[123] and took on regular employment in the predominately male electrical engineer profession, 'working extremely hard and eventually rising to become the most highly qualified woman electrical engineer in the London area'.[124] Indeed, her earnings massively outstripped Mr Stack's earnings.[125] When it came to considering the conduct in relation to the property in dispute, Ms Dowden provided by far the greater financial contribution and even had the utilities bills in her sole name, 'although Mr Stack claimed to have paid some of these'.[126] Importantly, the parties always had separate bank and savings accounts, despite their relationship lasting from 1975 to 2002.

Applying the law to the facts, after considering the parties' respective financial contributions, Baroness Hale stated that the contributions must be looked at in the context of the parties' relationship. Not only was this 'not a case in which it can be said that the parties pooled their separate resources, even notionally, for the common good',[127] but it was a case where Mr Stack did not commit himself sufficiently to the family home, not even undertaking to pay for consumables and child minding.[128] Consequently this was

---

[119] *ibid*, para [69].
[120] *ibid*, para [87].
[121] See *ibid*, para [86].
[122] *ibid*, para [74].
[123] *ibid*, para [74].
[124] *ibid*, para [74].
[125] *ibid*, para [76].
[126] *ibid*, para [81].
[127] *ibid*, para [90].
[128] *ibid*, para [91].

'a very unusual case' justifying a departure from equal ownership: 'There cannot be many unmarried couples who have lived together for as long as this, who have had four children together, and whose affairs have been kept as rigidly separate as this couple's affairs were kept'.[129] In other words, in real relationships parties do not intend to maintain individual property interests and consequently an equal sharing of the beneficial interest is unlikely to be appropriate. In *Stack* this amounted to Baroness Hale stating that Ms Dowden and Mr Stack's relationship was a charade, despite living together for 27 years and having had four children.[130]

In his dissenting judgment Lord Neuberger provides an interesting critique of the factors on which Baroness Hale relies, in particular on the relevance of family finances. Although the pooling of finances may provide strong evidence that the sums in the pooled account were intended to be owned equally, it does not follow that the parties intended the beneficial interest in property acquired in joint names to be shared equally.[131] Equally, the fact that the parties keep their finances separate is of little evidential value in determining their common intentions with regard to their beneficial interests.[132] The point is that, for Lord Neuberger, the family home is a significantly different investment to other family resources. Consequently it is erroneous to infer from non-acquisitive conduct relating to the running of the family home how the family home itself was intended to be shared. The point to note is that the range of interpretations to be placed on such factors as joint bank accounts is very wide; almost any intention can be construed on the basis of the factors listed by Baroness Hale, as demonstrated by Lord Neuberger's analysis. The problem is that unlike contract, where the context is admitted in order to interpret intention as manifested in the text of the contract, there is no hanger on which to hang the context in common intention constructive trusts, as the context *is* the text. The lack of explicit constraints on the interpretation of intention is not a problem if there is a homogeneity of hidden assumptions and generalisations working as background, or implicit, constraints on the judiciary. However, as the difference of opinion between Baroness Hale and Lord Neuberger demonstrates, this may not always be the case.

The scope of the search has been widened to such an extent that the search often appears subjective and arbitrary, with results not objectively justifiable. For example, in *Adekunle v Ritchie*[133] property was transferred into the joint names of mother and son without an express declaration

---

[129] *ibid*, para [92].
[130] *cf Frost v Clarke* [2008] EWHC 742 in which the nature of the relationship played a central role. *cp Fowler v Barron* [2008] EWCA Civ 377.
[131] *Stack v Dowden* [2007] UKHL 17, para [133].
[132] *ibid*, para [134] and *cf* [141].
[133] *Adekunle v Ritchie* [2007] WTLR 1505.

of their respective beneficial interests. The mother died intestate, with the flat being her only real asset. The question was as to the extent of the son's beneficial interest. Given that they were joint tenants, the son claimed that he was the sole legal and beneficial owner by virtue of the doctrine of survivorship. His Honour Justice Behrens held that this case was 'very different from that of the normal cohabiting couple',[134] justifying a departure from the strong presumption of joint beneficial ownership. In particular, the mother had accumulated a generous discount on the price of the property under the right-to-buy scheme but could not afford the balance alone, which provided the context for the property being placed in joint names, although the 'primary purpose of the acquisition was to provide a home for Adassa Ritchie'. The parties' finances were separately held rather than pooled for the common good. Moreover, the mother had nine other children, with whom she was on good terms. The judge held that '[t]here is no reason to believe that she would have wanted the whole of her estate to pass to her youngest son, Richard Richie'.[135] These factors made this a very unusual case and 'strongly indicative that the parties did not intend their shares in the property to be equal (still less that they intended a beneficial joint tenancy with the right of survivorship should one of them die before it was severed)'.[136] As to the specific shares, the judge held that on a strictly arithmetical basis the son could not claim more than 25 per cent, but he awarded him 33 per cent of the beneficial interest on the basis of the holistic approach to the parties' intentions. The basis on which HHJ Behrens arrived at 33 per cent is a matter for conjecture. He provided no explanation or justification, apart from the fact that he took an holistic approach to determining the parties' intentions. Indeed, he recognised the 'subjectivity and uncertainty of the task' in making this assessment.[137] As Gardner has said, 'Discretionary justice ... cannot be seen to be done unless the judge gives an account of how he or she arrived at the response in question'.[138] This is clearly unconstrained discretionary justice, where the principle of intention provides little to no guidance, which confronts the property paradigm in a more pervasive way than the recognition of imputed intentions. This may, however, have been the intention of Baroness Hale in promulgating a factors-based approach to intention. Discretion is usually used when the facts or policy involved is nuanced and individualised. This is particularly the case in family law

---

[134] *ibid*, para [66].
[135] *ibid*, para [66].
[136] *ibid*, para [67].
[137] *ibid*, para [68]. Cp *Laskar v Laskar* [2008] EWCA Civ 347.
[138] S Gardner, 'The Remedial Discretion in Proprietary Estoppel—Again' (2006) 122 *Law Quarterly Review* 492, 510. *cf* S Gardner, 'The Remedial Discretion in Proprietary Estoppel' (1999) 115 *Law Quarterly Review* 438.

where 'discretionary resolution is par excellence the technique'.[139] Indeed, some have also considered a discretionary regime to be appropriate at the end of intimate relationships, notably one Brenda Hale, who some time ago considered that a discretionary approach similar to that under the Matrimonial Causes Act 1973 ought to govern all family home disputes:

> [C]ontinued examination and reform of the discretionary remedies on marital or family breakdown is more likely to bear fruit than attempts to introduce new rules of substantive law which will affect [the] whole population—especially in the property law area where, however misguidedly, this may be seen as benefiting certain (usually less powerful) groups at the expense of others (usually more powerful).[140]

It is suggested that if Baroness Hale intended to adopt such an approach, or at least a weak version of such an approach, she should have done so explicitly rather than widening the meaning of intention to the point of uncertainty. Indeed, Barlow and Lind have suggested that such a discretionary scheme, even if introduced by statute, faces the problem of making settlement difficult and provides little guidance to those decision-makers.[141]

C. A More Limited Approach to Intention?

Two recent cases suggest that facts that may have been sufficient to construct a common intention pre-*Stack* but post-*Rosset* may no longer be sufficient to construct an intention.[142] In *James v Thomas*[143] and *Morris v Morris*[144] the claimant was in each case not a legal owner, and in both cases the relationship between the claimant and the legal owner had developed long after the initial acquisition of the property.[145] In both cases the claimants undertook work without remuneration for the family business, which was carried out at the family home. In both cases the Court of Appeal

---

[139] S Gardner, 'The Element of Discretion' in P Birks (ed), *The Frontiers of Liability Volume 2* (Oxford, Oxford University Press, 1994) 199.

[140] B Hale, 'Family Law Reform: Whither or Wither?' [1995] *Current Legal Problems* 217, 229.

[141] A Barlow and C Lind, 'A Matter of Trust: the Allocation of Rights in the Family Home' (1999) 19 *Legal Studies* 468, 476.

[142] I discuss these cases in more detail in 'A Common Intention of a Rare Bird? Proprietary Interests, Personal Claims and Services Rendered by Lovers Post-Acquisition' (2009) 21 *Child and Family Law Quarterly* 104.

[143] *James v Thomas* [2007] EWCA Civ 1212.

[144] *Morris v Morris* [2008] EWCA Civ 257.

[145] *Morris* is complicated by the fact that the property was in the sole name of Olive Morris, the mother of the claimant's husband Richard, but was leased to Olive and Richard as joint tenants for the purpose of running the family farm.

rejected the claim to a beneficial interest. In *James v Thomas* Chadwick LJ accepted that

> as a matter of law, the common intention may be formed at any time before, during or after the acquisition of the property; and that the common intention may be inferred from evidence of the parties' conduct during the whole course of their dealings in relation to the property.[146]

However, 'in the absence of an express post-acquisition agreement, a court will be slow to infer from conduct alone that parties intended to vary existing beneficial interest at the time of acquisition'.[147] In this case, the claimant's conduct was 'wholly explicable on other grounds'.[148] The Court of Appeal was even more explicit in *Morris*. After emphasising Chadwick LJ's comments in *James v Thomas*, Gibson LJ gave a strict interpretation to *Stack*, limiting it to the quantification issue, and then stated that '[t]he authorities make clear that a common intention constructive trust based only on conduct will only be found in exceptional circumstances'.[149] This was a case where the evidence was 'wholly inadequate to establish any such common intention',[150] as the claimant's conduct was exactly what would be expected in the circumstances and not 'of such an exceptional nature as to lead to any inference ... that the claimant must have acted in the belief that she was acquiring an interest in the farm'.[151]

These cases suggest that despite the possibility of broader approach to intention in *Stack*, the construction of intentions remains rooted in the need for a 'real bargain' which will only be inferred where there is compelling evidence, ie evidence which cannot be explained on grounds other than an acquisitive intention. The cases also demonstrate that a strict approach to intention may be to the detriment of the non-legal owning claimant; the imposition of a heavy burden combined with the removal of the necessary inference from financial contribution in *Stack* has rendered the finding of a common intention much narrower than it was even in the aftermath of *Burns*. However, the cases can perhaps be explained on the ground that in both the land was acquired prior to the claimant meeting the defendant[152] and that, if the question really is one of ownership, then it is necessary to consider whether there has been any post-acquisition variation. In both these cases the behaviour of the parties was not sufficient to demonstrate any form of post-acquisition variation of ownership interests.[153]

---

[146] *James v Thomas* [2007] EWCA Civ 1212, para [19].
[147] *ibid*, para [24].
[148] *ibid*, para [27].
[149] *Morris v Morris* [2008] EWCA Civ 257, para [23].
[150] *ibid*, para [23].
[151] *ibid*, para [26].
[152] *cf Williamson v Sheikh* [2008] EWCA Civ 990 and *Thomson v Humphrey* [2009] All ER(D) 280 (Jun).
[153] *cf Webster v Webster* [2009] 1 FLR 1240 and *George v Szyczak* [2009] EW Misc 5.

VI. FROM CONTRACT TO STATUS?

Ten years ago Ursula Riniker asked 'why should the courts continue to insist on the fiction of "common intention"?'[154] Lon Fuller explains that the motive of most fictions is to reconcile a legal result with an express or an unexpressed premise:[155]

> Generally a fiction is intended to escape the consequences of an existing, specific rule of law. But occasionally the matter is more obscure. In some cases a fiction seems to be intended to avoid the implications, not of any specific and recognised rule of law, but of some unexpressed and rather general and vague principle of jurisprudence or morals.[156]

This is most likely to occur in 'developing fields of the law, fields where new social and business practices are necessitating a reconstruction of legal doctrine', which is nearly always done by way of 'artificial constructions' but in many cases through 'outright fictions'.[157]

Arblaster has noted the 'rooted pervasiveness' of liberal ideology,[158] and it is not inappropriate to state the same of the property paradigm. The unexpressed premise in this context is the continuing influence of the property paradigm, which forces property questions to be answered in terms of intention. The question arises, however, as to what the normative basis of the constructive trust in these cases is, if not intention. Fuller suggests that one advantage of legal fictions is that they can be used like scaffolding for the development of new laws, which can then be taken down once the law has been constructed.[159] If we can find the normative basis for the intervention of the courts in the distribution of property rights, then we may be able to dismantle the scaffolding of intention.

A. Dismantling Intention: Status as a Causative Event

According to Peter Birks's taxonomy of private law, rights and obligations arise from real events that happen in the real world which can be classified as consent, wrongs, unjust enrichment or arising in the miscellany. The common intention constructive trust is usually understood as arising from

---

[154] U Riniker, 'The Fiction of Common Intention and Detriment' [1998] Conv 202. *cf* L Fuller, *Legal Fictions* (Stanford, Stanford University Press, 1967) 88–9.

[155] Fuller, above n 77, at 51.

[156] *ibid*, 53.

[157] *ibid*, 68. *cf* Henry Maine's definition of a legal fiction in *Ancient Law* (London, JM Dent and Sons, 1917) 16.

[158] Arblaster, above n 5, at 9.

[159] Fuller, above n 77, at 70.

the category of consent.[160] However, recognition that the intention is constructed by the courts and does not necessarily correspond with the parties' subjective intended meanings weakens this argument. It has recently been suggested by Sir Terence Etherton that *Stack* can be interpreted as a case of unjust enrichment,[161] but this suffers from a similar problem to the consent category to the extent that it relies on the notion of intention. In order for rights and obligations to arise from the category of wrongs a duty must have been breached, but in most of these cases the parties are not in any form of relationship recognised by law or equity as incurring duties. In this final section I will tentatively suggest that the rights and obligations arising under the constructive trust are responding to an event in the miscellany: status.

With the rise of the welfare state at the beginning of the twentieth century the legislature and the judiciary reconceived the purpose of law as a tool in the regulation and active participation in economic and social organisation. Graveson notes that 'a movement from contract to status' had become apparent by 1941.[162] In his introduction to Graveson's *Status in the Common Law*, Roscoe Pound wrote that 'more and more the adjustment of relations is removed from the domain of free contract',[163] and that an understanding of 'status' in modern law is essential to understanding the relationship between State and the individual.[164] However, as Graveson notes, the term 'status' has rarely been used in English law, and the nature of the concept rarely examined. However, '[i]n one form or another problems of status are constantly before the courts'.[165] The Oxford English Dictionary defines status as '[t]he legal standing or position of a person as determined by his membership of some class of persons legally enjoying certain rights or subject to certain limitations'. However, Graveson concedes that it is not possible to define status in black and white, as it is a highly contextual concept.[166] Examples of status include spouse, civil partner, bankrupt and convict, all of which bring certain rights or limitations on rights. As Graveson explains,

> [w]hen a person becomes endowed with a new status his legal position undergoes a substantial alteration. His former legal capacity may be increased or reduced: the

---

[160] For example, R Chambers, 'Constructive Trusts in Canada Part II' (2002) 16 *Trust Law International* 2.

[161] T Etherton, 'Constructive Trusts: a New Model for Equity and Unjust Enrichment' (2008) 67(2) *Cambridge Law Journal* 265, 280–84.

[162] RH Graveson, 'The Movement from Status to Contract' (1941) 4 *Modern Law Review* 261, 268–9.

[163] RH Graveson, *Status in the Common Law* (London, Athlone Press, 1953) ix.

[164] It is interesting to note that Baroness Hale has also noticed a movement in family law from contract to discretion. See B Hale, 'Family Law Reform: Whither or Wither?' [1995] *Current Legal Problems* 217.

[165] Graveson, above n 163, at 2.

[166] *ibid* 3.

mass of his former legal rights and duties may be varied: he may receive new powers, and may be subjected to new disabilities.[167]

It can therefore be said that status is already a recognised causative event in the English legal system.

B. Cohabitation: From Common Intention to Status?

We have seen that the common intention constructive trust is rooted in the ideology of liberalism and the property paradigm, the search consequently being for intentions and bargains. The problem is not that the bargains supposedly found are in fact created by the courts, but rather that talk of a bargain at all in the context of the family home is inappropriate. The family home is built on different ideological foundations to the property paradigm. Rather than individualism and autonomy, family relations are built on notions of community, consideration, and trust and confidence.[168] Those who recognise this have suggested that an alternative means of regulating ownership in this area should be focused on the nature of the relationship, that rights and obligations should arise from status rather than contract. Gardner, for example, suggests that 'a doctrine centred on the fact of the relationship would allow the law to bypass such specific reference to the parties' thinking'.[169] Barlow and Lind suggest that the law should recognise 'that the home is a special type of property which ought to be governed by the same principles governing other (notably business) property',[170] and that 'the fact of the family relationship must be an important consideration in settling legal entitlements'.[171] Both Gardner and Barlow and Lind recommend the introduction of a community of property scheme, which would align legal principle with the ideological and factual foundations of the family unit.[172]

But is it possible to find the text of such scheme built upon the status of the parties' relationship in *Stack*? I suggest that it can. Although on the facts it was held that the parties' relationship was not sufficiently 'communal' to create the necessary status relationship, the suggestion is that where there

---

[167] *ibid*, 136

[168] See generally S Gardner, 'Rethinking Family Property' (1993) 109 *Law Quarterly Review* 263.

[169] S Gardner, 'Rethinking Family Property' (1993) 109 *Law Quarterly Review* 263, 282. *cf* S Gardner, 'Family Property Today' (2008) 124 *Law Quarterly Review* 422.

[170] A Barlow and C Lind, 'A Matter of Trust: the Allocation of Rights in the Family Home' (1999) 19 *Legal Studies* 468, 472.

[171] *ibid*, 473.

[172] S Gardner, 'Rethinking Family Property' (1993) 109 *Law Quarterly Review* 263, 287. *cf* E Cooke, A Barlow and T Callus, *Community of Property: A Regime for England and Wales?* (Nuffield Foundation, 2006) and further J Simon, 'With all My Worldly Goods ...' (1964) *Holdsworth Club Lecture*.

is a pooling of resources for the common good the court will recognise the community of property. The rights do not arise from the existence of a cohabitation relationship per se, but rather give legal effect to a de facto community of property. Where this is the case, the court is likely to find the beneficial shares are held equally. This was implied in *Stack* itself, and explicit in *Abbott*, a sole legal owner case, and *Edwards v Edwards*,[173] a legal co-owner case. In those cases not only were the parties married—a prima facie indicator of a community—but they organised their finances together through a joint bank account and, in *Abbott*, also undertook joint responsibility on the mortgage and interest. As such it was held that the property was held equally. It can also be found in the Court of Appeal's decision in *Holman v Howes*.[174] In that case property was purchased in Mr Howes's sole name with a view to joint occupation and reconciliation between the parties, who had formerly been married. The trial judge held that the parties held in equal shares. In the Court of Appeal Miss Holman sought a share greater than 50 per cent. Lloyd LJ held that the parties held in equal shares. Despite giving judgment on the basis of a lack of intention that Miss Holman should have more than an equal share, it is clear that this was not a sufficiently unusual case; the purchase was for their joint occupation and reconciliation, undertaken as a 'joint and equal venture'. *James v Thomas* and *Morris* can also be analysed within the terms of community. In those cases the acquisition of the property predated the existence of any community. This suggests that only property purchased in the course of the relationship will fall into the community of property. Community of property also explains why cases involving parent and child will rarely give rise to equal shares.[175] Community of property was also central to *Fowler v Barron*.[176] The facts of that case were remarkably similar to those in *Stack*. However, Arden LJ held that in this case the party seeking to rebut the presumption of joint ownership had failed to establish a common intention. Distinguishing *Stack*, Arden LJ pointed out that in this case 'the parties largely treated their incomes and assets as one pool from which household expenses will be paid'.[177]

The question that needs to be addressed is whether or not status provides a sufficient normative foundation for interfering with property rights. The community of property interpretation directly confronts the property paradigm, as it arises through an operation of law rather than the intentions of the parties, and is rooted in an ideology in conflict with our common ideas of property. This necessarily entails asking how the constructive trust

---

[173] *Edwards v Edwards* [2008] All ER (D) 79 (March).
[174] *Holman v Howes* [2007] EWCA Civ 877. cf *Fowler v Barron* [2008] EWCA Civ 377.
[175] cp *Adekunle v Ritchie* [2007] WTLR 1505 and *Laskar v Laskar* [2008] EWCA Civ 347.
[176] *Fowler v Barron* [2008] EWCA Civ 377. Also see *Jones v Kernott* [2009] EWHC 1713.
[177] *ibid*, para [46].

arising in the context of communal property ought to affect third parties. Given that property's binding effect arises from the notion of pre-existing self-imposed obligations, it is questionable whether or not a community of property ought to bind third parties. However, as Martin Dixon has demonstrated, beneficial interests in the home are increasingly proprietary rights in name only, and that '[e]quitable co-ownership without legal title is, for all practical intents and purposes, a claim on a pot of money, not a claim to an interest in land'.[178]

VII. CONCLUSIONS

The problems surrounding the distribution of the family home on the breakdown of intimate and familial relationships have been framed by property questions: who owns the home and in what shares? Consequently the answers to these questions are framed in terms consistent with property norms, where pre-existing property entitlements are discovered by looking to some prior 'transaction' that will inform us as to how the parties regulated their affairs. On the face of it *Stack* presents a single text rooted firmly within the property paradigm. However, I have argued that the property paradigm is challenged at a number of levels. First, the interpretation of the facts in the construction of intention itself implicates the court in the process of determining property interests. Secondly, the broad evidential basis and unconstrained nature of the construction of intention is symptomatic of a discretionary approach to the re-arrangement of property rights, which challenges the notion of property as entitlement. However, the discretion is inherently constrained by liberal notions of both property and the family unit. Finally, I have tentatively suggested that the normative basis for the re-arrangement of rights in *Stack* is status, and presents the greatest challenge to the property paradigm. The extent to which the constructive trust will be used to determine property rights according to status will depend on the extent to which the judiciary is willing to depart from the traditional understanding of property. However, as Craig Rotherham has said, 'the classic liberal understanding of property has a place in our consciousness as an immutable truth'.[179] As the recent case law has demonstrated, intention may also be an immutable truth in the context of ownership of the family home.

---

[178] M Dixon, 'Equitable Co-ownership: Proprietary Rights in Name Only?' in E Cooke (ed), *Modern Studies in Property Law: Volume 4* (Oxford, Hart Publishing, 2007) 46.
[179] C Rotherham, 'Proprietary Relief for Enrichment by Wrongs: Some Realism about Property Talk' (1996) 19 *University of New South Wales Law Journal* 378, 382.

10

Bankrupt Husbands and the Application of the Doctrine of Exoneration in Australian Law: Moving into the 21st Century[*]

JUSTICE BERNA COLLIER[**]

I. INTRODUCTION

FOLLOWING THE MARRIED Women's Property Acts of the late nineteenth century, property law principles specific to the protection of married women have been few and far between.[1] A concept which traditionally satisfied this description beyond the enactment of those Acts is the equitable doctrine of exoneration, which historically applied, in respect of the interest of a wife in property jointly owned with her husband, to debts incurred by the husband in relation to that property.

A succinct description of the equity is found in *Halsbury's Laws of England* as follows:

> If the property of a married woman is mortgaged or charged in order to raise money for the payment of her husband's debts, or otherwise for his benefit, it is presumed, in the absence of evidence showing an intention to the contrary, that she meant to charge her property merely by way of security, and in such case she is in the position of surety, and is entitled to be indemnified by the husband, and to throw the debt primarily on his estate to the exoneration of her own.

> The right to exoneration is, however, a presumptive right only; it depends on the intention of the parties to be ascertained from all the circumstances of each particular case. It may be rebutted by evidence showing that the wife

---

[*] Biennial Conference on Property Law, Queens' College, Cambridge University, 2 April 2008.

[**] Judge, Federal Court of Australia.

[1] One noted exception in Australia being the so-called rule in *Yerkey v Jones* (1939) 63 CLR 649, applied and broadened in recent times by the High Court of Australia in *Garcia v National Australia Bank* (1998) 194 CLR 395.

intended to make a gift of the property to her husband; and it has been held to be rebutted where the money was raised to pay debts which, though legally the husband's, had been contracted by reason of the extravagant mode of living of both parties. No presumption of a right to exoneration arises where the money is raised to discharge the debts or obligations of the wife, otherwise for her benefit.[2]

The doctrine of exoneration, in its application to jointly-owned property of husband and wife, can be explained through a simple hypothetical example:

> A married couple (*H* and *W*) own real property as joint tenants. The matrimonial home is located on that property. No mortgage exists over the property.
>
> *H* operates a business as an electrician, as a sole trader. He wishes to expand the business, however the business requires an injection of capital.
>
> At *H*'s request, *W* agrees that an approach be made to the Bank for a loan of $175,000 for use in *H*'s business. The Bank agrees to this loan, provided it is secured by a first registered mortgage over the matrimonial home.
>
> *H* and *W* execute a mortgage in favour of the Bank, which advances the $175,000.
>
> Unfortunately, *H*'s business is unsuccessful. He becomes bankrupt.
>
> The matrimonial home is sold for $580,000. The Bank is paid $175,000 from the proceeds of sale to discharge the mortgage. The balance remaining from the sale is $405,000.
>
> *H*'s trustee in bankruptcy, *T*, claims that the sum of $405,000 should be equally divided between *H*'s bankrupt estate and *W*. This would mean that both T (on behalf of the creditors of *H*) and *W* would each receive $202,500.
>
> The doctrine of exoneration in this case however applies. Subject to discharge of the mortgage to the Bank, each of *H* and *W* are entitled to half of the sale price of the matrimonial home, being $290,000 each (half of $580,000). The doctrine of exoneration applies so that *H*'s interest in the matrimonial property is the primary fund from which the debt of $175,000 is discharged.

---

[2] 19 *Halsbury's Laws of England*, 3rd edn, para 1375 (footnotes omitted). See also D Browne (ed), *Ashburner's Principles of Equity*, 2nd edn (London, Butterworths, 1933, republished Sydney, Legal Books, 1983) 170.

> $290,000 minus $175,000 is $115,000. Accordingly, of the surplus of $405,000 remaining from the sale of the property following the discharge of the mortgage to the Bank, *T* on behalf of *H*'s creditors is entitled to *H*'s interest in $115,000 (not $202,500 as claimed) while *W* is entitled to $290,000.

Despite the relative obscurity of this equity, the principle that the wife was presumed to intend to charge her interest in the property as surety only for the husband's debts and could thus claim the 'exoneration' of her interest in the property in the event of the husband's bankruptcy, appears to have been recognised by English law for at least three centuries.[3] Further, as the cases demonstrate, not only does the principle continue to represent good law with respect to married women, but it appears to extend beyond that class. Indeed the principle has been the subject of reliance by married men from an early time, and beyond the matrimonial relationship applied to co-ownership of property more generally.

The expansion of this principle is of particular interest from a legal perspective (and of perhaps potential alarm to creditors) in that it is said to give rise to a *presumption* in relevant circumstances that the wife/co-owner was in the position of a surety.[4] The alarm to creditors derives from the terms of section 116(2)(a) of the Bankruptcy Act 1966 (Cth), which enacts the long-standing principle[5] that property of a bankrupt divisible among the creditors of a bankrupt does not include property held by the bankrupt in trust for another person. The relief afforded to the wife/co-owner by the doctrine in circumstances of the bankruptcy of the principal debtor is similarly of long standing.[6]

This paper will consider issues including:

1. The parameters of the doctrine.
2. Who can rely on the doctrine and
3. The elements of the doctrine and issues relevant to its application.

II. PARAMETERS OF THE DOCTRINE

The words 'exonerate' and 'exoneration' bear a number of meanings, all referable to relief from liability. For the purposes of this paper, 'exoneration'

---

[3] See, for example, *Pocock v Lee* (1707) 2 Vern 604, 23 ER 995.

[4] This issue is considered in detail later in the paper.

[5] See, for example, *Scott v Surman* (1743) Willes 400, 125 ER 1235 (Willes CJ), and cases discussed in P McQuade and M Gronow, *McDonald, Henry and Meek Australian Bankruptcy Law and Practice* (Sydney, Lawbook Co, 1996) para 116.2.05 *et seq.*

[6] See, for example, D Browne (ed), *Ashburner's Principles of Equity*, 2nd edn (London, Butterworth, 1933, republished Sydney, Legal Books, 1983) 170.

will be considered in the property law context, which contemplates—in certain cases—relief of a person or an estate from a liability *but so as to throw that liability on to another person or estate.*[7] Common examples of the use of the word in the property law context include the following:

— The right of trustees to appropriate trust assets to discharge a trust-related liability is known as 'the right of exoneration', which takes priority over the rights in or in reference to the assets of beneficiaries.[8]
— Historically in the testamentary context:
    — a specific legatee had the right to have his specific legacy exonerated from debts and liabilities of a testator existing at the testator's decease;[9]
    — in circumstances where mortgaged lands descended, the heir was entitled to exoneration out of the first two classes of property in the administration of assets;[10] and
    — only a specific intention from the testator would exonerate the personality from its primary liability in relation to satisfaction of the testator's debts.[11]

This paper, however, does not examine these formulations of exoneration principles. As made clear earlier, this paper focuses on the right of exoneration vesting in a co-owner of property—in the case law traditionally (although not exclusively) the wife—which is presumed to arise in the circumstances where jointly-owned property is mortgaged to secure money raised for the benefit of *the other* joint owner, and the principles which, over time, have developed specific to those circumstances.

The concept of an owner of jointly owned property—married or otherwise—relying on an equitable concept relevant to mortgages and guarantees raises the question of the extent to which the principles under examination intersect with traditional rules applicable to mortgages, guarantees, and more generally applicable equitable principles. In this respect it is useful at this point to make the following observations.

First, as identified in a number of decisions,[12] the recognition of the co-owner as a surety for the purposes of the doctrine has in more recent

---

[7] *Jowitt's Dictionary of Judicial Law.*

[8] *Commissioner of Stamp Duties (NSW) v Buckle* (1998) 192 CLR 226, 246–7, *CPT Custodian Pty Ltd v Commissioner of State Revenue* (2005) 224 CLR 98, 120–21, and see discussion in HAJ Ford and WA Lee, *Principles of the Law of Trusts* (Sydney, Thomson Lawbook Co, 2006) para 14010.

[9] *Fitzilliams v Kelly* (1852) 10 Hare 266, 68 ER 926 and see the discussion in HS Theobald, *A Concise Treatise on the Law of Wills*, 6th edn (London, Stevens & Sons, 1905) 168–9.

[10] *Yonge v Furse* (1855) 20 Beav 380, 52 ER 649 and see discussion in Theobald, above n 9, at 170.

[11] *Kilford v Blaney* (1885) 29 Ch D 145, and see discussion in Theobald, above n 9, at 800.

[12] For example *Parsons v McBain* (2001) 109 FCR 120, 127 and *Re Berry* [1978] 2 NZLR 373, 377.

times resulted in the doctrine falling within the third class of surety cases described by Lord Selborne LC in *Duncan, Fox & Co v North and South Wales Bank*,[13] namely those kinds of cases

> in which, without any ... contract of suretyship, there is a primary and a secondary liability of two persons for one and the same debt, the debt being, as between the two, that of one of those persons only, and not equally of both, so that the other, if he should be compelled to pay it, would be entitled to reimbursement from the person by whom (as between the two) it ought to have been paid.[14]

It is not necessary[15] for the creditor to be a party to this 'constructive'[16] suretyship. Further, it is clear that the concept of suretyship extends beyond that of personal liability in respect of the debts of a third party and includes circumstances where a person pledges, mortgages or charges their property for the debts of another as well as those who pledge their personal credit.[17]

Secondly, the doctrine appears to constitute an exception to the principles of contribution recognised both at law and in equity.[18] The right of contribution, which is based on principles of natural justice, arises in circumstances where several persons are debtors[19] and extends to, for example, co-sureties, co-insurers under contracts of indemnity insurance, co-contractors, parties liable to the holder of a bill of exchange, partners, joint tenants and tenants in common.[20] There are elements of pre-conditions to contribution inherent in the doctrine of exoneration in this context, in the sense that:

1. The relevant property is co-owned.
2. The property is mortgaged jointly by the co-owners and

---

[13] *Duncan, Fox & Co v North and South Wales Bank* (1880) 6 App Cas 1, 11.

[14] Other examples of this third class of suretyship given by O'Donovan and Phillips are in respect of put options (para 1.980), and the right of an indorser of a bill of exchange to indemnity from the acceptor (para 12.300).

[15] *Duncan, Fox & Co v North and South Wales Bank* (1880) 6 App Cas 1 (HL) 12.

[16] J O'Donovan and J Phillips, *Modern Contract of Guarantee* (looseleaf, Sydney, Thomson Lawbook Co, 2004) para 1.500.

[17] See for example *Re Conley* [1938] 2 All ER 127 (CA) 131–2, 132–3, and 138–9, *Dickson v Reidy* [2004] NSWSC 1200, [33].

[18] This was certainly the view of Cohen J in *Chase Corporation (Australia) Pty Ltd v North Sydney brick and Tile Co Ltd* (1994) 35 NSWLR 1, 22 and Hamilton J in *Oamington Pty Ltd (Receiver and Manager Appointed) v Commissioner of Land Tax* (1997) 98 ATC 5051. Further, Fisher and Lightwood are of the view that the doctrine of contribution may be displaced by the doctrine of exoneration: *Fisher and Lightwood's Law of Mortgage*, 12th edn (Sydney, LexisNexis Butterworths, 2006) 846, para 45.4; ELG Tyler, PW Young and C Croft, *Fisher and Lightwood's Law of Mortgage*, 2nd Australian edn (Sydney, LexisNexis Butterworths, 2005) 680, para 30.4.

[19] See, for example, Kitto J in *Albion Insurance Co Ltd v Government Insurance Office (NSW)* [1969] 121 CLR 342, 351.

[20] R Meagher, D Heydon and M Leeming, *Meagher, Gummow & Lehane's Equity Doctrines & Remedies*, 4th edn (Sydney, Butterworths LexisNexis, 2002) 387.

3. On its face, the co-owners have a co-ordinate liability under a mortgage
    to meet the liability secured by the mortgage, however
4. One of the co-owners is absolved from the need to contribute equally
    to that liability.

Thirdly, the doctrine is in some ways akin to the traditional concept of marshalling,[21] the purpose of which is to prevent one creditor depriving another of its security,[22] and rests 'upon the principle that a creditor who has the means of satisfying his debt out of several funds shall not, by the exercise of his right, prejudice another creditor whose security comprises only one of the funds'.[23] Interestingly in *Re a Debtor (No 24 of 1971), ex parte Marley v Trustee of the Property of the Debtor* Foster J observed that, had the principal debtor not become bankrupt,

> on a sale of the property the bank's debt would necessarily have been paid off out of the proceeds of sale and the [surety], as a matter of marshalling, could have insisted upon the debt being discharged out of the bankrupt's share.[24]

Finally, the principles with respect to *indemnity* of sureties by principal debtors are, in specific ways, relevant to the position of the co-owner in these circumstances. Subject to any agreement between the parties to the contrary, as a general rule at common law, a surety's right to claim an indemnity from the principal debtor will not arise until a surety has paid the principal debt or some part of it.[25] The nature of the doctrine of exoneration is that, once the obligation to the mortgagee of the jointly owned property is discharged, the 'surety' can then claim exoneration of his or her estate in respect of that property. However, it is equally clear that the

---

[21] Indeed in circumstances where there are multiple debtors and multiple securities, both the equity of exoneration and marshalling principles may apply—see, for example, *Knight v Lawrence* [1993] BCLC 215, 231.

[22] See, for example, comments of Lord Eldon in *Aldrich v Cooper* (1803) 8 Ves 382, 395; 32 ER 402, 407.

[23] *Fisher and Lightwood's Law of Mortgage*, 12th edn, above n 18, at 848, para 45.8; Tyler, Young and Croft, above n 18, at 686, para 30.9. See also Meagher, Heydon and Leeming, above n 20, at 417 *et seq* and GE Dal Pont and DRC Chalmers, *Equity and Trusts in Australia and New Zealand* (Sydney, LBC Information Services, 2000) 379 *et seq*.

[24] *Re a Debtor (No 24 of 1971), ex p Marley v Trustee of the Property of the Debtor* [1976] 1 WLR 952, 955.

[25] See, for example, G Moss and D Marks, *Rowlatt on Principal and Surety*, 5th edn (London, Sweet & Maxwell, 1999) 148, para 7-09 and O'Donovan and Phillips, above n 16, at para 11.350. Conversely, the general rule is that a guarantor who has not paid the principal debt cannot require the creditor to proceed against the principal debtor *before* having recourse to the guarantor: Lord Westbury in *Ewart v Latta* [1865] SC 36, discussed in O'Donovan and Phillips at para 11.350. (Interestingly the right of a guarantor to an "indemnity" from the debtor in circumstances where the guarantor has paid all or some of the principal debt is referred to as the guarantor's right of "exoneration" in the US—see, for example, SW Symons, *A Treatise on Equity Jurisprudence as administered in the United States of America (by John Norton Pomeroy)*, 5th edn, vol IV, (Union NJ, The Lawbook Exchange Ltd, 2002) p 1070 para 1417.

doctrine can apply in the absence of prior payment by the surety of any part of the principal debt, for example where one of the parties seeks a declaration from the court as to their rights inter se in respect of the relevant property.[26] Indeed, the right of the co-owner has been described as an inchoate right of indemnity.[27] The position was summarised by Campbell J in *Rossfreight Holdings Pty Ltd v Unipep Australia Pty Ltd*[28] as follows:

> It's part of the justification for the equity of exoneration that, when the obligations between surety, creditor and principal debtor are worked out, one can say with confidence, at the time the court makes an order, that it is the principal debtor who will end up being liable to pay. Equity avoids multiplicity of actions, by ordering that the inevitable eventual outcome of two different actions by creditor against surety, and then by surety against principal debtor, be achieved straight away, without going through those two different actions, and without the surety suffering any financial disruption involved in first paying the creditor and then seeking reimbursement from the principal debtor.

Further, the interest of the person relying on the doctrine of exoneration against their co-owner has in numerous cases been described as a charge upon the estate of the co-owner by way of *indemnity* for the purpose of enforcing against that co-owner the right to have that estate first resorted to for the payment of the debt.[29]

Considered in the surety context, it is useful to note at the outset that this doctrine is not relevant to:

1. Cases where a joint mortgagor is *specifically* recognised by the relevant agreement to be a surety, and rights and remedies flow from the relevant agreement. In this case the general laws of guarantee will apply and the surety may be entitled to seek an order that the other mortgagor is primarily liable for the debt.[30]
2. Cases associated with such equitable doctrines commonly applied in transactions involving the marital relationship, including unconscionability,[31] undue influence[32] or the rule in *Yerkey v Jones*.[33]

It is appropriate now to turn to the manner in which the equity operates.

---

[26] See, for example, the orders sought in *Re Pittortou* [1985] 1 WLR 58.

[27] Foster J in *In re a Debtor (no 24 of 1971), ex parte Marley v Trustee of the Property of the Debtor* [1976] 1 WLR 952, 955, and *Re Pittortou*, above n 26, at 61.

[28] *Rossfreight Holdings Pty Ltd v Unipep Australia Pty Ltd* [2002] NSWSC 1074, [18].

[29] *Gee v Liddell* [1913] 2 Ch 72, 76, *Farrugia v Official Receiver in Bankruptcy* [1982] 58 FLR 474, 477 and *Parsons and Parsons v McBain* (2001) 109 FCR 120, 128.

[30] For example, *Tate v Crewdson* [1938] 3 All ER 43.

[31] See, eg, *Commercial Bank of Australia v Amadio* (1983) 151 CLR 447.

[32] See, eg, *Barclays Bank plc v O'Brien* [1994] 1 AC 180.

[33] *Yerkey v Jones* (1939) 63 CLR 649.

III. WHO CAN RELY ON THE DOCTRINE?

A. Exoneration of Wife's Estate

As noted earlier in this paper, the traditional application of the doctrine was to exonerate the estate of the wife from the debts of the husband. Tyler, Young and Croft identify numerous cases involving the application of the doctrine in such circumstances, dating from the early eighteenth century.[34] By way of illustration, an example of the principle can be seen in the report of *Pocock v Lee*,[35] which is as follows:

> A. and his wife mortgage the wife's estate, and A. covenants to pay the money, but the equity of redemption is reserved to them and their heirs. A. dies and his wife survives. The mortgage shall be discharged out of the husband's estate.
>
> Mr *Alexander* and his wife, who was the daughter and heir of one *Dayly*, made a mortgage of the wife's estate; the husband covenanted to pay the money, but the equity of redemption was reserved to them and their heirs. Mr *Alexander* the husband died, and made the defendant his executor. The wife surviving, after a decree to account.
>
> The question was upon exceptions to the Master's report, whether the mortgage-money should stand charged upon the land, or the land be exonerated out of the husband's personal estate.
>
> *Per Cur.* The husband having had the money, is in equity the debtor, and the land is to be considered but an additional security; and so decreed it according to the judgment in the House of Peers, in the case of *Lord* and *Lady Huntington.*

The genesis of the doctrine in its application to the matrimonial relationship was explained by Richardson J in *Re Berry*:[36]

> Under the old law applied to married women's property preceding the enactment of the *Married Women's Property Act 1882* (UK) a payment to husband and wife was a payment to the husband. And, even though the wife might have been partly or wholly interested in it, it belonged to the husband (*Hudson v Carmichael*; *Hall's* case pp 494–495).[37]

Further, as Bryson J observed in considering the equity,

> [t]he doctrine of exoneration became established in an earlier age when a wife's property existed only in equity, and equity, in a number of rules including this one, protected property interests of wives against the legal and social dominance of husbands.[38]

---

[34] Tyler, Young and Croft, above n 18, at 681, para 30.7. Cases cited by the learned authors cite *Huntington v Huntington* (1702) 2 Vern 437, 23 ER 881; *Tate v Austin* (1714) 1 P Wms 264, 24 ER 382; *Peirs v Peirs* (1750) 1 Ves Sen 521, 27 ER 1180 and *Lancaster v Evors* (1846) 10 Beav 154, 50 ER 541; *Thomas v Thomas* (1855) 2 K & J 79, 69 ER 701.

[35] (1707) 2 Vern 604, 23 ER 995.

[36] *Re Berry* [1978] 2 NZLR 373.

[37] *ibid*, 377.

[38] *Official Trustee in Bankruptcy v Citibank Savings Ltd* (1995) 38 NSWLR 116, 129–30.

The historical background to the development of the doctrine has, on occasion, caused courts to reflect on the continuing relevance of the doctrine in the matrimonial relationship. Judges have, in particular, noted that the legal and social contexts in which the doctrine developed are now very different,[39] and that the guidance that Victorian era (and, indeed, pre-Victorian era) cases can provide to the inferences which should be drawn from the dealings with one another of husbands and wives today is often not very valuable.[40] As Walton J expressed the position succinctly in *re Woodstock AP (Bankrupt)*:[41]

> It seems to me that that case [*Hall v Hall*] was decided in the days when the wife did nothing except sit at home and run the household and boss the servants about and the husband was expected to be, and indeed was, the provider. Times have now changed.

Notwithstanding these reservations however, it is clear that the courts have no difficulty in accepting the continued application of the doctrine in the context of the matrimonial relationship. Indeed, in those cases where reservations have been expressed by courts, the courts have then proceeded to consider the applicability of the doctrine to the facts of the relevant case. A significant number of cases in which the doctrine was applied, or at least its application was considered, since the end of the nineteenth century have involved married women claiming the benefit of the doctrine, with varying degrees of success depending on the facts of the case.[42]

An important illustration of this point can be seen from the decision of the Full Court of the Federal Court in *Parsons and Parsons v McBain*,[43] where the court held that the doctrine of exoneration applied in the wife's favour. It is informative to briefly consider the facts of that case, and the reasons for the court's decision.

---

[39] Bryson J, *ibid*, 130.

[40] Scott J in *Re Pittortou* [1985] 1 WLR 58, 62, and see similar observations of Richardson J in *Re Berry* (1978) 2 NZLR 373, 377 and comments of the Court of Appeal for British Columbia in *Re Bankruptcy of Kostiuk* [2002] BCCA 410, [58].

[41] Unreported, Walton J, in the High Court (Ch D), 19 November 1979. The author would like to express her sincere thanks to Mr GS Moss QC, of Gray's Inn, for his assistance in making available the unreported (and generally unavailable) transcript of the decision of his Lordship in this case.

[42] Cases include *Paget v Paget* [1898] 1 Ch 470, *In re Cronmire* [1901] 1 QB 480 and *Hall v Hall* [1911] 1 Ch 487. Relatively recent cases from a variety of jurisdictions in which married women have been successful include *Parsons and Parsons v McBain* (2001) 109 FCR 120 (discussed below); *Lin v Official Trustee in Bankruptcy (No 1)* (2002) 187 ALR 220; *Re Pittortou* [1985] 1 WLR 58 (in relation to payments made for business purposes and for the husband's sole benefit); *Ken Glover & Associates Inc v Irwin* [2005] BCJ No 2080 (Master McCallum); *Re Bankruptcy of Kostiuk* [2002] BCCA 410; *Farrugia v Official Receiver in Bankruptcy* (1982) 58 FLR 474; and *White v Dortenzio* [2004] VSC 381. Relatively recent cases from a variety of jurisdictions in which, despite judicial acceptance of the existence of the doctrine, married women have unsuccessfully claimed the benefit of the doctrine include *Re Berry* [1978] 2 NZLR 373 and *Official Trustee in Bankruptcy v Citibank Savings Ltd* (1995) 38 NSWLR 116.

[43] *Parsons and Parsons v McBain* (2001) 109 FCR 120.

(i) Parsons v McBain

Peter Parsons and Geoffrey Parsons, were partners, with their parents, in a family transport business in Tasmania. In 1977 each brother separately purchased property. Peter Parsons acquired a property at 80 King Street, Smithton. Geoffrey Parsons purchased a vacant block at 2 Leesville Road, and a house at 22 Simpson Avenue, Smithton.

In 1979 Geoffrey marred the appellant, Cathryn Parsons. They agreed that the property at 22 Simpson Avenue would be their matrimonial home to be owned by them equally, however before moving into that property they decided to build a house at 2 Leesville Road where they would live.

In 1987 Peter married the appellant, Bronwyn Parsons. They agreed that the property at 80 King Street would be their matrimonial home owned by them equally. Bronwyn Parsons made contributions towards the loan taken out by Peter Parsons in respect of that property.

The transport business of the Parson family fell into financial difficulties. In June 1992, Peter Parsons, with the consent of his wife, mortgaged 80 King Street to secure a loan of AUS$36,000, which he advanced to the partnership. At the same time, Geoffrey Parsons mortgaged 2 Leesville Road to secure a loan of AUS$58,000 to contribute to the partnership.

Some time thereafter, the property at 80 King Street was transferred to Bronwyn Parsons, and the property at 2 Leesville Road was transferred to Cathryn Parsons.

The Parsons family transport business failed, and both Peter and Geoffrey Parsons were declared bankrupt.

The trustee in bankruptcy of Peter and Geoffrey Parsons commenced proceedings against Bronwyn Parsons and Cathryn Parsons to recover the two properties, on the basis that the transfer of each was void against him pursuant to section 120 or 121 of the Bankruptcy Act 1966 (Cth). Both section 120 and 121 apply to avoid certain antecedent transactions of a bankrupt as against the trustee in bankruptcy.

The proceedings commenced by the trustee in bankruptcy were heard together. Bronwyn Parsons and Cathryn Parsons each alleged, in summary, that:

1.   She was entitled to an equitable interest as to one moiety in the transferred property and that a transfer of the legal title to that interest was outside sections 120 and 121; and
2.   She had an equity of exoneration in respect of the 1992 mortgage of the relevant property, which equity entitled her to cast the burden of the debt upon her husband's interest. Since the amount of the loan secured by the mortgage exceeded the value of her husband's interest, his interest in the property had been extinguished.

At first instance the trial judge dismissed the claims of Bronwyn Parsons and Cathryn Parsons, and found in favour of the trustee.

The Full Court of the Federal Court of Australia upheld the first claim of Bronwyn Parsons and Cathryn Parsons to an equitable interest as to one moiety in the relevant properties. In relation to the remaining moiety, the court considered the claims of the appellants with respect to equity of exoneration. The court noted that, although the doctrine was originally considered to be limited to the relationship between husband and wife, the authorities clearly showed that this was not the case. Further, their Honours held (in summary at 127–8):

— the equity of exoneration is an incident of the relationship between surety and principal debtor;
— it usually arises where a person has mortgaged his property to secure the debt of another, whether or not that other has covenanted to pay the debt, although it also arises where the relationship is *treated* as one of suretyship as discussed in *Duncan, Fox, & Co v North and South Wales Bank* (1880) 6 App Cas 1, 10;
— the equity operates in the nature of a charge upon the estate of the principal debtor by way of indemnity for the purpose of enforcing against that estate the right which the co-owner has, as between co-owner and the principal debtor, to have that estate resorted to first for the payment of the debt: *Gee v Liddell* [1913] 2 Ch D 62, 72;
— where co-owners mortgage their property so that money can be borrowed for the benefit of one mortgagor, the other has an interest in the property of the co-mortgagor whose property is to be regarded as primarily liable to pay the debt;
— if a surety received a benefit from the loan, the equity of exoneration may be defeated: *Paget v Paget* [1898] 1 Ch 470;
— in this case, any benefit received by either Bronwyn or Cathryn Parsons was both too remote to defeat the equity, and incapable of valuation.

Although each appellant was entitled to exoneration, this did not give her ownership of her husband's property, but merely a charge over it. Accordingly, the court held it would be necessary for each appellant to transfer a one half interest in the property to the trustee who would hold it subject to each appellant's charge.

B. Exoneration of Husband's Estate

Interestingly, given what appears to have been the historical foundation of the doctrine in equity protecting the property interests of wives against the legal and social dominance of husbands, there are a number of cases where husbands have claimed exoneration in the nature of a surety in circumstances where the wife was the primary debtor. While by no means comparable in number to the cases involving wives claiming reliance on the equity—which, at least prior to the Married Women's Property Acts, reflected the legal disabilities of married women at that time discussed earlier in this paper, and perhaps more recently reflects real-life relationships[44]—the existence of these authorities suggests a broader foundation for the doctrine than the equitable protection of married women only. This hypothesis applies equally to circumstances involving claims of exoneration outside the matrimonial relationship.

(i) Early Cases

Three early cases where it appears the principle was applied to the benefit of a husband are *Bagot v Oughton*,[45] *Gee v Smart*[46] and *Gray v Dowman*.[47]

In *Bagot v Oughton* Sir Edward Bagot married the daughter and heir of Sir Thomas Wagstaff, who died having mortgaged part of his estate for £3,500 and leaving his daughter his heir. Lady Bagot settled her estate on her husband and herself and her male children. Sir Edward Bagot subsequently joined an assignment of the mortgage and covenanted that he or his wife or one of them would pay the money owing on the mortgage. Sir Edward later died, and Lady Bagot remarried Colonel Oughton but then she also died.

Cowper LC held that the covenant from Sir Edward Bagot for the repayment of the £3,500 should not oblige his personal estate to go in ease of the mortgaged premises. The debt was originally that of Sir Thomas Wagstaff, and continued to be so. The additional security given by Sir Edward Bagot did not alter the nature of that debt.

In *Gee v Smart* a husband and wife mortgaged lands to the plaintiff, as security for money lent by the plaintiff to them for the purpose of, inter alia, repaying a debt of the wife contracted before marriage. Coleridge J observed:

> There are many cases where, money having been borrowed on the security of the wife's estate for the discharge of the husband's debt, relief has been given and the wife's estate exonerated, at least until the husband's has been exhausted ... The same principle seems clearly applicable in the converse case, where the object of the proceeding is to charge the personal estate of the husband primarily, and exoneration is sought for that, by throwing the primary charge on the wife's estate, on the ground of the covenant having been only for a discharge of her debt.[48]

---

[44] Note the observation to this effect by Peter Smith J in *Hurst v BDO Stoy Hayward LLP* [2006] EWHC 791, [69].

[45] *Bagot v Oughton* (1717) 1 P Wms 347, 24 ER 420.

[46] *Gee v Smart* (1857) 8 El & Bl 313, 120 ER 116.

[47] *Gray v Dowman* (1858) 27 LJ Ch 702.

[48] *Gee v Smart* (1857) 8 El & Bl 313, 319–20; 120 ER 116, 119.

Accordingly, the husband was entitled to rely on the doctrine of exoneration.

In *Gray v Dowman* Mrs Dickerson received certain estates on her marriage, vested in trustees for such uses and trusts as she should by deed or will appoint, and in default of appointment for her for life, the proceeds to be for her sole and separate use and not to be subject to the debts, control or engagements of her husband. In execution of her power, Mrs Dickerson later mortgaged her property to secure a sum of £400. Mr Dickerson was made a party to that mortgage, and both husband and wife covenanted that they would pay the mortgagee the money so advanced with interest. The mortgage stated that the £400 was borrowed by Mrs Dickerson for the benefit of her sister to enable the sister to pay off her mortgage. Mr Dickerson later died, and the issue arose as to whether the mortgagee could look to his estate in settlement of the mortgage debt owing.

Kindersley VC held that, although on the face of the deed the mortgage purported to have been made by Mr and Mrs Dickerson, on the evidence the money was obtained for the use of the wife in order that she might be able to benefit her sister. The covenant to pay entered into by Mr Dickerson was in the nature of a suretyship. Accordingly, the husband's estate was entitled to be indemnified in respect of that debt.

Each of these cases involved decisions by the court as to the application of the estates of deceased husbands in satisfaction of mortgages entered by the husband for, it appears, the benefit of the wife. Each case also involved litigation following the death of the husband, which in turn raises the question whether these cases can be explained as peculiar to testamentary law as distinct from the equitable doctrine of exoneration currently under consideration. However this seems unlikely. The general rule in England prior to 1926[49] was that in the case of death the personal estate of a deceased person was the primary fund for the payment of debts, but the testator could appropriate a specific portion of his personal estate for the payment of debts; alternatively a testator could specifically make the realty the primary fund or create a mixed fund for the payment of debts.[50] Neither *Bagot*, *Gee*, nor *Gray* considered this issue—rather the issue in each case was whether the husband's estate should be exonerated from the debt by reason of arrangement with the wife. The direct application of exoneration principles in *Gee* is noted above. Further, in *Bagot* the report of the case concludes:

> From hence, as it seems, it may be inferred, that if a feme sole makes a mortgage, and receives the money, and marries, and then the mortgage is transferred,

---

[49] And the enactment of the Administration of Estates Act 1925 (UK).
[50] For further explanation of these principles see 16 *Halsbury's Laws of England*, 3rd edn, para 676 *et seq*.

the husband joining in the assignment, and covenanting to pay the money, the wife, or the heirs of the wife, upon the death of the husband, shall not compel an application of the husband's personal estate for the payment of the mortgage-money.[51]

More directly, Kindersley VC in *Gray* found:

> I think it clear that parol evidence may be admitted in such a case as this to show for whose benefit the money was really advanced; and upon the evidence I am satisfied that the money was obtained for the use of the wife in order that she might be able to benefit her sister, and the covenant to pay entered into by the husband was in the nature of a suretyship ... The husband was the surety on his covenant for the wife, and there was nothing in the security given by Mrs Lake which affected the question in favour of the wife's estate ... Mrs Lake's property, after satisfying the first mortgage, turns out to be worthless, and I think that the husband is therefore entitled to be indemnified in respect of so much as he is liable to pay.[52]

(ii) Dickson v Reidy

Of more contemporary interest and relevance in relation to reliance by a married man on the doctrine is the decision of Nicholas J of the Supreme Court of New South Wales in *Dickson v Reidy*.[53]

In this case Mr and Mrs Dickson were the registered proprietors as joint tenants of property which was their matrimonial home. Mrs Dickson wanted to invest money in her employer's business and become a part-owner of that business. Mr Dickson reluctantly agreed to join with Mrs Dickson in borrowing the sum of AUS$343,000, the money being secured by a mortgage over the property, of which AUS$70,000 would be paid to a creditor of the business, AUS$100,000 to the vendor of the matrimonial home who had originally provided a vendor mortgage to the Dicksons, and the balance to the wife's employer for the acquisition by the wife of an interest in the business. Without the knowledge of Mr Dickson (indeed the court found that Mrs Dickson had forged his signature to the relevant document), Mrs Dickson subsequently arranged for refinancing of the loan from Lawteal Pty Ltd, and increased the amount borrowed, secured by a mortgage over the property.

Unfortunately the business failed and, inter alia, a sequestration order was made against the estate of Mrs Dickson. The defendant was appointed trustee in bankruptcy of her estate.

---

[51] *Bagot v Oughton* (1717) 1 P Wms 347, 348; 24 ER 420, 421.
[52] *Gray v Dowman* (1858) 27 LJ Ch 702, 704.
[53] *Dickson v Reidy* [2004] NSWSC 1200.

The matrimonial home was sold for AUS$747,000 by the plaintiff and the defendant as the wife's trustee in bankruptcy. After the discharge of mortgage and other liabilities the net proceeds of sale were AUS$230,616. Half of this amount—AUS$115,313—was paid to Mr Dickson, with the balance paid to the trustee in bankruptcy. Mr Dickson claimed the balance from the defendant on the basis that:

the jointly owned property was mortgaged to secure the loan which was wholly for the benefit of the wife and , in the circumstances, the doctrine of exoneration applies so that her interest in the property was subject to a charge to secure his right of exoneration from liability for the loan. He claims that her interest in the property which passed to the Defendant was subject to that charge, and thus he was entitled to the whole of the net proceeds of sale rather than to one half thereof.[54]

Nicholas J held: 'the doctrine of exoneration depends on the presumed intention of the parties and continues to exist to supply a presumption of the intention of parties as to who should be principal and who should be surety'.[55]

His Honour accepted the husband's submissions, namely that the evidence established that all the loans were arranged on the wife's initiative, and that she prevailed on the husband to join with her in providing their property as security for them. Accordingly,

[t]he circumstances of each transaction show that in agreeing to his wife's proposal he intended to stand in the position of a surety to support the loan with the understanding, as was the fact, that the whole of it was for her use and benefit and not for his.[56]

Mr Dickson had a right of exoneration in respect of, inter alia, the loan from the mortgagee, and the plaintiff has established a charge on the wife's interest in the property to secure that right, which property has passed to the trustee in bankruptcy subject to the charge. His Honour therefore ordered that the trustee in bankruptcy pay Mr Dickson the balance from the sale of the matrimonial home remaining in the hands of the trustee in bankruptcy.

A further question, however, is whether *Dickson v Reidy* is simply an example of a broader application of the doctrine to persons other than married women. Indeed, in *Dickson v Reidy* it is clear that Nicholas J based his decision on the proposition that the doctrine was of general application rather than confined to the marital relationship.

---

[54] *ibid*, [6].
[55] *ibid*, [27].
[56] *ibid*, [32].

C. Other Relationships

In *Official Trustee in Bankruptcy v Citibank Savings Ltd*[57] counsel for the plaintiff submitted that an application of the doctrine of exoneration to facts beyond those involving reliance by a married woman, was an unwarranted extension—not authorised by authority—of the doctrine.[58] On the facts of the case Bryson J did not need to decide this issue. However, in any event it is clear that the application of the doctrine to situations other than as between husband and wife, while possibly an extension of the application originally contemplated by the courts, is not 'unwarranted' and has not been unwarranted for some time.

In *Parsons v McBain* the Full Court of the Federal Court observed that it was once thought that the doctrine was limited to husband and wife; however, the authorities showed that the doctrine was not so limited and would apply in other cases. Their Honours cited *Gee v Liddell*[59] and *Caldwell v Ridge Wholesale Acceptance Corporation (Australia) Ltd*[60] in support of this proposition.[61]

In *Parsons v McBain*, the facts of the case did in fact involve married women relying on the doctrine in relation to the debts of their husbands. However, as indicated by the court, there is authority, both modern and extending historically beyond *Gee v Liddell* in 1913, where the courts have been prepared to apply the equity so as allow relief from a debt. So, for example:

— in *Lee v Rook*[62] the court held that a minor who borrowed money from a married couple, where the married couple mortgaged their estate to raise the money, was primarily liable for the debt after he came of age, and the married couple were entitled to have their estate disencumbered of the debt by the borrower;
— in *Stokes v Clendon*[63] the court held that a mortgagor or a provider of collateral security was entitled to be a party to a bill of foreclosure against the principal mortgagor to prevent the burden of the mortgage falling inappropriately on the collateral mortgagor's estate;
— in both *Peirs v Peirs*[64] and *Re the estate of John Keily the elder Owner; ex parte John Keily the younger, Petitioner*[65] a son who had joined

---

[57] *Official Trustee in Bankruptcy v Citibank Savings Ltd* (1995) 38 NSWLR 116.
[58] *ibid*, 129–30.
[59] *Gee v Liddell* [1913] 2 Ch 62.
[60] *Caldwell v Ridge Wholesale Acceptance Corporation (Australia) Ltd* (1993) 6 BPR 13, 539.
[61] *Parsons and Parsons v McBain* (2001) 109 FCR 120, 127.
[62] *Lee v Rook* (1730) Mos 318, 25 ER 415.
[63] *Stokes v Clendon* (1790) 3 Swans 158n, 35 ER 812.
[64] *Peirs v Peirs* (1750) 1 Ves Sen 521, 27 ER 1180.
[65] *Re the estate of John Keily the elder Owner; ex p John Keily the younger, Petitioner* (1857) Ir Ch Rep 394.

his father in a mortgage of an estate where the father received all the money advanced was held to be a surety only and that the son's assets were not to be held primarily liable in relation to the mortgage. Significantly in *Peirs v Peirs* the Lord Chancellor drew an analogy with the situation where a wife claimed exoneration:

> If a father tenant for life, wants to raise a sum, and gets his son to join for the security, but the father receives the money, it is the debt of the father, who will be bound to exonerate the son's estate from this incumbrance ... for the son will be considered as having pledged his estate for that purpose; *just as if wife joins with husband in raising money on her estate, it will be considered as pledging her estate for that, and the husband is bound to exonerate it.*[66] (emphasis added);

— in *Robinson v Gee*[67] the principle was held to apply between two brothers, the Lord Chancellor drawing an analogy with the principle where a wife joined in a mortgage of her inheritance for a debt of her husband and was entitled for her estate to be exonerated;[68]

— in *Gee v Liddell*[69] the court, relying on *Stokes v Clendon*, applied the principle in respect of two men who entered into a mortgage with a third man, where the third man was primarily liable as principal debtor;

— in *Re a Debtor (no 24 of 1971) ex parte Marley v Trustee of the Property of the Debtor*[70] a father, who co-owned a house with his son, was held entitled to rely on the doctrine in circumstances where the son became bankrupt;

— in *Caldwell v Ridge Wholesale Acceptance Corporation (Australia) Limited*[71] a woman who was the joint proprietor of a housing unit with a married couple (who in turn held their half share as between themselves as joint tenants) was held able to rely on the doctrine of exoneration so that, when the housing unit was sold, repayments in respect of the mortgage over the property for which the married couple were primary debtors came first from their interest in the property;

— in *Dinsdale by his tutor the Protective Commissioner v Arthur*[72] the court applied the principal in favour of the former de facto spouse of the principal debtor's daughter.

---

[66] *Peirs v Peirs* (1750) 1 Ves Sen 521, 522; 27 ER 1180, 1181.
[67] *Robinson v Gee* (1749) 1 Ves Sen 251, 27 ER 1013.
[68] ibid, 252; 1014.
[69] *Gee v Liddell* [1913] 2 Ch 62.
[70] *Re a Debtor (no 24 of 1971) ex p Marley v Trustee of the Property of the Debtor* [1976] 1 WLR 952.
[71] *Caldwell v Ridge Wholesale Acceptance Corporation (Australia) Ltd* (1993) 6 BPR 13, 539.
[72] *Dinsdale by his tutor the Protective Commissioner v Arthur* [2006] NSWSC 809.

Given the accepted breadth of the doctrine in respect of the parties who can invoke its operation, the next issue for consideration is the circumstances in which the doctrine operates.

IV. PRE-CONDITIONS TO APPLICATION OF THE DOCTRINE

The courts in *Re Berry*[73] and *Parsons v McBain*[74] identified three pre-conditions to the application of the doctrine of exoneration:

A. A person must charge his property.
B. The charge must be for the purpose of raising money to pay the debts of another person or to otherwise benefit that other person.
C. The money so borrowed must be applied for that purpose.

It is useful to examine each of these requirements in light of the reported cases.

A. 'A Person Must Charge his Property'

The court in *Parsons v McBain* held that this requirement was satisfied where a person claiming reliance was the beneficial owner of the relevant property and the charge was by his or her trustee.[75] As the cases demonstrate, the principle applies to circumstances where a person pledges, mortgages or charges their property for the debts of another as well as those who pledge their personal credit,[76] although most of the cases in relation to the doctrine of exoneration involve circumstances where the surety joins with the principal debtor in the mortgage of a jointly-owned property.

The doctrine will have no application where the claimant has not charged his or her property. This was demonstrated in *In the matter of James Alan Peasegood (a bankrupt) and Edwin Francis Hunt (trustee in bankruptcy) v Hannah Susan Peasegood*[77] where the relevant property was the sole property of the husband. The Court of Appeal held that the equity of exoneration claimed by the wife had no application in relation to such property because it was not *her* property which was the subject of a charge.

---

[73] *Re Berry* [1978] 2 NZLR 373, 376–7.
[74] *Parsons and Parsons v McBain* (2001) 109 FCR 120, 127.
[75] *ibid*, 127.
[76] See, eg, Luxmoore J in *re Conley* [1938] 2 All ER 127, 138–9 (cf Clauson LJ at 132–3), *Dickson v Reidy* [2004] NSWSC 1200, [33].
[77] *In re JA Peasegood (a bankrupt) and EF Hunt (trustee in bankruptcy) v HS Peasegood* [1997] EWCA Civ 1589.

B. 'The Charge Must Be for the Purpose of Raising Money to Pay the Debts of Another Person or to Otherwise Benefit that Other Person'

This requirement in turn raises three inter-related issues:

— first, it is clear that, in order for the doctrine to apply, *another person* must benefit from the transaction;
— secondly, the *purpose* of the 'surety' charging his or her assets must be to benefit that other person;
— thirdly, the surety must obtain *no benefit* from so charging their assets.

(i) Benefiting Another Person

It is clear from consideration of cases in which the doctrine of exoneration has been applied that the 'other person' whom the 'surety' intends to benefit from their action in charging their property is, effectively, the principal debtor. The fact that the transaction is for the principal debtor's benefit is, indeed, the rationale for the burden of the debt being primarily cast on that person's estate. As the Lord Chancellor stated plainly in *Re Keily*,

> [w]hen two persons join in an instrument to secure a sum of money, and a question arises as to who is the principal and who is the surety, there being no evidence of contract, the common test is, who got the money?[78]

This situation was recognised by the Federal Court in *Parsons v McBain*, where the example was given:

> [W]here co-owners mortgage their property so that money can be borrowed for the benefit of one mortgagor, the other has an interest in the property of the co-mortgagor whose property is to be regarded as primarily liable to pay the debt.[79]

However, it is also clear that, if the purpose of raising the money is that it is actually to be paid to a third party at the direction of the principal debtor, the doctrine is not excluded. So, for example, in *Dickson v Reidy*[80] Nicholas J observed:

> In my view the fact that the funds were raised and applied for the use of the wife without benefit to the Plaintiff is sufficient to attract the doctrine ... The equity is not confined to a situation in which the liability is incurred to discharge a debt or obligation personal to the co-owner of the secured property. Thus, for example, in the circumstances of this case, it is not of significance that the wife caused the $70,000.00 to be made available for the payment of Mr Page's rent ... Insofar as the evidence does not establish the destination of some part of a particular loan,

---

[78] *Re Keily* (1857) Ir Ch Rep 394, 405.
[79] *Parsons v McBain* (2001) 109 FCR 120, 127–8.
[80] *Dickson v Reidy* [2004] NSWSC 1200.

nevertheless when the whole of the evidence is taken into account there is ample basis for the inference that it was probably spent in furtherance of the wife's interests.[81]

Similarly in *Gray v Dowman*[82] the fact that the moneys were raised by mortgage for the purpose of assisting the sister of the principal debtor rather than for the specific benefit of the principal debtor herself in no way affected the right of the husband to claim exoneration from the mortgage at a later date.

That the 'surety' will be unable to rely on the equity of exoneration if he or she has received a benefit from the transaction is not contentious. This principle has been recognised by a large number of recent cases including *Parsons v McBain*,[83] *Re Pittortou*,[84] *Farrugia v Official Receiver in Bankruptcy*,[85] *Dickson v Reidy*,[86] *Dinsdale by his tutor the Protective Commissioner v Arthur*,[87] *Lin v Official Trustee in Bankruptcy (No 1)*,[88] and *Re Bankruptcy of Kostiuk*.[89] It also represents the traditional position as made clear in such earlier cases as *Paget v Paget*,[90] *Re Keily*,[91] *Hudson v Carmichael*,[92] and *Clinton v Hooper*.[93] In many ways the issue of whether the surety receives— or does not receive—a benefit from the transaction is the key to the application of the doctrine in any particular case. If the 'surety' receives a benefit from, for example, a loan transaction, the immediate question is whether he or she is actually a 'surety' or is in reality a principal debtor. If the 'surety' receives a benefit, it will be difficult, if not impossible, to demonstrate the purpose of raising money for another person, or to demonstrate that the money was so applied for that other person's benefit. Finally, the presumption in relation to married women which the courts traditionally recognised could not apply if the wife had received a benefit from the transaction.

(ii) Purpose

While closely related to the issue whether the 'surety' has received a benefit, it is also necessary, for the doctrine to apply, that the purpose of the

---

[81] *ibid*, [33]–[34], and see also *Dinsdale by his tutor the Protective Commissioner v Arthur* [2006] NSWSC 809, [23].
[82] *Gray v Dowman* (1858) 27 LJ Ch 702.
[83] *Parsons and Parsons v McBain* (2001) 109 FCR 120.
[84] *Re Pittortou* [1985] 1 WLR 58.
[85] *Farrugia v Official Receiver in Bankruptcy* (1982) 58 FLR 474.
[86] *Dickson v Reidy* [2004] NSWSC 1200.
[87] *Dinsdale by his tutor the Protective Commissioner v Arthur* [2006] NSWSC 809.
[88] *Lin v Official Trustee in Bankruptcy (No 1)* (2002) 187 ALR 220.
[89] *Re Bankruptcy of Kostiuk* [2002] BCCA 410.
[90] *Paget v Paget* [1898] 1 Ch 470.
[91] *Re Keily* (1857) Ir Ch Rep 394.
[92] *Hudson v Carmichael* (1854) Kay 613, 69 ER 260.
[93] *Clinton v Hooper* (1791) 3 Bro CC 201, 29 ER 490.

transaction by which the surety has raised money was to benefit the principal debtor or another person at the principal debtor's direction. Interestingly, if such a purpose exists, the traditional rule involving the position of a married woman was that it was *presumed, in the absence of evidence showing an intention to the contrary*, that she meant to charge her property merely by way of security, and could therefore seek exoneration of her own estate, from the debts of her husband.[94]

In *Paget v Paget*,[95] Lindley MR, delivering the judgment of the Court of Appeal, explained the principle in the following terms:

> The authorities bearing on the subject, beginning with *Huntingdon v Huntingdon* (1702) 2 W & T 6th ed 1147 and coming down to *Hudson v Carmichael* (1854) Kay 613, 620 shew that if a married woman charges her property with money for the purpose of paying her husband's debts and the money raised by her is so applied, she is prima facie regarded in equity, and as between herself and him, as lending him and not giving him the money raised on her property, and as entitled to have her property exonerated by him from the charge she has created. This doctrine is purely equitable, and the authorities which establish it shew that it is based on an inference to be drawn from the circumstances of each particular case; the prima facie inference being in such a case as that supposed that both parties intended that the wife's assistance should be limited to the necessity of the case and should not go beyond such necessity.[96]

Interestingly his Lordship then went on to say:

> But even where the wife charges her property to pay her husband's debts incurred without reference to her there may be circumstances which prevent any inference from arising in her favour ... It was long ago settled that, although under the old law a husband became liable for the ante-nuptial debts of the wife, she had no right in equity to compel him to exonerate property of hers charged with those debts, even although he had expressly covenanted to pay them ... This shews the importance of ascertaining and not confounding the wife's debts with the husband's debts when considering such cases as those to which I am alluding. *To say that in all such cases there is a presumption in favour of the wife, and that it is for the husband to rebut it, is, in our opinion, to go too far and to use language calculated to mislead. The circumstances of each case must all be weighed in order to see what inference ought to be drawn; and until an inference in favour of the wife arises there is no presumption for the husband to rebut.* It this is forgotten, error may creep in.[97] (emphasis added)

The position as stated by Lindley MR therefore constitutes a somewhat circular proposition—namely that the inference that the 'surety' has loaned, rather than given, the money raised on the surety's property to the principal

---

[94] See 19 *Halsbury's Laws of England*, 3rd edn, para 1375.
[95] *Paget v Paget* [1898] 1 Ch 470 (CA).
[96] ibid, 474.
[97] ibid, 474–5.

debtor will not arise at all unless the purpose of benefiting the principal debtor is first demonstrated, and the money raised has been so applied. The Court of Appeal in *Paget v Paget* clearly rejected any suggestion that there was a rebuttable presumption in favour of a wife, or any other surety, in such circumstances. It is clear from the terms of that case that the circumstances of each case must *first* be considered to determine whether the court can draw the inference which allows the claimant to rely on the doctrine of exoneration.

As explained in *Paget v Paget*, the inference in relation to married women has been a traditional incident of the doctrine, and continues to be accepted with varying degrees of caution in academic writings on this subject[98] and later judicial decisions.[99] Significantly, however, a number of leading commentators accept an extended articulation of the proposition, namely that the inference extends to *anyone*—not just married women—who so pledges, mortgages or charges their property.[100] Similarly, courts in a number of more recent decisions have indicated that the inference is generally applicable, only with more frequent application in cases where a wife's property is charged for her husband's benefit.[101] Bryson J said in *Official Trustee in Bankruptcy v Citibank Savings Ltd*:[102]

> The legal and social contexts are now very different, but the doctrine of exoneration continues to exist to supply a presumption of the intention of parties as to who should be principal and who should be surety ... The doctrine serves to illustrate that the intention of a party may establish which is to stand as surety and which as principal even though both appear to incur substantially the same legal obligation.[103]

In relying on the doctrine of exoneration, the claim will fail if the purpose of the 'surety' in raising the money is not to benefit another. Consideration of this issue will, almost inevitably, blur with the consideration of whether the 'surety' has received a benefit, and whether the moneys were applied in accordance with the alleged purpose, both matters are discussed later in this paper. However, identification of the requisite intention of the parties is a prior issue for consideration in each case, and establishment of the requisite

---

[98] See, for example, ELG Tyler, PW Young and C Croft, *Fisher and Lightwood's Law of Mortgage*, 2nd Australian edn (Sydney, LexisNexis Butterworths, 2005) p 681, para 30.7, D Browne (ed), *Ashburner's Principles of Equity*, 2nd edn (London, Butterworths, 1933, republished Sydney, Legal Books, 1983) 170.

[99] For example *Farrugia v Official Receiver in Bankruptcy* (1982) 58 FLR 474, 476.

[100] G Moss and D Marks, *Rowlatt on Principal and Surety*, 5th edn (London, Sweet & Maxwell, 1999) 156, para 7-26, *Fisher and Lightwood's Law of Mortgage*, 12th edn (London, LexisNexis Butterworths, 2006) 847, para 45.7.

[101] *Re Berry* [1978] 2 NZLR 373, 376 and see, for example *In re a Debtor (no 24 of 1971), ex parte Marley v Trustee of the Property of the Debtor* [1976] 1 WLR 952 where Foster J held that the surety relationship should be implied from the circumstances.

[102] *Official Trustee in Bankruptcy v Citibank Savings Ltd* (1995) 38 NSWLR 116.

[103] *Ibid*, 130.

intention is essential to the success of the claim; similarly, absence of the requisite intention will prove immediately fatal. Bryson J further observed in *Official Trustee in Bankruptcy v Citibank Savings Ltd*:[104]

> Although contemporaneous agreements, arrangements and expressions of intention are the usual sources of evidence about the intentions of parties on such a subject, there is no reason why their intentions may not be inferred from the circumstance in which they acted. Intentions, like other facts, may be proved from circumstances. Circumstances could conceivably furnish very clear proof of intention as to who was to be principal and who was to be surety, and the intended and actual application of funds raised when two persons incur a common liability would often have an important, even predominant part in the proof of the relevant intention.[105]

So, as his Honour observes, contemporaneous expressions of intention are useful sources of evidence. For example:

— in *Parteriche v Powlet*,[106] although the husband and wife joined in a bond, the husband wrote on the bond 'I own this to be my debt'. The Lord Chancellor held that the natural construction of this concession was that the wife merely became surety for this debt;

— in contrast, in *Caldwell v Bridge Wholesale Acceptance Corporation (Australia) Ltd*,[107] where property was owned by Mrs Caldwell as to one-half, as tenant in common with Mr and Mrs Thomson, although all co-owners joined in a mortgage to the bank, only the Thomsons were described in the mortgage as debtors. Cole J held that an agreement could clearly be implied between the Thomsons and Mrs Caldwell that, as between themselves, the Thomsons' half interest in the property would first bear the obligation of repayment of the loan to the Bank and that Mrs Caldwell stood only in the position of surety;

— further, in *Paget v Paget*,[108] the Court of Appeal specifically attached more importance to statements of the wife in contemporaneous documents in support of her application for a mortgage, than to statements she made 15 years later before the court, in particular to references by the wife to the debts contracted by her husband and herself as 'our debts'. The court therefore formed the view that the purpose of the wife in joining in the relevant mortgage was to address debts of both herself and her husband, and not to benefit her husband alone, as she had claimed.

---

[104] *Ibid.*

[105] *Ibid*, 130.

[106] *Parteriche v Powlet* (1742) 2 Atk 383, 26 ER 632.

[107] *Caldwell v Bridge Wholesale Acceptance Corporation (Australia) Ltd* (1993) 6 BPR 13, 539.

[108] *Paget v Paget* [1898] 1 Ch 470 (CA).

Interestingly in *Re Berry*,[109] although the evidence before the court was that overdraft facilities were arranged on a joint account for which the matrimonial home was used as security, the account remained overdrawn because of the business drawings of the husband, the wife had no part in arranging the security for the overdraft and the wife's deposits into the account were both small and infrequent, the New Zealand Court of Appeal held that the wife could not rely on the doctrine of exoneration in relation to her interest in the matrimonial home. The reason was that the court was not persuaded that the intentions of the parties was that, in relation to this transaction, the husband was to be the principal debtor and the wife was to be the surety. Richardson J observed:

> So in each case husband and wife mortgaged property which they owned jointly, and they did so in consideration of advances of accommodation made or given to them jointly and received by them jointly. To put it another way, the transactions in each case were two-party transactions, between the lender (the bank or the nominee company) on the one hand and the borrower (husband and wife) on the other. They did not involve three distinct parties (the lender, the principal debtor, and the surety) which is the essence of the surety situation ...

> Here, husband and wife were at all times co-debtors to the bank and later to the nominee company. There is nothing in that relationship of co-debtor to warrant the implication that as between themselves, one is principal debtor and the other is secondary debtor. It is not a case where a wife charged her property or pledged her credit and the husband received the loans moneys. They entered into the transactions jointly. They were jointly liable and they incurred liability in consideration of advances made and accommodation given to them jointly. And there is no evidence of any agreement between husband and wife that one should be principal debtor. In my opinion the mortgage transactions, whether taken on their own or in conjunction with the operation of the joint account, did not give rise to any obligations by the husband to the wife. In these circumstances I consider there is no room for the application of the principle of exoneration.[110]

In *Re Berry*, the findings of their Honours were clearly influenced by factors relevant to the existence of a joint account between the husband and wife. However, to the extent that *Re Berry* is authority that a security given in respect of a joint account, being an account concerned with 'a vital feature of the family life—the earnings of the husband',[111] cannot be the subject of a claim in exoneration by one account holder where the drawings from the account are primarily for the purposes of the other account holder, the authority of the decision must be questioned—in Australia at least—in light of such decisions as *Parsons v McBain*.

---

[109] *Re Berry* [1978] 2 NZLR 373.
[110] *ibid*, 377–8, and *cf* Woodhouse J (at 383–5).
[111] *ibid*, 385.

(iii) No Benefit to Surety

As is clear from such cases as *Paget v Paget*,[112] any inference as to role of the co-owner as 'surety' will be negated if the 'surety' receives a benefit from the transaction. In cases where the moneys raised by the relevant transaction are unequivocally obtained and used by the principal debtor for his or her own purposes, the courts have no difficulty in identifying the absence of 'benefit' derived by the surety from the loan transaction. Similarly, where the surety clearly receives a benefit from the transaction, as was conceded in *Re Bankruptcy of Kostiuk*,[113] or where it is clear that the surety 'received the money'[114] or where the debts were contracted, not for purposes of the husband with which the wife had little to do, but in order to enable them both to live in the style they both thought suitable, and perhaps necessary, to enable them to maintain and enjoy that high social position which they both so greatly desired,[115] the refusal of the court to permit reliance on the doctrine is unremarkable.

One contentious issue in this regard, however, is the meaning of 'benefit' for the purposes of the doctrine in more ambiguous cases. This is of particular interest in the matrimonial context—if, for example, the jointly-owned property of the couple is mortgaged to secure a business account of one spouse, but the family relies on the business for its living expenses, does that mean that the other spouse is deriving a 'benefit' from the mortgage transaction?

Notwithstanding the decision in *Re Berry*, as a general rule the courts have not been prepared to go that far. In *Parsons v McBain* the Full Court of the Federal Court overturned the decision of the trial judge that the wives in that case had received a 'tangible benefit' from the mortgage each had given, which benefit could be described as 'an expected benefit, [namely] that, by putting money into the partnership business, the business might survive and, as put by counsel for the trustee, that would bring "home money to put food on the table and clothe the children"'.[116] The Full Court held that that 'tangible benefit' referred to by the trial judge did not defeat the equity of exoneration—it was too remote, and in any event was incapable of valuation or a valuation which bore any relationship to the amount received by the principal debtor.[117] Similarly in *Re Pittortou*, although Scott J considered that the conduct of the wife in working in the family business without pay was 'similar to the conduct of many wives assisting their

---

[112] *Parsons and Parsons v McBain* [1898] 1 Ch 470.
[113] *Re Bankruptcy of Kostiuk* [2002] BCCA 410.
[114] Cf Wood VC in *Thomas v Thomas* (1855) 2 K & J 79, 85; 69 ER 701, 704, and the Lord Chancellor in *Re Keily* (1857) Ir Ch Rep 394.
[115] *Paget v Paget* [1898] 1 Ch 470, 472.
[116] *Parsons and Parsons v McBain* (2001) 109 FCR 120, 128.
[117] *ibid*, 128.

husbands in the conduct of the business on which the livelihood and support of the family depend',[118] with the result that payments made out of the account for the benefit of the family were, for relevant purposes, for the 'benefit' of the wife, his Lordship was prepared to differentiate such payments from payments made by the husband purely for business purposes, which were not for the wife's benefit.

Interestingly, in a number of recent cases the courts have been prepared to recognise 'partial' exoneration in circumstances where joint property is charged partly for the benefit of the principal debtor alone, and partially for the benefit of both parties. In *Farrugia v Official Receiver in Bankruptcy*,[119] for example, Deane J noted:

> The present case is not, however, the simple one where the whole of the moneys borrowed jointly by husband and wife on the security of their joint property have been applied for the benefit of the husband. As has been mentioned, $12,500 of the amount borrowed was applied for the joint benefit of Mr and Mrs Farrugia upon the discharge of the previous mortgage under which they were jointly liable. It was only the balance of $10,500 that was applied for the benefit of Mr Farrugia alone. A question which arises is whether the one borrowing can, for the purposes of the application of the relevant equitable principles, be in effect subdivided into what was borrowed and applied for the joint benefit of Mr and Mrs Farrugia and what was borrowed and applied for Mr Farrugia's benefit alone. In my view it can.[120]

Similarly, in *Re Pittortou*,[121] Scott J observed:

> The present is a case in which, as is plain from the evidence, the family, until the sad departure of the bankrupt in 1981, acted as a family unit in its family and business affairs ... In my view payments made out of the bankrupt's National Westminster Bank account for the benefit of the family are of a character as to make it impossible to impute to the parties the intention that as between the husband and the wife the payments should be regarded as falling on the share in the mortgaged property of the husband. In my view the equity of exoneration should be confined to payments out of the account which do not have the character of payments made for the joint benefit of the household.

> On the other hand, save for payments made for the joint benefit of the household, it does not seem to me that the equity of exoneration has any less part to play now than it had in the days when the equitable doctrine was being formulated. Accordingly, payments made by the husband purely for business purposes and, a fortiori, any payments made by the husband for the purposes of the second establishment it seems he was supporting, should as between the bankrupt and the second respondent be treated as charged primarily on the bankrupt's half share in the mortgaged property.[122]

---

[118] *Re Pittortou* [1985] 1 WLR 58 (Ch) 62.
[119] *Farrugia v Official Receiver in Bankruptcy* (1982) 58 FLR 474.
[120] *ibid*, 477.
[121] *Re Pittortou* [1985] 1 WLR 58.
[122] *ibid*, 62–3.

If the purpose of the parties in raising the money is to benefit only one of them, however, the money so raised must be applied for that purpose.

C. 'The Money so Borrowed Must be Applied for that Purpose'

The question whether the money so raised is actually applied for the purpose of benefiting the 'principal debtor' is invariably determined on the evidence before the court. In cases of uncertainty, the courts have been prepared traditionally to admit extrinsic evidence to establish whether or not the money was so applied: *Hudson v Carmichael*,[123] *Gray v Dowman*,[124] *Earl of Kinnoul v Money*,[125] and *Clinton v Hooper*[126] (although not allowed in *Parteriche v Powlet*[127]) or even to order an inquiry as to whom and for whose use money raised by a mortgage was paid and applied: *Thomas v Thomas*.[128] So, for example, in finding that the estate of the wife could rely on the doctrine of exoneration in *Hall v Hall*,[129] Warrington J observed that the true result of the evidence was that the money raised was controlled by the husband and used to purchase property for the husband, and that there was 'absolutely no evidence at all of the expenditure of any part of that money for the benefit of the wife, nor [were] there any circumstances shewing that it might have been so expended'.[130] Interestingly, in those circumstances, Warrington J held that the proper inference to be drawn from the absence of any affirmative evidence was that the money was not applied for the benefit of the wife.[131]

Once again, the helpful question posed by the Lord Chancellor of Ireland in *Re Keily*, namely 'who got the money?'[132] is the critical enquiry.

V. CONCLUSION

In conclusion, a number of observations may be made in relation to the equitable doctrine of exoneration.

First, the doctrine appears to have particular relevance to, inter alia, mortgage of jointly-owned property by *individuals*. It is not a doctrine in relation to which there has been litigation involving corporate debtors and

---

[123] *Hudson v Carmichael* (1854) Kay 613, 69 ER 260.
[124] *Gray v Dowman* (1858) 27 LJ Ch 702.
[125] *Earl of Kinnoul v Money* (1767) 3 Swan 202n, 36 ER 830.
[126] *Clinton v Hooper* (1791) 3 Bro CC 201, 29 ER 490.
[127] *Parteriche v Powlet* (1742) 2 Atk 383, 26 ER 632.
[128] *Thomas v Thomas* (1855) 2 K & J 79, 85; 69 ER 701, 704.
[129] *Hall v Hall* [1911] 1 Ch 487.
[130] *ibid*, 500.
[131] *ibid*, 500.
[132] *Re Keily* (1857) Ir Ch Rep 394, 405.

sureties, although in theory there is no reason why corporate entities should be excluded if the appropriate pre-conditions for operation of the doctrine, including purpose and benefit, are satisfied. One reason for the absence of such litigation involving persons other than natural persons may be that, like many equitable doctrines, the doctrine arises by inference, often from an arrangement between parties who are not at arms length such as husband and wife, rather than by overt contractual provision.

Secondly, traditionally, the doctrine has been considered to be an equity applicable for the benefit of married women. However the analysis of the doctrine in this paper indicates that, although the doctrine may have had its most frequent *application* for the benefit of married women, the doctrine is not—and has never been—confined to claims by married women in respect of the debts of their husbands. The doctrine clearly extends to claims by husbands in relation to the debts of their wives, and beyond that relationship to claims by third party co-owners of property. The genesis of the doctrine may have been equity's aspiration to protect married women and their proprietary interests at a time when married women had little legal control over their property, however, as this paper demonstrates the Courts of Equity were quick to recognise injustices in equivalent circumstances involving husbands and others, and to invoke the doctrine for their protection. While cases prior to the enactment of the Married Women's Property Acts do need to be read with caution in relation to the rights of a wife to rely on the doctrine of exoneration, many principles found in such cases are replicated in other decisions, which do not involve the claim of a married woman. Indeed, it could be said that the third class of surety in *Duncan, Fox & Co v North and South Wales Bank*[133] is an acknowledgement of the relationship of principal debtor and surety, which had been inferred by application of the doctrine of exoneration for two centuries prior to that decision.

Thirdly, the effect of the application of the doctrine is that the estate of the 'surety' in the relevant property is exonerated, to the extent possible, once the relevant debt is repaid. Practically, the doctrine does not completely relieve the surety to the extent that the surety is not liable for the debt at all—in relation to a contract of loan secured by a registered mortgage, for example, the surety remains liable on the loan to the extent provided in the contract, and the interest of the surety in the relevant property is similarly bound.

Fourthly, as pointed out by Warrington J in *Gee v Liddell* (and specifically followed by the Federal Court in both *Farrugia v Official Receiver in Bankruptcy* and *Parsons v McBain*), if the 'principal debtor' is bankrupt and the bankrupt's estate is insufficient to satisfy the relevant debt, the

---

[133] *Duncan, Fox & Co v North and South Wales Bank* (1880) 6 App Cas 1, 11.

interest of the surety in any remaining interest of the bankrupt in the co-owned property is that of a charge upon the estate of the bankrupt by way of indemnity for the purpose of enforcing against that estate the right which the surety has, as between the surety and the principal debtor, to have that estate resorted to first for the payment of the debt.[134] The benefits of the doctrine for the claimant include:

— as discussed throughout this paper, the primary obligation for the debt is placed upon the principal debtor, and if the interest of the principal debtor is adequate to satisfy the debt the interest of the surety will be completely relieved from liability for the debt, and

— importantly in practice: in the event of the bankruptcy of a co-owner of property (such as the matrimonial home) where the co-owners have jointly charged their interest in the property, the co-owner is able to maximise his or her interest in the property to the detriment of other creditors of the bankrupt. It was pointed out at the commencement of this paper that a trustee in bankruptcy is subject to the same equities as those which bound the bankrupt. As observed by one writer, creditors should not become too excited about the results of a title search revealing property in the name of the bankrupt—there is sometimes little utility in a trustee in bankruptcy pursuing any claim where the bankrupt's loan exceeds his remaining equity in the property, as the co-owner could have a charge on the bankrupt's interest in the land by way of exoneration.[135]

Finally, notwithstanding concerns expressed in a number of decisions about the relevance of the doctrine in the twenty-first century, the courts have continued to find the doctrine of exoneration relevant and applicable in appropriate circumstances. The strengthening of equitable principles through such decisions as *Garcia v National Australia Bank*,[136] where the High Court of Australia reinforced the rationale of the so-called rule in *Yerkey v Jones* as being based on trust and confidence, in the ordinary sense of the word, between marriage partners, lends support to the validity of principles such as exoneration in relation to marriage partners. If anything, the principle is likely to remain valid in its broader application applying across relationships, and not merely those involving solvent wives and bankrupt husbands.

---

[134] *Gee v Liddell* [1913] 2 Ch 62, 72. The surety does not have 'ownership' of the principal debtor's interest: *Parsons and Parsons v McBain* (2001) 109 FCR 120, 128.

[135] R O'Sullivan, 'Whose Mortgage is it anyway? Jointly owned property and the equity of exoneration', paper, Worrells Insolvency Conference 2002 (www.worrells.net.au/library/insolvency/Jointly%20owned%20property%20and%20exoneration.pdf).

[136] *Garcia v National Australia Bank* (1998) 194 CLR 395.

11

The Elderly, Their Homes and the Unconscionable Bargain Doctrine

LORNA FOX O'MAHONY AND JAMES DEVENNEY[*]

I. INTRODUCTION

B RITAIN HAS AN aging population: although overall population growth in the last 35 years was just eight per cent, the elderly population (persons aged over 65) grew by 31 per cent,[1] and with birth rates falling, and increasing numbers of people living into very old age, recent statistics have shown that the proportion of the population of England who are aged over 65 years of age is likely to have grown from 15.6 per cent in 2000 to 19.2 per cent by 2021.[2] As the 'baby-boomer generation'[3] reaches retirement age, policy analysts are increasingly concerned with the implications for economic and social policies:[4] '[t]he economic and social well-being of the growing elderly population is, therefore, an important issue for society in general and for policy-makers in particular'.[5]

Policy questions relating to the elder population are recognised in a range of legal contexts—from medical law to estate planning, housing and social

---

[*] Durham Law School, University of Durham.

[1] Social Trends 37, (available online at http://www.statistics.gov.uk/cci/nugget.asp?ID=949).

[2] Statistics available online at http://www.statistics.gov.uk/cci/nugget.asp?id=949.

[3] 'Baby boomers' is the term used to describe those people born between 1946 and 1964, when post-World War II optimism led to a surge in population; see eg, J Harkin and J Huber, *Eternal Youths: How the Baby boomers are having their time again* (London, Demos, 2004).

[4] See eg, SA Nyce and SJ Schieber, *The Economic Implications of Aging Societies: The Costs of Living Happily Ever After* (Cambridge, Cambridge University Press, 2005); A Tinker, 'The Social Implications of an Aging Population' (2002) 123 *Mechanisms of Aging and Development* 729; P Wallace, *Agequake: Riding the Demographic Rollercoaster Shaking Business, Finance and Our World* (London, N Brearley Publishing, 1999); J Tavares Alvarez, *Reflections on an Agequake* (New York, UN-NGO Committee on Aging, 1999).

[5] NK Kutty, 'The Scope for Poverty Alleviation among Elderly Home-owners in the United States through Reverse Mortgages' (1998) 35 *Urban Studies* 113.

welfare to guardianship and disability rights[6]—where it is recognised that the elderly may be vulnerable to discrimination, disadvantage, neglect or abuse. Yet, in addition to the vulnerability associated with aging per se, a range of social, economic and political trends in recent decades has also ensured that this elderly population may face a specific set of risks in relation to financial transactions affecting their homes. This paper considers elderly homeowners as a potentially 'vulnerable population' in relation to financial transactions. While recent research has challenged the suggestion that economic decision-making is impaired by age,[7] this paper argues that, distinct from the question of capacity for decision-making, a series of contextual factors has exposed elderly homeowners to a new type of systemic vulnerability around financial transactions.

II. ELDER VULNERABILITY IN FINANCIAL TRANSACTIONS

It is, of course, not only elders who face risk in respect of home-ownership, even before the credit crunch and mortgage meltdown that has followed the sub-prime lending crisis since 2006. Following the boom and slumps in the UK housing market from the 1980s to the mid 1990s, Ford et al argued that a series of circumstances including economic recession, but also relating to changes to social, economic and political structures, had rendered home-ownership a much riskier undertaking that it hitherto had been.[8] Even in a benign economic climate, with historically low interest rates, there was evidence of 'a set of more enduring socio-economic transformations which have raised the "normal" level of risk associated with home-ownership compared to that which pertained in earlier periods'.[9] Adding to this the impact of the 'credit crunch' and the threat of global recession, the 'riskiness' of entering financial transactions affecting the home has been brought into particularly sharp relief.

This paper suggests that, besides being susceptible to these 'typical' risks, the elderly can be viewed as a particularly vulnerable population in

---

[6] For example, in the UK, Solicitors for the Elderly is a national organisation of lawyers who specialise in elder law, and who describe their key objectives as: 'to develop expertise in areas of public and private law relevant to our clients' needs and where there is at present a skills shortage. These include: Consent, capacity and substituted decision-making; Financial planning, including retirement and long-term care; Housing and social and health care issues; Dealing with abuse'. see http://www.solicitorsfortheelderly.com/public/index.php.

[7] S Kovalchik, CF Camerer, DM Grether, CR Plott and JM Allman, 'Aging and Decision Making: A Comparison between neurologically healthy elderly and young individuals' (2005) 58 *Journal of Economic Behaviour and Organisation* 79; *cf* E Peters, ML Finucane, DG McGregor and P Slovic in PC Stern and LL Carstensen (eds), *The Aging Mind: Opportunities in Cognitive Research* (Washington DC, National Academy Press, 2000).

[8] J Ford, R Burrows and S Nettleton, *Home Ownership in a Risk Society: A social analysis of mortgage arrears and possessions* (Bristol, Policy Press, 2001) Preface, vi.

[9] *ibid*, 44.

relation to financial transactions. The business of financial services for elderly consumers is booming in Britain. Old age can be a time of low income, as life events including retirement or the death of a spouse can considerably reduce the income of these elders, giving rise to a 'pension gap' between pensioners' incomes and their cost of living.[10] Furthermore, increasing longevity has created a large population of fixed-income citizens of moderate means, with fewer wage earners, and more likely to be reliant on public or private pensions, private investments or savings. This period of life may also coincide with increasing costs, which UK elders are increasingly expected to fund through private means rather than relying on social welfare.[11]

Another important characteristic of the aging baby-boomers is that, while for much of the twentieth century the elderly were *less* likely to own their own homes than other demographic groups, this figure has been increasing steadily, with many elder households now owning their homes mortgage free: 56 per cent of those aged over 75 are outright owners, with a further three per cent owning subject to a mortgage; while 64 per cent of the 65–74 cohort are outright owners, with a further nine per cent owning subject to a mortgage.[12] Overall, 75 per cent of retired persons are owner-occupiers (against 70 per cent in the general population).[13] Yet, alongside significant asset-holding, elderly homeowners may find themselves 'house-rich but income-poor'.[14] This creates a substantial population for whom release of equity from their homes will be a potentially attractive (or useful or necessary) strategy to generate income in their elder years.[15] Wealth tied up in the home is currently regarded as: 'more "spendable" now than it will be ever again'.[16] Owned homes are increasingly regarded as a repository of financial value, with the expectation that 'the asset value

---

[10] For studies analysing the economic needs of elders, see S Middleton, R Hancock, K Kellard, J Beckhelling, V Phung and K Perren, *Measuring Resources in Later Life: a review of the data* (York, Joseph Rowntree Foundation, 2007); and K Hill, K Kellard, S Middleton, L Cox and E Pound, *Understanding Resources in Later Life: views and experiences of older people* (York, Joseph Rowntree Foundation, 2007).

[11] Thus, in relation to nursing care, for example, in many cases, private means must be exhausted before public funds become available; see generally, SJ Smith, *Banking on Housing: Speculating on the role and relevance of housing wealth in Britain* (Paper prepared for the Joseph Rowntree Foundation Inquiry into Home Ownership 2010 and Beyond, 2005).

[12] Social Trends 31 (London, Office for National Statistics, 2001) Table 10.7; see also R Forrest, P Leather and C Pantazis, *Home Ownership in Old Age: The Future of Owner-Occupation in an Ageing Society* (Oxford, Anchor Trust, 1997).

[13] Social Trends 34 (2004) Table 10.9.

[14] K Rowlingson, ' "Living Poor to Die Rich"? Or "Spending the Kids' Inheritance"? Attitudes to Assets and Inheritance in Later Life' (2006) 35 *Journal of Social Policy* 175; J Bull and J Poole, *Not Rich, Not Poor: A Study of Housing Options for Elderly People on Middle Incomes* (Oxford, SHAC/Anchor Housing Trust, 1989).

[15] See generally, R Hancock, 'Can Housing Wealth Alleviate Poverty among Britain's Older Population?' (1998) 19 *Fiscal Studies* 249.

[16] Smith, above n 11, at 2.

of housing ... accumulates over the life course, provides a cushion (in the form of low housing costs) for old age, and flows on to the next generation through inheritance';[17] or, if the next generation cannot wait for inheritance, by providing equity for release, for capital gifts, or to enable a parent to act as surety for the debts of their adult children.[18]

While there are many reasons—financial, political and personal—why elders may wish to release capital or income from their homes to fund expenses in later life, the use of an owned home in this way also raises interesting issues about the tensions between the preservation of the home as a dwelling place for old age—extensively analysed in the 'aging in place' literature[19]—and the use of the home as a financial asset, for the elder or for inheritance. Notwithstanding the importance of retaining their 'place' for elders' autonomy, independence, identity, and continuity in the community,[20] empirical research has recently highlighted the pragmatism with which elders typically approach issues relating to equity release and the need to use their homes as an asset, to release capital or income for expenses in their old age:[21]

> Previous research suggested that people wished to keep their housing assets intact during their later life, not so much in order to pass on these assets to the next generation but because they feel they have an 'inalienable right' to their housing wealth. People in this position might be living a frugal lifestyle in order to preserve their housing assets. They will be 'living poor in order to die rich'.[22]

Rowlingson notes that '[t]he social policy concern here is that people might be impoverishing themselves and potentially damaging their health by not

---

[17]   *ibid*, 11.

[18]   This is described by Fiona Burns as 'intergenerational debt'; see eg, F Burns, 'Protecting elders: Regulating intergenerationally transmitted debt in Australia' (2005) 28 *International Journal of Law and Psychiatry* 300.

[19]   For example, GD Rowles and H Chaudhury, *Home and Identity in Late Life: International Perspectives* (New York, Springer, 2005); G Mowl, R Pain and C Talbot, 'The ageing body and homespace' (2000) 32 *Area* 189; PC Kontos, 'Resisting Institutionalization: Constructing Old Age and Negotiating Home' (1998) 12 *Journal of Aging Studies* 167. Rowles and Chaudhury suggested, eg, that: 'Especially with the loss of social roles, retirement, physical frailty, and environmental changes, for many older adults the past experience of home may hold different meanings' p 11. For a discussion of the relationship between aging in place and housing law, see J Pynoos, C Nishita, C Cicero and R Caraviello, 'Aging in Place, Housing, and the Law' (2008) 16 *Elder Law Journal* 77.

[20]   See GD Rowles and H Chaudhury, 'Home and Identity in Late Life: International Perspectives' in Rowles and Chaudhury, above n 19; Frank Oswald and Hans-Werner Wahl, 'Dimensions of the Meaning of Home in Later Life' in Rowles and Chaudhury, above n 19; Robert L Rubinstein and Kate de Medeiros, 'Home, Self, and Identity' in Rowles and Chaudhury, above n 19.

[21]   K Rowlingson and S McKay, *Attitudes to inheritance: A Literature Review and Secondary Analysis of Data* (York, Joseph Rowntree Foundation, 2004); Rowlingson, above n 14; see also IF Megbolugbe, J Sa-Aadu and JD Shilling, 'Oh, Yes, the Elderly Will Reduce Housing Equity under the Right Circumstances' (1997) 8 *Journal of Housing Research* 53.

[22]   Rowlingson, above n 14, at 176.

taking advantage of the assets they have'.[23] However, the elders interviewed in this 2004 study typically took a balanced approach to the tensions between 'home as asset' and 'home as inheritance', leading Rowlingson to conclude that

> people are more pragmatic about their property. Ideally, they would like to be able to maintain their property intact—both for their own purposes and in order to bequeath—but they are aware that their income in later life is likely to be fairly low. Rather than expecting the state to resolve this issue by substantially increasing pension incomes, people seem to expect that they themselves may have to access their housing equity at some point in the future to maintain a reasonable living standard.[24]

This conclusion appeared to point to greater scope for the use of equity release products, if consumers were to become sufficiently confident in the products on offer: '[t]he options currently available to access equity are generally undesirable to many people at present, but they are not strictly averse to the principle of unlocking housing equity'.[25]

While lack of consumer confidence in the sector has long acted as a barrier to market growth in this area,[26] recent changes in the regulatory framework relating to equity release products has meant that consumer confidence seems likely to rise. This paper argues, however, that notwithstanding the increase in regulation, there are a number of important issues relating to legal responses—particularly in light of the particular and specific vulnerabilities that elderly homeowners experience in relation to financial transactions affecting their homes—which could be usefully considered. Financial products such as equity release schemes are often explicitly targeted at elderly consumers, and this also raises important questions about the ways in which any protection which might be available under the law is suitable to meet the needs of vulnerable elders. While current legal approaches to vulnerable elders in the context of financial transactions are limited, we argue that there is considerable potential within existing legal doctrine, to better map law's response onto the reality of the elder's contextual experience of using their homes to raise capital, to ensure adequate legal protection against unscrupulous or unconscionable transactions. In section III we outline the regulatory context within which creditors are governed in England and Wales, and assess the extent to which recent developments in the jurisdiction of the Financial Services Authority will effectively address

---

[23] *ibid.*

[24] *ibid*, 187.

[25] *ibid*, 187–8.

[26] See D Hirsch, Consultation Response to HM Treasury: 'Regulating home reversion plans' (February 2004); available online at www.jrf.org.uk/knowledge/responses/docs/homereversion. asp; see also R Terry and R Gibson, *Overcoming obstacles to equity release* (Joseph Rowntree Foundation, Ref 1939, 2006).

the vulnerability which has been acknowledged in this context. Section IV then proceeds to examine the role which the doctrine of undue influence and the unconscionable bargain doctrine might play in this context.

III. THE REGULATORY APPROACH

In Parliamentary debates preceding the extension of the Financial Services Authority's regulatory 'umbrella' to include equity release, a number of key headlines were emphasised, including:

> We must bear it in mind that the purchase of a home is the biggest financial investment that any individual or family makes. Given that the problem affects people who have already paid off a mortgage and are now in retirement, it compounds the vulnerability of the people taking out the schemes.[27]

Yet with equity release per se increasingly recognised as an important mechanism for improving quality of life for elderly homeowners,[28] much depends on the nature of the product, the context and terms of the transactions, and, the present authors would argue, on the 'conscionability' of the bargain struck between the creditor and the elderly homeowner.

Equity release schemes are generally marketed as products to enable elderly home-owners to tap into the value of their homes—their 'equity'—without having to sell up altogether and move out. Although the terms of equity release products vary, the general idea is that the homeowner receives a payment of capital, the 'loan', which is not scheduled for repayment by instalments, but which is secured against the equity which the borrower holds clear of any other secured debt in the owner-occupied home, and which accumulates until the property becomes 'available', when the elderly homeowner dies or decides to sell, at which point the creditor is entitled to execute its claim against the capital. There are as many equity release products on the market as the imaginations of credit suppliers can create, but two principal *types* of scheme have tended to dominate the UK market in recent years: (1) home reversion plans and (2) lifetime mortgages.

'Home reversion plans' involve the sale of a portion of the total value of the property to the product provider in exchange for a lump sum payment, or an income for life, or, in some cases, a combination of lump sum *and* income. This type of scheme utilises a form of co-ownership, since the 'vendor' continues to own a portion of the property as tenant in common with the 'purchaser' company. Both co-owners will benefit from any increase in value, proportionate to their shares, and the elderly occupier's share continues to be an inheritable asset for the purposes of his or her estate.

---

[27] *ibid.*
[28] See discussion in section II.

These arrangements typically include an agreement as to occupation between the co-owners (the vendor-occupier and the purchaser-credit company) that allows the occupier to continue to live in the property, paying a peppercorn 'occupation rent', until they die or until the house is sold.[29] A 'lifetime mortgage', in contrast, is more readily comparable to a standard interest-only mortgage against equity in the property, although the 'borrower' does not make any repayments of interest during their lifetime; rather, the 'repayments' due are 'rolled up'—or added to the mortgage capital, with the whole debt to be paid off when the borrower dies or when the property is sold.

Until relatively recently, British consumers approached the prospect of equity release with some trepidation. It is likely that this lack of consumer confidence was significantly influenced by the negative publicity that followed the upsurge in reverse mortgages during a period of 'boom and bust' in the British housing market in the late 1980s and early 1990s, when many households lost their homes through repossession.[30] However, in recent years there has been a major growth in the equity release market in Britain, which is attributable to several factors. The first is the rise in self-regulation amongst equity release providers in Britain, the majority of whom (approximately 90 per cent) are members of Safe Home Income Plans (SHIP). SHIP, which was launched in 1991, describes itself as 'dedicated entirely to the protection of planholders and promotion of safe home income and equity release plans'.[31] All participating companies pledge to observe the SHIP Code of Practice, which binds the companies to provide a fair, easy-to-understand and full presentation of their plans, and these providers also give their customers a 'no negative equity guarantee', which means that they are assured that they will never owe more than the value of their homes.[32] Founded with four member companies, there are now 21 member companies, estimated to supply about 90 per cent of equity release funds by volume in the United Kingdom.[33] The equity release sector is now big business in Britain, with the market share of SHIP members to reach £1.279 billion in 2007, an 11 per cent increase on full-year figures for

---

[29] In some cases the property may be sold in order to release the remaining equity to fund further expenses, for example the costs of nursing care.

[30] 'During the 1980s [in the UK], equity release came under scrutiny and suffered a bad reputation due to poorly designed and marketed products that led to several court cases': C Huan and J Mahoney, 'Equity Release Mortgages' (2002) 16 *Housing Finance International* 29, 33. This analysis uses the examples of home income plans and interest roll-up loans to identify weaknesses in equity release products in the UK, which led to escalating debt, left consumers vulnerable to rising interest rates and falling house prices, and led to forced sale of their homes.

[31] See http://www.ship-ltd.org/about/index.shtml.

[32] A worst case scenario which would leave homeowners exposed to not only repossession but further personal actions to recover additional outstanding debt.

[33] See http://www.ship-ltd.org/bm~doc/08-dec-2007a.pdf.

2006.[34] Indeed, a recent survey of SHIP members has predicted that their total market share for 2010 could reach £2.19 billion.[35]

Alongside this self-regulation, considerable attention has recently been focused on government regulation of equity release. The 'lifetime mortgage' or 'reverse mortgage' sector has been regulated by the Financial Services Authority (FSA)[36] since it took over responsibility for regulation of the mortgage industry in October 2004,[37] and in April 2007 the FSA umbrella extended to cover home reversion plans through the Regulation of Financial Services (Land Transactions) Act 2005,[38] with a view to filling a gap that existed in the regulation of equity release products. In considering this legislation, the government recognised that purchasing an equity release product is a major decision, with tax, inheritance and long-term financial planning implications,[39] and also, crucially, that the function of regulation in this context is specifically targeted at providing *information* and *advice*. On introducing the second reading of the Bill, Lord McKenzie stated:

> Regulation is not designed to discourage people from purchasing these products, but to help them make informed choices, offer valuable consumer protection and ensure there is a level playing field in the equity release market, most of which already falls within the scope of the FSA mortgage regulation ... these are not simple products to understand, hence the need to ensure that potential purchasers receive an appropriate level of advice.[40]

The touchstone of the legislative policy of this Act was emphasised once again in Lord McKenzie's closing comments when he claimed that the Bill would

> open the door to important consumer protections to be extended to vulnerable and minority consumers, level the playing field in mortgage regulation, ensure that no artificial distortions go forward, bolster consumer confidence in those products and thus help to ensure that the markets continue to develop.[41]

---

[34] See SHIP Press Release, 8 December 2007, available online at http://www.ship-ltd.org/bm~doc/08-dec-2007a.pdf.

[35] *ibid.*

[36] The FSA is an independent, non-government body, given statutory powers by the Financial Services and Markets Act 2000, to regulate the financial services industry in the UK and it has four objectives under the Financial Services and Markets Act (FSMA) 2000: maintaining market confidence; promoting public understanding of the financial system; securing the appropriate degree of protection for consumers; and fighting financial crime.

[37] Brought under the FSMA 2000 by the Financial Services And Markets Act 2000 (Regulated Activities) Order 2001.

[38] Regulation of Financial Services (Land Transactions) Act 2005.

[39] 'Buying a home reversion plan is a huge financial decision involving the most important and sometimes only significant asset of elderly people. It can have significant implications for tax, benefits, inheritance and long-term financial planning, which need to be considered very carefully'. HL Deb 17 October 2005, col 554 (Lord McKenzie).

[40] *ibid.*

[41] HL Deb 17 October 2005, col 558 (Lord McKenzie).

As Lord McKenzie acknowledged in his speech, equity release products are generally both complex and expensive, and the provision of clearer information and advice for consumers—especially elderly consumers—to ensure that they are able to make informed decisions, is undoubtedly welcome. In addition, the requirements concerning the quality of information supplied by the equity release provider are copper-fastened by giving borrowers greater recourse to apply to the Financial Ombudsman Service to claim compensation if they believe they have been mis-sold a product.[42]

Yet while this shift to a stronger regulatory framework for equity release products will go a long way to addressing many of the (sometimes catastrophic) difficulties encountered by British consumers who purchased these products in the 1980s and 1990s, the regulatory framework has limited scope. In particular, legal regulation through the FSA is directed primarily at disciplining the behaviour of the *creditor*. Under the Financial Services and Markets Act 2000, creditors sign up to the FSA's scheme in order to become 'authorised'—receiving the quality 'kite-mark' to signify products which consumers can trust. While the compensation scheme purports to provide a safety net for users of regulated services, there are three important points to note regarding the scope of the regulatory scheme: (1) the emphasis of the FSA scheme is on clear information and advice, to ensure an *informed* decision can be made; (2) the function of the regulatory protection offered by the FSA is largely to *avoid* claims by regularising the activities of the credit provider, although in cases where an authorised creditor breaches the rules of the scheme—for example rules requiring clear information—the remedy for the claimant is compensation only; and (3) that social and economic factors at work in this context, sometimes coupled with relational pressures, may still leave an *informed* elder in a vulnerable position. In other words, there remains a separate set of issues, not adequately addressed through regulatory schemes (which focus on governing creditor activities and the content of products), which is rooted in the social, economic and cultural contexts in which the 'purchase' of equity release products by elderly homeowners has been mainstreamed in Britain.

It is, therefore, pertinent to consider the wider protection—beyond regulation—afforded to the elderly in connection with equity release schemes. Indeed, the suggestion that the FSA is enjoying some considerable success in improving consumer confidence[43] makes this task particularly apposite. In section IV we explore the nature, and extent, of the protection given to the elderly by the doctrine of undue influence and the unconscionable bargain doctrine in equity release schemes. In particular, we argue that the unconscionable bargain doctrine—a doctrine which is particularly

---

[42] See Financial Services and Market Regulation Act 2000, Pt XV.

[43] 'Equity release—time to grow?' *Mortgage Finance Gazette* (May 2007), available online at http://www.mfgonline.co.uk/ccstory/20235/130/Equity_release_%E2%80%93_time_t.

sensitive to the terms of the transaction, the effectiveness of any independent advice, informational inequalities and the vulnerabilities of the parties— may provide an appropriate vehicle for the protection of the elderly in this context.

IV. UNDUE INFLUENCE, THE UNCONSCIONABLE BARGAIN DOCTRINE AND THE PROTECTION OF ELDERS IN EQUITY RELEASE SCHEMES

A. Introduction

The doctrine of undue influence may afford elders with a measure of protection in relation to financial transactions involving their home.[44] Indeed, although the doctrine of undue influence is often closely associated with relationships of trust and confidence,[45] it is clear that the operation of the doctrine is not confined to such relationships.[46] Thus in *Royal Bank of Scotland v Etridge*[47] Lord Nicholls, in the context of relational undue influence, noted that:

> there is no single touchstone for determining whether the principle is applicable. Several expressions have been used in an endeavour to encapsulate the essence: trust and confidence, reliance, dependence or vulnerability on the one hand and ascendency, domination or control on the other. None of these descriptions is perfect. None is all embracing. Each has its proper place.[48]

However, the precise nature, and extent, of the protection given to the elderly by the doctrine of undue influence in relation to financial transactions involving their home will, of course, depend on the jurisprudential basis, and hence the essence, of the doctrine of undue influence. For

---

[44] It has been noted above that the motivations for equity release may vary, to encompass pressure as a result of both the needs of the elder themselves, and the needs of adult children who may wish that the elder use an owned home to release equity to enable the adult offspring to 'cash in' their inheritance early, often to fund their own house purchase. In this regard, it is interesting to note that where a transaction has been procured by undue influence, or unconscionability, on the part of the other party thereto, the party subject to the influence, or unconscionable conduct, will, subject to certain bars, be entitled to have the transaction set aside. By contrast, where the transaction has been procured by the undue influence, or unconscionability, of a third party—perhaps the children of the elder—the position is more complex and may depend on the principles of notice as set out in *Royal Bank of Scotland v Etridge* [2001] UKHL 44. For an analysis of those principles in the context of transactions with the elderly see FR Burns, 'The elderly and undue influence inter vivos' [2003] 23 *Legal Studies* 251 and *Portman Building Society v Dusangh* [2000] 2 All ER (Comm) 221.

[45] cf *Barclays Bank plc v O'Brien* [1994] AC 180 (HL).

[46] See *Allcard v Skinner* (1887) 36 Ch D 145 and *Re Craig (decd)* [1970] 2 All ER 390.

[47] *Royal Bank of Scotland v Etridge* [2001] UKHL 44.

[48] *ibid*, [11].

example, *if* the doctrine of undue influence focuses *solely* on the *capacity* of the elderly person,[49] the protection provided by the doctrine of undue influence in equity release schemes is likely to be peripheral.[50] The vulnerability of elders in this context is more likely to stem from social and economic factors[51] rather than from a lack of capacity;[52] and an important question in this context is whether or not it is deemed appropriate for legal doctrine to respond to these social and economic contextual factors.

Yet, despite the Brobdingnagian amount of academic literature on the subject,[53] the jurisprudential basis of the doctrine of undue influence remains obscure.[54] Indeed in *Niersmans v Pesticcio*[55] Mummery LJ stated:

> The striking feature of this appeal is that fundamental misconceptions [about the doctrine of undue influence] persist, even though the doctrine is over 200 years old and its basis and scope were examined by the House of Lords in depth ... less than 3 years ago in the well known case of Royal Bank of Scotland Plc v Etridge (No.2) [2002] 2 AC 773. The continuing confusions matter. Aspects of the instant case demonstrate the need for a wider understanding, both in and outside the

---

[49] *cf.* M Chen-Wishart, 'Undue Influence: Beyond Impaired Consent and Wrongdoing towards a Relational Analysis' in A Burrows and A Rodger (eds), *Mapping the Law: Essays in Memory of Peter Birks* (Oxford, Oxford University Press, 2006) 207–11.

[50] See FR Burns, above n 44, at 253–5.

[51] See Section II, above.

[52] See the text to n 7 above.

[53] See, eg, P Birks and Y Chin, 'On the Nature of Undue Influence' in J Beatson and D Friedmann (eds), *Good Faith and Fault in Contract Law* (Oxford, Clarendon Press, 1995); R Bigwood, 'Undue Influence: "Impaired Consent" or "Wicked Exploitation"' (1996) 16 *Oxford Journal of Legal Studies* 503, J O'Sullivan, 'Undue Influence and Misrepresentation after O'Brien: Making Security Secure' in F Rose (ed), *Restitution and Banking Law* (Oxford, Mansfield Press, 1998) 42–69, B Fehlberg, *Sexually Transmitted Debt* (Oxford, Clarendon Press, 1997) 24–25, S Smith, *Atiyah's Introduction to the Law of Contract*, 6th edn (Oxford, Clarendon Press, 2002) 288–91, M Pawlowski and J Brown, *Undue Influence and the Family Home* (London, Cavendish, 2002) 7–17, 27–30 and 205–12, M Oldham, ' "Neither borrower nor lender be"—the life of O'Brien' (1995) *Child and Family Law Quarterly* 104, 108–9, M Chen-Wishart, 'The O'Brien Principle and Substantive Unfairness' [1997] *CLJ* 60, D Capper, 'Undue Influence and Unconscionability: A Rationalisation' (1998) 114 *Law Quarterly Review* 479, Price, 'Undue Influence: finis litium' (1999) 115 *Law Quarterly Review* 8, L McMurtry, 'Unconscionability and Undue Influence: An Interaction?' [2000] 64 *Conveyancer and Property Lawyer* 573, Chen-Wishart, above n 49, and J Devenney and A Chandler, 'Unconscionability and the Taxonomy of Undue Influence' [2007] *Journal of Business Law* 541.

[54] See, generally, J Elvin, 'The Purpose of the Doctrine of Presumed Undue Influence' in Giliker (ed), *Re-examining Contract and Unjust Enrichment: Anglo-Canadian Perspectives* (Leiden, Martinus Nijhoff Publishers, 2007). In *Portman Building Society v Dusangh* [2000] 2 All ER (Comm) 221, 233, Ward LJ stated: 'Professors Birks and Chin ... see undue influence as being "plaintiff-sided" and concerned with the weakness of the plaintiff's consent owing to an excessive dependence upon the defendant, and unconscionability as being "defendant-sided" and concerned with the defendant's exploitation of the plaintiff's vulnerability. I do not find it necessary to resolve this debate'.

[55] *Niersmans v Pesticcio* [2004] EWCA Civ 372.

legal profession, of the circumstances in which the court will intervene to protect the dependant and the vulnerable in dealings with their property.[56]

In their seminal paper on the jurisprudential basis of the doctrine of undue influence, Professors Birks and Chin[57] argued that 'the doctrine of undue influence is about impaired consent, not about wicked exploitation'.[58] In so doing, Birks and Chin identified two models by which undue influence might be classified.[59] Under the first model—the so-called 'claimant-sided' approach—the emphasis is on the vulnerability of the claimant. In the context of equity release schemes, such an approach would focus on the potential vulnerability of the elder. By contrast, the second model identified by Birks and Chin—the so-called 'defendant-sided' analysis—is more concerned with the conduct of the other party to the transaction. In the context of equity release schemes, such an approach would often[60] focus on the conduct of the equity release provider. Thus, while concerns with 'wicked exploitation' resonate with a defendant-sided view of undue influence, the claimant-sided approach would arguably be more responsive to the context in which the elder entered into the transaction, so that 'it is not necessary for the party claiming relief to point to fraud or unconscionable behaviour on the part of the other'.[61]

Birks and Chin's thesis in support of a claimant-sided approach to undue influence has gained *some* support in the case law.[62] Yet their *overall* thesis is not unproblematic: for example, it arguably tends towards a pathological view of 'trust',[63] and, within a claimant-sided framework, it may take an unduly restrictive, capacity-driven, view of undue influence.[64] It also contrasts uncomfortably with the language employed both by the House of Lords in its landmark decisions of *National Westminster Bank plc v Morgan*,[65] *Barclays Bank plc v O'Brien*[66] and *Royal Bank of Scotland v Etridge (No 2)*,[67] and with more recent opinions of the Judicial Committee

---

[56] *ibid*, [2].

[57] Birks and Chin, above n 53.

[58] *ibid*, 126.

[59] It should, however, be noted that these models are contested: see, eg, Bigwood, above n 53.

[60] Although not always: see n 44 above.

[61] Birks and Chin, above n 53, at 126.

[62] See, eg, *Hammond v Osborn* [2004] EWCA Civ 885, *Turkey v Awadh* [2005] EWCA Civ 382 and *Jennings v Cairns* [2003] EWCA 1935. *cf Macklin v Dowsett* [2004] EWCA Civ 904 and *Dunbar Bank plc v Nadeem* [1998] 3 All ER 876 (discussed in A Chandler, 'Manifest Disadvantage: Limits of Application' (1999) 115 *Law Quarterly Review* 213).

[63] See Chen-Wishart, above n 49, at 208.

[64] *ibid*.

[65] *National Westminster Bank plc v Morgan* [1985] AC 686 (HL).

[66] *Barclays Bank plc v O'Brien* [1994] AC 180 (HL).

[67] *Royal Bank of Scotland v Etridge (No 2)* [2001] UKHL 44. In that case Lord Nicholls (at [6]–[7]) stated: 'Undue influence is one of the grounds of relief developed by courts of equity *as a court of conscience*. The objective is to ensure that the influence of one person

of the Privy Council,[68] which adopt an unconscionability-based approach to undue influence.[69]

Perhaps the most troublesome aspect of Birks and Chin's thesis is the linking of the concept of unconscionability to a notion of 'wicked exploitation'. Unconscionability is a delicate concept and although few would argue that unconscionability requires malign intent, it is (perhaps) less obvious, given the connotations of conscience, that relief on the grounds of unconscionability can be claimant-sided relief and so focused on the potential vulnerability of, for example, an elder.[70] Nevertheless, relief on the ground of unconscionability *can* be claimant-sided relief, and this, as we shall see, can be demonstrated by reference to the case law on the unconscionable bargain doctrine—a doctrine which has both contextual and historical links with the doctrine of undue influence[71]—where many of the leading cases adopt a clear claimant-sided orientation.[72]

Indeed, one of the current authors has argued[73] that the doctrine of undue influence is based on a notion of unconscionability which finds resonance in the unconscionable bargain doctrine in general, and specifically with cases such as *Evans v Llewellin*,[74] *Baker v Monk*,[75] *Fry v Lane*,[76] and *Cresswell v Potter*.[77] In particular, although we would argue that there is an (often overlooked) overriding unconscionability requirement to the

---

over another is *not abused*. In everyday life people constantly seek to influence the decisions of others. They seek to persuade those with whom they are dealing to enter transactions, whether great or small. The law has set *limits to the means properly employable for this purpose* ... Equity extended the reach of the law to other *unacceptable forms of persuasion*. The law will investigate the manner in which the intention to enter into the transaction was secured: "how the intention was produced", in the oft repeated words of Lord Eldon LC, from as long ago as 1807 (*Huguenin v Basely* (1807) 14 Ves Jun 273, 300; [1803–13] All ER Rep 1, 13). If the intention was produced by *unacceptable means*, the law will not permit the transaction to stand. The means used is regarded as an exercise of *improper or "undue"* influence, and hence *unacceptable*, whenever the consent thus procured ought not fairly to be treated as the expression of a person's free will' (emphasis added). Lord Hobhouse added (at [103]) that undue influence 'is an equitable wrong committed by the dominant party against the other which makes it unconscionable for the dominant party to enforce his legal rights against the other'. Lord Bingham agreed with Lord Nicholls.

[68] See *R v Attorney-General for England and Wales* [2003] UKPC 22 and *National Commercial Bank (Jamaica) Ltd v Hew's Executors* [2003] UKPC 51. The late Professor Birks acknowledged the difficulties that these decisions created for his thesis: see P Birks, 'Undue Influence as Wrongful Exploitation' (2004) 120 *Law Quarterly Review* 34.

[69] See further Devenney and Chandler, above n 53, at 541–2.

[70] Devenney and Chandler, above n 53.

[71] See, eg, *Evans v Llewellin* (1787) 1 Cox CC 333.

[72] See below, nn 124–35 and text thereto.

[73] Devenney and Chandler, above n 53.

[74] *Evans v Llewellin* (1787) 1 Cox CC 333, 29 ER 1191.

[75] *Baker v Monk* (1864) 4 De GJ & S 388, 46 ER 968.

[76] *Fry v Lane* (1888) 40 Ch D 312.

[77] *Cresswell v Potter* [1978] 1 WLR 255n.

doctrine of undue influence,[78] it can be argued that the existing elements of undue influence serve as a covert means of distinguishing between conscionable and unconscionable dealings.[79] For example, as we have noted, a finding of trust and confidence, reliance, dependency or vulnerability *may* be central to a finding of undue influence; but *how much* trust and confidence, reliance, dependency or vulnerability is required? Professors Birks and Chin were of the opinion that the influence needed to be 'excessive'[80] and they were apparently adopting a high threshold.[81] Yet it is not at all clear that the relevant case law supports such an approach.[82] Indeed the relevant case law appears to take a more fluid approach to this aspect of undue influence[83] and it can be argued that this (quantitative) aspect of undue influence is used by the courts to covertly distinguish between conduct which they believe to be acceptable and conduct which they believe to be unacceptable.[84] Such a conclusion is made more tempting given that this quantitative enquiry is a question of law,[85] it is context-specific[86] and it is said to be informed by 'public policy'.[87] Support for such a view can be found in *Bank of Scotland v Bennett*:[88] 'At the end of the day the question of whether or not there has, in any particular case, been actual undue influence involves a *value judgment*'[89] (emphasis added). Given the controversy surrounding the jurisprudential basis of the doctrine of undue influence, in the remainder of this paper we will explore the nature, and extent, of the protection given to the elderly, in relation to financial transactions involving their home, by the unconscionable bargain doctrine. In particular, we will consider the protection which this doctrine might provide in the context of elders entering into equity release schemes.

---

[78] See, eg, *National Westminster Bank plc v Morgan* [1985] 1 AC 686 (HL) 709F–H where Lord Scarman stated: 'I would wish to give a warning. There is no precisely defined law setting the limits to the equitable jurisdiction of a court to relieve against undue influence. This is the world of doctrine, not of neat and tidy rules ... A court in the exercise of this jurisdiction is a court of conscience. Definition is a poor instrument when used to determine whether a transaction is or is not unconscionable: this is a question of fact which depends on the facts of the case'. See also *Dunbar Bank plc v Nadeem* [1998] 3 All ER 876 and *Lloyds Bank plc v Lucken* [1998] 4 All ER 738.

[79] See further Devenney and Chandler, above n 53, at 562–7.

[80] Birks and Chin, above n 73, at 87.

[81] Chen-Wishart, above n 69, at 208.

[82] See, eg, *Tate v Williamson* (1866) LR 2 Ch App 55.

[83] In *Bank of Scotland v Bennett* [1997] 3 FCR 193, 216C, James Munby QC, sitting as a Deputy Judge of the High Court, stated: 'It is impossible to define, and difficult even to describe, at what point influence becomes, in the eye of the law, undue'.

[84] Devenney and Chandler, above n 53, at 562–4.

[85] *Re T (An Adult: Medical Treatment)* [1992] 2 FCR 861 (CA) 883B (Staughton LJ).

[86] *Mrs U v Centre for Reproductive Medicine* [2002] EWCA Civ 565.

[87] *Mutual Finance Ltd v John Wetton & Sons Ltd* [1937] 2 KB 389, 394–5 (Porter J). See also J Devenney and R Morgan, 'Mrs U v Centre for Reproductive Medicine' (2003) 25 *Journal of Social Welfare and Family Law* 74.

[88] *Bank of Scotland v Bennett* [1997] 3 FCR 193 (High Court).

[89] *ibid*, 220D.

B. The Cartography of the Unconscionable Bargain Doctrine

The unconscionable bargain doctrine is of considerable antiquity[90] and, in recent times, it has undergone a renaissance in Australia and New Zealand.[91] By contrast, during the same period, the unconscionable bargain doctrine has operated more modestly in England and Wales,[92] although, as we have seen, it is arguable that the doctrine of undue influence has been, to an extent, mimicking the unconscionable bargain doctrine. Indeed, one commentator has described the unconscionable bargain doctrine as a 'living fossil'[93] in England and Wales. Moreover, the parameters of the unconscionable bargain doctrine are faint,[94] although in *Alec Lobb (Garages) Ltd v Total Oil GB Ltd*,[95] Peter Millett QC, sitting as a Deputy Judge of the High Court, was able to distil three elements from the case law:

> [I]f the cases are examined, it will be seen that three elements have almost invariably been present before the court has interfered. First, one party has been at a serious disadvantage to the other ... secondly, this weakness of the one party has been exploited by the other in some morally culpable manner ... and thirdly, the resulting transaction has been, not merely hard or improvident, but overreaching and oppressive. Where there has been a sale at an undervalue, the under-value has almost always been substantial, so that it calls for an explanation ... In short, there must, in my judgment, be some impropriety, both in the conduct of the stronger party and in the terms of the transaction itself (though the former may

[90] See *Chesterfield v Jansen* (1750) 2 Ves Sen 125, 130 and, generally, LA Sheridan, *Fraud in Equity* (London, Pitman, 1957). See also *Proof v Hines* (1735) Cases Talbot 111 and DEC Yale (ed), *Nottingham's Chancery Cases* 72 Seldon Society xcvi, fn 3. Many of the early cases involved 'expectant heirs': see, eg, *Earl of Ardglasse v Muschamp* (1684) 1 Vern 273. It is clear that the doctrine in favour of 'expectant heirs' and the general unconscionable bargain doctrine developed separately: see, eg, *Webster v Cook* (1866–67) LR 2 Ch 542 and the Sale of Reversion Act 1867 (now Law of Property Act 1925 s 174). However, it is not clear whether or not these two doctrines had a common genesis: in *O'Rourke v Bolingbroke* (1877) App Cas 814, the Lord Chancellor was of the opinion that the general doctrine was borne of the rule in favour of 'expectant heirs', but the converse is not unarguable—see Fletcher, 'Unconscionable Transactions' [1974] *QLJ* 1. Today it seems that 'expectant heirs' will not be treated as *sui generis*: see *Re Brocklehurst (deceased)* [1978] 1 AC 438. cf *Benyon v Cook* (1875) LR10 Ch App 389.
[91] See D Capper, 'Undue Influence and Unconscionability: A Rationalisation' (1998) 114 *Law Quarterly Review* 479, I Hardingham, 'The High Court of Australia and Unconscionable Dealing' (1984) 4 *Oxford Journal of Legal Studies* 275 and A Finlay, 'Unconscionable Conduct and the Business Plaintiff: Has Australia Gone too Far?' [1999] *Anglo-American Law Review* 470.
[92] See Devenney and Chandler, above n 53 and cf *Cresswell v Potter* [1978] WLR 258n, *Portman Building Society v Dusangh* [2000] 2 All ER (Comm) 221, 233, *Credit Lyonnais Bank Nederland NV v Burch* [1997] 1 All ER 144, *Royal Bank of Scotland v Etridge (No 2)* [2001] EWCA Civ 1466, *Irvani v Irvani* [2000] 1 Lloyd's Rep 412, *Barclay's Bank plc v Goff* [2001] EWCA Civ 635, and *Jones v Morgan* [2002] EWCA Civ 565.
[93] J Ross-Martyn, 'Unconscionable Bargains' (1971) 121 *New Law Journal* 1159.
[94] See J Devenney, 'A Pack of Unruly Dogs: Unconscionable Bargains, Lawful Act (Economic) Duress and Clogs on the Equity of Redemption' [2002] *JBL* 539.
[95] *Alec Lobb (Garages) Ltd v Total Oil GB Ltd* [1983] 1 All ER 944.

often be inferred from the latter in the absence of an innocent explanation)—which in the traditional phrase 'shocks the conscience of the court,' and makes it against equity and good conscience of the stronger party to retain the benefit of a transaction he has unfairly obtained.[96]

However, as this passage suggests, these elements should not be viewed in an excessively technical manner; the courts adopt a holistic, qualitative approach to determining whether or not a transaction is unconscionable.[97] Moreover, as we will argue below, the application of these elements is loaded with normative assumptions.

C. Vulnerability

Central to the operation of the unconscionable bargain doctrine are conceptions of vulnerability,[98] sometimes referred to in the relevant case law by the nomenclature of 'special' or 'serious' disadvantage.[99] Thus relief *may* be granted under the unconscionable bargain doctrine where a person has entered into a contract as the result of drunkenness[100] or mental deficiency.[101] Yet, as we have already suggested,[102] *if* relief hovers around questions of capacity, the protection provided by the unconscionable bargain doctrine to elders, in the context of financial transactions involving their home, is likely to be limited. For example, in *Investors Compensation Scheme v West Bromwich Building Society*[103]—a case with particular

---

[96] *ibid*, 961e–g. The Court of Appeal largely avoided discussion of the unconscionable bargain doctrine: see [1985] 1 All ER 585.

[97] Capper, above n 91, at 496, approved in *Portman Building Society v Dusangh* [2000] 2 All ER (Comm) 221.

[98] It is reasonably clear that inequality of exchange ('substantive unconscionability') is insufficient, per se, to ground relief under the unconscionable bargain doctrine: see, eg, *Maynard v Moseley* (1676) 3 Swans 651; *Wood v Fenwick* (1702) Pr Ch 206; *Floyer v Sherard* (1743) Amb 18; *Lukey v O'Donnel* (1805) 2 Sch & L 395; *Longmate v Ledger* (1860) 2 Giff 157; *Burmah Oil Co Ltd v Governor of Bank of England* (1981) 125 *Solicitors Journal* 528 (where Walton J reinforced the primary principle of *pacta sunt servanda*; *Rowan v Dann* (Unreported) 21 February 1991, Ch D; *Clarion Limited v National Provident Institution* [2002] 1 WLR 1888. *cf Keen v Stuckely* (1721) Gil 155 and *Walter v Dalt* (1676) 1 Ch Ca 276 where an alternative view is advanced. See also LA Sheridan and G Keeton, *Fraud and Unconscionable Bargains* (Chichester, Barry Rose, 1985) 9–10; *cf* C Barton, 'The Enforcement of Hard Bargains' (1987) 103 *Modern Law Review* 118. Gross inequality of exchange may, however, give rise to a presumption of fraud: *Rowan v Dann* (Unreported) 21 February 1991, Ch D.

[99] See, eg, *Alec Lobb (Garages) Ltd v Total Oil* [1983] 1 WLR 87. See also LA Sheridan, *Fraud in Equity* (London, Pitman, 1957) 73–86; *cf Boustany v Pigott* (1993) 69 P & CR 298, where relief was granted without an explicit identification of a 'special disadvantage'.

[100] See, eg, *Dunnage v White* (1818) 1 Swan 137; *Griffin v Devenille* (1781) 3 P Wms 130.

[101] See, eg, *Price v Berrington* (1851) 3 Mac & G 486 and *York Glass Co Ltd v Jubb* (1925) 134 LT 36.

[102] See above section II.

[103] *Investors Compensation Scheme v West Bromwich Building Society* [1999] Lloyd's Rep PN 496.

significance in the context of equity release schemes, as it involved 'Home Income Plans' executed with elderly consumers—the court stressed that:

> although able to understand concepts such as the borrowing of money on security and the payment of interest, the claimants were not financially sophisticated people and not in a position, without the advice of persons more expert than themselves, properly to judge the risks involved in embarking on a Home Income Plan.[104]

Moreover, as we have already noted,[105] it is important to appreciate that the vulnerability which an elder might experience in this context may stem from a variety of social and economic factors. It is equally important to recognise that the provision of *information* and *advice*—as envisaged under the statutory regulation of this area—is not a panacea for the range of social and economic vulnerabilities in this area.[106]

It is, however, clear that the unconscionable bargain doctrine is sensitive to socio-economic factors. Thus in *Fry v Lane*[107] Kay J felt able to extract the following principles from previous case-law:

> [W]here a purchase is made from a poor and ignorant man at a considerable undervalue, the vendor having no independent advice, a Court of Equity will set aside the transaction. This will be done even in the case of property in possession and *a fortiori* if the interest is reversionary.[108]

The relevance of socio-economic factors is also vividly demonstrated by *Cresswell v Potter*,[109] where Megarry J sought to update the guidance laid out in *Fry v Lane*: 'the euphemisms of the 20th century may require the word "poor" to be replaced by "member of the lower income group" or the like, and the word "ignorant" by "less highly educated"'.[110] It is also clear that old age is a relevant, if perhaps unquantifiable, factor in the case law.[111]

Notwithstanding the foregoing it will be fascinating to observe how, if at all, some of the ideas discussed above—such as the idea that the homes of the elderly are repositories of capital to fund their expenses in old age—impact on the court's conceptions of vulnerability in this context.[112] Certainly in the context of the analogous doctrine of undue influence, Burns

---

[104] *ibid*, 513.
[105] Above, section II.
[106] See section III.
[107] *Fry v Lane* (1888) 40 Ch D 312.
[108] *ibid*, 322.
[109] See also *Mountford v Callaghan* (unreported, 29 September 1999, QBD) and, in particular, *Growden v Bean* (unreported, 26 July 1982, QBD).
[110] *ibid*.
[111] See, eg, *Clark v Malpas* (1862) 4 De GF & J 401, 45 ER 1238; *Baker v Monk* (1864) 4 De GJ & S 388, 46 ER 968; and *Portman Building Society v Dusangh* [2000] 2 All ER (Comm) 221.
[112] *cf* Burns, above n 44, at 272–3.

has noted ostensible differences in the case law in respect of the court's approach to establishing a relationship of trust and confidence between an elder and their offspring.[113] In particular, Burns notes that in some cases an elderly parent-child relationship was sufficient to establish a relationship of trust and confidence;[114] whereas in other cases more was required.[115]

D. Transactional Outcomes

The unconscionable bargain doctrine is also sensitive[116] to the terms of the transaction.[117] This may be particularly significant in the context of equity release schemes where the focus of statutory regulation is on the provision of information and advice, rather than transactional outcomes. Moreover, the analogy with the former manifest disadvantage requirement in the context of undue influence suggests that the assessment of transactional outcomes will be influenced by normative assumptions.[118] If so, it will be intriguing to observe how some of the ideas discussed above—such as the idea that the homes of the elderly are repositories of capital to fund their expenses in old age—impact on the application of the unconscionable bargain doctrine in this context.[119] Likewise, in situations where an elderly parent attempts to assist adult offspring onto the housing ladder, it will be intriguing to observe how ideas, such as the advancement of the interests of offspring, impact on the application of the unconscionable bargain doctrine in this context. A glimpse of these socio-culturally charged issues can be seen in *Portman Building Society v Dusangh*.[120] In that case an old, illiterate man mortgaged his home to support the business ventures of his son. In refusing to utilise

---

[113] *ibid.*

[114] See, eg, *Love v Love* (unreported, 11 March 1999, CA).

[115] See, eg, *Davies v Dobson* (unreported, 7 July 2000, Ch D).

[116] In *Alec Lobb (Garages) Ltd v Total Oil GB Ltd* [1983] 1 All ER 944, Peter Millett QC, sitting as a Deputy Judge of the High Court, felt that substantive unconscionability was a prerequisite of relief under the unconscionable bargain doctrine. However, it appears that this is not necessarily the case: see, eg, *Cooke v Clayworth* (1811) Ves 12, 34 ER 222.

[117] See J Devenney, *An Analytical Deconstruction of the Unconscionable Bargain Doctrine in England and Wales* (unpublished Ph D thesis, Cardiff, University of Wales, 2003) 287–312. There is some uncertainty as to whether or not the unconscionable bargain doctrine is relevant in the context of gifts. In *Langton v Langton* [1995] 2 FLR 890—a case involving an elder— AWH Charles, sitting as a Deputy Judge of the Chancery Division, held that the unconscionable bargain doctrine was not relevant in the context of gifts: see the discussion at [1995] 2 FLR 890, 907–910. Indeed there is earlier authority, which was not considered by the learned judge, supporting both positions: see *Henshall v Fereday* (1873) 29 LT 46 and *Mousley v Reid* [1974] EG 17. It seems that the unconscionable bargain doctrine does apply to suretyship transactions: see *Credit Lyonnais Bank Nederland NV v Burch* [1997] 1 All ER 144. In such transactions the surety *may* not get any benefit from the transaction and, therefore, such transactions *might* be regarded as analogous to gifts.

[118] Devenney and Chandler, above n 53, at 564–6.

[119] See Burns, above n 64, at 272–3.

[120] *Portman Building Society v Dusangh* [2000] 2 All ER (Comm) 221 (CA).

the unconscionable bargain doctrine, the court placed heavy reliance on its view that the transaction was not to the manifest disadvantage of the father. Simon Brown LJ stated:

> [I]t was not manifestly disadvantageous to this appellant that he should be able to raise money ... so as to benefit his son ... I would agree ... But I simply cannot accept that building societies are required to police transactions of this nature to ensure that parents ... are wise in seeking to assist their children ... In short, the conscience of the court is not shocked.[121]

This was echoed by Ward LJ, who added that:

> it was a case of father coming to the assistance of the son. True it is that it was a financially unwise venture ... and the father's home was at risk. But there was nothing ... which comes close to morally reprehensible conduct or impropriety. No unconscientious advantage has been taken of the father's ... paternal generosity ... The family wanted to raise money: the building society was prepared to lend it. One shakes one's head, but with sadness ... alas not with moral outrage.[122]

E. Independent Advice

Many of the leading cases on the unconscionable bargain doctrine make some reference to the relevance of independent advice, although there is very little discussion of the precise role of independent advice in this context.[123] For present purposes, it will suffice to note that independent advice is not regarded as a panacea in this context.[124]

F. Theoretical Framework

The precise nature, and extent, of the protection given by the unconscionable bargain doctrine to the elderly in relation to financial transactions involving their home is, of course, linked to the theoretical framework within which the foregoing elements operate. In *Hart v O'Connor*[125] the Privy Council located the unconscionable bargain doctrine under the umbrella of the rather elusive notion of procedural unconscionability.[126] Birks and Chin, as noted above, argued that unconscionability is defendant-sided relief and, in so doing, they linked the concept of unconscionability

---

[121] *ibid*, 228–30.

[122] *ibid*, 234.

[123] See J Devenney, *An Analytical Deconstruction of the Unconscionable Bargain Doctrine in England and Wales* (unpublished Ph D thesis, Cardiff, University of Wales, 2003) 271–83.

[124] See, eg, *Backhouse v Backhouse* [1978] 1 All ER 1158, 1166 (Balcombe J).

[125] *Hart v O'Connor* [1985] 2 WLR 944, 958.

[126] *ibid*, 958. See also R Clark, 'The Unconscionability Doctrine Viewed from an Irish Perspective' (1980) 31 *Northern Ireland Legal Quarterly* 114, especially at 122.

to a notion of 'wicked exploitation'. Yet, as one of the current authors has argued elsewhere,[127] many of the cases on the unconscionable bargain doctrine—particularly, although by no means exclusively,[128] those from the eighteenth and nineteenth centuries[129]—reveal a strong claimant-sided flavour. Whilst we do not wish to rehearse those arguments here, the words of Turner LJ in *Baker v Monk*[130] bear repetition given the valuable insight they offer into the operation of the unconscionable bargain doctrine:

> *I say nothing about improper conduct on the part of the Appellant; I do not wish to enter into the question of conduct.* In cases of this description there is usually exaggeration on both sides, and I am content to believe that in this case there has been no actual moral fraud on the part of the Appellant in the transaction; but, for all that, in my judgment an improvident contract has been entered into.[131]
> (emphasis added)

Such a view seems to find some resonance with the notion of 'passive acceptance' outlined by the Privy Council in *Hart v O'Connor*.[132] In fact, if the cases which adopt a claimant-sided approach are further analysed, at least two different approaches are evident within them: the 'causal-connection' approach and the 'status' approach.[133] The essence of the causal-connection approach is that the resultant bargain is causally linked to the claimant's vulnerability.[134] By contrast, the essence of the status approach is that a court has the power to relieve particular sections of society from *some* forms of improvident bargain despite the fact that there is not necessarily a causal connection between the resultant bargain and the claimant's position.[135] Such an approach is, perhaps, surprising although there are also hints of it within the doctrine of undue influence in relation to relationships formerly described as 2A relationships.[136] It remains to be seen, in the context of the

---

[127] Devenney and Chandler, *ibid*, 544–8.

[128] See, eg, *Cresswell v Potter* [1978] 1 WLR 255n.

[129] See M Chen-Wishart, *Unconscionable Bargains* (Sydney, Butterworths, 1989) 18, who argues that the conduct of the defendant was 'largely irrelevant' in these cases.

[130] *Baker v Monk* (1864) 4 De GJ & S 388, 46 ER 968.

[131] *ibid*, 425. See also *Evans v Llewellin* (1787) 1 Cox CC 333 and *Clark v Malpas* (1862) 31 Beav 80; 54 ER 1067; affirmed on appeal, (1862) 4 De GF & J 401, 45 ER 1238. It is not impossible to argue that a defendant-sided approach is evident in *Alec Lobb (Garages) Ltd v Total Oil GB Ltd* [1985] 2 WLR 944 although that is questionable: see Devenney and Chandler, above n 73, at 547–8.

[132] *Hart v O'Connor* [1985] 2 WLR 944 (PC) 958.

[133] See Devenney, above n 94.

[134] See, eg, *Multiservice Bookbinding Ltd v Marden* [1979] 1 Ch 84.

[135] See Devenney & Chandler, above n 53. See further, eg, *Cresswell v Potter* [1978] 1 WLR 255n and *Evans v Llewellin* (1787) 1 Cox CC 333.

[136] It has been argued elsewhere that there are questions surrounding the legitimacy of this category of relationships, see Devenney and Chandler, above n 53, at 556–8; *cf* Burns, above n 44, at 264–5. Yet, *if* the law is to recognise a category of '2A relationships' there are cogent arguments to suggest that the relationships between an elder and their adult offspring, an elder and their financial adviser and an elder and their carer should be, for the reasons outlined in sections II and III, included in such a category, at least in the current context.

unconscionable bargain doctrine, whether or not a 'status approach' will be adopted in relation to elders and equity release schemes.

V. CONCLUSION

There is a growing awareness of issues relating to the elderly, their homes and the transactions into which they enter. In particular, there has been increased concern in relation to the use of equity release schemes. Such schemes have dramatically increased in recent years and, given the social and economic factors at work here, an elder may be vulnerable in this context. Although recent statutory regulation of this area is to be welcomed, it is important to appreciate the limitations of this regulation. In particular, the statutory regulation of this area is targeted at providing *information* and *advice* whereas it is crucial to recognise that the social and economic factors at work here, sometimes coupled with relational pressures, may still leave an *informed* elder in a vulnerable position. As a result the equitable doctrine of undue influence *may* have an important role to play in providing a measure of legal protection for elderly homeowners who engage in these financial transactions. However, the jurisprudential basis of the doctrine of undue influence is keenly disputed and *if* the views of Birks and Chin prevail, the doctrine of undue influence will hover around questions of capacity. Moreover, *if* the doctrine of undue influence focuses *solely* on the *capacity* of the elderly person, the protection provided by the doctrine of undue influence in such situations is likely to be limited. Accordingly, this paper has suggested that the unconscionable bargain doctrine—a doctrine which is particularly sensitive to the terms of the transaction, the effectiveness of any independent advice, informational inequalities and the vulnerabilities of the parties—has an important role to play in this context. However, the precise protection afforded by the unconscionable bargain doctrine in this context will, for example, depend on the application of the normative assumptions underpinning the assessment of transactional outcomes; and these *may* be informed by ideas such the contemporary political idea that the homes of the elderly are repositories of capital to fund their expenses in old age.

IV

Different Conceptions of Property

12

Selling the Land: Should It Stop?

A Case Study from the South Pacific

SUE FARRAN[*]

I. INTRODUCTION

CENTRAL TO CONTEMPORARY property law, certainly in the United Kingdom but also in many other common law jurisdictions, is the idea of land as a marketable commodity, and that the role of property law is to facilitate this. Indeed so commonplace is the notion that land should be freely alienable that the wisdom of the underlying policy or philosophy is rarely questioned. However, there may be places or circumstances where land sale and purchase is not always beneficial and where the common law assumptions need to be scrutinised. This paper looks at one case where the introduction of common law conceptions and values not only is at odds with indigenous perceptions and values in relation to land, but where the continued pursuit of the marketability of land could have grave consequences.

The case study is based on empirical and academic research undertaken in the Pacific island country of Vanuatu. Many of the dilemmas encountered here are experienced in other parts of the Pacific and the wider developing world.[1] Moreover, many of the features of this case study are illustrative of phenomena which are or have occurred elsewhere, from the fishing villages of Cornwall to the coastal belt of Spain and the Mediterranean. At a time when house prices and mortgage finance seem to be key indicators of national and global economies it is hoped that this paper may provide food for thought and a moment to reflect on the assumptions we make about land as a market-place item.[2]

---

[*] Senior Lecturer, University of Dundee; Visiting Lecturer University of the South Pacific.
[1] See eg K Dixon, 'Mobilising Customary Land in Papua New Guinea the Melanesian Way' (2007) 31 *Harvard Environmental Law Review* 219–77.
[2] Since writing this paper the shaky foundations on which such economies are based has become self-evident.

II. A CASE STUDY FROM THE SOUTH PACIFIC

Land has become a tradeable commodity with a concomitant demand for easy transferability of title.[3]

One of the central features of contemporary property law is the way in which it operates to facilitate property transactions, to protect property interests of third parties against purchasers and to protect purchasers. The idea of land as a marketable commodity is so commonplace today that it may be easy to lose sight of the consequences of land alienation for the vendors.

These may be of particular concern where land or real estate is the sole or prime resource available for alienation, as is the case in some of the least developed or underdeveloped regions and countries of the world. Where people have the opportunity to relocate and reinvest the material gains of land alienation the consequences may not be entirely negative. Where, however, this is not possible, and there are pressures to engage in a cash economy and attract inward investment in order to participate in global markets, then the negative consequences may be greater, especially if a high percentage of land alienation is to outsiders or foreigners and land is acquired as second home/holiday/retirement property, with little or no intention to generate employment or engage in commercial activity.

In the South Pacific land alienation is not a recent phenomenon. Indeed the region has a history of dispossession of land, first by warring clans and chiefdoms and later, as contact with westerners grew, through dispossession by planters, colonial government and grants to missionaries and churches. In many of the island countries of the region one of the key motivating factors in the period leading up to independence was the desire to reclaim the land. Certainly this was the case in the islands of the New Hebrides which were to become Vanuatu, the country with which this case study is concerned. Here, in the decade before independence it was estimated that over half the country had been alienated, primarily as agricultural land to foreigners during the years of Anglo-French colonial government.

Consequently, when the Republic of Vanuatu gained its independence in 1980, all land was restored to custom owners, title to which was to be determined by diverse custom laws according to the provisions of the written constitution which conferred new national status on the country as the Republic of Vanuatu.[4]

---

[3] G Ward and E Kingdom (eds), *Land, Custom and Practice in the South Pacific* (Cambridge, Cambridge University Press, 1995) 37.
[4] Constitution of the Republic of Vanuatu arts 73–77.

III. VANUATU: EFATE

The Republic of Vanuatu is situated in the Pacific Ocean. There are approximately 80 islands in Vanuatu, not all of them inhabited. They vary considerably in size and population. Most are volcanic in origin with steeply rising interiors. Consequently, population density tends to be greatest along the coastal belt and near inland waters.

As an independent state and member of the family of nations, the Republic of Vanuatu is a young nation. In fact it is on the United Nations list of least developed nations of the world.[5] Its economy is based primarily on small-scale agriculture, which provides a living for 65 per cent of the population,[6] fishing, financial services (offshore) and tourism. Nevertheless it aspires to development, to membership of the World Trade Organization and other regional and international trading frameworks. To do this not only must it put in place the necessary facilitating legal framework but it must also attract inward investment. One way of doing this is to attract foreign investment in land, by encouraging either tourism operators such as hotel chains, or individuals seeking second or holiday homes.

This case study focuses on one island: Efate. This is where the capital, Port Vila, is located. Efate is the third largest island in the archipelago of islands which make up Vanuatu and has a land mass of approximately 915 square kilometres. This island has the highest population concentration and largest urban development in the country.

By air the island is around three hours from the east coast of Australia, and the same from Auckland, New Zealand. The country's international airport is located here and passenger cruise ships make frequent visits, usually stopping for just a few hours to disgorge their passengers for a quick look at Port Vila, and perhaps some of the island. Tourism is an important revenue source for Vanuatu. Some visitors come and want to stay. Others come because they are on contracts with various aid agencies dedicated to the 'improvement' of the country. They too may want to stay, perhaps just for a little while, perhaps for longer. They are keen to acquire homes in islands made famous by musicals, Michener and more recently reality television. They are tempted by the glossy advertisements in the airline magazine, by the photos of beach frontage and aquamarine seas in estate agents windows in the main street of the capital, and by the cachet of having an 'island home'. They are used to the idea of second homes and the philosophy of 'if you want it, buy it'.

---

[5] United Nations list of Least Developed Countries http://www.un.org/special-rep/ohrlls/ldc/list.htm (18 October 2008).

[6] Some sources claim this percentage to be as high as 80. See opening speech at the National Land Summit by the Minister of Lands.

In 2000–2001, while based at the University of the South Pacific in Vanuatu, I undertook a field study into the extent of land alienation on Efate. Research into registered land lease records indicated that the approximate total land area of the island held under lease was 24,205h 46a 95ca. This land area—which excluded the urban area of Port Vila—represented about 25 per cent of the land area of the island but, importantly, covered a considerable percentage of the coastal land. These findings received considerable local publicity at the time and were presented at a public conference in Port Vila. In 2007, with the assistance of funding from the Society of Legal Scholars, I returned to Vanuatu to find out what developments there had been. This paper draws on that research.

IV. LAND, CUSTOM AND LAW

The ethno-centric perception of land held by many visitors to Vanuatu is different from that held by most indigenous inhabitants (ni-Vanuatu). To them, land is everything: 'It is a place where ni-Vanuatu can find food and his other basic needs. Land is linked with culture and family relationships. Many people talk about land as our mother'.[7]

Bonnemaison, writing in 1984, stated:

> In Vanuatu custom land is not only the site of production but it is the mainstay of a vision of the world. It represents life, materially and spiritually. A man is tied to his territory by affinity and consanguinity. The clan is its land, just as the clan is its ancestors. The clan's land, its ancestors and its men are a single indissoluble reality—a fact which must be borne in mind when it is said that Melanesian land is not alienable.[8]

As has been indicated, by the time Vanuatu gained independence a considerable area of land had been alienated. Land clearance and especially incursion into native bush land or 'dark bush' led to insurgence and the rise of political parties supporting the move towards independence.[9]

As so much land had been alienated transitional provisions had to be put in place. Foreigners who had acquired freehold titles and were in occupation no longer held such titles, as freehold was abolished entirely. However, these settlers could remain in possession of the land they occupied until they were either paid compensation by the custom owners, or granted a lease, or a combination of these if the custom owners wished to reclaim some, but

---

[7] R Nari, Director-General of the Ministry of Lands, address to the National Land Summit, 25–29 September 2006.

[8] J Bonnemasion, 'Social and Cultural Aspects of Land Tenure' in Peter Larmour (ed), *Land Tenure in Vanuatu*, (Port Vila, Vanuatu, Institute of Pacific Studies, University of the South Pacific, 1984) 1–2.

[9] Represented in particular by the *Nagriamel* movement in Santo and the New Hebrides National Party.

not all, the land.[10] Where the land was not occupied—and there were many absentee planters, then the land reverted to the custom owners who had originally alienated it. Any custom owner wishing to enter into a lease with a tenant had to be recognised as the appropriate person or persons to negotiate such a lease. There were, however, problems. After a period of over 100 years, it was not always possible to trace the custom owners of land, most of whom had had to move elsewhere once planters took over, and who in any case may not have cultivated the land but simply used its natural resources. This led to disputed claims. The Constitution, envisaging such possibilities, provided that where title was in dispute or unclear then the land vested in the appropriate representative of the government—the Minister of Lands, until the dispute was resolved.[11] The Minister in the interim had the power to manage the land. A further problem was that there was no national law governing leases. Any leases entered into were therefore governed either by custom, or by French or English law in force at the date of independence, as provided for in the constitutional rules on interim laws. It was not until four years after independence that the Land Leases Act (Cap 163) was put in place. Since then other legislation has followed to facilitate land alienation, for example, in the 1990s restrictions on sub-division were lifted and in 2000 Strata Title was introduced.

No time limit was provided in the various legal provisions which were intended to transfer title back to customary owners who had alienated the land, and govern the payment of compensation or the granting of leases to foreigners or non-customary owners who were in occupation. This had a number of consequences, some of which are still of significance 28 years after independence. First it seems likely that a number of settlers remained in occupation in a legal limbo, not yet having a lease but being no longer entitled to hold the freehold title to land.[12] Where agricultural leases were granted—and the lands records indicate that these were the majority of leases in the 1980s—the lease was for a much shorter period than the maximum permitted under the law, and tended to be for 30 or 40 years. These leases will therefore be reaching maturity in the next decade, if not sooner, which is a matter of some concern, as will be indicated. Secondly, because leases had to be entered into by the appropriate, original alienator or his descendants, it was often unclear who these were. In a number of cases title had been acquired by foreigners by unscrupulous means.[13] Although

---

[10] The Land Reform Act (Cap. 123) s 3. This replaced a Joint Regulation passed before independence. Joint Regulations were laws passed by the Anglo-French Condominium government—usually for indigenous people.

[11] Constitution of Vanuatu art 87(1).

[12] The fact that a number of leases are backdated—some to 1980—suggests that this may have been the case.

[13] See H Van Trease, *The Politics of the Land in Vanuatu* (Institute of Pacific Studies, University of the South Pacific, 1987).

the Joint Court, which was in place under Anglo-French Condominium rule prior to independence, had endeavoured to sort out disputes relating to title in the years 1906–80, and had indeed resolved a number of cases, it nevertheless remained the situation that at independence there was land without ascertainable custom owners.[14] The consequence of this was that a considerable area of land was held and managed by the Government until custom owners could be ascertained or disputes between them resolved. Even where the custom owners could be ascertained and they had granted leases to the alien occupier, in some cases disputes subsequently arose regarding the status of the grantor as the true custom owner or representative of the custom owners, leading either to cautions being registered against the lease, or the forfeiture or surrender of the lease, or the intervention of the Minister of Lands. As a result the first decade of independence saw a rapid escalation of land title claims, some of which are still pending before the courts. Failure to clear this back-log and dissatisfaction about the lack of custom and customary law being considered in the process, led to reforms in the courts structure and procedure to deal with land issues. In 2001 the Lands Tribunal Act set up a new tier of courts to consider and rule on customary land claims. At present there is no appeal from the decisions of the highest Customary Land Tribunal to the ordinary courts. Moreover not all areas yet have customary tribunals and the efficiency of those that do exist has been questioned.[15] In the meantime the Minister of Lands continues to manage and administer land subject to dispute. In particular the Minister has the power to lease land. The fact that he can give good title to a lease means that land developers far prefer to acquire land held under the Minister's powers than to go to the bother of trying to deal with custom owners. Ministers of Lands have therefore been key players in granting a large percentage of the total number of leases.[16]

The constitutional provisions put in place to provide for the transition from colony to republic remain in place and although probably intended to be used for a relatively short interim period, continue to be used, and to be used in circumstances for which they were probably not intended. The laws which give them practical effect are essentially based on introduced concepts, language and institutions relating to property, the successful transplant of which is at the very least questionable.[17]

---

[14] Some land was also left abandoned or had never been developed despite being alienated.

[15] See Republic of Vanuatu Department of Lands, 'Land Tribunal Progressive Report 2003', Ref No: LD:/AHKM/ahkm, 12 December 2003.

[16] See S Farran, 'Ministerial Leases in Vanuatu: A Working Paper' (2002) 6 *Journal of South Pacific Law* http://www.vanuatu.usp.ac.fj/jspl.

[17] See further S Farran, 'Land in Vanuatu: Moving Forwards, Looking Backwards' (2002) II *Revue Juridique Polynesienne* 213–24.

V. LAW RELATING TO LEASES

Leases of land are regulated by the Land Leases Act (Cap 163). The Act imports into Vanuatu law the paraphernalia and concepts of western land law. It establishes the administrative machinery for the recording, surveying and registration of leases and the creation of management posts such as the Director of Lands Records and Land Surveys to oversee this administration. No lease of longer than 75 years may be granted and those of three years or more have to be registered. These registers provide some factual evidence of the total area of land held under lease. For example, data collected in 2001 from the paper records filed in the Lands Registry Office in Port Vila indicated that there were around 1,070 registered leases for land in Efate, outside the municipal area of the capital of Vanuatu, Port Vila.[18] Any figure obtained from the records is necessarily approximate owing to the back-log of leases waiting to be processed, missing leases, and some cases where there seems to be more than one lease for the same parcel of land. Moreover, formal leases which are registered represent only a fraction of land taken out of the hands of the original customary owners. Non-owners assert rights of occupation and cultivation through informal licences and the granting of privileges—sometimes in return for political support, and increasingly through squatting. There is also, no doubt, a number of unregistered leases of under three years' duration.

VI. STRATA TITLE

The sub-division of single plots by means of strata title was introduced under the Strata Title Act 2000. The purported aim of the legislation was to facilitate the sub-division of buildings into separate lots by registering a strata title plan. Certainly the language and detail of the legislation indicated that this was the purpose. Had the use of strata titles been so limited then it could have provided a useful means for small businesses to raise mortgage loan finance on the security of strata title held in commercial premises. However it is evident that the Act has been used for sub-division of undeveloped land and that this is in fact facilitated by amendments made to the original Act in 2003. As the Land Leases Act already provides for sub-division it is suspected that the Strata Title Act has been used because it lacks the safeguards for lessors—the custom owners—found in the former. Under the Strata Title Act, the lessee does not have to seek the consent of the lessor for sub-division but has to apply to the relevant authority—the municipal council or provincial government. Each lot under a strata title is

---

[18] This was at December 2001. The municipal area was excluded from the research because of the very large number of sub-leases that occur.

issued with its own separate certificate of title, thereby removing the tie of a head-lease. Abuse of the Act is self-evident. The provisions require that any lease from which strata title is granted must have at least 75 years to run. This is the maximum period for all leases with the exception of renewable 75-year leases granted under the Land Leases (Amendment) Act 2003. These renewable leases are only possible over public land, which is overwhelmingly restricted to urban areas. Sub-divisions under strata title are however being advertised outside the municipal areas and in respect of rural land.

VII. THE VANUATU RESPONSE

Vanuatu is not oblivious to the problems of rapid land alienation. Land conferences have been held annually at the University of the South Pacific since 2002. During the course of 2006 a number of provincial meetings and consultations took place to consider land issues.[19] These culminated in a National Land Summit in September 2006. The National Summit provided the forum for a wide expression of views, including those resulting from provincial-level consultations. The aim was to review issues of land management and development. In particular a need to address questions of land ownership, fair dealing, and the role of Government in the management and development of land were identified as key issues.

A. Questions of Ownership

It became evident from the Land Summit that this was an issue of considerable and continuing confusion 26 years after independence. Although the Constitution returned land to custom owners and stated that the rules of custom should form the basis of ownership, there were no clear guidelines on who the indigenous custom owners were and how they were to be ascertained, or what custom rules were to apply. There was also no consideration of what forms of proprietary interests were to be considered or how they should be ranked. Within the Constitution there is implied reference to both group rights and individual rights.[20] The problem was further compounded by the fact that in custom there was no 'owner', only a spokesperson or representative of a tribe, clan or family.[21] At the same time there were, and

---

[19] S Tahi, *National Land Summit, Final Report* (Government of Vanuatu, 2007) 15–19.

[20] See Art 73 compared with Art 79(2)(b).

[21] The problem of language and legal concepts has been commented on elsewhere, see K Brown, 'The Language of Land: Look Before You Leap' (2000) 4 *Journal of South Pacific Law* http://www.paclii.org/journals/fJSPL/vol04/; and S Farran, 'The Language of Property Law and the Construction of Property Interests: Common Ground or Conflict' paper presented at the Australasian Law Teachers Conference, Canberra, Australia (July 2000).

continue to be, complicating factors such as temporal and spiritual rights, use and access rights, succession rights and suspended rights.[22] There is also the difficulty of reducing oral custom to written rules and reducing the fluidity of a highly adaptable form of land tenure to writing. Customs are not codified, although there are collections of statements of custom for some islands. For example there is a statement of custom for Tanna, and more recently a statement of customary land law has been written by the Efate Council of Chiefs (Efate Vaturisu). This was published in February 2007 after the Land Summit, and perhaps marks the beginning of a wider movement to codify customary land law so that custom rules can emerge and be applied by the appropriate tribunals. However this process may well be resisted, as codification may make it much easier to amend or abolish such rules by legislation.

A further question of ownership which arose at the summit, and one that has been an issue for some time in Vanuatu, was the question of ownership of reefs and the sea. Unlike the situation in some Pacific island countries, the coastline does not vest in the state. Customary tenure deems custom land to extend to the reefs that fringe the islands. This is logical, as the reefs at low tide provide a rich harvest of marine resources and a place from which the spear fishermen can dive for larger fish. Legislation in the form of the Foreshore Development Act permits the development of the foreshore with the required consent of the Minister.[23] This Act, however, was a Joint Regulation prior to independence and therefore applied before all land was returned to custom ownership. As the foreshore has been held to be customary land for the purposes of the Act,[24] and as the Constitution provides that

> the rules of custom shall form the basis of ownership and use of land in the republic of Vanuatu (Article 74),

it appears that there is an incompatibility between the powers conferred on the Minister under the Foreshore Development Act and these constitutional provisions, because permitted development may take the beneficial ownership of foreshore land out of the hands of custom owners. By virtue of Article 95 of the Constitution, this pre-independence legislation must be construed

> with such adaptations as may be necessary to bring them into conformity with the Constitution.

---

[22] Where for example, there is no eldest son, so patrilineal land must temporarily pass matrilineally.

[23] Foreshore Development Act—Joint Regulation No 31 prior to independence (now Cap 90)—s 2 states: 'No person shall undertake or cause or permit to be undertaken any development on the foreshore of the coast of any island in Vanuatu without having first obtained the written consent of the Minister to such development'. Development is defined in s 1 as: 'the carrying out of any building, engineering, mining or other operations in, on, over or under the land, or the making of any material change in the use of buildings or other land whether or not such land is covered by water'.

[24] *Brown v Bastien* [2002] VUSC 2.

To do this it would probably be correct to say that no development of the foreshore can take place where that affects customary land. The lease boundary of any coastal lease should therefore only extend to the high water mark. Despite this, however, the National Land Summit heard many examples of beaches, rivers, lakes and other recreational sites being fenced off by individuals, especially foreigners, and public and customary access denied. Among the resolutions of the Summit—see below—were a number relating to coastal areas, in particular the need for public access to the sea, rivers and lakes, the recognition and safeguarding of public and custom owner rights to areas above the high water mark and to the reef, as well as concerns about the environmental protection of rivers and beaches.

B. Fair Dealing

The report of the 2006 National Land Summit identified a number of concerns with land dealings. In principle land held under customary land tenure can only be dealt with in two ways: either in custom or by lease. In practice there may be some overlap. First, customary owners may negotiate what either appear to be or are understood as leases over their land with other indigenous occupants but these arrangements turn out to fall short of a lease. Alternatively customary owners may think that they are agreeing to various rights and privileges recognised in custom, such as the right to access the beach or the right to take sand or timber, but find that they have entered into leases of some kind. Sometimes there are genuine misunderstandings between parties; at other times there is duplicity or fraud.

Where custom is used as the basis for land dealing it may be unclear what customary rules are to be applied or indeed what these are. Custom is flexible and subject to manipulative interpretation. Customary transactions are also not required to be registered. They are therefore potentially uncertain and insecure. There is also some uncertainty whether a non-ni-Vanuatu can enter into any transaction governed by custom—for example, banks being approached for loans secured against customary land.

Predominantly therefore land alienation takes place by way of leases. Lease transactions confront custom owners with a range of alien concepts which are not always easily understood and which can leave customary owners vulnerable. Issues identified at the Land Summit included ignorance about the market value of land (compared to its customary value) especially in advance of considering whether to lease it; lack of understanding about the nature of a lease; lack of any regulation of estate agents and middle men—usually ex-patriates—operating in Vanuatu; unfair and undervalued rentals and premiums which custom owners have insufficient participation in negotiating; and failure of representatives of groups to take into account the interests of the whole group in making land management decisions.

Similarly, concerns were expressed about lack of accountability when the Minister exercised his powers to manage lands over which there was a dispute.

The Constitution states that

> land transactions between an indigenous citizen and either a non-indigenous citizen or a non-citizen shall only be permitted with the consent of the Government. [This] ... shall be given unless the transaction is prejudicial to the interests of—
>
> (a) the custom owner or owners of the land;
> (b) the indigenous citizen where he is not the custom owner;
> (c) the community in whose locality the land is situated; or
> (d) the Republic of Vanuatu.[25]

Arguably these considerations should apply whether the Minister is managing land under dispute, or state/public land. However, it is unclear if, and to what extent, the above provisions empower government to act independently. If they do, then returning land to custom owners may have been meaningless in the current climate of land alienation. If they do not, then any decisions of government which involve land management should be assessed against the above conditions.

C. Sustainable Development

Sustainable development is not a new concept to customary land-owners, although the contemporary phrasing of it may be unfamiliar. Customary traditions of cultivation, harvesting, land and marine resource-use have been in place for centuries. However there is a difference between the use of resources for subsistence economies and the exploitation of these for cash. Rapid land clearance, sand, coral and gravel mining, road construction and building construction all have a grave impact on sustainability, as does increased cultivation, especially in water catchment areas or coastal zones. Often customary land-owners are not aware of the long-term impact of these changed usages. Developers are keen to play down any adverse environmental impact and although there are requirements for environmental impact statements to be presented prior to development, the policing and enforcement of these appears to be weak and often the environmental damage is taking place away from the actual development, for example where sand is being bulldozed out of beaches or coral being mined from hills. Population increase and urban drift is leading to native bush land being cleared for gardening—often by squatters—and as coastal areas become more developed this process is moving inland. Vanuatu also lacks any effective or co-ordinated zoning plan. Although registered leases must indicate

---

[25] Art 79.

an approved use, often this is changed or abused. For example, the limited construction of buildings allowed on agricultural leasehold may be ignored and extra buildings constructed. Density of building on residential plots may be uncontrolled and little attention given to the longer-term effect of land drainage, or land infill, or the efficiency of raw sewage treatment or storm drainage systems.

There is also virtually no awareness of the social impact of taking customary land out of customary hands, or how development is affecting people both within its immediate vicinity and further afield. One of the impacts which has been poorly studied is that of depriving people of coastal access. Others are the impact—both positive and negative—of improved infrastructure. For example, in 2006 the Republic of Vanuatu and the United States of America agreed that one of the projects of the Millennium Challenge Corporation would be to develop the transport infrastructure of Vanuatu. An aid fund of US$65,690,000 was set aside for this purpose. The aim is to 'reduce poverty and increase incomes in rural areas by stimulating economic activity in the tourism and agricultural sectors'.[26] In Efate this means improvement to the round island road, which is only tar-sealed for a very short distance near Port Vila, and in places is sometimes impassable due to rainwater erosion. Islanders from the north of the island wishing to bring produce to the Port Vila market have to hire taxi trucks and buses. This road will make their journey easier, although whether the Port Vila market can absorb a great increase in produce may be more questionable. There is, however no evidence of social impact assessments having been made on the villages through which this much faster road will pass, whether easier access by tourists to the North of the island is being encouraged with sustainability in mind, or whether the new road will simply facilitate and accelerate the alienation of the entire perimeter of coastal land in Efate.

D. Land Summit Resolutions

The National Land Summit arrived at a list of 20 resolutions. In summary these were:

— the law should recognise and give effect to communal ownership of land;
— the central and provincial governments and the National Council of Chiefs should work together to document the custom (*kastom*) that determine ownership, land policies, boundaries and land dealings;

---

[26] *Vanuatu Daily Post*, 7 July 2007.

— greater awareness of the existing (plural) legal and economic framework should be undertaken;

— the current law of leases should be reviewed;

— lease agreements should be made comprehensible and inclusive in their negotiation and agreement;

— certificates of negotiation should be subject to increased scrutiny and publicity, especially at the local level;

— the Minister should cease to have the power to approve leases over disputed land;

— abuses of the use of strata title should cease and land owners should be involved in their approval;

— real estate agents should be regulated;

— lease rental and premium rating should be reviewed and reformed;

— should be put in place and effectively enforced;

— physical planning and zoning laws should be strengthened and a subdivisions policy adopted at national and provincial level, and

— efforts should be made at all levels and to all sectors of the community to raise awareness of sustainability issues.

Given that over 1,000 proposals were made, to reduce these to 20 resolutions was quite a feat. It is still, however, an ambitious list. What is not clear yet is how greater awareness of customary land tenure (Land Ownership) will inform and improve dealings in land especially under leases (Fair Dealings) or how regulation will accommodate custom.[27] Much also depends on the support and drive of central government as well as co-operation between provincial governments—some of whom currently benefit considerably from development and some of whom derive very little benefit and would probably like more development.

The 20 resolutions of the National Land Summit were included in a document: 'Interim Transitional Strategy and Future Plans to Implement the Resolutions of the National Land Summit 2006' and endorsed by the Council of Ministers.[28] An interim strategy was approved. This was to endorse the resolutions of the National Land Summit (which had been modified slightly by the Council);[29] to endorse an interim transitional strategy and the appointment of a Steering Committee; and an indication of

[27] On the integration of custom and informal economies into legal systems and formal economies see H de Soto, *The Other Path: The Invisible Revolution in the Third World* (New York; London, Harper & Row, 1989) but also the failure of the Land Groups Incorporation Act 1974 in Papua New Guinea: L Kalinoe, 'Incorporated Land Groups in Papua New Guinea' (2003) *Melanesian Law Journal* 4.

[28] Decisions 138/2006: Outcome of the National Land Summit and the Interim Transitional Strategy, 21 November 2006.

[29] The original resolutions were written in Bislama—the *lingua franca* of the country. These differ slightly from those published in the Final Report written in English.

government commitment to seek support and funding for implementation of the resolutions (ie seek external aid funding).

Following the Summit the proposed Steering Committee was established;[30] funding was secured and—as is often the case with any matter requiring reform in the region—a call for a review team to consider how to implement the resolutions, was put out to tender. After two visits to Vanuatu in early 2007,[31] the selected review team (an Australian-based consortium) published its report in March 2007. This indicated that:

> [t]o remedy the problems raised at the Land Summit, policies need to be clarified, new legislation introduced, and some existing legislation amended. What is required is not a sweeping revolution, but a reinstatement of sound land tenure and land use principles, as well as fairness and social equity. There is also a pressing need for strengthening the land administration and land use management arrangements. Partly this can be done by institutional reform, partly by better co-ordination, partly by training and capacity-building. Decentralisation is also important, but in order to be effective it must be accompanied by organisation and management reforms.[32]

Key weaknesses were lack of a national land policy, the system of land administration and the current legal framework.

E. Land Policy

The very clear policy at independence was to return land to custom owners and to thereby reduce the amount of land held by foreign settlers, including absentee owners.[33] At the same time, however, the new state had to develop its economy and attract investors, especially as pre-independence turmoil had driven away a number of these. What was not clear, however, was the intended or anticipated relationship between central government and custom owners. The latter were given the freedom to deal with their own land as they wished while the former was responsible for ensuring

---

[30] The Steering Committee members consisted of the Director-General of Lands, the Director-General of Trade, the Director-General of Finance, the Director-General of Agriculture, Forestry and Fisheries, a representative from the State Law Office, the Secretary General of the Council of Chiefs, a delegate from the Vanuatu Cultural Centre, the Chief Executive Officer of the Vanuatu National Council for Women, a representative from Women's Affairs, a representative for youth from Wan Smol Bag theatre group, a representative from the private (estate agents and developers') sector, and the Secretary to the Committee, Ausaid has observer status.

[31] A total of three weeks.

[32] *Vanuatu: Review of National Land Legislation, Policy and Land Administrations* (March 2007) p ii.

[33] This represented about 20% of all rural land. Other land was public land, mostly in urban areas and used for public purposes, and urban land, located in Port Vila and Luganville, which was originally to be under the administration of the Urban Land Corporations of those two towns.

that land transactions prejudicial to custom owners, the national interest or local communities would be prevented. The Constitution envisaged that a national land law would be put in place after consultation with the Council of Chiefs.[34] In fact this never happened. Clearly Vanuatu needs a new land policy, and it needs a national policy which will override or inform the policy and decisions of people at a local level but which is supported by such people.

What the Review Report does not address is whether the government of Vanuatu is in a position to formulate a national policy on land when it is pressured from within and without to 'develop' and maintain economic growth. In an IMF publication entitled 'Doing Business in 2007' the delay and cost of registering land in Vanuatu was criticised—presumably because it delays the setting up of business ventures—often by ex-patriates.[35] In an AusAid funded report on the South Pacific region, entitled 'Pacific 2020', problems of customary land tenure were highlighted as being an obstacle to economic development in the region.[36] In a paper published in 2006 Claire Slatter highlighted the difficulties Pacific islands face if they impose too many restrictions or conditions on tourism development, because of the commitments under the WTO General Agreement on Trade in Services not to introduce unnecessary barriers to trade.[37] This therefore makes it difficult to insist that beach resorts catering for tourists permit local people to freely exercise customary rights over the beach, or that the benefits of tour operators are shared with local communities. She points out that the likelihood of Vanuatu retaining its own policy space is becoming increasingly constrained by the conditions of trade agreements such as European Economic Partnership Agreements, accession to the WTO (for which Vanuatu has recently recommenced negotiations) and commitment to PACER,[38] the proposed free trade zone linking Pacific island countries with their larger neighbours.

Elsewhere, where land is at a premium, a range of policies has been adopted to restrict land alienation. These include moratoriums on all development—as has occurred in coastal parts of Spain; strict requirements of residence, nationality and investment before a person can acquire a home in a particular location—as in the Channel Islands; repatriation and redistribution of land by government decree—as has happened in parts of East Africa; or state control of all land transactions—as is happening in parts of

---

[34] Art 76.

[35] IMF Country Report 07/93.

[36] Pacific Islands 2020 Report by AusAid http://www.ausaid.gov.au/publications/pdf/pacific2020.pdf (3 March 2008).

[37] C Slater, 'The Con/Dominium of Vanuatu? Paying the Price of Investment and Land Liberalisation—a case study of Vanuatu's Tourism Industry', *Vanuatu Daily Post*, 19 August 2006.

[38] Pacific Agreement on Closer Economic Relations.

South Africa where land must be sold to the state rather than private purchasers. While not all of these policies may seem attractive or even feasible
in the context of Vanuatu, what should be clear to the Review Team or any
other body making recommendations for reform is that the formulation of
the policy is the first and essential step.

F. Legislation

Although there has been a considerable body of legislation passed since
independence relating to land—including law to create freehold titles of
urban land[39]—the basic legislative framework which remains in place was
one to facilitate the changed status of land holding at independence.[40] While
the Land Summit identified defects in the existing legislation, many of the
safeguards that are there are simply not enforced. The complexity of legislation such as the Land Leases Act does not lend itself to easy comprehension
and in any case the concepts on which it is based are foreign to customary
tenure. Often customary owners who have granted leases fail to appreciate
that they have lost all rights to their land for a period of 75 years, or that registration of leasehold title is generally indefeasible, or that rights of way or
profits should be secured by registration if they are to bind subsequent successors in title—especially where there is subsequent multiple sub-division
of a plot. There are provisions in the existing laws which could be used
more effectively. For example, there is provision for forfeiture of leases, for
the imposition of conditions as to use of land, for review of rentals and for
compulsory acquisition of land for the public benefit.

At the same time it is clear that provisions which were made for a period
of transition and therefore intended to be interim ones have remained
unaltered and in many instances been used for purposes for which they
were not intended. Two important examples suffice. First, the power of the
Minister to manage lands where custom owners could not be ascertained
or where there was a dispute as to who these were, was intended to be a
power exercised over alienated land. It was necessary as an interim measure
to ensure that those to whom land had been alienated and who were still
in possession of the land could, if they so wished, lease the land and keep
it in production. Ministerial power, however, has continued to be exercised
not only over land which was originally alienated but over other, non-
alienated land as well. Secondly, again as part of the transitional process,

---

[39] Freehold Titles Act 1994, which has never been used.

[40] Post-independence legislation includes: Lands Acquisition Act 1992 (which has never
been used); Urban Lands Act 1993 (repealed in 2003); Freehold Titles Act 1994; Land Referee
Act 1983 (repealed in 2002); Valuation of Land Act 2002; Land Valuers Registration Act
2002; Environmental Management and Conservation Act 2002 and Forestry Act 2001.

under the Alienated Land Act 1982 any person claiming to be an alienator had to apply to be registered as such. If the custom owners were willing to negotiate with settlers on their land, then the Minister issued a Certificate of Registered Negotiator. If the custom owners did not wish to negotiate a lease, the land had to be vacated. This procedure is still being used today to negotiate leases over customary land which has never been alienated to colonial settlers.[41]

Legislation put in place to control and manage development and land use, to protect the environment and ensure sustainability has simply been ignored or by-passed in many instances or found to be unworkable either because of poor drafting or because of weak enforcement. For example the Physical Planning Act 1986 potentially provides a means of zoning through the declaration of Physical Planning Areas. However, not only does responsibility fall under the Minister of Internal Affairs—rather than that of land—but the legislation does not impose land use restrictions, breach of which would be an offence. Instead non-compliance with the Act requires the serving of an enforcement notice within a limited time period with the right of appeal to a Magistrates' Court. There is no penalty for non-compliance with a discontinuation notice. Similarly weak enforcement is found in the Foreshore Development Act 1975, where non-compliance is subject to the paltry fine of Vt 200,000 (approximately £1,000), which is easily affordable by overseas developers. In the case of the Environmental Management and Conservation Act 2002 there is no right of enforcement officers to enter land, with the consequence that officers trying to enforce environmental protection measures have found themselves involved as defendants in civil litigation, and been held personally liable when they have expressed an opinion on the undesirability of certain developments.[42]

G. Land Administration

The early land legislation established an administrative machinery to give effect to the law. The efficiency of this has depended very much on individual office-holders, the resources allocated to Departments under national governments and the facilities provided to support the work required. There has been confusion for a number of years over the respective responsibilities of the various office-holders and also on the division of tasks between central and provincial government, especially in determining and controlling land use, planning and zoning. It has also not been clear whether the administration of land is to be carried out in the interests of

---

[41] For an example of the abuse of these two provisions see *Ifira Trustees Ltd v Family Kalsakau* [2006] VUCA 23.

[42] See *Kakula Island Resorts Ltd v Government of the Republic of Vanuatu* [2006] VUSC 3.

custom owners, the developers, the individual minister or the government of the day. Often these various stakeholders have competing and conflicting interests.[43] While the division of roles and tasks across different departments prevents the vesting of power, and potentially the abuse of that, in the hands of a single unit, it can also result in overlap or lacunae.

A more fundamental problem is the underlying weakness of public administration and the challenges of enhancing private sector economic development in the face of public sector inefficiency. Despite a huge injection of cash from the Asian Development Bank to fund a Comprehensive Reform Programme, which started in 1997, it is clear that there is still considerable need to improve the quality and delivery of government services.[44] Many of the posts which have been created to support land management are unfilled. Often senior posts are subject to political influence, or competent members of staff are relocated to other departments. The Department of Lands, Survey and Records within the Ministry of Lands and Natural Resources has key responsibility for the administration of land management in Vanuatu and also represents the interface between customary land owners, developers and the government. Within it, however, are a number of different units not all of which operate with the same level of efficiency. There is also the problem that most of these services are located in Port Vila, with very little decentralisation to provincial government. However, decentralisation, although in line with greater local input into land development, could aggravate the weaknesses of the current system.

The Review Team suggested that the weaknesses of the current administration of land management need to be addressed by a study of the organisation, management and operations to review structures, roles and responsibilities. It identified as necessary: staff training; recruitment and retention; clarification of role responsibilities; and increased monitoring.

Capacity building, good governance in the public sector and institutional strengthening are the frequently stated mantra of aid-funded projects. This is understandable in so far as these themes lend themselves to projects with clear objectives, which can be managed within a stipulated time frame and the cost of which can be relatively easily assessed. However, what is not addressed but which might be fundamental to poor delivery of public services, is the local approach to public service. Pacific island countries inherited the legacy of colonial administrations. In Vanuatu in fact there were two colonial administrations, French and British, which operated

---

[43] See eg D Paterson, 'Ifira Trustees Ltd v Family Kalsakau [2006] VUCA 23; Vanuatu Copra and Cocoa Exporters Ltd v Maison De Vanuatu [2007] VUCA 24: Two instructive cases for ministers of government, their political advisers, and public servants' (2008) 12 Journal of South Pacific Law 128–37.

[44] See report by the Ministry of Finance and Economic Management, entitled 'Priorities and Action Agenda 2006–2015 (June 2006) p 3 and concerns expressed in the final Report of the National Land Summit.

separately and with very different public sector civil service philosophies. At independence it appears to have been assumed that these models would continue to work and were compatible not only with the new status of the nation but also with Pacific values. The post-independence experience raises questions about these assumptions. Certainly in many Pacific island countries the public sector is a significant employer. With limited private sector development the state is an important source of income and there are many related benefits to be derived from state employment, for example housing, pension schemes and health care. Despite this there is little sense of ownership of central government services, and consequently there is little sense of accountability by employees.[45] However, corruption in the public sector is endemic, ranging from the misuse of government vehicles and telephones to nepotism. Indeed, the Vanuatu Ombudsman has published a number of reports on breach of the Leadership Code and misuse of public office.[46] Such publications cause a ripple but no long-term impact and prosecutions rarely, if ever, follow.

Although a number of the resolutions of the Land Summit indicate that the appropriate response lies in improved public administration, in many ways this is at odds with resolutions advocating more involvement by customary land owning groups, a greater role for chiefs, and non-governmental agencies such as the Vanuatu Cultural Centre. The proposed administrative reform is indicated as a 'short-term' initiative by the Review Team, to be accomplished in a period of three to 12 months. This may be optimistic.

VIII. THE 2007 PICTURE

In 2007 I was unable to update my statistical data regarding the number of leases registered in the period 2000–07 because the Lands Records Department had been relocated and the hard copy records were still in the packing cases waiting to be transferred to a sophisticated electronic data base, which unfortunately was found to be unable to cope with the plot maps.[47] Information had to be obtained in other ways. The latest survey map of Efate indicated that many more leasehold plots had been marked out. It was also evident that many of the original larger leaseholds had been subject to sub-division and were being advertised and developed. Revenue figures from the Land Leases Records Office indicate that lease

---

[45] An example can be found in the *Kakula* case where the government parties (defendants) failed to file a defence, to cross-examine the claimant witnesses or pay trial fees as required.

[46] Established under the Leadership Code Act 1998 amended in 1999. The reports of the Ombudsman can be found on PacLII http://www.paclii.org.

[47] Part of an aid-funded digitisation project.

transactions generated considerable income for government in 2006.[48] There was considerable visual evidence of land clearance, and in some cases indigenous bush had completely disappeared. Beaches which had formerly been open to the public were fenced off, and several had been privatised and incorporated into tourist developments. In some places local people were now being charged a fee if they wished to access the beach. Beach excavation and construction was also evident, with natural sea pools being blasted out of coral coast land, thereby changing the natural wall of sea defences and contributing to silting elsewhere. Around the capital there were several large building supply depots with piles of sand, crushed coral and hardwood timber ready for use. The local paper carried reports of illegal logging taking place on land controlled by the Minister of Lands in a location where a land management area had been established at the request of the island's Council of Chiefs and the provincial government. On prime sites large villas were being constructed, many with high walls topped with razor wire, electric gates and security lighting. In some developments barriers had been erected across roads and access controlled by security staff. More positively, small building and service firms were springing up and more material wealth was evident in the amount of road traffic congesting the capital. On the other hand I heard stories of violence and civil unrest in the peri-urban areas, inter-island land disputes, especially among squatters, and a sense of pessimism among young, unemployed urban dwellers matched by the increasingly hard-line views by traditionalists, including restricting freedom of movement from rural areas to urban areas, sending young people back to the rural areas and giving chiefs more powers to punish those guilty of anti-social behaviour.

IX. THE OUTLOOK

The population of Vanuatu is not huge by international standards. In 2007 it was estimated to be around 212,000, with a growth rate of 1.46 per cent. Thirty two per cent of the population is under the age of 14.[49] Employment opportunities are limited and outward migration almost zero. Vanuatu, unlike some other Pacific island countries, lacks outward migration links to Australia, New Zealand or the United States of America.[50] Ni-Vanuatu have nowhere to go. Increasingly they drift to the urban centres. Many young people are now second or third generation urban dwellers. They have no

---

[48] There were 1,155 leases transferred and 817 new leases granted, generating Vt 153,819,123 (approx £7,690,956).

[49] CIA World Factbook: Vanuatu https://www.cia.gov/library/publications/the-world-factbook/geos/nh.html#People (10 March 2008).

[50] Cf for example, the relation of Cook Islands and Niue with New Zealand; Marshall Islands and the Federated States of Micronesia with the United States of America.

inclination to return to their island roots. Urban poverty and urban crime is on the increase. Property crime is common. Recently the editor of one of the local newspapers suggested that given the ineffective police service, ex-patriates should form vigilante patrols, road blocks should be set up on roads leading to areas where ex-patriates live, and ex-patriates should arm themselves to deal with intruders and trouble-makers.[51] This suggests little confidence in the strengthening of law and order services, which has been ongoing for many years with the assistance of aid funding. Indeed, the Australian Federal Police have a permanent presence in the Australian High Commission, which is housed in new premises on land leased from the government, in a building which resembles a high-security jail.[52]

2008 is envisaged by the Lands Steering Committee as the year in which there will be increasing public awareness of the land issues highlighted at the 2006 summit, leading to a new Land Law Act in 2009. A number of projects are underway. Immediately following the Summit a moratorium was imposed on the granting of new sub-divisions and the surrendering of agricultural leases. Detailed draft laws have been formulated to govern land use, as have guidelines for land sub-division. Fieldwork has been started to establish customary boundaries and case studies have been undertaken to establish a factual understanding of customary tenure at ground level.[53] Funding has been secured from New Zealand to foster public awareness, to review and strengthen the Customary Land Tribunals and to improve the recording of land leases and to digitalise the records. Australian financial assistance has been promised for undertaking a land lease audit and for reforming the Strata Titles Act 2000. Some proposals have failed. For example the resolution that the powers of the Minster for Lands to manage contested land be curtailed required the Minister himself to introduce the proposal in Parliament. As the Lands Ministers in Vanuatu have a fairly well-established track record on taking advantage of this power—as evidenced by Ombudsmen reports—this never happened. Indeed there has been very little legislative activity. Although an amended Land Lease Act came into effect in 2007 these amendments had in fact been passed in 2004. To date nothing appears to have been done about the Strata Title Act, or to regulate estate agents and developers operating in Vanuatu or to clarify foreshore rights. There is no record of any leases being forfeited because they have not complied with conditions or because the land use is damaging to the public interest.

---

[51] Marc Neil Jones, 'Crime is Out of Control—It is time to Stop the Talk and Act', *Vanuatu Daily Post*, 12 January 2008.
[52] I interviewed one of my sources within the building, under the scrutiny of surveillance cameras.
[53] These have been undertaken in Mele and Ifira. The former lies outside the Port Vila municipal area, the latter largely within it.

Recently the government in Vanuatu has changed and so a new Minister of Lands is in place. While the Director-Generals are not direct political appointees and so can survive changes in government, they are not immune to these. There is a danger therefore that some of the impetus of the National Land Summit and its resolution will be lost. In the meantime there is real concern among local people, especially those who are not benefiting from the economic profits of land alienation, or who have made short-term gains but see longer-term misery ahead.

X. CONCLUSION

This case-study, while particular to a certain time and place, is also illustrative of a phenomena occurring in other places. It is hoped that presentation of this research will prompt consideration of comparative studies elsewhere and an opportunity to reflect on the policies which informed land law reforms in the United Kingdom and other common law countries from the early twentieth century, as well as to critically consider the human and social dimension of land commoditisation when this is transplanted in foreign soil. On islands, in particular, land is not limitless. Yet in many countries with undeveloped economies, the majority of the population remains dependent on the land for subsistence, and may have nowhere else to go. There are difficult dilemmas. When I presented this paper at the Modern Studies in Property Law Conference in April 2008, I used an illustration drawn by a Vanuatu teenager. The heading was 'Decisions have Consequences'. It depicted a sad ni-Vanuatu with many children and a contented Australian standing behind a barbed wire fence from which hung the advertisement for sub-divisions of land. The narrative was as follows:

> In January 2006 James sold his land to an Australian. The Australian subdivided the land he bought from James and sold it for ten times the price per plot that he had given James (for the whole plot). He was very rich indeed. Nine years later James's children and grandchildren have nowhere to build a house.

I was asked, 'Why did James sell the land?' The answer is not profound. He wanted the money. He needed money for shoes, for school fees and health care,[54] for transport and increasingly, especially in urban areas, for food. Perhaps at the time he had other land he could live on, or relatives who were willing to accommodate him on their land. Perhaps he had fewer children, better health, a job. Perhaps he bought a taxi bus with the money or hoped to start a small business, little realising that there is a glut of taxi-buses and small shops all selling identical imported Chinese goods. In the shift from subsistence economies to monetary ones, people want money. Moreover, if

---

[54] Neither of these are free in Vanuatu.

it was James's land, why should he not exercise his autonomy as an owner to make, what turned out in the long run, to be an unwise decision? The illustration, however, poses many wider questions. Should those who can afford to take advantage of the legal framework that facilitates alienation refrain from doing so? Should those who benefit from the short-term gain of that alienation be counselled not to alienate their land? Should the international community have an obligation not to exhort underdeveloped countries to 'make the most of their natural resources'? Is buying second homes in small islands a 'crime against humanity'? Indeed, should potential buyers be counselled not to buy land? Should selling the land stop? These are difficult questions and there are no easy answers. Western perceptions of land are often very different from those of indigenous people. The language and concepts used to describe the relationship of people with land are not the same. Along with colonialism went legal imperialism. While the former may have all but disappeared, the latter has not. There continue to be initiatives to, for example, introduce the Torrens system into South Pacific island countries and to establish ownership by way of cadastral survey and registration. The recommendations of the Review Team being deployed in Vanuatu illustrate a range of these ethno-centric approaches. Focus on process, mechanics and procedure fails to take into account differences of underlying philosophy informing the relationship of people with land. The rhetoric of owner-occupation, mortgage finance and the economic advantages of privatisation of land has been so long with us that perhaps it is time to pause and consider the ethical dimensions of that perspective, especially when we are tempted to acquire second homes in countries where we, and our ideas, may be foreign.

13

Ownership, Possession, Title and Transfer: Human Remains in Museum Collections

CHARLOTTE WOODHEAD[*]

I. INTRODUCTION

THIS PAPER CONSIDERS the nature and extent of any property rights which may be attached under English law to human remains held within museum collections. Consideration will be given to three issues relevant to the determination of these rights. These are:

(a) the various applications of the exception to the supposed 'no-property' rule found in English law in respect of human remains;

(b) the hierarchy of rights relating to human remains and in particular the implication of letters of administration on any property rights which might exist in respect of human remains; and

(c) the nature and extent of transfers which can take place under section 47 of the Human Tissue Act 2004.

A number of cases, most notably *R v Kelly*,[1] have considered property rights in respect of human remains in the context of the exception (to the supposed no-property rule) relating to body parts which have undergone some process of work and skill.[2] However, the scope of this exception and the precise nature of the rights possibly enjoyed in respect of human remains falling

[*] Barrister; Lecturer in Law, School of Law and Criminology, University of Derby. An earlier version of this paper was delivered at the 7th Biennial Property Law Conference held at Cambridge University, April 2008. Thanks are due to Nicholas Taggart for the initial discussion which gave rise to the idea for this paper and to Kevin Bampton for discussions relating to the section *The various approaches to the work and skill exception* (p 322) and his suggestions concerning the separation of the use and significance approaches.
[1] *R v Kelly* [1998] 3 All ER 741 (CA).
[2] See R Hardcastle, *Law and the Human Body: Property Rights, Ownership and Control* (Oxford, Hart Publishing, 2007).

within it are far from clear. Four approaches or rationales are put forward to interpret the principal decisions relating to this exception in an attempt to clarify the nature of its application.

The decision *In re an application by the Tasmanian Aboriginal Centre Inc and In re the estates of 17 deceased Tasmanian Aboriginals*[3] once again highlights the uncertainty relating to the precedence which should be afforded to the rights of the personal representatives to possession of a body for the purposes of burial, in comparison with the rights, if any, of a museum currently holding human remains within its collection.

The trustees of certain, named, national museums now have a power to transfer human remains from their collections.[4] If one analyses property as a bundle of rights, then the precise nature of the rights which are transferred by the institution holding the remains to the successful claimant (who has made a repatriation request) needs to be established. It is argued that this legislative provision can only refer to the transfer of the physical remains themselves, rather than to the rights in respect of them, due to the uncertainty surrounding the nature of the property rights in the wide range of human remains held by museums.

The application of the exception to the common law rule, that there can be no property in a corpse, to remains held within museum collections can produce arbitrary and inconsistent results. This paper argues that a more appropriate approach to rights in respect of human remains held by such institutions would be the notion of custodianship, akin to the personal representative's right to a body for the purposes of burial.

II. BACKGROUND/CONTEXT

A. Human Remains in Museum Collections

Many museums and other institutions within England and Wales hold collections of human remains.[5] The sizes of collections range from one or two skeletons which have been unearthed in archaeological excavations, to the world-renowned collections of thousands of remains at the Natural

---

[3] *In re an application by the Tasmanian Aboriginal Centre Inc and In re the estates of 17 deceased Tasmanian Aboriginals* [2007] TASSC 5.

[4] Human Tissue Act 2004 s 47. This power only applies to human remains which the trustees reasonably believe to be the remains of someone who died less than one thousand years before the date on which the provision came into force: Human Tissue Act 2004 s 47(2).

[5] The phrase 'other institutions' is used to refer to institutions such as universities and other teaching collections which house human remains. Throughout this paper the term 'holding institution' will be used to refer to these institutions, together with museums housing collections of human remains.

History Museum.[6] The nature of the collections is equally diverse. Egyptian mummies grace the exhibition halls of the British Museum; preserved bog bodies are viewed in awe; shrunken Peruvian heads delight the young visitors of the Pitt Rivers Museum at Oxford; and Aboriginal skulls, other body parts and mokomokai[7] gradually move from being exhibited, to being stored, to being repatriated. Additionally, scientific collections of body parts, tissue and organs are essential for teaching and learning at institutions such as the Royal College of Surgeons and provide important data for researchers.

Human remains naturally conjure up a variety of emotions in people and there is a variety of attitudes towards the dead.[8] Many human remains are held by museums and similar institutions with little or no controversy.[9] However, a number of contentious issues surround the holding of Aboriginal human remains from the Americas and Australasia. Debates have arisen as to the proper treatment of these remains, since research or exhibition of them can be at odds with the wishes of the present-day communities whose ancestors they are.[10] The circumstances of the acquisition of the remains held by holding institutions have also been the cause of concern and raise questions regarding the entitlement to retain the remains within their collections.[11]

Over recent years there has been an increase in the number of repatriation requests which have been made to holding institutions.[12] As early as 1990 both Maori and Australian and Tasmanian Aboriginal remains were returned from university museums.[13] Non-national museums, such as local authority museums and university collections, have not been prohibited from removing remains from their collections and have been able to repatriate them to claimants where appropriate to do so. However, several national museums, which are governed by statute, were precluded from acceding to any repatriation request since the governing statute only provided for the

---

[6] The first full survey of these collections was commissioned by Re:Source and the Working Group on Human Remains in 2003.

[7] Maori tatooed heads.

[8] See R Grimes, 'Breaking the glass barrier: the power of display' (1990) 4 *Journal of Ritual Studies* 239, cited in M Simpson, *Making Representations* (London, Routledge, 2001) 242.

[9] For example, the remains which have been unearthed during archaeological excavations in London and which now form part of the collections of the Museum of London. Although, note the concerns of organisations such as *Honouring the Ancient Dead* which represents the views of Pagan groups: http://www.honour.org.uk, accessed 16 October 2008.

[10] See generally Department of Culture, Media and Sport (DCMS), Report of the Working Group on Human Remains, November 2003, in particular ch 10.

[11] Such as removal from burial grounds in contravention of expressed wishes: see the Report of the Working Group on Human Remains (*ibid*, 20).

[12] Report of the Working Group on Human Remains, above n 10. This may be due to claimant communities gaining an increased political voice.

[13] Report of the Working Group on Human Remains, above n 10, at 15.

power to dispose of objects in very limited circumstances.[14] The repatriation of human remains to individual claimants, claimant communities or governments did not fall within these categories. It took the recommendations of the Report of the Working Group on Human Remains and the enactment of section 47 of the Human Tissue Act 2004 to give the power to the trustees of six named national institutions to transfer certain categories of human remains from their collections.[15]

Remains which are less than 100 years of age fall within the ambit of the licensing scheme established by the Human Tissue Act 2004. The treatment of these remains is regulated by statute and their treatment is influenced by the general tenor of the Human Tissue Act 2004: that of the concept of consent.[16] This paper focuses on remains which fall outside the licensing scheme.

III. COMMON LAW POSITION REGARDING HUMAN REMAINS

A. The General Rule

It appears to have been long accepted by the courts that there can be no property in a corpse or part thereof.[17] The judicial origin of this common law rule has been subject to academic debate,[18] and it was acknowledged by the Court of Appeal in *Kelly*[19] that the rule had questionable origins. Nevertheless, the Court stated that despite this, the common law is 'that neither a corpse, nor parts of a corpse, are in themselves and without more capable of being property protected by rights'.[20]

---

[14] For example, the British Museum Act 1963 s 5. Disposal is only possible in respect of duplicates, printed matter made post-1850 and of which a copy can be made and where 'in the opinion of the Trustees an object is unfit to be retained in the collections of the Museum and can be disposed of without detriment to the interests of students'. This provision is similar in scope and application to those found in the Museums and Galleries Act 1992 and the National Heritage Act 1985, which relate to other national museums. The prohibition on disposal is founded on the premise that the trustees of these national museums hold the collections on trust for the nation and focuses on the need to protect the interests of the students.

[15] To aid the exercise of this power by the trustees, the DCMS produced guidance in the form of *Guidance for the Care of Human Remains in Museums* (DCMS, October 2005).

[16] The Act came about in response to the inquiries concerning Bristol Royal Infirmary and Alderhey.

[17] *Handyside's case* (1749) 2 East PC 652, where 'Lord CJ Willes held that action [in trover in respect of a conjoined twins] would not lie, as no person had any property in corpses'. In respect of the already buried, Blackstone in *Commentaries*, Book II 'Of Things' stated (at 429): 'But though the heir has a property in the monuments and etchutcheons of his ancestors, yet he has none in their bodies or ashes; nor can he bring any civil action against such as indecently at least, if not impiously, violate and disturb their remains, when dead and buried'.

[18] See, eg P Matthews, 'Whose Body? People as Property' [1983] *Current Legal Problems* 193.

[19] *Kelly*, above n 1.

[20] *Ibid*, 749. More recently in *Re Organ Retention Group Litigation* [2005] QB 506 Gage J started from the 'firm ground of a proposition which is not disputed. This is the principle that there is no property in the body of a deceased person'.

There appears to be a philosophical difficulty with treating the dead as being the subject of property rights, since it seems in some way distasteful to use concepts of property to discuss former people. Gage J emphasised this point in the litigation which followed the British Royal Infirmary and Alderhey organ scandals in the early 2000s,[21] where he talked of the dislike of talking about possession and ownership rights of a body or parts thereof and of it being particularly inappropriate to the parents of children.

The so-called 'no-property' rule does not have the strongest of judicial foundations and appears to have arisen from a hotchpotch of cases and commentaries. Paul Matthews's research shows that one of the cases was not actually heard and others tended to be obiter comments about the no-property rule.[22] On these shaky foundations have been built two exceptions.

B. The Exceptions

(i) Possession for the Purposes of Burial

The first concerns the right of possession enjoyed by the personal representatives[23] of the deceased for the purpose of disposal of the body.[24] This has been categorised as a right of possession and therefore in the nature of a property right.[25] However, the view has been taken by some that it amounts to a right of custody.[26] This right is limited in scope, since it is only in respect of the duty to dispose of the body and cannot be assigned to third parties. It is, however, enforceable against those who interfere with the personal representative's possession for the purpose of disposal.[27] It is perhaps better termed as a limited possessory right.[28]

[21] *Re Organ Retention Group Litigation, ibid.*

[22] Matthews, above n 18.

[23] That is to say the executors or administrators of the estate (where a person died intestate).

[24] *Williams v Williams* (1882) 20 Ch D 659 and see *Dobson*, below n 37.

[25] Although, despite being classed as a possessory right, Hardcastle includes a discussion of this right under 'Non-proprietary interests': Hardcastle, above n 2, at 46.

[26] *Ibid*, 50 and R Atherton, 'Who owns your body?' (2003) 77 *Australian Law Journal* 178, 184, who also described it as a 'protective right'. This would presumably fall short of being proprietary in nature.

[27] Presumably if the personal representative decided to put the body on display or to keep the body, preserved, then an action against an interloper would not necessarily be successful since the action would not be for the return of the body for the purpose of disposal.

[28] See Matthews, above n 18 and the Report of the Working Group on Human Remains, above n 10.

(ii) The Work and Skill Exception[29]

The second exception relates to work or skill which has been undertaken on human remains. There have been four principal decisions which have dealt with the skill and work exception. None has fully refined the principle or made its application entirely clear.

(a) Doodeward v Spence[30]

This decision of the High Court of Australia concerned the display of a preserved two-headed foetus, which had been confiscated by the Inspector of Police. The person who had been displaying the foetus brought an action in detinue against the Inspector.

Griffith CJ said:

> I do not know of any definition of property which is not wide enough to include such a right of permanent possession. By whatever name the right is called, I think it exists, and that, so far as it constitutes property, a human body, or a portion of a human body, is capable by law of becoming the subject of property.[31]

The Chief Justice was minded to treat such a right as having been acquired

> when a person has by the lawful exercise of work or skill so dealt with a human body or part of a human body in his lawful possession that it has acquired some attributes differentiating it from a mere corpse awaiting burial, he acquires a right to retain possession of it, at least as against any person not entitled to have it delivered to him for the purposes of burial.[32]

Griffith CJ did not envisage that the only circumstances in which a body could become the subject of property were those detailed in the passage above, since he deemed it unnecessary to give an exhaustive enumeration of the circumstances under which such a right may be acquired.[33]

The decision in *Doodeward* was not the strongest of authority for establishing an exception to the no-property rule, since the other judge in the majority, although apparently agreeing with the reasoning of the Chief Justice, was influenced by the fact that the foetus was still-born and had not lived.[34] Furthermore, Higgins J provided a strong dissenting judgment.[35]

---

[29] See generally Hardcastle, above n 2, at 28–40.
[30] *Doodeward v Spence* (1908) 6 CLR 406.
[31] *ibid*, 414.
[32] *ibid*.
[33] *ibid*.
[34] Barton J, in a judgment, perhaps of its age, said 'can such a thing be, without shock to the mind, associated with the notion of the process that we know as Christian burial?' He therefore doubted whether a 'dead-born foetal monster, preserved in spirits as a curiosity ... can be regarded as a corpse awaiting burial'. Whilst he agreed with the Chief Justice, he did not 'cast the slightest doubt upon the general rule that an unburied corpse is not the subject of property': *ibid*, 416.
[35] *ibid*, 417–24. See generally Matthews, above n 18.

The so-called exception in *Doodeward* arises where a person undertakes a 'lawful exercise of skill' in respect of remains of which he already has lawful possession. Griffith CJ appears to suggest that that person would then acquire a right to retain the remains. It is unclear whether the exercise of the skill actually creates the right to acquire lawful possession in the first place or rather focuses on legitimising the existing state of affairs. It could even be suggested that if one already has lawful possession then the identification of this right on the facts of the case is otiose, since presumably lawful possession would, in itself, give rise to a right to challenge anyone who interfered with that right.

A further point to note is that Griffith CJ indicated that the right would be enforceable against all but the person entitled to the body for the purpose of re-burial. This suggests the right to retain possession to be inferior to that of the personal representative and consequently the latter has better title. However, an unqualified right to possession, as a property right, should take priority over a limited right of possession for the purpose of burial, and in any event certainly over a right of custody, if such a label is more appropriate.[36]

(b) *Dobson v North Tyneside Health Authority*[37]

Peter Gibson LJ was prepared to accept 'as properly argued' the passage in *Clerk and Lindsell on Torts* (17th edition, 1995) that

> once a body has undergone a process or other application of human skill, such as stuffing or embalming, it seems it can be the subject of property in the ordinary way hence it is submitted that conversion will lie for a skeleton or cadaver used for research or exhibition, and the same goes for parts of and substances produced by, a living person.[38]

Although his Lordship did not accept *Doodeward* as authority for this passage, he was prepared to accept it in light of the academic offerings of Matthews and Magnusson.[39] This formulation of the exception requires there to have been some 'human skill' involved in the process and consequently human remains such as 'bog bodies'[40] would not appear to fall within the ambit of this exception since the process by which they were preserved was natural rather than by human skill. The decision treats the human body as being capable of being the 'subject of property in the ordinary way' and appears to deal with property in the sense of the object, rather than the property rights in respect of the object. However, the Court

---

[36] See p 317 above.
[37] *Dobson v North Tyneside Health Authority* [1996] 4 All ER 474.
[38] *ibid*, 478.
[39] Matthews, above n 18, and R Magnusson, 'Proprietary Rights in Human Tissue' in N Palmer and E McKendrick (eds), *Interests in Goods*, 2nd edn (London, LLP, 1998).
[40] An example being the Lindow Man exhibited in the British Museum.

of Appeal left open the question of the nature of any subsisting property rights.

(c) R v Kelly[41]

The well-known case of *R v Kelly* arose from the convictions of the artist Anthony Noel Kelly and a technician from the Royal College of Surgeons, Lindsay. Lindsay, at the request of Kelly, removed some 35–40 body parts from the college's collections.[42] These varied from human heads, legs and feet to parts of human torsos. Kelly then made casts of these remains and subsequently exhibited the casts in a gallery.

The Court of Appeal heard the defendants' appeals against conviction and sentence and had to determine whether Kelly and Lindsay were guilty of theft under section 1(1) of the Theft Act 1968 (the 1968 Act). Since the offence required the dishonest appropriation of property belonging to another with the intention of permanently depriving the other of it, it was necessary to establish whether parts of the human body could be classified as property for the purposes of section 4(1) of the 1968 Act.

The defendants advanced a number of arguments including one that body parts could not be property and therefore could not be stolen. Furthermore, it was argued that body parts belonged to no one. For the purposes of the 1968 Act something could not be property unless there existed a permanent right of possession.

Rose LJ, giving the judgment of the Court of Appeal stated that

> parts of a corpse are capable of being property within section 4 of the Theft Act, if they have acquired different attributes by virtue of the application of skill, such as dissection or preservation techniques, for exhibition or teaching purposes.[43]

A number of points are raised by this purported exception to the no-property rule. First, Rose LJ referred to 'parts of a corpse', which suggests that entire corpses would not fall within its scope. This would seem to lead to the situation whereby a leg bone or torso which had undergone the relevant application of skill would amount to property for the purposes of section 4, yet a whole body, even though it had undergone exactly the same process, would fall outside the statutory definition. Such a conclusion concentrates on the extent of the treatment or application of skill rather than the purpose for which the skill was applied. It is unlikely that the court sought to create such an arbitrary distinction.[44] Whilst the issue of rights in respect of a

---

[41] *Kelly*, above n 1.

[42] Kelly had befriended the technician whilst being granted privileged access to the college's collections in order to make drawings of some of the anatomical specimens.

[43] *Kelly*, above n 1, at 749.

[44] Furthermore, the decision in *Doodeward* related to an entire body and the Court of Appeal in *Dobson* was content to approve the approach taken in *Clerk and Lindsell on Torts*,

whole corpse was not before the court, it is interesting that the term 'parts of corpse' was used. It could be that the Court of Appeal had a conceptual difficulty with treating the whole of someone's body as being capable of being property. This could stem from the philosophical reluctance to treat the human body, in its entirety, whether dead or alive, as being capable of being owned.[45] Secondly, the application of skill was articulated as being for exhibition or teaching purposes. Presumably, if the skill were applied for alternative purposes, such as embalming as part of any funeral rites, then this would fall outside the scope of the exception.[46] Despite this reading of the case, it would seem that in the context of the obiter dicta of the Court of Appeal, together with the decisions in *Dobson*, *Doodeward* and *Re Organ Retention Group*, the exclusion of mummies and other anatomical specimens in museum collections from the work and skill exception was not the intention of the Court. Furthermore, *Doodeward* is one of a number of occasions over the years where suggestions have been made that the Egyptian mummies which are housed in many museums are capable of being property—presumably of the holding institutions—or that it is at least arguable.[47] Pollock and Wright query in a footnote whether 'surgical or other preparations' and 'mummies or bones imported from abroad' could in law be capable of being subjects of property.[48] Thirdly, it appears that the remains need to have acquired 'different attributes' by virtue of the application of the skill. Presumably these different attributes would need to distinguish it from a mere corpse awaiting burial, as suggested in *Doodeward*. A number of issues arise from this decision, but were not resolved. These are the level of skill which would be regarded as sufficient, the relevance of the purpose for which the skill is undertaken and the nature of the rights which are recognised in respect of remains which fall within the exception.[49]

which referred to the whole body as well as parts thereof. It is therefore unlikely that the court in *Kelly* intended to make this distinction.

[45] See eg, H Steiner, 'Property in the body: a philosophical perspective' in K Stern (ed), *Property Rights in the Human Body* (London, Kings College London, Centre for Medical Law and Ethics, 1997).

[46] See C Woodhead, 'A debate which crosses all borders. The repatriation of human remains: more than just a legal question' [2002] 8 *Art Antiquity and Law* 317, 319.

[47] Griffith CJ described it as 'idle' to suggest that the possession by museums of mummies or other body parts is unlawful because otherwise many collections would violate the law: *Doodeward*, above n 30. This appears to be a cart-before-the-horse style argument, since one cannot legitimise otherwise unlawful action by arguing that if it were not legitimate it would be illegitimate. This suggestion by the court was simply condoning the current state of affairs and legitimising it.

[48] Pollock and Wright, *An Essay on Possession in the Common Law* (Oxford, Clarendon Press, 1888). Quite why bones imported from abroad might be capable of being the subject of property, yet bones from England and Wales could not, is unclear.

[49] See Hardcastle's five key questions in respect of the exception to the work and skill exception: Hardcastle, above n 2.

Rose LJ suggested that there might well be possible development in the future due to the dynamism of the common law:

> [T]he common law does not stand still. It may be that if, on some future occasion, the question arises, the courts will hold that human body parts are capable of being property for the purposes of section 4, even without the acquisition of different attributes, if they have a use or significance beyond their mere existence.[50]

This suggests an absence of a need for the existence of different attributes and that use and significance may well be sufficient. The use of the phrase 'significance beyond their mere existence' could apply to any human remains of the recent dead since, for example, the proper treatment or disposal of the dead could be said to be an essential component of the grieving process. Equally, instances may occur where older human remains have a use or significance beyond their mere existence.[51]

(d) *Re Organ Retention Group Litigation*[52]

Gage J stated: 'In my judgment the principle that part of a body may acquire the character of property which can be the subject of rights of possession and ownership is now part of our law'.[53] He accepted that *Kelly* establishes the exception to the no-property rule in situations where part of the body has been the subject of the application of skill, such as dissection or preservation techniques.

Whilst the judge here was prepared to state that parts of the body can be the subject of rights of both possession and ownership, he accepted the defendants' contention that they only needed to establish a right of possession rather than a right of ownership in order to bring a successful claim in the tort of wrongful interference. Gage J talked about the remains as being 'the subject of possession',[54] although he then referred to the hospital acquiring 'proprietary and possessory rights'.[55]

IV. THE VARIOUS APPROACHES TO THE WORK
AND SKILL EXCEPTION

The above discussion reveals that the courts have failed to adopt a unified approach to the nature or extent of the property rights under the work and

---

[50] *Kelly*, above n 1, 750.

[51] See, for example, White who suggests that this could well have been the case in the saga relating to the alleged relics of Edmund the Martyr: S White, 'The Law relating to dealing with dead bodies' [2000] *Medical Law International* 145, 167. See below p 325.

[52] *Re Organ Retention Group Litigation* above n 20.

[53] *ibid*, 541.

[54] *Re Organ Retention Group*, above n 20, at 544.

[55] *ibid*, 566.

skill exception. However, the cases reveal four approaches to, or rationales for, the exception to the no-property rule.

The first approach can be labelled the *transformation approach*. It is evident in the cases of *Doodeward* and *Dobson v North Tyneside* and seems to be alluded to in *Kelly*. This focuses on the attributes which now endow the corpse. It objectifies the dead in the sense of having created something new.[56] This creation of an object permits the common law to treat it as the subject of property—in *Dobson* 'in the usual way' but in *Doodeward* in terms of giving rise to a right of possession. The courts appear to be concerned with the subject-matter of property, that is to say the object itself. In theory, regardless of the manner in which the attributes befell the object (whether due to human intervention or a natural process), the human remains are now capable of being the subject of property.[57]

Since this first approach has as its centre the notion of objectifying the dead, presumably there should be no philosophical problem with treating the dead as property 'in the usual way'[58] in the sense of creating rights of ownership. It follows that since such rights are possible in respect of objects of personal property, the remains are now such objects and can be so-treated. If, through work and skill, one has created an object of property (in a non-legal sense)—since attributes differentiate it from a mere corpse awaiting burial—then there appears to be no justification for refusing to treat any rights as rights of ownership. The effect of this approach is that human remains which have acquired different attributes in effect rendering them as objects would be capable of being bought and sold under the Sale of Goods Act 1979. Furthermore, they could be recovered by an action in conversion since the owner would obviously have an immediate right of possession.

Furthermore, the interpretation in *Kelly* of the definition of property within the context of the Theft Act 1968 focuses on the object of property, rather than the property rights existing in respect of it.[59] One does not necessarily have to be the owner of the property (perhaps even going so far as saying that the object does not therefore need to be capable of being owned, given that possession is the essential requirement), since property is regarded as belonging to a person who has possession or control of it.

The second approach, which could be termed the *intervention approach*, is based on the act of intervention by the person undertaking the work or skill. This intervention amounts to an act of possession sufficient to give rise to a right of possession against the whole world. This approach is based on the

---

[56] See Hardcastle's discussion of the specification doctrine: Hardcastle above n 2.

[57] Nevertheless, in *Dobson*, in approving the *Clerk and Lindsell* formulation, the need for a process of human skill was articulated.

[58] As per *Clerk and Lindsell on Tort* and *Dobson*.

[59] The Theft Act 1968s 5(1) states that '[p]roperty shall be regarded as belonging to another having possession or control of *it*' (emphasis added).

idea of possession being the origin of property.[60] The act of taking possession or occupancy of objects results in rights of property in a similar vein to the way in which taking an object of lost property found on land into one's custody or possession gives rights which are good against everyone except the true owner.[61] One problem is that whilst it is sufficient to take into possession certain objects, the exception seems to require a further act rather than merely the act of taking into possession.[62] In the context of human remains, until some kind of work or skill has taken place in respect of them, they remain *res nullius* in the same way as living wild animals.[63] The intervention approach focuses on the human skill used rather than the act of taking into possession. The notion of rewarding work and skill in this manner is akin to the recognition of intellectual property rights. In copyright law, in the context of authorial works,[64] the author acquires certain rights by creating original works.[65] In patent law, the validity of a patent requires there to be have been an inventive step, again requiring human skill.[66] In a similar manner to the recognition of property rights in the four cases under consideration in this paper, copyright law and patent law demonstrate human intervention in the form of skill being rewarded through the allocation of property rights.

Grubb's[67] requirement of an intention to create a novel item links both the *transformation* and *intervention* approaches. He states:

> It is not just a matter of what is done but also the purpose for which the work or skill is deployed. There must be an intention to create a novel item with a use of its own. It is the deliberate creation of a novel item which justifies the common law in conferring proprietary status on the 'item' in order to give legal protection to the artificer as reward for his expended effort.[68]

This reflects the Lockean concept of just deserts or mixing labour with land, which effectively rewards labour with the granting of property rights.[69]

The third, *usefulness approach* is evident in the decision of the Court of Appeal in *Kelly*. The focus of this is the purpose for which the work was

---

[60] See generally C Rose, 'Possession as the Origin of Property' (1985) 52 *University of Chicago Law Review* 73.

[61] See *Armory v Delamirie* (1722) 1 Strange 505; *Parker v British Airways* [1982] QB 1004 (CA). Obviously this is in the absence of the occupier of the land having manifested an intention to control everything on the ground as per Lord Donaldson in *Parker* (at 1014).

[62] Note Hardcastle's rejection of the first possession analysis: Hardcastle above n 2, at 131.

[63] See *Young v Hitchens* (1844) 6 QB 606 and *Pierson v Post* (1805) 2 Cai R 175.

[64] Such as musical, literary, dramatic and artistic works.

[65] Which means that it originates from the author: see generally Copyright Designs and Patents Act 1988 and *University of London Press Ltd v University Tutorial Press Ltd* [1916] 2 Ch 601 (Ch).

[66] Patent Act 1977 s 3.

[67] A Grubb, ' "I, Me, Mine": Bodies, Parts and Property' (1998) *Medical Law International* 299.

[68] *Ibid*, 311.

[69] J Locke, 'Of Property', *The Second Treatise of Civil Government* (1690).

undertaken and the notion, albeit implicit in the application to the facts of that case, of usefulness beyond its status as a mere corpse in the context of exhibition or teaching. The concept is more strongly articulated by Griffith CJ in *Doodeward*, where he stated that: 'possession is not unlawful if the body possesses attributes of such a nature that its preservation may afford valuable or interesting information or instruction'.[70]

This usefulness approach was developed further by Rose LJ in *Kelly* in his discussion of the possible future extension of the exception to situations absent any work undertaken endowing the remains with different attributes, but where the remains had a usefulness or significance beyond their mere existence. This is very much a utilitarian approach to human remains and is one of the arguments used by scientists who see the value of human remains as being in terms of research potential. The concept of usefulness in terms of remains having a value was highlighted in *Dobson v North Tyneside* by Peter Gibson LJ who talked about the value of remains for exhibition purposes.[71] When drawing an analogy with the facts of *Doodeward*, he was of the view that nothing in the pleadings suggested that the preservation of a brain post-mortem was on a par with stuffing or embalming.

Whilst Rose LJ in *Kelly* suggested that remains might have a use *or* significance beyond their mere existence, the notion of significance is worthy of separate treatment. The fourth approach is therefore termed the *significance* approach. Here, remains might have a cultural or religious significance to an individual or a group, which gives them a value different from that of a corpse of unknown origin. It could be argued that remains might acquire a significance purely by being displayed in a museum. The Egyptian mummies, for example, might well be seen as being synonymous with the British Museum and have a significance for the British people, or the visiting public, which is different from the significance to the Egyptian people (past and present). Marcel DuChamp's reinterpretation of a urinal by means of the addition of a word and the display of it as an artwork might be seen as a situation where the significance of an object is altered by a change in context. Furthermore, although it is more controversial[72] as to whether such rights would arise, it could be said that this changed context[73] gives rise to certain rights under copyright law and moral rights.[74]

---

[70] *Doodeward* above n 30 at 414 Furthermore, in the same case Barton J highlighted the point that the foetus had acquired a monetary value.

[71] *Dobson* above n 37 at 479.

[72] It is debatable whether there is sufficient originality to qualify for copyright protection as an artistic work under the Copyright Designs and Patents Act 1988 s 1.

[73] Obviously this is with the benefit of human intervention and thus links back to the second *intervention* approach discussed above.

[74] Under the Copyright Designs and Patents Act 1988. These moral rights would be the right of integrity and paternity.

V. PROPERTY: OWNERSHIP, POSSESSION AND TITLE OF HUMAN REMAINS

The focus now shifts to the nature of the property rights which might be necessary in respect of human remains. Throughout the following analysis it is worth bearing in mind the approach taken by Grubb in connection with the notion of property describing the relationship between a thing and an individual. He sets out the following as 'plausible categories of rules' which describe this relationship. First, *user entitlements*; secondly, *exclusionary control over the thing*; and thirdly, *dispositional liberties*.[75] This focuses on the reasons why we need a proprietary analysis in the context of human remains. With regard to human remains within museum collections, it is submitted that one should consider the user entitlement for non-commercial purposes in terms of the displaying and access to remains for research, and the exclusionary control and the dispositional liberties in order to establish what rights can be transferred if de-accessioning is deemed appropriate.

As discussed above, the treatment of human remains in the context of property law concepts can been seen as distasteful.[76] However, as Magnusson points out, 'A proprietary analysis need not be regarded as distasteful or unseemly, but as an honest recognition of the importance of protecting the deceased's body until it is properly disposed of'.[77] Whilst this was said in the context of the limited possessory rights enjoyed by the personal representatives, such a sentiment should be extended more widely to the treatment of human remains. In any event, in the context of the work and skill exception, the courts have adopted the concepts of property law, albeit in an inconsistent manner. Therefore, it is appropriate to consider in turn each of the various approaches to property taken by the courts in the four principal decisions.

A. Human Remains as the 'Subject of Property'

The first sense in which the courts have approached the nature of the human remains within the exception has been to treat them as the 'subject of property'. This focuses on the object of the property (in the sense of the *transformation* approach) as the final product, rather than the property rights. In *Doodeward* Griffith CJ talked in these terms and this was echoed in *Dobson* where Peter Gibson LJ accepted the proposition, set out in the then current edition of *Clerk and Lindsell on Torts*, that remains which fell under the

---

[75] Grubb, above n 67, at 301.

[76] See above p 317 and the judgment of Gage J in *Re Organ Retention Group*, above n 20.

[77] R Magnusson, above n 39 at 37.

exception could be 'the subject of property in the usual way'. This phrase appears to suggest these remains would be subject to rights of ownership, since in considering property in the usual way, one imagines in the context of personal property, the existence of rights of ownership and possession.

Again, in *Kelly* the focus is on the subject-matter or the object of property since the case revolved around the statutory definition of property under the Theft Act 1968. It was not at issue what rights would flow from the recognition of the object as property.

In *Re Organ Retention Group* Gage J's interpretation of the work and skill exception was that part of a body may acquire 'the character of property' and this can be the 'subject of rights of possession and ownership'. Gage J accepted counsel's contention that it was unnecessary to categorise precisely the nature of the rights enjoyed in respect of human remains which fell within the work and skill exception, since a right of possession was sufficient for a claim for unlawful interference.

B. Right of Possession

In *Doodeward* Griffith CJ referred to the right resulting from the application of work and skill as being the 'right to retain possession'. This is a continuing right, which effectively legitimises the existing status of being in lawful possession. As discussed above, this seems curious since lawful possession is required in the first instance in order to establish a right of continuing possession, although the case really revolved around establishing whether there existed a right of possession. Such a right would be sufficient to found an action for conversion and trespass and so deals with the exclusionary control issue above.

C. Ownership

As Lawson and Rudden point out: 'The strongest and clearest form of ownership occurs where a tangible thing belongs to, and is in the possession of, a single person, with no one else laying claim to it or to any share in it'.[78] In *Re Organ Retention Group* Gage J talked about 'Proprietary and possessory rights' and that part of the body may be the subject of both rights of possession and ownership. If the exclusionary control is the main concern, then one might ask what is the wisdom of insisting on rights of ownership in respect of human remains which fall within the work and skill exception, when rights of possession would suffice by providing a means by which the

---

[78] Lawson and Rudden, *The Law of Property*, 2nd edn (Oxford, Oxford University Press, 2002) 90.

possessor could prevent third-party interlopers from interfering with his rights. Furthermore, one could argue that even a right of possession might not be necessary since lesser rights have been shown in the context of real property to be sufficient to found an action for the recovery of land.[79]

VI. HUMAN REMAINS WITHIN MUSEUMS

The foregoing discussion of the approaches to the work and skill exception will now be applied to the context of those remains held within museums and other holding institutions.

A. Sufficiency of Skill

Hardcastle[80] articulates several unresolved questions concerning the work and skill exception. One relates to whether there is a need for an intention to create a novel item and another is whether work alone, rather than work and skill, would suffice. The wide range of human remains within museum collections gives a focus for a consideration of the sufficiency of skill required. First, the very nature of the term 'skill' seems to require human intervention. However, the 'bog bodies', which have undergone a natural process, would appear to fall outside the ambit of a requirement of human skill. However, the nature of such a body would be something other than a mere corpse awaiting burial and would benefit from additional attributes, in line with the transformation approach discussed above. Secondly, issues arise in respect of the purpose for which the exercise of work and skill was undertaken. If the courts were to adopt a strict interpretation of the Court of Appeal's decision in *Kelly* then work or skill carried out other than for the purposes exhibition or teaching would be insufficient to render the remains the subject of property and subject to rights of property.[81] Thirdly, if a new object must be created then arguably certain preservation procedures would fall short of this, regardless of how skilled an activity was involved.[82]

---

[79] *Manchester Airport plc v Dutton* [2000] QB 133 (CA). Here, an occupational licensee, who had not even yet gone into occupation of land, mounted a successful action against protestors who were trespassing on land which was the subject of the licence.

[80] Hardcastle, above n 2, at 39.

[81] This was discussed above in the context of *R v Kelly* and the application to the Egyptian mummies at p 321. In *Doodeward* it was argued by counsel for the respondent that: '[Mummies] may be considered to have been changed in nature by some special process, so as to be no longer a mere human body, and the length of time that has elapsed since death is so great as to remove it from the category of things held sacred by the living': above n 30, at 409.

[82] It has been suggested that a novel object needs to result from the application of the work or skill: Grubb, above n 67, at 311.

The application of the different interpretations of the work and skill exception creates a variety of results, not altogether consistent with one another. Some remains might have been the subject of careful, skilled treatment in order to maintain their current preserved status, yet this might be by means of environmental controls rather than any physical intervention towards the remains. The absence of direct physical treatment might be insufficient to amount to the requisite work and skill required by the decisions, certainly if the first approach to the exception discussed above (the *transformation* approach) is adopted wholesale. This is because it has at its core the notion that the remains acquire attributes differentiating them from a mere corpse awaiting burial. Placing remains in a climate-controlled environment would not have sufficient direct impact on the remains and would not endow them with characteristics or attributes which would render them anything other than a whole or part of a corpse. In contrast, if one adopts the *intervention approach*, which recognises the skill rather than the outcome, this would be sufficient. In *Re Organ Retention Group* Gage J was satisfied that the dissection and fixation of organs 'requires work and a great deal of skill, the more so in the case of a very small baby'.[83] Furthermore, 'the subsequent production of blocks and slides is also a skillful operation requiring work and skill of trained scientists'.[84] In contrast, in *Dobson*, Peter-Gibson LJ was not content to treat a preserved brain as being 'an item to possession of which the plaintiffs ever became entitled'.[85] Adopting the *usefulness approach*, one can see that any climatic or environmental procedure which has the effect of preserving the remains for the purpose of exhibition or teaching could well amount to work or skill sufficient to fall within the exception as articulated by the Court of Appeal in *Kelly*. It would therefore bring the 'bog bodies' and the mummies within the exception.

B. Acquisition and Enforceability of Rights

It has been suggested by the authors of *Clerk and Lindsell on Torts* that the person who exercises the skill would be the first in possession and therefore property would be vested in him.[86] If one rewards the person who has undertaken work or skill on human remains then one is effectively rewarding individuals for interference with the dead. However, in *Doodeward* it was

---

[83] Above n 20, at 541.
[84] *Ibid.*
[85] Above n 37, at 473.
[86] *Clerk and Lindsell on Torts*, 19th edn (London, Sweet & Maxwell, 2006) para [17–39]. This seems to be the approach taken by Gage J in *Re Organ Retention Group*, above n 20, at 566, although this seems to have been muddied somewhat by his suggestion that a parent might bring a claim for conversion where they had asked for the return of an organ, above n 20 at 544. See Hardcastle, above n 2, at 37.

clear that the application of work and skill had to be lawful and presumably applying work and skill to remains which were subject to the personal representative's right of possession would be a wrongful interference with that right. If, in the museum setting, a prior holder of the remains undertook the necessary work and skill, the question arises as to whether the current holding institution would acquire those rights by reason of any act of transfer of the remains to the museum.

'The law will protect a good title against a bad one, and a bad one against a worse one'.[87] With the words of Peter Birks in mind, museums can perhaps take solace in the fact that on the basic principles of the relativity of title, it is more likely than not that a museum would be able to show a better entitlement to human remains than an interloper.[88] However, it would seem from the decision in *Doodeward* that any rights acquired by virtue of the application of skill would be subject to the rights of personal representatives entitled to possession for the purposes of burial. Seemingly museums would not enjoy the best title to the remains where someone was entitled to letters of administration in respect of the estate of the deceased.

VII. LETTERS OF ADMINISTRATION AND THE EFFECT ON A MUSEUM'S RIGHTS

The decision *In re an application by the Tasmanian Aboriginal Centre Inc and In re the estates of 17 deceased Tasmanian Aboriginals*[89] highlights a particular issue relevant to museums. This relates to the precedence which should be afforded to the limited rights of possession enjoyed by personal representatives in comparison with the rights, if any, of a holding institution currently holding the remains.

In November 2006 the Natural History Museum announced that it would use its power under section 47 of the Human Tissue Act 2004 to transfer certain Tasmanian Aboriginal remains to the Tasmanian Aboriginal Centre (TAC), but would only do so once they had undertaken certain procedures on the human remains which included collection of data and DNA analysis.[90] TAC brought proceedings in the High Court in London seeking an injunction to prevent the tests and in Australia applied for letters of administration in respect of the estates of the 17 deceased Tasmanian

---

[87] P Birks, 'Five Keys to Land Law' in Bright and *Dewar, Land Law: Themes and Perspectives* (Oxford, Oxford University Press, 1998).

[88] See *Manchester Airport plc v Dutton* [2000] QB 133 (CA) and the discussion above p 328.

[89] Above n 3.

[90] Press release of 17 November 2006, 'Human remains to be returned from Natural History Museum's Collection' http://www.nhm.ac.uk/about-us/press-office/press-releases/2006/press_release_10031.html accessed 16 October 2008.

Aboriginals. Underwood CJ granted limited letters of administration to TAC in order to commence legal proceedings seeking the return of human remains or to prevent the disturbance of human remains and/or to take possession of the remains and/or to afford the deceased proper burial according to Aboriginal Law and custom.[91] Ultimately, no determination was made in an English court as to the enforceability of the letters of administration, since the dispute between the Tasmanian Aboriginal Centre and the Natural History Museum was resolved out of court.

It appears that where letters of administration are granted in a foreign jurisdiction a grant must also be obtained in England in order for a foreign personal representative to represent the deceased in England.[92] Therefore the foreign decision in itself would not give a better entitlement to the remains. However, it is more likely that a museum would be prepared to exercise its power to transfer remains where letters of administration had been granted abroad. In the case of a head of a Maori warrior, consigned for auction at Bonham's in London, the granting of letters of administration in New Zealand, it seems, persuaded the auction house to remove the head from sale and therefore an action in the High Court in London was unnecessary.[93] However, as pointed out in the Report of the Working Group on Human Remains, it is unclear whether an English court would grant letters of administration to seemingly 'remote descendants or cultural affiliates of a person who died many decades ago'.[94]

VIII. TRANSFER: HUMAN TISSUE ACT 2004, SECTION 47

This provision gives the trustees of nine, named, national museums the power to transfer human remains from their collections.[95] According to section 47(2) only the remains of people who died less than 1,000 years before the section came into force can be transferred. Consequently, remains such as the Egyptian mummies and the Lindow Man 'bog body' currently on display in the British Museum cannot be transferred.[96] The trustees can return human remains 'if it appears to them to be appropriate to do so for any reason, whether or not relating to their other functions'.[97]

---

[91] *Ibid*, [12].

[92] Morris, *The Conflict of Laws*, 6th edn (London, Sweet and Maxwell, 2005).

[93] P O'Keefe, 'Maoris claim head' (1992) 1 *International Journal of Cultural Property* 393.

[94] Report of the Working Group on Human Remains, at 195.

[95] These include the British Museum and the Natural History Museum: Human Tissue Act 2004 s 47(1) and (2).

[96] This 1,000-year cut off point was not in the original draft bill. Concerns were expressed during the passage of the bill that museums such as the British Museum might be subject to 'gratuitous claims' in respect of the Egyptian mummies: see Lords Hansard 22 July 2004, col 372.

[97] Human Tissue Act 2004 s 47(2). The power to de-accession also extends to remains which have been mixed or bound with something else and where it is undesirable or impracticable to separate them (Human Tissue Act 2004 s 47(3)).

The word 'transfer' is not defined in the Human Tissue Act 2004. It therefore needs to be established whether the word 'transfer' relates to the transfer of the physical remains themselves, or to the rights in respect of those remains. If the wording of the statute were expressly to state that the power relates to the transfer of property, then this would clearly mean the transfer of the bundle of rights, rather than the physical object. This point arose in *R v Chief Land Registrar, ex parte the Lord Chancellor*,[98] where the Courts Act 2003 referred to the transfer of 'property, rights or liabilities'. Stanley Burnton J refused to construe the word 'property' in the Act as referring to the physical buildings or premises, an interpretation which had been argued for by the Lord Chancellor. He stated: 'The context I am considering is the transfer of "property, rights or liabilities", and in this context it would be anomalous to construe "property" as meaning something physical, when there is a clear non-physical genus'.[99] This interpretation of 'property' affords with the traditional, legal, approach to property emphasised to undergraduate law students at an early stage in their legal education, and evident in the writing of Hohfeld in terms of property being a bundle of rights and duties.[100]

Other examples of statutes which involve the word 'transfer' include the Sale of Goods Act 1979, which refers in section 2 to the 'transfer of property in goods'.[101] This clearly refers to the rights in respect of goods, rather than to the physical objects themselves. In terms of the word transfer in section 47 of the Human Tissue Act 2004, a traditional view of property would suggest that it relates to the transfer of the rights, since the notion of property in the legal sense of the word is firmly based on the notion of the rights in respect of things, rather than the things themselves. 'Transfer' should, in theory, refer to a transfer of rights. However, the uncertainty surrounding the rights which can exist in respect of remains renders this questionable, rather than certain.

If the legislature envisaged that all remains which might be de-accessioned under section 47 would qualify as being the subject of property (that is to say falling within the work and skill exception), then it may well be the case that 'transfer' referred to the transfer of those rights or interests which arose out of the exercise of skill. However, this author suggests that this is unlikely to have been the case. It is by no means clear that all remains held by museums would necessarily have undergone the necessary processes of skill required by the work and skill exception.[102] It would have been flawed

---

[98] [2005] EWHC 1706 (Admin).

[99] *Ibid*, [23].

[100] WN Hohfeld, 'Fundamental Legal Conceptions as Applied in Judicial Reasoning' (1913) 23 *Yale Law Journal* 16.

[101] Again, 'transfer' is not defined in the 1979 Act.

[102] As to which, see above p 328.

logic if such a major assumption had been made in the first place, let alone had it informed the drafting of a statutory provision. The uncertainty relating to the application of the work and skill exception was articulated in the Report of the Working Group on Human Remains in November 2003 (the recommendations of which led to the enactment of section 47), where it was said that the situations in which the *Kelly* exception applied were far from clear. Furthermore, the Report made a specific recommendation that guidance should be produced in order to inform museums and other holding institutions as to the sufficiency of skill needed to activate the exception.[103] To make assumptions that all remains would qualify for this exception and therefore be treated in law as being the subject of property would be a leap too far so soon after doubts as to the ambit of the exception had been expressed.

It is trite law that when a transfer of property is made and title to the property passes, the principle of *nemo dat quod non habet* applies, meaning that the transferee will enjoy no more superior rights than those enjoyed by the transferee (assuming the absence of any pre-existing rights superior to those of the holding institution).[104] If a museum, through the application of skill, has acquired rights of property in respect of the remains one must consider whether these rights can be transferred to the transferee. If so, presumably the rights would be enforceable against third parties since they are in the nature of property rights. This is assuming that they can be transferred to third parties and subsequently enforced by the transferee against other third parties.[105] Furthermore, a point to be considered is whether the museum retains any rights in respect of the remains in question.

If full rights of ownership were to be transferred to successful claimants following a repatriation request and the exercise of the section 47 power, then claimants could sell the remains to third parties. They could also make a gift of the remains to another museum and could then lend them to a museum as well under a bailment agreement. The lender would then have a right of possession against someone who interfered with the possession of those remains, thus fulfilling the exclusory aspect of property rights. Whilst these seemingly commercial endeavours could well be carried out in respect

---

[103] Recommendation III of the Report of the Working Group on Human Remains, above n 10. To date, no such guidance has been produced.

[104] As to which see above p 319. The word 'transfer' used in the Courts Act 2003 in the context of a property transfer scheme which was construed as transferring only those rights which already existed, rather than permitting the creation of new rights by granting leases. It perhaps seems slightly unnecessary to make the point, but it would seem that, therefore, a court interpreting the word 'transfer' in the Human Tissue Act 2004 would hold that a museum would only be able to transfer to the transferee any rights which it enjoyed prior to the transfer, rather than being able to create any new rights in respect of the remains.

[105] See generally Hardcastle, above n 2.

of remains returned by means of section 47, in most cases the real reason for repatriation requests is so that the remains can be re-buried or kept in a sacred keeping place.

IX. CUSTODIANSHIP—A WAY FORWARD?

Rather than trying to force notions of ownership or possession onto some human remains but not others, it might be more appropriate to recognise a right of custody in respect of all human remains akin to the right enjoyed by personal representatives for the purpose of disposal of the body. Whilst full rights of ownership could give rise to various commercial possibilities in respect of remains, the main consideration in terms of exclusion from interference could still be met by lesser property rights or even rights of custody, if not property rights properly so-called.

This right would be acquired through acts of custody and the holder could prevent others from interfering with it and could transfer it to third parties, who would then enjoy a similar right against third-party interlopers. This would focus on the exclusory control aspect discussed above. However, this right of custody would be subject to the rights of claimants who had an interest in having the remains buried/re-buried. In short, it is suggested that such a right would have the following features:

1. It would apply equally to all human remains taken into lawful custody by museums and other holding institutions. There would be no distinction between human remains which had undergone some process of work or skill and those which had not.
2. It would be enforceable against third parties who interfere with that right.
3. It would be subject to the rights of persons entitled to possession of the remains for the purposes of re-burial (whether established under English law or in a foreign jurisdiction).[106]

Recognition of a right of custody, or even stewardship rather than full rights of ownership has the advantage of acknowledging the special status of human remains in terms of being former people. So long as the remains and the rights enjoyed in respect of them can be fully enforced against interlopers then there is not necessarily an impetus to recognise rights of ownership in preference to rights of custody or possession.

---

[106] So long as the granting of any letters of administration were duly recognised in an English court.

X. CONCLUSION

The foregoing discussion demonstrates that currently there are uncertainties regarding exactly when remains have undergone sufficient skill in order to render them capable of being the subject of property and shows that there is no consistent approach to this. The discussion of the various underlying rationales or approaches to the cases provides a conceptual solution to the differing approaches, but only a pragmatic solution in a change in the law (by fully articulating the nature of the rights) will remedy the current uncertainty in a necessarily decisive manner.

14

Protection of Cultural Property in Times of Armed Conflict: UK Ratification of the Hague Convention 1954

SARAH WILLIAMS[*] AND JAMIE GLISTER[†]

I. INTRODUCTION

T HE HAGUE CONVENTION for the Protection of Cultural Property in the Event of Armed Conflict 1954[1] was the first international agreement to provide comprehensively for the protection of cultural property during armed conflicts. The convention, together with its two protocols, requires state parties to take measures to protect cultural property during both peacetime and times of armed conflict or military occupation. In 2004, 50 years after it had originally signed the convention, the UK Government announced its intention to ratify the convention and to accede to the protocols. Ratification will require primary implementing legislation and to this end the government introduced the draft Cultural Property (Armed Conflicts) Bill in early 2008. The provisions of this draft bill will now form part of a wider Heritage Protection Bill that is due to be laid before Parliament in the 2008–09 session.

This paper provides an overview of the key provisions of the convention and the two protocols. It explores the concerns of the United Kingdom that originally prevented ratification and the changing circumstances that led to the recent shift in policy. Finally, we outline and assess the current proposals for legislative implementation.

[*] Dorset Fellow in Public International Law, British Institute of International and Comparative Law. The research for this paper was carried out while a Visiting Fellow at the Sydney Centre for International Law, University of Sydney.
[†] Lecturer, Faculty of Law, University of Sydney.
[1] 249 UNTS 240–88 ('the convention', unless the context requires 'Hague Convention').

II. THE HAGUE CONVENTION 1954

A. Background

Cultural property is protected as part of the common heritage of all mankind: by protecting the items of historic, artistic, scientific and religious importance to various cultures, we protect our own common heritage. But cultural property is easily destroyed by shelling, bombing and looting. The damage may be inadvertent if the property is located close to a military target, or the cultural property may be deliberately targeted as an attack on the culture with which it is associated. A recent example of the latter is the deliberate targeting of historic buildings within the UNESCO-protected city of Dubrovnik during the conflict in the former Yugoslavia. In 2005 the International Criminal Tribunal for the former Yugoslavia found that the deliberate destruction of such property constituted a war crime.[2]

For over 100 years states have been developing legal rules to protect cultural property from these threats. However, such protection was formerly found within more general provisions applicable during armed conflicts—specifically those concerning the protection of civilian property. During the American Civil War, the Lieber Code protected cultural property by categorising it as a form of private property subject to higher protection.[3] The 1907 Hague Convention[4] attempted to introduce further specific rules for the protection of cultural property, but those provisions failed dismally in the midst of the damage and destruction of the two world wars.[5] The Fourth Geneva Convention on the protection of civilians during armed conflict, adopted in 1949,[6] does not mention cultural property specifically but does prohibit

---

[2] *Prosecutor v Strugar*, ICTY Case No IT-01-42-T, Judgment, 31 January 2005.

[3] Instructions for the Governance of Armies of the United States in the Field, General Order 100, 1863. This code was the basis for the 1899 Hague Convention that included some provisions for the protection of cultural property: for example, art 27 (armies to take all necessary steps to spare edifices devoted to religion, art, science and charitable purposes, hospitals and places where there were sick and wounded, provided the buildings were not used for military purposes).

[4] 1907 Hague Convention IV Respecting the Laws and Customs of War on Land (1908) 2 *American Journal of International Law (Supplement)* 90–117. This convention adopted the provisions found in the 1899 Convention, but added 'historical monuments' to the list of protected edifices in arts 27 and 56.

[5] In the First World War the most significant incidents were the burning of the library at the University of Louvain and the bombing of the Cathedral at Rheims. There were some attempts to apply the provisions of the 1907 Hague Convention in the Second World War, particularly by the Allies. See eg, the Declaration of London of 1943, which permitted the Allies to nullify any transfer or traffic in property in occupied territories during the war. The Nuremberg trials also characterised the plunder of art as a war crime.

[6] Geneva Convention IV Relative to the Protection of Civilian Persons in Time of War (1950), 75 UNTS 287–417. The UK signed this convention on 8 December 1949, but did not ratify until 23 September 1957.

extensive destruction and appropriation of property, not justified by military necessity and carried out unlawfully and wantonly.[7]

In 1945 the United Nations Educational, Scientific, and Cultural Organization (UNESCO) was founded and charged with the international protection of cultural property. At its fifth annual meeting in 1950 a new convention was proposed to deal solely with the protection of cultural property in armed conflict. After four years of preparatory work the text was adopted at a diplomatic conference at The Hague on 14 May 1954.[8] Forty-five states, including the United Kingdom, signed the adopted text. The convention and the first protocol (which was drafted and adopted at the same time as the convention) entered into force on 7 August 1956. As of 16 December 2008, 121 states have ratified or acceded to the convention and 100 states have adopted the first protocol.

B. Application

(i) Definition of Cultural Property

'Cultural property' is defined in article 1 of the convention as including three types of property:

(1) movable or immovable property of great importance to the cultural heritage of every people;[9]
(2) buildings whose main and effective purpose is to preserve or exhibit the movable cultural property in category one; and
(3) centres containing a large amount of cultural property, to be known as 'centres containing monuments'.

Thus the convention protects monuments, works of art, manuscripts, buildings of historical or artistic interest, archaeological sites, museums, libraries and art galleries. The definition is restricted to physical objects and does not include the natural environment or natural resources. Additionally, the convention makes clear that cultural property is protected 'irrespective of origin or ownership'.[10]

---

[7] Art 147 makes such conduct a 'grave breach' of the Geneva Conventions.

[8] Final Act of the Intergovernmental Conference on the Protection of Cultural Property in the Event of Armed Conflict, The Hague, 14 May 1954.

[9] There is some degree of uncertainty as to what constitutes 'every people'. States taking a restrictive view consider that the property must be of significance internationally, that is to 'every people'. Other states consider that property that is of national importance is sufficient, since the property of each state contributes to the heritage of all. See further R O'Keefe, *The Protection of Cultural Property in Armed Conflict* (Cambridge, Cambridge University Press, 2006) 104–6.

[10] Convention art 1.

It is left to individual states to determine which items of property in their territory meet the definition and are therefore to be protected.[11] In practice, most states tend to protect all, or a significant portion, of their officially-listed monuments and sites as immovable cultural property and the contents of museums and art galleries as movable cultural property.[12]

(ii) Meaning of 'Armed Conflict'

The convention applies

> in the event of declared war or of any other armed conflict which may arise between two or more of the High Contracting Parties, even if the state of war is not recognised by one or more of them.[13]

This is the same definition that is used in common article 2 of the Geneva Conventions, and it is interesting that in neither case is 'armed conflict' defined. A state of war recognised by all sides will clearly be sufficient, but is not necessary. The prevailing view is that an armed conflict will exist when a 'difference arising between two States [leads] to the intervention of members of the armed forces'.[14]

For most purposes of the convention the armed conflict must be international in nature: that is, it must involve hostilities between states,[15] at least two of which must be parties to the convention. However, certain provisions also apply in situations of non-international armed conflict within a state.[16] In this context an armed conflict will exist if there is 'protracted armed violence between governmental authorities and organised armed groups within a State'.[17] The 'protracted' and 'organised' requirements would preclude most criminal activity, riots, and isolated or low-level acts of violence from being categorised as armed conflicts. The activities of some terrorist groups might be thought to meet the threshold.[18] Interestingly, in

---

[11] States are required to exercise this discretion 'reasonably and in good faith': see art 26 of the 1969 Vienna Convention on the Law of Treaties.

[12] For a summary of how many pieces are protected in various states see O'Keefe, above n 9, at 106–7.

[13] Convention art 18.

[14] J Pictet, *Commentary to Geneva Convention I* (Geneva, International Committee of the Red Cross, 1952) 32. See also J Pictet, *Commentary: Geneva Convention II* (Geneva, ICRC, 1960) 28; J Pictet, *Commentary: Geneva Convention III* (Geneva, ICRC, 1960) 23; and J Pictet, *Commentary: Geneva Convention IV* (Geneva, ICRC, 1958) 21.

[15] The Convention also applies to all cases of partial and total occupation of the territory of one state party by another state party, even if the occupation is not resisted—see Convention, art 18(2).

[16] Art 19 provides that the parties to the conflict must endeavour to bring into force all of the Convention provisions, and that at a minimum the provisions involving respect for cultural property shall apply.

[17] See *Prosecutor v Tadic* (1996) 105 ILR 419, 488 (ICTY Appeals Chamber).

[18] The US considers that the ongoing military and security operations against Al Qaeda constitute an armed conflict.

the context of the Geneva Conventions, the United Kingdom has stated that 'armed conflict is not constituted by the commission of ordinary crimes including acts of terrorism whether concerted or in isolation',[19] and the government has specifically indicated that it does not consider the Hague Convention to apply to acts of terrorism.[20] Thus the characterisation of the legal framework applicable to a particular situation will be highly significant in relation to the application of the convention.

It should be noted that acts that are unconnected to an armed conflict, for example 'normal' theft, or destruction of property on religious grounds, will be outside the ambit of the convention. O'Keefe points to the example of the destruction of the Buddhas of Bamiyan in 2001 by the Taliban government: while this event took place during an internal armed conflict, being based on religious grounds it was not connected to that conflict and would not have been subject to the convention.[21]

C. Key Provisions

(i) General Protection

Under the convention there are two levels of protection that may be afforded to cultural property: general protection and special protection. Placing cultural property under general protection imposes two duties on states: to safeguard the property in times of peace, and to respect the property in times of armed conflict.

In peacetime states are required to take measures for the safeguarding of cultural property within their own territory against the foreseeable effects of armed conflict.[22] The precise measures to be taken are left to the discretion of the territorial state, although at a minimum states will identify property that is subject to general protection and provide inventories of that property to UNESCO for distribution to other state parties. Further measures may include the construction of special refuges to protect cultural property during armed conflict, the adaptation of buildings to ensure greater protection against fire or collapse, and the establishment of civilian authorities responsible for removing movable items and transporting them

---

[19] Reservation to Additional Protocol I, discussed below in section III.B.(i).

[20] Department for Culture, Media and Sport (DCMS) press release 138/06, 3 November 2006, available online at http://www.dcms.gov.uk/reference_library/media_releases/2492.aspx, accessed 16 December 2008.

[21] O'Keefe, above n 9, at 98–9. Compare F Francioni and F Lenzerini, 'The Destruction of the Buddahs of *Bamiyan* and International Law' (2003) 14 *European Journal of International Law* 619. This is a hypothetical example: Afghanistan is not a state party to the convention.

[22] Convention art 3.

to safety should an armed conflict arise.[23] A blue shield emblem may also be displayed,[24] although this practice appears to be waning with the recognition that modern weapons are targeted remotely and do not necessarily depend on visual confirmation.[25]

In times of armed conflict states must respect cultural property subject to general protection: they must not use protected property or its immediate surroundings for purposes which are likely to expose it to damage or destruction, and they are generally precluded from attacking it. However, the obligation to respect is not absolute: it is suspended 'in cases where military necessity imperatively requires'. Thus cultural property may, in specific circumstances, be a legitimate military target. There is no definition of what constitutes 'imperative military necessity' in any given situation, which leaves this issue to be determined by customary international law. As with many obligations found in international humanitarian law, the obligation to respect cultural property is not based on reciprocity. Thus a state remains bound even if its opponents do not respect its cultural property and subject it to attack.[26]

(ii) Special Protection

Under the convention a much higher degree of protection may be extended to a limited number of refuges to shelter movable cultural property and to centres containing monuments and other immovable cultural property of very great importance.[27] The threshold for granting this immunity, which can only be withdrawn in strictly limited circumstances,[28] is extremely high, and by the late 1990s only five sites worldwide (four cultural property refuges and the Vatican) were subject to special protection. A new regime of 'enhanced protection' has now effectively replaced the special protection scheme.[29]

(iii) Exportation of Cultural Property

The first protocol to the convention sets out provisions concerning the exportation of cultural property from occupied territory and the safeguarding

---

[23] See also Convention art 15.

[24] Convention arts 6, 16, 17.

[25] More sinisterly, there is evidence that buildings displaying the blue shield were deliberately targeted for destruction during the conflict in the former Yugoslavia: see the 1995 UNESCO Implementation Report, Report ref CLT-95/WS/13 (UNESCO, Paris 1995) 22–3.

[26] Convention, art 4(5). Although note the possibility of a state entering a reservation to the effect that obligations will only be based on reciprocity.

[27] Convention art 8.

[28] Immunity is only lost if one party commits a violation (ie uses the property for military means), or if the commander of a military division withdraws immunity in 'exceptional cases of unavoidable military necessity': Convention, art 11.

[29] Discussed below, section III.B.(ii).

and return of property that has already been exported. States accept four obligations: first, to prevent the exportation of cultural property from territory where that state is an occupying power; secondly, to take any exported cultural property currently within its territory into custody; thirdly, to return any such property at the end of hostilities; and fourthly, if the state fails in its duty to prevent exportation, to pay compensation to good-faith holders who are required to surrender honestly-acquired items.

III. THE UNITED KINGDOM AND THE HAGUE CONVENTION

A. Initial Involvement

The United Kingdom participated in the diplomatic conference leading to the adoption of the convention and the first protocol, and was a signatory to the adopted text. During the conference the United Kingdom was concerned that the text should not unduly restrict its military options during an armed conflict: in fact the waiver of protection in cases of imperative military necessity was included at the insistence of the United Kingdom and the United States, who argued that some acts may be rendered militarily unavoidable.[30] The United Kingdom was also influential in the drafting of article 8 and the original special protection regime: it considered that the amount of property entitled to special protection should be limited to avoid the need to raise the issue of immunity frequently and thus debasing the effect and import of the regime. This position was controversial but was ultimately accepted in order to secure adoption of the text by the United Kingdom and the United States.

Despite adopting the text of the convention, neither the United Kingdom nor the United States proceeded to ratify the convention or the first protocol. Detailed reasons for the UK policy do not appear to have been made public, although it has been suggested that the United Kingdom was persuaded by the United States not to ratify.[31] It is likely that both states were concerned about how the provisions of the convention would sit with the use of nuclear weapons and, given the state of technology at the time, there may also have been concerns that even conventional weapons would be unable to discriminate sufficiently between legitimate military targets and

---

[30] Records of the Conference convened by the United Nations Educational, Scientific and Cultural Organisation, The Hague, 21 April–14 May 1954. See also P Boylan, *Review of the Convention for the Protection of Cultural Property in the Event of Armed Conflict*, Report ref CLT-93/WS/12 (Paris, UNESCO, 1993) 56.

[31] Boylan, above n 30, at 103–4; K Eirinberg, 'The United States Reconsiders the 1954 Hague Convention' (1994) 3 *International Journal of Cultural Property* 27, 29.

cultural property.[32] As the United Kingdom was a party to other relevant instruments that incorporated provisions on the protection of cultural property, and its military already took steps to protect cultural property, it may also have been felt that adopting the more specific provisions of the convention was not necessary. Certainly the United Kingdom now considers that the fundamental principle of the convention represents customary international law and is therefore binding.[33]

The failure of the United States and the United Kingdom to ratify the convention and the first protocol resulted in two states with large and active armies not being subject to their provisions. It also meant that three permanent members of the United Nations Security Council were not parties to the convention.[34]

B. Subsequent Events

There have been several key developments since the adoption of the convention in 1954 and its entry into force in 1956: the additional protocols to the Geneva Conventions, the second protocol to the Hague Convention, and the recent invasion and occupation of Iraq.

(i) The Additional Protocols to the Geneva Conventions

In 1977 a diplomatic conference adopted two optional protocols supplementing the Geneva Conventions: Additional Protocol I (API) concerning international armed conflicts and Additional Protocol II (APII) concerning non-international armed conflicts. The additional protocols reflect, for the most part, developments in customary international law. They contain both specific provisions regarding the protection of cultural property and more general provisions that have implications for protection of cultural property.

---

[32] These have been outlined as the concerns of the US Government; it is likely that they would have also applied to the UK. See Boylan, above n 30, 104; Eirinberg, above n 31; C Colwell-Chanthaphonh and J Piper, 'War and Cultural Property: The 1954 Hague Convention and the Status of US Ratification' (2001) 10 *International Journal of Cultural Property* 217. A US State Department analysis provided to President Clinton in 1998 indicates misguided early US concern that the Kremlin would be placed under special protection and would therefore be immune from attack: see analysis accompanying the letter of submittal from Strobe Talbot to President Clinton, 12 May 1998.

[33] See the UK Manual on the Law of Armed Conflict (MLAC), para [5.25]. For discussion as to whether the Convention in its entirety constitutes customary international law, see D Meyer, 'The 1954 Hague Cultural Property Convention and its Emergence into Customary International Law' (1993) 11 *Boston University International Law Journal* 349.

[34] The USSR ratified the convention on 4 January 1957 and France ratified on 7 June 1957. China, despite being a signatory to the convention, did not ratify until 5 January 2000.

In terms of the general provisions, articles 51 and 52 of API reflect the established principle of distinction: the civilian population and civilian objects should not be the object of indiscriminate attack or reprisals.[35] Only military objectives should be the object of attack.[36] Civilian objects are defined as all objects that are not military objectives. Military objectives are in turn defined as objects which by their nature, location, purpose or use make an effective contribution to military action and whose total or partial destruction in the circumstances at the time offers a definitive military advantage.[37] Articles 57 and 58 set out provisions on precautions to be taken in attack and against the effect of an attack, which would apply to attacks on cultural property as civilian objects. They include obligations to verify the use of objectives, to minimise incidental damage to civilian objects, and to refrain from attacks where incidental damage would be excessive.[38] It is clear that this provision applies to cultural property, although there is no guidance as to how the nature of the cultural property itself would be factored in to the assessment of whether the incidental damage is proportionate. API also introduces criminal sanctions for violations.

In terms of the specific provisions, article 53 of API sets out a regime for the protection of cultural property without prejudice to the provisions of the Hague Convention and other international legal instruments. Under article 53 it is prohibited:

(a)   to commit any acts of hostility directed against the historic monuments, works of art or places of worship which constitute the cultural or spiritual heritage of peoples;
(b)   to use such objects in support of the military effort;
(c)   to make such objects the object of reprisals.

While the language used does differ, it was intended that article 53 would apply to the same cultural property as the Hague Convention and that it would apply to both immovable and movable property. Unlike the Hague Convention, article 53 provides protection that is absolute; that is, there is no exception for military necessity. However, immunity from attack will be lost if the object is used so as to render it a military objective as defined in article 52(2).

APII, which applies to non-international armed conflicts, prohibits in article 16, acts of hostility against cultural property and the use of such objects in support of the military effort.

---

[35]   API arts 51(2), 52(1).
[36]   API art 52(2).
[37]   API art 52.
[38]   API art 57(2).

The United Kingdom ratified both Additional Protocols on 28 January 1998, following implementing legislation in the Geneva Conventions (Amendment) Act 1995. This is significant because the United Kingdom therefore accepted treaty obligations in similar terms to those contained in the Hague Convention. However, the UK reservations to API contain important indicators for how obligations under the Hague Convention will be interpreted. First, the United Kingdom made a general reservation such that 'armed conflict is not constituted by the commission of ordinary crimes including acts of terrorism whether concerted or in isolation'. As mentioned above, this reservation may indicate the circumstances in which the United Kingdom will consider the Hague Convention to apply. Secondly, the United Kingdom made a reservation in relation to articles 51 and 57, stating that 'military advantage is the advantage anticipated from the attack considered as a whole and not from isolated or particular parts of the attack'. Thirdly, a reservation to article 52 provides that it is the understanding of the United Kingdom that land may be a military objective solely because of its location. Fourthly, as to article 53 the United Kingdom stated that 'use ... in support of the military effort' includes use for military protection and so considers that any buildings used to shelter opposing forces will lose protection. Finally, in relation to articles 51 to 55, the United Kingdom will only accept these obligations on the basis of reciprocity. Given that in ratifying the Hague Convention and protocols the United Kingdom will undertake similar obligations, it is possible that similar reservations may be made.[39]

(ii) The Second Protocol to the Hague Convention

By the late 1990s there was considerable concern regarding the usefulness of the convention. Only five items were listed on the Register for Special Protection and states were not submitting the required implementing reports. Events including the Iran/Iraq conflict, the Iraqi invasion of Kuwait, and the destruction of important items of cultural property during the conflict in the former Yugoslavia, illustrated the ineffectiveness of the regime. In March 1999 the Netherlands Government sponsored a diplomatic conference (held again in The Hague) at which a new protocol was adopted. The United Kingdom attended the negotiations as an observer.

---

[39] The convention does not prohibit the making of reservations, nor does it restrict the type of reservations that may be made. Thus it is open for the UK to lodge a reservation with its instrument of ratification, provided the reservation is not incompatible with the object and purpose of the Convention: Vienna Convention on the Law of Treaties art 19. However, no proposed instrument of ratification has been made available, and the public documents and comments issued by the government do not indicate that reservations will be made. The vast majority of state parties to the convention have not lodged reservations, although it appears that the US intends to lodge an 'understanding' with its instrument of ratification.

The second protocol to the convention entered into force on 1 January 2006 and has 51 state parties as of 16 December 2008.

The second protocol supplements the convention in several important ways. First, it provides greater guidance as to what constitutes 'imperative military necessity'.[40] The protocol adopts the modern approach found in API, such that cultural property is civilian property and should not be the subject of attack unless by its function it has become a military objective and there is no feasible alternative available to obtain a similar military advantage. The decision to invoke military necessity so as to attack cultural property may only be taken at a senior level and an effective warning must be given whenever circumstances allow. An army may also waive protection and use cultural property so as to place it at risk of damage or destruction as long as there is no other choice possible for obtaining a similar military advantage.[41]

Secondly, the protocol develops an institutional framework and machinery for implementation. This includes provision for regular meetings of state parties and the establishment of the Committee for the Protection of Cultural Property in the Event of Armed Conflict (the Committee), plus a fund for providing financial and other assistance during peace time and for emergency assistance during an armed conflict.[42]

Thirdly, it introduces a new level of protection to be known as 'enhanced' protection. This level of protection is only available where the property in question meets the following conditions:[43]

1. It is cultural heritage of the greatest importance for humanity;
2. It is protected by adequate domestic legal and administrative measures recognising its exceptional cultural and historic value and ensuring the highest level of protection;
3. It is not used for military purposes or to shield military sites and [the state] has declared that it will not be so used.

The enhanced protection system should prove more effective than the old special protection system because unanimity of states is no longer required before a site can be included on the register. Instead the Committee will determine the cultural property eligible for enhanced protection.[44] Once

---

[40] Second Protocol art 6.

[41] J Hladik, 'The 1954 Hague Convention for the Protection of Cultural Property in the Event of Armed conflict and the notion of military necessity' (1999) 835 *International Review of the Red Cross* 621.

[42] Second Protocol arts 23–33.

[43] Second Protocol art 10.

[44] A request for enhanced protection must come from the state concerned, although the Committee may request a state to submit an application and there is also role for other states and non-governmental organisations, in particular the International Committee of the Blue Shield, to recommend specific cultural property to the Committee for inclusion.

included, the relevant property is immune from attack and the property or its immediate surrounds must not be used so as to make the property an object of attack.[45] Other than by deregistration, this protection is only lost if the property has by its use become a military objective. Even then any attack must be the only feasible way of terminating the military use, all feasible precautions must be taken to avoid or minimise harm, and, unless circumstances do not permit due to immediate self-defence, the decision must be taken at the highest level of operational command.[46]

Finally, the new protocol introduces a comprehensive system of penal sanctions, requiring states to criminalise various actions and to exercise jurisdiction, including in some circumstances on the basis of universal jurisdiction.[47]

The second protocol addresses the United Kingdom's concerns in that it clarifies the concept of military necessity and introduces the concept of enhanced protection, considered to be a better regime than that for special protection. In 2003 the then Secretary of State for Culture, Media and Sport, the Rt Hon Tessa Jowell MP, said that

> the UK reached a conclusion about the ineffectiveness of [the convention and first protocol]. UNESCO then recognised that a second protocol was required to improve the shortcomings in the original convention, particularly to establish a more effective system of protection for specially designated cultural property, and negotiations on this protocol in which the UK played a leading part were completed in 1999. In the light of that, UK ministers ... have agreed that we should negotiate with a view to ratifying both the convention and the second protocol.[48]

(iii) Invasion and Occupation of Iraq

In 2003 the United Kingdom and the United States invaded the territory of Iraq and subsequently acted as occupying powers of Iraqi territory. During the invasion and the occupation, wide-scale looting and destruction of Iraqi cultural property occurred. In particular, the Iraqi National Museum was looted extensively, with a loss of some 13,000 items,[49] and the National Library was burned down, destroying thousands of rare manuscripts,

---

[45] Second Protocol art 12.
[46] Second Protocol art 13.
[47] Second Protocol arts 15–21.
[48] Minutes of Evidence, 8 July 2003, Select Committee on Culture, Media and Sport, Q36.
[49] The looting of the National Library occurred between 8 April 2003 and 12 April 2003, when museum staff managed to return to salvage remaining items. While initial estimates of the loss suggested that some 170,000 items were missing, later estimates suggest that 13,000 items were stolen, including 33 key items, with 3,000 recovered by September 2003. For more detailed discussion of the impact of the armed conflict on Iraq's cultural heritage see P Stone and J Farchakh Bajjaly (eds), *The Destruction of Cultural Heritage in Iraq* (Woodbridge, Boydell Press, 2008).

maps and photographs. United States forces were the subject of heavy criticism for their failure to protect the National Museum, particularly given the warnings from numerous experts that valuable collections would be endangered by the invasion. While the US military did place the National Museum and other key sites on a list of prohibited targets, it did not dispatch troops to protect the museum, despite the direct plea of the museum's curator.[50] Instead US efforts were concentrated on securing palaces and the Iraqi oil ministry. Officials were reluctant to assume any responsibility for the failure to protect the museum, arguing that the protection of cultural property was the responsibility of the Iraqi authorities and that the United States had never promised to protect items—it had merely agreed to refrain from targeting them.[51]

The British Government was also criticised for failing to protect Iraqi cultural property. In April 2003 the Secretary of State for Culture, Media and Sport announced measures aimed at the recovery and, where possible, restoration, of looted Iraqi cultural property.[52] The UK Government, as with the US Government, indicated that its responsibility was to work with the Iraqi authorities, who bore the primary responsibility for protecting cultural property.[53]

Would the United Kingdom's obligations have been different if it had been a party to the convention in 2003? In terms of targeting during the military campaign, it probably would not have changed the practice and policy of the UK armed forces. The United Kingdom was already a party to API, which, as noted above, contains specific provisions for the protection of cultural property. The United Kingdom took steps to comply with its obligations under article 53, including issuing guidance reflecting the provisions of article 53 to all military personnel[54] and planning to ensure that the risk of damage to sites of historic, archaeological and cultural heritage was minimised.[55] It also consulted experts before the conflict.[56] The

---

[50] US troops did disperse a crowd of looters by firing shots on 10 April 2003, but the soldiers did not remain to prevent further attack.

[51] For further analysis, see C Phuong, 'The Protection of Iraqi Cultural Property' (2004) 53 *International Comparative Law Quarterly* 985 and M Thurlow, 'Protecting Cultural Property in Iraq: How American Military Policy Comports with International Law' (2005) 8 *Yale Human Rights & Development Law Journal* 153. This position is reflected in the understanding to be lodged with the US instrument of ratification, para 4 of which provides that primary responsibility for protection rests with the party controlling the property.

[52] Statement of 30 April 2003 at http://www.culture.gov.uk/reference_library/media_releases/2655.aspx, accessed 16 December 2008.

[53] DCMS Statement of 11 June 2003 regarding 'Safeguarding Iraq's Cultural Heritage' available online at: http://www.culture.gov.uk/reference_library/media_releases/2718.aspx, accessed 16 December 2008. See also Minister of State for Defence, 7 February 2005, Hansard 1249W and Secretary of State for Culture, Media and Sport, 8 May 2007, Hansard 66W.

[54] Hansard, 28 April 2003, WA64, Under-Secretary of State for Defence.

[55] Hansard, 26 March 2003, WA81, Under-Secretary of State for Defence.

[56] The government responded to letters from various bodies including the UK Institute for Conservation of Historic and Artistic Works, the Society of Antiquaries of London, and the

difference in the obligations would most likely have been later, when the coalition forces acted as occupying powers: the second protocol contains specific obligations to prevent looting, unlawful excavations etc that are not included in API.[57] As has been noted, the United Kingdom has not assumed any responsibility to protect cultural property within Iraq.

(iv) The Change in the Position of the United States

In September 2008 the US Senate consented to US ratification of the convention subject to the following four understandings:[58] first, the provisions on special protection codify customary international law in that they prohibit the use of cultural property to shield military targets and allow cultural property to be attacked by lawful and proportionate means if required by military necessity.[59] Secondly, any subsequent examination of the decision of a military commander should be on the basis of that commander's assessment of the information reasonably available to them at the time, and not in the light of information that subsequently becomes available. Thirdly, the convention provisions 'apply only to conventional weapons, and are without prejudice to the rules of international law governing other types of weapons, including nuclear weapons'. Finally, the primary responsibility for the protection of cultural property rests with the party controlling the object. The change in policy[60] was the culmination of a decade of lobbying by various groups, including the US Committee of the Blue Shield, the Lawyers' Committee for Cultural Heritage Preservation, the Archaeological Institute of America, and the American Bar Association.[61] The United

---

International Council on Monuments and Sites. On the other hand, recent evidence suggests that UK practice in Iraq may have been considerably influenced by a meeting between an academic and a naval officer in a Northumberland pub: see evidence given by Professor Peter Stone and Brigadier Gordon Messenger DSO OBE at Ev 7 and Ev 10 in Culture, Media and Sport Committee, 'Draft Cultural Property (Armed Conflicts) Bill', HC (2007–08) 693 (2008 CMS Committee Report).

[57] Second Protocol, art 9.

[58] The convention was included in a 'package' of five treaties (all of which concern international humanitarian law) presented to the Senate for consent as part of the Administration's Treaty Priority List for the 110th Congress on 7 February 2007.

[59] It is doubtful that this is what the convention means, given that art 11(2) provides that the immunity given by special protection may only be withdrawn in 'exceptional cases of unavoidable military necessity'. This wording is clearly meant to reflect a higher threshold than the reference in art 4(2) to when 'military necessity imperatively requires', in the context of general protection. Both convention phrasings are stronger than the US understanding's 'military necessity'.

[60] The reasons justifying the change in policy were set out by the Departments of State and Defense in evidence before the Senate Foreign Relations Committee on 15 April 2008.

[61] See, eg, the Statement of the Archaeological Institute of America (and 14 others) before the Senate Foreign Relations Committee on 15 April 2008, in support of the ratification of the Convention, available at http://www.culturalheritagelaw.org/advocacy/1954% 20Hague%20Testimony.doc, accessed 16 December 2008. The American Bar Association also

States has not yet indicated its intention to become a party to the first and second protocols, but, in suggesting that 'both protocols require further review', leaves open the possibility of further action.[62]

Ratification by the United States is obviously politically significant, but it also raises interesting legal points. For example, in only ratifying the convention itself and not adopting either protocol, the United States will be accepting different obligations to the United Kingdom—particularly in respect of the duties of occupying powers. Article 5 of the convention only imposes an obligation on occupying powers to 'as far as possible' assist local authorities in protecting cultural property, whereas the provisions in the first and second protocols are far more extensive.[63] Also, unlike the United Kingdom, the United States is not a party to API of the Geneva Conventions so has not already accepted treaty obligations in similar terms to those found in the Hague Convention.

IV. THE UNITED KINGDOM'S PROPOSALS FOR IMPLEMENTATION

In order to ratify the convention and accede to the two protocols, the United Kingdom had to consider both the practical and legal implications of becoming a party and the steps required to ensure that it would comply with the obligations being assumed. In summary, implementation has three aspects: peacetime safeguarding, military considerations, and legislative requirements.

A. Peacetime Safeguarding

The government's 2005 consultation process highlighted five themes.[64] First, it was necessary to determine the types of cultural property that should receive general protection under the convention. The United Kingdom has in the past adopted a narrow interpretation of 'cultural property',

---

submitted a report in support of ratification, available at http://www.abanet.org/intlaw/policy/armscontrol/conventionculturalproperty.pdf, accessed 16 December 2008.

[62] See Testimony of John B Bellinger, Legal Adviser, Department of State, to the Senate Foreign Relations Committee, 15 April 2008.

[63] See First Protocol arts 1–4; Second Protocol art 9. Not having adopted the second protocol, the US will also be unable to use the enhanced protection regime.

[64] See the original DCMS 'Consultation Paper on the 1954 Hague Convention on the Protection of Cultural Property in the Event of Armed Conflict and its two Protocols of 1954 and 1999', September 2005 (2005 DCMS Consultation Paper) and the summary of responses, DCMS '1954 Hague Convention on the Protection of Cultural Property in the Event of Armed Conflict and its two Protocols of 1954 and 1999, A Summary of Responses Received to the Government's Consultation', October 2006 (2006 DCMS Response Summary).

considering that the property to be protected must be of wider importance and international stature.[65] Under the current proposals general protection will only be extended to listed buildings, parks and gardens of Grade I or Category A status, the collections of museums and galleries that are directly sponsored or funded by the government, certain other museums, galleries and universities with important collections, and designated libraries and archives in England.[66]

Secondly, the government initially proposed that the decision on whether any particular cultural property should be protected should be left to the individual choice of the property's owners;[67] that is, that the system of protection should be voluntary.[68] This issue was the most controversial during the consultation process: those opposed to a voluntary scheme argued that it would lead to inconsistent coverage and that the government had a duty to protect cultural property, while supporters felt that it was inappropriate to compel owners to accept protection and were concerned that a compulsory regime would impose significant financial and administrative costs.[69] The government has now amended its initial proposal and intends that all cultural property satisfying the definition in article 1 of the convention will be automatically included on the United Kingdom's list of protected property.[70]

Thirdly, the government proposes that it should be the existing owner of the cultural property who will be responsible for the peacetime safeguarding measures including the preparation of inventories, planning of emergency measures in the event of fire or collapse, and preparation for the removal and safe storage of movable property. The government argued that most items of cultural property were already subject to such requirements and, moreover, that the owner would be in the best position to determine the best means of protection.[71] The government does not propose to stipulate any mandatory forms of safeguards beyond those already required by existing legislation or schemes.[72]

Fourthly, affixing the blue shield emblem to cultural property will also be at the discretion of the property's owner.[73] The government will provide a list of all protected cultural property—both general and enhanced protection—to UNESCO together with maps utilising GPS technology.

---

[65] The UK MLAC states that 'every people' means 'items of international rather than local importance': para [5.26.2] fn 116.

[66] Because of the absence of a designation system in Scotland, Wales and Northern Ireland, the government is undertaking further discussions with those administrations.

[67] Owners, guardians or trustees.

[68] 2005 DCMS Consultation Paper, 14–15.

[69] 2006 DCMS Response Summary, paras [51]–[57].

[70] *ibid*, para [58].

[71] 2005 DCMS Consultation Paper, 17.

[72] 2006 DCMS Response Summary, para [67].

[73] 2005 DCMS Consultation Paper, 20.

Property under protection will be marked with the emblem on these maps, which are to be confidential and password protected so as to ensure the security of the cultural property. The password will then be released to any party engaged in an armed conflict involving the United Kingdom.[74]

Finally, the government will only seek enhanced protection for World Heritage Sites designated as cultural property, for the collections of the museums and galleries that are Non-Departmental Public Bodies (NDPBs) or Assembly-Sponsored Public Bodies (ASPBs), for the National Archive Bodies and the five legal deposit libraries.[75]

B. Military Considerations

The United Kingdom must declare that no property under enhanced protection will ever be used for military purposes, and it must also agree not to expose property under general protection to the risk of damage or destruction in the event of an armed conflict. Military issues must therefore be considered when deciding which UK-based cultural property to protect. However, it will be the actions of the British military when engaged in occupation or armed conflict abroad that will be most important, given that UK operations abroad are more likely than an armed attack by another state on the United Kingdom's territory.

The government must ensure that military personnel are familiar with the requirements of the convention and the two protocols. The existing Manual on the Law of Armed Conflict (MLAC) already sets out instructions for the protection of cultural property and all British troops have received some training on the obligation to protect and respect cultural property. As outlined above, the United Kingdom has already accepted various obligations for the protection of cultural property, and the MLAC provides that cultural property is to be protected beyond the protection given to general civilian property and that the use of cultural property for military purposes is to be discouraged. The MLAC also contains guidance on the precautions to be taken on targeting[76] and the principle of proportionality.[77] However, there is no specific mention of how proportionality is to be assessed in relation to cultural property. In recent evidence given to the Committee on Culture, Media and Sport, a senior army officer confirmed that current training would need to be reviewed to ensure compliance, but that there would be no resource implications.[78]

---

[74] *ibid*, 19.
[75] *ibid*, 30–33. This is subject to the Ministry of Defence being satisfied that the sites will never be needed for military purposes.
[76] MLAC para [5.32].
[77] *ibid*, para [5.33].
[78] 2008 CMS Committee Report, Ev 11–12.

Given the current provisions of MLAC regarding targeting in an armed conflict, it is true that little more than a review and deepening of current training will be required before the United Kingdom can be confident of fulfilling those convention obligations. The British military considers that the general protection for cultural property is customary international law and so already binds the United Kingdom even though it is not yet a party to the convention. However, it is argued that current practice in respect of actions taken while an occupying power may have to be altered: the MLAC says nothing about any affirmative obligations of the occupying power to prevent theft and damage,[79] whereas both the first and second protocols contain such positive obligations.[80] However, the United Kingdom adopts a narrow view as to what constitutes occupation, defining it as where the former government has been rendered incapable and the occupying power is in a position to substitute its own authority for that of the government.[81] Recognition of occupation will therefore depend on the actual exercise of authority by the occupying power and not just on the military defeat of the host nation. This is relevant to when the United Kingdom will view itself as acting as an occupying power and hence obliged to protect property, and also in relation to when the United Kingdom will view property as having been removed from an occupied territory.

C. Legislative Aspects

After considering the existing laws on the protection of cultural property, the government decided that new primary legislation was needed to ensure the United Kingdom would meet its obligations under the convention and protocols. The draft Cultural Property (Armed Conflicts) Bill was released in January 2008 and was subjected to close scrutiny by the House of Commons Culture, Media and Sport Committee, which generally welcomed the Bill.[82] The government responded to the July 2008 committee report in a response paper in October 2008.[83] In this response the government confirmed that the provisions of the draft Cultural Property (Armed Conflicts) Bill would be included within a single Heritage Protection Bill

---

[79] MLAC para [11.87.1].

[80] First Protocol arts 1–4; Second Protocol art 9.

[81] MLAC para [11.3].

[82] See the 2008 CMS Committee Report. Some minor drafting changes were suggested but the only significant criticism concerned the lack of guidance from the government on which territories were 'occupied'.

[83] Department for Culture, Media and Sport, 'Government Response to the Culture, Media and Sport Committee Reports on the Draft Heritage Protection Bill and Draft Cultural Property (Armed Conflicts) Bill' (Cm 7472, 2008) (2008 DCMS Government Response).

that would—subject to the availability of parliamentary time—be laid before Parliament in the 2008–09 session.

(i) Criminal Sanctions for Offences Related to the Protection of Cultural Property During Armed Conflict

Several criminal offences concerning the protection of cultural property in armed conflict already exist. First, the Geneva Conventions Act 1957 incorporates the act of wanton destruction of civilian property, as found in article 147 of the Fourth Geneva Convention, as a criminal offence under domestic law. It also criminalises in the United Kingdom the act of attacking and damaging protected cultural property where the property is not located in the immediate proximity of military objectives.[84] In addition, the International Criminal Court Act 2001 makes it an offence for a person to commit a war crime. The jurisdiction of the courts of England and Wales extends to war crimes committed on UK territory by a UK national or resident, or by a person subject to UK service jurisdiction.[85] War crime is given the same meaning as in article 8 of the ICC Statute,[86] and an attack against cultural property could be prosecuted before the UK courts as a grave breach,[87] as a serious violation of the law and customs of war,[88] and also—possibly—as a crime against humanity.[89]

---

[84] Protected property is defined according to art 85(4)(d) of API. It would include property protected under the Hague Convention and protocols.

[85] ICC Act 2001 s 51.

[86] ICC Act 2001 s 50.

[87] Art 8(a)(iv) provides that it is a grave breach to commit the extensive destruction of property not justified by military necessity and carried out unlawfully and wantonly. The UK recognises, based on arts 53 and 85(4)(d) of API, that targeting clearly recognised cultural property will constitute a grave breach if the property is the subject of special protection, extensive destruction is caused, the property has not been used for military purposes, and it is not within the immediate proximity of a military objective: MLAC para [5.25.2].

[88] The following provisions of article 8 of the ICC Statute may be relevant: art 8(b)(ii) attacks against civilian objects; art 8(b)(iv), disproportionate attacks—ie incidental damage—against civilian objects excessive to military advantage; and art 8(b)(ix) attacks against buildings dedicated to religion, education, art, science or charitable purposes, historic monuments etc provided not military objectives.

[89] The ICTY has convicted defendants of the crime against humanity of persecution for unlawful attacks on civilian objects, in particular 'attacks on towns and villages [and] the destruction and plunder of property and, in particular, of institutions dedicated to religion and education': *Blaskic Trial Judgment*, No IT-95-14-T Part VI Disposition. See also *Kordic Trial Judgment*, No IT-95-14/2-T. For further discussion, see: H Abtahi, 'The Protection of Cultural Property in Times of Armed Conflict: The Practice of the International Criminal Tribunal for the Former Yugoslavia' (2001) 14 *Harvard Human Rights Journal* 1; and G Mose, 'The Destruction of Churches and Mosques in Bosnia-Herzegovina: Seeking a Rights-Based Approach to the Protection of Religious Cultural Property' (1996–97) 3 *Buffalo Journal of International Law* 180.

The United Kingdom ratified the 1970 UNESCO Convention in 2002.[90] Prior to this there was no specific legislation concerning the import and trade in illegally-obtained cultural objects and so the United Kingdom had become a target market. The Dealing in Cultural Objects (Offences) Act 2003 creates an offence of dealing in tainted cultural objects.[91] A cultural object is an object of historical, architectural or archaeological interest, which has been removed or excavated contrary to the law of the United Kingdom or another state.[92] In addition, article 8 of the Iraq (United Nations Sanctions) Order 2003 introduces new offences of dealing in any item of illegally removed Iraqi cultural property.[93] It implements Security Council resolution 1483.[94]

One of the main criticisms of the convention and the first protocol was the omission of detailed provisions for criminal jurisdiction in respect of violations.[95] This omission was rectified by the second protocol, and the Bill would introduce into domestic law the offence of a serious breach of the second protocol. An offence is committed where a person intentionally commits one of the acts listed in article 15(1)(a)–(e) of the second protocol,[96] where the act would be a violation of the convention or the two protocols (ie because the states concerned are parties to the convention and the two protocols), and where he or she knows or has reason to suspect that the property in question is cultural property protected by the convention and the two protocols. The Bill also provides for prosecution of company officers in some circumstances, and for command and superior responsibility for the acts of subordinates. Under section 7 the maximum penalty for all offences will be 30 years imprisonment.

The UK courts may exercise universal jurisdiction in respect of three offences: making cultural property under enhanced protection the object of attack; using cultural property under enhanced protection or its immediate surroundings in support of military action; and extensive destruction

---

[90] Convention on the Means of Prohibiting and Preventing the Illicit Import and Transfer of Ownership of Cultural Property.

[91] Cultural Objects (Offences) Act 2003 s 1.

[92] Cultural Objects (Offences) Act 2003 s 2.

[93] The article applies to persons within the UK and British nationals elsewhere: art 1(4).

[94] UN SC Res 1483 (22 May 2003) UN doc S/RES/1483. Para 7 requires member states to take steps to facilitate the return and to prohibit the trade or transfer of items where there is a reasonable suspicion that they have been illegally removed.

[95] MC Bassiouni, 'Reflections on Criminal Jurisdiction in International Protection of Cultural Property' (1983) 10 *Syracuse Journal of International Law and Commerce* 281.

[96] Art 15 provides that a person shall commit an offence by intentionally '(a) making cultural property under enhanced protection the object of attack; (b) using cultural property under enhanced protection or its immediate surroundings in support of military action; (c) extensive destruction or appropriation of cultural property protected under the Convention and this Protocol; (d) making cultural property protected under the Convention and this Protocol the object of attack; (e) theft, pillage or misappropriation of, or acts of vandalism directed against cultural property protected under the Convention'.

of cultural property protected by the convention and two protocols. However, the person must come within UK territory in order to be prosecuted. In respect of two other offences—making property under general protection the object of attack; and theft, pillage or misappropriation of, or acts of vandalism directed against, cultural property protected by the Convention—UK courts may only exercise jurisdiction where the offender is a UK national or a person subject to UK service jurisdiction.

(ii) Use and Protection of the Cultural Property Emblem

Part 3 of the Bill sets out provisions to regulate the authorised use of the cultural property emblem and includes the offence of unauthorised use of the cultural property emblem. The provisions are based on article 17 of the convention and section 6 of the Geneva Conventions Act 1957 and are designed to give the blue shield emblem the same protection as that enjoyed by the red cross and red crescent. It will be an offence for a person to use the cultural property emblem other than as authorised, or to use any other design that so closely resembles the emblem as to be capable of being mistaken for it. Unauthorised use of the emblem will be punished by a fine and will render the relevant property liable to forfeiture.

(iii) Property Exported from Occupied Territory

As outlined above, acceding to the first protocol would require the United Kingdom to take into its custody cultural property that has been exported from occupied territory and imported into the United Kingdom, and to return such property to the competent authorities at the close of hostilities. Article 21 of the second protocol also requires the United Kingdom to take measures to suppress any illicit export, removal or transfer of ownership of cultural property from occupied territory in violation of the Convention or the second protocol. Part 4 of the Bill will enable the United Kingdom to satisfy these obligations by creating the offence of dealing in unlawfully exported cultural property and providing for the forfeiture of unlawfully exported cultural property (whether in connection with the dealing offence or not).

Property will be unlawfully exported when it has been exported from territory that is occupied by a party to the first or second protocols and that exportation was in contravention of the laws of the territory from which it was exported or in contravention of any rule of international law. The proposed offence of dealing in unlawfully exported cultural property requires the person to 'deal'[97] in such property when he knows or has

---

[97] The acts that would constitute dealing are detailed in sub-s 3, and include acquiring, disposing of or importing; agreeing to deal or making arrangements so that a third person would deal. 'Acquires' and 'disposes of' are further defined in sub-ss (4) and (5).

reason to suspect that the property has been unlawfully exported. The British Art Market Foundation and the select committee thought that this would place dealers in cultural property in an invidious position: how would an art dealer know whether or not a particular territory was occupied at a certain time, or whether the export was contrary to local regulations at the time? In response the government pointed out that the proposed legislation would require a dealer to know or have reason to suspect that exportation was unlawful, that the burden of proof would rest on the prosecution, and that in its view dealers would not need to do anything more than their current due diligence would already require. The government also noted that no other country maintained a list of occupied territories.[98]

The maximum penalty for the offence of dealing in unlawfully exported cultural property will be seven years imprisonment (or 12 months on summary conviction),[99] and the relevant property may be forfeited.[100] Additionally, cultural property that has been unlawfully exported may be forfeited even if no conviction for an offence has been secured.[101]

Although these criminal law provisions are necessary, it must be admitted that it is unlikely that they will often be needed. The Bill refers to property exported from an occupied territory, but a territory will only have been 'occupied' at the relevant time if the occupying army was actually exercising authority over the territory.[102] This is a rather restrictive test: the United Kingdom considers only the Israeli-occupied territories to be currently 'occupied'.[103] It should also be noted that the Act will not have retroactive application and that to date there have been no prosecutions under the similar sections contained in the Dealing in Cultural Objects (Offences) Act 2003 or the Iraqi (United Nations Sanctions) Order 2003. The restrictive definition of an occupied territory will also limit the risk that the United Kingdom will have to pay compensation to holders in good faith where property has been unlawfully exported from an occupied territory and must be returned.[104]

(iv) Property Removed for Safekeeping

Article 14 of the convention requires the United Kingdom to grant immunity from seizure to any cultural property that enjoys special protection

---

[98] 2008 DCMS Government Response, paras [97]–[99].

[99] Draft Bill cl 18(6).

[100] Draft Bill cl 19.

[101] Draft Bill cl 22.

[102] Clause 17 of the Draft Bill refers to art 42 of the 1907 Hague Regulations, which provides for the same 'actual authority' test as the UK currently employs: see MLAC para [11.3].

[103] The Draft Bill's Regulatory Impact Assessment provides on p 88 that 'the only territories which the United Kingdom would now regard as being unequivocally occupied are the West Bank, East Jerusalem and the Golan Heights'. On p 90 it states that the only three occupied territories are 'the West Bank, the Gaza Strip, and the Golan Heights'.

[104] *ibid*, 90.

under article 12 of the convention.[105] This provision would apply to the transport of cultural property which has been removed from its original territory for safekeeping. UK law already extends immunity from seizure to certain diplomatic and state property, but this does not extend to cultural property.[106] Clause 27 of the Bill thus provides that cultural property may not be seized or forfeited where it is protected under article 12 of the convention. This includes property brought into the United Kingdom, property transiting through the United Kingdom, and property where the United Kingdom is the depository.

V. CONCLUSION

The first thing we might say is that there is a general consensus that the proposed ratification is a good thing and will not carry any disadvantages: the peacetime safeguarding of cultural property should not require substantial changes in the way that museums or important buildings already operate, and the military is happy that ratification will not involve much in the way of extra training and will not hamper them in theatre. Moreover, the United Kingdom has already been applying many of the principles found in the convention in practice, either due to its obligations pursuant to API or under customary international law. The domestic legislation in respect of dealing in unlawfully exported property—although necessary to give effect to obligations under the convention—will probably not have much of an impact simply because the likelihood of these sections being used is low. First, the definition of 'occupied' territory is very restrictive; secondly, the act will not have retroactive application; and thirdly there have not yet been any prosecutions under similar provisions in existing laws.

But is there a positive benefit of ratification? One popular argument is that it positions the United Kingdom as a 'leading standards-setter', sending a strong signal about how seriously the United Kingdom takes its international legal obligations, and that it is particularly significant since the Hague Convention is the last major humanitarian law treaty that the United Kingdom is not party to.[107] However, as one member of the select committee noted,[108] it is rather a stretch to see the United Kingdom as a standards-setter when it will now be the last permanent member of the Security Council to ratify and when it will do so 50 years after such

---

[105] Note that this is not quite the same as 'special protection' under arts 8–11 of the convention (now practically obsolete following the 'enhanced protection' scheme in the second protocol). Under art 12 a piece of cultural property that is not normally covered by special protection may acquire that protection when it is being transported.

[106] See the State Immunity Act 1978.

[107] See the witness evidence recorded in the 2008 CMS Committee Report, Ev 26–27.

[108] *ibid*, Ev 27 (Alan Keen MP).

diversely-resourced countries as France, Romania and the Democratic Republic of Congo. Despite this, it is possible that ratification will provide the United Kingdom with more credibility, thus enhancing its negotiating position with respect to other international humanitarian law instruments in the future.

A senior policy officer at English Heritage made the more subtle argument that ratification and implementation will have the indirect effect of improving public awareness of the need to safeguard important items.[109] This would indeed be a beneficial consequence, but is arguably not important or examinable enough to carry much weight—especially since the government does not envisage a huge change in the current practices of museums, libraries and art galleries. Ratification does reflect the government's commitment to preventing the United Kingdom remaining a popular destination country for illegally obtained and traded items of cultural property, particularly as links between such activities and organised crime and terrorism continue to emerge.

As a practical matter, ratification will bring the obligations of the United Kingdom in line with coalition partners, many of whom are parties to the convention and the two protocols. This may facilitate better co-ordination and co-operation on cultural property matters. It also reinforces the need to include sessions concerning the sensitivity of cultural property in the training of the military and the importance of considering cultural property at all stages in planning and conducting military operations. However, as noted above, the United Kingdom has, to a large extent, already been doing this.

A stronger point in favour of ratification was made by Brigadier Messenger, the Ministry of Defence's Director of Joint Commitments (Military). He argued that respecting cultural property was in fact militarily sensible, given the effect that such respect had on issues of consent.[110] Working in co-operation with local authorities to protect and to recover valuable items may develop a relationship of trust and confidence between the military and local actors, which should have beneficial effects on other areas of co-operation. Professor Stone, a professor of heritage studies, agreed and also noted that the trade in antiquities currently appeared to be funding the Iraqi insurgency.[111] Ratification should lead to greater efforts

---

[109] *ibid*, Ev 26.

[110] *ibid*, Ev 12.

[111] *ibid*, Ev 6. Individuals with strong links to the US Military have admitted publicly that income from the unlawful export of stolen Iraqi antiquities has been used to fund insurgents see E Becatoros, 'Artifact Smuggling Aids Iraq Insurgents', *The Seattle Times*, 19 March 2008. The author quotes Marine Reserve Col Matthew Bogdanos, the US investigator who led the initial probe into the looting of the Baghdad's National Museum, as saying 'The Taliban are using opium to finance their activities in Afghanistan. Well, they don't have opium in Iraq. What they have an almost limitless supply of is antiquities. And so they're using antiquities'.

to stop this trade, and that may in turn contribute to the suppression of insurgents.

Becoming a party to the convention and the protocols will also mean that the United Kingdom is better-placed to participate fully in meetings of the state parties and therefore to contribute directly to the development of practice concerning the interpretation and implementation of the convention. Similarly, ratification will allow the United Kingdom to exert greater influence if further protocols are negotiated in the future. It might be that this is the deciding factor: given the close relationship between the convention and relevant customary international law, and taking into account the new engagement of the United States in the convention, the United Kingdom's alternative position would be very unsatisfactory. Indeed, if the United Kingdom did not ratify it would be the only permanent member of the United Nations Security Council not to be a party to the convention, and it would be in a very small minority amongst NATO and EU countries.[112]

---

[112] Iceland (NATO), and Ireland and Malta (EU), are the only countries not to have ratified the convention.

15

The Extension of Land Registration Principles to New Property Rights in Environmental Goods

PAMELA O'CONNOR[*]

I. INTRODUCTION

ENVIRONMENTAL REGULATION IS now a major impetus for the creation of new property rights and the extension of existing categories of property. Current regulatory approaches favour the use of market-based methods of managing many environmental problems. Markets need products or packages of rights that can be the subject of trade. Where the rights do not already exist, legislatures need to create them. In some cases this need results in the introduction of new property rights, which may comprise a new type of property right previously unknown to the law, the fragmentation of an existing property right into a new set of component rights, or the extension of an established category to accommodate a new object of property. The innovations are driven by a conception of property as commodity, or as a means of wealth-creation, which Alexander calls 'commodification'.[1] By extension, the term is also used to mean the processes by which property rights are created to provide commodities to be traded in markets.

In various countries, legislatures have been active in creating new private property rights in environmental resources such as fisheries, flora and fauna, flowing and stored water and even carbon. This is commonly undertaken to promote the sustainable and productive use of existing

[*] Associate Professor, Faculty of Law, Monash University, Victoria, Australia. The author acknowledges the assistance of Professors Sharon Christensen, Bill Duncan and Doug Fisher and Mr Ross Ashcroft, all of Queensland University of Technology, for their comments. The author also acknowledges that this article was written with the assistance of a grant from the Australian Research Council.
[1] GS Alexander, 'Propriety Through Commodity: Why Have Legal Environmentalists Embraced Market-Based Solutions?' in HM Jacobs (ed), *Private Property in the 21st Century: The Future of an American Ideal* (Cheltenham, Edward Elgar, 2004) 75.

resources, and to encourage investment in new resources such as forestry plantations. New property may be created in several ways for regulatory purposes. First, it may arise through fragmentation, such as where a right to the ownership of trees growing on land is carved out of the landowner's title. Secondly, new property rights are created through privatisation when natural resources that were formerly enjoyed as a commons are brought into a private property regime. Thirdly, regulatory schemes may create 'hybrid property'—transferable rights which arise as a product of administrative regulation, such as transferable permits to develop land, to pollute, to generate waste, to degrade land or to emit greenhouse gases.[2] Although the rights arise through regulatory dispensation, they may be designed to function like property rights.[3] Some regulatory schemes combine elements of hybrid property and privatisation, such as arrangements to manage water or fisheries by allocating to individuals transferable quotas to take water or catch fish.[4]

The proliferation of new property rights presents challenges for property law, which is centrally concerned with co-ordinating multiple rights in the same asset and managing the information burden that property rights place on third parties—strangers to the transaction which created the rights.[5] Since property rights are enforceable *in rem* against third parties, anyone wishing to acquire or deal with a resource incurs information costs in discovering and measuring any private property rights that may be held in the resource.[6]

Systems of land registration are used in many countries to reduce the information costs of real property, by generating publicity for rights and limiting enforcement of unpublicised rights. Legislators are beginning to think more imaginatively about adapting land registration principles to manage the transaction costs of new property. Since many commodified resources are geo-spatially related to land parcels, recording them in some way in the land title register offers a convenient method of lowering information costs. Questions then arise as to how the new property rights should be defined for purposes of recording them, how they should be recorded and with what legal effects.

---

[2] CM Rose, 'The Several Futures of Property: Of Cyberspace and Folk Tales, Emissions Trades and Ecosystems' (1998–2000) 83 *Minnesota Law Review* 129, 165. Rose attributes the term to Stewart: R Stewart, 'Privprop, Regprop and Beyond' (1990) 13 *Harvard Journal of Law & Public Policy* 91, 93.

[3] For example, Australian legislation provides for rights to take water to be to be recorded in a register, to be assignable permanently or temporarily, and to be security for a mortgage loan.

[4] Regulation by quota management is discussed below, text accompanying n 24.

[5] TW Merill and HE Smith, 'Optimal Standardization in the Law of Property: The *Numerus Clausus* Principle' (2000) 110 *Yale Law Journal* 1, 26–34.

[6] *ibid.*

This article commences, in Part II, by surveying the economic theories that are driving the international vogue for market-based methods of managing environmental resources. Part III shows how the theories have influenced regulatory practices and resulted in the creation of new property. Part IV compares legal and economic perspectives on the optimal degree of fragmentation of property rights. The potential for land registers to reduce co-ordination problems and transaction costs of new property is outlined in Part V. Part VI evaluates diverse statutory approaches used in Australia to record novel property rights in water, trees and vegetation, and carbon stored in forests. While some of these legislative approaches are flawed, they provide some pointers to a more systematic framework for recording new property rights on land title registers.

II. THE ECONOMIC THEORY DRIVING THE CREATION OF NEW PROPERTY

The interest of economists in private property as an instrument of regulation can be traced to Ronald Coase's 1960 article, 'The Problem of Social Cost'.[7] Coase was concerned with the problem that a person, in deciding whether to engage in an activity, does not take into account the resulting environmental harm to the extent that it falls upon other people. The environmental harm is said to be a 'negative externality', in the sense that it is external to the person's assessment of the costs and benefits of the activity. Economists view the existence of externalities as a major cause of pollution and other environmental harms.

Before Coase, administrative regulatory methods were used to prohibit pollution, or at least to make the polluter bear the environmental cost of his activities through taxes so that the costs would be 'internalised' or taken into account in his decision to pollute. Coase hypothesised that in an ideal world where rights were clearly defined and there were no transaction costs, the polluter and the neighbours affected by the environmental harms would bargain until they agreed on the allowable level of pollution.[8] The externality would disappear, as the polluter would have to pay to pollute, and would therefore have an incentive to take the cost of the environmental harm into account and to abate the pollution.

Coase acknowledged that in the real world, poorly defined rights and high transaction costs distort price signals and inhibit the ability of voluntary exchange to arrive at an efficient allocation of resources.[9] Since

---

[7] R Coase, 'The Problem of Social Cost' (1960) 3 *Journal of Law and Economics* 1–44: S Norton, 'Property Rights, the Environment and Economic Well-Being' in RJ Hill and RE Meiners (eds), *Who Owns the Environment?* (Lanham, Rowman & Littlefield, 1998) 37.

[8] Coase, above n 7.

[9] *ibid.*

Coase's ideal world is an abstraction that does not exist, his analysis focused the attention of economists on institutional factors which affect the level of transaction costs and impede private bargaining. One school of post-Coasean economics, the new institutional economics, emphasises the importance of clearly specified and transferable rights, and institutional reforms to reduce transactions costs (which broadly include the costs of measuring the rights, bargaining and enforcement).[10]

Coase's demonstration of the importance of transaction costs was incidental to his main purpose, which was to challenge the centralised and prescriptive methods of welfare economics and the regulatory state.[11] He sought to show those methods were much less effective than regulators believed. Faith in the ability of government to manage environmental resources in the public interest was further shaken by public choice theorists such as Stigler, who sought to show that bureaucratic regulation is systematically subverted by rent-seeking special interest groups.[12] This school held that politicians and officials who are entrusted with powers to regulate resources in the public interest are inexorably captured by vested interests which bias decision-making in their own favour.

As evidence of the failure of state ownership and central planning, the critics of welfare economics could point to environmental degradation and poor economic performance in China and former Eastern bloc countries under socialism.[13] By the end of the twentieth century, many economists were prescribing environmental regulation through mutually beneficial agreement, markets and price signals to control externalities, with corrective taxes and other measures of direct interventions playing a subsidiary role.[14]

A. The Tragedy of the Commons

A major economic justification for converting resources from common ownership to private property ('commodification') relies on the notion of the tragedy of the commons. Hardin used an externality analysis to explain why resources held in a commons tend to be degraded through over-exploitation.[15] In a commons, nobody has the right to exclude others,

---

[10] F Parisi, 'Coase Theorem and Transaction Economics in the Law' in JG Backhaus (ed), *The Elgar Companion to Law and Economics* (Cheltenham UK and Northampton MA, Edward Elgar, 2005) 7, 7–10.

[11] *ibid*, 28–9.

[12] G Stigler, 'The Theory of Economic Regulation' (1971) 3 *Bell Journal of Economics and Management Science* 3.

[13] T Bethell, *The Noblest Triumph: Property and Prosperity Through the Ages* (New York, St Martin's Press, 1998) 272–3.

[14] M Faure and G Skogh, *The Economic Analysis of Environmental Policy and Law: An Introduction* (Cheltenham UK and Northampton MA, Edward Elgar, 2003) 2.

[15] G Hardin, 'The Tragedy of the Commons' (1968) 14 *Science* 1243.

and individuals can establish private property rights in the resource only to the extent that they use or capture it. Each person who uses the commons captures the full marginal value of his or her use or taking, but bears only a proportionate share of the cost to all users represented by the degradation of the resource through over-exploitation. The environmental cost is an 'externality' which the user cannot be expected to factor into his or her decision to use the resource. Individual users lack an incentive to postpone or moderate their use, as they have no way of excluding others from taking what they leave for future use. Therefore resources held under open access regimes are exploited more intensively and are pushed inexorably to exhaustion.

While Hardin did not propose commodification of the resources as the solution to the tragedy of the commons, other economists observed that to a private owner, the environmental cost of over-use would not be an externality. The expected future stream of income from a resource is capitalised into its present market value, and experienced by the owner as a price signal.[16] Private owners would generally have an incentive to use the resource sustainably, since they bear the full economic consequences of their decisions and have the right to exclude other users.[17]

Coase's theory of social cost and Hardin's Tragedy of the Commons are both regularly cited to support the argument that scarce environmental resources are likely to be managed more productively and sustainably if transferred from open access or state ownership regimes to private ownership. Instances of private owners exploiting their resources to exhaustion are explained as a consequence of inadequately defined property rights, or special cases where the discount rate of the capital of the resource exceeded its maximum growth rate.[18]

III. THE USE OF NEW PROPERTY IN ENVIRONMENTAL REGULATION

Commodification of natural resources and the creation of new types of hybrid property are global trends with considerable momentum.[19] In 2004, Alexander observed that most environmental lawyers and policy analysts were embracing regulatory methods based on commodification and markets 'to a degree not anticipated a decade ago'.[20] The vogue for

---

[16] L De Alessi, 'Private Property Rights as the Basis for Free Market Environmentalism' in Hill and Meiners, above n 7, at 10.

[17] *ibid*, 10,12.

[18] *ibid*, 31; TW Merrill, 'Private Property and the Politics of Environmental Protection' (2005) *Harvard Journal of Law & Public Policy* 69, 69.

[19] Alexander, above n 1, at 77–81; Rose, above n 2, at 163–9.

[20] Alexander, *ibid*, 76

commodification and hybrid property can be attributed to the convergence of a number of factors. First, as shown above, developments in economic and regulatory theory since Coase show a strong preference for private or limited commons property regimes and decentralised decision-making in place of open access resource regimes and central planning. Secondly, many natural resources that were formerly open access are now at risk of degradation through over-exploitation due to population growth, more intensive harvesting methods, greater commercial competition, and climate change.[21] More resources have reached the threshold where the environmental benefits of commodification outweigh the costs of establishing new property regimes.[22] Technological change affects the cost-benefit calculation by lowering the costs of property-based regulation.[23] For example, a system of tradeable emission permits is facilitated by the development of technology that allows regulators to identify the point sources of emissions and to measure the overall level of emissions.[24]

A third reason for the trend to commodification is that it enables governments to achieve broader regulatory objectives. Markets can bring about structural readjustment of industry and agriculture at minimal political cost to governments. Resistance to the initial step of commodifying a common resource is relatively easy to overcome, as existing users normally share in the initial allocation of property rights, and may even receive a windfall. Once they hold property rights in the resources, externalities disappear as all owners must take account of opportunity costs.[25]

A. The Example of Regulating Fisheries

The application of this theory can be seen in the development of market-based methods for regulation of fisheries. Fisheries are a paradigm case of a commons that is liable to over-exploitation due to competition among users. Traditional methods of limiting the total fish catch level relied on administrative controls on access to the fish stock, such as limiting the number of boats, type of equipment or time spent fishing.[26] This method of regulation through proxy measures tends to distort industry practice and equipment purchasing decisions, without limiting the overall catch.[27]

---

[21] Rose, above n 2, at 132–5; Alexander, *ibid*, 79.
[22] Rose, *ibid*, 132, Alexander, *ibid*.
[23] Rose, *ibid*, 137, 167.
[24] *ibid*.
[25] De Alessi, above n 16, at 17, 29; Bethell, above n 13, at 284; K Guerin, *Property Rights and Environmental Policy: A New Zealand Perspective*, NZ Treasury WP 03/02 (2003) 18.
[26] Guerin, *ibid*, 21.
[27] *ibid*.

In 1986, New Zealand introduced Individual Transferable Quotas (ITQ), a market-based method of regulation that is now used in several countries. The regulator determines a total allowable catch within each fishing zone for a year, taking into account the sustainability of the stock. Each fishing operator is allocated a quota of fish which can be taken in the year. Since the quota is transferable, operators who catch less or more fish than their quota entitlement can sell or buy additional quota from other operators. Because the ITQ is a transferable capital asset, operators have a stake in the sustainability of the fishery. Guerin reports that the method is easier to police because operators help enforce the quotas.[28]

In embracing market-based regulation, New Zealand faced the problem of how to define a property right to a resource in fluctuating supply that must be managed sustainably. Initially the ITQ was expressed in volumetric terms, entitling the holder to take a specified quantity of fish, but this led to a need for government to buy back quota when the available stock was insufficient to satisfy the quotas.[29] A later version of the scheme specified ITQs as a right to a specified percentage of the stock available in a given period, as determined administratively from time to time.[30] Specifying quota in ambulatory terms places the risk of fluctuations in supply upon the holders of quota.

B. Market-Based Regulation of Water Property in Australia

New Zealand's experience with ITQs showed that a right specified as a proportionate share of a resource could be the subject-matter for market trade. A similar approach was adopted by the Australian States when they legislated for the introduction of water property titles from the mid 1990s. A statutory scheme to commodify rural water was introduced as part of a national plan to manage a critical scarcity of water in certain regions. The scheme is made applicable to a defined area by ministerial determination. In a defined area, usually a river system or rural water catchment area, water may not be taken from a waterway or lake except in accordance with a water property title, known in Victoria as a 'water share',[31] expressed as a right to draw a specified percentage of the water available in the relevant water system in a water season. The volume of water that the holder of a water share is entitled to receive in a water season is determined administratively. Water shares

---

[28] *ibid.*
[29] K Guerin, *Theory vs Reality: Making Environmental Use Rights Work in New Zealand,* NZ Treasury WP 04/06 (2004) 8.
[30] *ibid.*
[31] As the legislative terminology varies between States, the term 'water share' is used in this article as a generic term.

can be transferred permanently or temporarily, and can be mortgaged. The holder of a water share can sell his or her seasonal water allocation, subject to Ministerial approval. All transactions involving water shares must be recorded in a register kept separately from the land register. Water titles are hybrid property that has been legislatively designed to function in much the same way as conventional property rights in land, while remaining subject to a significant degree of administrative control over allocations and transfers.

The purpose of commodifying rural water is to facilitate the development of a market for water property, which is expected to redirect the limited supply of water to more productive uses.[32] It is assumed that the opportunity cost of water will tend to persuade less efficient users that they will be better off selling or leasing their water share than using the water to irrigate their crops. These structural adjustments will occur through the decentralised decisions of individual users responding to impersonal market signals, without the need for governments to make invidious choices between competing claims upon the water supply.

IV. DETERMINING THE OPTIMAL DEGREE OF FRAGMENTATION OF PROPERTY RIGHTS

When market-based approaches to environmental regulation were first mooted, some environmentalists took strong objection to the idea that natural resources might be better conserved and managed in private hands.[33] This paradoxical proposition is now more widely accepted. Alexander finds that most of the recent critiques are internal to commodification theory rather than a challenge to its premises.[34] Current debates focus on the scope and implementation of market-based regulatory methods.

A major issue is determining what use rights should be allocated in particular types of resources. Some environmentalists are concerned that commodification of natural resources is too partial, selective and incomplete to protect all the interdependent environmental services of a holistic ecosystem.[35] Rochford provides an example from Victoria, where the legislation to commodify the water in lakes and watercourses originally left unchanged the common law rule that landowners were entitled to capture, store and use rainwater and surface run-off that flows across their land in no defined

---

[32] Australia, Productivity Commission, 'Rural Water Use and the Environment: The Role of Market Mechanism' (Canberra, 2006) xxii, 45.

[33] Rose, above n 2, at 169; Alexander, above n 1, at 87.

[34] Alexander, above n 1, at 85–8.

[35] *ibid*, 86; Rose observes that the argument that property is too partial is an argument for more property rather than more 'command and control' regulation: Rose, above n 2, at 175.

channel.[36] A subsequent water audit found that diversion of surface water run-off that would otherwise have reached waterways had caused a decline in the environmental health of rivers and a reduction in the volume of water available for users.[37] The commodification of only part of the total water in the catchment area had created an incentive for landowners to divert water, which frustrated the regulatory objective.

Economists and regulators too are concerned about the unintended effects arising from partial or incomplete commodification. De Alessi cautions that the absence of some private property rights may distort price signals and give rise to externalities, with possible adverse consequences for the environment.[38] Since new property rights are costly, they tend to be established only when growing scarcity or new technology renders it cost-effective to do so.[39] Therefore at any given time, the property rights in a resource are likely to be incomplete or, in economic parlance, 'inadequately specified'.[40]

A. Economic Perspectives on Optimal Specification of Property Rights

Modern economics follows Coase in regarding property as a bundle of use rights that can be combined or partitioned in various ways.[41] From this perspective, the key question is how to determine the optimal division of property rights in a resource to promote environmental quality.[42] Hill and Meiners have called for more empirical research to guide decisions regarding the degree of property rights specification, the form of the property rights and to whom they should initially be allocated.[43]

Economic theory recognises that beyond a certain point, fragmentation of property rights will not necessarily maximise economic value. If too many people hold property rights in a given resource, the transaction costs of

---

[36] F Rochford, '"Private" Rights to Water in Victoria: Farm Dams and the Murray Darling Basin Commission Cap on Diversions' (2004) *Australasian Journal of Natural Resources Law and Policy* 229.

[37] *ibid*, 236, citing Murray-Darling Basin Ministerial Council, *An Audit of Water Use in the Murray-Darling Basin* (June 1995).

[38] De Alessi, above n 16, at 1; Norton, above n 7, at 38–40.

[39] H Demsetz, 'Towards a Theory of Property Rights' (1969) 59 *American Economic Review* 347, 350; C Veljanovski, *Economic Principles of Law* (Cambridge, Cambridge University Press, 2007) 61, 69–70.

[40] Merrill, 'Private Property', above n 18, at 68; Productivity Commission, above n 32, at xxxv.

[41] Merrill and Smith show that this 'bundle of rights' conception has gained considerable support among post-Coasean economists and scholars of law and economics, eclipsing the traditional conception of property as rights in rem: TW Merrill and HE Smith, 'The Property/Contract Interface' (2001) *Columbia Law Review* 77, 357.

[42] PJ Hill and RE Meiners in Hill and Meiners (eds), above n 7, at xi.

[43] *ibid*.

collecting their consents to a proposed use will overwhelm the benefits. The likely result is that the resource will be under-utilised or wasted. Heller popularised the use of the term 'anti-commons' to describe the problem arising from too many people having rights of exclusion, since it is the mirror opposite of Hardin's tragedy of the commons in which resources are over-exploited because nobody has rights of exclusion.[44]

A related concern is that commodification and division of property rights are difficult and costly to reverse if they fail to achieve their purpose.[45] Alexander sees the process as 'a one-way ratchet from non-commodity to commodity'.[46] Parisi and Depoorter agree that property division is subject to a law of unidirectional inertia.[47] Reuniting fragmented property rights presents higher transactions costs than the original partitioning, due to co-ordination problems, hold-outs and other strategic behaviour by rights-holders who find themselves in the position of a bilateral monopoly.[48]

B. Legal Perspectives on Optimal Specification of Property Rights

Starting from the legal realist conception of property as a bundle of specific use rights, economists assume that rights to resources are or should be freely customisable.[49] Lawyers know that while parties can create whatever rights they wish by agreement and enforce them against each other, the law will not enforce the rights against successors in title and other third parties unless they conform to an established category of property.[50] Legislatures can of course create new property rights, but private parties cannot do so through private ordering. Rudden finds that although common law systems have no explicit doctrine corresponding to the civil law's *numerus clausus* (closed list), the basic categories of property rights recognised by

---

[44] MA Heller, 'The Tragedy of the Anti-Commons: Property in the Transition from Marx to Markets' (1998) 11 *Harvard Law Review* 621.

[45] B Ziff, 'The Irreversibility of Commodification' (2005) 16 *Stellenbosch Law Review* 283, 283.

[46] Alexander, above n 1, at 80.

[47] F Parisi and B Depoorter, 'Commons and Anticommons' in JG Backhaus, above n 10, at 77.

[48] *ibid*, 77; J Stake, 'Decomposition of Property Rights' in B Bouckaert and G De Geest (eds), *Encyclopedia of Law and Economics* (Cheltenham UK, Edward Elgar, 2000) 42–3. A bilateral monopoly means that there is only one buyer and one seller.

[49] Veljanovki, above n 39, at 65; TW Merrill and HE Smith, 'What Happened to Property in Law and Economics?' (2001) 111 *Yale Law Journal* 357, 373, 385; De Alessi, above n 16, at 12. The 'bundle of rights' metaphor can be traced to Hohfeld, who used it descriptively or analytically, but is often used by economists in a normative sense: S Bright, 'Of Estates and Interests: A Tale of Ownership and Property Rights' in S Bright and J Dewar (eds), *Land Law: Themes and Perspectives* (Oxford, Oxford University Press, 1998) 529, 533.

[50] B Rudden, 'Economic Theory v Property Law: The *Numerus Clausus* Problem' in J Eekelaar and J Bell (eds), *Oxford Essays in Jurisprudence: Third Series* (Oxford, Clarendon Press, 1987) 239, 241.

the judiciary in both systems are confined to a catalogue of about a dozen standard types, and new rights are admitted only rarely.[51]

The idea of property as a bundle of rights that can be freely customised conflicts with the closed list principle, but is normative for economists because it accords with their faith in the power of markets, free alienability and private ordering to maximise aggregate welfare.[52] This raises the questions whether the closed list principle serves any useful purpose, and whether it should continue to constrain the recognition of new property rights. The most persuasive functional explanation for the principle is that by standardising property rights, it limits the transaction costs that property rights impose upon third parties as an externality.[53] Since property rights are enforceable as rights *in rem*,[54] third parties must search for the rights and measure them in order to verify ownership before acquiring them, or to avoid trespassing upon them.[55] Haansman and Kraakman observe that verification helps to co-ordinate rights by avoiding mistakes that might otherwise lead to conflicts of rights, and reduces enforcement costs.[56]

Merrill and Smith emphasise the role of the closed list principle in limiting the measurement component of transaction costs. Transactions costs are of three kinds: information costs, bargaining costs and enforcement costs. Information costs include the costs of searching for existing property rights (search costs) and ascertaining the validity and extent of the rights (measurement costs).[57] According to Merrill and Smith, the closed list principle limits the measurement costs of third parties by ensuring that property rights come in a limited range of highly-standardised packages.[58]

---

[51] Rudden, *ibid*, 241–4; Merrill and Smith, 'Optimal Standardization', above n 5, at 3–4, 10–16.

[52] Stake says that the economic rationale for fragmentation is synergy—the sum of the parts can be worth more than the whole: Stake, above n 48, at 4.

[53] Merrill and Smith, 'Optimal Standardisation', above n 5, at 26–34; Rudden, above n 50, at 253–61, discusses several possible explanations but finds no clear functional justification for the principle. Haansman and Kraakman argue that the common law does not limit the categories of property, but limits enforcement of non-standard rights without notice: Henry Hansmann and Reinier Kraakman, 'Property, Contract and Verification: The Numerus Clausus Problem and the Divisibility of Rights' (2002) 11 *Journal of Legal Studies* 373.

[54] Merill and Smith, 'What Happened to Property in Law and Economics?', above n 49, at 385.

[55] Merrill and Smith, 'Optimal Standardization', above n 5, at 8, 26–27. Haansman and Kraakman argue that standardisation of the categories of rights does not help third parties to avoid trespass: above n 53, at 374.

[56] Haansman and Kraakman, above n 53, at 382–3.

[57] Merrill and Smith, 'Optimal Standardization', above n 5, at 26–7, 69; Merill and Smith, 'What Happened to Property in Law and Economics?', above n 49, at 385–8.

[58] Merrill and Smith, 'Optimal Standardization', above n 5, at 26–34; .see also Merrill and Smith, 'The Property/Contract Interface', above n 41, at 793–802. The problem of measurement cost is distinct from the anti-commons problem, where the productive potential of an asset may be sterilised by transaction costs because too many rights-holders have power of exclusion. Obtaining the consents is costly, even if all the rights are identical and measurement costs are minimal.

Merrill and Smith argue that there is an inherent trade-off between the 'frustration cost' of limiting the categories of property and the measurement costs associated with extending the categories; and an optimal point of balance at which efficiency is maximised.[59] If other methods can be used to reduce information costs, the optimal point of balance shifts towards accommodating a greater number of property rights.[60] One method is to provide a system of instrument recording (or 'recordation', as it is called in the United States). Merrill and Smith hypothesise that the US recording statutes lower information costs by giving notice of rights, and that this shifts the optimal point in favour of allowing more property rights.[61] The shift can be enhanced by use of digital technology to further reduce the costs of providing information about rights.[62]

V. THE ROLE OF REGISTERS IN LIMITING INFORMATION COSTS

It has long been recognised that providing notice or publicity for property rights reduces information cost externalities,[63] as shown by the refusal of courts to enforce equities against bona fide purchasers who take without notice. Land registration systems reduce third-party information costs by providing a means of publicity for property rights. By altering the priority rules in favour of recorded interests, the systems also give rights-holders an incentive to obtain publicity for their interests by recording or registering them.[64] The priority rule varies, but typically prevents or restricts the enforcement of unrecorded interests against holders of recorded interests.[65] Recorded interests usually rank for priority by the date order of registration rather than by the date of the instrument or transaction.[66]

Land registration systems may take the form of interest recording systems (also known as registration of deeds), or systems of registered title.[67] While

---

[59] Merrill and Smith, 'Optimal Standardization', above n 5, at 38–40 and graph in fig 2, p 39.

[60] *ibid*, 40–42.

[61] *ibid*, 41–2 and fig 3.

[62] *ibid*, 42.

[63] B Arruñada, 'Property Enforcement as Organised Consent' (2003) 19 *Journal of Law, Economics and Organization* 401, 411.

[64] *ibid*, 414; P O'Connor, 'Information, Automation and the Conclusive Land Register' in D Grinlinton (ed), *Torrens in the Twenty-first Century* (Wellington, LexisNexis, 2003) 249, 254–6.

[65] Although the benefit is reduced to the extent that the law continues to enforce unrecorded rights. For discussion of the different types of priority rules found in recording systems, see O'Connor, *ibid*.

[66] Arruñada, above n 63, at 414.

[67] In England and Wales, which had no deeds register outside a few counties, the term 'land registration' is equated with a system of registered title.

both systems use similar methods to limit search costs by providing publicity for rights, they differ in their approach to measurement costs. Recording systems require that deeds and conveyances, or a memorial of them, be placed on the public record, but the record is merely evidentiary. Enquirers bear the measurements costs of ascertaining the nature, extent, validity and currency of the interest which a deed purports to convey. Title registration statutes reduce measurement costs more effectively by providing an authoritative statement of all property rights subsisting in a given parcel. The authoritative statement usually takes the form of a statutory warranty that the property rights relating to a parcel of land are as stated in the register, subject to a limited range of known exclusions and exceptions.[68]

Edgeworth argues that as title registers reduce transaction costs more efficiently than systems of deeds registration or recording, they shift the optimal point of balance between frustration costs and measurement costs more decisively towards less standardisation in property rights.[69] While this is undoubtedly correct in theory, it is submitted that title registration often leads to *more* standardisation due to the unwillingness of the state to assume the cost of new property. In order to provide authoritative title information, the state takes upon itself much of the measurement costs previously borne by purchasers. It assumes the responsibility to examine, register and warrant titles and, on first registration, to extinguish unproven claims.

In order to limit its own measurement and error costs, the state usually confines its warranty to categories of rights which are relatively standard in their incidents, and records them in simplified and standardised form. Consequently, title registration systems generally register a much narrower range of interests than deeds registration systems, which do not provide measurement services.[70] The category of registrable interests is generally confined to legal estates and interests, with the addition of second and subsequent mortgages, and excluding some lesser non-possessory interests and short-term leases. The rationale for particular inclusions and exclusions is often unstated. Some interests are, by force of statute, enforceable without being registered or recorded.

The enforcement of unregistered interests outside the registration system has masked the restrictive *numerus clausus* of title registration.[71] Equitable estates and interests are generally excluded from registration, although most systems provide a method for recording claims which either reserves

---

[68] JE Hogg, *Registration of Title to Land Throughout the Empire* (Sydney, Law Book Co, 1920) 96.

[69] B Edgeworth, 'The *Numerus Clausus* Principle in Contemporary Australian Land Law' (2006) 32 *Monash University Law Review* 387, 405–7.

[70] O'Connor, above n 64, at 259.

[71] S Cooper, 'Equity and Unregistered Land Rights in Commonwealth Registration Systems' (2003) 3 *Oxford University Commonwealth Law Journal* 201.

their priority, or entitles the claimant to be warned when a rival disposition is lodged, or has both effects.[72]

Merrill and Smith suggested that digital technology may prompt a relaxation of the common law's closed list principle, since it lowers the cost of recording rights.[73] Current indications are that this potential may not be realised, and that we may actually see more rather than less standardisation of property rights.[74] The introduction of digital technology is initiated by states, which are generally more interested in using it to reduce their own measurement and error costs than to register additional types of property rights. Under electronic conveyancing, states are moving towards allowing licensed network users to register their own instruments without expert examination by the Registry,[75] while requiring them to assume much of the measurement and error costs.[76]

VI. LAND REGISTRATION PRINCIPLES
AND NEW PROPERTY RIGHTS

Recent Australian experience with legislation for new property suggests other ways in which land registers might be used to lower the information costs associated with new property rights. The Australian States have begun to extend modified land registration principles and methods to new environmental goods in rural water, forestry plantations and 'carbon sequestration rights'.

A. Registers of Water Rights

Since water property titles are now personal property held and traded separately from land, the Australian States have established separate water

---

[72] O'Connor, above n 64, at 262–4, 266–7.

[73] Merrill and Smith, 'Optimal Standardization', above n 5, at 42–3.

[74] Once electronic conveyancing is implemented in England and Wales, it will not be possible to create an interest by formal means other than by simultaneously registering or recording it: Lord Chancellor's Dept, *Explanatory Notes to the Land Registration Act 2002* (London, HMSO, 2002) paras 67–9; Land Registration Act 2002 s 93. This may result in the disappearance of some categories of unregistered interests: E Cooke, 'E-conveyancing in England: Enthusiasms and Reluctance' in D Grinlinton (ed), above n 64, at 290–91.

[75] Cooke, *ibid*, 290.

[76] The shifting of costs and risks to licensed users may occur through business or system rules or through certification requirements. For discussion of how this operates in New Zealand, see R Thomas, 'Fraud, Risk and the Automated Register' in Grinlinton, above n 64, at 353–6, 362–6; R Muir, 'Electronic Registration: The Legislative Scheme and Implications for the Torrens System in New Zealand' in Grinlinton, above n 64, at 318–20 (discussing the New Zealand provisions).

registers, which are modelled upon land registers.[77] In Queensland, for example, any instrument or dealing which may be registered for land under the Land Title Act may be registered for a 'water allocation' (water share) on the State's water register.[78] This means that dealings such as a transfer, mortgage or lease of a water allocation may be registered.[79] An instrument or dealing is not effective to create or transfer the interest at law until it is registered.[80] None of the State water registers presently confers a statutory warranty of title upon registered interests, although New South Wales has indicated an intention to introduce indefeasibility of title (that is, a title warranty) for registered water titles, after allowing a transition period for registration of existing rights.[81] Once this occurs, water titles will be held as securely as land titles, although the volume of water to which the holder is entitled is defined in ambulatory terms.[82]

B. Registering Forestry and Carbon Rights

Forestry and carbon rights are new property rights, which have been carved out of the fee simple owner's endowment by a process of fragmentation or further specification. Since persons dealing in the land would normally expect those rights to be part of the registered owner's bundle of rights, it is necessary for the land title to show that the rights are held by another. All Australian States have legislated to create forestry and carbon rights and to record them in some way on the land title register, although no consensus has emerged as to what the mode of recording or registration should be.[83]

---

[77] The States and Territories have agreed to develop compatible water registers: National Water Commission, *Compatability of Water Registers: A Report Prepared by the NWC Working Group on Compatible Registers* (2005) 59. Since the provisions and terminology are far from uniform among the States, this discussion provides only a general overview.

[78] Water Act 2000 (Qld) s 150(1). This is subject to some exceptions in s 151(1). Note that the Queensland Act uses the term 'water allocation' to mean water share, and 'seasonal assignment' to mean seasonal allocation.

[79] S Schoen, 'Taking a Security Over Water Allocations: Implications of the Water Act 2000 (Qld) for Financiers' (2003) 14 *Journal of Banking Law and Finance* 194, 195.

[80] Water Act 2000 (Qld) s 150(5). This leaves open the possibility that the transaction may be effective at equity, on the basis of equitable enforcement of a specifically enforceable contract for the creation of an interest: Schoen, *ibid*. The New South Wales provision excludes this possibility by providing that a dealing has no effect until recorded: Water Management Act 2000 (NSW) ss 71B, 71D, 77IL(1).

[81] G Ryan, 'Water Licences and Land Come Adrift' (2004) 42 *Law Institute Journal* 55, 57. The National Water Initiative, to which all States have agreed, requires that water access rights should be mortgageable and that mortgages have similar status as in freehold land: National Water Commission, above n 77, at 14.

[82] The States have various frameworks for specifying water rights with varying degrees of security of supply and compensation,

[83] Note that the terms 'recording' and 'registration' cannot be distinguished semantically: AJ Garro, *The Louisiana Public Records Doctrine and the Civil Law Tradition* (Baton Rouge L?, Paul M Herbert Law Centre Publications, 1989) 76, fn 6.

Two modes of recording the rights can be observed in the State statutes. The first mode is that the rights are 'substantively' registered with warranty of title,[84] by forcing them into the closest available category of registrable interest, the profit à prendre. The second approach is to provide for the rights to be recorded on the land title in a way which does not attract a title warranty, but which makes them enforceable to some extent against successors in title to the registered owner. This is a form of interest recording.

Since forest property and carbon rights are novel, some explanation of their nature and purpose is required. In the 1980s, the Australian States wished to encourage forestry to promote environmental benefits.[85] To enable capital formation for forestry plantations, it was envisaged that landowners would enter into agreements with forestry companies or state forestry authorities to plant, maintain and harvest a plantation on their land. Such an agreement did not give rise to a profit à prendre at common law, since the subject-matter required for a profit is confined to things taken out of the soil and the natural produce of the land (*fructus naturales*) and does not extend to a right to tend or grow crops and plantations (*fructus industriales*).[86] It was left to legislation to accommodate the new right.[87]

Since 1998, the Australian States decided to create a further derivative of forest property, namely the 'carbon sequestration right' or 'carbon right'.[88] There are different views as to what a carbon right is, and this diversity is seen in the statutory definitions. On one view it is a type of hybrid property—the right to claim credit under an emissions trading scheme for the carbon (dioxide) absorbed and stored from the atmosphere by forests.[89] Other statutory definitions appear to conceptualise it as a physical commodity, such as a right to the carbon stored in forest vegetation,[90] or an

---

[84] Since the Land Registration Act 2002 s 132(1) provides that 'registered' means 'entered in the register', the term 'substantively registered' is to distinguish the effect of registered dispositions under Pt 3 from the effect of the entry of a notice or restriction under Pt 4.

[85] Senate Rural and Regional Affairs and Transport References Committee Australian Parliament, *Australian Forest Plantations: A Review of Plantations for Australia—the 2020 Vision* (2004) para 1.45.

[86] *Permanent Trustee Australia Ltd v Shand* (1992) 27 NSWLR 426, 331 (Young J in Eq): *Clos Farming Estates Pty Ltd v Easton* (2002) 11 BPR 20, 605; [2002] NSWCA 389, [51]–[62] (Santow JA, Mason P and Beazley JA agreeing); *Race v Ward & Ors* (1855) 4 El & Bl 702; 119 ER 259, 709 (Campbell CJ).

[87] Edgeworth argues that there is no sound policy justification for the courts' refusal to extend the category of the profit à prendre to include rights to tend crops and forests: Edgeworth, 'The *Numerus Clausus Principle*', above n 69, at 415–17.

[88] Both terms are found in the State statutes establishing the right.

[89] This understanding is incorporated into the definitions of 'carbon sequestration right' in Forestry Rights Act 1996 (Vic) s 3; Conveyancing Act 1919 (NSW) s 87A; and Forestry Rights Registration Act 1990 (Tas) ss 3, 5(4).

[90] Forestry Act 1959 (Qld) Sch 3 defines a 'natural resource product' to include carbon stored in or sequestered by a tree or vegetation. Forests store carbon in trees, soil (through

attribute of growing plants, namely, 'the capacity of forest vegetation to absorb carbon from the atmosphere'.[91]

The enactment of carbon rights legislation was prompted by the desire of the Australian States to position themselves as potential suppliers in the emerging international market for carbon credits in forestry. It was anticipated that some greenhouse gas mitigation programmes would allow investments in forestry carbon sinks to earn transferable credits to be offset against emissions of greenhouse gases for purposes of determining the level of emissions permitted.[92] Since the market regards carbon credits as a different investment product to timber harvesting and other forestry rights, it was necessary to provide for the carbon rights to be assignable separately from the tree rights and other 'forest property'.[93]

(i) Extension of a Category of Registrable Interest

All Australian States legislated to provide for new rights with respect to trees and their products ('forest property') to be recorded on title in some way. Queensland, New South Wales and Tasmania, each of which allows profits à prendre to be substantively registered under its general registration statute, accommodated forest property rights by deeming them to be a profit à prendre.[94] The statutes extended the category of a profit to encompass a right ('tree profit')[95] granted to a person to plant and maintain, as well as to harvest, trees on another's land and to carry out works on the land for that purpose, thereby extending the profit to *fructus industriales* as well as *fructus naturales*.[96]

Some of the statutes allow the owner of land to grant to another person the ownership of trees growing on the land ('tree rights').[97] Since growing

---

root abscission), floor litter and understorey vegetation: J Bredhauer, 'Tree Clearing in Queensland—A Cost-Benefit Analysis of Carbon Sequestration' (2000) 17 *EPLJ* 383, 384.

[91] Forest Property Act 2000 (SA) s 3A(1). Surprisingly, the definition classes this attribute of growing plants as a 'chose in action'. The Carbon Rights Act 2003 (WA) s 6 defines a carbon right as a 'hereditament and an encumbrance' and as a separate interest in the affected land.

[92] Art 3.3 of the Kyoto Protocol authorises carbon sinks planted since 1990 as a way to meet targets for reduction in greenhouse gas emissions: Bredhauer, above n 90. Much of the detail of the allowances for carbon credits is yet to be worked out: N Durrant, 'Emissions Trading, Offsets and Other Mitigation Options for the Australian Coal Industry' (2007) *Environment & Planning Law Journal* 361, 367.

[93] The Queensland Minister's second reading speech said that international investors were awaiting the introduction of just such a legislative scheme providing ownership of transferable carbon rights: Qld LA, *Hansard*, 19 June 2001, 1536–7.

[94] Conveyancing Act 1919 (NSW) ss 87A, 88AB; Forestry Act 1959 (Qld) s 61J(3), (5); Forestry Rights Registration Act 1990 (Tas) s 5(1).

[95] The term is my own. The States are not consistent in their terminology, and some generic terms are used here to aid clarity.

[96] See provisions cited above n 94.

[97] Conveyancing Act 1919 (NSW) ss 887A, 88AB; Forestry Rights Registration Act 1990 (Tas) s 3; Forestry Act 1959 (Qld) s 61J(3)(a), (5). The term 'tree rights' is my own, used generically because of the variety of terminology used in the State legislation.

trees are a corporeal hereditament,[98] it would seem to follow that the grant of the tree rights would create an interest in the land. The Tasmanian and Queensland Acts deem the tree rights to be a profit à prendre,[99] although the Queensland Act inconsistently states that the vesting of the tree rights does not create an interest in land.[100] The Queensland provisions do some violence to the conventional understanding of a profit as an interest in the servient land rather than an interest in the things that may be taken off the land.[101]

When carbon rights were later separated out from forest property, Queensland Tasmania and New South Wales were drawn into a further incremental extension of the category of a profit to include a carbon right.[102] This presented a conceptual challenge particularly for New South Wales, the only State which defined the carbon right in terms of hybrid property rather than real property.[103] The New South Wales Act strives to reconcile its definition of the carbon right with the concept of a profit. It equates the 'profit' with the commercial benefit of the carbon, and the right to take something from the land is deemed to be the right to the benefit conferred by the right.[104]

The Australian statutes show that the extension of land registration to new property by strained analogies with an existing category of registrable interest can lead to incoherence of the category and confusion as to the scope of the analogy.

(ii) Interest Recording by Analogy with Another Category of Right

Profits à prendre are not registrable in the other States,[105] and there is no other existing category of registrable interest that could accommodate forestry

---

[98]   P Butt, 'Carbon Sequestration Rights: A New Interest in Land?' (1999) 73 *Australian Law Journal* 235, 235.

[99]   Forestry Rights Registration Act 1990 (Tas) ss 3, 5(1), (2); Forestry Act 1959 (Qld) s 61J(3)(a), (5) and sch 3.

[100]   Forestry Act 1959 (Qld) s 61J(3)(a), (4) and sch 3.

[101]   *R v Toohey: ex parte Meneling Station Pty Ltd* (1982) 158 CLR 327, 352 (Wilson J stated that a profit is an incorporeal hereditament in the servient land). New South Wales does not extend the category of profit to encompass tree rights. The Conveyancing Act 1919 s 3 excludes from the definition of a 'forestry right' a covenant providing for the ownership of trees to vest in the owner of a forestry right. Provision is made for tree rights to be granted to the holder of a tree profit under an incidental covenant which may be recorded on title: ss 87, 88EA.

[102]   Conveyancing Act 1919 (NSW) ss 87A, 88 AB; Forestry Rights Registration Act 1990 (Tas) s 3; Forestry Act 1959 (Qld) s 61J and sch 3.

[103]   See text accompanying n 89, above.

[104]   Conveyancing Act 1919 (NSW) s 88AB(2).

[105]   A Bradbrook, SV McCallum and AP Moore, *Australian Real Property Law*, 4th edn (Sydney, Lawbook Co, 2007) 780.

rights. Rather than create a new category of registrable interest, other States have chosen to protect forest property rights in another way.

In Victoria and some other States, restrictive covenants cannot be registered with a warranty of title, but may be recorded on title in such a way that they are enforceable against successive registered owners of the burdened land, to the extent that they are valid and effective under the ordinary rules of unregistered conveyancing.[106] It is not generally recognised that this is a provision for a form of interest recording within the title registration system.[107] Victoria's Forest Property Act 1996 extends the same mode of recording to agreements that grant forest property rights.[108] The Act provides that a landowner may enter into a written agreement with another person, called the 'forest property owner', to vest ownership of the tree rights and carbon sequestration rights in the forest property owner, and to grant him or her the right to plant, maintain and harvest forest property on the land and to have access to the land for the purposes of those activities.[109]

Notwithstanding that the rights granted under a forest property agreement are deemed *not* to be an interest in land,[110] the agreement may be 'registered' or 'recorded' on the title to the land.[111] Upon registration, the burden of any covenant in the agreement runs with the land and is enforceable against any successor in title to the covenanting landowner as if it were a restrictive covenant, even if the covenants are positive in nature, and whether or not they are for the benefit of any land of the forest property owner.[112] The forest property owner's rights are assignable and are enforceable by an assignee against the covenantor and his or her successors in title.[113]

As with the profit analogy used in the Queensland, Tasmanian and New South Wales legislation, Victoria's device of legislating by analogy with the restrictive covenant is confusing and strained. The Act has modified

---

[106] Transfer of Land Act 1958 (Vic) ss 88(1), (3) and 42(1). Statutory easements, charges and rights can also be recorded in the same way: s 88(2). Similar modes of recording covenants are found in some other States: Conveyancing Act 1919 (NSW) ss 88, 88EA; Land Titles Act 1980 (Tas) s 102; Transfer of Land Act 1893 (WA) s 129A.

[107] Although Whalan points out that this is a form of deeds registration: DJ Whalan, *The Torrens System in Australia* (Sydney, Law Book Co, 1982) 97.

[108] See also Conveyancing Act 1919 (NSW) ss 77, 88EA, which allow for recording and enforcement of certain covenants incidental to 'forestry rights', including the vesting of tree rights in the owner of the tree profit.

[109] Forestry Rights Act 1996 (Vic) ss 5, 6. The wording indicates that the rights can only be granted as a package, the only choice being whether to confer the right to plant: Butt, above n 98, at 235. In other States the rights can be granted severally or in combination.

[110] Forestry Rights Act 1996 (Vic) s 11(b).

[111] Note that the Act uses both terms, apparently interchangeably, to refer to the same process: Forestry Rights Act 1996 (Vic) ss 8, 9.

[112] Forestry Rights Act 1996 (Vic) s 9.

[113] This is the combined effect of Forestry Rights Act 1996 (Vic) s 9(b) (forest property owner may enforce the right) and the s 3(1)(b) definition of 'forest property owner', which includes an assignee of the right.

some requirements for a restrictive covenant that would otherwise apply, but leaves unanswered other questions about the scope of the analogy, such as whether the equitable rules on extinguishment of restrictive covenants apply in the same way to a covenant in a registered forest property agreement.[114]

(iii) Interest Recording as a Sui Generis Category

Unlike Victoria, South Australia does not have interest recording for restrictive covenants. The South Australian legislature appears to have had difficulty in integrating the special statutory regime of forestry rights with the general registration statute, and has resorted to some confusing analogies. The Forest Property Act 2000 (SA) provides that forest property agreements may be 'registered' in the form of a declaration of trust (notwithstanding that declarations of trust are otherwise 'deposited', not registered).[115] While registration laws apply to a carbon right agreement as if it were a profit à prendre, this is expressed to be 'subject to this Part'.[116] Reliance on the analogy with the profit is residual, as the Part itself specifies the scope and incidents, creation, variation, termination, recording, enforcement and transfer of the carbon right. Although the agreement is registered on the land title under the State's title registration statute,[117] the legal effect of the registered agreement is as provided by the Forest Property Act.

The Act establishes a special registration regime with its own mode of registration and priority rules.[118] Upon registration, the agreement is deemed to be binding and enforceable by and against successors in title to the original parties in accordance with the priorities set out in the Act, which even specifies the priority of the transferee under an unregistered agreement.[119] There is no statutory warranty of title.

The South Australian Act represents an attempt to create an interest recording rule by special legislation rather than by amendment to the general registration statute. This has led to difficulties in specifying how the recording was to be made, and in limiting the normal operation of the registration statute. Many of the complexities and anomalies in the South

---

[114] The Law Commission's proposed new legislative scheme of 'Land Obligations' would not overcome the difficulties presented by the legislative intention to create an obligation which need not be appurtenant to land and which is deemed not to be an interest in land. See Law Comm, CP No 186, *Easements, Covenants and Profits à Prendre* (2008), see esp paras 8.63–8.65.

[115] Forest Property Act 2000 (SA) s 7(1), (4).

[116] Forest Property Act 2000 (SA) s 12.

[117] Registration under the Real Property Act 1886 (SA) is authorised by the Forest Property Act 2000 (SA) s 7(4).

[118] Forest Property Act 2000 (SA) ss 7–9. Note that under s 7(4), when an agreement is registered under the Act, the effect of the agreement or dealing is 'as specified in this Act'.

[119] Forest Property Act 2000 (SA) s 9.

Australian Act could have been avoided if provision were made in the general registration statute for a mode of recording a property right with the desired legal effects.[120]

It would be preferable for the State's general registration statute to incorporate provision for a system of interest recording that could then be made applicable to new property rights by other legislation. The centralisation of provisions for interest recording would also promote standardisation. To create special statutory regimes of interest recording each time a statute creates a new property right could lead to variations which increase information costs for third parties.[121]

VII. CONCLUSION

We can expect to see more new property created through commodification of natural resources and transferable permits. Economists and regulators are increasingly persuaded that private property and market-based regulatory methods are effective in promoting the sustainable and productive use of resources at minimal political and financial cost to governments. These methods will play an important role in co-ordinating the international response to climate change, since markets transcend the jurisdictional limits of the regulatory state.

Economists generally subscribe to the conception of property as a bundle of rights that can, and in some cases should, be divided in different ways in order to maximise the economic use value of the resource. Legal perspectives on fragmentation of property are more cautious, as new categories of private rights entail information costs and co-ordination problems which fall to be managed by property law. An example of the differing legal and economic perspectives is presented by the Australian initiative in first severing tree rights and other forest property rights from the fee simple ownership of land, and then further fragmenting them into carbon rights and other forest property rights. The second layer of fragmentation, while optimal from an economic point of view, increases the complexity of the co-ordination and information problem.

Land title registration systems reduce the transaction costs of property by providing publicity for interests, authoritative title information and clear priority rules to co-ordinate competing rights. Since the provision of title warranties involves a transfer of measurement and error costs from

---

[120] New South Wales is the only State in which the forest property provisions are an amendment to the general registration statute rather than the subject of a separate Act.

[121] Merrill and Smith, 'Optimal Standardization', above n 5, at 44–5, observing that non-standard rights are costly to process.

purchasers to the state, most systems of land title registration adopt a strict *numerus clausus* of registrable interests. While the introduction of digital technology into land registries offers the capacity to extend the categories of registrable interests, it seems that states have little interest in providing title warranties for additional classes of interests.

New property rights that are severed from land may be accommodated in land registers by deeming them to conform to an existing category of registrable interests, but this method can become strained if the analogy is weak or over-extended. For example, deeming tree profits to be profits à prendre merely relaxed the distinction between *fructus naturales* and *fructus industriales*, but the concept of the profit lost coherence when first, tree rights and subsequently, carbon rights were forced into the same category.

A method that offers potential for accommodating new property rights is the use of title registers for interest recording. This is a method of publicly recording an interest in a non-authoritative way that reserves its priority but does not affirm or validate or guarantee the right. Most systems of title registration presently incorporate a subsidiary form of interest recording, although it is not often recognised as such.[122] For example, some Australian States allow restrictive covenants to be recorded or 'notified' on a land register with priority effects, but without a warranty of title.[123] Victoria has extended this limited existing form of interest recording by providing that agreements that create forest property rights and carbon rights may be recorded on the land register in a similar way, and with similar effects, to a restrictive covenant.[124]

Interest recording is an attractive option to a state that wishes to limit the information costs of new property rights without taking upon itself the measurement and error costs of registering them with a title warranty. The measurement costs reside with purchasers, who need to inspect the recorded agreement to measure the rights, but can at least discover the rights more cheaply if the documents are retained by the registry.[125] More variable and idiosyncratic rights may be better suited to recording by this method, since an evidentiary system of interest recording demands less standardisation than an authoritative system of title registration.

Some will deplore interest recording as a backward step that detracts from the security of property rights in registered land. There is much to be said for the view that new property rights derived from the fee simple title

[122] O'Connor, above n 64, at 260, fn 64. An example is the provision in Land Registration Act 2002, Pt 4 for entry in the register of notices and restrictions: *ibid*, 267–75.

[123] See, eg, Transfer of Land Act 1958 (Vic) s 88; Conveyancing Act 1919 (NSW) s 88(3); Land Titles Act 1980 (Tas) s 102(3); Transfer of Land Act 1893 (WA) s 129A.

[124] Foresty Rights Act 1996 (Vic) ss 8, 9; see also Conveyancing Act 1919 (NSW) ss 87A, 88B (recording of forestry covenants).

[125] See, eg, Forestry Rights Act 1996 (Vic) s 8(2).

should be registered on the land title by expanding the class of registrable interests. But if states prove unwilling to take on the measurement costs of new property, it is preferable that the recording of new property on land registers be accommodated in a systematic way, avoiding the ad hoc and inconsistent approaches seen in some of the Australian legislation for forest property and carbon rights.

V

The Nature of Property Rights

The Role of Expectation in the Determination of Proprietary Estoppel Remedies

JOHN MEE[*]

I. INTRODUCTION

THE DECISION OF the Court of Appeal in *Jennings v Rice*[1] signalled an important shift in the approach of the English courts to the role of expectation in the determination of proprietary estoppel remedies. The implications of this case have yet to be fully worked through and the position has been further clouded by the speech of Lord Scott in *Yeoman's Row Management Ltd v Cobbe*,[2] where his Lordship made certain assumptions about the remedial question without referring to *Jennings v Rice* or other relevant Court of Appeal decisions.[3] In light of the fact that the law is arguably in a state of transition (or, perhaps, in a state of confusion), the primary focus of this chapter will be on analysing the various possible roles for expectation[4] and attempting to identify the most satisfactory approach

---

[*] J Mee, Associate Professor, Law Faculty, University College Cork. This chapter is based on papers delivered at the Modern Studies in Property Law Conference, Queens' College Cambridge, April 2008 and the Obligations IV Conference, National University of Singapore, July 2008. I am grateful for the comments I received from participants at these conferences. I also wish to thank Professor Andrew Robertson and Dr Mary Donnelly for their comments on an earlier draft of this chapter. The usual caveats apply.

[1] *Jennings v Rice* [2002] EWCA Civ 159.

[2] *Yeoman's Row Management Ltd v Cobbe* [2008] UKHL 55.

[3] Note also the more recent decision of the House of Lords in *Thorner v Major* [2009] UKHL 18. For further discussion of the impact of these cases, see text to nn 30–42 below.

[4] The concept of 'expectation' is understood in this chapter in an objective sense, to mean the expectation which the claimant has reasonably formed on the basis of the inducement or encouragement of the defendant. The term is not intended to encompass a subjective expectation of the claimant which has no reasonable relationship to any inducement or encouragement of the defendant (compare n 22 below). An alternative terminological option would be to refer to a remedy which requires the defendant to make good his representation rather than to one which fulfils the claimant's expectation. However, this terminology is not always apt, since it does not cover cases where the defendant has merely encouraged, or acquiesced in, an assumption made independently by the claimant.

as a matter of principle. The central argument of the chapter will be that the only role for expectation should be to provide a cap or upper limit on a remedy which must be determined by reference to other factors which do not include the question of expectation.

The foundation of a proprietary estoppel claim is that the claimant (C) was induced to incur detriment on the basis of an expectation created or encouraged by the defendant (D). At first sight, it seems logical to suggest that D should be able to satisfy the claim by erasing the detriment or, if this is more favourable to D, by satisfying the expectation. In either case, the foundation for C's appeal to justice is removed and D cannot be said to have acted unconscionably.[5] If the detriment exceeds the expectation, C has no grounds for complaint because D cannot be said to have acted unfairly if the expectation he has created is satisfied. Thus, on this model, the expectation would act as a cap or upper limit on the extent of a remedy based on detrimental reliance.[6]

While the 'reliance-based' remedial approach enjoys not inconsiderable academic support,[7] it has not yet found acceptance in the English case law. Judges have preferred the view that the court must determine the appropriate remedy by exercising 'a wide judgmental discretion'.[8] In *Jennings v Rice*, Robert Walker LJ explained that a range of relevant factors could be considered by the court, including misconduct on the part of C, particularly oppressive conduct by D, the need in some circumstances to ensure a clean break between the parties, changes in the benefactor's circumstances over the years, the likely effect of taxation, (to a limited extent) the other legal and moral claims on the benefactor or his estate, and 'many other factors which it may be right for the court to take into account in particular factual situations'.[9] On this discretionary approach also, it is logical that the expectation should operate as an upper limit on the remedy (because its fulfilment eliminates C's cause of complaint) and this emerges with reasonable clarity from the English case law.[10]

---

[5] Although this complex question will not be pursued in this chapter, it should be noted that there could be a case for a remedy which would be measured by D's gain, where this exceeds the level of C's detriment but does not exceed the level of the expectation.

[6] See eg S Bright and B McFarlane, 'Proprietary Estoppel and Property Rights' (2005) 64 *Cambridge Law Journal* 449, 456–8.

[7] See eg A Robertson, 'Reliance and Expectation in Estoppel Remedies' (1998) 18 *Legal Studies* 360; Spence *Protecting Reliance—The Emergent Doctrine of Equitable Estoppel* (Oxford, Hart Publishing, 1999); Bright and McFarlane, above n 6; D Jensen, 'In Defence of the Reliance Theory of Equitable Estoppel' (2001) 22 *Adelaide Law Review* 157.

[8] *Jennings v Rice* [2002] EWCA Civ 159, [51] (Robert Walker LJ).

[9] *ibid*, [52].

[10] See eg *Dodsworth v Dodsworth* (1973) 228 EG 1115 (CA) 1115 (Russell LJ); *Watson v Goldsbrough* [1986] 1 EGLR 265, 267 (Browne-Wilkinson V-C); *Baker v Baker* [1993] 2 FLR 247 (CA) 251 (Dillon LJ); 253 I (Beldam LJ); 256G–H (Roch LJ); *Parker v Parker* [2003] EWHC 1846 (Ch), [210] (Lewison J). It is sometimes assumed, eg by Aldous LJ in *Jennings v Rice* [2002] EWCA Civ 159, [22], that the court in *Crabb v Arun UDC* [1976] Ch 179

The primary purpose of this chapter is not to champion the reliance-based remedial paradigm. Instead, the chapter seeks to advance the debate through a close examination of the role of expectation in the remedial inquiry. It accepts the relatively uncontentious proposition that the expectation must serve as the upper limit on C's remedy. However, it also advances the more significant claim that the expectation should have no further role in the remedial inquiry. Proponents of both the discretionary approach and the reliance-based approach to remedies have argued that the expectation has an important role to play in the determination of the remedy, whether as the starting point in the remedial inquiry, or as a factor to be considered in the exercise of the court's discretion, or as providing a 'proxy' for the detriment incurred by C. Furthermore, there is also a third possible view on the remedial question—which is arguably bolstered by Lord Scott's unconventional approach in *Yeoman's Row v Cobbe*[11]—which would suggest that the fulfilment of the expectation should be the invariable remedial response. This chapter interrogates these various positions on the proper role of expectation, seeking to demonstrate that none is defensible in principle.[12] Prior to undertaking this analysis, it will be necessary to prepare the ground by considering the evolution of the law to date.

II. THE DEVELOPMENT OF THE LAW ON PROPRIETARY ESTOPPEL REMEDIES

A. The Position before *Jennings v Rice*

As has already been mentioned, the courts have traditionally emphasised the extent of their discretion in determining the appropriate remedy for proprietary estoppel. For example, in *Crabb v Arun District Council*,[13] Lord Denning MR explained that it was up to the court to determine how to satisfy the equity which arises in favour of a successful claimant,

---

(CA) gave a remedy which went beyond the expectation. However, this overlooks the fact that a potentially important element of the claimant's expectation is the time when it is to be fulfilled. In *Crabb*, C's expectation was to obtain a vital easement within a short time frame for a relatively modest sum, so that the remedy of granting C the easement without payment a number of years later was, on the facts of the case, a remedy valued at much less than the expectation, properly understood.

[11] *Cobbe* [2008] UKHL 55. For discussion, see text following n 30 below.

[12] This area has been illuminated by the contributions of a number of leading scholars, whose works are referred to throughout the chapter. It should be stressed that the emphasis of this chapter is, for the most part, on what the law *should* be. Equally legitimately, other commentators on the subject are often concerned (though rarely exclusively) with establishing the current state of the law. To the extent that the arguments of others represent an attempt to rationalise the authorities, criticisms in this chapter of those arguments should be understood as aimed at the cases rather than the commentator wrestling with them.

[13] *Crabb v Arun District Council* [1976] Ch 179 (CA).

equity being displayed here 'at its most flexible'.[14] It might be argued that, because the relevant issues are complex and the courts were not in a position to state a convincing set of principles to govern the determination of remedies, they fell back on a wide discretion which would allow them to avoid counter-intuitive results without having to explain their reasoning too closely. However, it seems difficult to justify, as a matter of principle, a broad discretion which does not even provide the court with a clear objective in framing a remedy.[15]

At an earlier point in the development of the case law, it was plausible to argue that, notwithstanding the tendency of the courts to give lip-service to the existence of a wide remedial discretion, the court's invariable response was to fulfil the expectation. In 1997, Cooke noted that, in a survey of all the decided cases, she was only able to find, at most, four decisions which departed from the expectation remedy model.[16] However, writing at around the same time, Smith detected the early beginnings of a move away from the previously prevailing position.[17] A key turning point has been *Jennings v Rice*,[18] where the Court of Appeal accepted that it would not be appropriate to give a remedy based on the expectation where this would be disproportionate in comparison with the extent of the detriment incurred by C.

B. *Jennings v Rice*

The claimant in *Jennings* had begun to work as a part-time gardener for Mrs Royle in 1970. Over the years, he took on a greater role in assisting her, running errands for her, taking her shopping and helping to maintain

---

[14] *ibid*, 189.

[15] Note the work of Gardner in highlighting the difficulties associated with an excessive level of discretion: S Gardner, 'The Remedial Discretion in Estoppel' (1999) 115 *Law Quarterly Review* 438; S Gardner, 'The Remedial Discretion in Proprietary Estoppel—Again' (2006) 122 *Law Quarterly Review* 492. See also N Hopkins, 'Understanding Unconscionability in Proprietary Estoppel' (2004) 20 *Journal of Contract Law* 210. The idea of an approach to estoppel remedies which is broadly discretionary does, however, have its academic supporters. See eg M Thompson, 'The Flexibility of Estoppel' [2003] *Conveyancer* 225.

[16] E Cooke, 'Estoppel and the Protection of Expectations' (1997) 17 *Legal Studies* 258, 271–3. See also E Cooke, *The Modern Law of Estoppel* (Oxford, Oxford University Press, 2000) 150ff. In each case, Cooke's views were expressed in the context of a study which considered other forms of estoppel as well as proprietary estoppel. This chapter makes no attempt to pursue the question of whether expectation plays, or should play, a different role in relation to remedies outside the context of proprietary estoppel.

[17] R Smith, 'How Proprietary is Proprietary Estoppel?' in F Rose (ed), *Consensus Ad Idem: Essays on Contract in Honour of Gunter Treitel* (London, Sweet and Maxwell, 1996) 242–3.

[18] *Jennings v Rice* [2002] EWCA Civ 159. See also *Sledmore v Dalby* (1996) 72 P & CR 196; *Gillett v Holt* [2001] Ch 210; *Campbell v Griffin* [2001] EWCA Civ 990.

the house. By the late 1980s she had ceased to pay him. After a burglary in the house in 1993, the claimant was persuaded to stay in the house to provide security for Mrs Royle and he slept on a sofa in the sitting room almost every night from some time in 1994 until her death in 1997. She had at various times given him to understand that she would leave him some or all of her property on her death. In fact, she died intestate. At first instance, the claimant was awarded £200,000. He appealed on the basis that the remedy in proprietary estoppel should fulfil the claimant's expectation, which in this case was either that he would inherit the entire estate of Mrs Royle valued at £1,285,000 or the house and furniture valued at around £435,000. This appeal was rejected by the Court of Appeal. Two judgments were given, by Aldous LJ and Robert Walker LJ (who agreed with each other's judgments), with Mantell LJ agreeing with both judgments.

In terms of establishing general principles in relation to the remedial inquiry, the judgment of Robert Walker LJ is of the greater interest, although it is not always easy to interpret. Robert Walker LJ summed up his approach in the following terms:

> To recapitulate: there is a category of case in which the benefactor and the claimant have reached a mutual understanding which is in reasonably clear terms but does not amount to a contract. I have already referred to the typical case of a carer who has the expectation of coming into the benefactor's house, either outright or for life. In such a case the court's natural response is to fulfil the claimant's expectations. But if the claimant's expectations are uncertain, or extravagant, or out of all proportion to the detriment which the claimant has suffered, the court can and should recognise that the claimant's equity should be satisfied in another (and generally more limited) way.[19]

Read literally, this passage (and Robert Walker LJ's earlier reasoning)[20] appears to divide up the possible scenarios into two categories. The first category involves cases where the parties have reached a mutual understanding in reasonably clear terms (what have been called 'bargain' cases)[21]—here the court's natural approach is to fulfil C's expectation. The second category includes cases where C's expectations are uncertain or extravagant[22] or out of all proportion to the detriment which C has suffered—in such cases, the court will normally give C a lesser remedy than the fulfilment of his expectation. It is obvious, however, that Robert Walker LJ's dichotomy is a strange one, since his second category is not

---

[19] *ibid*, [50].

[20] See *ibid*, [45]–[49] (with a curious transition between paras [45] and [46]).

[21] See eg Bright and McFarlane, above n 6, at 458.

[22] In referring to 'extravagant' expectations, Robert Walker LJ had in mind ([2002] EWCA Civ 159, [47]) cases where the court 'is not satisfied that the high level of the claimant's expectations is fairly derived from his deceased patron's assurances'. Thus, he was using the term 'expectation' in a looser sense than the one in which it is used in this chapter: see above n 4.

the converse of his first. It is somewhat as if he had divided up the class of all animals into (i) cats and (ii) those animals which are not mammals. To understand Robert Walker LJ's meaning, it is necessary to fill in some gaps.

Robert Walker LJ's assertion that the court will not generally fulfil C's expectation in cases where this expectation is 'uncertain, or extravagant, or out of all proportion to the detriment which the claimant has suffered' seems to suggest that the court *will* generally fulfil C's expectation in the converse case where that expectation is not uncertain, extravagant or disproportionate to the detriment. Stronger support for this conclusion derives from Robert Walker LJ's explanation of why it would be natural for the court to fulfill C's expectation in a 'bargain' case. His Lordship explained that, in such a case, 'the consensual element of what has happened suggests that the claimant and the benefactor probably regarded the expected benefit and the accepted detriment as being (in a general, imprecise way) equivalent, or at any rate not obviously disproportionate'.[23] This reasoning points to a view that the expectation should be fulfilled where it is not disproportionate to the detriment incurred by C. As a final indicator in this direction, it should be noted that Robert Walker LJ explicitly accepted 'the principle of proportionality (between remedy and detriment)'.[24] This principle was also accepted by Aldous LJ.[25]

Thus, it appears to emerge from *Jennings* that, in general, the court should fulfil the expectation of C unless this would be disproportionate to the detriment suffered by C.[26] If an expectation remedy would be disproportionate, then it would be necessary for the court 'to exercise a wide judgmental discretion'.[27] The approach in *Jennings v Rice* has since been approved on a number of occasions in the Court of Appeal, and in two of the more significant authorities, *Ottey v Grundy*[28] and *Powell v Benney*,[29] the proportionality principle was invoked to justify giving C a remedy which fell short of the expectation.

---

[23] *ibid*, [45].

[24] *ibid*, [56]. See text to and following n 54 below for discussion of an alternative understanding of *Jennings v Rice* and of the proportionality principle.

[25] *ibid*, [38]. See below n 55 for discussion of how Aldous LJ phrased his support for the principle.

[26] Note that Robert Walker LJ's judgment might, in places, be interpreted to suggest that an expectation remedy should be denied only if it would be *very* disproportionate. See *ibid*, [45], [50]. However, at the conclusion of his judgment (*ibid*, [56]) he emphasised that it cannot be right to give 'a disproportionate remedy' and this seems to represent a more defensible position.

[27] *ibid*, [51]. See text to n 9 above for Robert Walker LJ's list of some of the factors relevant to the exercise of this discretion.

[28] *Ottey v Grundy* [2003] EWCA Civ 1176.

[29] *Powell v Benney* [2007] EWCA Civ 1283.

C. *Yeoman's Row Management Ltd v Cobbe* and *Thorner v Major*

In the recent case of *Yeoman's Row Management Ltd v Cobbe*,[30] the House of Lords overturned the generous decision of the Court of Appeal[31] in favour of an experienced property developer who had relied on an incomplete 'agreement in principle', which he knew to be binding only 'in honour'. Two leading speeches were delivered in the case, by Lord Scott (with whom Lords Hoffman, Mance and Brown agreed) and by Lord Walker (with whom Lord Brown also agreed). While the final result was a reasonable one, the speeches in the case appear to reflect a flawed understanding of the doctrine of proprietary estoppel as it had previously been applied by the courts.

In his speech, Lord Scott argued that:

> [a]n 'estoppel' bars the object of it from asserting some fact or facts, or, sometimes, something that is a mixture of fact and law, that stands in the way of some right claimed by the person entitled to the benefit of the estoppel. The estoppel becomes a 'proprietary' estoppel—a sub-species of a 'promissory' estoppel—if the right claimed is a proprietary right.[32]

This passage takes too literally the label 'proprietary *estoppel*'. As is explained in *Megarry and Wade*, '[i]t is perhaps unfortunate that proprietary estoppel should be so called. Although the equitable doctrine shares some characteristics with estoppel at common law, it differs fundamentally from it'.[33]

Lord Scott's unorthodox view of proprietary estoppel appears to have led him to assume that the remedy for proprietary estoppel will inevitably be the fulfillment of the expectation of C;[34] if proprietary estoppel is regarded as preventing D from asserting certain facts which would otherwise defeat C's proprietary claim, the implication is that that claim will then simply succeed, leaving C with a proprietary remedy reflecting his expectation. Lord Scott did not address the remedial question directly nor did he make any reference to the line of Court of Appeal authority, including *Jennings v Rice*,[35] which is clearly inconsistent with the assumption that the remedy

---

[30] *Cobbe* [2008] UKHL 55. For commentary, see B McFarlane and A Robertson 'The Death of Proprietary Estoppel?' [2008] *Lloyds Maritime and Commercial Law Quarterly* 449; T Etherton 'Constructive Trusts and Proprietary Estoppel: The Search for Clarity and Principle' [2009] *Conveyancer and Property Lawyer* 104, 116–20, J Getzler 'Quantum meruit, estoppel, and the primacy of contract' (2009) 125 *Law Quarterly Review* 196.

[31] *Cobbe* [2006] 1 WLR 2964 (CA).

[32] *Cobbe* [2008] UKHL 55, [14].

[33] C Harpum, S Bridge and M Dixon, *Megarry and Wade: The Law of Real Property*, 7th edn (London, Sweet & Maxwell, 2008) 699 (footnotes omitted).

[34] *Cobbe* [2008] UKHL 55, [4], [14], [16], [38].

[35] *Jennings* [2002] EWCA Civ 159. See also *Gillett v Holt* [2000] EWCA Civ 66; *Campbell v Griffin* [2001] EWCA Civ 990; *Ottey v Grundy* [2003] EWCA Civ 1176; *Powell v Benney* [2007] EWCA Civ 1283.

will automatically reflect C's expectation. It seems that Lord Scott's rejection of the proprietary estoppel claim in *Cobbe* can be satisfactorily explained on more limited grounds,[36] so that his apparently misconceived views as to the nature of proprietary estoppel, with their implications for the remedial question, could be seen as falling outside the ratio of the case.

Interestingly, Lord Walker's speech, whilst also taking an unexpectedly restrictive view of the scope of proprietary estoppel,[37] did recognise the existence of a discretion in the court in relation to the appropriate remedy in proprietary estoppel cases.[38] It is noteworthy that Lord Brown agreed with both Lord Walker and Lord Scott, despite the differences in their two speeches in relation to the remedial question. This suggests that the House of Lords was not really focused on that question and that too much should not be read into the case in this regard.

The more recent decision of the House of Lords in *Thorner v Major*[39] appears to represent a retreat from some of the more controversial aspects of *Cobbe*. In *Thorner*, the House of Lords unanimously upheld the claim of a Somerset farmer to inherit the farm of his father's first cousin, the claimant having worked unpaid on the farm for many years on the strength of oblique assurances that he would inherit. Once again, the issue of remedies was not central to the case. Significantly though, when one compares *Thorner* with *Cobbe*, it is clear that the balance of support in the House of Lords has switched away from the views of Lord Scott to those of Lord Walker.[40] Given that, in *Thorner*, Lord Walker adhered to the traditional position that the court has a discretion in relation to the remedy for proprietary estoppel,[41] it appears probable that this position now represents the law.[42]

---

[36] Lord Scott emphasised that the proprietary interest expected by C was too uncertain to form the basis for a claim in proprietary estoppel, in that it was dependent on the successful conclusion of future negotiations on certain essential contractual terms: *Yeoman's Row* [2008] UKHL 55, [18]–[20], [23]; see also *ibid*, [87]–[89] (Lord Walker).

[37] See *ibid*, [63]–[68] (asserting that C must believe that D is legally bound by his assurance).

[38] *ibid*, [55], [82].

[39] [2009] UKHL 18. See generally, J Mee 'The Limits of Proprietary Estoppel: *Thorner v Major*' (2009) 21 *Child and Family Law Quarterly* (forthcoming).

[40] Five speeches were given in *Thorner*. Lord Neuberger agreed with Lord Walker, although he made a substantial speech of his own. Lord Rodger also agreed with Lord Walker, making a short separate speech. Lord Scott made a comparatively short speech, having stated that he was 'in broad agreement' with the reasons of Lords Walker and Neuberger. Lord Hoffman also made a short speech.

[41] [2009] UKHL 18, [66].

[42] In *Thorner*, Lord Scott did not resile from the views he had expressed in *Cobbe* on the nature of proprietary estoppel. However, he suggested that, by utilising the 'remedial constructive trust' recognised in *Gissing v Gissing* [1971] AC 886, the court could exercise a remedial discretion in certain cases that would conventionally be regarded as falling under proprietary estoppel. With great respect, it appears that Lord Scott's views are not consistent with the orthodox understanding of either proprietary estoppel or the *Gissing v Gissing* constructive trust. For discussion, see Mee 'The Limits of Proprietary Estoppel' n 39 above.

III. THE ROLE OF EXPECTATION

Having considered the current state of the law, it is now possible to move on to examine the various possible roles which expectation could play in the determination of the remedy for proprietary estoppel.

A. Expectation as Determinant of the Remedy

(i) Expectation as Remedy

While the case law (up until *Cobbe* at any rate) has turned away from this approach, it is relatively coherent from a logical point of view to suggest that the fulfilment of C's expectation should be the aim of the court in devising a proprietary estoppel remedy.[43] The idea would be that C's detriment would be the key which would 'unlock the impulse to compel men to make good their promises'.[44] One advantage of this approach is that it would be as certain and easy to apply as one could reasonably hope.[45]

A difficulty with this approach lies in reconciling it with the fact that, in the absence of any detriment, the court will give no remedy on the basis of an unfulfilled promise. If the claimant has incurred detriment to the extent of X, the court requires the promise to be satisfied, leading to a remedy valued at (say) $X + Y$. The claimant who has incurred some detriment seems to get a bonus to the value of Y, which is denied to the claimant who has incurred no detriment. One possible answer to this point would be to argue that the existence of detriment takes the case into a different category, from 'unenforceable promise' to 'promise enforceable due to detriment incurred by promisee'. It remains unclear, however, why the injection into the equation of C's detrimental reliance leads to the enforcement of the promise, rather than simply entitling C to a remedy valued by reference to the detriment

---

[43] For practical reasons, it would not be possible to achieve this in every case and, in some instances, it would be necessary to substitute a monetary award which would, to the extent practicable, be valued at the level of the expectation. See Gardner (1999) above n 15, at 446–52.

[44] L Fuller and W Perdue, 'The Reliance Interest in Contract Damages: I' (1936–37) 46 *Yale Law Journal* 52, 69. This approach would require the application of a threshold principle, whereby detrimental reliance which was regarded as too insignificant would be disregarded and would fail to trigger any remedy.

[45] E Cooke ('Estoppel, discretion and the nature of the estoppel equity' in M Bryan (ed), *Private Law in Theory and Practice* (London, Routledge, 2006) 189) argues that the courts are given a strong incentive to favour expectation relief in estoppel cases by the fact that such relief is normal under the common intention constructive trust analysis. However, it would be most unsatisfactory if the principled development of the law on estoppel remedies were to be impeded by a requirement to ensure uniformity with the theoretically incoherent common intention analysis (criticised in J Mee, *The Property Rights of Cohabitees* (Oxford, Hart Publishing, 1999) ch 5).

(the reliance-based remedial approach) or to the remedy which seems appropriate to the court in light of all the circumstances of the case (the discretionary approach to remedies).[46]

(ii) The Problem of Countervailing Benefits

A different objection to the 'expectation as remedy' approach relates to the question of countervailing benefits which may have been received by C. Unlike consideration in the context of a contract, detrimental reliance by C in the estoppel context does not constitute the agreed price of D's promise. Since such detrimental reliance is deemed sufficient to trigger an estoppel remedy, it would seem inconsistent not to take account of countervailing benefits received by C from D, notwithstanding the fact that the provision of such benefits has not been formally agreed upon by the parties as compensation for C's detrimental reliance. Although the question has not been sufficiently analysed, it seems to be generally accepted that it is necessary to take such benefits into account.[47] The issue is often presented in terms of the need for C to show 'net' detriment, so that C will receive no remedy if the detriment on which he is relying is offset by the benefits he has received. Applying this in the context of the approach discussed above, the receipt of countervailing benefits would be fatal to a claim if C has suffered no significant net detriment; however, if the net detriment remains significant, it appears that the countervailing benefits would have no effect and C would still receive his expectation remedy.

This approach, however, leads to results which are very difficult to defend. Consider a case where C has incurred detriment to the value of three units, in reliance on an expectation of receiving 10 units. Assume that this level of detriment exceeds the minimum threshold for an estoppel claim and that, in the absence of any other relevant factor, C would stand to have his expectation fulfilled. Imagine, however, that C has received three units worth of countervailing benefits. This brings his net detriment to zero and he is no longer entitled to any remedy. The question is why receiving

---

[46] Nonetheless, the 'expectation as remedy' approach has proven attractive to a number of scholars. See eg S Moriarty, 'Licences and Land Law: Legal Principles and Public Policies' (1984) 100 *Law Quarterly Review* 376; J Edelman, 'Remedial Certainty or Remedial Discretion in Estoppel after *Giumelli*?' (1999) 15 *Journal of Contract Law* 179. Cooke, above n 41, favours a variation whereby expectation remedies are the norm but the existence of an underlying discretion permits 'a sensitivity to moral and economic factors which the courts use, however sparingly and carefully' (*ibid*, 190), though she does also acknowledge (*ibid*, 183) the 'renewed stress on the need for proportionality between detriment and remedy' after *Jennings*. See also Gardner (1999) above n 15.

[47] See eg *Jennings v Rice* [2002] EWCA Civ 159, [51] (Robert Walker LJ); *Watts v Storey* (1983) 134 *NLJ* 631; K Gray and S Gray, *Elements of Land Law*, 5th edn (Oxford, Oxford University Press, 2009) 1230; RA Pearce and J Stevens *The Law of Trusts and Equitable Obligations*, 4th edn (Oxford, Oxford University Press, 2006) 343.

three units is sufficient to destroy his claim to the ten units which he would otherwise have received. It is possible to modify the example so that the receipt of the countervailing benefits occurs after the detriment of 3 units has been incurred. Thus, at one point in the chronology, C would stand to receive 10 units; then he receives three units and his entitlement goes down to zero. This appears illogical.

It is possible, also, to set up the example so that the countervailing benefits, in fact, represent the beginning of the enjoyment of the expected benefit. Consider the following scenario, based loosely on the facts of *Sledmore v Dalby*.[48] D promises that C can live rent-free in a house belonging to D for the rest of C's life. C takes up occupation of the house and incurs significant detriment in reliance on D's promise by making improvements to the premises (or, say, by giving up secure accommodation elsewhere). If D were to resile from the expectation at this point, C would be able to establish a claim in proprietary estoppel and, applying the remedial approach under discussion, would stand to benefit from the fulfilment of the expectation. Imagine, however, that no dispute arises for a number of years, during which time C is permitted to enjoy the occupation of the house rent-free. At this point, the value of these countervailing benefits (let it be said) cancels out the detriment, and C no longer has any basis for an estoppel claim. D would then be permitted to resile from the expectation and recover possession of the house. However, this seems an entirely indefensible result. How can it be that enjoyment of part of the expected benefit will eliminate a claim, which would otherwise have been available, to the remainder of that benefit?

When one considers the matter further, it appears that (in the context under discussion) the principled approach might be to deduct the countervailing benefits from the expectation remedy, rather than comparing them to the detriment. Countervailing benefits do not generally undo detrimental reliance but rather constitute something which C has received in return. Thus, it seems that they fall into the same category, and should (as it were) be entered in the same column for accounting purposes, as the possible fulfilment of C's expectation. This approach would work well where the countervailing benefits took the form of enjoyment of the expected benefit; the 'reduced' expectation remedy would simply be to enjoy the property for the remainder of the period envisaged, with the period of enjoyment which has already occurred being notionally deducted from the total time period originally envisaged. This would avoid the counter-intuitive result discussed in the previous paragraph.

However, where the countervailing benefits are unrelated to the satisfaction of the expectation, one would be left with a remedial approach which

---

[48] *Sledmore v Dalby* (1996) 72 P & CR 196.

is much harder to justify. When framing a remedy, one would in principle have to deduct the value of the countervailing benefits from the expectation. This would require the quantification of both the expectation and the countervailing benefits, reducing the advantage of simplicity which is normally associated with the 'expectation as remedy' approach. The result would also be that a remedy could be available to C even where the countervailing benefits exceeded C's detriment. For example, if the expectation was valued at 10 units and the detriment at four units and the countervailing benefits at five units, C would still be entitled to a remedy of five units despite already having received benefits which are more valuable than the detriment incurred.

Overall, in the context of the remedial approach under discussion, it does not seem possible to find a way of dealing with the issue of countervailing benefits which is both consistent and satisfactory.[49]

(iii) Conclusion on 'Expectation as Remedy' Approach

It has just been argued that, while it has certain attractions, the approach under discussion runs into difficulties in relation to the question of countervailing benefits. In addition, the approach has another obvious problem: the fact that it requires the court to grant an expectation remedy even where the detriment, though sufficiently large to entitle C to a remedy, is much less valuable than the expectation. Ultimately, the courts were not prepared to tolerate this type of outcome. As Robert Walker LJ put the point in *Jennings*, '[t]he essence of the doctrine of proprietary estoppel is to do what is necessary to avoid an unconscionable result, and a disproportionate remedy cannot be the right way of going about that'.[50]

Recognition of the need to ensure proportionality has led the courts to a different approach to the role of expectation in the remedial inquiry, relegating it from the more or less automatic choice to the status of a starting point, subject to testing on the basis of a comparison with the detriment incurred by C. Significantly, the introduction of detriment into the equation reduces

---

[49] Under a detriment-based remedial approach, these difficulties would not arise, since one would simply seek to determine the net detriment incurred by C and would base the remedy on this. Note, however, that the net detriment issue appears to create difficulties for the argument, in Bright and McFarlane, above n 6 (building on B McFarlane, 'Proprietary Estoppel and Third Parties after the Land Registration Act 2002' (2003) 62 *Cambridge Law Journal* 661), that property rights arising under proprietary estoppel take effect immediately without any need for a court order. On this analysis, a property right will come into existence as soon as C has incurred sufficient detriment for the grant of that property right to be proportionate (assuming other conditions for the creation of a property right are satisfied). But what happens if C subsequently enjoys countervailing benefits which reduce his net detriment such that it would no longer be proportionate to grant the property interest in question? Does that property right flicker out of existence again?

[50] *Jennings* [2002] EWCA Civ 159, [56].

the dimensions of the countervailing benefits problem, since the court would not grant an expectation remedy if this would be disproportionate to the (net) detriment of C.[51] The discussion now turns to a consideration of the merits of this different view of the role of expectation.

B. Expectation as a Starting Point in Framing the Remedy

As has already been mentioned, this is the role for expectation which emerges from the leading case of *Jennings v Rice*. This is similar, in broad outline at any rate, to the position currently prevailing in Australia in light of the decision of the High Court in *Giumelli v Giumelli*[52] (notwithstanding the assertion in *Jennings* that the Australian courts favour a remedial approach which focuses exclusively on detriment).[53]

It is important to note that the essence of the approach under discussion, which gives a role to expectation as a starting point in the inquiry, is that there is a two-stage approach to determining the remedy for estoppel, with somewhat different criteria being applied at each stage. The first question is whether the expectation remedy would be 'disproportionate' to C's detriment. If it would not be disproportionate, then the expectation remedy will be granted. Robert Walker LJ's judgment is silent on the question of whether, in judging whether the expectation is proportionate to the detriment, the court should take into account the full range of discretionary factors that come into play if the court is obliged to reject the expectation remedy and devise an appropriate lower remedy.[54] It is quite possible that the court would not disregard (say) serious misconduct on the part of C but it seems improbable that, in considering the focused question of proportionality between expectation and detriment, the court is intended to exercise the same wide discretion as when devising a non-expectation remedy. In any event, if the expectation remedy is deemed to be disproportionate, then the court goes on to exercise its 'wide judgmental discretion' by reference to all the relevant factors. The key point is that this involves applying a somewhat different set of criteria in 'proportional' cases, as against 'non-proportional' cases. This is because in the latter cases there can be no element of effectively rounding up the remedy to the level of the expectation on the grounds that this would not be 'disproportionate' and, also, because it is probable

---

[51] Compare n 49 above.

[52] *Giumelli v Giumelli* (1999) 196 CLR 1011. Note also Deane J's reference to 'the prima facie entitlement to relief based on the assumed state of affairs' in *Commonwealth of Australia v Verwayen* (1990) 170 CLR 394, 442. See A Robertson, 'The Reliance Basis of Proprietary Estoppel Remedies' [2008] *Conv* 295, 297.

[53] *Jennings* [2002] EWCA Civ 159, [42], [54] (Robert Walker LJ). See also *ibid*, [30] (Aldous LJ).

[54] See text to n 9 above for Robert Walker LJ's list of some of these factors.

that a lesser range of discretionary factors is relevant to the proportionality inquiry as compared to the determination of an alternative remedy if the expectation remedy is adjudged to be disproportionate.

It would, of course, be possible to envisage an approach whereby the same criteria would be applied in all cases. However, such an approach would not actually accord the type of role to expectation which is currently under discussion. Consider an approach whereby one determined the appropriate remedy by applying a specified set of factors in every case. It would be superfluous to add the qualification that, if the universally applicable test pointed in favour of an expectation remedy, then an expectation remedy would be granted. The applicable test could fully be described without reference to expectation and an expectation remedy could not sensibly be described as the starting point in the inquiry. Similarly, if the expectation is merely operating as a cap on a remedy which is determined by reference to other factors, it would not be accurate to describe the expectation as a starting point. For example, a test whereby the remedy is based on the detriment unless it exceeds the expectation could, at the cost of some artificiality, be phrased as a test whereby the remedy is based on the expectation unless this exceeds the detriment, in which case the remedy will be based on the detriment. However, if this were the applicable test, it would be unhelpful for analytical purposes to present the expectation remedy as the starting point.

The previous paragraph laboured the point that, in order to have independent significance, the 'expectation as starting point' approach must involve applying a different remedial approach where an expectation remedy is proportional, compared to that applicable if proportionality is found to be lacking. This point is being emphasised because it represents the key problem, from a principled point of view, in the 'expectation as starting point' approach.

(i) The Flaw in the 'Expectation as Starting Point' Approach

Consider a hypothetical case where D has promised to leave C a certain house and where, in reliance on this, C has incurred detriment which is substantial but is difficult to quantify. On the approach under discussion, the court should grant an expectation remedy unless this would be disproportionate to the detriment incurred by C. A crucial variable in the hypothetical scenario is, therefore, the value of the house. The argument will proceed by examining the consequences of adjusting the example by increasing the value of the hypothetical house, while holding constant the level of C's detriment and the other features of the case.[55] Let it first be said

---

[55] It is not easy to make a reasoned criticism of a particular approach to estoppel remedies, since apparent inconsistencies in the treatment of different factual situations can be dismissed on the basis that the choice of remedy responds to unique features in a specific scenario. The

that the house is worth (say) £100,000 and that, on the facts, it would not be disproportionate for the court to fulfill C's expectation when it is set at this level. In these circumstances, the court would grant the house to C by way of remedy.

Consider next a case where the value of the house is adjusted upwards to the highest level whereby it would still not be disproportionate to fulfill C's expectation. Let it be said that this value of the house is £400,000. In the version of the example where the house has this value, the court will once more fulfill C's expectation and grant him the house worth £400,000 (although the case is at the outer limit of proportionality and, if the level of the expectation had been meaningfully higher, the court would have found it disproportionate to give an expectation remedy). Consider finally a variation on the example where all the facts are the same except that the house is now worth £1,000,000. In this situation, it would be disproportionate to order that C should receive the house, given the disparity in value between the expectation and C's detriment. Therefore, the court must devise a remedy in the exercise of its 'wide judgmental discretion'. Depending on the way in which the relevant factors operate in the particular circumstances of the case, the court might award a monetary remedy valued at (say) £200,000 or £300,000 or £400,000. It cannot be argued that the remedy will inevitably be greater than or equal to £400,000, the expectation remedy which was given to C in the previous example. In fact, as was mentioned in the discussion of that example, that figure effectively represents the maximum possible remedy in light of the level of C's detriment, given that any higher remedy would be disproportionate to that detriment.[56] Imagine that, in the circumstances of the case, the court exercises its discretion to choose a remedy of £300,000.

Thus, with an expectation valued at £400,000, C received a remedy valued at £400,000 (the fulfilment of the expectation); however, when the expectation was greater, being valued at £1,000,000, the award was only £300,000. That cannot be right. It is not possible to defend a position where, with all the other facts in the scenario being held constant, a *higher* expectation on the part of C can lead to a *lower* remedy.[57] It is necessary

methodology in the text seeks to surmount this difficulty by considering variations on the same hypothetical situation, making it possible to isolate and analyse the impact of just one factor, the expectation of C.

[56] The court could not be regarded as having a discretion if it was obliged in every case to grant the highest possible remedy which would not be disproportionate to the detriment. If the court were so obliged, one would be dealing with a very different remedial approach, ie a variation on the model whereby the remedy is determined by reference to the level of the detriment.

[57] If anything, one might expect the opposite—that sometimes a higher expectation might justify an increased remedy for C, even where the remedy does not take the form of fulfilling the expectation completely. However, it will be argued in the next section that such an approach is not appropriate.

to treat like cases alike and this principle is violated where C can be treated less favourably where the only difference in the scenario is one which in no way weakens his claim to a remedy. Yet this anomaly is the inevitable consequence of an approach which seeks to privilege the expectation remedy as 'the starting point' in the remedial inquiry, ie as the prima facie remedy which will be granted unless it is disproportionate to C's detriment. Either one applies the same approach to determining the remedy in all cases—in which case the expectation remedy loses its status as the prima facie remedy—or else one faces the absurdity that C may be in a stronger position if he can show that the expectation induced in him by D was sufficiently low to count as 'not disproportionate' to his detriment.

C. Expectation as a Factor in the Determination of the Remedy

This section considers a different and wider understanding of the proportionality principle, which would allow expectation to be taken into account as a factor in the determination of a remedy, even if that remedy is lower in value than the expectation. The issue of proportionality, as it was described in the previous section, was a question of the relationship between detriment and remedy. In *Jennings*, Robert Walker clearly had in mind 'the principle of proportionality (between remedy and detriment)'.[58] Gardner, however, seems to argue for a different understanding of proportionality. He suggests that, while the statements in *Jennings* about proportionality are not always cleanly put, '[t]he idea, however, is probably that there must be proportionality between the expectation, the detriment *and the outcome*'.[59]

Since both the expectation and the detriment are fixed features of a particular case, the outcome (ie the remedy) is the only one of the three things mentioned by Gardner which can vary. Therefore, on Gardner's view, the court must ensure proportionality by taking the expectation, as well as the detriment, into account in determining the outcome. Where one

---

[58] *Jennings* [2002] EWCA Civ 159, [56]. This is confirmed by *Ottey v Grundy* [2003] EWCA Civ 1176, [57] where Arden LJ explained *Jennings v Rice* as having decided that: '[t]he remedy must be proportionate to the detriment suffered'. See also *ibid*, [62], in similar terms. This is also the understanding of proportionality which emerges from the judgment of Mason CJ in *Commonwealth of Australia v Verwayen* (1990) 170 CLR 394, 413, which Robert Walker LJ accepted in *Jennings* [2002] EWCA Civ 159, [56] as applicable in English law.

[59] S Gardner, 'The Remedial Discretion in Proprietary Estoppel—Again' (2006) 122 *Law Quarterly Review* 492, 498. Gardner *ibid* derives support for his interpretation of proportionality from a dictum of Aldous LJ in *Jennings* [2002] EWCA Civ 159, [36] that 'the task of the court is to do justice. The most essential requirement is that there must be proportionality between the expectation and the detriment'. Since the expectation and the detriment in a given case are matters of fact which cannot be made proportionate to each other by any action of the court, it is submitted that Aldous LJ meant that such proportionality must exist *if an expectation remedy is to be granted*. Note that Aldous LJ made his remarks in a case where the central issue was the claimant's argument that an expectation remedy must invariably be granted.

is considering a possible expectation remedy, there would be no difference between the two versions of proportionality because the expectation and the remedy under consideration are the same, so that the third variable introduced by Gardner's formulation disappears. The difference appears in cases where an expectation remedy is ruled out because it would be disproportionate to the detriment. On Gardner's version of proportionality, the court would take the expectation into account (alongside the detriment) as a factor in framing a remedy which is lower than the expectation.

Some aspects of Robert Walker LJ's judgment might indeed seem to envisage a role for expectation short of actually determining the remedy. For example, when he discussed cases where it is not appropriate to grant an expectation remedy, he commented that 'that does not mean that the court should in such a case abandon expectations completely'.[60] He also agreed with Hobhouse LJ in *Sledmore v Dalby*[61] that

> to recognise the need for proportionality '... is to say little more than that the end result must be a just one having regard to the assumption made by the party asserting the estoppel and the detriment which he has experienced".[62]

While not clear-cut, such dicta could be interpreted to mean that the level of the expectation can play a role in determining the remedy even in cases where the remedy is less than the expectation. It would involve a further step to conclude that the judges had in mind the version of proportionality favoured by Gardner, rather than envisaging a simpler approach under which expectation, along with all other matters, would be taken into account when the court is exercising its very broad discretion.[63]

Assuming that Gardner's approach finds some support in the case law, how would it work in practice? Consider the facts of *Jennings*, where the claimant acted to his detriment in the expectation of inheriting a house worth £435,000 and was awarded a remedy of £200,000. If the expectation had been to inherit a house worth £1,000,000, would this have justified an increase in the value of the remedy? In other words, in *Jennings* the defendant 'promised Mr Jennings the moon and left him nothing';[64] would Jennings have deserved a greater remedy if he had been promised the moon *and* the stars? If the expectation is relevant to the process of choosing a remedy, alongside other factors, it must be possible to envisage circumstances where adjusting the extent of the expectation, while not varying the status of other relevant factors, would lead to a change in the extent of the remedy to be granted. Yet it is difficult to see why, as a matter of principle,

---

[60] *Jennings* [2002] EWCA Civ 159, [51].
[61] *Sledmore v Dalby* (1996) 72 P & CR 196, 209.
[62] *Jennings* [2002] EWCA Civ 159, [56].
[63] This latter possibility is considered later in this section: see text to and following nn 70–72 below.
[64] *Jennings* [2002] EWCA Civ 159, [14].

the claimant in a case like *Jennings* should receive an ever greater remedy, on the basis of the same detriment, as one increases the extent of the hypo-thetical expectation. Such an approach would seem to offend unacceptably against the more straightforward proportionality principle discussed previ-ously, which stipulates that the remedy should not be disproportionate to the detriment (a principle not recognised on Gardner's analysis, since it is replaced by a complex understanding of proportionality which brings expectation into the question as well as detriment).

A central problem with an approach which gives a role to expectation as a factor in the determination of the remedy is that, unless it is to be an entirely arbitrary process, there must be some principled way of determin-ing the extent to which the expectation impacts upon the remedy. However, no such principled mechanism is available. One must ask how, as a matter of logic, the remedy can be made proportional to two different values, the expectation *and* the detriment? The only answer appears to be that one would have to resort to some defined rule which would relate the two values to each other, so as to generate one new value to which the remedy could be made proportionate. A simple example of this would be a rule which stipulated that the court should pitch the remedy at a point half-way between the detriment and the expectation.[65] Unless one imposes some arbitrary formula like this (which is surely not a viable option as a mat-ter of principle), the inevitable result would be that different courts would give different relative weightings to the expectation and the detriment. The result would be indefensibly inconsistent.

In terms of explaining how the expectation is to be taken into account in framing the remedy, Gardner argues that the remedy will normally be pitched somewhere between the value of the expectation and the value of the detriment.[66] He suggests that the aim of the court is 'to rectify uncon-scionability, of a particular kind' and that '[t]he claimant's expectation and reliance are relevant because they are the essential elements of the uncon-scionability'.[67] In Gardner's view, in order '[t]o redress the unconscionabil-ity, the outcome must therefore reflect *both* the claimant's expectation and reliance, *and* the degree to which these can be ascribed to the defendant, given his encouragement or acquiescence'.[68] Unfortunately, Gardner does not fully explain this argument concerning the ascription to D of responsi-bility for C's expectation and reliance.[69] His argument appears to involve the proposition that, as well as being a threshold issue for any liability in

---

[65] Perhaps adjusting this up or down depending on the play of other discretionary factors of the sort identified by Robert Walker LJ in *Jennings*.

[66] Gardner, 'The Remedial Discretion in Proprietary Estoppel—Again', above n 55, 498–500.

[67] *ibid*, 499.

[68] *ibid*, 500.

[69] Coming closest perhaps, *ibid*, 508.

proprietary estoppel, D's responsibility for C's expectation and detriment is also a question of degree which affects the remedial inquiry. Even if one accepts this proposition, however, it is unclear how Gardner's emphasis on ascription of responsibility can provide a non-arbitrary solution to the question of the relative weight to be given to detriment and expectation in the determination of the remedy.

Overall, Gardner's analysis does not appear to be convincing as a matter of principle. However, it does not represent the only way in which expectation could be taken into account as a factor in determining the extent of a non-expectation remedy. Rather than suggesting that the ultimate remedy must be proportional to the expectation as well as the detriment, it could simply be argued that the court is entitled to take the expectation into account alongside all the other factors relevant to the exercise of the court's discretion. In relation to the idea of taking expectation into account in determining a non-expectation remedy, one must consider why, as a matter of justice, it might be thought that a higher expectation should indicate a higher remedy. It seems that the argument would have to be that the larger the expectation, the more significant the 'disappointment' suffered by C when the expectation is not fulfilled. In *Powell v Benney*,[70] this point was considered in passing by Sir Peter Gibson, who noted that the trial judge 'chose to increase the sum of £8,830, which he found [the first claimant] had expended, by what appears to be an arbitrary amount "looking at the size of the estate and the disappointment [the claimants] had suffered"'.[71] Since there was no cross-appeal by the defendants against the modest award of £20,000 to the claimants, Sir Peter Gibson did not comment further on the judge's rounding up of the remedy to that sum to allow for the claimants' 'disappointment' but his use of the term 'arbitrary' might indicate disapproval of this approach.

Two comments can be made on the question of factoring 'disappointment' into the determination of the remedy. First, as Sir Peter Gibson implied, it is difficult to see how one would avoid arbitrariness when deciding how much allowance to make for the level of C's expectation. Secondly, along the lines of an argument put forward by Brennan J in *Commonwealth v Verwayen*,[72] it cannot be said that disappointment is something which C suffers *in reliance* on the expectation created by D. It is a consequence of the non-fulfilment of the expectation but does not appear to fall within the category of detrimental reliance on the expectation. The disappointed claimant who has incurred no detriment will not obtain any remedy when the promise is not fulfilled. Why should disappointment be compensatable when associated with detrimental reliance but not when it occurs on its own?

---

[70] *Powell v Benney* [2007] EWCA Civ 1283.
[71] *ibid*, [18].
[72] *Commonwealth v Verwayen* (1990) 170 CLR 394, 429.

On the whole, it does not seem to be defensible in principle to treat the expectation as a factor to be taken into account in devising a non-expectation remedy, whether through the adoption of Gardner's version of proportionality or otherwise.

D. Expectation as a Proxy for Detriment

Another role for expectation is suggested by Robertson in his latest contribution to the debate.[73] Robertson's general view is that the purpose of estoppel relief is to protect C against reliance-based harm. Seeking to explain the approach of recent English and Australian cases, he argues that C's detriment in estoppel cases is often difficult to quantify and that, in such cases, the expectation provides a reliable proxy for the reliance interest of C. He suggests:

> If the primary goal of proprietary estoppel is to protect the claimant against harm resulting from reliance on the representor's conduct, then the most complete way to provide that protection is to fulfil the claimant's expectations *in specie*. The claimant suffers no detriment as a result of his or her reliance on a particular assumption if that assumption is made good. The notion that a Court of Equity should grant specific relief where it can by that means provide better protection for a plaintiff than would be provided by a monetary award is consistent with the principle that a court will grant specific performance for breach of contract, 'when it can by that means do more perfect and complete justice'.[74]

The trouble, however, with this idea of doing 'more perfect and complete justice' to C is that this occurs at the expense of D.

Robertson concedes that the courts could attempt to quantify reliance loss but feels that they should not do so. This is because

> [w]here the reliance loss cannot accurately be quantified, the court is faced with a choice between running a risk of under-compensating the claimant by seeking to quantify the reliance loss, and running a risk of over-compensating the claimant by awarding relief in the expectation measure.[75]

It is submitted that these risks are not equally balanced. If the court tries conscientiously to quantify the reliance loss, there should be an equal risk that it will over-compensate or under-compensate C; thus it is favouring neither C nor D. If, on the other hand, it insists on taking the expectation as the determinant of the remedy, it is picking the highest possible measure (given that the expectation must operate as an upper limit on relief),

---

[73] A Robertson, 'The Reliance Basis of Proprietary Estoppel Remedies' [2008] *Conv* 295.
[74] *ibid*, 315–16, quoting from *Wilson v Northhampton and Banbury Junction Railway Co* (1874) 9 Ch App 279, 284.
[75] *ibid*, 317.

eschewing all risk of under-compensation but running a very clear risk of over-compensation since no attempt has been made to ensure that the detriment actually equals or exceeds the value of the expectation.

Robertson justifies this favouring of C on the basis that 'the court is, in effect, holding the representor responsible for the factual uncertainty brought about by his or her inconsistent conduct [ie in resiling from his promise]'.[76] However, it is important to note the manner in which it is proposed to hold D responsible for the factual uncertainty. Instead of declining to give D the benefit of the doubt in the process of quantifying the remedy on the basis of detriment, it is proposed that the court should discard detriment as the basis for quantification and settle instead on the expectation as the remedy (at least where this would not be 'disproportionate' to the detriment).

Furthermore, Robertson's argument seems to presuppose that, in all estoppel cases, D's behaviour can be regarded as sufficiently blameworthy to justify skewing the quantification of the remedy against him. One might be reluctant to give D the benefit of any doubt if he had never had any intention of fulfilling the expectation he had created and had deliberately engineered a benefit for himself by inducing C to act to his detriment. However, there are many cases where D is not acting in bad faith and where his failure to fulfil C's expectation may be due to an unforeseen change in circumstances or to a falling out between the parties for which D is no more to blame than C. In such circumstances, even if it may be appropriate to allow C a remedy in estoppel, it is not clear that all assumptions should be made against D in terms of quantification.

Robertson envisages as a protection for D the fact that the court will not fulfil the expectation where to do so would be disproportionate to the detriment suffered. In 'rare cases' where C's loss is 'is purely financial or is otherwise accurately quantifiable', the court can award financial compensation. However, '[i]n other cases, the focus is necessarily on fashioning an award that is *proportionate to* the claimant's reliance loss, rather than one that precisely corresponds to it'.[77] This argument makes it necessary to look more closely at what is meant by the somewhat slippery notion of 'proportionality'.

Proportionality is a concept which, at a superficial level, is difficult to quarrel with—we are accustomed to thinking of a proportional response as being, by definition, reasonable. Yet the attractiveness, in the abstract, of the concept masks certain difficulties. If you owe me £200 and you offer to repay me £150, suggesting that this amount is proportionate (or 'not

---

[76] *ibid.*

[77] *ibid,* 319. Note that, although at this point Robertson refers to a remedy which is proportionate to the detriment, what he seems to envisage is subtly different: a remedy which is merely 'not disproportionate' to the detriment.

disproportionate') to the amount of the debt, I would not be satisfied with this rough correspondence in terms of scale. Both the debt and the tendered payment are measured in the same currency and I would insist on full repayment. Even if we had agreed that you would repay me with natural produce from your garden, we would be thinking of a payment in kind which, as closely as possible, mirrored the amount of the debt. I would not be satisfied with a payment, even in kind, which was merely 'not disproportionate' to the debt. These analogies lead to the following question: Given that, on Robertson's view, the court's task is to erase the detriment of C, why should the court not simply fashion a remedy which represents its best endeavour to do that? In other words, why should the court be willing to give an expectation remedy where that remedy is greater than that indicated by the court's best attempt to quantify the detriment?

Significantly, as with the 'expectation as starting point' approach which was considered earlier in this chapter, further difficulties emerge with the approach under discussion if one considers what happens in a hypothetical scenario where the level of the expectation is increased. Consider a case where C's expectation is not regarded as being disproportionate to the detriment he has incurred. Therefore, rather than attempt the difficult task of quantifying the detriment, the court will opt for an expectation remedy—even if that would be greater than a detriment-based remedy. However, what if one changed the facts so that C's expectation was far higher, such that it would be disproportionate to give effect to it? The court would then have to resort to quantifying the detriment, possibly leading to a lesser remedy for C. Once more, one sees that C will potentially be in a less favourable position if he had a *higher* level of expectation. Note also that, where the expectation is disproportionate to the detriment, the court is forced to do its best to quantify the detriment and to determine the remedy on this basis. If this can be done in some cases, why should it not be done in all cases? It is true that it can be difficult to quantify certain forms of detriment and that it is possible to underestimate the significance of activities such as caring for an elderly defendant, investing emotionally in a home, sacrificing other financial opportunities or making 'life changing decisions of a personal nature'.[78] However, this merely highlights the importance of not quantifying the detriment-based remedy on a crude or unsympathetic basis. It does not justify favouring the expectation measure over the court's best estimate of the remedy appropriate to erase the detriment.[79]

To sum up, if one accepts (as Robertson does) that the purpose of the remedy is to erase C's detriment subject to a cap based on expectation, then one must be willing to quantify the detriment. Clearly, the court will

---

[78] See Robertson's discussion of these issues, *ibid*, 305–15.

[79] Unless, of course, the court's valuation of the detriment is such that the expectation comes into play as the upper limit on C's remedy.

sometimes be faced with difficult issues of quantification but these issues are identical to those which arise in cases where the expectation happens to be disproportionate to the detriment. These difficulties are a necessary consequence of an equitable jurisdiction, which is regarded, under Robertson's approach, as having the function of protecting detrimental reliance. It is submitted, therefore, that it is not appropriate to regard C's expectation as a proxy for the detriment which C has incurred.

E. Linking Expectation with Detriment by Reference to a Bargain

In *Jennings v Rice*, Robert Walker LJ felt that one justification for an expectation remedy would be that there has been something approaching a bargain between the parties. He referred to the possibility of a case where 'the assurances, and the claimant's reliance on them, have a consensual character falling not far short of an enforceable contract'.[80] He went on to explain:

> In a case of that sort both the claimant's expectations and the element of detriment to the claimant will have been defined with reasonable clarity. A typical case would be an elderly benefactor who reaches a clear understanding with the claimant (who may be a relative, a friend, or a remunerated companion or carer) that if the claimant resides with and cares for the benefactor, the claimant will inherit the benefactor's house (or will have a home for life). In a case like that the consensual element of what has happened suggests that the claimant and the benefactor probably regarded the expected benefit and the accepted detriment as being (in a general, imprecise way) equivalent, or at any rate not obviously disproportionate.[81]

In considering these remarks, it is first necessary to identify the possible significance of this attempt to link expectation with detriment in cases where there is 'a mutual understanding which is in reasonably clear terms but does not amount to a contract'.[82]

In the context of Robert Walker LJ's judgment, the 'bargain' analysis does not really represent an independent conception of the role of expectation in the remedial inquiry. It simply indicates a set of circumstances where, according to Robert Walker LJ, it will be reasonable to conclude that there is no lack of proportionality between expectation and detriment (presumably applying in cases where the detriment or the expectation, or both, are difficult to quantify in financial terms). Under Robert Walker LJ's analysis, this would justify the award of an expectation remedy on the basis of the principle that such a remedy should be awarded unless it is disproportionate

---

[80] *Jennings* [2002] EWCA Civ 159, [45].
[81] *ibid.*
[82] *ibid*, [50].

to the detriment.[83] Thus, the bargain analysis can be seen as merely an aspect of the wider 'expectation as starting point' approach, which has already been discussed.[84] Similarly, the bargain idea could be integrated into an approach which, unless the expectation were disproportionate to the detriment, regarded the expectation as a suitable proxy for the detriment.[85] Again, the existence of a bargain could be regarded as showing that there was no lack of proportionality, thus permitting the award of an expectation remedy. In both cases, the possible role for the concept of 'bargain' is dependent on the concept of 'proportionality' and it has already been argued in detail that this concept does not stand up to close scrutiny in the case of either approach.

Furthermore, there are serious difficulties with the idea of taking a bargain into account in the manner envisaged by Robert Walker LJ.[86] An important preliminary point is that there may well be an element of gift in an apparent bargain.[87] It is quite possible that D wished to make a gift to C while gaining some benefit from C in partial return. Therefore, it does not necessarily follow from the existence of a consensual arrangement between the parties, involving an apparent quid pro quo, that either party regards the promised benefit as equivalent, or not disproportionate, in value to the detriment which it is envisaged will be incurred by C.

This means that the possible relevance of a bargain is confined to a subset of consensual arrangements where there is no element of gift in the exchange between the parties. It should be emphasised, of course, that in the type of case which is under discussion there is no binding contract between the parties (or it would not be necessary for C to rely on proprietary estoppel). It seems clear that the parties' agreement as to the equivalence of the detriment and the expectation is part of the unenforceable bargain and, therefore, is unenforceable just like the bargain as a whole. Apparently accepting this, Robert Walker LJ does not suggest that the parties are bound, as such, by their consensual arrangement. Rather, he sees the fact that the parties were willing to exchange the detriment for the expectation simply as evidence of the fact that each regards the expectation as being roughly equivalent in value to the detriment or, at least, not disproportionately higher in

---

[83] Contrast the comments of Gardner (2006), above n 55, 494–7 on Robert Walker's 'bargain' analysis, which are conditioned by Gardner's different understanding of the concept of proportionality as it emerges from *Jennings* (see text to nn 58–69 above).

[84] See text to nn 52–57 above.

[85] See the discussion of this approach in the text to nn 73–79 above.

[86] Lord Walker's extra-judicial commentary suggests that he now has reservations concerning his 'bargain' analysis, at least in its original form: see R Walker 'Which Side "Ought to Win"?—Discretion and Certainty in Property Law' [2008] *Singapore Journal of Legal Studies* 229, 238–239. (His Lordship's article is also to be found at (2008) 6 *Trust Quarterly Review* 5).

[87] Consider, for example, the facts of *Baker v Baker* [1993] 2 FLR 247 (CA).

value. Thus, the existence of the bargain is regarded as assisting the court in comparing the value of the detriment to that of the expectation.

The plausibility of this approach depends on one's view as to the appropriate basis on which to value detriment for the purpose of determining estoppel remedies. In fact, untested questions arise in relation to this issue.[88] It is unclear whether one should be looking at the value of the detriment from the point of view of C, or of D, or from some 'objective' viewpoint (or on some other more complex basis). The resolution of this issue seems to impact on the possible relevance of a bargain in terms of valuing the detriment. If the valuation is to be, in some sense, 'objective', then it is not obviously decisive that the parties themselves regarded the detriment as being equivalent in value to the expectation. If, on the other hand, the appropriate test requires the court to consider the value of the detriment from C's or D's viewpoint (or, say, to take the higher of these two valuations where there is a difference), the existence of an unenforceable bargain might seem more relevant—not because either party is bound by it but because it might be thought to indicate the value which each party places on the detriment. However, even this proposition must be examined further.

Consider a case where X, an artist, agrees to sell one of his paintings to Y for £50,000. This does not actually show that each values the painting at £50,000. X might have been willing to sell for anything above (say) £30,000, while Y might have been willing to pay up to (say) £100,000. Thus, the bargain which they actually strike simply shows that £50,000 was greater than or equal to the value which X placed on the painting and less than or equal to the value Y placed on the painting. At what point the agreed price fell in the range of £30,000 to £100,000 would have depended on, amongst other things, the respective negotiating abilities of the parties. Thus, an informal agreement between the parties gives us no guidance as to how to value the detriment from C's viewpoint, which is one leading option in terms of how the court should be trying to value the detriment. Since C was willing to exchange the detriment for the expectation, we know that he does not value the detriment more highly than the expectation but that adds no information in terms of choosing a remedy because, in any case, there is a general principle that the remedy can never exceed the expectation. However, if the aim of the exercise is to value the detriment by reference to its value to D,[89] then the existence of a bargain might indeed seem to justify valuing the detriment at the level of the expectation. This is because D's agreement to exchange the expectation for the detriment shows that he values

---

[88] These issues have not been given much consideration to date since the valuation of detriment is not necessary within the expectation remedy paradigm nor does it feature prominently in the context of a strongly discretionary approach to remedies.

[89] Or if the idea is to value it by reference to whichever is the greater, its value from D's perspective or from C's perspective.

the detriment at the level of the expectation or higher, and the existence of the cap at the expectation level rules out the possibility of imposing a remedy greater than the expectation. However, one should also mention the difficulty that circumstances may have changed significantly between the time of the bargain and the time when the court must determine the remedy, so that the prior 'bargain' may not give an accurate indication of D's current view as to the relative value of the detriment and the expectation.

The preceding discussion has suggested that it does not follow simply from the existence of a consensual arrangement between the parties that it is appropriate to regard the detriment and the expectation as roughly equivalent or to assume that the expectation is not disproportionate to the detriment. It depends, first, on whether the apparent bargain between the parties involves an element of gift; secondly, on the viewpoint from which it is regarded as appropriate to value the detriment; and, thirdly, on the assumption that the circumstances have not changed significantly since the time of the bargain.

Further complications arise in a scenario where the 'bargain' between the parties is such that it is unclear what amount of detriment C will have to incur in return for the fulfilment of the expectation. Consider, for example, the type of scenario envisaged by Robert Walker LJ where D, who is (say) 70 years old, 'promises that if the claimant resides with and cares for [D], the claimant will inherit [D's] house'.[90] A key feature here is that it is unclear how long the obligation to care for D will last (given that it is uncertain when D will die), so that it is not possible to know in advance what C will have to do in order to obtain the house. What if D dies after two years, so that C incurs a relatively modest, but not trivial, amount of detriment? Robert Walker LJ's 'bargain' idea would suggest that the remedy should reflect the expectation. However, in these circumstances, the existence of the bargain actually gives no indication that either C or D valued the detriment which was subsequently incurred, ie two years of caring for D, as equivalent or not disproportionate to the expectation. All the existence of the bargain could show is an equivalence or lack of disproportion between a gift of the house and 'caring for D for as long as D may live, be it one year or 20 years'. That is irrelevant to the question of what value the parties place on the actual detriment, ie 'caring for D for two years'. Thus, the existence of the bargain is of no evidential significance in terms of assisting the court in comparing the value of the detriment incurred by C to the value of the expectation.

It might be thought that there is some unfairness to C in this refusal to take account of the bargain when comparing the detriment actually incurred with the expectation. The basis for this view would be that C might have had

---

[90] *Jennings* [2002] EWCA Civ 159, [45].

to care for D for 20 years (instead of for two years), incurring detriment at a much higher level than the value of the expectation, but would in those circumstances have had to be content with a remedy capped at the level of the expectation. Would it not be appropriate for the court to 'take account of the parties' perception of "the balance of risks and rewards" to [C] of performing his side of the bargain'?[91] This would involve fulfilling the expectation once C has done 'exactly what [D] agreed or suggested was necessary in order to acquire the promised right'.[92] However, this appears to involve an impermissible shift from the notion of using the existence of the bargain as evidence of the value placed by the parties on the detriment over to an approach which seeks to enforce the unenforceable bargain (once C has fulfilled his side of it). When one is applying the proportionality principle envisaged by Robert Walker LJ, what matters is the detriment which was actually incurred by D, not the amount of detriment he might have incurred if things had turned out differently. The bargain principle cannot justify awarding an expectation remedy where this would be disproportionate to the detriment.[93]

IV. CONCLUSION

This chapter has analysed the various roles which expectation could play in relation to the determination of proprietary estoppel remedies. It has been argued, by a process of eliminating the various alternatives, that the only appropriate role for expectation is as a cap on a remedy determined on the basis of other factors. This involves a rejection of the notion, supported by *Jennings v Rice*, that the fulfilment of the expectation should be the prima facie remedy, to be granted unless such a remedy would be disproportionate to the detriment suffered by C. This chapter has argued that such an approach does not stand up to close scrutiny and leads to demonstrably illogical results. It is interesting, however, to reflect on why this approach has become fashionable.

The answer seems to be that, understandably, courts and commentators feel uneasy with the idea of a completely discretionary approach to remedies. In a sea of discretion, the only two concepts to which one can cling are expectation and detriment. The approach of automatically fulfilling C's

---

[91] Bright and McFarlane, above n 6, 458, quoting Etherton J at first instance in *Cobbe v Yeoman's Row Management Ltd* [2005] EWHC 266 (Ch), [136].

[92] *ibid.*

[93] Interestingly, Bright and McFarlane, *ibid*, 459 concede that in a bargain case 'it may be that proportionality does have a minor role if B's expectation greatly exceeds his reliance', referring to the possibility of D dying 'very shortly' after the arrangement is made. However, once this concession is made, it is difficult to see why proportionality should have a role only if the expectation is 'out of all proportion to the reliance' (*ibid*, 460). Why does the normal proportionality principle not apply?

expectation, perhaps given a boost by the recent decision of the House of Lords in *Cobbe*,[94] affords no role whatsoever to the concept of detriment at the remedial stage. No convincing argument has been advanced as to why this should be so and, as well as allowing for the possibility of an award for C which is disproportionate to his detriment, this approach also runs into difficulties in dealing with the problem of countervailing benefits received by C (as pointed out in this chapter). The 'estoppel as starting point' approach of *Jennings* seems to represent an improvement, in that it gives a prominent role to expectation, while making a concession to the fact that C's detriment is central to the establishment of his cause of action and so, in principle, should not be ignored completely at the remedial stage. The difficulty is that upon analysis it turns out that, once it has been admitted to the remedial inquiry, it is not possible to keep the concept of detriment locked up in a box marked 'proportionality'. The attempt to do so leads to inconsistent results, as has been pointed out in this chapter by reference to hypothetical examples showing C being awarded a lower remedy based on a higher expectation.

If one rejects the attempt to give a role to detriment through the 'expectation as starting point' approach, what is the alternative? One obvious candidate is a detriment-based remedial approach. This can be seen as allocating an appropriate role to both of the two main elements in an estoppel claim, expectation and detriment. C's claim to justice is based on the combination of the expectation and the detriment and so it is logical that D can satisfy the claim either by erasing the detriment or by fulfilling the expectation. This suggests a remedial approach whereby the remedy is designed to erase the detriment, subject to an upper limit at the level of the expectation. It is true, of course, that the English courts have been hostile to this approach. This is presumably based, in part at least, on the complexity of trying to quantify C's detriment, which may not be financial in nature. Since it tends to be easier to fulfill C's expectation, the courts prefer to avoid the problem of quantifying detriment.

If this is the case, it highlights a potential difficulty with the whole proprietary estoppel jurisdiction. It would not seem acceptable to contend that, while justice to D requires the courts to limit the remedy by reference to C's detriment, the courts must lean towards the maximum possible remedy (one based on expectation) because of the practical difficulty in calculating a remedy based on detriment. Equity has arrogated to itself a very broad jurisdiction which, given the principles of justice which underlie it, sometimes requires the court to put a value on C's detriment. If this requirement were to make the doctrine too difficult to operate in practice, then the justification for its existence would be called into question.[95] At the least,

---

[94] *Cobbe* [2008] UKHL 55.
[95] For an argument in favour of abolishing proprietary estoppel, see S Gardner *An Introduction to Land Law* (Oxford, Hart Publishing, 2007) 121–2.

one might doubt the wisdom of the rapid expansion in the scope of the doctrine in recent years.[96]

It is probably too soon, however, to concede that it is impossible for the courts to take a principled approach to proprietary estoppel remedies. The law is still absorbing the lessons of cases such *Jennings v Rice*, which represent the beginning of a move to take account of detriment at the remedial stage. As the case law develops, one can hope for greater sophistication from the courts in terms of their understanding of the concepts of expectation and detriment, and of the relationship between them. In truth, there may not be all that much distance between the reliance-based remedial model and the traditional discretionary approach. While Robert Walker LJ did not include a reference to detriment in his non-exhaustive list of factors relevant to the exercise of the court's discretion,[97] it cannot sensibly be denied that the detriment incurred by C is an important factor relevant to the exercise of the court's discretion. After all, it is not difficult to imagine a case where none of the other (relatively peripheral) factors explicitly mentioned by Robert Walker LJ will be relevant. Thus, it might not be much of a stretch to recast the court's traditional discretionary approach in terms of the court being required to grant a remedy which is appropriate in light of C's detriment, viewed in conjunction with any other relevant factors of the sort identified by Robert Walker LJ, and which is subject to an upper limit based on the level of the expectation. While not all that radical on the face of it (and not yet representing a complete move to a reliance-based model), such a rethinking of the basis for estoppel remedies would seem to represent a step forward in terms of coherence and certainty.

Some observations have been offered at this concluding stage as to the possible future development of the courts' approach to proprietary estoppel remedies, betraying sympathy on the part of the author with the reliance-based remedial model. However, the primary intention has been to analyse the place of expectation in the remedial inquiry, trying to cast light on the possible roles of this concept, whether as the invariable measure of the remedy, or as a starting point in the remedial inquiry, or as a proxy for detriment, or as an element in an informal bargain between the parties. It is hoped that this analysis may be of value irrespective of the reader's doctrinal allegiances.

---

[96] Consider, for example, developments in relation to testamentary promises, including those which do not necessarily concern land. The speeches in *Cobbe* [2008] UKHL 55 suggested anxiety on the part of the House of Lords, not specifically related to the remedial question, as to the recent expansion in the reach of proprietary estoppel. However, in the subsequent decision in *Thorner v Major* [2009] UKHL 18, the House of Lords upheld a claim in the testamentary context which appeared to fall at the outer limits of the existing proprietary estoppel jurisdiction.

[97] See text to n 9 above.

17

Leases: Property, Contract or More?

JILL MORGAN[*]

I. INTRODUCTION

THE TRADITIONAL VIEW of a lease—which had crystallised by the end of the fifteenth century—is that it is primarily a proprietary interest, which involves the creation of an estate in land. Once the landlord has granted the tenant possession of the premises, he has carried out his primary obligation. However, societal and other changes have expanded the contexts in which leases are used and have transformed the expectations of the parties. Today, most leases—be they of commercial or residential premises or of agricultural land—involve far more than the grant of a legal estate and 'impose on the parties a whole range of covenants which can result in the common law incidents of estate being overwhelmed'.[1] As a result, the courts in a number of jurisdictions have been prepared to accept the lease as 'both an executory contract and an executed demise',[2] recognising that the grant of a legal estate is not necessarily the primary purpose of the lease. In consequence, they have adopted and applied contractual principles to leases, albeit with varying degrees of enthusiasm. At the same time, there has been extensive debate as to whether—and, if so, the extent to which—the landlord and tenant relationship should be extended to embrace principles of contract law. This debate exemplifies the significant amount of energy which is devoted in conventional legal doctrine to what Kevin Gray describes as 'patrolling the frontier between property and contract'.[3] He explains:

> Property lawyers keep especially vigilant watch for those fugitive varieties of contractual right which threaten to cross the frontier and settle in property

---

[*] J Morgan, School of Law, Swansea University.
[1] P Luxton, 'Termination of leases: from property to contract?' in J Birds, R Bradgate and C Villiers (eds), *Termination of Contracts* (London, Wiley Publishing, 1995) 179.
[2] *Progressive Mailing House Pty v Tabali Pty* (1985) 157 CLR 17, 51 (Deane J).
[3] K Gray, 'Property in thin air' (1991) 50 *Cambridge Law Journal* 252, 302.

territory. Much fuss is made whenever the conceptual border is realigned and rights of 'contract' are brought within the province of property.[4]

Today, we are witnessing further changes which impose different demands and pressures on land use. For example, the current Government policy of overseeing the provision of three million new homes by 2020[5] raises the question of how best to balance housing and transport needs in ways which minimise negative impacts on green space and natural habitats. Arguably, neither property or contract principles as they have been applied to leases by English law provide the answer, both of them simply being ways of regulating the parties' own selfish, private interests. Thus, as well as seeking to outline the development of, and the rationales for, contractual intervention into leases and the emergence of the consumer model, this paper seeks to explore whether a 'stewardship' approach might be developed which would help achieve more efficient land use and operate more obviously therefore in the 'public' interest. The notion of stewardship—that a person who has rights in property must hold that property for the public good—has traditionally been associated with the preservation of wetlands, coastlines and other natural phenomena,[6] but also more recently with the promotion and protection of urban green spaces. There is a strong argument, however, for extending a similar approach into the English law of landlord and tenant. The law relating to abandonment is taken as an example.

II. HISTORICAL DEVELOPMENT

Those who advocate the application of contractual principles to the landlord and tenant relationship often point to the origins of the term of years by way of justification—despite the fact that, as Professor Milsom puts it, 'the arrangement was about the profits rather than the land itself'.[7] Until the thirteenth century, the tenant was in a very weak position, largely because the term of years was used for purposes which were regarded as 'immoral and speculative',[8] namely the avoidance of the usury laws. Given that 'even a feudal economy ... could not flourish without some means of financing development' it became necessary to devise a means by which lenders were given not only security for, but also a return on, their loans. The solution

---

[4] *ibid*, 302.

[5] Department for Communities and Local Government, *Homes for the Future: More Affordable, More Sustainable* (2007) (Cmd 7191) 7.

[6] See C Redgewell, *Intergenerational Trusts and Environmental Protection* (Manchester, Manchester University Press, 1999), especially as regards the American public trust doctrine.

[7] SFC Milsom, *Historical Foundations of the Common Law* (London, Butterworths, 1981) 153.

[8] TFT Plucknett, *A Concise History of the Common Law* (Boston, Little, Brown & Co, 1956) 511.

was for the lender to take a lease of the land, and either to re-let it or to go into possession and farm or otherwise manage it. The term granted was of sufficient duration to enable the lender to use the revenue from the land to recover the principal sum and make a profit.

The transformation of the term of years into a proprietary interest came with the accumulation of various remedies which enabled dispossessed tenants to be restored to their land, thereby bringing them into line with freeholders. From the thirteenth century the action of trespass *quare clausum fregit* was available to dispossessed freeholders. By contrast, an interest limited to a term of years did not confer any estate and real actions were not available to protect it. Between lessor and lessee there was simply a contractual relationship. As a result, a lessee evicted by his lessor before the end of his term could only claim damages for breach of contract. The first stage in the 'transformation of a tenancy for a term of years into a property right' may be traced to about 1235 when a new action was formulated, *quare ejecit infra terminum*, which was designed to restore a tenant who had been ejected from the premises before the end of his term by a purchaser of the land from the lessor.[9]

As feudalism died out and 'commercialism grew up', the fourteenth century witnessed an increase in the number of people who, 'anxious to make a living by agriculture, preferred to take farms for terms of years at money rents, rather than become freehold tenants'.[10] At the same time the mortgage arose as a more satisfactory method of securing land in return for a debt, with lenders insisting on the land being conveyed to them in fee simple in return for the loan. The term of years was no longer associated with money-lending and the lessee was popularly regarded as a freeman whose capital [was] insufficient to buy the land but who [was] enterprising enough to work the land of other owners'.[11] Gradually the writ of *ejectione firmae* became available to protect a lessee for years who had been ousted by a stranger. Initially only damages were recoverable but it was developed during the second half of the fifteenth century so that the lessee could recover the remainder of the term. The earliest reported case in which a lessee was allowed in this action to recover both damages and possession was in 1499. The writ of *ejectione firmae* was thus converted into the action of ejectment which ultimately came to replace many of the old forms of action.[12] Once

---

[9] A Bradbrook, 'The application of the principle of mitigation of damages to landlord-tenant law' (1977) 8 *Sydney Law Review* 15, 16.

[10] Arthur Underhill, *A Concise Explanation of Lord Birkenhead's Act (The Law of Property Act 1922)* (London, Butterworth & Co, 1922) 15.

[11] FE Colbourn, 'A guide to problems in shopping center leases' (1961–62) 20 *Brook Law Review* 227, 232.

[12] While *quare clausum fregit* required forcible entry, *de ejectione firmae* required only wrongful possession. In due course it was extended to cases involving disputed title to freeholds. The claimant would enter on the land and grant a term of years to another person.

the lessee's right of possession was afforded legal protection, the leasehold interest acquired a predominantly property characteristic and the lessee came to be regarded as the holder of an interest in land rather than merely the holder of a contractual interest.

By the end of the fifteenth century therefore, the primary function of a lease had come to be regarded as the creation of an estate in land. In the rural society of the time and for many years afterwards, it was appropriate that the lease should be viewed as primarily proprietary in nature. Possession of the land was the essential element of the lease, allowing for the planting, cultivation and harvest of crops. Only rarely would the land contain buildings and, in any case, the average tenant would possess the skills to carry out any necessary repairs and 'would also expect to provide any amenities, such as the supply of heat or water'.[13] Tenants would seldom have any complaints unless there was interference with their possession of the land. Many of the property-based characteristics of the lease emerged from this period. For example, the rent, the consideration for the lease, was regarded as issuing out of the land which meant that, so long as the tenant had possession of the land, there could be no failure of consideration. Further, as the contract was regarded as executed, the doctrine of frustration did not apply. If, therefore, the premises were 'expropriated by a government authority during the term of a lease'[14] or 'destroyed by fire, flood or storm', the obligations imposed on both parties remained and the tenant was still obliged to pay the full rent even though the premises were incapable of occupation or had even been destroyed.

During the last 200 years however, cities have replaced farms as the places where most people live and work; the spatial concentration of much of the population has highlighted the importance of residential leases; for many households, houses have given way to flats, often in high-rise living complexes, the residents of which are concerned with the provision of services 'such as heating, lighting, plumbing, garbage disposal, security and recreation' and not just 'the right to possession of a plot of ground or a cubic area of airspace';[15] the business lease has become more common and of greater social importance than the agrarian lease; buildings (and 'their quality, condition, maintenance and terms of use') have become increasingly significant. In addition, the modern tenant does not expect—and is often unable—to do the sort of repairs which were carried out by 'his fifteenth

---

The lessee remained on the land, and the next person who entered was taken to be an ejector of the lessee, who then served upon him a writ of trespass and ejectment. Interestingly and unusually, the freeholder acquired the lessee's remedy.

[13] Bradbrook, above n 9, at 30.
[14] *Paradine v Jane* (1647) 82 ER 519.
[15] RF Hicks, 'The contractual nature of real property leases' (1972) 24 *Baylor Law Review* 443–547, 451.

century counterpart'. Indeed, in multi-unit dwellings or commercial premises, it would often be impossible for a tenant 'to make structural repairs without trespassing upon the premises of other tenants'.[16] As a result, modern leases usually impose on both parties a range of covenants, most of which are intended to endure for the lifetime of the lease. However, while

> the contents of leases have changed to reflect the needs of the parties ... the development of modern contract law in the nineteenth century to [accommodate] rapid commercial expansion and to satisfy the ethical principles of the time occurred too late to work as a sea-change on an already centuries-old law of leases.[17]

Subsequently, the English courts have taken a more muted approach to the infusion of contract into landlord and tenant law.

III. THE CONTRACTUAL PERSPECTIVE

Nonetheless, in several cases over the last 30 years the English courts have turned towards the contractual character of the lease. An early example was *United Scientific Holdings Ltd v Burnley Borough Council*,[18] in which the House of Lords took the view that the rights and obligations of the parties with regard to rent, particularly under rent review clauses, should be determined as a matter of the construction of the contract, just as payment obligations would be under any other contract. Lord Diplock explained that

> the mediaeval concept of rent as a service rendered by the tenant to the landlord has been displaced by the modern concept of a payment which a tenant is bound by his contract to pay to the landlord for the use of his land.[19]

A few years later, by accepting the potential application of the doctrine of frustration to leases (albeit only very exceptionally, and not on the facts of the particular case),[20] the House of Lords effectively paved the way for the application of ordinary contractual principles to leases. The courts were slow to make use of the opportunity to do so, however, and a decade was to pass before[21] Mr Assistant Recorder Sedley QC (as he then was) held in the county court that a lease could be brought to an end by the tenant's acceptance of a repudiatory breach by the landlord.[22] Since then, other

---

[16] Bradbrook, above n 9, at 30.
[17] Luxton, above n 1, at 179.
[18] *United Scientific Holdings Ltd v Burnley Borough Council* [1978] AC 904 (HL).
[19] *ibid*, 935.
[20] *National Carriers Ltd v Panalpina (Northern) Ltd* [1981] AC 1965 (HL).
[21] *Hussein v Mehlman* [1992] 2 EGLR 87.
[22] *ibid*. In *Total Oil Great Britain Ltd v Thompson Garages (Biggin Hill) Ltd* [1972] 1 QB 318 (HL), Lord Denning had said, obiter, that a lease was not capable of determination by repudiation and acceptance. His view was attributable in part to the fact that a lease was not then capable of determination by frustration so that contractual remedies in other cases could not apply.

courts in England have held, or assumed, that a lease can be brought to an end by acceptance of a repudiatory breach.[23] The fact that a joint periodic tenancy could be determined by any one of the joint tenants giving notice to the landlord without the knowledge (let alone the consent) of the other was established in *Hammersmith and Fulham London Borough Council v Monk*,[24] Lord Bridge stating that there was no reason why the question should receive any different answer in the context of the contractual relationship of landlord and tenant than that which it would receive in any other contractual context.[25]

However, lest it be thought that the English courts are surely—albeit slowly—catching up with their brethren in other jurisdictions, it should be remembered that the vitality of the contractual approach is doubtless attributable, at least in part, to the paucity of statutory landlord and tenant law elsewhere. By contrast, English law has a long history of conferring statutory security upon the majority of residential, commercial and agricultural tenants by providing that, unless the tenant vacates voluntarily, the landlord cannot lawfully recover possession without a court order. The court can only make an order in accordance with the scheme provided by the relevant statute. It appears that statutory security provides immunity to certain contract law challenges.[26] For example, a tenancy cannot be rescinded if it is subject to a statutory scheme which contains a ground allowing for recovery of possession by a landlord who has been induced to grant the tenancy by the tenant's fraudulent misrepresentation.[27]

The culmination of the contractual approach by the English courts can be found in the House of Lords decision in *Bruton v London & Quadrant Housing Trust*,[28] the consequence of which is that the existence of a lease or tenancy does not inevitably lead to the grant of a proprietary right. Rather, there appear to be two types of lease. The traditional type is based on a contractual arrangement between the parties but also involves a proprietary element, which not only exists between grantor and grantee but can also bind third parties according to the normal rules of registered and unregistered land. The other is based purely on a contractual arrangement between two parties and does not create a proprietary right. This personal, non-proprietary lease exists between grantor and grantee but cannot bind

---

[23] *Chartered Trust plc* v *Davies* (1997) 76 P & CR 397 and *cf Nynehead Developments Ltd v RH Fibreboard Containers Ltd* [1999] 1 EGLR 7.

[24] *Hammersmith and Fulham London Borough Council v Monk* [1992] 1 AC 478 (HL).

[25] *ibid*, 483.

[26] In *Hussein v Mehlman*, it was predicted that, if default in rent payments did amount to a repudiatory act on the tenant's part, the landlord's rights to accept it would be subject not only to the various statutory codes which 'hedge the right to recover possession' but also (where there is a term certain) 'to the provision contained in the contract of letting itself in relation to forfeiture. For a recent example of

[27] *London Borough of Islington v Uckac* [2006] 1 WLR 1303.

[28] *Bruton v London & Quadrant Housing Trust* [2000] 1 AC 406 (HL).

anybody else. As Bright explains, the acceptance in *Bruton* that there can be such a creature as a 'non-estate lease ... seems to shift the lease's centre of gravity away from the grant of a proprietary interest in land to a contractual relationship involving the grant of exclusive possession for a term'.

A side-shoot of contract law as applied to leases can be found in the emergence of consumer law which, in Bright's view, represents an 'even stronger doctrinal challenge'. Until recently, consumer-based arguments failed to bear much fruit in the context of landlord and tenant law. For example, in *Dunn v Bradford London Borough Council*,[29] in holding that consumer legislation[30] did not place a duty on a local authority to carry out repairs which it was not contractually obliged to do, the Court of Appeal reiterated the property-based nature of the landlord and tenant relationship. Chadwick LJ explained that 'in recognising the tenant's right to occupy the premises', the landlord was not carrying out a service but simply giving effect to the grant; the provision of any service and 'respecting existing property rights'. Thereafter the landlord's obligations were to be found in the terms of the tenancy.[31]

More recently, however, the Court of Appeal confirmed in *London Borough of Newham v Khatun*[32] that the Unfair Terms in Consumer Contracts Regulations 1999 apply to contracts dealing with interests in or rights of occupation over land (including tenancy agreements) and that local authority landlords must conform with the Regulations as regards the standard terms upon which they let accommodation. It held that when acting as landlords, local authorities are 'sellers' or 'suppliers' of the relevant consumer item (namely accommodation) and tenants are 'consumers'. While acknowledging that transfers of houses are most often effected between consumers rather than between consumers and traders, Laws LJ noted that tenancies are commonly granted by landlords who are in business, and was unable therefore to perceive any rationale for the exclusion of land transactions from the legislation's scope.

Another important step towards the assimilation of consumerist principles within the landlord and tenant relationship comes from the Law Commission's proposals for the reform of housing law. At the heart of the Commission's proposals lies a 'consumer perspective' of rented housing (or, at least its legal regulation), which involves a departure from the concept of a lease. It involves instead the conceptualisation of housing law as a branch of consumer law with the key component of the landlord-occupier relationship being the contract, which grants a right to occupy a property as a home. The nature of the contract—as lease or licence—would no longer

---

[29] *Dunn v Bradford London Bough Council* [2003] HLR 15 (CA).
[30] Supply of Goods and Services Act 1982 s.13.
[31] *Dunn v Bradford London Borough Council* [2003] HLR 15, para 52.
[32] *London Borough of Newham v Khatun* [2005] QB 37.

be important. All landlords and occupiers would have a written statement of their contract, setting out their rights and obligations, including those provided for by the Rented Homes Bill. The intention is to make a break with past 'legislative strategy', which has involved landlords and tenants entering into contractual arrangements which are then substantially ignored 'as details in the agreement are over-ridden by statute'.[33]

IV. THE SINGULARITY OF LAND

While both the contract- and consumer-based approaches may have much to commend them, they share the disquieting feature of appearing to treat land as simply another commodity. Certainly, land can be regarded as a commodity subject to the laws of the market-place. As such, it will be supplied if and when the supplier anticipates the probability of securing a reasonable return and it will be bought by those able and willing to pay the price which will yield that return. Accordingly, it is given no special treatment to differentiate it from any other commodity: state intervention is limited to 'general regulation guaranteeing the right of ownership and ... freedom of exchange in a capitalistic economy',[34] and no provision is made to give landlords and tenants any rights or obligations over and above those which are contractually agreed.[35] However, whilst land is indeed a vehicle whereby wealth can be stored and accumulated, it possesses a number of features which distinguish it from other commodities. First, the multiplicity of interests which can exist in land are unparalleled compared with other commodities and can give rise to complicated property relations. Secondly, land is necessarily connected with place, and a person who buys or rents land is accessing infrastructure services, as well as employment and leisure opportunities. Thirdly, and most importantly for the present discussion, although the law regards the ownership of land as extending up to the heavens and down to the depths of the earth, land is (almost) non-renewable, with no new frontiers to exploit. Whether taken separately or together, these factors mean that land warrants special treatment and its provision should not be left simply to the vagaries of the market.

Thus, while it may be more realistic in today's society to regard a lease as a contract for services rather than merely the grant of an estate in land, treating the lease as a contract under which both the parties have continuing obligations even after the conveyance of the estate in the land fails to take

---

[33] Law Commission, *Renting Homes 1: Status and Security*, Law Com Consultation Paper No 162 (London, The Stationery Office, 2002) para 1.33.

[34] B Bengtsson, 'Housing as a social right: implications for welfare state theory' (2001) 24 *Scandinavian Political Studies* 255–75, 262.

[35] D Donnison and C Ungerson, *Housing Policy* (Harmondsworth, Penguin, 1982) 1.

into account the special qualities of land. A useful example is the way in which English law deals with abandonment.

V. ABANDONMENT

Abandonment occurs where a tenant manifests an intention never to occupy the demised premises or, having gone into possession, vacates them with no intention of returning. Sometimes failure of the rent to materialise is the first intimation which a landlord has that its tenant has departed. A landlord faced with the tenant's abandonment has a number of options. First, it may choose to put an end to the lease; this could be by re-entry under a forfeiture clause (provided that the abandonment, or a consequence of the abandonment, is a breach of covenant in the lease, eg a breach of a keep-open covenant, a repairing covenant, or a covenant to pay rent), or by acceptance of what might be treated effectively as the tenant's offer to surrender the lease. If the landlord chooses either of these options, the tenant loses his right to possession of the property and he is no longer liable to pay rent for the unexpired portion of the term or to observe any other covenants. Secondly, and alternatively, the landlord may treat the term as continuing and sue for the instalments of rent as they fall due.

The application of contractual principles leads to a further possibility: the tenant's abandonment may be regarded as a repudiatory breach. Repudiation occurs if one party makes it clear that he no longer intends to be bound by the contract or he will fulfill the contract only in a manner substantially inconsistent with his obligations.[36] According to contract law, the innocent party again has a choice. It may accept the other party's conduct as terminating the contract. This ends the parties' rights and obligations as to further performance but the defaulting party must compensate the innocent party for any consequential loss. The innocent party has a 'duty' to mitigate its loss, meaning that it must not only take reasonable steps to minimise its loss but it must also refrain from taking unreasonable steps which increase it. By contrast, it can affirm and continue the contract. Here, because the contract remains alive, no question of damages or of mitigation arises. However, in *White and Carter (Councils) Ltd v McGregor*[37] the House of Lords indicated that if the innocent party can be shown to have 'no legitimate interest, financial or otherwise, in performing the contract rather than claiming damages, he ought not to be allowed to saddle the other party with an additional burden with no benefit to himself'.[38] To be a legitimate interest 'the innocent party must have reasonable grounds for keeping the

---

[36] *Ross T Smyth & Co Ltd v TD Bailey, Son and Co* [1940] 3 All ER 60, 72 (HL).
[37] *White and Carter (Councils) Ltd v McGregor* [1962] AC 413 (HL).
[38] *ibid*, 431.

contract open bearing in mind also the interests of the wrongdoer'.[39] In a string of shipping cases[40] the courts have held that an election to keep the contract alive would be wholly unreasonable where damages would provide an adequate remedy for any loss suffered.

The issue recently fell to be considered by the Court of Appeal in *Reichman v Beveridge*,[41] in which the tenants (a firm of solicitors) held a five-year lease of office premises. Having ceased to practise, they abandoned their offices and stopped paying rent. The landlords decided not to bring the lease to an end but to issue proceedings for the arrears, seeking only a money judgment for the sums due. The tenant sought to establish that it would be unreasonable to keep the contract alive in cases where the tenant had not only failed to pay rent and all other sums due under the lease, but had also abandoned the demised premises.

A. The Adequacy of Damages

In order to succeed the tenants had to persuade the court that damages would be an adequate remedy. This meant that, first it had to be established that damages for the loss of the future rent could be recovered where the landlord ended the tenancy because of the tenant's breach and then re-let the premises at a lower rent than that which would have been payable for the remainder of the original lease. If the landlord could sue the former tenant for the difference, then it could legitimately be argued that damages would be an adequate remedy. If damages could not be recovered at all, then they would clearly not be an adequate remedy.

Although there are a number of Commonwealth authorities which suggest that a landlord can recover loss of bargain damages,[42] the only English decision that appears to have any bearing on the matter is to the contrary. In *Walls v Atcheson*[43] a tenant took premises for a year, occupied them, paid rent for a quarter and then quit. After about four weeks the landlord re-let the premises, at a slightly lower rent. They remained let for some months but were empty for the last two months of the original term. The landlord failed in her attempt to recover the loss of rent under the original

---

[39] *Stocznia Gdanska SA v Latvian Shipping Co* [1996] 2 Lloyd's Rep 132 (CA) 138–9 (Hutchins LJ).

[40] *Attica Sea carriers Corp v Ferrostaal Posei don Bulk Reederei GMBH (The Puerto Buitrago)* [1976] 1 Lloyd's Rep 250; *Gator Shipping Corp v Trans-Asiatic Oil SA (The Odenfield)* [1978] 2 Lloyd's Rep 357; *Clea Shipping Corp v Bulk Oil International (The Alaskan Trader) (No 2)* [1984] 1 All ER 129.

[41] *Reichman v Beveridge* [2006] EWCA Civ 1659.

[42] *Highway Properties v Kelly, Douglas & Co* (1971) 17 DLR (3d) 710; *Progressive Mailing House Pty Ltd v Tabali* (1985) 157 CLR 17; *Wood Factory Pty v Kiritos Pty* [1985] 2 NSWLR 105.

[43] *Walls v Atcheson* (1826) 130 ER 591 (Court of Common Pleas).

lease, including both the amount by which the rent was less under the later lettings, and the whole of the rent for the later period when the premises were vacant. It was held that putting in another tenant amounted either to accepting a surrender or to eviction of the tenant, so as to put an end to the right to claim the rent. In *Reichman v Beveridge*, the Court of Appeal explained that 'it may be a logical development to hold that a landlord, having forfeited the lease, can recover damages for the loss of future rent, at least if the breach which led to the forfeiture was fundamental and repudiatory'.[44] However, it concluded that English law has not yet reached that stage and that damages would not be an adequate remedy.

The tenants argued that the landlords had failed to mitigate their loss: they had failed to instruct agents to market the premises, declined the offer of a prospective assignee and refused an offer to negotiate payment for a surrender of the lease. Nevertheless, Lloyd LJ believed that a landlord could not be described as 'wholly' unreasonable if it took the view that the tenant, whose default had caused the problem, should bear the burden of finding a new tenant.[45]

B. A Question of Reasonableness

The decision in *Reichman v Beveridge* is clearly based on the proprietary view of leases. Because the tenants owned an estate in the land for a defined period of time, the landlords did not need to concern themselves if, during that time, the tenants decided to under-utilise what could be regarded as their own property. If the tenants did not want to occupy the property themselves, it was up to them to sub-let or assign the remainder of the term (if the tenancy agreement allowed).[46] The Court of Appeal acknowledged that a tenant in a similar situation might encounter practical and economic problems in assigning or sub-letting, especially if the current rent were higher than the market rent. It would be difficult to find an assignee (except perhaps at a reverse premium) and a sub-tenant might not be prepared to pay enough rent to cover the obligations under the head-lease. Moreover, both the landlord and the prospective assignee would typically require all arrears to be paid off. Nonetheless, as we have seen, the Court decided that the landlord would not be acting wholly unreasonably by leaving the lease in place and suing for the rent instead of trying to find an alternative tenant.

---

[44] *Reichman v Beveridge* [2007] 1 P & CR 20 (CA) para 27.
[45] *ibid*, para 31.
[46] K Gray and S.Gray, *Elements of Land Law*, 4th edn (Oxford, Oxford University Press, 2005) para 14.202.

Two points may be made as regards the issue of reasonableness. First, even if the 'stewardship' approach is adopted, ie a solution is sought which seeks to optimise effective use of the land, it could be argued that the tenant bears as much responsibility in this regard as his landlord. However, in *Reichman*, even though the tenants had made clear their intention not to use the premises themselves, the possibility had arisen of a replacement tenant who, presumably, would actually have made use of the land. Was it really reasonable in such circumstances to allow the landlord to continue the lease and perpetuate the current tenants' liability? Indeed, if the current tenant were to find an prospective assignee, might the tenant succeed in arguing that the landlord could not treat the lease as continuing if, in circumstances such as in *Reichman*, the landlord had in fact unreasonably refused consent to assign?

Secondly, account should be taken of the length of the term. In *Reichman*, the lease (typical of commercial leases) was for five years. Had it been for longer, there might have been scope for regarding as unreasonable the landlord's decision to continue with it and sue for rent. In the Scottish case of *Salaried Staff London Loan Company Ltd v Swears and Wells Ltd*,[47] tenants under a 35-year lease repudiated the lease after five years. The landlords refused to accept the repudiation and held the tenants to their contract. The landlords' action for rent and service charges for a period of nearly a year subsequent to the repudiation succeeded. However, the court expressed reservations as to whether the landlords could have sued each year for the next 29 years, Lord Ross suggesting that 'it might be inferred that it would be manifestly unjust or unreasonable to allow the [claimants] to continue suing for rent'. Similarly, in its Report on *Remedies for Breach of Contract*,[48] the Scottish Law Commission proposed that a party to a contract who has been told that performance under the contract is no longer wanted but who has nonetheless carried it out would be precluded from recovering payment for post-notification performance if: (a) he could have entered into a reasonable substitute transaction without unreasonable effort or expense; or (b) it was unreasonable for him to proceed with the performance. In such cases the claimant's remedy would be to rescind the contract and claim damages. The rules on mitigation of loss would then apply. An example of a 'substitute transaction' put forward by the Commission is that of a landlord whose tenant repudiates a lease which has still many years to run. The landlord could not go on claiming rent for the whole duration of the lease if the [premises] could easily be re-let to another tenant on reasonable terms. The 'landlord would ... be able to rescind and claim damages

[47] *Salaried Staff London Loan Company Ltd v Swears and Wells Ltd* 1985 SC 189.
[48] Scottish Law Commission, *Remedies for Breach of Contract*, Scot Law Com No 174, SE 1999/59 (Edinburgh, 1999).

for the difference between the rent obtainable from the new tenant (if less) and the rent due under the repudiated contract'.[49]

In *Reichman*, the Court of Appeal suggested that the issue of mitigation would only be likely to arise if the landlord could not re-let (either at all or for the whole of the unexpired term) or could re-let but only at a lower rent. If the rental market were to improve, the landlord would be likely to forfeit (or to accept the surrender) and re-let at a profit. Such a view presupposes, of course, that landowners (including landlords) are rational economic agents. Even if they are, there may be situations in which—because there is 'an immediate profit to be made, future returns on investments in the resource are expected to be low, and the owner's subjective discount rate is high'[50]—the depletion or destruction of a resource is the most rational course of action. More importantly for the present discussion, 'an owner who would not intentionally destroy an asset ... might not manage it so as to maximise its social, as opposed to private [economic] value'.[51]

VI. CONCLUSION

Apart from a few limited exceptions, obligations relating to the maximisation of the potential usefulness of land are not a common law default position.[52] That role tends instead to be the preserve of statute.[53] Two particular criticisms may be levelled at the response of English law to abandonment. First, it tacitly encourages landlords to keep a usable asset out of the economy. Secondly, it provides them with an incentive to neglect their property after abandonment. Taking the first criticism, land may be viewed as fulfilling an economic function if the landlord is still entitled to insist upon payment even after abandonment. However, it is suggested that, given the short supply of land, as much (if not more) emphasis should be placed on its social as its economic use. The welfare of the whole community is

---

[49] *ibid*, para 2.8.

[50] DH Cole, *Pollution and Property* (Cambridge, Cambridge University Press, 2002) 147.

[51] *ibid*.

[52] One exception exists in the implied covenant of non-derogation from grant. Thus, where a lease is made for particular purposes, landlords are under an obligation not to use adjoining land which they have retained in such a way as to render the demised premises unfit or materially less fit for that purpose. As was said in *Birmingham Dudley & District Banking Co v Ross* (1888) 38 Ch D 295 (CA) 313: 'a grantor having given a thing with one hand is not to take away the means of enjoying it with the other' (Bowen LJ).

[53] Examples can be found in s.11 Landlord and Tenant Act 1985 (which imposes repairing obligations in certain circumstances on landlords of dwelling-houses) and the provisions of Part II of the Landlord and Tenant Act 1954, the Rent Act 1977 and the Housing Acts of 1985 and 1988, all of which allow for recovery of possession from a tenant on various 'estate management' grounds.

advanced by encouraging the productive use of property. As was stated by Pemberton J in *Martin v Siegley*,[54]

> [i]t is not in accordance with public policy to lay down a rule whereby the landlord would be required to permit the premises to remain idle over along term and thereafter recover damages for the full amount of the rentals stipulated for the term, because it is better for the parties to the agreement as well as to the public to have property put to some beneficial use.

Turning to the second criticism, maintaining the physical condition of the property may be of less concern where property is lying empty. The neglect of property following abandonment 'increases the likelihood of damage through vandalism, accidental fire, deterioration in appearance and decline in value. In extreme cases, this may lead to the surrounding neighbourhood declining in desirability, resulting in a fall in local property values'.[55]

Although a majority of jurisdictions still recognise the landlord's right to allow the premises to stand idle and sue for rent as it falls due, a substantial minority have adopted the 'mitigation of damages' principle and refuse to allow the landlord to recover damages he could have avoided by exercising real efforts to obtain a new lease. The current emphasis in the United Kingdom, in planning terms, is upon housing and other development in existing residential areas and on 'brown-field' sites. So far as the recycling of existing properties is concerned, the Housing Act 2004 makes provision for Empty Homes Development Orders. Against this backdrop of trying to maximise land use, surely an argument can be made for the English law of landlord and tenant to make its own small contribution by adopting an overarching principle of stewardship.

---

[54] *Martin v Siegley* (1923) 212 P 1057, 1059.
[55] Bradbrook, above n 9, at 20.

18

The Property Rights of Tribes

DR PG MCHUGH[*]

I. THE BREAKTHROUGH ERA OF THE 1980s: COMMON-LAW ABORIGINAL TITLE FROM CLOISTER TO COURTROOM

IN THE EARLY 1980s a band of academics—lawyers most of us—were arguing that the common law recognised the customary property rights of the tribal inhabitants of Canada and Australasia. The argument being made in Canada, Australia and New Zealand was that an underlying principle of common-law continuity applied to tribal property rights so much as it had been applied, say, to the property rights of the Quebecois French or Dutch population of Cape Colony. At that time the governing rule had been one of non-justiciability of Crown dealings with the tribes. Government relations with the tribal polities, in particular its management of land-related matters (including the enforcement of the terms of land cessions), were seen as a high political trust in which the courts would not intervene. That longstanding deference to the executive, with its exclusion of tribes from access to courts to vindicate their ancestral property rights and (in Canada and New Zealand) past deals made with the Crown facilitating white settlement, was then most egregiously embodied in the Australian principle of terra nullius. All three jurisdictions had a version of that exclusory stance. Indeed in the *Calder* case[1] (1973) a majority of the Supreme Court of Canada had appeared to accept the new revisionist legal principle of the continuity of all pre-existing property rights after Crown sovereignty. However even in that benchmark case, the non-justiciability bar ultimately prevailed, dressed up in the procedural need for a fiat in order to implead the Crown. Essentially that 'hands-off' stance by the courts

---

[*] PG McHugh, Reader in Law at the University of Cambridge.
[1] *Calder v Attorney-General of British Columbia* (1973) 34 DLR (3d) 145 (SCC). See generally Paul Tennant, *Aboriginal Peoples and Politics: The Indian Land Question in British Columbia, 1849–1989* (Vancouver BC, British Columbia Press, 1990) and for a good Canada-Australia comparison Peter H Russell, *Recognizing Aboriginal Title: The Mabo Case and Indigenous Resistance to English-Settler Colonialism* (Toronto, University of Toronto Press, 2005).

was the legal impediment that this band of academics sought to dissolve. At that time the intellectual mission of our scholarship was plain: We described the rights of tribal peoples in the present tense: 'the common law *recognises* the tribes' aboriginal title' (the term used to describe the set of tribal property rights inside Crown sovereignty). However there was no mistaking that it was actually an argument that 'the common law *should recognise*' those rights.[2]

Essentially, the scholarship of that era invited the courts to embark upon a process of doctrine-formation through development of a distinct customary property rights regime (termed 'aboriginal' and 'native' title) inside the introduced common-law legal system.[3] This invitation was issued out of frustration with the failures of the national political processes to devise an accommodation of aboriginal claims. Rising militancy by tribal activists seemed highlighted the unresponsiveness of governments to their claims even as national awareness and shame were rising. The retreat by Australia's Hawke Government in March 1986 from its earlier solemn commitment to a National Preferred Model of Aboriginal Land Rights was prompted by fear of its electoral cost. That political retreat was symptomatic of the feeling underlying that scholarship. It seemed to confirm our implicit belief that the courts were needed to nudge the political systems toward an accommodation that the executive branch (as embodiment of the Crown) would never take unprompted. The scholarship of that era therefore had a kind of ballast. Cynicism towards the political system and its historic pattern of indifference, on one hand, was counterbalanced on the other by a naïve and somewhat simplistic belief in the redemptive possibilities of the common law.[4] More leftist academics condemned this exhortation to the courts as Pollyanna-ish, given the oppressive function

---

[2] I give a personal retrospect of this scholarship in 'A History of the Modern Jurisprudence of Aboriginal Rights—Some Observations on the Journey So Far' in D Dyzenhaus, M Hunt and G Huscroft (eds), *A Simple Common Lawyer Essays in Honour of Michael Taggart* (Oxford, Hart Publishing, 2009) 209.

[3] Those scholars and some of their influential works included Cuming and Mickenberg, *Native Rights in Canada*, 2nd edn (Toronto, General Publishing 1972), esp parts II and IV; Kenneth Lysyk, 'The Indian Title Question in Canada: An Appraisal in the Light of *Calder*' (1973) 51 *Canadian Bar Review* 450; Thomas Berger, *Fragile Freedoms: Human Rights and Dissent in Canada* (Toronto, Clarke, Irwin, 1981); Douglas Sanders and Brian Slattery, *The Land Rights of Indigenous Canadian Peoples, as Affected by the Crown's Acquisition of Their Territories*, Doctoral Dissertation, University of Oxford (Reprinted, Saskatoon, University of Saskatchewan Native Law Centre, 1979); 'Understanding Aboriginal Rights' (1987) 66 *Canadian Bar Review* 727; Kent McNeil, *Common Law Aboriginal Title* (Oxford, Oxford University Press, 1987); Richard Bartlett in, for example, 'Indian and Native Rights in Uranium Development in Northern Saskatchewan' (1980–81) 45 *Saskatchewan Law Review* 13, and 'Making Land Available for Native Land Claims in Australia: An Example for Canada' (1983) 13 *Manitoba Law Journal* 73.

[4] R Bartlett, '*Mabo*: Another Triumph for the Common Law' (1993) 15 *Sydney Law Review* 183.

law had historically served as a tool of colonialism.[5] Perhaps they also saw the inherently conservative outcome that admission of tribes to the rights-place would eventually produce? Wrapped as it was in the language of property-right recognition, this newly-minted 'doctrine' carried an inherently conservative tendency (as I will explain) that was not really evident at the time. In the pre-breakthrough era, the transposition of the language of property into the legal vacuum of Crown-tribe relations was novel and entailed a reversal of the political branch's ingrained complacency. Perhaps because it was dressed in such familiar garb, the legal mainstream was ready to embrace that scholarship as the proverbial idea whose time had come. More controversially, it allowed the courts to seize the initiative, to address and assuage national guilt and to habilitate the tribes into a constitutional space that national law (ie Parliament) had until then resolutely refused to provide.

There was, then, the germ of an idea that was spreading in the early 1980s, encompassing the interplay of the world of scholarship and all branches of government. Aboriginal title began as an academic argument, which, in turn, became judicial doctrine and spread from Canada to New Zealand, then Australia and in the new century to South Africa,[6] Malaysia[7] and Belize.[8] It was essentially an argument about a species of previously 'overlooked' property rights. Since I was closely associated with that process and was drawn heavily into New Zealand's foreshore and seabed controversy, I attempt here a critical and to some extent personal assessment of what became of that mission. Since rights have lives, this is a biography from the perspective of a participant who was there before, during and after the heady days of the breakthrough cases.

The course of jurisprudential development that the doctrine has taken raises two broad questions addressed here. One concerns the scope of

---

[5] For instance, Jane Kelsey, *A Question of Honour? Labour and the Treaty 1984–1989* (Wellington, Allen & Unwin, 1990); DV Williams, '*Queen v Symonds* Reconsidered' (1989) 19 *Victoria University of Wellington Law Review* 385 and in the writings of Ward Churchill (fired in 2007 by the University of Colorado for 'research misconduct').

[6] *Alexkor Ltd & Another v Richtersveld Community* (Constitutional Court of South Africa, 14 October 2003). Online at http://www.austlii.edu.au/au/journals/AILR/2003/41.html. See Ozlem Ulgen, 'Developing the Doctrine of Aboriginal Title in South Africa: Source and Content' (2002) 46 *Journal of African Law* 131–54. Also see the timely (and pointed) warnings of Alex Reilly, 'The Australian Experience Of Aboriginal Title: Lessons For South Africa' (2000) 16 *South African Journal of Human Rights* 512.

[7] *Adong bin Kuwau & Ors v Kerajaan Negeri Johor & Another* [1997] 1 Malaysian Law Journal 418 (HC); *Nor Anak Nyawai & Ors v Borneo Pulp Plantation Sdn Bhd & Others* [2001] 6 Malaysian Law Journal 241 (HC); *Sagong bin Tasi & Ors v Kerajaan Negeri Selangor & Others* [2002] 2 Malaysian Law Journal 591 affirmed by Court of Appeal 2005. See Peter Crook, 'After *Adong*: The Emerging Doctrine of Native Title in Malaysia' (2005) 2 *Journal of Malaysian and Comparative Law* 71–98.

[8] *Maya Village of Santa Cruz v Attorney-General (Belize)* Supreme Court of Belize, 18 October 2007. Online at http://www.law.arizona.edu/depts/iplp/advocacy/maya_belize/documents/ClaimsNos171and172of2007.pdf.

the proprietary paradigm and its experience inside turbulent and highly-politicised tribal and national settings. At the beginning there was some faint suggestion that the aboriginal rights to land being articulated in the 'breakthrough' cases were not even proprietary but a special constitutional and personal interest—a view that had no traction at all.[9] The paradigm of most intense legal focus has been clearly proprietary; and it is that zone's experience I explore here today. The other related question concerns the nature of the academic enterprise when it is thrust into court and political settings—tribal and national—where purity of argument is a less cherished value or rubs against more pragmatic demands. There can be few other examples of how what started as a legal 'idea' tumbled so dramatically and profoundly out of the ivory tower and cloisters into the commotion of the national legal and political systems.

At its bluntest the message of that 80s' scholarship was that the tribes should have legal rights over their subsisting traditional lands based upon the simple principle that the Crown's mere assumption of sovereignty over their territory (*imperium*) did not displace their traditional property rights (*dominium*). The common law recognised a principle of continuity of local property rights, albeit qualified by the feudal principle of title by which only the Crown could mediate title between tribe and settler, so prohibiting direct transactions between the two sets of subject. Because the thrust was towards establishing the initial principle of common-law recognition, this scholarship did not attempt any sustained elaboration of the identity of the immanent property rights it was insisting were 'there' already, apart from claiming that they could only be extinguished by clear legislative measures. That was the detail *in futuro*—and in later years it proved to be where the devil lurked—but at the time an elaborate description of the prospective property right was not an intellectual priority. The mission was more basic. It sought judicial acceptance of the 'modified continuity' principle.[10] It was expected that the detailed amplification of that property right would play out later once the tribes were inside the rights-place. Frankly, I do not think any of us in this field in the early 1980s were thinking much beyond getting national courts across that threshold.

There was a tension implicit in this use of an ostensible proprietary paradigm to correct what was essentially a negative feature of national law. Aboriginal title—especially in Canada and Australia—was conceived and born as a form of public interest litigation, which was a distinct trend

---

[9] Brian Slattery, 'The Nature of Aboriginal Title' in Owen Lippert (ed), *Beyond the Nass Valley: National Implications of the Supreme Court's Delgamuukw Decision* (Vancouver, Fraser Institute, 2000) 11.

[10] The term used by Brian Slattery in *Ancestral Lands, Alien Laws: Judicial Perspectives on Aboriginal Title* (Saskatoon, University of Sastatchewan Native Law Centre, 1983) 11, 22–3.

in western public law of that time.[11] Those of us writing at the time were aware of the political impact judicial recognition might have, although we did not dwell on this. The scholarship underplayed both the political as well as proprietary dimensions of the doctrine, matters that lay beyond the primary and initial step of common-law recognition.

In a classic article Professor Abram Chayes used the term 'public law litigation' to refer to the emergent practice of American lawyers seeking to precipitate social change through court-ordered decrees to reform legal rules, enforce existing laws, and articulate public norms.[12] In the United States, this emergence of public law litigation has usually been linked with *Brown v Board of Education of Topeka*,[13] where the US Supreme Court declared unconstitutional state segregation of pupils on the basis of race. Many procedural features of *Brown* have become associated with public law litigation as a general phenomenon in western countries of the last quarter of the twentieth century: the defendant was a public institution; the claimants comprised a self-constituted group with membership that changed over time; relief was prospective, seeking to reform future action by government agents; and the judge played a leadership role, complemented by the parties' efforts at negotiation.[14] Those features distinguish public interest litigation from ordinary adversarial adjudication, where there is a private bipolar dispute marked by individual participation and the imposition of retrospective relief involving a tight fit between right and remedy.[15] That was—and remains—the gulf that common-law aboriginal title has had to bridge: a proprietary paradigm invoked at least initially for public interest ends.

At their outset, the national jurisprudences of aboriginal title had much in common with those features of public law litigation described by Professor Chayes. Those cases were brought to influence governmental behaviour as it affected a minority ethnic group that had experienced a history of legal neglect and marginalisation. Crucially, however, this one happened to be the indigenous inhabitants of each country. The notion of indigeneity or *aboriginality* was pivotal both to the judgments and in shaping the jurisprudence that ensued. The rights that aboriginal peoples obtained, being proprietary, *vested in* rather than *pertained to* them as tribal polities. As the jurisprudence of aboriginal title developed, that distinction became

---

[11] I discuss this in 'New Dawn to Cold Light: Courts and Common Law Aboriginal Rights' [2005] *New Zealand Law Review* 485.

[12] A Chayes, 'The Role of the Judge in Public Law Litigation' (1976) 89 *Harvard Law Review* 1281.

[13] *Brown v Board of Education of Topeka* 347 US 483 (1954).

[14] H Hershkoff, 'Public Interest Litigation: Selected Issues and Examples' (circa 2000) (online at http://www1.worldbank.org/publicsector/legal/access.htm#public). This and the following paragraph draw extensively on that essay.

[15] The classic description is L Fuller, 'The Forms and Limits of Adjudication' (1978) 92 *Harvard Law Review* 353.

the junction at which the doctrine varied from other forms of constitutional right. Aboriginal title rights developed not as an increasingly more elaborated norm for the protection of minority rights, so much as the refinement of proprietary rights vested in the tribal nation. These were rights of a different order to those held by minorities, not least because they entailed—or at least anticipated—the management of a considerable asset base by the group. Thus, the rights that started out as broad and with the flavour of public interest about them gradually by a process of refinement and amplification ramified into more concrete and ostensibly proprietary forms. Necessarily the proprietary element required closer inspection and articulation. Over time there grew a closer fit between the (aboriginal) right and the remedy, but those processes themselves led to more issues of right and remedy and so on. The tension between the proprietary and public threads of the doctrine became more and more evident in the hubbub of the national political systems where tribes, now seen as (potential) rights-bearers, were growing muscle. The legalism of aboriginal title accelerated and became more frenetic.

This is a tension that has been under-estimated yet it underlies the course of aboriginal-title jurisprudence in all jurisdictions. Looking at that legalism one can see just how the proprietary paradigm has been pulled and stretched. The ends which the aboriginal title serves are not those of a single-purpose ownership regime (like a matrimonial home) or even a general-purpose trust for a changing class of beneficiaries (a charity). In those regimes purpose and the law of property knit together. The notion of juridically identifiable purpose has been a central dynamic and momentum in the development of the common law in the past century, not just in the law of property (and equity at large) but other essentially parallel notions of *vires* in public and corporate spheres. Tribes, however, are political organisms, founded on genealogy rather than pooled for a particular purpose. There is no such thing as a single 'tribal' purpose. The tribe claiming aboriginal title is not a beast with a single will, or one helmed by trustees with a clear mandate and transparent legal situation. To put it in Maori terms, tribes are based on *whakapapa* (kinship) rather than *kaupapa* (purpose). Being a political organism of humans united by kin, the achievement of agreement is rare—the group's dynamic and vitality is lived through the natural internal processes of contestation and debate. Tribes are messier and more irresolute than families because they are bigger. They squabble, they argue amongst themselves and with one another. They are a human and not a juridical entity. From the start, then, there was destined to be a considerable strain in the notion of tribal ownership. This was largely unaddressed, so fixated was the scholarship of that era in getting over the basic doctrinal hump of modified continuity. But once that had occurred those immanent issues of 'tribal' ownership were uncorked and spilled into the national legal systems, as I will explain.

There is also the tribal perspective of the proprietary paradigm. To argue over one's sovereignty is an exercise of it and the tribes are clear that their rights over their territory are those of a sovereign, even if but a residual one. As persistently as the Howard Government in Australia characterised their remaining land-rights as those of 'self-management' accruing to all owners under law, Aboriginal representatives replied that they were actually rights to 'self-determination.' One sees that more than a claim to proprietary rights was being advanced, yet the juridical vehicle for those claims—the one that actually gave the tribes most (indeed, only) leverage in the national political systems—was proprietary. To reiterate, property was serving a highly-politicised role.

By the early 1980s Australasian scholars were looking closely at the post-*Calder* situation in Canada. Prime Minister Trudeau, that most dangerous of beasts—a law professor at the national helm—was canny enough to see at once that the actual *ratione* of the Supreme Court judgments on the question of Crown fiat were less important than the underlying acceptance of the principle of common-law continuity. The end was looming for non-justiciability and the free executive rein on aboriginal affairs. Whereas previously he had derided common-law aboriginal title as 'an historical might-have-been' after *Calder* and the Quebec Superior Court's injunction against the James Bay hydro project (1972), his federal Government commenced comprehensive land claims negotiations, realising that the courts were poised and about to begin articulation of such a set of rights. Whereas once he had advocated removal of vestigial statutory protection of aboriginal and treaty rights and status in the notoriously titled White Paper (1969),[16] he now faced the messy spectre of judicial intervention. *Calder* plainly had forced the Government's hand, bringing it to the negotiating table. By the time of his second term (1980–84), Prime Minister Trudeau was even willing, after considerable First Nations pressure, to enshrine constitutionally the (then still highly inchoate) rights that he had once disdained. The recognition and constitutional protection from executive and legislative abridgement of 'existing aboriginal and treaty rights' in section 35 of the Constitution Act, 1982, underlined the feeling in the antipodes that the Canadians were setting the legal pace. Even though the Canadian courts had barely embarked upon elaboration of common-law aboriginal title the nascent title-rights had still been protected, although prefacing recognition with the term 'existing' suggested that the Canadian governments did not regard them as extensive and wanted the courts to proceed likewise. This protection of the court-led process later contrasted with the willingness of Australasian legislatures to pre-empt their own and similar common-law courses of legal development as court-centred and prone to the vagaries and

---

[16] See SM Weaver, *Making Canadian Indian policy: the hidden agenda 1968–70* (Toronto, University of Toronto Press, 1981).

particularities of the adversarial setting. Instead they put in place legislative frameworks ostensibly housing the inchoate common-law right. But in the 1980s, the Native Title Act 1993 and its controversial 1998 Amendment (Commonwealth Aust) and the Foreshore and Seabed Act 2004 (New Zealand) were still a long way off.

It is well known that the courts accepted the invitation of that scholarship and began articulating national doctrines of common-law aboriginal title (called 'native title' in Australia). The argument now ran in the courts as well as the law journals and there, of course, its life and viability altered vastly. The most significant impact was transformation of the political theatre of Crown-tribe relations. By the early 1990s there was no doubt that common-law aboriginal title was an emergent—and very important—doctrine of proprietary entitlement in all three jurisdictions.

In Canada *Calder* was followed by a sequence of cases—the rather inconclusive *Baker Lake* and *Guerin* and other cases building to the *Van Der Peet* trilogy (1996) and *Delgamuukw* (1997). In the new century the Supreme Court continues to articulate the doctrine messily and to no one's evident satisfaction or apprehension. Privately my antipodean colleagues mutter that it might have been more sensible for the Dominion to have legislated something on Down Under lines, but that was never treated as a serious option, apart from a discarded proposal for a uniform (and interim) governance structure for Indian Act bands, many of whom held and still hold outstanding aboriginal title and treaty claims.

In the New Zealand setting, two papers circulated widely in 1983 argued that the common-law basis for Maori customary property had been notoriously ousted by statute in the early twentieth century.[17] Through the same statutory framework that codified the principle of non-justiciability, those customary rights had been transmuted into 'Maori freehold land', a statutory adaptation of the tenancy-in-common applied during the late-nineteenth and early-twentieth centuries by operation of the Maori (Native) Land Court. Nonetheless, the argument ran, there remained unextinguished customary property rights around the New Zealand coastline, 'non-territorial' rights (analogous to incorporeal hereditaments) which were less than claims to the statutory and non-justiciable form of exclusive 'territorial' title. Justice Williamson accepted that argument in *Te Weehi v Regional Fisheries*

---

[17] These papers built upon an exploratory paper I had written under the supervision of Professor Brian Slattery, my LLM supervisor in late 1980, who suggested I try 'to make sense of the New Zealand cases' published as the first essay in *Maori Land Laws of New Zealand* (Saskatoon, Native Law Centre, Studies in Aboriginal Rights No 7, 1983) 80. The 1983 papers, written as audition pieces for Research Fellowship competition in Cambridge, were eventually published the next year as 'Aboriginal title in New Zealand courts' (1984) 2 *University of Canterbury Law Review* 235–65 and 'The legal status of Maori fishing rights in tidal water' (1984) 14 *Victoria University of Wellington Law Review* 247–73.

Officer (1986), a judgment that the Crown declined to appeal.[18] It is now accepted (though the suggestion was controverted loudly by the executive branch at the time) that this was from fear of what was then perceived as an 'activist' Court of Appeal (presided over by Sir Robin Cooke (as he then was). As with *Calder* this recognition of common-law aboriginal title gave the tribes negotiating leverage, here enabling them to intervene in the Government's proposed carve-up of the commercial sea fisheries into transferable quota. A multi-million dollar settlement ensued, and with it came a biblical 10-year plague of intra-Maori litigation over application of the income generated by these assets. The quickness with which common-law aboriginal title found traction in New Zealand during the mid-1980s was remarkable. Not only the courts—though only in dicta after *Te Weehi* until 2003—endorsed it, but also the Waitangi Tribunal (New Zealand's Maori claims body), Law Commission and other academics. The Crown was disinclined to resist. Indeed, chastened by this exposure of the 'unconstitutional' codification of the exclusory principle, the Government committed itself to seeking Parliament's repeal of the offensive statutory provisions preventing judicial cognisance of the common-law territorial title. However, this was regarded as gesture politics since it was thought—at least until 2003 and the foreshore and seabed controversy—that after settlement of the fisheries dispute, common-law aboriginal title had little scope left in the country.

Although the politicians howled about 'activist' courts in Canada and New Zealand, this was nothing compared to the reception of the revisionist common-law principles in Australia. In New Zealand the coastline represented the only space over which such rights might have residual scope and even then, it was believed that the sea fisheries settlement had resolved their entirety. Australia, however, had vast tracts of outback land as well as coastal seas, thousands of square miles, over which Aboriginal communities continued to live in the traditional manner. By the comfortable standards of the white population perched precariously and (in environmental terms) ruinously on the littoral edges of the continent, this was harsh uninviting land of no interest to them other than for its very considerable mineral potential. For years the Australian Crowns (Commonwealth and State) had issued mineral exploration and extraction licences, grazing licences and other permissions in disregard of Aboriginal claims, acting on the implicit basis of the terra nullius fiction. This activity was stopped in its tracks by the High Court of Australia's judgments in *Mabo No 2* (1992) followed by *Wik* (1996).

These cases took the Australian legal system seemingly by surprise, yet a trans-jurisdictional glance should have anticipated that result. There were cries of judicial activism and political interference but, as in the other

---

[18] *Te Weehi v Regional Fisheries Officer* [1986] 1 NZLR 680 (HC).

jurisdictions, a negative outcome would have required more explanation from the courts in an era of extending judicial control of executive conduct. Terra nullius—which was more a supposition than an actual hardened rule *contra* native title—was intellectually indefensible. Given the momentum of Anglo-Commonwealth public law at that time, it would have been less credible for the courts to exclude tribal claimants from that wider trend. By the early 1990s the doctrine of aboriginal title was being intellectually fortified on such apparently sound and irrefutable common-law principles (respect for Crown sovereignty and property rights derived from prolonged physical presence and possession) that those hostile to it were outgunned. The cry of 'judicial activism' was not an intellectual argument against the doctrine so much as a vehement insistence on the rigidity of precedent, a position easily dismissed as old-school,[19] reactionary even, and out-of-touch in an era of expansive judicial review and which anyway crumbled before the meticulous scholarship of the proponents, particularly that of the influential Canadians Brian Slattery and Kent McNeil.

In Australia after *Mabo No 2*, the passage of the Native Title Act 1993 generated considerable controversy. Essentially, though not wholly, the Act sought to house the inchoate native title inside a statutory framework that allowed continued access to land subject to a claim whilst putting in place a mechanism to ascertain the title rights. Importantly the Act contained a definition of 'native title' in section 223 that slightly reconfigured the axis for the Commonwealth courts' articulation of the common law principles. The 1993 controversy was nothing compared to the protest that followed the Howard Government's response to the *Wik* case (1996) and the 1998 Amendments to the principal Act. There has been some suggestion that this statutory paring of native title was in the political pipeline already and that *Wik* provided the populist Prime Minister with an excuse. In any event, the Commonwealth's statutory framework for native title now 'houses' the common law property right and it is in that compound that the jurisprudence has developed.

I do not propose giving detailed histories of those national jurisprudences in which the Canadian and Australian routes started to diverge slightly; rather I want to look at what became of the common-law aboriginal title in terms of the proprietary paradigm. Remember we are dealing with what started off as a highly inchoate right vested in a fluid and inherently contestative political body—the tribe—organised by custom and membership arising from kinship. The intervention by the courts now inevitably meant also that the scholarship followed rather than led the courts, try as it might to regain the intellectual initiative. And politicians and tribes tried to exploit

---

[19] As representative see EJ Haughey, 'A Vindication of Sir James Prendergast' [1990] *NZLJ* 230 and Guy Chapman, 'The Treaty of Waitangi—Fertile Ground for Judicial (and Academic) Myth-making' [1991] *New Zealand Law Journal* 228.

those judicial and (to a much lesser and diminishing extent) academic sites for ongoing leverage in the tussle and pull of national politics. The key judicial interventions thus set in train not merely a national common-law site of doctrinal development but more importantly they also required political processes for the Crown to negotiate with the tribes and reach settlement. If anything dominated the aftermath of those cases it was that political consequence rather than the proprietary elements of a still-vague right. The political stage rather than the courtroom was the focus of attention and energy. Courts encouraged those political sites of resolution, a more intense parallelism that required institutionalised processes for commencement of Crown-tribe dialogue. To repeat, that extensive activity would not have occurred without the judicial pronouncements in the key 'breakthrough' cases. In Canada accommodation of the extant aboriginal-title claims in the Arctic necessitated the federal comprehensive claims policy, though that was a long time in the brewing into its 1985 form because of First Nations' dogged refusal to disengage their *imperium* from *dominium*. Plainly they were less enamoured with a purely proprietary paradigm. The *Te Weehi* case led to the commercial sea fisheries settlements in New Zealand, not least because the Government feared a judicial emulation of the so-called Boldt-case[20] and the award of a 50 per cent share to Maori. Sometimes politics did not fail so much as the constitutional might of the state prevailed, that is to say the Government's perception of its electoral position out-trumped its willingness to engage a prospective and uncertain legalism. This can be seen in the Australasian responses to *Mabo No 2*, *Wik* and *Ngati Apa* respectively. Leviathan legislated the inchoate right into a statutory compound widely regarded (despite the executive's contrary insistence) as constricting and straitening the nature of that indeterminate right.

II. 'LAWFARE': MAKING SENSE OF THE POST-BREAKTHROUGH LEGALISM

Once tribes had jolted into the rights-place, their political leverage vastly enhanced, downstream issues quickly arose. Litigation was rife involving tribe against Crown, but also intra-tribal and inter-tribal issues increasingly perplexed the courts. The juridical amplification of the aboriginal property right occurred also in negotiating rooms, as tribe and Crown agreed

---

[20] *United States v Washington*, 384 F Supp 312 (WD Wash, 1974). The Boldt judgment had been referred to by the Waitangi Tribunal in two reports *Report of the Waitangi Tribunal on the Manukau Claim* (Wai 8, 1985) para 9.2.8 and *Report of the Waitangi Tribunal on the Muriwhenua Fishing Claim* (Wai 22, 1988) para 9.1.2, and its currency in Maori argumentation of the period (see my article of that time 'Maori Fishing Rights and the North American Indian' (1985) 6 *Otago Law Review* 62) was plainly worrying the Government, anxious about the 'activist' Court of Appeal of Sir Robin Cooke, President.

formats for formal asset-vesting in the tribe. In these settings, both court and negotiating table, those latent issues of the 'tribe' as a juridical entity were now exposed in the cold and demanding light of the rights-place. The gesture of common-law recognition of aboriginal title for which that band of scholars had argued was only a beginning, rather than an apotheosis.

This frantic legalism has become a fact of tribal life in the last 20 years. Tribes are in the courts constantly, or they are locked in seemingly endless negotiation with Crown, corporations and municipalities (whose faces across the table seem to differ each sitting) or responding to yet another bureaucratic inquiry or notification (usually in the field of resource management). They are under a state of legal siege, leading one commentator to describe their contemporary condition as 'lawfare'.[21] The new legalism has had deep impact on many tribes, effecting fundamental changes of a type that would never have happened in the old era of juridical exclusion. As I will explain, much of this legalism has been an expression of the issues that arise when a proprietary regime is thrust into such a politicised and public role.

That lawfare is a phenomenon that national courts, politicians and public administrators have grappled with *ex necessitae*, unlike much of the scholarship (Canadian especially), which mostly remains in '80s mode mesmerised by rights-fetishism. However, it has been the tribes themselves who have felt the real brunt of that frantic post-breakthrough legalism. Entry into the rights-place has been debilitating and an ongoing effort inside multiple sites of legal engagement. For some it has even become a struggle, demanding the making of hard and often deeply divisive choices with tribal capacity and resources (human capital not least) being stretched to their limit. And as I have indicated much of that has been a consequence of the friction between custom-based tribalism and the demands of westernised proprietary regimes especially when cast in a political role.

This engulfing legalism has occupied three broad areas of activity. They are all a consequence of the legal systems response to and absorption of the prospect of significant asset-vestment in the tribe through aboriginal-title processes (be it legislated settlement, ILUA,[22] tribunal vesting or other) or historical claims settlement.[23] Throughout all this it must be recalled that the 'assets' about which we are talking generally speaking involve Crown

---

[21] The term is taken from John L Comaroff, 'Colonialism, Culture, and the Law: A Foreword' (2001) 26 *Law and Social Inquiry* 305, 306.

[22] Indigenous Land Use Agreement (Australia).

[23] This is the major vehicle for land title (re)-vestment in New Zealand Maori *iwi* (tribes), and to a much lesser extent in Canada (specific claims). In Australia and Canada the national processes of the Native Title Acts and comprehensive claims settlement respectively are oriented about transforming the common-law title rights. Nonetheless all jurisdictions experience issues surrounding rights-management and rights-integration which arise when significant assets are vested in a political kinship group (the tribe).

land, albeit subject to the aboriginal title. Since these assets are notionally in the public weal, albeit 'burdened' by the aboriginal entitlement, the Crown has set its own prerequisites for the formal vesting of such assets into tribal ownership:

1. rights-definition and amplification;
2. rights-management;
3. rights-integration.

III. DEVELOPING TRIBAL PROPERTY RIGHTS—SITES OF LEGAL ACTIVITY

A. Defining the Property Right: Rights-design or -fetishism?

Once the recognition in principle of the inchoate property right had issued in the breakthrough cases, the process of rights-design began. In terms of legal development this process of defining and designing the aboriginal-title property right operated through three often—though not wholly—interwoven legal mechanisms: contract, statute and common-law.

(i) Rights-Design Through Claims-Settlement Processes

Most importantly there were the 'political' sites where Crown and tribe negotiated asset-vestment through claims-resolution processes. In Canada and New Zealand those processes were extra-statutory, whilst in Australia the ILUA regime of the Native Title Act and associated processes provided a more juridified umbrella.[24] For the most part tribes, in reaching settlement, did not trust the law of contract of itself, a historical legacy from the past refusal of courts to apply the terms of the older land cessions of the nineteenth and early twentieth centuries. Getting a court to enforce those huge real estate transactions (from a property law perspective misleadingly called 'treaties' in Canada) had been an enduring grievance that the tribes would not repeat in the new era of claims-resolution. Consequently these Canadian and New Zealand settlements were put carefully into statutory form, including, sometimes, an apology from the Crown. These settlements were reached through grinding non-statutory administrative processes—including the culminating Parliamentary one—into which the courts declined to venture. In that zone anyway the old principle of

---

[24] For a good account of the Australian mechanisms see David Llewellyn and Mauren Teehan, 'Treaties', 'Agreements', 'Contracts', and 'Commitments'—What's in a Name? The Legal Force and Meaning of Different Forms of Agreement Making' (2005) 7 *Balayi: Culture, Law and Colonialism* 6

non-justiciability resurfaced as courts declined to exercise judicial review forms of intervention in the settlement process; but this, as I will explain, was as much an admission of their institutional incapacity (as well as reluctance) in that complex zone. The IULA and arbitration processes in Australia's native title legislation have provided a more structured format for negotiations, agreed outcomes and consensus mechanisms to recognise rights that might not emerge from the adjudicative processes of the Native Title Act.[25] Yet it is notorious that for most of their life, the consensual mechanisms of the Australian Act have been downplayed and overshadowed by the adversarial, compromising the capacity for a consensual process to facilitate more expansive and generous approaches to rights-design. There has never been a strong Commonwealth encouragement and accompanying resourcing of those consensual provisions, although the recent revision of policy (2007) on funding of PBCs (Prescribed Bodies Corporate) has been a positive move.[26] Moreover, and perhaps more than the other jurisdictions, governance issues have compromised the effectiveness of title-determination in Australia.

In all jurisdictions the idea of negotiation and settlement seems to have appealed to governments more than the actual experience of it. In their ways, the Canadian and New Zealand governments have been just as slow moving and indisposed as the Australian Commonwealth, the momentum dragged by under-resourcing not only in the financial sense, crippling as that is, but human capital. Crown negotiators and officials (lawyers not least) constantly jump off what is seen as an under-incentivised professional treadmill and dead-end. Few—though there are some distinguished exceptions—want to build a career in this area. Governments are not interested in encouraging any sense that there are any professional rewards, thus ensuring constant personnel turnover on the Crown side. These officials, many of them brave and with a strong sense of public service, are over-worked and their negotiating brief is often deliberately sketchy so that the process produces the least concession from government rather than one motivated by a more generous disposition. Aboriginal representatives, raised on highly-personalised forms of political engagement, are constantly re-educating and re-stating their position to a faceless bureaucratic Crown. The institutional memory of this Crown is usually poor and prone to the personal commitment of particular officials whose initiative, anyway, is

---

[25] Tony Corbett and Ciaran O'Faircheallaigh, 'Unmasking the Politics of Native Title: The National Native Title Tribunal's Application of the NTA's Arbitration Provisions' (2007) 33 *University of Western Australia Law Review* 153–171.

[26] Department of Families, Housing, Community Services and Indigenous Affairs (Commonwealth) *Guidelines for Support of Prescribed Bodies Corporate (PBCs). Policy and Legislative Framework. Funding Applications* (Canberra, Land Branch Native Title Program, 2007) 16. The new policy framework enables Commonwealth funding of PBC administrative costs either through Native Title Representative Bodies (NTRBs) or directly to PBCs.

subject to political oversight and agendas (where concessions to tribal claims are often seen as electorally costly). Governments talk contradictorily to the tribes of 'building relationships' through those agreements rather than using settlements as closure and exit,[27] yet needs must use the rhetoric of finality to sell the process to the claims-weary electorate. So governments consider issuing timetables for the conclusion of all these claims,[28] without addressing seriously and positively any of the concomitant resourcing issues that would at least increase the tempo of negotiated outcomes. There is a strong media tendency to depict tribes negatively, as fractious and administratively (as well as—and this racist disposition is never far from the surface—ethically) challenged. A tribe, to repeat, is not a purpose-driven corporation, trust or suchlike legal entity but a customary political formation of people of different outlooks, ages, incomes and education, united as kin. Yet in this area of claims-resolution it has been shown too often to be the Crown who is slippery, de-stabilising and incapable of commitment; hidebound in its own processes rather than seriously (much less, actively) advancing a programme of settlement. I have put this situation rather strongly, doing so not least as a counter to the usual tendency of the media to depict the tribes as bringing the problematic side of negotiations.

Therefore, the amount of concluded agreements since the door-opening breakthrough cases has been very small, certainly compared to the vast number of claims still inside the several systems buzzing (some would say droning) around the courts and other sites of institutional engagement. These agreements have barely emerged with the frequency envisaged at the time the processes were put in place over a decade (and sometimes, as Canada's federal policy, two) ago. All three jurisdictions hold up certain benchmark agreements as exemplary (such as the Argyle Participation ILUA and Burrup Agreement[29] in Australia; the Nisga'a Settlement in Canada and Tainui and Ngai Tahu Settlements in New Zealand). Spurts of apparent government commitment, such as the British Columbia Treaty

---

[27] I have been particularly associated with this rhetoric which has proven vastly easier in the governmental iteration than practice: 'Aboriginal Identity and Relations in North America and Australasia.' Policy advice commissioned by the New Zealand Ministry of Justice (1996) published with short commentaries as *Kokiri Ngatahi: Living Relationships—The Treaty of Waitangi in the New Millenium* (Wellington, Victoria University Press, 1998) 107–86.

[28] In New Zealand Cabinet has set the year 2020 for conclusion of all (historical) claims: see Office of Treaty Settlements (NZ) *Briefing for Incoming Minister Vote Treaty Negotiations* (October 2007) (online at http://www.justice.govt.nz/pubs/reports/2007/briefings-to-ministers/vote-treaty-negotiations/BIMTrea1.pdf). As at the end of 2007 there had been 14 settlements since 1995, of the hundreds formally lodged. In Canada at the beginning of the new century there had been only 13 comprehensive claims settlements since 1973 (for an account see Mary Hurley and Jill Wherrett, 'Settling Land Claims' (Ottawa, Parliamentary Information and Research Service, 1999).

[29] But even this has run into trouble with regard to the treatment of Aboriginal rock art: http://www.standupfortheburrup.com/doco/FARA_Press_Release_18_11_2007.pdf

Process, regularly run out of steam and aggravate rather than ease the frustration of the tribes trapped inside an inescapable, ongoing relationship with government that in a domestic context would be described as abusive. The reality is now a tired and fatigued one: It is that the exemplary settlements are mostly exceptions and more a reflection of what is actually not happening on the ground. That progeny of the breakthrough cases, *la bonne idée* of rights-design by claims-settlement, has found more acceptance than *l'actualité*—the grinding semi-paralysed graft of actually reaching resolution. A prospect that envisaged a renewal of the relationship between Crown and tribe has turned into something vastly less positive, some might say cancerous. Rights-design by agreement has been a very hard job to get done.

Further, the shape of the rights that are designed by political processes has changed over the years. One day someone will write a comparative history of the evolution and changing patterns of rights-design in claims-resolution agreements of the past 30 years. For instance, to use Canadian examples, put the James Bay (1975) and Nisga'a (1999) Agreements side by side and you will see two quite different approaches to rights-design. As I will explain briefly later, these agreements nonetheless have been oriented around issues of rights-integration; that is to say, they have been concerned with giving the tribes ongoing rights in matters of resource management compatible with other rights-holders' interests, such as those of conservation, municipalities, mineral exploration and extraction, etc. These rights tend to be procedural in character and often it is by that means—through a web of complex proceduralism—that any proprietary element is to be discerned. To switch to another jurisdiction, New Zealand, the Government has recently announced Agreement in Principle with the Ngati Porou tribe as to its 'ownership' rights along the tribe's coastline, a significant stretch of the East Coast of the North Island.[30] Those will entail certain veto rights over developments on the coast, the right to change place names, erect signs, the right to make fisheries regulations, greater influence over district council processes and rights of consultation with certain ministers.

(ii) Rights Designed Adversarially (ie In the Courts)

Necessarily the courts were drawn into considering the aboriginal-title property rights being talked about and the subject of long-winded negotiation, if only as part of a wider strategy inside the political sphere. Judges, of course, are not naïve and framed the breakthrough cases, more than anything else, as a spur to governments to embark upon those processes

---

[30] Announcement by Michael Cullen, 5 February 2008 (online at http://www.justice.govt. nz/foreshore/negotiations/te-runanga-o-ngati-porou/agreement-february-2008/index.html)

of claims-negotiation and -settlement. The judgments were intended to encourage that process and to put the tribes at the table with considerably more legal muscle. The inchoate nature of the property right was far from unwitting. The breakthrough represented a political so much as doctrinal outset. But the kick-starting intervention of the courts meant that further recourse to them was also a viable option, especially in forcing the hand and pace of negotiation. The key cases signaled the courts' willingness to embark upon that process of doctrine formation, though judicial patience (that precious commodity) was soon to be sorely tested in the litigation log-jams of the late 1990s. Though the tenor of the breakthrough judgments encouraged the political site of resolution, necessarily they invited more litigation as part of the tug and pull of the new dynamic of Crown-tribe relations. That litigation came with a real sting in the late 1990s in Canada and Australia, the most experienced aboriginal-title jurisdictions. Moreover the purple language of the breakthrough judgments—with the similar rhetoric of the exhortative scholarship before it, speaking in terms of a redemptive common law—led tribes to hope for the same courageous and sympathetic momentum in the ensuing case-law. In the early 1990s, tribes saw judges as their rescuers and protectors, a sure recipe for the disappointment that inevitably followed. Judges, mindful of the intense activity in the political sphere (and, doubtless, the tribes' insistence upon depicting their relations with the Crown as nation-to-nation), amplified the proprietary paradigm cautiously and gingerly. Retrenchment rather than boldness became the later theme of juridical development. That sense of mounting judicial impatience runs most strongly through the key judgments of the High Court of Australia in the late 1990s, where only the dissentient Justice Michael Kirby maintained the expansive spirit of *Mabo No 2* and *Wik*. For tribes, the golden sunrise of the breakthrough years soured into disillusion and an engulfing legalism where progress towards asset-vestment seemed further rather than nearer to hand.

By the beginning of the new century the Canadian and Australian courts in particular had given fuller doctrinal shape to the aboriginal-title property rights they had said they would recognise. Argument and litigation continue to wage about those shapes, which at least one aboriginal commentator quickly saw as having a shifting and slippery quality reminiscent of the tribes' own elusive trickster gods.[31] Many commentators, the Canadians in particular, have seen the case-law of the late 1990s as a betrayal of the

---

[31] John Borrows, 'Frozen Rights in Canada: Constitutional Interpretation and the Trickster' (1997) 22 *American Indian Law Review* 37 (1997), 'Re-Living the Present: Title, Treaties, and the Trickster in British Columbia' (1998/99) 120 *British Columbian Studies* 99 and 'The Trickster: Integral to a Distinctive Culture' (1997) 8(2) *Constitutional Forum* 27, 31–32 Also more generally in his book *Recovering Canada: The Resurgence of Indigenous Law* (Toronto, University of Toronto Press, 2002).

promise that the proprietary paradigm once seemed to be offering. This process of doctrine formation has been going on long enough now for an historical perspective to be taken of it, as I have suggested and outlined very generally in the previous paragraph.[32] To risk repeating, that picture is one in which the new dawn of the breakthrough era envisioning tribes as significant asset holders (the proprietary paradigm) was superseded by spluttering and very slight progress in the political sphere, rampant necine and internecine litigation and debilitating legalism, and—as I will now explain—any initial prospect of doctrinal coherence being compromised by what followed in the judicial retrenchments of the late 1990s. There emerged in the case-law an ill-conceived and disabling incrementalism (Canada) and conservatism (Australia) in the face of procedurally and evidentially difficult multi-million dollar claims. In those *fin de siècle* years the new dawn of the proprietary paradigm turned to a very cold light.

How, then, in very general terms, did the courts construct the aboriginal-title property rights? It must be said that the key Australian jurisprudence of the late 1990s carried more inherent coherence than the Canadian, but it was marked also by a deeper lying conservatism and impatience.

The scholarship had always been divided over the juridical basis for the common-law aboriginal title, although hardly to the point of schism. One school argued that the title derived from the continuity of aboriginal customary legal systems on the Crown's assumption of the territorial sovereignty over their territory (normative continuity). The other school founded the title on the fact of aboriginal use and occupation of their traditional lands at the time of Crown sovereignty. Kent McNeil took the latter position in his influential text *Common Law Aboriginal Title* (1989), building carefully and most persuasively upon deep-seated common-law notions of occupancy and presumptive possession. That became the basis for the Canadian aboriginal-title jurisprudence particularly as framed by the Supreme Court in the key case *Delgamuukw* (1997).[33] Australia, however, rested the common-law native title on principles of normative continuity.[34] That foundational difference did not of itself cleave the national jurisprudences, since the courts immediately realised the need to have regard to both factors—physical presence and tribal customary law—in amplifying the respective foundation.[35] The different shapes that the key Australian

---

[32] See also Karen Lochead, 'From Common Law Recognition to Judicial Confirmation: An Analysis of Native Title's Proof Criteria in Canada and Australia' Paper presented at the Annual Meeting of the Canadian Political Science Association, 1–3 June 2006, York University, Toronto ON, Canada.

[33] *Delgamuukw v British Columbia* [1997] 3 SCR 1010.

[34] Discussed in McHugh, 'Aboriginal Title in New Zealand: A Retrospect and Prospect' (2004) 2 *New Zealand Journal of Public and International Law* 139–202.

[35] For instance Brian Slattery, 'Nature of Aboriginal Title' above n 9, at 21–2 on role of custom in the Canadian test.

and Canadian jurisprudences took in the late 1990s were the product of other juridical factors.

(a) Canada

Most importantly the Canadian case-law drew a distinction between aboriginal *title* and aboriginal *rights*. In *Delgamuukw* (1997) Chief Justice Lamer famously described the First Nations' common-law proprietary paradigm as comprising a spectrum ranging from full exclusive ownership (title) through a range of non-exclusive proprietary rights that might arise as clusters (hunting and foraging, for instance) through to site-specific stand-alone rights. An aboriginal title described full exclusive ownership of land; and was marked by the exercise of the right to exclude. This title derived from aboriginal use and occupation of land at the time of Crown sovereignty. In the *Marshall* and *Bernard* cases (2005) the Supreme Court set the factual threshold for proof of exclusive use and occupation at a very high—some say virtually impossible—level.[36] Aboriginal *rights*, on the other hand, described a compendious category into which fell all rights other than those of title (though title was still to be regarded, unhelpfully, as a particular species of right). Thus, First Nation claims to a right to cross the Canadian border freely, to rights to gamble free of provincial regulation, to inherent self-government and to hunt and fish over unoccupied Crown land all represented a claim to a right. As can be seen, the category of *rights* comprehended more than non-exclusive property rights going to those of a political character, but plainly it had important ramifications for the aboriginal-title proprietary paradigm. The spectrum was now split between *title* and *rights*, the threshold from one to the other being the presence of the right to exclude. Title (exclusive ownership) and lesser proprietary rights (hunting and fishing being the key ones) thus acquired different tests.

The Supreme Court gave a controversial test for *rights* in the so-called *Van der Peet* trilogy (1996),[37] requiring the *right* to be integral to a distinctive culture at the time of European contact. Here the Supreme Court quickly found it had boxed itself into a very rigid and frosted intellectual corner, one that drew a lot of very justified criticism.[38] The different test for

---

[36] *R v Marshall; R v Bernard* [2005] 2 SCR 220. For useful comment see Bruce McKinnon, 'Aboriginal Title after *Marshall* and *Bernard* Parts I and II' (2007) 65 *The Advocate* 513 and 611. See *Tsilhqot'in Nation v British Columbia*, Judgment of Vickers J in the BC Supreme Court, 21 November 2007 (the Court's first look at aboriginal title since *Delgamuukw* over 10 years ago). Justice Vickers held that the claimants held aboriginal rights but not title to the land, so endorsing the high proof threshold of the Supreme Court.

[37] *R v Van Der Peet* [1996] 2 SCR 507: *R v NTC Smokehouse Ltd* [1996] 2 SCR 672; and *R v Gladstone* [1996] 2 SCR 723.

[38] RL Barsh and JY Henderson, 'The Supreme Court's *Van der Peet* Trilogy: Naïve Imperialism and Ropes of Sand' (1997) 42 *McGill Law Journal* 993; Leonard I Rotman, 'Hunting for Answers in a Strange Kettle of Fish: Unilateralism, Paternalism and Fiduciary Rhetoric in *Badger* and *Van der Peet*' (1997) 8(2) *Constitutional Forum* 40; Michael Asche,

title handed down soon after in *Delgamuukw* (1997) was plainly intended to thaw that test. The criticism of the *rights* test focused on its definition and confinement of the non-exclusive property right by reference to pre-contact ways. How, for instance, could a fishing right incorporate a non-subsistence element unless it could be shown that a commercial aspect had been distinctive to that tribe's pre-contact culture? The test was rightly seen as a mean-spirited fossilisation of the scope of non-exclusive aboriginal property rights, treating them as museum-pieces rather than viable dynamic rights vested in a tribal community in the twentieth century.

Nevertheless, in the decade since the *Van der Peet* case was decided, Brian Slattery believes the Supreme Court has shown mounting signs of discomfort with the test laid down there. In a series of important decisions, he argues that it has quietly initiated the process of reshaping the test's basic tenets. This process has taken place on three fronts. First, the Court has relaxed its exclusive focus on specific rights—rights distinctive to particular aboriginal groups—and allowed for the existence of generic rights—uniform rights that operate at an abstract level and reflect broader normative considerations. Secondly, the Court has recognised that the date of European contact is not an appropriate reference point in all contexts, and looked increasingly to the period when the Crown gained sovereignty and effective control (in title claims). Finally, the Court has placed ever-greater emphasis on the need for aboriginal rights to be defined by negotiations between the parties, tacitly signalling that aboriginal rights are flexible and future-oriented, rather than mere relics of the past.[39] Indeed, the emphasis in the *Haida Nation* case (2005) in the new millennium was upon the right to consult and the broad approach the Supreme Court has been taking towards it[40] is seen by some as an attempt to reconstruct in procedural terms a new version of right that the Court had previously botched on the proprietary front. Against that warmer trend, however, was the restrictive high-threshold test for proof of title given in *Marshall* and *Bernard* (2005). The Supreme Court's signals remain mixed and any guidance remains cloudy.

'From *Calder* to *Van der Peet*: Aboriginal Rights and Canadian Law, 1973–1996' in Paul Havemann (ed), *Indigenous Peoples Rights in Australia, Canada and New Zealand* (Oxford/Melbourne, Oxford University Press, 1999).

[39] Brian Slattery, 'The Generative Structure of Aboriginal Rights' (2007) *Supreme Court Law Review* forthcoming.

[40] *Haida Nation v British Columbia (Minister of Forests)*, 2004 SCC 73; *Taku River Tlingit First Nation v British Columbia (Project Assessment Director)*, 2004 SCC 74. In both cases, the Court held there was a duty for governments to consult with, and where appropriate, to accommodate the interests of Aboriginal peoples and that this might arise before claims of aboriginal rights and title had been determined. The basis of that duty, the Court indicated, was the 'honour of the Crown'. See the anticipation of this trend in S Lawrence and P Macklem, 'From consultation to reconciliation: Aboriginal rights and the Crown's duty to consult' (2002) 79 *Canadian Bar Review* 252. There is now a considerable amount of material available online—particularly by environmental consultants, on the duty to consult.

This incrementalism and the continued doubt over what should be clear principles emanating from the country's pinnacle court reveals one of the fundamental and (in my opinion) perverse features of the Canadian jurisprudence. For a good while Canadian scholars like Slattery and McNeil (*les éminences grises*) emphasised the *historical* nature of the aboriginal property spectrum, and that thread is picked up less subtly and reflectively by the courts. That characterisation runs through the case-law without a real grasp of where it leads or what it means. There seems to be an idea running through the Canadian jurisprudence that the historical character of the rights entails their restoration in something resembling the historical form. This is not very clear-headed thinking about what the law of property does and is designed to accomplish. Most fundamentally the Canadian jurisprudence has never grasped the point that the Australians saw immediately as self-evident. The point is that the law of property is concerned with the protection of extant rights. Property lives in the present rather than the past tense. Where property rights have been lost by some colourable means, equity has developed its complex remedial principles of restitution, but even those, for all the dark wizardry of this branch of law, cannot pretend to restore property rights of more than a century's vintage and longtime effective disappearance. Something of an antique quality has seemed to grip judges besieged in long trials with mountains of historical and anthropological evidence. Implicitly they think the nature of the evidence must somehow determine strongly the juridical outcome, in a sense like the doctrine of precedent. Tribes' property and cultural integrity in today's world become lodged fixatedly and imaginatively in the manner of their exhaustive presentation as historical authenticity, a backwards orientation where the past tense downplays speaking in the present. Thus courts, clinging to historical evidence and authenticity as a juridical life raft, articulate tribal property rights in a backward gazing manner that leaves them very cold in the present tense.

To return to a motif: Property lives in the present tense. The common-law property paradigm applies to protect extant tribal rights wherever they fall along the spectrum. It is concerned with preserving and recognising rights that are living and breathing now, and facilitating their life into the future. It is not a restorative doctrine, but an essentially protective one guarding what remnant rights the tribes still have (not inconsiderable in the Arctic north and Australian desert). Hence, the Australian courts have articulated a continuity test requiring the property rights that crystallised with Crown sovereignty to have been maintained in the exercise and practice through an ongoing normative association to the present day. That is property in its natural tense, the present.

Further, where those property rights have been impugned by Crown mis- or mal-administration the Canadian courts have on occasions used the doctrine of Crown fiduciary duty. This doctrine, though linked to the proprietary paradigm, sets standards for Crown accountability, and in that regard serves a supplementary, though essentially different, juridical function. It is able comfortably to talk in the past tense, though there its backward gaze also draws on notions like *laches* to guide and guard the extent of retrospection. To summarise, the common-law property paradigm was built to accommodate and protect extant tribal rights; the fiduciary duty established standards of Crown accountability for its management of tribal assets.

For a long while the thrust of Kent McNeil's scholarship was aimed at the courts and helping them draw the 'right' doctrinal basis for aboriginal title/rights from the common-law well. In that sense he was clutching the baton of the 80s scholarship and anchoring it into the 90s. His writing focused most strongly (though not wholly) on the proprietary zone. One reflection of that faith in the common-law mission was his insistence that conceptually the Canadian courts should continue to reject—and have rejected, he observed rightly—a continuity test on the Australian lines. This meant that the aboriginal title crystallised upon the establishment of European sovereignty over the relevant part of Canada whenever that was in the seventeenth or eighteenth century. Aboriginal title was formulated as an historically crystallised proprietary right rather than a subsisting entitlement in possession as a consequence of undisrupted customary use and occupation. The Supreme Court recently (2005) reiterated that position:[41]

> The common law theory underlying recognition of aboriginal title holds that an aboriginal group which occupied land at the time of European sovereignty and never ceded or otherwise lost [at law] its right to the land, continues to enjoy title to it.

McNeil uses the absence of a continuity test as a way of presenting aboriginal title as a restorative doctrine. If the First Nation claimants could prove title at that time of European sovereignty there would be no need for them to invoke continued use and occupation as presumptive proof working backwards in time. The implications of this are that an unextinguished title can arise like Lazarus from the seemingly dead, or rather it may subsist undetected, unused, unknown in fact but alive at law. This is common-law prestidigitation that no judge would ever allow, since it would destabilise land titles to an extent that no court would want to be seen to permit. Yet the Canadian courts will not take the conceptual bull by the horns. However, one may ask if there is any need. At the end of 2007 no First

---

[41] *R v Marshall; R v Bernard* [2005] 2 SCR 220, para 39 (McLachlin CJ and Major, Bastarache, Abella and Charron JJ); see also para 129 (minority).

Nation had ever proven title before them.[42] Since *Calder*, however, there have been 20 modern-day 'treaties' or settlements of title claims.

Nonetheless, the Canadian title conundrum remains. To give an example in which I was professionally involved, in the *Chippewas of Sarnia* case (2000),[43] it was seriously advanced that because the Crown had—it was argued—not followed minutely and exactly the surrender requirements of the Royal Proclamation 1763, much of downtown Sarnia was under an unextinguished aboriginal title. This whipped up a feeding frenzy for talk-back hosts and scare-mongering press. In the end the provincial Court of Appeal invoked the innocent third-party purchaser rule—equity's venerable and somewhat flyblown darling—to prevent the displacement of private titles that such a holding would have entailed. But it could have done that more simply and cleanly. Here the appropriate action, if any, was against the Crown on the fiduciary duty rather than against the titular land-owners of Sarnia on the purportedly unextinguished aboriginal title. The issue was one of Crown conduct not one of remnant and viable property rights. Kent continues to insist against any continuity test[44] and argues unblinkingly for the restitution of ancient unextinguished property rights as if that were possible on the pure logic of the common law. He is able—breathtakingly in my estimation—to extrapolate an unextinguished aboriginal title over vast reaches of eastern Canada from the customary rights of a few villagers in a few cases in olde England. This is a leap of legal imagination that no judge would ever make, yet just as steadfastly Canadian courts have refused to reject it directly through a continuity test. In the *Marshall* and *Bernard* cases (2005) the Supreme Court said that the present-day claimant group must display continuity with the group there at the time of European sovereignty, but that is not the same as requiring continuity of customary presence upon the land.

I have used Kent's position on the continuity test as indicative of the tenor of his scholarship in the post-breakthrough years. For a long while much of his scholarship was arguing that it was all now a matter of setting the correct legal design; and that the material for that was already inside the common law. He displayed consistent and considerable faith in the capacity

---

[42] This fact is noted on the official Indian and Northern Affairs website: http://www.ainc-inac.gc.ca/ai/mr/is/tcc-eng.asp (accessed 12 December 2008).

[43] *Chippewas of Sarnia* (2000) 195 DLR (4th) 135 (Ont CA) leave to appeal to the Supreme Court of Canada denied 8 November 2001, SCC Bulletin of Proceedings, 9 November 2001 (at 1998); application for reconsideration dismissed 13 June 2002, SCC Bulletin of Proceedings, 13 June 2002 (at 925) (Panel: L'Heureux-Dubé, Arbour and Le Bel JJ). For full discussion see Paul Perell and Jeff G Cowan, 'In Defence of *Chippewas of Sarnia Band v Canada*' (2002) 81 *Canadian Bar Review* 727, and James Reynolds, 'A Reply to "In Defence of *Chippewas of Sarnia Band v Canada*"' (2003) 82 *Canadian Bar Review* 122.

[44] 'Legal Rights and Legislative Wrongs: Maori Claims to the Foreshore and Seabed' in Claire Charters and Andrew Erueti (eds), *Maori Property Rights in the Foreshore and Seabed: The Latest Frontier* (Wellington, Victoria University Press, 2004).

of the common law to get it right, albeit with some nudging and fine-tuning which he supplied with his characteristically deep and gentle scholarly precision and care. More latterly, he has resiled from that position of faith,[45] a trend also in the work of Brian Slattery.

Brian Slattery's recent work has grasped the nettle and he is presently engaged in an attempt to redefine those rights (and title) as 'generative' rather than historical in nature.[46] He sees clearly the hidebound messiness that has come from dwelling almost nostalgically on the historical nature of the rights. Brian's notion of a generative right carries the admission that the common-law mission on which he and the rest of us embarked so idealistically has been unsuccessful (and perhaps over-ambitious). It is impossible for the courts satisfactorily (much less, comprehensively) to design the proprietary rights of tribes. In essence, he realises that their depiction as 'historical' rights suggested their judicial erection through processes of historical forensis; but for the tribes in a modern world that left their property restrictively and impotently in the past tense. Brian thus argues that as a generative right, aboriginal title exists in a dynamic but latent form, which is capable of partial articulation by the courts but whose full implementation requires agreement between the Indigenous party and the Crown. He believes that whilst the courts have the power to recognise the core elements of a generative right—sufficient to provide the foundation for negotiations and to ensure that the Indigenous party enjoys a significant portion of its rights pending final agreement, they are not in a position to give a detailed and exhaustive account of a generative right in all its facets. That result can be achieved only by negotiations between the parties.[47] In that sense the avowed goal of reconciling Crown sovereignty with aboriginal title and rights becomes one of acknowledging the ineradicable dialectic between the political and proprietary paradigms.

The pattern taken in the published work of Brian Slattery and Kent McNeil during the 1990s and into the new century was emblematic of Canadian scholars' broader and ongoing emphasis upon rights-design. In the years after the breakthrough cases, that disposition revealed the lurking tendency of the scholarship to reify and fetishise the notion of common-law

---

[45] For example K McNeil, 'The Vulnerability of Indigenous Land Rights in Australia and Canada' (2004) 42 *Osgoode Hall Law Journal* 271–301 where he argues that recourse to the courts might not be advisable for tribes given the impure percolation of economic and political factors into the courts' reasoning.

[46] Brian Slattery, 'The Generative Structure of Aboriginal Rights' (2007) Supreme Court Law Review forthcoming.

[47] Brian Slattery, 'The Metamorphosis of Aboriginal Title' (2006) 85 *Canadian Bar Review* 255–86. For an early and very similar analysis of the relationship between adjudicated and negotiated outcomes in this field see Eric Colvin *Legal process and the resolution of Indian claims* (Saskatoon, Native Law Centre, 1981) drawing on the famous work by Lon Fuller, 'The Forms and Limits of Adjudication' (1978) 92 *Harvard Law Review* 353 on the zero-sum nature of the adversarial process and its unsuitability for treatment of 'polycentric problems'.

tribal property. That, one might speculate, was nourished by the coincidence of this jurisprudence with the new Charter era (1982–). However, and again using Brian and Kent's more recent work as indicative, there is now a growing (and well-placed) wariness of the courts. No one seriously thinks nowadays that the doctrinal mess the Canadian courts have made will be resolved. The rights-fetishism of the 90s has begun to wane. The Canadian scholarship is entering a new period of realism and more critical engagement with the compass of the proprietary paradigm and its necessary engagement with the political, but that simply means they have caught up with the cold reality that has gripped First Nations. First Nations, including their scholars—John Borrows foremost amongst the lawyers—have always had reservations about the proprietary paradigm. It was never a tribal invention. One hopes that Canadian scholars, no longer mesmerised by rights-talk and less fixated with sorting out the mess made by the courts, will now turn their attention to the pressing and complex downstream issues of rights-management and -integration.[48]

Tribes everywhere, in all the common-law jurisdictions, have long since twigged to the reality that true, if any, progress towards asset-vestment lies less in the commentariat so much as the political will and impetus to resolve and resource that process. That has not prevented a constant opportunistic recourse to the courts by tribes but this furious activity is not imbued with the shining hope of the 1980s that the courts will deliver as dramatically as then. The scholarship had its potency in the breakthrough era and early afterwards, but its ongoing influence on legal development is now vastly less. In all jurisdictions the limits of the judicial imagination and (in)capacity of a wholly proprietary paradigm have been shown, especially one that pulls courts into such a problematic engagement with history and the idea of the past.[49] It was always more than a matter of getting the design of the property right right.

(b) Australia

In Australia, however, there has been never been such an encompassing disposition towards putting the notion of native title on a constitutional pedestal tying the legislative hand. From the start politicians made it plain that they would legislate and house the inchoate right first recognised in *Mabo No 2* in a statutory framework that kept Crown land available for

---

[48] Though in 'Aboriginal Governments and the Canadian Charter of Rights and Freedoms' (1996) 34 *Osgoode Hall Law Journal* 61–99, Kent raises issues of rights-integration. Also the Canadian experience with the Indian Act s 12(1)(b), the *Lovelace* litgation and the passage of Bill C-31 has been a classic and highly-problematic (as well as high-profile) issue of rights-integration that has drawn considerable scholarly attention.

[49] Important writers on the topic of 'juridical history' are Andrew Sharp, Bain Attwood, Damen Ward, Alex Reilly.

exploitation (mineral extraction especially). Whatever the nature of the native-title property right, the politicians were not prepared to leave its articulation to the beaks (and boffins). From the start they took a robust attitude that did not flinch from circumscribing the potential of the key judgments in *Mabo No 2* and *Wik*. This was particularly the case with the controversial 1998 Amendments which drew negative international attention to Australia. Whilst the amending Act had some positive features in the ILUA provisions, it truncated the right to negotiate[50] and other aspects of the 1993 Act seen by the Howard Government as 'congesting' the efficiency of the statutory machinery. The Commonwealth was happy to up the tempo of legal development considerably, bringing suddenly to Aboriginal clan nations a new and swamping legalism under the grinding machinery of the Native Title Acts.

The major question that the key High Court of Australia cases of the late 1990s dealt with concerned the basis of native title as 'ownership' or a 'bundle of rights'. The question for the jurisprudence at its early stage was whether native title was capable of being a form of exclusive ownership analogous to freehold ownership or was it something less, at most a 'bundle of rights' which might—or, more usually, might not—include a right to exclude? Putting this in Canadian terms, the question became one of whether Australian law recognised *title* as well as *rights*. The answer it gave was that native title was a bundle of rights, each of which had to be identified and proven, including any right to exclude. From that it followed that any such exclusivity could be no more than partial, since a general right to exclude was the hallmark of full titular ownership. Exclusivity was thus linked, if at all, to exercise of the particular right. This diminished the scope and, for Aboriginal nations, potential of native title considerably, since it meant they were denied the key attribute of ownership by which to protect their land, a general right to exclude all-comers.

The High Court continued in the diminishing vein by resting the native title on the principle of normative continuity—the continuance of tribal customary legal systems on Crown sovereignty—but with a rigorous continuity test requiring the right as practised now to be virtually the same as at the moment of sovereignty. Notionally anyway, since the test was one of continued normative association (as opposed to physical) this has meant that downtown Perth might be subject to subsisting native-title rights.[51] The approach of the High Court, however, carries the same disposition as the

---

[50] For detailed analysis of the amended right to negotiate provisions, see GD Meyers and S Raine, 'Australian Aboriginal land rights in transition (Part II): The legislative response to the High Court's native title decisions in *Mabo v Queensland* and *Wik v Queensland*' (2001) 9(1) *Tulsa Journal of Comparative & International Law* 95.

[51] *Bennell v State of Western Australia* [2006] FCA 1243. The judgment of Wilcox J is under appeal. See 'Nyoongar people win native title over Perth', 19 September 2006; http://www.abc.net.au/news/newsitems/200609/s1744596.htm.

Canadian to use the concept of historically-validated rights as a means of constricting the property right in its present incarnation. In this Australian continuity test the judicial idea of history as a museum holds the bundle of rights tightly by the ankle. Rights become relics, their utility defined and limited by their very age. Justice Kirby had pleaded for a less onerous and more generous test that gave the property right the elasticity to adapt to changing conditions and technologies, but the museum-piece mentality prevailed. Again, the notion of aboriginal property rights as historical in character was used in a reductive manner. There can be few other property rights the present-day character and exercise of which are defined by reference to their state of being at the time of Crown sovereignty. It was for precisely this reason that some endorsed the Kirby approach as one driven by principles of equality drawn from international human rights norms.[52] That is to say, property was in the present tense and all ownership rights should rest on principles of equality to allow each person without discrimination (the ethnic basis of the right) the fullest use of the right in the light of modern conditions.

However, rail as one might against the doctrinal strictures articulated by the High Court of Australia in its native title jurisprudence of the late 1990s,[53] those impediments to the successful execution of a claim were nothing compared to the practical issues and sheer effort required to mount a claim. Many of those hoops related to questions of rights-management, as I will explain in the next section; however, there were also fundamental issues concerning the placing of claims into a juridical forum.

Eight years ago Alex Reilly warned South Africa. He observed that the presentation of claims raised fundamental evidentiary issues that put the authenticity of tribal culture under a juridical microscope:[54]

> By not accepting that claimants have a connection to the land based on traditional laws and customs, or by finding that the people's laws and customs are not sufficiently 'traditional' [ie too westernised], the law makes a judgment not only about the legal rights of the community, but also about their cultural integrity. The acquiring and recording of indigenous laws and customs might be conceived to be the final act of colonialism.

Finally he noted with observations that remain as ringing today:[55]

> The eight years of Aboriginal land claims in Australia have seen the potential content of native title diminish, the types of interest that extinguish native

---

[52] Notably Richard Bartlett, *Native Title in Australia* (Sydney, Butterworths, 1999) ch 7.

[53] For a trenchant account see Alex Reilly, 'From a Jurisprudence of Regret to a Regretful Jurisprudence: Shaping Native Title from *Mabo* to *Ward*' (2002) 9 *Murdoch University E-Law Journal*.

[54] Alex Reilly, 'The Australian Experience Of Aboriginal Title: Lessons For South Africa' (2000) 16 *South African Journal of Human Rights* 512, 532.

[55] *Ibid*, 533–4. His observation that no claims have been finally determined no longer holds.

title increase, and no claims finally determined through the court process. This spectacular failure may be due to the way the legislative process has been implemented, to the slow development of common law principles through the courts, to confusion over amendments to the Act, and to the negative attitude of many State governments to the existence of Aboriginal title rights.

Whilst there has been movement in the use of ILUAs in the new century, his observations remain applicable today, as one finds reading the HRESOC *Native Title Reports*[56] of recent years. Whilst the doctrinal strictures have stunted the potential reach of native title in Australia, another and greater curb has been the operational one arising from absence of political commitment by Commonwealth and States to the process. There has been recent movement in the field of governance, but official attitudes towards native title remain tight-fisted and more oriented towards the least- rather than the most-generous bundle.

(c) New Zealand

In 2003 the New Zealand Court of Appeal agreed that Maori tribes might hold unextinguished aboriginal-title property rights around the coastline.[57] The judgments made it plain that this legal possibility was subject to factual proof of extant customary usage on a basis of exclusivity. Nonetheless the admission of the legal possibility, though couched in terms of being actually remote because of the level of proof needed, set off the most heated political controversy of the new century. The Labour Government nearly fell and its historic link with Maori was severed as they exited to form their own political party (which, to rub the (sea) salt into the wound, has entered into a coalition agreement with the recently elected conservative National Government of Prime Minister John Key). Much of the heat came from the Government's resolution to emulate the Australian pattern of putting the inchoate common-law right inside statutory housing. Accusations flew, including condemnation of the perceived extinguishment of actual property rights that entailed 'Maori ownership' of coastline through to rule-of-law anxieties about the statutory pre-emption (and second-guessing) of eventual court ruling.

---

[56] Online at http://www.hreoc.gov.au/social_justice/native_title/index.html. Under the Native Title Act 1993, the Aboriginal and Torres Strait Islander Social Justice Commissioner is required to: prepare an annual report to the Attorney-General on the operation of the NTA and its effect on the exercise and enjoyment of human rights of Aboriginal and Torres Strait Islander peoples; and report, when requested by the Attorney-General, on any other matter relating to the rights of Indigenous people under the NTA. The objectives of the Commissioner are to provide and promote a human rights perspective on native title; assist in developing more efficient native title processes; and to advocate for the co-existence between Indigenous and non-Indigenous interests in land, based on compatible land use.

[57] *Attorney-General v Ngati Apa* [2003] 3 NZLR 643 and see Richard Boast, 'Maori proprietary claims to the foreshore and seabed after *Ngati Apa*' (2004) 21 *New Zealand Universities Law Review* 1.

The Foreshore and Seabed Act 2004 took the concept of the common-law aboriginal title spectrum, but (unlike the Australian interpretation) did not effectively rule out the utmost possibility of exclusive or 'territorial' title. Identification of any territorial title was, in the first instance, to be pursued through political negotiation (ostensibly insulated from judicial review) and agreement then endorsed by the High Court as meeting the statutory criteria for territorial title.[58] Lesser non-exclusive rights, so-called 'non-territorial rights' ranging from a bundle through to stand-alone site-specific customary rights, were to be ascertained through a new Customary Rights Order (CRO) jurisdiction given to the Maori Land Court.[59] The Act codified a test for the ascertainment of territorial and non-territorial rights; one that synthesised the Australian and Canadian approaches (normative continuity plus physical presence). The statute gave a continuity test requiring both unbroken normative and physical association, leaving no room for a claim based solely on the first continuity ground.

These new jurisdictions are now playing out in the New Zealand legal system. Undoubtedly the statutory framework has transformed the possibilities of Maori ownership rights around the coastline. Paradoxically the Act might have enlarged rather than circumscribed Maori prospects. Two Agreements in Principle were reached in February 2008, agreements inconceivable without the statutory framework. The suggestion that this statute might give Maori more than the common law alone would have provided[60] seems to have been realised, making life tricky for a new conservative Government committed to reviewing the statute.[61] Also the Maori Land Court has approached its new statutory jurisdiction in an expansive manner that surely will eventually be reviewed by the country's new Supreme Court.[62] Although the New Zealand courts have yet to consider the statutory tests for proprietary entitlement, a clear direction has appeared towards talking up those rights. Given the way the scene is presently being set, the kiwi courts may be headed towards an interpretation of aboriginal property rights on the coastline that is less fixated with tying those rights

---

[58] See McHugh, 'Setting the Statutory Compass: The Foreshore and Seabed Act 2004' (2005) 3 *New Zealand Journal of Public and International Law* 255–83 and McNeil, 'Legal Rights and Legislative Wrongs', above.

[59] See S Dorsett and L Godden, 'Interpreting Customary Rights Orders under the Foreshore and Seabed Act: The New Jurisdiction of the M ori Land Court' (2005) 36 *Victoria University of Wellington Law Review* 229–56.

[60] PG McHugh, 'Setting the Statutory Compass: The Foreshore and Seabed Act 2004' (2005) 3 *New Zealand Journal of Public and International Law* 255.

[61] The new Government has endorsed the Agreement: *The Gisborne Herald*, 15 November 2008.

[62] See the outstanding Whakatohea application and press coverage online at http://www.nzherald.co.nz/section/1/story.cfm?c_id=1&objectid=10117881. See also the first Customary Rights Order (CRO) Application online at http://www.courts.govt.nz/maorilandcourt/panui/NP-November-2006.pdf. To date there have been less than a dozen CRO applications.

to some historical and limiting quality, notwithstanding the clear invitation of the statutory language to do exactly that.

(d) Historical Rights Vest in Historical Polities

Another important consequence stemmed from the historical character of aboriginal rights, and this was one that fundamentally reconfigured the world of aboriginal politics. Since those rights vested in the tribe, the radical prioritising of aboriginal rights that came with the breakthrough cases also repositioned the tribe as the fundamental political unit in aboriginal life. If the pull of urbanisation and demographic change had been weakening the profile of the territorial tribe in aboriginal identity-practices, the attention being given to historical rights as the foundation for (eventual) asset-vestment reversed that. Retribalisation became a feature of aboriginal politics and a corollary of the proprietary paradigm. Arguments based on social welfare and citizenship (addressing aboriginal peoples' poverty, health and educational disadvantages) were regarded as a separate theatre where aboriginality was less the foundation of right as a means of delivery of basic services. Many de-tribalised urban aboriginals fell outside the reach of the new legalism.

I am not putting that outcome negatively so much as descriptively. It has meant that the tribe has been reinvigorated as the political heart of aboriginal culture, an orbit from which many aboriginal individuals are excluded, many it must be said by choice. This, like situation of their rights inside a proprietary paradigm, has an inherently conservative tendency. Old forms of leadership have been reinvested with more authority. Historical patterns of relations with the settler state—at least in Canada and New Zealand with their patterns of treaty-making[63]—have resumed.

(e) Patterns of Adversarial Rights-Design: Summary

In summary, once the breakthrough judgments gave the tribes the prospect of entry into a proprietary paradigm, there necessarily ensued court-driven processes of rights-design, especially with the tribes' recourse to the courts as negotiations with governments faltered. In the late 1990s the highest courts of Australia and Canada handed down key judgments examining the scope of the common-law right recognised in principle in the earlier breakthrough cases. In those downstream cases the courts signalled their unwillingness to extend the scope of the proprietary paradigm beyond an essentially protective function tied in to the historical character of the rights. For tribes, extending the present-day economic possibilities of the

---

[63] Richard Boast, 'Recognising Multitextualism: Rethinking New Zealand's Legal History' (2006) 37 *Victoria University of Wellington Law Review* 547 on the New Zealand 'treaties'.

aboriginal title property right became a matter of political negotiation rather than an outcome of active judicial encouragement.

B. The Management of Tribal Property Rights

For courts the proprietary paradigm began as an idea, nourished by the scholarship of the 1980s, starting out as recognition in principle that the pull of the adversarial process eventually and necessarily required them to examine more closely. Yet common-law recognition was not a rights-vesting machinery. If one looks, for instance, at the Canadian case-law, only one case *Baker Lake* (1978)[64] resulted in a finding and vesting of common-law title.[65] Most of the cases have involved a statement of legal principle, sending the case back to trial—and the resumption of political negotiation.[66] An under-acknowledged positive feature of the Australian and New Zealand statutes discussed above is their recognition that the adjudicative process of itself is a poor title-determining and -vesting jurisdiction. Since aboriginal-title rights arise technically as burdens on Crown titular ownership of land, those rights subsist in that burdening form at common law; a half-life for both Crown and tribe that inherently invites transformation of the spectre of title into more meaningful forms that clarify the respective positions of the parties. No developer will enter into a joint venture with a tribe on the basis of their alleged common-law property rights or attempt some deal with the Crown where the land is subject to an outstanding aboriginal claim. Common-law tribal property rights do not have enough legal purchase in their own right, those to title most especially. In that sense the common-law proprietary paradigm is a precursor to title-vestment rather than an actual accomplishment of it.

The Crown plays a central role in this process of title-vestment. Just as once the Crown held the sole capacity to obtain the purchase or cession of the tribal title, so too it is now the sole means to a full unfettered title for tribes. This continues to flow from the technical position that the land subject to the aboriginal title 'burden' is in Crown ownership. Yet because this land is technically in the public weal, the Crown quite properly sets terms and requirements before relinquishing its ownership, however 'technical', to tribes.

---

[64] *Hamlet of Baker Lake v Minister of Indian Affairs* (1979) 107 DLR (3d) 513 (FCTD).

[65] See McKinnon, 'Aboriginal Title after *Marshall* and *Bernard*', and text accompanying n 5 above.

[66] See McNeil, 'The Onus of Proof of Aboriginal Title' (1999) 37 *Osgoode Hall Law Journal* 775–803 suggesting that First Nations might have more success in court bringing actions in trespass or to recover possession than to claim an aboriginal title.

A tribe might be a sufficient juridical entity to commence proceedings and enforce certain obligations against the Crown but it is not an all-weather entity recognised by the legal system. Canadian law, for instance, has had a slippery struggle with the unincorporated Indian bands under the Indian Act when it comes to their status under the law of contract and tort (employment relations especially). Likewise in the United States, Congress has had to intervene to abbreviate the sovereign immunity of Indian tribes in the same key areas of contract and tort. Tribes want to be economic players, which means assuming a full rights-bearing legal profile. In that regard the common-law legal personality of the tribe is vague and so elusive that it cannot suffice. Asset-vestment has required the juridical filling in of the tribe and this process has been fraught and difficult since it entails the replacement—or at least the overlaying—of a customary system based on the informality and flexibility of actual practice with a textualised system that has been drawn up deliberatively. For many tribes 'corporatisation' has been a difficult and divisive process, yet governments consistently set erection of a legal title-holder as an absolute precondition for formal asset vestment. This is not an unreasonable requirement, since it would serve no benefit anywhere to have such an elusive legal creature holding and managing huge assets. It would not be consistent with governments' broader duties to the stability of the legal system to facilitate such a situation. If the tribal ownership is to have any meaning and economic potential, there must be a legally effective rights-bearer.

The formation of a juridical identity for the tribe has involved more than statutory incorporation or adoption of corporate vehicles. Tribes have had to address, and almost always they have had to revise, the conduct of their internal affairs in order to facilitate asset-vestment. Again, matters of custom have had to become textualised in the name of transparency and at the altar of managerialism. Here, again, one returns to the basic nature of the tribe as a political organism linked by kinship rather than as a purpose-driven being. Disagreement is the stuff of political life no less in tribal long-rooms and *marae* than in parliamentary chambers and corridors. Yet, governments set additional specific requirements for asset-vestment in addition to the basic requirement of legal personality. Tribes need to have clear rules for identification of their leadership (usually by election), the mandating of those leaders and verification of important decisions reached by them. Tribes are also required to put in place fully audited processes of financial reporting and accounting and they are expected to make these publicly available not least because public funds are often involved. Their political processes are required to be organised on principles of equality, transparent decision-making recorded in minutes of properly convened meetings and on principles of individual participation that prioritise the individual over the tribal. Governments impose these requirements because of the public moneys and assets involved and their desire that these asset-vestment agreements with tribes stick, particularly given the financial stakes and the imbalanced history that claims-resolution is intended to close.

The bitter irony is that in attempting to redress that historical pattern, the outcome has often—though not always—been its perpetuation rather than amelioration. In this bustling and busy new age of life inside the rights-place tribes are desperately short of the human capital necessary for them to participate fully. Capacity-building has become one of the new buzzwords amongst policy-makers (such as the World Bank) as tribal groups are bombarded with legalism. Under these stresses and with the lure of richesse, leadership becomes more exposed. Rifts and factionalism are accentuated, old rivalries and feuds revive with added potency. Ill-trained and untrained individuals are put in crucial posts where their over-parting is cruelly exposed, cultural seniority and experience not necessarily translating into the minutae of management. And since for the tribes this is an enlarged world of textualism and legalism, courts get drawn into these necine and internecine battles. Of course, the courts and their western ways lack the institutional experience and equipment to resolve such disputes. Judges heave their shoulders wearily as they say so. Tribal parties leave the court-room with their grievance intact rather than addressed. Yet, the customary sphere has also become equally incapable of accommodating these disputes given the inroad into courtroom and corporation of western legalism and the proliferation of sites for tribal disputation. Custom, textualised, ossifies and re-forms outside the text in conduct that now is prone to characterisation as ulta vires. As the stakes have risen, political life for tribes has got decidedly messier, more bureaucratic and entangled.

Membership is another area that has been put under strain. Governments insist that tribes have clear rules for identification of their members and their entitlement to participate in the economic benefits of asset-vestment. This is an example of the spread of textualism. Whereas once membership was a matter of self-defining practices, increasingly it has become a matter of substantive entry onto a tribal roll. Since entitlement arises through defined criteria—usually and most simply genealogical descent—this has meant that the natural customary filters have been turned off. Persons who have had little involvement with the life and politics of the tribe have been put on the list and share as much entitlement to scholarships and other distributions as active members. Moreover, the application of membership criteria means that positive rather than customary decisions have to be made as to who is in the tribe and who is not. The self-consciousness as to membership that this necessitates runs against the customary grain. Once upon a time tribal membership rolls were drawn up in North America as a prelude to the dissolution of the tribe and the allocation of its land to individual members. Nowadays tribal rolls are necessary for the tribe to be able to hold those assets on a secure, economically-integrated basis.

Issues of rights-management have, therefore, a legal and a human dimension. Tribes have had to adapt and compromise a purely customary system in the interest of asset-vestment and the economic development it promises.

On the legal front, all three jurisdictions have faced this question of the design of rights-management vehicles for tribes with some progress being made, although its success remains to be seen. There has been a recognition that these vehicles need to be culturally sympathetic as well as fulfilling the commercial and other demands that the legal system imposes upon rights-players; however, the actual construction of such vehicles has proven problematic. The tribes have emphatically rejected the one-size-fits-all approach of the IRA boiler-plate tribal constitutions (United States), ill-fated Runanga Iwi Act 1990 (New Zealand), First Nations Governance Bill C-7 2002 (Canada)[67] and the template entities in the (repealed) Aboriginal Councils and Associations Act 1976 (Commonwealth, Aust).[68] The major initiatives have been the Harvard Project on Indian Governance under Professors Stephen Cornell and Joseph Kalt,[69] the New Zealand Law Commission's *Waka Umanga* project[70] and the Australian audit of the Aboriginal Councils and Associations Act 1976[71] (ACA), which led to recent replacement legislation, the Corporations (Aboriginal and Torres Strait Islander) Act (Cth) 2006.

The question of tribal governance has occupied the sustained attention of policy-makers and aboriginal peoples. Other than in Australia,[72] however, academic attention has lagged. One recently updated and long-term Australian study has criticised the separation of title-determination from governance, the former being treated as a step before and apart from the latter. In resolving native title 'the structure of the title-holding

---

[67] See the commentary by Mary C Hurley, 'Bill C-7; The First Nations Governance Act' (Ottawa, Law and Government Division, 10 October 2002, Revised 18 December 2003).

[68] For a critique of the Aboriginal Councils and Associations Act see C Mantziaris and D Martin, *Native Title Corporations: a legal and anthropological analysis* (Sydney, The Federation Press, 2000) especially at 183–232, explaining how the ACA was unable successfully to incorporate customary group recruitment mechanisms and decision-making processes.

[69] See the overview of the Project at http://www.hks.harvard.edu/hpaied/overview.htm.

[70] At the end of 2007 consultations were being convened on a draft bill for Maori legal entities: http://www.lawcom.govt.nz/ProjectMiscellaneousPaper.aspx?ProjectID=115.

[71] *Review of the Aboriginal Councils and Associations Act 1976*. Review Team headed by Corrs Chambers Westgarth Lawyers (the Corrs Review) January 2002 online at www.oratsic.gov.au/publications/ legislation/Summary_of_Discussion_Paper.doc. See Nicole Watson, 'The Corporations (Aboriginal and Torres Strait Islander) Bill 2005 (Cth): Coming Soon to a Community Organisation Near You' [2006] *Indigenous Law Bulletin* 32.

[72] Not least in the published output of Dr Lisa Strelein, Director of the Native Title Research Unit at the Australian Institute of Aboriginal and Torres Strait Islander Studies (AIATSIS), Canberra. See also Paul Memmott and Peter Blackwood, *Holding Title and Managing Land in Cape York—Two Case Studies* (Canberra, Native Title Research Unit Australian Institute of Aboriginal and Torres Strait Islander Studies, 2008).

corporation is often the last aspect to be considered'. The authors made this conclusion:[73]

> In our view the preferred approach is to work with claimants from the outset on designing and establishing their PBCs and land trusts. This would shift the initial focus from the frustratingly lengthy and legalistic processes leading to a determination, to consideration of what are the optimal corporate structures that will meet the long-term outcomes which Aboriginal communities wish to achieve from their native title. As the claimants pursue their claim, important dynamic aspects of their political processes and social structuring are likely to be revealed and may hold valuable clues as to how their title-holding corporations might and should operate in reality.

Rather than being a 'downstream' issue, as I have been describing it here, governance may turn out to be the initial and preliminary requirement: The property rights are tailored to the pre-constituted right-bearer rather than other way around. In other words, the shaping of viable tribal governance mechanisms may require anthropological considerations to precede and shape, rather than be subordinate to, what is at present an over-dominant legalism. Nonetheless the overall tone of the Australian study is pessimistic, observing that 'while there have been encouraging movements forward at local, state and Commonwealth levels, the existing PBCs and land trusts in both regions are under-resourced, under-supported and are functionally dormant'.[74]

No one pretends there is a single-fix solution in this area because of the intersecting issues not merely of legal design—which has tended to predominate—but of group disposition and human capacity (as the above passages disclose). Property management is an ongoing process, and, to reiterate, that becomes fraught where the manager is a kin-based rather than purpose-driven entity. It is all very well to wrap that management in an ostensibly culturally sympathetic legal regime, if such can be found, but the inevitable disputation and internal jockeying typical of political systems cannot be eradicated by the pacifying processes of the proprietary paradigm. Leaving aside the key—though essentially non-legal—issues of capacity and resourcing, the search for, and failure of unsatisfactory, governance structures can compromise any benefit derived from the vesting of the property right. The exit mechanism of partition of title is not a viable option for a kin-based assemblage, even supposing the resourcing issues can be addressed satisfactorily. Hence the designers of these regimes have also looked at ADR, and the possibility of authorising special officials—registrars (the Australian device) and courts (the New Zealand)—to act as internal mediators and arbitrators. In other words, these officials

---

[73] Memmott and Blackwood, *ibid*, 39.
[74] *ibid*.

might act as sites where the two dynamics of custom and textualisation are synthesised into a discrete tribal jurisprudence that provides tribal entities with running repairs.

That is an emergent idea anyway. It might have legs. In New Zealand, Maori freehold land represents a distinct regime of land tenure for the highly fragmented tenancies-in-common into which the landward aboriginal title was transmuted a century ago. Because that process of title transmutation had long-since been completed, it was thought there was no residual common-law aboriginal title in the country. As I have indicated the *Ngati Apa* case (2003) shook that understanding as applied to the coastline; but inland the governing regime for Maori ownership is the statutory tenure of Maori freehold land. A generation ago this jurisdiction, under the aegis of the Maori Land Court, was seen as dying,[75] yet it has been revivified and today is a flourishing site of Maori *mana* (cultural standing). There has been a distinct trend towards enlarging rather than downsizing the Court's jurisdiction. In the New Zealand setting, then, the Court's sturdiness and stature suggest that it is possible to devise mechanisms where custom, textualism and legalism can all converge. Of course, kin will always argue, and some will never agree. However, provision of a forum in which that natural disposition is recognised, validated (rather than negated), ritualised and resolved is not necessarily so impossible.

The major problem with establishing officers or courts with special ADR jurisdiction is that parties, fractious ones especially, might not be disposed to recognise the exclusivity of its jurisdiction. Whilst the jurisdiction can be made exclusive for matters of an internal character, third-parties will want access to the general courts system (unless they have agreed beforehand to particular ADR mechanisms). This is a right of access to the ordinary courts that traditionally common-law legal systems have prioritised. Generally speaking, persons suing or being sued by a tribe in contract or tort will want that claim heard by an ordinary court, not one of special jurisdiction defined by the ethnicity of one party.

C. Rights-Integration

The scenario just described is an example of 'rights-integration'. Once it has been determined what property rights and entitlement a tribe has (rights-definition), and those assets have been vested in a suitable ownership regime (rights-management), there will be an ongoing need to square tribes'

---

[75] This was the supposition of the Royal Commission Report in 1980. Sir TP McCarthy (chairman), *The Maori Land Courts: Report of the Royal Commission of Inquiry* (Wellington, Government Printer, 1980).

rights with those of other rights-bearers outside the kin group.[76] Other rights-bearers include employees, municipalities, other property-owners and -licence holders, the environment (conservation), recreationalists, gender and related non-tribal minorities, to name a few of the more obvious.

Legal systems accomplish this process of rights-integration consensually by contract or adversarially in the courts. Rights will rub against one another and there need to be processes to accommodate and resolve the inevitable friction.

The phenomenon of land-claims settlements has been mentioned. This is not only a form of rights-definition but also of rights-integration. For instance, there has been a massive rise in the use of co-management structures in these agreements. These give tribes various rights in the management of national parks, marine resources etc and there is now a substantial literature in this area. So far as one can generalise, the theme of this literature now tends to be less concerned with the matter of legal design so much as the issue of human capacity. Co-management works where it is resourced adequately and there is the human capital to make it work (on both the bureaucratic as well as tribal sides).

The rise of aboriginal-rights jurisprudence has required national resources management policy-makers to accept movement away from earlier notions of a blanket national regime. Instead, in the new world of claims-settlement and co-management, that blanket is becoming quilted with regionalism.

Another related feature of recent years has been the rise of joint venture projects between tribes and corporations. Again the success of these vehicles seems to be less legal design, which is always done most carefully, than the human factors.

Inevitably, too, rights-integration has occurred in the courts, where these days tribes regularly appear in all range of matters from employment relations, debt recovery, to planning and local government matters. This is a perfectly natural pattern and in this sphere, so much as one can generalise broadly, the legal system makes little play of the tribal nature of one of the parties.

Courts and consensus are obvious sites of rights-integration about which not much more need be said here. However, it is not usually appreciated that rights-integration must also be tackled by the Crown. Inevitably in the constitutional exercise of government, the Crown will need to balance and regard competing rights-bearing interests. How do aboriginal rights factor into that mix? The Canadian courts have been particularly vigorous in establishing standards by which the Crown must demonstrate that its decision-making and exercises of discretion take appropriate account of

---

[76] This class can include tribe members claiming non-kin rights, such as gender or employment rights.

tribal interests, especially those of a proprietary character. In Canada the entrenchment of aboriginal rights has accentuated that necessity, lifting it from an obligation in administrative law to a deeper-lying constitutional obligation reaching to the legislative power. Hence in the leading case *Sparrow* (1990) the Supreme Court drew up a list of interests and the order of their prioritisation by the Crown in formulating legislative and executive conduct likely to impair the exercise of aboriginal property rights (fishing and hunting). Once it had been determined that an impairment was involved the Court agreed that a justificatory test applied.[77] The Court ranked the aboriginal interest below fair measures of conservation, but ahead of other non-aboriginal interests (recreational most especially):[78]

> The significance of giving the aboriginal right to fish for food top priority can be described as follows. If, in a given year, conservation needs required a reduction in the number of fish to be caught such that the number equalled the number required for food by the Indians, then all the fish available after conservation would go to the Indians according to the constitutional nature of their fishing right. If, more realistically, there were still fish after the Indian food requirements were met, then the brunt of conservation measures would be borne by the practices of sport fishing and commercial fishing.

The Court explained the justificatory test as it applied to the executive and legislative branches:

> The objective of this requirement is not to undermine Parliament's ability and responsibility with respect to creating and administering overall conservation and management plans regarding the salmon fishery. The objective is rather to guarantee that those plans treat aboriginal peoples in a way ensuring that their rights are taken seriously.

The Crown's compliance with this obligation involved procedural as well as substantive elements:

> These include the questions of whether there has been as little infringement as possible in order to effect the desired result; whether, in a situation of expropriation, fair compensation is available; and, whether the aboriginal group in question has been consulted with respect to the conservation measures being implemented. The aboriginal peoples, with their history of conservation-consciousness and interdependence with natural resources, would surely be expected, at the least, to be informed regarding the determination of an appropriate scheme for the regulation of the fisheries.

---

[77] Expressly adopting the approach of Professor Brian Slattery, 'Understanding Aboriginal Rights', (1987) 66 *Canadian Bar Review* 727.
[78] *Sparrow* [1990] SCR 1075

The Court made it plain in *Sparrow* that there was not an overriding and broad 'public interest' element in the justificatory test.[79] The identification had to be made of specific countervailing interests that might out-trump the high-priority aboriginal set. This flowed from both the constitutional position of the Crown (in its executive and legislative branches) and its special fiduciary duties to the tribes.

Whilst *Sparrow* cannot travel to other jurisdictions in the legislative sphere, it raised the prospect of a doctrine of executive accountability and justification in the development of administrative law Down Under.[80] This has not happened, or at least, it has not happened yet. The Australian courts declined to draw upon such principles in the 'Stolen Generation' case, where an action was brought against the Crown for the forcible removal of mixed-race children into residential schools.[81] Likewise New Zealand courts have not bitten into any similar notion of Crown fiduciary duty; mainly because the cases before them have not really provided any opportunity. The litigation has mostly concerned the claims-settlement processes towards which the courts have taken an unintrusive stance. Lacking the emboldening Canadian constitutional platform, antipodean courts have been much more deferential to executive discretion in the conduct of its relations with tribes. Outside the comfort—and late 1990s' discomforts—of elaborating the tribes' proprietary paradigm, old judicial habits die hard.

IV. CONCLUSION

One of the most significant legal developments in the common-law jurisdictions of Canada and Australasia in the last 25 years has been the admission of tribes into the rights-place of the national legal systems, reversing a cold century (often more) of neglect and marginalisation. In particular the courts have recognised the ancestral property rights of the tribes (common-law aboriginal title), using the proprietary paradigm to transform the political and legal leverage of the tribes. This set in train downstream and ongoing processes of rights-definition and raised the need for effective tribal vehicles of rights-management, given the vague legal status of the tribe. It has also necessitated the ongoing integration of tribal ownership rights with those of other rights-players. The result has

---

[79] See Gordon Christie, '*Delgamuukw* and the Protection of Aboriginal Land Interests' (2000–01) 32 *Ottawa Law Review* 85 suggesting the Court's post-*Sparrow* jurisprudence has produced by the backdoor such a text.

[80] PG McHugh *Aboriginal Societies and the Common Law* (Oxford, Oxford University Press, 2004) 535–6

[81] *Cubillo and Gunner v Commonwealth* (2000) 174 ALR 97 (FC, Full Court; leave to appeal declined 3 May 2002). Also *Thorpe v Commonwealth (No 3)* (1997) 144 ALR 677 (HCA).

been a busy and frequently frantic legalism engulfing tribes, taking them from one extreme—legal irrelevance—to the other.

On a personal note, this is a legalism that has occurred in a period co-terminous with my academic career. I came to this field in the late 1970s when the scholarship and jurisprudence were very thin on the ground. The field is now extremely busy. The 'lawfare' that surrounds the tribes these days is so complex and multiplex that drawing any general conclusion is hazardous, as plainly there are positive and negative features. The proprietary paradigm has been cast into a highly politicised arena where its inward tendencies have become more apparent over time. By their very nature property rights cannot remain indeterminate; but in the rub of the everyday they will become more defined (and perhaps limited), the principles for their management more specific, and there will be ongoing clarification and integration of their situation alongside other rights-bearers. As this happens the outcomes will have an increasingly conservative tendency.

Index

abandonment *see under* leasehold
Abbott v Abbott 211
Aboriginal Councils and Associations
  Act 1976 466
aboriginal title *see* tribal property rights
acknowledgment and repudiation 16–25
  personal remedies 24–5
  proprietary remedies 16–24
Adekunle v Ritchie 226–7
Administration of Estates Act 1925 106
Alderhay organ scandal 317
Alec Lobb Ltd v Total Oil GB Ltd 279
Alexander, GS 363
Alfred, King 112–13, 114
Alienated Land Act 1982 (Vanuata) 305
American Civil War 338
Anscombe, GEM 215
Arblaster, A 204, 230
armed conflict, meaning 340–1
Atter v Atkinson 164–5
Attorney-General v Odell 57
Australia
  easements
    definition 65
    equitable obligations 74–5
    implied 66
    law reform 72–3
    legislative/judicial approaches 73–8
    no uniform approach 71–2
    prescriptive 65–6
    statutory prescription 77–8
    virtual abolition 75–7
    see also Torrens jurisdictions
  exoneration *see* exoneration doctrine,
    Australia
  forestry and carbon rights 377–83
    by analogy 380–2
    extension of category 379–80
    as sui generis category 382–3
  tribal property rights 433–44*passim*,
    445–8, 449–51, 457–60, 463–8*passim*
  water property
    market-based regulation 369–70
    registers 376–7

baby-boomer generation 265
Bagot v Oughton 246, 247
Bahr v Nicolay (No 2) 16–25, 28
Baker, JH 99–100
Baker Lake case 463
Baltimore, Lord 190

Bant, E 14, 15
Barclay's Bank plc v O'Brien 28
Beloved Wilkes' Charity, Re 150
beneficiaries, right to information 145–58
  background 145–6
  commercial sensitivity 151
  conclusions 157–8
  confidentiality 150–1
  court's inherent jurisdiction 153–4
  defences 149–52
  exclusion 151
  letters of wishes 151–2
  main issues 146–7
  proactive/reactive issues 147–8
  proprietary approach 152–3
  Rosewood principle 154–7
  sanctity of reasoning 150
  trust documents, definition 148–9
  see also trustees
beneficiary-made wills *see* suspicious wills
Bernard case 451, 452, 455
Berry, Re 242–3, 258, 259
Birk, P 230, 278, 283
Birks, P 276
Bogdanor, V 113
bona vacantia 106, 107–8
Bonnemaison, J 292
breach of trust/fiduciary
  obligation 26–32
  background 26
  personal remedies 31–2
  proprietary remedies 26–30
Breakspeare v Acland 152, 156
British Columbia Treaty Process 447–8
British Royal Infirmary 317
*Brown v Board of Education of
  Topeka* 437
Brussels I 183–4
*Bruton v London & Quadrant Housing
  Trust* 424–5
Buckenham v Dickinson 174
Buddhas of Bamiyan 341
Burn, EH 100
Burrup Agreement 447
Butt v Kelson 151

Calder case 433, 439–41*passim*, 455
Canada
  title registration fraud (Ontario) 20
  tribal property rights 433–43*passim*,
    445–8, 449–57, 463–8*passim*, 469–71

Chambers, R   13
Charitable Trusts Amendment Act
   1855   129
Charities Act 1993   125, 126–8, 142–4
charity land, dispositions   125–44
   background   125
   conclusion   144
   context for rules   138–42
   cy-pres schemes   139–40
   definition   126*n*
   deregulation   137
   historical context   128–32
   investment pattern changes   137–8
   land registration   134
   non-land investments   132–4
   permanent endowment   140
   prevention of abuse   140–1
   price information   139
   reporting/transparency   135
   statutory regime   126–8, 141–4
   trustees *see* trustees
Charles I   116
Charles II   190
Chayes, A   437
Chin, Y   276, 278, 283
Chippewas of Sarnia   455
Civil List Act 1697   117
Coase, R   365–6, 371
cohabitation   232–4
commodification   363, 366–8, 370–1
Commonwealth v Verwayen   407
Conaglen, M   31–2
Constable v Tufnell   163–4
Constitution Act 1982 (Canada)   439
constructive trusts   203–34
   background   203
   cohabitation   232–4
   conclusions   234
   ideology of liberalism   203–5
   intention
      approach   211–12
      boundaries   215–20
      centrality of   209–13
      constraints on interpretation   222–9
      discretion   222–8
      fairness or   209–10
      imputed   213–14, 220–2
      inference or invention   212–13
      legal fictions and   213–14, 220–1, 230
      limited approach   228–9
   property paradigm   203–9, 230
   real bargains   215–20
   status   230–2
      cohabitation   232–4
contentious probate practitioners   161–2
contribution doctrine   239–40
conveyancers' investigations   49–52
   excessive risk-taking   54–8

Conveyancing Act 1919 (NSW)   95
copyhold tenure   109
Cornwall, Duchy of   118–20
Courts Act 2003   2003
Cresswell v Potter   281
Croft v Day   163
crown land   112–21
   case for reform   120–1
   categories   112–13
   Duchy of Cornwall   118–20
   Duchy of Lancaster   115–18
   political capacity   113–14
   private capacity   114–15
Crown Lands Act 1702   114, 115, 116–17
Crown Private Estates Act 1862   114
crown sovereignty, tribal property
   and   433–4, 457–9, 463–4, 469–71
cultural property
   definition   339–40
   emblem   357
   exportation   342–3
Cultural Property (Armed Conflicts)
   Bill 2008   337, 354
cy-pres schemes   139–40

Dalton v Angus   64
*Daraydan Holdings v Solland International
   Ltd*   155
De Alessi, L   371
Dealing in Cultural Objects (Offences)
   Act 2003   356
deferred indefeasibility   8–9
Delgamuukw case   450–2
Depoorter, B   372
Deschamps v Miller   193–4
d'Eye v Avery   175
Dickson v Reidy   248–9, 253–4
discretionary indefeasibility   9–11
Dixon, M   234
*Dobson v North Tyneside Health
   Authority*   319–20, 321, 325, 329
Doodeward v Spence   318–19, 321, 325,
   327, 329–30
DuChamp, Marcel   325
Duke v Andler   200
*Duncan, Fox & Co v North and South Wales
   Bank*   239, 245
Dunn v Bradford LBC   425

easements and servitudes   61–97
   Australia *see* Australia, easements
   background   61–2
   conclusion   96–7
   diverse reactions   88–9
   human rights *see* European Convention for
      the Protection of Human Rights
   prescriptive/implied   62–9
   statutory rights   92–3

statutory user rights 94–6
title *see* title-by-registration
Edelman, J 14, 15
Edgeworth, B 375
Edward III 118
Edward IV 118
Edwards v Edwards 233
Efate 291–2
ejectione firmae 421–2
elderly population 265–85
  equity release see equity release products
  financial vulnerability 266–70
  growth 265
  homes as asset/inheritance 267–70
  policy issues 265–6, 285
  unconscionable bargain doctrine
    276–8
    elements 279–80
    independent advice 283
    theoretical framework 283–5
    transactional outcomes 282–3
    vulnerability and 280–2
  undue influence 274–6
Elizabeth II, 120
England and Wales
  easements 62–5
    definition 62–3
    implied 64–5
    legislation 79–80
    prescriptive 63–4
    proposals 80–3
    uniform approach 78–9
  human rights *see* European Convention
    for the Protection of Human Rights
  title registration fraud 20–2, 29–30
environmental goods, new property rights
  background 363–5
  commodification 363, 366–8, 370–1
  conclusion 383–5
  creation 363–4
    economic justification 365–7
  fisheries regulation 368–9
  forestry and carbon rights *see under*
    Australia
  interest recording 374–5, 384–5
  land registers
    principles 376–83
    role 374–6
  optimal fragmentation 370–4
    economic perspectives 371–2
    legal perspectives 372–4
  water property *see under* Australia
Environmental Management and
  Conservation Act 2002
  (Vanuata) 305
Epstein, RA 206
equity release products 269–70
  regulatory approach 270–4

escheat 105–8
  application 106
  meaning 105–6
  modern case law 106–7
  reform options 107–8
European Convention for the Protection of
  Human Rights 89–92
  Article 1 89–90
    influence 90–2
  manorial rights and 111–12
  Scotland and 92
Ewing v Orr Ewing 197–9
exoneration doctrine, Australia
  another person benefit requirement
    253–4
  bankrupt's estate 262–3
  benefit purpose requirement 254–8
  charging property requirement 252
  conclusion 261–3
  description 235–6
  example 236–7
  extension of 250–2
  husband's estate 245–9
  jointly owned property and 238–41
  married women's benefit 262
  money borrowed purpose
    requirement 261
  no benefit to surety requirement
    259–61
  preconditions 252–61
  property context 237–8
  relevance to individuals 261–2
  surety's relief 262
  wife's estate 242–5
expectation *see* proprietary estoppel
  remedies determination

*Farah Constructions Pty Ltd v Say-Dee
  Pty Ltd* 26–32
Farrelly v Corrigan 165
feudal law
  background 99
  basic principles 99–104
  escheat *see* escheat
  leasehold 420–1
  manor *see* manorial rights
  pyramid system 101–3
  residual categories 105
Financial Services (Land Transactions)
  Act 2005 272
Financial Services and Markets
  Act 2000 273
First Nations 443, 454–5
fisheries regulation 368–9
Foreshore Development Act 1975
  (Vanuata) 297, 305
Foreshore and Seabed Act 2004
  (New Zealand) 440, 461

forestry and carbon rights *see under*
  Australia
Forfeiture Act 1870   106
forgery, title registration   5–16
  background   5–6
  personal remedies   13–16
  proprietary remedies   6–13
Fowler v Barron   233
Franks v Sinclair   179, 180–1
fraud
  definition   4
  forgery *see* forgery, title registration
  responses   4–5
  statutory   16–18, 26–7
  see also title registration systems, fraud
Fried, C   204
Fry v Lane   281
Fuller, L   214, 222, 230
Fuller v Strum   177
Fulton v Andrew   160

Garcia v National Australia Bank   263
Gardner, S   23, 24, 209–10, 404–8
Gee v Smart   246–7
Geneva Conventions   338
  Additional Protocols I and II   344–6
Geneva Conventions Act 1957   355
George II   197
George III   117
Gibbs v Messer   58
Gissing v Gissing   212–13, 220
Giumelli v Giumelli   401
Goodacre and Taylor v Smith   165
Graveson, RH   231
Gray, K   96–7, 419
Gray, SF   96–7
Gray v Dowman   247–8, 254
Greville v Tylee   163
Grubb, A   324

Haansman, H   373
Hague Convention 1907   338
Hague Convention for the Protection of
  Cultural Property in the Event of Armed
  Conflict 1954
  armed conflict, meaning   340–1
  background   337–9
  cultural property *see* cultural property
  enhanced protection   347–8
  general protection   341–2
  property exported from occupied
    territory   357–8
  property removed from safekeeping
    358–9
  Second Protocol   346–8
  special protection   342
  terrorism and   341
  United Kingdom
    criminal sanctions   355–7
    cultural property emblem   357
    initial involvement   343–4
    invasion/occupation of Iraq   348–50
    legislative proposals   354–9
    military considerations   353–4
    peacetime safeguarding
      proposals   351–3
    ratification   346, 359–61
    subsequent events   344–51
    US position change   350–1
Haida Nation case   452
*Hammersmith and Fulham BC v
  Monk*   424
Hardcastle, R   328
Hardin, G   366–7, 372
Hardwicke, Lord   187, 190, 197
Hart v O'Connor   283–4
Hartigan Nominees Pty Ltd v Rydge   151
Hawke, Robert   434
Hayton, D   153
Heller, MA   372
Henry III   115
Henry IV   116
Heritage Protection Bill 2008–09   337,
  354–5
Hicks, A   208
Hoffmann, L   216, 218
Holdsworth, WS   106
Holman v Howes   233
home reversion plans   270–1
Houlditch v Donegal   200
Housing Act 2004   432
Howard, John   442, 458
HRESOC, *Native Title Reports*   460
human remains, property rights   313–35
  background   313–14
  burial purposes   317
  conclusion   335
  custodianship   334
  in museums
    acquisition/enforceability of
      rights   329–30
    letters of administration   330–1
    named collections   313–15
    repatriation requests   315–16
    sufficiency of skill   328–9
    transfer   331–4
  nature of   326–8
  no-property rule   313, 316–17
    exceptions   317–22
    intervention approach   323–4, 329
    transformation approach   323, 324
    usefulness approach   324–5
  ownership   327–8
  right of possession   327
  subject of property   326–7
  work and skill exception   318–22

human rights *see* European Convention for the Protection of Human Rights
Human Tissue Act 2004   313, 314, 316, 330–4

ideology of liberalism   203–5
ILUAs (Indigenous Land Use Agreements) (Australia)   444, 445–7, 458, 460
immediate indefeasibility   6–8
in personam
   claim   18–20
   obligations   74–5
   Scotland   197–9
   specific performance   184–7, 190–3, 196
indefeasibility
   deferred   8–9
   discretionary   9–11
   easement exceptions   74, 77–8
   immediate   6–8
   qualified   11–13
Indigenous Land Use Agreements (ILUAs) (Australia)   444, 445–7, 458, 460
indigenous people *see* tribal property rights
individual transferable quotas (ITQs)   369
information
   price   139
   right to *see* beneficiaries, right to information
Ingram v Wyatt   163–4
intention *see under* constructive trusts
International Criminal Court Act 2001   355
investment
   charity land   132–4, 137–8
   trustees' duties   132–4
Investors Compensation Scheme v West Bromwich Building Society   218–19, 280–1
Iraq, invasion/occupation   348–50
Iraq (United Nations Sanctions Order) 2003   356
ITQS (individual transferable quotas)   369

James Bay Agreement   439, 448
James I   116, 188
James v Thomas   228–9, 233
Jennings v Rice   390, 391–4, 400, 401, 404–6

Kensington Palace   114
Key, John   460
Kirby, Judge Michael   449, 459
Kostiuk, Re Bankruptcy of   259
Kraakman, R   373

Lancaster, Duchy of   115–18
land
   alienation *see* Vanuata, land alienation
   charity *see* charity land, dispositions

crown *see* crown land
   singularity of   426–7
   title registration   70–1
Land law Act 2009 (Vanuatu)   309
Land Leases Acts (Vanuata)   295, 304, 309
land registration
   charity land, dispositions   134
   comprehensiveness   59
   conveyancers' investigations   49–52
   costs suppression   40–2, 52–3
   promoting acceptance   37–9, 44, 49
   registry examination of instruments   39, 49
   see also title registration
Land Registration Act 2002   22–4, 30, 79–80, 81
   crown lands   114
   escheat   107
   manorial rights   110–12
Land Registry Act 1862   44
Land Transfer Act 1875   44–5
Land Transfer Act 1897   42, 45
Land Transfer Act (New Zealand) 1952   38
Lands Tribunal Act 2001 (Vanuata)   294
Law Commission, *Easements* Consultation Paper
   background   80
   implied easements   82–3
   prescriptive easements   80–2
Law of Property Act 1922   109–10
lawfare   443–5
Lawrence v Wright   5–14, 32
Lawson, FH   327
leasehold changes   419–32
   abandonment
      background   427–8
      conclusion   431–2
      damages' adequacy   428–9
      reasonableness   429–31
   background   419–20
   contractual approach   423–6
   as estate in land   421–2
   feudal   420–1
   historical development   420–3
   modern   422–3
   residential   422
   singularity of land   426–7
legal fictions   213–14, 220–1, 230
letters of wishes   151–2
liberalism, ideology of   203–5
Lindow Man   331
Lloyd's Bank v Rosset   209–10, 211
Londonderry's Settlement   149, 150
Lord of the Manor   109–10
Loughlin, M   205
Loxston, Re   175–6
Lumley v Gye   24–5

Mabo No 2   441–2, 449, 457–8
MacCallum, GC   222–3
McKenzie, Lord   272–3
McNeil, K   442, 450, 453–6, 457–8
MacQueen, H   104
Magnusson, R   326
Maitland, FW   100, 184, 195
manorial rights   108–12
  background   108
  human rights issues   110–12
  Lord of the Manor   109–10
  manor's role   108–9
  purchase   110
Maori (Native) Land Court   440, 461, 468
Marley v Trustee, ex p   240
Married Women's Property Acts   235, 246
Marshall case   451, 452, 455
marshalling concept   240
Martin v Siegley   432
Matrimonial Causes Act 1973   211, 228
Matthews, P   317
Megarry v Wade   395
Merill, TW   373–4, 376
Messenger, Brigadier G   360
Milsom, SFC   420
Moçambique case   193
Morris v Morris   229
Murphy v Murphy   148
museums, human remains in *see under*
  human remains, property rights

Native Tile Act 1993 and 1998
  (Australia)   440, 445, 446, 458
Native Title Reports (HRESOC)   460
Neave, M   210
nemo dat quod non habet   333
New Zealand, tribal property rights
  433–43*passim*, 445–8, 460–2,
  463–8*passim*, 471
Newham (LB) v Khatun   425
Ngai Tahu Settlement   447
Ngati Porou tribe   448, 468
Niersmans v Pesticcio   275–6
Nisga'a Settlement   447, 448
Nolan, R   31–2
Nova Scotia, title registration
  fraud   20–2

*OBG v Allan; Mainstream Properties v
  Young*   25
O'Connor, P   32–3
*Official Trustee in Bankruptcy v Citibank
  Savings Ltd*   256–7
O'Keefe, R   341
Ontario, title registration fraud   20
Organ Retention Group, Re   321, 322,
  327, 329
O'Rourke v Darbyshire   148, 152

Osment, In the Estate of   164
Oxley v Hiscock   209, 210

Paget v Paget   254, 255–6, 257, 259
Parisi, F   372
Parsons v McBain   243, 244–5, 250, 252,
  254, 259, 262
*Peasegood (JA) and EF Hunt v HS
  Peasegood, In re*   252
Penn v Baltimore   186, 183, 185, 187–9,
  190–3
Penn, William   190
Penner, JE   206
Peterstone Wentloog   110
Pettitt v Pettitt   212–13
Physical Planning Act 1986 (Vanuata)   305
Pittortou, Re   259–61
Pocock, JGA   100
*Portman Building Society v
  Dusangh*   282–3
Pound, R   231
Powell v Benney   407
Prescription Act 1832   63
property
  paradigm   203–9, 230
  sanctity of   40, 47, 59
  trust law and   205–9
Property Law Act 1974 (Queensland)   94–5
proprietary estoppel, remedies
  determination
  background   389–91
  conclusion   415–17
  development of law   391–6
  expectation
    concept   389*n*
    countervailing benefits   398–400
    as factor   404–8
    as proxy for detriment   408–11
    with reference to a bargain   411–15
    as remedy   397–8, 400–1
    as starting point   401–4

qualified indefeasibility   11–13
qualified surveyor, definition   126*n*
Quia Emptores, Statute   102

R v Chief Land Registrar   332
R v Kelly   313, 316, 320–9*passim*, 333
real bargains   215–20
Real Property Act 1858 (South Australia)   3
Registrar of Titles (WA) v Franzon   14–16
Reichman v Beveridge   428, 429–31
Reilly, A   459–60
repudiation *see* acknowledgment and
  repudiation
reverse mortgage sector   272
*Richard West & Partners (Inverness) v
  Dick*   197, 199

Richards v Allan 174–5
Ridge, P 160
right to information *see* beneficiaries, right
  to information
Riniker, U 230
Robertson, A 408–11
root of title
  examinations at first registration 44–6
  removal of blemishes 46
Rosewood Trust 153–7
Rossfreight Holdings Pty Ltd v Unipep
  Australia Pty Ltd 241
Rotherham, C 203–4, 234
Royal Bank of Scotland v Etidge 274, 278
Rudden, B 327, 372

Safe Home Income Plans (SHIP) 271–2
Salaried Staff London Loan Company Ltd v
  Swears and Wells Ltd 430
Sale of Goods act 1979 323, 332
sanctity
  of property 40, 47, 59
  of reasoning 150
Saunders v Vautier 187
Schmidt v Rosewood Trust Ltd 153–7
Scotland
  feudal system 103–4, 111–12
    abolition 104–5
  in personam 197–9
  servitude
    context 83–5
    definition 66–8
    European human rights and 92
    implied 69
    prescriptive 68–9
    reform recommendations 85–8
servitudes *see* easements and servitudes;
  Scotland, servitudes
Settled Land Act 1925 132
Sifri v Clough & Willis 178
Simpson, AWP 100
singularity of land 426–7
Slattery, Brian 442, 453, 456–7
Sledmore v Dalby 403
Smith, HE 373–4, 376
social cost theory 365–6, 367
Somerville, R 116
South Pacific *see* Vanuata, land alienation
Sparkes, P 113
Sparrow case 470–1
specific performance 183–200
  conclusion 200
  in Europe 183–7
  exclusivity 184, 187
  extra-territoriality limits 197–200
  foreign title 193–7
  in personam 184–7, 190–3, 196
  possession order 187–9

Stack v Dowden 209–13, 223–9, 231,
  232–4
state indemnity provisions 35–60
  background 35
  conclusion 59–60
  first registration losses 43–7
  future event deprivations
    counterpolicies 40–2
    policies 36–9
  limits on indemnity 41–2, 53–4
  past-event defects
    counterpolicies 52–60
    policy objectives 47–52
  premiums/awards correlation 41
  proprietors' dangers 35–6
    self-protection 42–3
  sanctity of property 40, 47, 59
  title *see* root of title
status *see under* constructive trusts
Steyn, J 218
Stigler, G 366
Stone, Professor P 360
Stott, Re 173–4
Strata Title Act 2000 (Vanuata) 295–6,
  309
subinfeudation 102
Sugden's Act 1830 189
sureties' indemnity 240–1
suspicious wills
  background 159–60
  contentious probate practitioners
    161–2
  draftsmen *see* will draftsmen
  lawyers 160–2
    interaction 163–4
  post-1980 cases 172–81
  pre-1960 cases 164–5
  solicitors' rules 170–1
  will draftsmen 162, 176–7
  Wintle v Nye 164, 165–70, 171, 179
  see also will draftsmen
sustainable development,
  Vanuata 299–300

Tainui Settlement 447
Tasmanian Aboriginal Centre, In re an
  application 314, 330
Te Weehi v Regional Fisheries Officer
  440–1, 443
Tenant in Chief 100–1, 108–9
tenant's abandonment *see* leasehold,
  abandonment
Tenures Abolition Act 1660 102
terra nullius principle 433–4
terrorism 341
Theft Act 1968 320
Thorner v Major 395–6
Tierney v King 150

title registration
  fraud
    acknowledgment *see* acknowledgment
      and repudiation
    background   3–5
    breach of trust *see* breach of trust/
      fiduciary obligation
    conclusion   32–3
    forgery *see* forgery, title registration
    repudiation *see* acknowledgment and
      repudiation
  see also land registration; root of title
title-by-registration   70–88
  Australia *see* Australia, easements
  England *see* England and Wales,
    easements
  land title registration   70–1
  Scotland *see* Scotland, servitude
  Torrens jurisdictions   3–4, 16–20, 33
    fraud and   4–5
      statutory   16–18, 26–7
    in personam claim   18–20, 28–9
    notarised execution of transfers   40
    past-event defects   48
    proprietors' self-protection   42–3
    sanctity of property   47
    in South Pacific   311
    volunteer status   27–8
    see also Australia, easements
tragedy of the commons   366–7
Transfer of Land Act 1893
  (Western Australia)   14
Transfer of Land Act (Victoria) 1958   15
tribal property rights   433–72
  activist militancy   434–5
  Australia   433–44*passim*, 445–8,
    449–51, 457–60, 463–8*passim*
  Canada   433–43*passim*, 445–8, 449–57,
    462, 463–8*passim*, 469–71
  claims-settlement processes   445–8
  as common law right   434, 436, 439–44
  conclusion   471–2
  court processes   448–51, 462–3
  crown sovereignty and   433–4, 457–9,
    463–4
  historical leadership patterns   462
  integration   468–71
  lawfare   443–5, 472
  management/governance   463–8
  New Zealand   433–43*passim*, 445–8,
    460–2, 463–8*passim*, 471
  proprietary paradigm   436, 438–9
  as public law litigation   436–8
  recognition   435–6
  terra nullius principle   433–4, 442
Trudeau, Pierre   439
trust documents, definition   148–9
Trustee Act 2000   132–4

trustees
  autonomy   135–6
  investment duties   132–4
  restrictions on   138–9
  see also beneficiaries, right to
    information
Tudor, OD   188
Twining, William   216–17

unconscionable bargain doctrine *see under*
  elderly population
undue influence   274–6
UNESCO   339, 341
  Convention on Means of Prohibiting
    and Preventing the Illicit Import and
    Transfer of Ownership of Cultural
    Property   356
United Kingdom *see* England and Wales;
  Hague Convention for the Protection
  of Cultural Property in the Event of
  Armed Conflict, United Kingdom;
  Scotland
*United Scientific Holdings Ltd v Burnley
  Borough Council*   423
unjust enrichment   14, 15

Van der Peet cases   451–2
Vanuata, land alienation   289–311
  background   289
  as case study   290
  conclusion   310–11
  custom/law   292–4
  Efate   291–2
  fair dealing   298–9
  future   308–10
  land administration   305–7
  land policy   302–4
  land summit resolutions   300–2
  lease law   295
  legislation   304–5
  ownership questions   296–8
  response   296
  situation in 2007   307
  strata title   295–6
  sustainable development   299–300
Victoria, Queen   120
villeinage   101–2, 109
Virgo, G   15
volunteer status   27–8

Walls v Atcheson   428–9
Walsh v Lonsdale   195
water property *see under* Australia
Webb v Webb   186–7
Wells, Re   106–7
Wheeldon v Burrows   64
White and Carter Ltd v McGregor   427–8
White, FT   188

Wik case 442, 449, 458
will draftsmen
  clients unseen 173–4
  costs 177–9
  fault 172–3
  instructions from beneficiaries 174–7
  suspicious wills 162, 176–7
William of Orange 113
wills *see* suspicious wills

Wills Act 1837 159
Wilson v Law Debenture Trust Corporation 150
Windsor Castle 115
Wintle v Nye 164, 165–70, 171, 179

Yeoman's Row Management Ltd v Cobbe 389, 391, 395–6, 397
Yerkey v Jones 263